ROOTS *of* REBELLION

ROOTS
of
REBELLION

*Workers' Politics and
Organizations in St. Petersburg
and Moscow, 1900–1914*

Victoria E. Bonnell

University of California Press / *Berkeley, Los Angeles, London*

University of California Press
Berkeley and Los Angeles, California
University of California Press, Ltd.
London, England
© 1983 by
The Regents of the University of California

Library of Congress Cataloging in Publication Data
Bonnell, Victoria E.
    Roots of rebellion.
        Bibliography: p.
    Includes index.
        1. Trade-unions—Russian S.F.S.R.—Leningrad—
History.   2. Trade-unions—Russian S.F.S.R.—Moscow—
History.   I. Title.
HD6735.L4B66   1983   331.8′09473′12   83-1084
ISBN 0-520-04740-0
ISBN 0-520-05114-9   (pbk.)

Printed in the United States of America

1   2   3   4   5   6   7   8   9

To My Parents

Contents

Tables

Illustrations

the century. *(Materialy k istorii Prokhorovskoi trekhgornoi manufaktury*, Moscow, 1913, p. 312.)

5. St. Petersburg bakers in the 1890s. *(Ocherki istorii Leningrada*, Moscow and Leningrad, 1956, III, p. 83.)

6. Tobacco workers in St. Petersburg in the early 1900s. *(Istoriia rabochikh Leningrada*, Leningrad, 1972, I, following p. 352.)

Photos 7–11 Follow page 184

7. Factory Committee at the Baltiiskii shipbuilding plant in St. Petersburg in 1905. (Kuznetsov, Livshits, and Pliasunov, eds., *Baltiiskii sudostroitel'nyi*, p. 317.)

8. Participants in the First All-Russian Conference of Trade Unions held in Moscow on September 24 and October 1, 6, and 7, 1905. (P. Kolokol'nikov and S. Rapoport, eds., *1905–1907 gg. v professional'nom dvizhenii: I i II Vserossiiskie konferentsii professional'nykh soiuzov*, Moscow, 1925, p. 152.)

9. Participants in the Second All-Russian Conference of Trade Unions held in Moscow, February 24–28, 1906. (Kolokol'nikov and Rapoport, eds., *1905–1907 gg.*, p. 250.)

10. Aleksandr Osipovich Iatsynevich, a metalfitter at the Odner plant, served as president of the St. Petersburg metalworkers' union from 1906 to 1910. (F. Bulkin, *Na zare profdvizheniia: Istoriia Peterburgskogo soiuza metallistov 1906–1914 gg.*, Moscow and Leningrad, 1924, following p. 200.)

11. V. P. Nogin, the leading Bolshevik union organizer in Moscow in 1906–1907. *(Krasnaia Moskva 1917–1920 gg.*, Moscow, 1920, p. 36.)

Photos 12–15 Follow page 328

12. Library of the St. Petersburg metalworkers' union, 1907. (Bulkin, *Na zare*, following p. 328.)

13. Workers active in the St. Petersburg textile workers' union, 1907–1911. *(Istoriia rabochikh Leningrada*, I, following p. 352.)

14. Members of the directing board of the St. Petersburg Union of Men and Women in the Tailoring Trades on an excursion to Shuvalovo, a suburb of the city, in May 1911. (S. M. Gruzdev, *Trud i bor'ba shveinikov v Petrograde 1905–1916 gg.*, Leningrad, 1929, p. 81.)

15. Four leading Moscow trade unionists who were informants for the Okhrana on the eve of the First World War: A. Poskrebukhin, union of sales employees; A. K. Marakushev, union of metalworkers; S. I. Sokolov, union of metalworkers; A. N. Nikolaev, union of printers. (I. Menitskii, *Revoliutsionnoe dvizhenie voennykh godov [1914–1917]: Ocherki i materialy*, Moscow, 1924, I, pp. 352, 384.)

Acknowledgments

My greatest debt is to Professor Barrington Moore, Jr., formerly my dissertation advisor, who has done so much to stimulate my thinking and to support my research. His high standards have been a model to me, and I hope this study carries forward the tradition of scholarship I have learned from him. I am also very appreciative of the advice and encouragement unstintingly provided by my friend and colleague Professor Reginald E. Zelnik. His erudition, generosity, and critical spirit have helped me to make many improvements in the manuscript. I shall always remember with gratitude the guidance and support provided by the late Professor Merle Fainsod at the inception of this project. Since my arrival at the University of California, Berkeley, in 1977, I have come to know Professor Reinhard Bendix and to benefit from his rare combination of historical knowledge and sociological imagination. Our discussions have made this a better book.

I want to thank Mark David Steinberg, my Research Assistant. With a gift for meticulous scholarship and a strong background in Russian labor history, he has assisted me in many tasks, both large and small. I am particularly indebted to him for his assistance in collecting labor force data and assembling the appendices. Without his help, the book would have been far longer in preparation.

Many colleagues and friends have read parts or all of the manuscript. They are too numerous by now to be thanked individually, but I should like to express special appreciation to Abraham Ascher, Laura Engelstein, Rose Glickman, Leopold Haimson, William G. Rosenberg, Steve Smith, and Allan K. Wildman. I also appreciate the assistance provided by V. Ia. Laverychev during the initial phase of my research in the Soviet Union.

Research for this project has taken me to many libraries and archives. I am grateful to the staffs at the State historical archives in Leningrad and Moscow; the Lenin Library, in Moscow; the Bibliothèque de Documentation Internationale Contemporaine, Nanterre, France; the Helsinki University Library; the New York Public Library; the libraries at Harvard University, Columbia University, and the University of California at Berkeley; and the Library and Archive of the Hoover Institution on War, Revolution, and Peace.

The International Research and Exchanges Board (IREX) supported my travel to the Soviet Union in 1970–1971 and 1977. In 1977 I was further assisted by a Fulbright-Hays Faculty Research Abroad Fellowship. Grants from the American Council of Learned Societies and the National Endowment for the Humanities enabled me to carry out research in London, Paris, Helsinki, Moscow, New York City, and Cambridge, Massachusetts. I appreciate the year of uninterrupted research and writing provided by the National Fellows Program at the Hoover Institution, Stanford University, and the release time from teaching made possible by a Career Development Grant, a Regents Faculty Fellowship, and the Institute of International Studies at Berkeley. Valuable research assistance was supported by the Center for Slavic and East European Studies, the Institute of International Studies, and the Committee on Research at Berkeley.

Nadine Zelinski at the Institute of International Studies expertly typed the first draft of the manuscript. I wish to thank Dorothy Heydt at the Institute of Urban and Regional Development for her superb inputting and formatting of the manuscript on the word processor. I am also grateful to Grant Barnes and Sheila Levine at the University of California Press. They have waited patiently for the manuscript and have provided every possible encouragement and assistance along the way. My husband Gregory Freidin was a source of support throughout the years I was working on this project.

Note on Dates and Transliteration

All dates are given according to the Old Style (Julian) calendar, which was thirteen days behind the Western (Gregorian) calendar in the twentieth century. The Western calendar was introduced into Russia in February 1918.

The system of transliteration used here is the Library of Congress system. Names and places that are well known are presented in their more familiar English form.

Abbreviations

Introduction

This book explores the roots of rebellion among workers who participated in voluntary associations—especially trade unions—during the final decades of Russia's autocratic regime. In undertaking this study, I wanted to understand the circumstances that shaped the social identity of Russian workers and influenced their political attitudes and aspirations. My investigation has led me to focus on the interaction among organized workers, employers, parties, and the state in an effort to ascertain the constellation of social and political relations that precipitated three revolutions in Russia at the beginning of the twentieth century.

THE HISTORICAL ROLE OF TRADE UNIONS IN TRANSITIONAL SOCIETIES

Notwithstanding notable differences among Western European states, trade unions have historically played several important roles. Above all, they have enabled workers to defend and assert their interests and rights in the workplace and society at large. In the course of these struggles, trade unions have funda-

1

mentally altered the alignment of forces in countries making the transition from an agrarian to an industrial economy, fortifying the power of labor in class and political relations. Over the long term, trade unions have often promoted among workers a commitment to, or at least a tolerance of, the existing institutional arrangements.

Workers' combinations first arose in Western Europe among skilled craftsmen attempting to defend themselves against an actual or a threatened deterioration in their position. The presence or absence of trade unions emerges as one of the decisive factors determining the impact of industrial development on groups whose skills, status, and standard of living were adversely affected by the development of a factory system.[1]

Through collective association, workers have endeavored—in varying degrees—to achieve the right to bargain collectively and to negotiate a collective labor contract, to improve (in some cases maintain) wages, hours, and working conditions, and to control the work environment and opportunities for employment (including entry into apprenticeship and hiring and firing). The "collective civil rights" of labor, as T. H. Marshall has called them, were preceded in most Western European countries by the attainment of individual civil rights.[2] These individual rights—particularly the individual freedom of contract—stood in the way of collective rights claimed by workers, and it was only after a protracted struggle that workers obtained state and employer recognition of their freedom to unite and to act as a collectivity.[3]

State and employer resistance to workers' demands for collective rights has been a virtually universal phenomenon and the reasons for this are not difficult to comprehend. Trade unions have been instrumental in altering the balance of forces in transitional societies. They have encroached in various ways on what employers considered to be their traditional prerogatives, and they have signaled the entry of workers into political life. As Reinhard Bendix has put it:

Trade unions seek to raise the economic status of their members. The workers organize in order to attain that level of economic reward to which they feel entitled. . . . These

---

[1] E. P. Thompson, *The Making of the English Working Class* (New York, 1964), makes a convincing argument on this point. See especially pp. 225, 321. The best general historical survey of Western European unions remains Walter Galenson, ed., *Comparative Labor Movements* (New York, 1952).

[2] T. H. Marshall, *Class, Citizenship and Social Development* (New York, 1965), pp. 103–104, 122.

[3] Reinhard Bendix, *Nation-Building and Citizenship: Studies of Our Changing Social Order* (Berkeley, 1977), pp. 98–102.

practical achievements of trade unions have a far-reaching effect upon the status of workers as citizens. For through trade unions and collective bargaining the right to combine is used to assert "basic claims to the elements of social justice." In this way the extension of citizenship to the lower classes is given the very special meaning that as citizens the members of these classes are "entitled" to a certain standard of well-being, in return for which they are only obliged to discharge the ordinary duties of citizenship.[4]

From the vantage point of the workers themselves, the struggle to achieve freedom of combination has been waged not only to gain protection and improvement of the terms and conditions of labor, but also to attain social justice and full equality in civil society where, as individuals, workers could not adequately contend with the power of employers and the state. The struggle for associational rights was therefore also a struggle for citizenship in the broadest sense and for dignity and respectability in the polity and in society. The obstacles to these demands have been formidable, and it was only after an extended period that Western European workers finally won the right to form legal trade unions, to bargain collectively, and to secure a collective labor contract.

The acquisition of these rights has contributed, over the long run, to gradualist trends in Western European labor movements. There have been many reasons for this "strong tendency to come to terms with the status quo,"[5] and it is not possible to examine them here. Repression and the defeat of revolutionary movements have played their part, as has the growing prosperity of the advanced industrial nations. But there can be no doubt that the material improvements and the extension of workers' power and rights which were achieved, in large measure, under union auspices, have helped to promote reformist rather than revolutionary solutions to labor problems.[6]

This study seeks to explain why prerevolutionary Russian trade unions, despite their initial promise, ultimately failed to duplicate this pattern during their short-lived existence; or, more specifically, why the organized labor movement

---

[4]Ibid., p. 104; for similar arguments, see Marshall, *Class, Citizenship and Social Development,* pp. 122–123.

[5]Barrington Moore, Jr., *Injustice: The Social Bases of Obedience and Revolt* (White Plains, N. Y., 1978), p. 473.

[6]The reformist potential of trade unions had already been recognized by the end of the nineteenth century in Germany by Karl Kautsky and Eduard Bernstein and in Russia by Lenin. On these points, see Vernon L. Lidtke, *The Outlawed Party: Social Democracy in Germany, 1878–1890* (Princeton, 1966), Carl E. Schorske, *German Social Democracy 1905–1917: The Development of the Great Schism* (New York, 1972), and, for Lenin's views, chapter 4, below.

in Russia became a vehicle for revolutionary rather than reformist aims. This issue has received little attention from Western and Soviet scholars.[7]

If we are to grasp the political and social implications of Russian trade unions and their impact on the workers who participated in them, several issues need to be addressed. First, it is a matter of great consequence whether individual and collective civil rights have been achieved sequentially or concurrently. In Western Europe these developments generally occurred sequentially, whereas in Russia the struggle for individual and for collective civil rights proceeded concurrently at the beginning of the twentieth century, and the working class took a leading part (together with other social groups) in advancing both these claims on the autocratic regime.

Second, the priorities of the organized labor movement deserve careful consideration. In particular, it is important to distinguish between workers' demands concerning the issues of wages and hours and those involving the control of conditions within the enterprise and access to employment. This distinction is a critical one. Anthony Giddens has pointed out that

any sort of extension of industrial conflict into the area of control poses a threat to the institutional separation of economic and political conflict . . . because it serves to bring into the open the connections between political power in the polity as such, and the broader "political" subordination of the working class within the economic order.[8]

---

[7]No comprehensive and systemic study of Russian trade unions exists in Western historiography. Some early studies that discussed these organizations include S. P. Turin, *From Peter the Great to Lenin: A History of the Russian Labour Movement* (London, 1935); Manya Gordon, *Workers Before and After Lenin* (New York, 1941); Selig Perlman, *A Theory of the Labor Movement* (New York, 1949); Isaac Deutscher, *Soviet Trade Unions* (London, 1950). More recent Western research on prerevolutionary Russian labor, with the exception of Engelstein's study, deals only peripherally with trade unions. See especially J. L. H. Keep, *The Rise of Social Democracy in Russia* (Oxford, 1963); Leopold Haimson, "The Problem of Social Stability in Urban Russia, 1905–1917," *Slavic Review*, pt. 1, 23, no. 4 (December 1964); Solomon Schwarz, *The Russian Revolution of 1905* (Chicago, 1967); Gerald Surh, "Petersburg Workers in 1905: Strikes, Workplace Democracy, and the Revolution," Ph.D. dissertation, University of California, Berkeley, 1979; Laura Engelstein, *Moscow, 1905: Working-Class Organizations and Political Conflict* (Stanford, 1982). Soviet scholars writing since the 1920s have also neglected the study of trade unions. Despite the appearance of a number of surveys, collections of documents, and essays, Soviet treatment of the subject has benefited little from the use of archival materials. *Revoliutsiia 1905–1907 godov v Rossii i profsoiuzy* (Moscow, 1975) exemplifies standard Soviet treatments of the subject. An exception is U. A. Shuster, *Peterburgskie rabochie v 1905–1907 gg.* (Leningrad, 1976).

[8]Anthony Giddens, *The Class Structure of the Advanced Societies* (New York, 1975), p. 206.

In Russia, as this study will show, organized workers were exceptionally bold in demanding *control* over key aspects of factory life. This was a matter of considerable significance in shaping labor-management relations during the Revolution of 1905 and the years that followed.

A third issue centers around the capacity of trade unions to register significant improvements for workers. The success of unions in ameliorating conditions has been an important factor in inducing workers to accept, or at least tolerate, the prevailing arrangements. While the failure of the organized labor movement to attain such improvements cannot alone be considered a sufficient condition for the development of revolutionary ideas or activities, the inability of unions to register tangible improvements would, a fortiori, indicate inauspicious prospects for the peaceful resolution of labor problems.

ROOTS OF REBELLION

Working-class movements that acquire a revolutionary dimension have been the exception rather than the rule. As Barrington Moore has observed, no basis exists for supposing that workers have had any innate "desire to overhaul the society."[9] Resentment, frustration, and anger can be discerned at many historical junctures, but it is only on very rare occasions that such sentiments culminate in mass mobilization and the spread of revolutionary ideas. Russia at the beginning of the twentieth century presents one such occasion, and it remains, to date, the only instance of a successful social revolution in which urban workers have played a major part.

The literature on workers and revolutionary consciousness offers a great variety of theoretical approaches, not all of them equally useful for understanding the concrete historical circumstances that have induced lower-class groups to reject the existing sociopolitical arrangements. Just as the category "working class" is too broad and undifferentiated to serve as a useful heuristic device, so the term "consciousness" must also be broken down into a number of more or less distinct categories, such as craft consciousness, class consciousness, and revolutionary consciousness.

Consciousness of class among workers has often been preceded or accompanied by craft consciousness—the awareness of belonging to a specialized

[9]Moore, *Injustice*, p. 474.

occupational group. In Western Europe, craft consciousness was prevalent not only among artisanal groups but also among skilled workers in a factory setting.[10] The transition from craft to class consciousness—and the formation of class consciousness among groups without prior craft traditions—has generally taken place through conflicts that sharpened the awareness of class antagonisms and extended the bases of solidarity among workers through common struggle.[11] The phenomenon of craft consciousness has often been thought to have been absent in Russia, where corporate traditions were comparatively weakly developed. This assumption warrants further investigation, and is discussed in the chapters that follow.

In this study, the term "class consciousness" will be used descriptively, to denote the awareness of belonging to a broad social collectivity that is different from, and often perceived to be antagonistic to, other social groups.[12] Historically, class consciousness has tended to coincide with a common position in the relations of production. But a strict definition of this kind does not always adequately reflect the composition of groups with a common class identification. In early twentieth-century Russia, contemporary workers included highly diverse elements as part of the Russian "working class," extending the concept not only to those employed in the manufacturing sector (both factory and artisanal groups), but also to hired workers in sales-clerical and service occupations and many others.

If the shift from craft to class consciousness—from particularism to universalism—has been a characteristic feature of European labor, the transition from

[10]On this point see Bernard Moss, *The Origins of the French Labor Movement: The Socialism of Skilled Workers, 1830–1914* (Berkeley, 1976); William G. Sewell, *Work and Revolution in France: The Language of Labor from the Old Regime to 1848* (Cambridge, England, 1980); Michael P. Hanagan, *The Logic of Solidarity: Artisans and Industrial Workers in Three French Towns* (Urbana, 1980); Joan Wallach Scott, *The Glassworkers of Carmaux: French Craftsmen and Political Action in a Nineteenth-Century City* (Cambridge, Mass., 1974).

[11]For a valuable discussion of class consciousness and class struggle, see E. P. Thompson, "Eighteenth-Century English Society: Class Struggle Without Class?" *Social History* 3, no. 2 (May 1978), pp. 146–150.

[12]There is a vast literature on the nature of class and class consciousness. In general, I subscribe to E. P. Thompson's view that the concept has both a historical and a heuristic usage. My own use of the term, discussed in chapter 1, emphasizes the way in which a specific historical group came to view their own collective identity as different from, and often opposed to, other groups. Thompson, *The Making of the English Working Class*, p. 9. A useful survey of various concepts of class can be found in Reinhard Bendix and Seymour Martin Lipset, eds., *Class, Status, and Power: A Reader in Social Stratification* (Glencoe, Ill., 1953).

class to revolutionary consciousness can scarcely be considered typical. Many stages may intervene, moreover, between the attainment of class identity and the adoption of a revolutionary perspective. Giddens has suggested an intermediary form of awareness, which he calls "conflict consciousness," involving a recognition of the opposition of class interests.[13] I would sharpen this interesting concept by limiting it to a recognition of the *irreconcilability* of one's own class interests with the interests of those who belong to other antagonistic classes.

A belief in the irreconcilability of class interests does not, in itself, represent a commitment to revolutionary change. It is possible, and indeed it has often been the case, that workers come to view their interests as ultimately opposed to those of the "capitalists" or employers and at the same time continue to accept or at least tolerate the existing arrangements. Nevertheless, a belief in the irreconcilable nature of class antagonisms represents, in my view, an important stage in the development of workers' consciousness. In the case of Russia, I will argue that this belief began to gain acceptance among workers as the result of a combination of circumstances, not the least of which was the dissemination of the idea by radical intellectuals acting, in part, through the trade union movement.

Revolutionary consciousness among workers must be distinguished from the foregoing categories because neither an awareness of class identity nor a belief in the irreconcilability of class interests necessarily involves a commitment to the fundamental restructuring of society and the state. What distinguishes revolutionary consciousness, then, is the conviction that grievances can be redressed *only* by a transformation of the existing institutions and arrangements, by the establishment of an alternative form of social and political organization.

But how do workers arrive at this rejection of the prevailing arrangements, and how do they develop an alternative vision? These issues are often conflated, but from an analytic point of view they represent distinct if interrelated problems. It is conventional in the literature to draw a distinction between two basic approaches to these issues: theories that focus primarily on revolutionizing circumstances external to the workers themselves and to their milieu, and those that locate the roots of rebellion in the workers' own experiences acquired at the workplace, in the community, or in society. For the sake of brevity, I will call them exogenous and endogenous, respectively. They are not mutually exclusive, and elements of both can be found in some studies.

---

[13]Giddens, *The Class Structure of the Advanced Societies*, pp. 114–115. For another provocative discussion of this issue, see Michael Mann, *Consciousness and Action Among the Western Working Class* (London, 1973), p. 13.

Exogenous theories share a common assumption that workers cannot develop revolutionary consciousness on their own. To become revolutionary, workers require outside help in the form of a political party or the intervention of radical intellectuals. Lenin exemplifies this perspective, but similar conclusions can also be found in the work of Selig Perlman and Barrington Moore.[14] Where these theories differ is in their explanations of the conditions that make workers receptive to revolutionary ideas imparted to them by nonworkers. In some cases, class struggles provide the precondition (Lenin), in others it is state policy (Perlman), and in still others it is a violation of the social contract that exists between workers and superordinate authorities (Moore).

Endogenous theories, by contrast, argue that workers are revolutionized by their own experiences, without the intervention of an outside agency. Marx was an exponent of this theory, as was Trotsky, but the approach is hardly confined to the Marxist tradition. Some scholars, such as Reinhard Bendix and Seymour Martin Lipset, emphasize the revolutionizing effect of workers' exclusion from society and the polity.[15] In a different version of this argument, Charles Tilly focuses on the impact of workers' new "proactive" claims for power in the polity and the consequences that ensue when these claims are not met.[16] Neil Smelser and Chalmers Johnson assert that massive structural changes in a society deprive workers of their traditional values and dispose them toward revolutionary ideas and movements.[17] Ted Robert Gurr stresses the social-psychological consequences of frustrated expectations that result when workers anticipate greater progress than is actually achieved.[18]

As the foregoing suggests, a dual classification of the literature actually conceals a variety of explanatory models that try to account for the circumstances that dispose workers to embrace revolutionary solutions to labor problems. In this study, I have found it helpful to identify five variables that focus our attention on different (though not necessarily incompatible) dimensions of

[14]V. I. Lenin, *Sochineniia*, 3rd ed., 30 vols. (Moscow, 1928–1937), vol. 4, pp. 359–508; Perlman, *A Theory of the Labor Movement;* Moore, *Injustice.*

[15]Bendix, *Nation-Building*, pp. 86–89; Seymour Martin Lipset, *Political Man: The Social Bases of Politics* (Garden City, N.Y., 1963), pp. 70–73.

[16]Charles Tilly, "Revolutions and Collective Violence," in *Macropolitical Theory*, ed. Fred I. Greenstein and Nelson W. Polsby (Reading, Mass., 1975).

[17]Neil J. Smelser, *Theory of Collective Behavior* (New York, 1963); idem, *Social Change in the Industrial Revolution: An Application of Theory to the British Cotton Industry* (Chicago, 1959); Chalmers Johnson, *Revolutionary Change* (Boston, 1966).

[18]Ted Robert Gurr, *Why Men Rebel* (Princeton, N.J., 1969).

working-class life: the workplace environment, the characteristics of the work force, the interaction between workers and politically-minded intellectuals, social contracts between workers and superordinate authorities, and, finally, the integration of workers into established institutions. These are briefly summarized below.

The Workplace

One explanatory model, originating in Marx's theory, emphasizes the role of the workplace in shaping workers' consciousness and organizations. For Marx, two features of the workplace in a capitalist society were decisively important: the elaborate division and the high concentration of labor. Marx argued that workers would develop class and revolutionary consciousness partly as a consequence of their day-to-day experiences of "spiritual and physical misery" at the workplace, where

not only is the detail work distributed to different individuals, but the individual himself is made the automatic motor of a fractional operation, and the absurd fable of Menenius Agrippa, which makes man a mere fragment of his own body, becomes realized.[19]

The elaborate division of labor under capitalism was, for Marx, a key element in the workers' estrangement from the act of production within the labor process.[20] As a result, the worker "does not feel content but unhappy, does not develop freely his physical and mental energy . . . feels himself outside his work, and in his work feels outside himself."[21] Both labor power and the product of labor confront the worker as an "alien power," a power that the worker comes to comprehend as issuing not from the gods or from nature but from "man himself."[22] This identification of the *human* causes of suffering was, in Marx's view, a basic advance toward a full comprehension of the capitalist system and the historical necessity for its abolition.

Marx further emphasized the importance of labor concentration in facilitating class solidarity and collective action. Thus, he wrote that the working class

[19]Marx, *Capital,* vol. 1 in *Karl Marx: Selected Writings,* ed. David McLellan (Oxford, 1977), p. 477.

[20]For Marx's view on this subject, see Karl Marx, *Economic and Philosophic Manuscripts of 1844* (Moscow, 1961), pp. 67–83; Marx and Engels, *The German Ideology,* ed. with an introduction by C. J. Arthur (New York, 1970).

[21]Marx, *Economic and Philosophic Manuscripts,* p. 72.

[22]Ibid., p. 79.

becomes ever more "trained, united, and organized by the very mechanism of the capitalist process of production."[23] The first step toward combination grows out of the conditions in large-scale enterprises:

Large-scale industry concentrates in one place a crowd of people unknown to one another. Competition divides their interests. But the maintenance of wages, this common interest which they have against their boss, unites them in a common thought of resistance—combination.[24]

Marx's theory offers two important propositions: first, that the large-scale enterprise with an elaborate division of labor will provide the locus for labor organization and political radicalism, and second, that workers have a capacity to generate an alternative (revolutionary) vision of society on the basis of their own experiences acquired at the workplace and through class and political struggles. The first of these propositions, though not the second, has become axiomatic in Soviet scholarship. Workers employed in large-scale, technologically advanced enterprises are reputed to have provided the social basis both for labor organizations and for the revolutionary workers' movement led by the Bolshevik party. Thus, P. Volobuev, a leading Soviet historian, asserts that prerevolutionary workers with the most highly developed political consciousness were drawn from factories with more than five hundred workers.[25] Another Soviet scholar has written, "The large and very large enterprises were the strong point of Bolshevik organizations that spread their influence over the entire working class."[26]

In contrast to Marxist theory, Mancur Olsen argues that small-scale work environments, rather than large ones, are most conducive to collective association.[27] Other scholars have noted that isolated and even dispersed workers sometimes display a high level of organization and militance.[28] A growing body of literature demonstrates that Western European artisans in small unmechanized workshops in the nineteenth century were among the first to initiate trade unions

[23]Marx, *Capital*, vol. 1 (New York, 1977), p. 929.

[24]Karl Marx, "The Poverty of Philosophy," in *Karl Marx: Selected Writings*, p. 214.

[25]P. Volobuev, *Proletariat i burzhuaziia Rossii v 1917 g.* (Moscow, 1964), pp. 29, 39.

[26]S. I. Antonova, *Vliianie stolypinskoi agrarnoi reformy na izmeneniia v sostave rabochego klassa* (Moscow, 1951), p. 211.

[27]Mancur Olson, *The Logic of Collective Action: Public Goods and the Theory of Groups* (Cambridge, Mass., and London, 1975).

[28]Clark Kerr and Abraham Siegel, "The Interindustry Propensity to Strike—An International Comparison," in *Industrial Conflicts*, ed. Kornhauser et al. (New York, 1954).

and to embrace socialist and revolutionary ideologies.[29] From these and other studies, we find that workers in a small workplace environment with a limited division of labor have shown a high propensity for labor activism and political radicalism in certain contexts.

This study will devote considerable attention to workers in small, dispersed, and unmechanized work environments, particularly artisanal groups. Although most accounts of Russian labor focus almost exclusively on industrial workers, especially those in very large plants in technologically advanced branches of industry, workers in artisanal trades and other sectors of the urban economy sometimes played a significant role in the country's labor and revolutionary movements.

Research linking consciousness to experiences at the point of production has shown the importance of investigating aspects of the workplace other than size and the division of labor.[30] The stratification of workers in an enterprise, social relations, hierarchies of authority and control, shop traditions and customs, as well as changes in any of these areas or in the labor process, may influence the way workers think and act.

Characteristics of the Work Force

A second major approach centers not on the workplace per se, but on the characteristics of the workers employed there, including their origins, background, life history, and other attributes (skill, literacy, urbanization, gender, and so on). Trotsky relies on this type of explanatory model, which connects consciousness and activism to specific characteristics of the workers themselves.

Trotsky argues that peasants who were "snatched from the plow and hurled straight into the factory furnace" were disposed to develop revolutionary consciousness. These workers, he asserted, were "without any artisanal past, without craft traditions or prejudices."[31] In his view, it was out of the deracinated peasant

---

[29]Recent studies on this subject include Scott, *The Glassworkers of Carmaux*, Ronald Aminzade, *Class, Politics and Early Industrial Capitalism: A Study of Mid-Nineteenth-Century Toulouse, France* (Albany, N.Y., 1981); Hanagan, *The Logic of Solidarity;* Moss, *The Origins of the French Labor Movement.*

[30]For an interesting discussion of the effect of different workplace settings on worker consciousness, see Robert Blauner, *Alienation and Freedom: The Factory Worker and His Industry* (Chicago, 1964). Historical studies focusing on such factors include Scott, *The Glassworkers*, and Hanagan, *The Logic of Solidarity;* Alain Touraine, *La Conscience Ouvrière* (Paris, 1966).

[31]Leon Trotsky, *1905*, trans. by Anya Bostock (New York, 1972), p. 291.

population, bereft of common corporate traditions, that Russia's revolutionary proletariat emerged. In this connection, he wrote that

in Russia the proletariat did not arise gradually through the ages carrying with itself the burden of the past as in England, but in leaps involving sharp changes of environment, ties, relations, and a sharp break with the past. It is just this fact—combined with the concentrated oppressions of tsarism—that made the Russian workers hospitable to the boldest conclusions of revolutionary thought.[32]

This line of argument has much in common with a Durkheimian approach which also stresses the radicalizing effects of disorientation produced by sudden discontinuities and rapid social changes. Smelser sums up this idea when he asserts that the "theoretical and empirical evidence suggests that social movements appeal most to those who have been dislodged from old social ties by differentiation but who have not been integrated into the new social order."[33]

A modified version of this approach can be found in Leopold Haimson's essay "The Problem of Social Stability in Urban Russia, 1905–1917." In that essay, Haimson draws a connection between the mounting revolutionary disposition of workers on the eve of the First World War and the influx into the factories of young workers who were disoriented and lacked the traditions and sobering experiences that had been acquired by older, more seasoned workers in the aftermath of the 1905 revolution.[34]

Tilly, a consistent critic of the Durkheimian approach, reaches quite different conclusions about the attributes of Western European workers in the nineteenth century who formed collective organizations and adopted radical ideas. Rapid social change, Tilly writes,

withdrew discontented men from communities in which they had already had the means for collective action and placed them in communities where they had neither the

---

[32]Leon Trotsky, *The Russian Revolution,* selected and edited by F. W. Dupee (Garden City, N.Y., 1959), p. 9. It is noteworthy that Trotsky's emphasis on the link between abrupt deracination and receptivity to revolutionary consciousness represented one of his major departures from the mainstream of Menshevik thought. For most Mensheviks, deracination and the absence of working-class traditions led not to the development of genuine class and revolutionary consciousness but to *buntarstvo,* elemental rebelliousness, which was said to stand in the way of a mature working-class movement.

[33]Neil J. Smelser, "Toward a Theory of Modernization," in *Social Change: Sources, Patterns, and Consequences,* ed. Eva Etzioni-Halevy and Amitai Etzioni, 2nd ed. (New York, 1973), p. 281.

[34]Haimson, "The Problem of Social Stability," pt. 1.

collective identity nor the means necessary to strike together. . . . It took considerable time and effort both for the individual migrant to assimilate to the large city, and thus to join the political strivings of his fellows, and for new forms of organization for collective action to grow up in the cities.[35]

Research by Tilly and others indicates that a high incidence of skill, literacy, and prolonged urban residency characterized the working-class participants in revolutionary upheavals of nineteenth-century Europe.[36] Thus, two quite different arguments can be found in the literature concerning the characteristics (demographic and otherwise) of radical workers, one emphasizing their uprootedness, uncertain identity, and lack of common traditions; the other stressing their long-term urban roots, collective identity, and preestablished bases of collective action.

Political Parties and Intellectuals

A third explanatory model, closely associated with Lenin's theory but by no means confined to it, emphasizes the role of an outside agency—a political party or intellectuals—in shaping the ideology and collective activities of workers. Whereas Marx expected workers to acquire revolutionary consciousness as a result of their own experiences, Lenin argued that workers had to be "trained" to develop "political consciousness and revolutionary activity":

In no way except by means of [comprehensive political] exposures *can* the masses be trained in political consciousness and revolutionary activity. . . . Working-class consciousness cannot be genuine political consciousness unless the workers are trained to respond to *all* cases of tyranny, oppression, violence, and abuse . . . to respond from a Social Democratic point of view and no other.[37]

---

[35]Charles Tilly, "Collective Violence in European Perspective," in *A History of Violence in America: Historical and Comparative Perspectives*, ed. Hugh Davis Graham and Ted Robert Gurr (New York, 1969), p. 11.

[36]Charles Tilly and Lynn Lees, "Le Peuple de juin 1848," *Annales: économies, sociétés, civilisations* 29 (1974), pp. 1061–1091; Mark Traugott, "The Mobile Guard in the French Revolution of 1848," *Theory and Society* 9, no. 5 (September 1980), pp. 683–720; P. H. Noyes, *Organization and Revolution: Working Class Associations in the German Revolutions of 1848–1849* (Princeton, 1966).

[37]This translation is from "What Is To Be Done?" in V. I. Lenin, *Selected Works*, 3 vols. (New York, 1967), vol. 1, p. 154. Italics are in the original. The verb "to train" is a translation of the Russian *priuchit'*, a word that can also mean "to inculcate."

A vanguard party, composed of dedicated professional revolutionaries, was in Lenin's view the instrument for implanting revolutionary consciousness in the minds of workers.

Lenin assigned to the party the task of training workers "to respond from a Social Democratic point of view and no other," an equivalent in Lenin's lexicon to Marx's notion of revolutionary consciousness. But in contrast to Marx, Lenin tied the concept of revolutionary consciousness to the fate of a single political party—indeed, to a particular point of view within a party. Thus the concept is narrowed to encompass only the policies, programs, and doctrines sanctioned by a political organization which, at the turn of the century when Lenin first presented these ideas, scarcely included any genuine workers at all. These Leninist arguments, once the foundation for Bolshevik party practice, now serve as unchallenged assumptions in Soviet scholarship where the Bolshevization of the labor movement is equated with the spread of revolutionary consciousness.

Perlman's *Theory of the Labor Movement* also proceeds from the assumption that workers will not develop a radical transformative outlook if left to their own devices. Perlman emphasizes the historical role played by intellectuals in the labor movement, diverting workers from their natural inclination for gradualism and incremental material improvement to the politics of revolutionary change.[38]

In his recent study *Injustice,* Moore argues that revolutionary ideas, especially a socialist vision of the future, must reach workers through the intervention of an outside agency. Like Lenin, he believes that workers are unlikely to move on their own beyond industry-specific demands to develop a comprehensive radical critique of society.[39] Insofar as workers have a vision of a better society, it is likely to be backward-looking, or a version of the present stripped of its most painful features.[40]

The socialist orientation of many organized workers was a distinctive feature of the labor movement in Russia from 1905 on. But it remains to be seen how these ideas originated among workers and what they meant to different groups at different times. If an outside agency was indeed responsible for implanting revolutionary concepts among Russian workers, then we still must explain the appeal of drastic and far-reaching solutions to labor problems. Two other explanatory models, based on social contracts and on worker integration, suggest ways to answer this question.

[38]Perlman, *A Theory of the Labor Movement,* especially chap. 8.
[39]Moore, *Injustice,* p. 477.
[40]Ibid., pp. 208–216, 476.

Social Contracts

In *Injustice,* Moore presents a social contract theory to explain the "social bases of obedience and revolt" among workers in Germany from 1848 to the Nazi era. Moore contends that social contracts, subject to continual testing and re-negotiation, exist at all levels of society between dominant and subordinate groups—not only between rulers and subjects, but also between employers and workers.[41] Workers derive their standards of justice and condemnation from preexisting mutual expectations and obligations, particularly, though not ex-clusively, at the workplace. Violations of these reciprocal relations by superordi-nate authorities provide an important cause of moral outrage among workers.

For moral outrage to develop into a basic critique or even rejection of the status quo, something else must take place. Specifically, Moore notes three circumstances: workers must learn to identify the human causes of suffering as distinct from an inevitable order of things; their escape to traditional forms of security must be blocked; and their reliance on paternalistic authority must be transcended.[42] Even then, no certainty exists that workers will develop revolu-tionary ideas on their own or will embrace such ideas when they are imparted by radical parties and groups. In his view, "some precipitating incident in the form of a new, sudden, and intolerable outrage" must occur before moral indignation is likely to find expression in a revolutionary movement.[43]

Alexis de Tocqueville's analysis of the French Revolution also places great importance on the violation of expectations in generating lower-class rebellion. Tocqueville's argument contains the crucial idea that people become enraged when their expectations are first heightened and then disappointed. He contends that lower-class revolt in eighteenth-century France was most intense where some prior improvements in the situation had taken place, creating new expectations:

Patiently endured so long as it seemed beyond redress, a grievance comes to appear intolerable once the possibility of removing it crosses men's minds. For the mere fact that

---

[41]Ibid., pp. 18, 19, 23, 202–203.

[42]Ibid., p. 125. Moore's argument that workers must learn to identify the *human causes* of suffering as distinct from an inevitable order of things bears close resemblance to Marx's view that workers need to comprehend that power issues not from the gods or from nature but from "man himself." Marx, *Economic and Philosophical Manuscripts,* p. 79.

[43]Ibid., p. 321. Moore makes this same argument in his discussion of peasant rebellion in *Social Origins of Dictatorship and Democracy: Lord and Peasant in the Making of the Modern World* (Boston, 1966), pp. 474–475.

certain abuses have been remedied draws attention to the others and they now appear more galling; people may suffer less, but their sensibility is exacerbated.[44]

Tocqueville's argument focuses on the circumstances that induce people to alter their conception of what constitutes tolerable misery by making them aware of alternatives. Marx and Moore make similar points when they call attention to the shift in consciousness that occurs when workers cease to view certain kinds of suffering as part of the laws of nature. For Tocqueville, the catalyst for this change in consciousness is an improvement in conditions, exposing the mutability of existing arrangements and the possibilities for amelioration.

Integration

A linkage between frustrated expectations and workers' rebelliousness also underlies integration theories. But unlike explanatory models based on the idea of a social contract, integration theories emphasize the frustration that workers experience when they are excluded from the dominant institutions.

The concept of integration has been subject to highly variable usage in the literature, sometimes by scholars with a functionalist perspective. But in general it has been associated with the view that in transitional societies, workers have advanced new claims for rights and for participation in key institutions.[45] To the extent that workers have been accorded these rights, they are likely to develop at least a minimal attachment to the existing institutions (political, economic, social, and cultural) and a willingness to accept the ground rules for the continuation of these institutions, possibly in a modified form.

Integration theories, as put forward by Bendix, Lipset, and others, are based on the assumption that workers will acquire a stake in the prevailing system to the extent that they can achieve tangible improvements through an exercise of their rights to participate in society and the polity. From this perspective, state policies and actions, and more generally the "flexibility and rigidity with which

[44]Alexis de Tocqueville, *The Old Regime and the French Revolution*, trans. Stuart Gilbert (New York, 1955), p. 177. Tocqueville's argument has served as the basis for several recent theories. See Gurr, *Why Men Rebel*, and James C. Davies, "Toward a Theory of Revolution," *American Sociological Review* 27, no. 1 (February 1962), pp. 5–15.

[45]Bendix, *Nation-Building*, pp. 86–89; Lipset, *Political Man*, pp. 70–73; Guenther Roth, *The Social Democrats in Imperial Germany: A Study of Working-Class Isolation and National Integration* (Totowa, N.J., 1963).

the dominant groups . . . were prepared to meet the challenge from below,"[46] are accorded a decisive influence over the political direction of workers in transitional societies.

Guenther Roth's *Social Democrats in Imperial Germany* uses integration theory to explain the political outlook of German workers in the late nineteenth and early twentieth centuries. The German case is particularly relevant to Russia, for here too industrialization proceeded under the auspices of a monarchical system, but with very different government policies and results for the working class.

According to Roth, workers in Imperial Germany faced a situation of "negative integration," that is, economic and partial cultural inclusion into society combined with political and social isolation. Beginning in 1890, German workers acquired the right to organize mass-membership trade unions, and through them to mount a collective struggle against employers. The consequences of this development have been analyzed by Roth:

It was of great importance for the theory and practice [of the labor movement] that the authoritarian state did not completely repress the labor movement, but that it permitted a parliamentary framework within which the movement could achieve tangible success. This provided [trade unions] a strong incentive to pursue moderate policies and an equally strong interest in legal status, though moderation appeared, of course, also advisable in view of the overwhelming power of the state.[47]

To analyze a complex phenomenon, a single theory, however rich and multivariate, will seldom suffice. Complex events usually have multiple causes, and in the discussion of workers' politics and organizations that follows, I shall have occasion to pose questions and to offer analyses drawing on some of the foregoing approaches and criticizing others. I shall also make use of a comparative approach, focusing attention on the similarities and differences between the two leading cities in the Russian Empire—St. Petersburg and Moscow—and more generally, between early twentieth-century Russia and the industrializing nations of Western Europe at earlier periods. Comparisons with Western Europe will be presented for the purpose of highlighting those features of tsarist society that present contrasting or common patterns with other European societies and to identify the factors that explain different outcomes in organized labor move-

---

[46]Bendix, *Work and Authority*, p. 441. The state also occupies an important place in Tilly's explanatory model. Charles Tilly, *From Mobilization to Revolution* (Reading, Mass., 1978), especially chap. 7.

[47]Roth, *The Social Democrats in Imperial Germany*, p. 170.

ments. Western European labor practices and relations, moreover, had a profound influence on all the participants in Russian industrial life, including
governmental authorities, employers, political activists, and the workers themselves. Without an appreciation of these influences, it is not possible to understand the mentality and the conduct of these diverse groups at the beginning of
the twentieth century.

The organization of the book combines chronological and thematic approaches. The basic framework consists of four parts subdivided chronologi-
cally, but the chapters within each section are arranged thematically. Part One
(chapters 1 and 2) examines the composition of the labor force and selected
aspects of working-class life at the beginning of the twentieth century, as well as
workers' organizational experiences before 1905. In Part Two (chapters 3 and 4),
I turn to the organizations created by workers in the First Russian Revolution
and the impact of the revolution on workers' political attitudes and aspirations.
Part Three (chapters 5, 6, 7, and 8) focuses on the era of legal labor organization
following the promulgation of the law of March 4, 1906, which accorded trade
unions a legal status for the first time. These chapters cover the years 1906 to
1911 and trace the internal development of workers' organizations and their
external relations with employers, the state, and political parties. This period, in
my estimation, represents the critical turning point in the history of Russian
labor, allowing us to see the circumstances that stood in the way of a peaceful
resolution of the country's labor problems. Finally, Part Four (chapters 9 and
10) covers the prewar years, 1912 to mid-1914, when trade unions revived and
became radically transformed into organizations for revolutionary change. A
summation and analysis can be found at the end of most chapters, while the
conclusion is devoted to a discussion of the historical findings and their sociological implications.

Part One

The Background

Chapter 1

The St. Petersburg and Moscow Working Class, Circa 1900

> In the spring of 1895, when I was sixteen years old,
> father drove me to Moscow, where he placed me in an
> apprenticeship at the Gustav List metalworking factory.
> I remember the stunning impression Moscow made on
> me. My father and I, sitting in our cart, walked our grey
> horse along brightly lighted streets. Huge multistoried
> houses—most of them with lighted windows—stores,
> shops, taverns, beer halls, horse-drawn carriages going
> by, a horse-drawn tramway, and all around us—crowds
> of bustling people, rushing to unknown destinations for
> unknown reasons.
>
> *S. Kanatchikov*[1]

In the second half of the nineteenth century the face of traditional Russian society began to change. Many villages and towns became transformed into factory centers, and mills started to appear where once there had been only peasant huts. In the leading urban centers of the Russian Empire—St. Petersburg, the modern capital, and its predecessor, Moscow—the pace of industrialization was rapid and intense. Factories and shops were springing up as never before, spilling over into the outskirts of each city, and creating jobs for thousands of people in the expanding urban economy.[2]

St. Petersburg and Moscow became meccas for impoverished peasants. During the 1890s—the decade of industrial "takeoff"—400,000 people, most of them peasants, migrated to the capital, bringing an average of 40,000 new

---

[1] S. Kanatchikov, *Iz istorii moego bytiia*, Book 1 (Moscow and Leningrad, 1929), p. 8. This and subsequent passages from Kanatchikov's memoir are translated by Reginald E. Zelnik and appear in Victoria E. Bonnell, ed., *The Russian Worker: Life and Labor under the Tsarist Regime* (Berkeley and Los Angeles, 1983), chap. 1. All translations are by the author, unless otherwise indicated.

[2] James H. Bater, *St. Petersburg: Industrialization and Change* (London, 1976).

inhabitants each year. Moscow also grew at an impressive if slower pace, absorbing an average of 26,000 migrants every year between 1892 and 1902. By 1900 Petersburg had a population of 1.4 million, and Moscow's inhabitants had exceeded 1.1 million by 1902, which made the two cities the most populous in the Russian Empire.[3]

The migrants who came to St. Petersburg and Moscow in these years were destined for jobs not only in factories and workshops but also in the rapidly expanding construction, transportation, communications, and service sectors of the economy. Still others joined the large population of casual day-laborers, beggars, and drifters. Not all of the migrants made a permanent home in the city. There were many who retained a house or land in the countryside and expected to return to the village following a sojourn in the urban labor force. At the turn of the century, however, more and more workers were spending a significant part of their working lives in an urban center.

Who were these workers, and how did their sojourn in the city affect their self-image? To what extent did they perceive themselves as part of a working class, instead of the peasantry from which most had come? And how did workers develop bases of commonality in the new and bewildering atmosphere of the big city, enabling them to act collectively and to form organizations, such as trade unions? To answer these questions, we must begin by examining the definition and composition of the working class.

DEFINING THE WORKING CLASS

Soviet studies in the Russian labor field, particularly those published after the 1920s, generally apply a narrow definition of the working class, virtually equating it with factory workers. Adhering to Marxist-Leninist assumptions concerning the progressive historical role of the "proletariat," Soviet scholars have

---

[3]A. G. Rashin, *Formirovanie rabochego klassa Rossii: Istoriko-ekonomicheskie ocherki* (Moscow, 1958), pp. 353–354; *Istoriia Mosvky*, vol. 5 (Moscow, 1955), p. 15. For two recent studies of Russian migration patterns, see Barbara A. Anderson, *Internal Migration During Modernization in Late Nineteenth-Century Russia* (Princeton, 1980), and Robert Eugene Johnson, *Peasant and Proletarian: The Working Class of Moscow in the Late Nineteenth Century* (New Brunswick, N.J., 1979). After the turn of the century, the population influx continued, and on the eve of the First World War there were 2.2 million inhabitants in the capital and 1.7 million in Moscow.

concentrated on workers employed in factories to the exclusion of most other groups within the urban hired labor force.[4]

This highly circumscribed definition of the working class does not take into account workers in sectors of the urban economy other than manufacturing, or even all of the workers in the manufacturing sector. In the capital, factory workers constituted only 25 percent of the total hired labor force at the beginning of the twentieth century, and in Moscow, a mere 21 percent.[5] Even within the manufacturing sectors, the number of factory workers did not exceed a bare majority of the labor force. At the turn of the century, there were more Moscow workers in artisanal shops than in factory employment, and in the capital, artisans were almost as numerous as factory workers (see table 1). To exclude artisanal workers from the working class is to ignore one half of the printers and binders

[4]The standard procedure in Soviet works is to provide a perfunctory survey of the labor force, followed by a substantive discussion of workers' activities which concentrates almost exclusively on the role of factory groups. Illustrative of this pattern are L. M. Ivanov, M. S. Volin, et al., eds., *Rossiiskii proletariat: oblik, bor'ba, gegemoniia* (Moscow, 1970); *Rabochii klass i rabochee dvizhenie v Rossii, 1861–1917 gg.* (Moscow, 1966); G. A. Arutiunov, *Rabochee dvizhenie v Rossii v periode novogo revoliutsionnogo pod"ema 1910–1914 gg.* (Moscow, 1975), and E. E. Kruze, *Peterburgskie rabochie v 1912–1914 godakh* (Moscow and Leningrad, 1961). Studies of the 1905–1907 period are particularly prone to distortion as a consequence of this narrow conceptualization of the working class. Thus, the collection *Revoliutsiia 1905–1907 godov v Rossii i profsoiuzy: Sbornik statei* (Moscow, 1975), with contributions by V. Ia. Laverychev and others, makes only passing reference to the involvement of nonfactory groups in the trade union movement, despite the overwhelming evidence of their participation in these organizations. Iu. I. Kir'ianov's recent study of working-class life, *Zhiznennyi uroven' rabochikh Rossii* (Moscow, 1979), while rich in documentation, deals exclusively with factory groups. Notable exceptions to the dominant approach in Soviet historiography are U. A. Shuster, *Peterburgskie rabochie v 1905–1907 gg.* (Leningrad, 1976), N. I. Vostrikov, *Bor'ba za massy: Gorodskie srednie sloi nakanune oktiabria* (Moscow, 1970), S. N. Semanov, *Peterburgskie rabochie nakanune pervoi russkoi revoliutsii* (Moscow and Leningrad, 1966). Rashin's important statistical compilation, *Formirovanie rabochego klassa Rossii,* also applies a broad definition of the working class and includes data on such groups as artisans, sales-clerical employees, household servants, day laborers, and workers in transportation, communications, and construction.

[5]At the turn of the century, according to municipal censuses, there were 641,656 workers in St. Petersburg and 537,522 workers in Moscow in the following categories: manufacturing, sales-clerical, transportation, communications, construction, and service. *Perepis' Moskvy 1902 goda,* chast' 1, vyp. 2 (Moscow, 1906), pp. 46–197; *S.-Peterburg po perepisi 15 dekabria 1900 g.,* vyp. 2 (St. Petersburg, 1903), pp. 1–173. There were 161,924 workers employed in private and state-owned factories in St. Petersburg in 1902, or 25 percent of the total hired labor force noted above. In 1902 there were 111,719 workers in Moscow factories and plants, or 21 percent of the total hired labor force. For a discussion of labor force data, see the footnote to table 1.

Table 1

Factory and Artisanal Workers in
St. Petersburg and Moscow at the Turn of the Century

City	Factory Workers	Percent of Total	Artisanal Workers	Percent of Total	Total Factory and Artisanal Labor Force
St. Petersburg	161,924 (1902)	52	150,709 (1900)	48	312,633
Moscow	111,719 (1902)	42	151,359 (1902)	58	263,078

Sources: This table is based on data from *Perepis' Moskvy*, pp. 116–161; Rashin, *Formirovanie*, p. 354; Pogozhev, *Uchet*, pp. 148–151; *S.-Peterburg po perepisi*, vyp. 2, pp. 38–137. Unlike the Moscow city census, which distinguished between factory and artisanal workers, the St. Petersburg city census combined both groups into one undifferentiated total. The approximate number of Petersburg artisans has been calculated by the following method. First, I have determined the number of workers in private and state-owned factories in St. Petersburg and its industrial suburbs of Petergof, Shlissel'burg, Poliustrov, and Lesnoi. These data are based on figures calculated by Pogozhev for 1902. Pogozhev relies primarily on statistics collected by the Ministry of Finance and its subordinate agency, the Factory Inspectorate, and published in the *Spisok fabrik i zavodov evropeiskoi Rossii* (St. Petersburg, 1903). Pogozhev has expanded the data in the *Spisok* to include several state-owned firms (mainly shipbuilding and munitions plants), some railroad workshops of the Nikolaevskii and Warsaw railways, firms subject to the excise tax (especially vodka and wine factories), and firms omitted by the Factory Inspectorate because their owners contended they were artisanal despite their large size. Even with Pogozhev's additions, the data are incomplete because they do not include *all* of the workers in state-owned metalworking plants and railroad workshops. To correct this deficiency, I have disregarded Pogozhev's labor-force data on metalworkers and have calculated my own total based on enterprises listed in the *Spisok fabrik i zavodov evropeiskoi Rossii*, with the addition of the following state-owned metalworking enterprises and workshops: the Obukhov plant (4,300 workers in 1898), the Novoe Admiralteistvo plant (3,000 workers in 1905), the Orudiinyi plant (700 workers in 1905), the Patronnyi and Trubochnyi artillery plants (6,693 workers in 1905), and the Warsaw and Nikolaevskii railroad workshops, including the Aleksandrovskii plant (8,000 workers in 1900). The state-operated Baltiiskii plant, it should be noted, is already included in the *Spisok*. The sources for these data are as follows: *Istoriia rabochego klassa Leningrada*, vyp. 2 (Leningrad, 1963), pp. 25, 117–118; A. L. Sidorov et al., eds., *Vysshii pod"em revoliutsii 1905–1907 gg.*, chast' 1 (Moscow, 1955), pp. 360–361; Semanov, *Peterburgskie rabochie*, p. 33. Furthermore, in those cases where Pogozhev's figures are less than shown in the *Spisok* for a given category, I have used the *Spisok* figures. Finally, it has been necessary to add the large state-owned paper and printing factory, Ekspeditsiia zagotovleniia gosudarstvennykh bumag, whose workers were excluded from both the *Spisok* and Pogozhev's data. The addition of all these workers to Pogozhev's figures brings the total Petersburg factory labor force in 1902 to 161,924. This figure was then subtracted from the total number of workers in the St. Petersburg city census, giving us the approximate number of artisanal workers. Individual garret-masters *(odinochki)* have been added to the artisanal category, making a total of 150,709 artisanal workers in the capital at the turn of the century. Apprentices are included in the data for both cities. The figures for the total labor force in manufacturing apply only to workers in production; sales and clerical employees in the manufacturing sector are excluded from the table. Additional information on methods used to obtain these data can be found in tables 2 and 3.

in St. Petersburg, more than two-fifths of the Moscow metalworkers, and nearly all the workers in the Petersburg and Moscow apparel trades, representing the second largest aggregate group in the manufacturing sector of each city.[6]

Some recent studies—both Soviet and Western—have attempted to expand the definition of the Russian working class to include *all* workers in the manufacturing sector (factory and artisanal), as well as those employed in construction.[7] This approach provides a more comprehensive picture of the working class, but workers in other sectors of the urban economy are still excluded.

From the point of view of the present study, neither of these definitions will suffice for an understanding or even a description of the collective behavior of the heterogeneous groups that took part in the workers' movement after the turn of the century. Workers' collective organizations and activities drew the participation of far more diverse segments of the urban labor force than can be encompassed by the factory population alone or even by workers in the manufacturing sector as a whole. The participants in the Soviets of Workers' Deputies, trade unions, strikes, and demonstrations included not only workers from metal and textile factories, but also printers and tailors, carpenters and plumbers, salesclerks and coachmen. A definition of the working class that does not incorporate all of these constituent elements cannot do justice to the scope and significance of the events that polarized Russian society at the beginning of the twentieth century and challenged the very foundations of the autocratic system.

This study takes as its point of departure a definition of the urban working class that is broader than either of those discussed above, and more attentive to the problem of disaggregating the constituent elements within this social category. In adopting a broader definition than is customary in the literature, I am seeking to establish an approximate congruence between the analytical category of class and the meaning of that term within the context of contemporary social, economic, and political life. The composition of the working class, as defined here, includes a multiplicity of groups in manufacturing, sales-clerical, construction, transportation, communication, and service occupations who belonged to the hired labor force and were engaged in manual or low-level white-collar jobs.

---

[6]See tables 2 and 3.

[7]Semanov, *Peterburgskie rabochie,* and Shuster, *Peterburgskie rabochie,* are two Soviet works that apply this broader definition. Among Western scholars, this definition is applied by Gerald Surh, "Petersburg Workers in 1905: Strikes, Workplace Democracy, and the Revolution," Ph.D. dissertation, University of California, 1979.

By virtue of their statements and actions, all of these groups can be construed as part of a larger social collectivity that contemporaries called the *rabochii klass* (working class). My definition of the working class takes into account, therefore, both the shared characteristics of this group and the common experiences that induced highly diverse segments of the Petersburg and Moscow labor force to "feel and articulate the identity of their interests as between themselves, and as against other men whose interests [were] different from (and usually opposed to) theirs."[8]

WORKERS IN THE MANUFACTURING SECTOR

There were two major groups within the manufacturing sector of the urban economy at the beginning of the twentieth century: factory workers *(fabrichno-zavodskie rabochie)* and artisans *(remeslenniki)*. Generally speaking, factory and artisanal workers could be distinguished by a variety of circumstances, including the size of the enterprise, the character of the labor force, the extent of mechanization and division of labor, and conditions at the workplace. When contemporaries contrasted factory and artisanal workers, they were describing not only differences in labor force composition, labor process, and working conditions, but also juridical distinctions with important practical consequences for workers. Those employed in firms designated as "factories" by the Factory Inspectorate—an agency of the Ministry of Finance prior to 1905 and of the Ministry of Trade and Industry thereafter[9]—were subject to government legislation regulat-

[8]E. P. Thompson, *The Making of the English Working Class* (New York, 1964), p. 9.

[9]The Factory Inspectorate was established by the law of June 1, 1882, but it was not until the promulgation of the law of June 3, 1886, that the functions of the Factory Inspectorate were fully elaborated. In this law, the Inspectorate was charged with examining and approving wage rates and rules of internal factory order, adopting measures to prevent disputes and misunderstandings between factory owners and workers, and initiating court action against those who violated the rules. M. I. Tugan-Baranovsky, *The Russian Factory in the 19th Century*, translated from the 3d Russian edition by Arthur Levin and Claora S. Levin (Homewood, Ill., 1970), pp. 329–330. Another important task of the Factory Inspectorate was to collect data on factories and the factory labor force. These data were published in summary form in the annual *Svod otchetov fabrichnykh inspektorov* (St. Petersburg, 1900–1915), the *Spisok fabrik i zavodov evropeiskoi Rossii* (St. Petersburg, 1903), and the *Spisok fabrik i zavodov Rossii 1910 g. Po ofitsial'nym dannym fabrichnogo, podatnogo i gornogo nadzora* (Moscow, St. Petersburg, Warsaw, n.d.).

ing working time, child labor, and various terms and conditions of employment. These regulations placed restrictions on employer prerogatives and provided factory workers with opportunities for legal redress that were not available to artisanal groups.

Although the contrast between factory and artisanal workers occupied a central place in contemporary descriptions of the labor force, the criteria used to distinguish these two categories were often vague and inconsistent. Before 1901 the Factory Inspectorate defined a "factory" as any manufacturing enterprise that employed fifteen or more workers or utilized engine-powered machinery. In 1901 the Ministry of Finance instructed the Inspectorate to modify its classification system to include as a "factory" any manufacturing enterprise with twenty or more workers, regardless of the type of machinery.[10] This definition was exceedingly broad, allowing for the inclusion of highly diverse enterprises with widely differing characteristics and conditions. An unmechanized bakery with twenty workers, and a giant metalworking plant with five thousand workers and extensive mechanization, both qualified as "factories" according to either of the definitions noted above. Moreover, the Inspectorate did not apply these criteria consistently throughout the Empire, or even within each city or district.[11]

To make matters worse, other contemporary data collections, such as municipal censuses, sometimes ignored the distinction between factory and artisanal workers altogether.[12] These circumstances present formidable obstacles in the path of a labor historian seeking to differentiate factory and artisanal groups. And yet it would not do justice to the realities of working-class life at the turn of the century to ignore the significant differences that separated these two types of workers and workplace situations.

Using contemporary data collections, particularly the Factory Inspectorate reports and municipal censuses, it is possible to arrive at an approximation of the number of factory and artisanal workers in each city at the beginning of the

[10]For a discussion of the problems and limitations of Factory Inspectorate data, see Semanov, *Peterburgskie rabochie,* pp. 10–31; Shuster, *Peterburgskie rabochie,* pp. 6–17, especially p. 7, n. 4; V. Alymov, "K voprosu o polozhenii truda v remeslennom proizvodstve," *Narodnoe khoziaistvo,* Book 6 (November-December, 1904), pp. 3–6.

[11]See A. V. Pogozhev, *Uchet, chislennost' i sostav rabochikh v Rossii: Materialy po statistike truda* (St. Petersburg, 1906), pp. 17–18, for a discussion of these inconsistencies.

[12]In the 1900 St. Petersburg city census, for example, both factory and artisanal workers are combined into one category, *rabochie.* Only individual garret-masters *(odinochki)* are listed separately. On the discrepancies in the criteria applied by contemporary data collections, see Pogozhev, *Uchet,* pp. vii-xxvi.

twentieth century (table 1). While these figures are not precise, they illustrate the relative size of these two important groups. Workers in both privately owned and state-owned enterprises (that is, munitions and shipbuilding plants, railroad workshops, the government-operated printing firm, and factories producing alcohol) have been included in the factory totals. The data on artisanal workers are discussed below, but suffice it to note that table 1 includes workers employed in artisanal workshops and skilled construction trades, as well as garret-masters, who carried on their trade in their own lodging under a putting-out system.[13]

In assessing table 1, we must keep in mind that an indeterminate number of enterprises were arbitrarily placed in one category or the other by contemporary data collections. More than merely a statistical problem, the uncertain status of these enterprises is indicative of the difficulties in drawing clear boundaries between factory and artisanal workers. As we shall see further on, there were many firms that occupied an ambiguous position in these transitional urban economies, combining features of both artisanal and factory situations.

The Artisanal Labor Force

Little is known about the tens of thousands of workers who labored in artisanal trades, although they exceeded the number of factory workers in Moscow and nearly equalled them in the capital. Artisans were an elusive group, bypassed by most data collections and seldom eager to draw attention to their activities. In the hope of evading taxation, they fled the census-takers and local police registration procedures, sometimes leaving no statistical trace of their existence. At the turn of the century there were 150,709 artisanal workers in St. Petersburg and 151,359 in Moscow (table 1). These figures probably err on the conservative side, and it is likely that the total number of artisanal workers in these cities was even higher.

Artisanal trades had three common characteristics. First, production was carried on mainly by hand with little division of labor. Second, the tasks of the trade required considerable skill acquired by means of lengthy apprenticeship

---

[13]Only garret-masters who worked alone *(odinochki)* or with family members are included in the artisanal labor force. The position of the garret-master was frequently temporary. Because of the loss of employment or the desire to remain with other family members (the cramped conditions in workshops did not easily accommodate entire families), some workers set up shop on their own. As outworkers, their position was exceedingly precarious, and they often moved in and out of workshops and subcontracting shops in the course of their working lives.

training. Finally, the labor force was stratified hierarchically, with apprentices *(ucheniki)*, journeymen *(podmaster'ia)*, and master craftsmen *(mastera)*. For virtually all artisanal workers, including garret-masters, this hierarchical subdivision remained the basic, though not the only, line of stratification within the labor force of a given trade.

The tripartite division of artisans into apprentices, journeymen, and master craftsmen originated in the guild system, first introduced into Russia by government decree in the early eighteenth century.[14] By the beginning of the twentieth century, the guilds were in steep decline, and whereas twenty-one guilds had once functioned in the capital, only eight remained in 1900.[15] Guild membership was confined to a small proportion of the artisans. Excluding master craftsmen, who were generally workshop owners and employers of labor, guild artisans (journeymen and apprentices) constituted 28 percent of the total artisanal labor force in the capital and 16 percent in Moscow at the turn of the century.[16]

With the onset of industrialization in the second half of the nineteenth century and the spread of large-scale capitalist production, two important developments took place in artisanal trades: the shift of some artisanal activities into a factory setting, and the proliferation of subcontracting arrangements. The printing industry provides a good illustration of the first phenomenon. Beginning in the 1870s, mechanical as opposed to hand-operated printing presses were introduced into the Petersburg and Moscow printing industry.[17] The availability of mechanical printing presses did not coincide, however, with the mechanization of typesetting. The first typesetting machines were introduced only in 1906, and until that time typesetting remained a highly skilled, labor-intensive occupation.

A rapid expansion of the printing industry during the closing decades of the nineteenth century increased the demand for typesetters. On the eve of 1905,

[14]Reginald E. Zelnik, *Labor and Society in Tsarist Russia: The Factory Workers of St. Petersburg, 1855–1870* (Stanford, Cal., 1971), pp. 12, 15; K. A. Pazhitnov, *Problema remeslennykh tsekhov v zakonodatel'stve russkogo absoliutizma* (Moscow, 1952), chap. 3. See below, chapter 2, for further discussion of artisanal guilds.

[15]*Trudy pervogo vserossiiskogo s"ezda po remeslennoi promyshlennosti v Peterburge*, vol. 3 (St. Petersburg, 1900), p. 131.

[16]*Remeslenniki i remeslennoe upravlenie v Rossii* (Petrograd, 1916), p. 32; *Obzor po gorodu Moskve za 1905* (Moscow, 1907), p. 25. There were 41,800 guild journeymen and apprentices in the capital and 24,500 in Moscow at the turn of the century.

[17]V. V. Sher, *Istoriia professional'nogo dvizheniia rabochikh pechatnogo dela v Moskve* (Moscow, 1911), pp. 7–8; *Istoriia Leningradskogo soiuza rabochikh poligraficheskogo proizvodstva*, Book 1: 1904–1907 gg. (henceforth ILS), (Leningrad, 1925), pp. 66–67; B. P. Orlov, *Poligraficheskaia promyshlennost' Moskvy: Ocherk razvitiia do 1917 goda* (Moscow, 1953), chap. 5.

about one out of every three or four printing workers was a typesetter.[18] Typesetting persisted as an essentially artisanal occupation, but it was now increasingly carried on in large firms where mechanical presses were extensively utilized. The typesetters belonged to a category that we shall designate as "factory artisans" because they preserved many of the traditions and practices of craftsmen, including the three characteristics enumerated above. For statistical purposes, the "factory artisans" are classified with the factory rather than the artisanal labor force, but these highly skilled workers shared a number of common features with those employed in artisanal workshops.

While some artisanal trades shifted out of the traditional small workshop and into the factory setting, other trades moved from the workshop into the subcontracting shop *(masterskaia khoziaichikov)*. The proliferation of subcontracting arrangements was especially evident in the apparel and shoemaking trades at the end of the nineteenth century.[19] But this type of modified putting-out system could also be found in metalworking, woodworking, and other industries.[20]

Subcontracting arrangements in the apparel and shoemaking trades coincided with the growing demand for the mass production of ready-made, low-quality goods. As elsewhere in Europe during the initial phase of industrialization, the increased volume of production in apparel and shoemaking was not initially achieved by means of the introduction of a factory system. Instead, subcontracting shops and garret-masters proliferated, working on contract for large wholesale and retail marketing firms and producing inexpensive ready-made commodities for the new mass market.

Despite the many changes taking place in artisanal trades at the beginning of the twentieth century, the traditional workshop *(masterskaia khoziaev)* catering to the retail market was still widespread in both St. Petersburg and Moscow on the

[18]P. V. Vasil'ev-Severianin, "Tarifnaia bor'ba soiuza rabochikh pechatnogo dela v 1905–1907 gg.," *Materialy po istorii professional'nogo dvizheniia v Peterburge za 1905-1907 gg.: Sbornik* (henceforth *MIPDP*) (Leningrad, 1926), p. 3. V. A. Svavitskii and V. Sher, *Ocherk polozheniia rabochikh pechatnogo dela v Moskve (Po dannym ankety, proizvedennoi obshchestvom rabochikh graficheskikh iskusstv v 1907 godu)* (St. Petersburg, 1909), table 1, provides data for 1907 showing that typesetters constituted 23 percent of the Moscow printing workers (all categories).

[19]For a description of this development in the Moscow apparel trades, see E. A. Oliunina, *Portnovskii promysel v Moskve i v derevniakh Moskovskoi i Riazanskoi gubernii: Materialy k istorii domashnei promyshlennosti v Rossii* (Moscow, 1914), chap. 2. See also S. M. Gruzdev, *Trud i bor'ba shveinikov v Petrograde 1905-1916 gg.* (Leningrad, 1929), chap. 1.

[20]For an account of this type of arrangement in metalworking, see Kanatchikov *Iz istoriia*, pp. 64–68. On woodworking, see Iu. K. Milonov and M. Rakovskii, *Istoriia Moskovskogo professional'nogo soiuza rabochikh derevoobdelochnikov*, vyp. 1 (Moscow, 1928).

eve of 1905. Owned by a master craftsman and producing custom-made, high-quality goods, mainly for the more prosperous urban consumers, these work-shops could be found in tailoring, shoemaking, jewelrymaking, watchmaking, carpentry, and other trades.[21]

The largest employer of artisanal labor was the garment industry. In each city, more workers labored in the apparel trades than in any other branch of manufac-turing, except for metalworking in the capital and textiles in Moscow. The construction trades ranked as the second largest employer of artisanal labor in St. Petersburg, followed by leatherworking and shoemaking, woodworking, and metalworking. In Moscow, the leatherworking, woodworking, construction and metalworking trades also employed many artisanal workers (tables 2 and 3).

Metalworking presents an interesting case from the point of view of artisanal labor. The metalworking industry usually conjures up an image of enormous plants with many hundreds or even thousands of workers. And indeed, if one considers only those firms large enough to be covered by the Factory Inspector-ate, the degree of labor concentration in this industry was considerable. But metalworking was both an artisanal and a factory industry, especially in Moscow, where 14,645 out of 32,647 metalworkers (45 percent) belonged to the artisanal rather than the factory sector.

Virtually all artisanal trades required some degree of skill acquired through apprenticeship training. But in trades where subcontracting shops had prolif-erated, such as apparel and shoemaking, there was a gradual decline in the level of skill and the quality of training. Nevertheless, in comparison with factory industries, the artisanal labor force was still relatively homogeneous at the turn of the century in the sense that almost everyone had to serve an apprenticeship and acquire at least minimal skills of the trade.

Skill and gender were closely related. Women workers almost universally held jobs requiring lower levels of skill than their male counterparts. In the apparel trades, for example, where women constituted about two-thirds of the labor force in each city, female labor was concentrated in subspecialties with relatively low skill requirements.[22] Some artisanal trades, such as baking, leatherworking

---

[21]In addition to sources cited above in notes 19 and 20, see N. Mamontov, "Dvizhenie rabochikh po obrabotke blagorodnykh metallov v Moskve," in *Materialy po istorii professional'nogo dvizheniia v Rossii* (henceforth *MIPDR*), 5 vols. (Moscow, 1924–1927), vol. 5, pp. 180–184; Ivan Belousov, *Ushedshaia Moskva: Zapiski po lichnym vospominaniiam s nachala 1870 godov* (Moscow, 1927); A. S. Kurskaia, *Proizvodstvo chasov v Moskve i Moskovskoi gubernii: Materialy k istorii kustarnoi pro-myshlennosti v Rossii* (Moscow, 1914).

[22]*S.-Peterburg po perepisi*, pp. 66–69, 134–137, and *Perepis' Moskvy*, pp. 130–131, 153–154. On the position of women in the Moscow apparel trades, see Oliunina, *Portnovskii promysel*, pp. 171–

and shoemaking, jewelrymaking, printing, and woodworking, were almost exclusively male in the early 1900s.

Unlike their factory counterparts, most artisanal workers were widely dispersed in a multitude of small shops and garrets. To some extent, the geographical clustering of shops in commercial neighborhoods served to counteract this dispersion. Workshops catering to the retail trade, in particular, tended to be concentrated in certain inner-city neighborhoods, such as the City (Gorodskaia) District in Moscow near the Kremlin (Kitai-Gorod) and St. Petersburg's Nevskii Prospect. Subcontracting shops and garret-masters, by contrast, were usually situated on the outskirts of the city in working-class districts where rooms and apartments could be rented inexpensively and a garret-master could set up shop in the corner of a room.[23]

The Factory Labor Force

There were 161,924 factory workers in the capital at the turn of the century and 111,719 in Moscow, constituting 52 percent and 42 percent of the manufacturing labor force in each city, respectively. One out of every nine Petersburg inhabitants, and one out of every eleven in Moscow, was employed in a factory, and their number was steadily increasing. Between 1881 and 1900—but primarily in the 1890s—the factory population in the capital grew by 82 percent, while Moscow's industrial labor force increased by 51 percent.[24]

Unlike their counterparts in artisanal workshops, factory workers were often employed in enterprises with a high concentration of labor (table 4). Approximately one out of three factory workers in each city could be found in an enterprise with more than one thousand workers. Nearly half were located in firms with one hundred to one thousand workers. The degree of labor concentration per enterprise in St. Petersburg and Moscow exceeded that of European Russia as a whole and was far higher than in neighboring Germany, where only 6.6 percent of the factory labor force was employed in firms with more than a thousand workers in 1895.[25]

Labor concentration in individual enterprises was further accentuated by

---

172, and Bonnell, ed., *The Russian Worker*, chap. 4. Women in the Russian labor force are discussed in Rose L. Glickman, *Russian Factory Women: Workplace and Society 1880-1914* (Berkeley and Los Angeles, 1984).

[23]See *Sovremennoe khoziaistvo goroda Moskvy* (Moscow, 1913), p. 16, and Bater, *St. Petersburg,* especially maps 43 and 44, for the location of Petersburg jewelry workshops and bakeries.

[24]Surh, "Petersburg Workers in 1905," p. 7.

[25]Pogozhev, *Uchet,* p. 46.

Table 2

Distribution of Petersburg Factory and
Artisanal Workers by Branch of Production,
1900–1902

Industry	Total Workers	Factory Workers	Artisanal Workers
1. Apparel	45,839	55	45,784
2. Chemicals and minerals	15,136	12,997	2,139
3. Construction (skilled trades)	32,287	0	32,287
4. Food and tobacco	23,186	14,049	9,137
5. Leather and shoes	22,583	3,586	18,997
6. Metal and machine	80,834	70,032	10,802
7. Paper	5,261	5,236	25
8. Precious metals	3,509	211	3,298
9. Printing and binding	18,048	8,831	9,217
10. Textiles	36,716	36,036	680
11. Wood	24,146	6,080	18,066
12. Miscellaneous (no designation)	5,088	4,811	277
Total	312,633	161,924	150,709

Sources: The method used to compile the data in table 2 is described in table 1. Several additional comments are in order here. The city census data *(S.-Peterburg po perepisi,* pp. 38–137) have been reorganized to provide more useful categories and to coincide with data for Moscow (table 3). Workers employed in precious metalworking, for example, have been removed from the metalworking category; electrical workers have been added to metalworkers (the census already includes railroad shop workers in this category); bindery workers have been classified together with printers, and leather workers with shoemakers. Unlike the Moscow census, the St. Petersburg census does not provide a separate listing for workers in gas and water plants. I have added to Pogozhev's figures the workers employed in the large, state paper-and-printing-factory, Ekspeditsiia zagotovleniia gosudarstvennykh bumag. In 1899, the Ekspeditsiia factory employed 3,700 individuals in all classifications. Of these, 2,427 were workers employed in both the printing and paper sections of this large firm; there were, in addition, 59 apprentices. I have been unable to locate a breakdown of the Ekspeditsiia labor force into printing and paper workers, although the subdivision of white-collar employees into the paper and printing sections of the firm is available *(Entsiklopedicheskii slovar',* vol. 40 [St. Petersburg, 1904], p. 283). Using this as a guide, I have estimated that approximately 1,500 of the Ekspeditsiia workers were employed in the printing departments and about 900 in paper. These workers have been added to the total number of factory workers in each category. In two cases, paper and textiles, the number of factory workers (based on the *Spisok* and on Pogozhev's calculations) actually exceeded the total number of workers shown in the St. Petersburg city census. Whereas the census recorded only 2,040 workers in the paper and carton industry, the *Spisok* shows a total of 3,564 factory workers in these categories. Similarly there are 12,875 factory workers in cotton-spinning mills listed by the census, but the *Spisok* shows a

Table 2, Sources *(continued)*:

considerably higher number—17,342. Since it is not possible to resolve this discrepancy on the basis of available sources, I have used the larger total provided by the *Spisok*. The only artisanal workers in these categories, therefore, are those listed separately in the census as individual garret-masters *(odinochki)*.

Table 3
Distribution of Moscow Factory and Artisanal Workers by Branch of Production, 1902

Industry	Total Workers	Factory Workers	Artisanal Workers
1. Apparel	53,397	1,823	51,574
2. Chemicals and minerals	7,841	6,056	1,785
3. Construction (skilled trades)	12,555	258	12,297
4. Food and tobacco	24,164	14,627	9,537
5. Leather and shoes	22,309	3,107	19,202
6. Metal and machine	32,647	18,002	14,645
7. Paper	1,857	1,748	109
8. Precious metals	6,554	2,017	4,537
9. Printing and binding	12,384	7,186	5,198
10. Textiles	59,540	51,932	7,608
11. Wood	17,443	2,541	14,902
12. Water and gas	1,673	395	1,278
13. Miscellaneous	10,714	2,027	8,687
Total	263,078	111,719	151,359

Source: *Perepis' Moskvy*, pp. 116–161. Included in the category of "artisanal" are the following groups as listed in this city census: nonfactory hired workers, individual garret-masters *(odinochki)*, and garret-masters working only with members of their families, together with these family members. Certain categories shown in this table differ slightly from the ones used by the census. Workers in precious metals have been removed from the metalworking category and listed separately; electrical workers and workers in railroad shops have been included in the metalworking category; leather workers have been grouped together with shoemakers (instead of with apparel workers); bindery workers have been transferred from paper to printing; plumbers have been moved from gas and water to construction; and finally, sanitation workers, workers in scientific and artistic manufacture, and undesignated workers have been classified as miscellaneous. In all cases, these alterations have been made so that the categories in this table and in table 2 correspond.

geographical concentration within each city. Factory workers tended to live in certain districts, for example, the Vyborgskaia, Vasil'evskaia, Aleksandro-Nevskaia, and Peterburgskaia districts of the capital, the Presnenskaia, Lefortovskaia, and Zamoskvorech'e (Iakimanskaia and Piatnitskaia) districts of Moscow. These industrial neighborhoods, often situated on the periphery of the city, had a grim character that set them off from the rest of the urban environment. As one Petersburg worker put it:

You can always tell when you are getting close to a factory because of the buildings: the dirty taverns, and the even dirtier shops and beer halls. A little further on you notice smoke rising from the factory chimneys, then you see the chimneys and finally the factory building itself.[26]

In the capital, the metalworking industry was the largest employer of factory labor. There were 70,000 metalworkers in enterprises classified as factories, and nearly 11,000 in artisanal firms (see table 2). Divided into five major branches—munitions, shipbuilding, railroad construction, machine building and electrical engineering—the Petersburg metalworking industry included a number of plants with exceptionally high concentrations of labor, such as the Putilov plant in the Narvskii district, with 12,000 workers, and the Nevskii shipbuilding and machine plant in the Aleksandro-Nevskaia district, employing about 4,000 workers.

The Nevskii and Putilov plants operated under private ownership, but there were a number of major enterprises owned and operated by the state. The Baltiiskii shipbuilding plant, for example, employed about 5,000 workers and was directed by the Ministry of the Navy.[27] Even enterprises in private hands were closely connected to the government by virtue of their heavy reliance on state orders.

A distinctive characteristic of the capital's metalworking industry (and Moscow's as well) was the predominance of skilled workers, nearly all of them male. At the turn of the century, as many as four out of every five metalworkers in some plants belonged to the ranks of skilled labor.[28] These workers, like their counterparts in artisanal trades, required prolonged training to master the specialized skills demanded of a patternmaker, metalfitter, lathe operator, or smelter.

---

[26]P. Timofeev, *Chem zhivet zavodskii rabochii* (St. Petersburg, 1906), p. 19. On the residential patterns of factory workers, see Bater, *St. Petersburg; Sovremennoe khoziastvo goroda Moskvy*, p. 16.

[27]Other large state-owned metalworking enterprises are listed in table 1.

[28]Timofeev, *Chem zhivet*, p. 11.

Table 4

*Distribution of Factory Workers by Size of
Enterprise (in Percent) in Petersburg
Province, Moscow, and European Russia*

NO. OF WORKERS PER ENTERPRISE

	0–49	50–99	100–499	500–999	1,000 +
Petersburg province (1901–1905)	6.7	8.1	31.8	15.5	37.9
Moscow city (1910–1911)	8.0	10.4	30.4	17.3	34.2
European Russia (1901–1905)	14.1	9.8	28.5	16.4	31.2

Sources: Data on the concentration of factory workers per enterprise in St. Petersburg and Moscow at the turn of the century are not available, because Factory Inspectorate statistics on this point apply only to the province as a whole, rather than to each city. The data for Petersburg province do, however, provide an approximation of the extent of labor concentration in city enterprises during the period 1901–1905. This cannot be said of Moscow province, where a multitude of very large textile mills were situated outside city boundaries. Moscow city data are available for 1910–1911, and although labor concentration had undoubtedly increased somewhat since the turn of the century, the 1910–1911 figures furnish a very rough estimate of the earlier situation. Semanov, *Peterburgskie rabochie*, p. 37; S. I. Antonova, *Vliianie stolypinskoi agrarnoi reformy na izmeneniia v sostave rabochego klassa: Po materialam Moskovskoi gubernii, 1906-1913 gg.* (Moscow, 1951), p. 156. Semanov's data are based on Factory Inspectorate reports for the years 1901–1905. Antonova's source is *Statisticheskii ezhegodnik goroda Moskvy* (Moscow, 1913); her data on Moscow total 100.3 percent.

The textile industry occupied first place in Moscow's industrial economy, employing 46 percent of the factory labor force, or nearly 52,000 workers (table 3). Some of the mills had an extremely high concentration of labor. The largest mill, the Prokhorovskaia Trekhgornaia firm in the Presnenskaia district, employed 6,000 workers, but there were eleven other mills in the city with 1,000 or more workers. Only a small proportion of the labor force in the textile industry consisted of skilled workers, such as knitters, ribbonweavers, and machinists. Most mill hands in cotton, wool, silk, and other textile factories were unskilled or semiskilled workers who needed little training to acquire competency in their jobs. Forty-four percent of the Moscow labor force in this industry was female, and women were concentrated in the lowest-skilled and lowest-paying jobs.

Notwithstanding the importance of metalworking in the capital and of textiles in Moscow, these were not the only major employers of factory labor in each city at the beginning of the twentieth century. St. Petersburg had a sizable labor force in textile production, while metalworking ranked second highest as an employer of factory labor in Moscow. In both cities, the food and tobacco processing industries also accounted for large contingents of factory labor. This branch of manufacturing encompassed large, highly concentrated firms in candymaking, teapacking, and tobacco processing with five hundred to one thousand workers and numerous small firms in baking, sausagemaking, and other food-related industries. Candymaking employed many adult women workers who performed unskilled and semiskilled jobs; teapacking relied primarily on the labor of young women and juveniles.[29] Tobacco processing was also carried on primarily in large firms. More than half of the labor force was female, most of them unskilled and semiskilled.[30] Here, as elsewhere, men predominated in jobs requiring greater training and specialization.

The baking industry was still largely artisanal at the turn of the century, despite the appearance of a few large firms, such as the Filippov bakery in Moscow, employing more than 350 workers in 1899.[31] In 1902, 1,546 Moscow bakers were classified as factory workers and 7,929 as artisans.[32] Nearly all bakery workers (both factory and artisanal) were male.

Other leading employers of factory labor in both cities included the chemical, mineral, paper, and printing industries (see tables 2 and 3). The printing industry, with nearly nine thousand factory workers in Petersburg and more than seven thousand in Moscow, deserves particular attention because of the important role played by printers in the events of 1905 and afterward. This industry encompassed two distinct subbranches: printing (typographical and lithographical trades) and binding. A large number of printing workers in both cities were employed in firms designated as factories, particularly in Moscow where 91

---

[29]*Professional'noe dvizhenie Moskovskikh pishchevikov v gody pervoi revoliutsii*, sbornik 1 (Moscow, 1927), p. 42. According to municipal census data, women constituted 30 percent of the labor force in the Petersburg candymaking industry, 53 percent in Moscow. Data on the female contingent in teapacking are not available, because the censuses do not list this group in a separate category.

[30]Women made up 85 percent of the 7,318 factory workers in the capital's tobacco industry, and 60 percent of the 3,397 factory workers in this industry in Moscow. In addition to the large tobacco factories, there were cigaretmakers, the so-called *chubuki*, who were employed in small artisanal-type enterprises. Ibid., p. 190.

[31]Shuster, *Peterburgskie rabochie*, p. 7. Changes in this industry are described in *Professional'noe dvizhenie Moskovskikh pishchevikov*, pp. 101–102.

[32]*Perepis' Moskvy*, chast' 1, vyp. 2, pp. 128–129, 150–151.

percent were so classified. Most binders, by contrast, were employed in artisanal firms (table 5).

A relatively high level of labor concentration could be found in printing establishments within the factory sector. In Moscow, for example, 63 percent of the printing firms classified as factories employed one hundred or more workers, 13 percent employed fifty-one to one hundred workers, and the remaining 23 percent employed fifty or fewer workers.[33] Most of the workers in these large printing houses were employed in typographical and lithographical occupations, and nearly all of them were skilled and male. Bindery workers constituted a more diversified group, which included both skilled craftsmen and a large contingent of unskilled and semiskilled workers, some of them female.

The factory labor force in St. Petersburg and Moscow at the turn of the century—like the manufacturing labor force as a whole—was characterized by contrasts in composition and concentration. The capital's metalworking industry and Moscow's textile industry exemplify differences in skill and gender, although both shared a similar high level of labor concentration. Other important industries, such as food and tobacco processing and printing, illustrate the variability of labor concentration and labor-force composition within a single branch of production.

These contrasting features of key factory industries had important consequences for the men and women who labored within them. "The world of the textile factory," observed one contemporary, "is completely different from that of the large metalworking plant . . . and these two groups of workers should never be confused."[34] There was no such thing as *the* factory worker at the turn of the century. Instead, St. Petersburg and Moscow harbored a great diversity of factory groups, facing many different kinds of work situations and internally differentiated along such lines as skill and gender.

WORKERS IN SALES-CLERICAL OCCUPATIONS

Sales-clerical workers, like the artisans, constitute a vague and elusive category. The multiplicity of sales-clerical occupations belonged to five major subgroups:

[33]Mark David Steinberg, "Moscow Printing Workers: The September Strikes of 1903 and 1905." Unpublished seminar paper, University of California, Berkeley, Spring 1980, p. 6.

[34]Timofeev, *Chem zhivet*, p. 4. For a similar statement, see Aleksei Buzinov, *Za Nevskoi zastavoi: Zapiski rabochego* (Moscow and Leningrad, 1930), p. 20. The Buzinov memoir, published in 1930, was written after the October Revolution, about 1919.

Table 5

Distribution of the Factory and Artisanal
Labor Force in the Petersburg and Moscow
Printing Trades, 1900–1902

| | FACTORY | | ARTISANAL | | TOTAL |
	Number	Percent	Number	Percent	
	St. Petersburg				
Total	8,831	48.9	9,217	51.1	18,048
Printing	7,859	60.7	5,086	39.3	12,945
Binding	972	19.0	4,131	81.0	5,103
	Moscow				
Total	7,186	58.0	5,198	42.0	12,384
Printing	6,720	91.3	644	8.7	7,364
Binding	466	9.3	4,554	90.7	5,020

Sources: Data for this table are derived from the 1900 St. Petersburg municipal census and the 1902 Moscow municipal census, using methods described in tables 1 and 2.

(1) salesclerks *(prikazchiki)*, (2) cashiers *(kassiry)*, (3) bookkeepers *(bukhgaltery)*, (4) clerks *(kontorshchiki)*, and (5) apprentices *(ucheniki)*. Workers in all these groups together numbered 109,479 in the capital and 85,821 in Moscow at the beginning of the twentieth century (table 6).

Salesclerks represented the largest of the five subgroups. There were nearly 60,000 salesclerks in St. Petersburg and more than 40,000 in Moscow, employed in a multitude of retail, wholesale, industrial, and cooperative firms.[35] Thus, approximately one half of the sales-clerical workers in each city were employed as salesclerks. About 90 percent of the salesclerks were men. Women could be found mostly in retail stores, where they performed low-skilled jobs.[36]

[35]*S.-Peterburg po perepisi*, pp. 1–167, and *Perepis' Moskvy*, pp. 46–115. The different categorizations of data in the Petersburg and Moscow censuses have made it necessary to use different approaches for estimating the number of salesclerks in each city. For Moscow, I have included all *prikazchiki* in commercial firms, garret-masters, peddlers, family-employed workers in sales occupations, and workers *(rabochie)* in sales firms. For St. Petersburg, where occupational categories are not as disaggregated, the figure for salesclerks includes all workers *(rabochie)* and garret-masters *(odinochki)* in sales occupations, as well as peddlers and vendors.

[36]When the Imperial Russian Technical Society collected data from various cities on the conditions of sales workers, three categories were used: "salesclerks [male] of the first rank," "salesclerks [male] of the second rank," and "female salesclerks." Rashin, *Formirovanie*, p. 167.

Table 6
Distribution of the Labor Force in
St. Petersburg and Moscow at the Turn of the Century

	St. Petersburg	Moscow
Factory Workers	161,924	111,719
Artisanal Workers	150,709	151,359
Sales-Clerical Workers	109,479	85,821
Unskilled Construction Workers	2,893	3,127
Transportation Workers	46,483	49,799
Service Workers	166,479	133,167
Communications Workers	3,689	2,530
Total Hired Labor Force	641,656	537,522

Sources: *S.-Peterburg po perepisi,* pp. 1–167, and *Perepis' Moskvy,* pp. 46–115. Workers in skilled construction trades—32,287 in St. Petersburg and 12,297 in Moscow—are included in the figures for artisanal workers for reasons discussed below. The figures for transportation workers exclude those employed in railroad workshops, who have been placed together with metalworkers in factory enterprises. Included under the rubric of sales-clerical workers are office employees in industrial establishments and all sales and clerical workers in commercial, financial, professional, and governmental firms and institutions. Clerical workers in the transportation, communication, and service sectors are not included here; they are counted, instead, with other workers in those industries. Municipal census data for St. Petersburg make it impossible to separate the small number of directors, supervisors, and technical personnel from sales-clerical employees.

Bookkeepers, clerks, cashiers, and salesclerks in fashionable retail establishments were a significant cut above the mass of salesclerks. Almost exclusively male, they occupied an intermediary position between the "worker" and the "professional," prompting one contemporary labor activist to describe them as a "semiproletarian stratum."[37] Their ambiguous class position, both in the way they viewed themselves and the way other, more distinctly "proletarian," elements viewed them, came to the surface in the course of 1905.

Sales-clerical workers, like their artisanal counterparts, were widely dispersed in a multitude of firms. Most retail shops were very small, employing no more than a handful of salesclerks and other personnel. Roughly two-thirds of all the retail commercial establishments in St. Petersburg and Moscow sold foodstuffs,

[37]V. Sviatlovskii, *Professional'noe dvizhenie v Rossii* (St. Petersburg, 1907), p. 105.

and these firms were situated throughout the city. A few large retail firms were established at the end of the nineteenth century, such as the Muir and Merrilees department store in Moscow, but most transactions still took place in small shops.

Sprawling public markets could also be found in each city at the turn of the century, with stalls selling everything from food to apparel. The street vendor, with his horse- or hand-drawn cart, was another important channel for commercial transactions. A colorful part of the urban scene, street vendors hawked their wares in all neighborhoods of the city.

Of course, not all sales-clerical workers were employed in retail commerce. Many found jobs in wholesale firms, industrial enterprises, banks, insurance companies, and municipal and state offices. They were present, in fact, in nearly all parts of urban life, and their number was steadily increasing with the expansion and diversification of the economy.

WORKERS IN THE CONSTRUCTION, TRANSPORTATION,
COMMUNICATION, AND SERVICE SECTORS

The labor force in the construction industry consisted of migrant workers, most of them unskilled, and a permanent core of workers, most of them skilled. During the spring and summer months, when the weather improved and construction could proceed at full pace, the labor force expanded with the influx of semipeasant workers from the surrounding countryside. Most of the seasonal workers were unskilled laborers who arrived in the city each spring at the start of the construction season and departed for their villages the following autumn when construction work subsided. The exact number of seasonal workers cannot be established, since only the relatively small contingent of year-round unskilled construction workers was included in the municipal census (table 6).

Apart from migrant laborers, each city had a more or less permanent core of skilled construction workers: 32,287 in St. Petersburg and 12,297 in Moscow around the turn of the century.[38] They practiced such trades as carpentry, masonry, plumbing, marble and granite carving, and decorative plastering. Each of these subspecialties was an artisanal trade in its own right, with the characteristics earlier ascribed to artisanal workers, namely, a production process based mainly on hand labor with little division of labor, skills acquired through

[38]*S.-Peterburg po perepisi,* pp. 10–11, and *Perepis' Moskvy,* pp. 132–133, 154–155.

prolonged apprenticeship training, and a skilled work hierarchy. Some of these workers, such as the plumbers who were mainly metalfitters, moved between construction and metalworking firms.[39]

In one important respect, the craftsmen in construction trades differed from their counterparts in artisanal enterprises. Since the construction site changed with each new assignment, construction workers lacked a fixed workplace or a stable contingent of co-workers. The plumbers constituted one important exception to this pattern. Unlike most other construction workers, they were concentrated in large construction shops, a circumstance that affected their subsequent disposition for collective activity.[40]

The transportation sector of the urban economy had a large and variegated labor force that included dockworkers, teamsters, coachmen, cabmen, and employees on state railroads and municipal tramways. For statistical purposes, machinists employed in railroad shops have been classified together with metalworkers because of the close similarity in labor-force composition and workplace conditions. In all the remaining categories of transportation, there were 46,483 workers in the capital and 49,799 in Moscow at the beginning of the twentieth century.[41]

Most intracity passenger transportation around 1900 was by horse-drawn vehicle; the electric tram was not introduced into St. Petersburg until 1907, when it quickly became a major competitor of horse-trams, horse-buses, public steam-boats, and ferries.[42] In addition, there were numerous horse-drawn cabs and, for the more prosperous inhabitants, the horse-drawn coach. At the end of the nineteenth century, privately owned horse-trams and horse-buses began to be taken over by the municipalities, and their drivers came under the aegis of the city administration.[43] The cabmen, on the other hand, remained in the private sector. About one-third of the Moscow cabmen were self-employed or working for family members; others worked for an employer who owned the vehicles and sometimes also provided room and board.[44]

[39]*Pervaia konferentsiia professional'nykh soiuzov rabochikh po metallu Moskovskogo promyshlennogo raiona* (Moscow, 1907), p. 22.

[40]T. V. Sapronov, ed., *Iubileinyi sbornik: Po istorii dvizheniia stroitel'nykh rabochikh Moskvy* (Moscow, 1922), pp. 10, 12–14.

[41]*S.-Peterburg po perepisi*, pp. 88–93, 156–161, and *Perepis' Moskvy*, pp. 160–161.

[42]Bater, *St. Petersburg*, pp. 270, 276.

[43]Ibid., pp. 272–273, for a history of this transition to a municipal transportation system. A description of the Moscow tram system can be found in *Sovremennoe khoziaistvo goroda Moskvy*, pp. 400 ff.

[44]*Perepis' Moskvy*, pp. 160–161. No comparable data are available for St. Petersburg.

Freight was still moved over land by horse-drawn wagons at the beginning of the twentieth century. In the capital, an elaborate network of canals was utilized for freight-hauling. Workers in these occupations were often seasonal, arriving in the city each spring and departing in the fall for their villages in the countryside. As a port city, St. Petersburg also included a substantial number of dockworkers. Like the freight-haulers, the dockworkers were often seasonal migrants from the surrounding countryside.[45]

Railroad workers made up the single largest group within the transportation industry of each city. Excluding those employed in railroad workshops, there were 5,389 railroad workers in St. Petersburg and 21,281 in Moscow at the turn of the century, including conductors, ticket-takers, office-workers, engineers, and unskilled laborers.[46] Like sales-clerical workers, some railroad workers occupied an ambiguous class position, and it was only in the crucible of 1905 that specific subgroups defined their relationship to the "working class" and its collective aspirations.

Service workers constituted another very large segment of the hired labor force in both St. Petersburg and Moscow. In all categories subsumed under this general rubric, there were 166,479 in the capital and 133,167 in Moscow.[47] Domestic servants represented the largest single subgroup within the service sector, comprising 128,045 workers in St. Petersburg and 78,728 in Moscow.[48] Most of the domestic servants were women, and nearly all had migrated to the city from villages in the surrounding countryside.

Hotels, restaurants, taverns, and inns also employed many workers in the service sector. Numbering about 19,289 in St. Petersburg and 33,700 in Moscow, these cooks, waiters, janitors, maids, and others displayed a wide range of skills and specializations.[49] Cooks and waiters, for example, required apprenticeship training, and in the more prosperous establishments they were almost always men. Other occupations in the service sector were unskilled and employed mostly female labor. A very diverse group, the labor force in the service sector also included barbers, chimney sweeps, laundresses, gardeners, and many others.

Finally, the urban economy included communications workers employed in

---

[45]P. Dorovatovskii, *Soiuz transportnykh rabochikh: Ocherk istorii Leningradskoi organizatsii 1905–1918 gg.* (Leningrad, 1927), pp. 8–10.

[46]*S.-Peterburg po perepisi*, pp. 88–93, 156–161, and *Perepis' Moskvy*, pp. 160–161.

[47]*S.-Peterburg po perepisi*, pp. 21–23, 31–35, and *Perepis' Moskvy*, pp. 52–53, 92–93, 137–197.

[48]*S.-Peterburg po perepisi*, pp. 21–23, 31–35, and *Perepis' Moskvy*, pp. 137–197.

[49]*S.-Peterburg po perepisi*, p. 21, and *Perepis' Moskvy*, pp. 52–53, 92–93.

the telegraph, telephone, and postal systems. Operating under municipal and state auspices, communications systems employed 3,689 workers in St. Petersburg and 2,530 in Moscow.[50] Like some of their counterparts in sales-clerical and transportation sectors of the economy, these workers often occupied an ambiguous class position. Low-level white-collar workers sometimes chose to identify themselves as part of the working class, whereas others sought bases of solidarity within professional groups. These lines did not emerge clearly until 1905 and afterward, when workers had their first opportunity to form independent collective organizations.

In sum, the St. Petersburg and Moscow working class consisted of widely diverse elements drawn from the various sectors of the urban economy. Within and among these sectors, there were many contrasts in labor force composition and differentiation along the lines of skill, gender, and concentration per enterprise. But workers employed in factories, artisanal workshops, commercial firms, and elsewhere did not inhabit entirely separate worlds. There was considerable interoccupational mobility, as workers moved between factories and workshops, from sales occupations to factory employment, and so on. It was not uncommon for members of a single family to find employment in different sectors and occupations within the urban economy. Cooperative living arrangements (artels) brought together workers who often shared a common place of origin but were employed in a variety of different occupations, and a room or an apartment might provide lodging for a salesclerk, a shoemaker, and a factory worker. Through intertwining patterns of work and residency, all of these workers had points of contact. They inhabited some of the same grey, squalid, and overcrowded neighborhoods, they encountered each other in the streets and shops, in the local taverns and beer halls, and their children played together in the alleyways before they, too, entered the factory, workshop, or commercial firm at an early age.

THE FORMATION OF SOCIAL IDENTITIES

At the turn of the century, most urban workers had been born in the countryside, and many of them retained a connection with their native village. The importance of workers' rural social origins and ties to the countryside can scarcely be underestimated. And yet it is far easier to document the rural-urban nexus than

[50] *S.-Peterburg po perepisi,* pp. 88–93, 156–161, and *Perepis' Moskvy,* pp. 160–161.

to explain its significance for the formation of a worker's social identity. How, it may be asked, did workers acquire a conception of their position in Russian society? At what point in an individual's career, if at all, did the new identity as an urban worker supplant the older self-definition as a peasant? Were some elements in the urban labor force more inclined than others to adopt a worker self-image? These problems are especially relevant to the study of workers' politics and organizations. Workers who felt a shared social identity tended to join in associational efforts from 1905 on, and these commonalities furnished the bases for solidarity in the organized labor movement.

It is often assumed by Soviet and Western scholars alike that a worker's relationship to the countryside holds the key for understanding the process of identity formation. Soviet historians have emphasized the rapidity with which urban workers were becoming disengaged from rural life and assimilated into the world of the factory at the beginning of the twentieth century.[51] Their accounts document the appearance of an expanding core of permanent urban "proletarians" who had lost or relinquished all ties with the countryside. This process, already under way in the closing decades of the nineteenth century, is said to have become accelerated in the wake of the Stolypin land reforms enacted in 1906–1907.[52]

Citing Lenin's statement that the formation of a "proletarian psychology" is "impossible without many years of employment in a factory," the Soviet scholar E. Kruze has noted a growing proportion of workers with protracted urban living and working experience, having been born in a city or resided there for many years.[53] This development was already apparent at the turn of the century, as is illustrated by data drawn from the 1902 Moscow city census (table 7).

Combining columns three and five in table 7, we find that 42 percent of the factory workers, 46 percent of the artisanal workers, 53 percent of the sales-clerical workers, 35 percent of the service workers, and 55 percent of the total city population either was born in Moscow or had resided there for more than ten years by 1902. In fact, the proportion of workers with prolonged urban living and working experience was even higher than that shown in table 7 when the phenomenon of interurban migration is taken into account. Workers not only

[51]E. Kruze, *Polozhenie rabochego klassa Rossii v 1900–1914 gg.* (Leningrad, 1976), pp. 131–159; L. M. Ivanov, "Preemstvennost' fabrichno-zavodskogo truda i formirovanie proletaria v Rossii," in *Rabochii klass i rabochee dvizhenie v Rossii 1861–1917 gg.* (Moscow, 1966), pp. 58–140.

[52]S. I. Antonova, *Vliianie stolypinskoi agrarnoi reformy na izmeneniia v sostave rabochego klassa: Po materialam Moskovskoi gubernii, 1906–1913 gg.* (Moscow, 1931), chap. 3.

[53]Kruze, *Polozhenie*, p. 136.

Table 7

Moscow-born Workers and Length of
Residency of Workers in Moscow, 1902
(in percentages)

	NOT MOSCOW-BORN, LENGTH OF RESIDENCY					
Occupational Category	Less than 2 years	2–10 years	More than 10 years	Not known	Moscow-born	Total
Factory workers (N = 107,781)	16.9	40.9	34.4	0.4	7.4	100.0
Artisanal workers (N = 104,899)	12.7	40.3	36.7	0.6	9.7	100.0
Apprentices (N = 32,656)	35.2	46.3	2.2	0.3	16.0	100.0
Sales-clerical employees (N = 71,264)	12.3	33.9	33.8	0.4	19.6	100.0
Service workers (N = 110,375)	23.7	41.0	30.2	0.8	4.3	100.0
All categories of the population (N = 1,092,360)	15.4	29.2	27.2	0.6	27.6	100.0

Source: *Perepis' Moskvy*, p. 10. The aggregate number of workers in each category differs from the total shown in table 6 and in the text because it was necessary to use somewhat different methods of categorizing workers when extracting these data from the municipal census. The artisanal category includes only workers *(rabochie)* employed in nonfactory enterprises in the manufacturing sector, together with construction workers, both skilled and unskilled. The inclusion of unskilled construction workers in these figures lowers slightly the percentage of urban-born and long-time urban residents. Excluded from the artisanal category (but included in data on artisans in table 6 and elsewhere) are garret-masters and their families, putting-out workers, and apprentices. The apprentices shown above were employed in artisanal, sales-clerical, and service establishments.

moved from the countryside to the city and back; many of them also migrated from one city to another in the course of their working lives. A peasant from Tver province, for example, might begin his working life in a Moscow metal-working plant, and after several years there, migrate to St. Petersburg. A study of Moscow printers in 1907 revealed that one out of six typesetters had worked in two cities, and one out of sixteen had spent time in three.[54] Thus, even among

[54]Svavitskii and Sher, *Ocherk*, p. 11.

workers who are shown in table 7 to have spent fewer than two years in Moscow, there were some who had a prior experience living and working in another of Imperial Russia's urban manufacturing centers before arriving in Moscow between 1900 and 1902.[55]

A recent study by Robert E. Johnson confirms the trend toward long-term urban employment at the turn of the century, but contends that it "was not necessarily an obstacle to maintaining rural ties."[56] Although factory workers seldom actually participated in agricultural cultivation by 1902, they nevertheless continued to maintain nominal ownership of land and to return periodically to the village in times of adversity or to reunite with family members.

Johnson places great importance on the retention of rural ties and on the tendency of some workers to form social networks in the city with others originating from the same village or district.[57] These networks are said to have "helped to maintain village traditions and folkways in the new setting, thereby helping to perpetuate the migrant's identification with peasant society."[58] Johnson concludes that "the typical worker had one foot in the village and one in the factory but showed little inclination to commit himself irrevocably to either alternative."[59]

To assess the effect of workers' continuing rural ties on identity formation, it is necessary to investigate not only the urban worker's contacts with the peasant village but also the worker's position in the urban labor force. An individual's links to the countryside had different implications—both practical and psychological—depending on the place he or she occupied in the new world of the urban factory, workshop, or commercial establishment. From a quantitative perspective, the incidence of landholding or periodic returns to the village appears the same, regardless of whether the worker was a metalfitter, a subcontracting-shop tailor, a spinner, or a salesclerk. But in reality, landholding and visits to the village had varied significance, depending on a worker's placement in the urban work hierarchy.

Stratification of the labor force took many forms, but most fundamental of all was the hierarchical subdivision within each industry and trade in accordance with skill and occupational specialization. This aspect of urban working-class life

[55]For further evidence on trends toward a prolongation of urban residency, see Antonova, *Vliianie*, pp. 188–189.

[56]Robert E. Johnson, *Peasant and Proletarian*, p. 37.

[57]Ibid., chap. 4.

[58]Ibid., p. 79.

[59]Ibid., p. 50.

had a far-reaching effect on the way in which workers came to perceive themselves and the meaning that they accorded to their relationship with the countryside from which most had come.

SKILL AND THE WORKER'S SELF-IMAGE

Peasant migrants who entered a St. Petersburg or Moscow workplace for the first time encountered a highly stratified hierarchical arrangement. Not only were there bosses and managers, foremen and supervisors with varying degrees of direct and indirect authority over the hired labor force, but the workers themselves were stratified hierarchically along the lines of skill and occupational specialization. The most important and basic dividing line, though not the only one, was drawn in accordance with skill. At the top of the hierarchy stood a small but highly qualified substratum in each industry and trade, such as metal patternmakers in metalworking plants, fabric cutters in the garment industry, and engravers and chromolithographers in the printing trades. This group, which has been called the "labor aristocracy,"[60] also included guild journeymen in some trades. Below this group ranged a variety of skilled occupations: metalfitters, lathe operators, smelters, and tinsmiths in metalworking, garment workers in custom tailoring shops, and typesetters and press operators in printing houses. They were followed by the semiskilled and unskilled workers.

In virtually all skilled occupations, there was a hierarchical division of the labor force into apprentices and qualified adult workers. In artisanal workshops, the latter group was sometimes further subdivided into journeymen and master craftsmen. This arrangement, originating in the guilds, remained in effect at the turn of the century, despite the fact that most journeymen could anticipate only lateral mobility into other workshops, not vertical mobility into the ranks of workshop owners.

Until the mid-1880s, the term *masterovoi* (pl. *masterovye)* was used both officially (by the government and by factory administration) and by the workers themselves to refer to a skilled worker in a factory enterprise. The term *masterovoi,* derived from the traditional guild hierarchy, was carried over into the

---

[60]Discussion of the "labor aristocracy" by a Soviet author can be found in U. N. Netesin, "K voprosy o sotsial'no-ekonomicheskikh korniakh i osobennostiakh 'rabochei aristokratii' v Rossii," in *Bol'shevistskaia pechat' i rabochii klass Rossii v gody revoliutsionnogo pod"ema 1910–1914 gg.* (Moscow, 1965).

factory setting to describe workers who were skilled, a group that included the "factory artisans."[61] Semi- and unskilled strata of the labor force were called *rabochie*.[62] Among skilled metalworkers, this designation had such pejorative connotations that it was often used as an expression of opprobrium.[63] Attempts by factory management to alter the traditional designations provoked bitter opposition from skilled workers, who fought to retain their dignified classification as *masterovye*.[64] By the turn of the century, the term *masterovye* was still employed by the workers themselves, but the factory administration now increasingly called skilled workers *rabochie*, while the remainder of the work force was classified as *chernorabochie*.[65]

The working life of most skilled workers began with apprenticeship training. This first and formative encounter with the urban workplace played a far more important role in a worker's life than is generally acknowledged in the literature, and helped to shape the individual's conceptions of class and status in Russian society.

In artisanal workshops, one typically began apprenticeship training at a very young age. State regulatory laws concerning artisanal apprenticeship had long

[61]The words *masterovoi* and *master* are derived from the Latin *magister* by way of the German *Meister*. These terms were originally used within the guild system to denote the attainment of the highest level of skill within a given trade, one qualified not only to practice the craft but to teach it. A contemporary definition of *masterovoi* is as follows: a craftsman *(remeslennik)*, or more generally, a worker, in some kind of craft, e.g., factory *(zavodskie) masterovye*. *Tolkovyi slovar' zhivogo velikorusskogo iazyka V. Dalia*, 3rd ed., vol. 2 (E-O) (St. Petersburg and Moscow, 1905).

[62]The word *rabochii* (pl. *rabochie*) is etymologically a descendant of the Old Church Slavic word *rab",* meaning servant, servitor, or slave, which in turn can be traced to the Indo-European **orbhus,* meaning "bereft of father" or "deprived of free status." Max Fasmer, *Russisches etymologisches Wörterbuch* (Heidelberg, 1950–1958), "Rabochii," and *The American Heritage Dictionary of the English Language,* ed. William Morris (New York, 1969), p. 1532. It is noteworthy that *rabstvo* (slavery) is the second definition of *rabota* (work) in V. Dal' *Tolkovyi slovar' velikorusskogo iazyka,* vol. 3 (St. Petersburg and Moscow, 1907). It is not farfetched to suppose that at the beginning of the twentieth century the word *rabochii* still carried a distant echo of *rab",* or slave. This unpleasant connotation may have prompted skilled workers to reject the term in preference for *masterovoi* or a specific occupational designation. Thus, a turn-of-the-century worker-activist in St. Petersburg recalls that "the title of 'worker' *[rabochii]* . . . sometimes jarred me and I disguised [it] with the more pleasant-sounding word— 'mechanic' *[mekhanik].*" Cited by Surh, "Petersburg Workers in 1905," p. 120, from N. M. Varnashev, "Ot nachala do kontsa s gaponovskoi organizatsiei (Vospominaniia)," in *Istoriko-revoliutsionnyi sbornik,* ed. V. I. Nevskii, vol. 1 (Leningrad, 1924), p. 180.

[63]Timofeev, *Chem zhivet,* p. 5.

[64]Ibid., pp. 5–6.

[65]The prefix *cherno,* meaning black, was affixed to the word *rabochii* to signify the lowest position within the ranks of workers.

since ceased to be enforced, and in some trades, such as shoemaking and apparel, it was not uncommon for children to enter an apprenticeship at the age of ten or eleven.[66] The average age of a beginning Moscow typesetter's apprentice in 1902 was 13.2 years, and 14.3 years in 1904.[67] A survey of Moscow printers in 1907 reported that seven out of ten workers in the printing industry had entered the labor force before reaching the age of fourteen.[68] Generally speaking, apprentices in artisanal trades commenced work between the ages of twelve and fifteen.

Artisanal apprentices tended to "begin work earlier in life than [was] generally the case among proletarians in big factories."[69] The belated onset of apprenticeship among factory workers was due to government regulations prohibiting factories from employing children younger than twelve years of age, and restricting the employment of children between the ages of twelve and fifteen to eight hours a day, at a time when factory shifts generally lasted about eleven hours, excluding overtime.[70] As a consequence of these restrictive regulations, factory owners were often reluctant to take on apprentices under the age of sixteen.[71]

[66]*Vpered*, no. 4 (May 30, 1906), p. 3, reported that owners of shoemaking shops in the capital "bought" nine- and ten-year-old boys in Iaroslavl Province and kept them "in virtual slavery."

[67]Svavitskii and Sher, *Ocherk*, p. 47. For additional material on the subject of artisanal apprenticeship, see G. Gordon, "K voprosu o polozhenii detei voobshche i remeslennykh i torgovykh uchenikov v chastnosti," *Trudovaia pomoshch'*, no. 1 (January 1908); Oliunina, *Portnovskii promysel*, p. 258; Alymov, "K voprosu o polozhenii truda v remeslennom proizvodstve," pp. 14–16; A. A. Kolychev, "K voprosu ob uregulirovanii polozheniia remeslennykh rabotnikov," *Vestnik znaniia*, no. 3 (1904), pp. 65–66, 68–69; S. O. Margolin, "Usloviia truda v remeslennoi i domashnei promyshlennosti," *Vestnik fabrichnogo zakonodatel'stva professional'noi gigieny*, no. 2 (February 1905), p. 43.

[68]Svavitskii and Sher, *Ocherk*, p. 10; Gruzdev, *Trud i bor'ba*, p. 27, notes that apprenticeship in the St. Petersburg tailoring trade typically began at the ages of twelve or thirteen.

[69]Sher, *Istoriia*, p. 10.

[70]The average workday in Russian factories in the years between 1899 and 1902 fell within the range of 11 to 11.4 hours. In St. Petersburg and its industrial suburbs, the average length of the workday in 1902 was 11 hours. Kir'ianov, *Zhiznennyi uroven'*, p. 56, especially n. 40; see also Iu. I. Kir'ianov, "Ekonomicheskoe polozhenie rabochego klassa Rossii nakanune revoliutsii 1905–1907 gg.," *Istoricheskie zapiski*, no. 98 (Moscow, 1977), p. 150.

[71]Sher, *Istoriia*, p. 158. Data on apprentices in St. Petersburg metalworking plants at the turn of the century provide further evidence of the employers' reluctance to take on factory apprentices under the age of sixteen. In 1900, children under sixteen constituted a mere 1.1 percent of those employed in St. Petersburg metalworking plants; children under the age of seventeen constituted 5.6 percent of the total labor force. Thus, an influx of child-apprentices occurred when boys reached the age of sixteen. According to F. Bulkin, employers did not want to employ children under sixteen years of age, whose working time was considerably restricted by labor legislation. F. Bulkin, *Na zare profdvizheniia: Istoriia Peterburgskogo soiuza metallistov 1906–1914 gg.* (Moscow and Leningrad, 1924), pp. 46–47.

Of course, not all children and juveniles in factories were serving an apprenticeship. In textile mills and teapacking firms, for example, there were many young boys and girls between the ages of twelve and seventeen performing unskilled tasks that involved no training or preparation for more complex future work. A survey of workers at the Tsindel' textile mill in Moscow at the turn of the century reported that 24 percent of the workers had begun employment before the age of fifteen, and 37 percent between the ages of fifteen and seventeen.[72]

Most contemporary sources did not distinguish between children performing unskilled work and those serving an apprenticeship.[73] Nevertheless, apprenticeship was the usual requirement for skilled occupations within a factory setting; and in metalworking and woodworking enterprises subject to the Factory Inspectorate, most boys began their apprenticeship when they reached their sixteenth birthday. It was therefore a typical situation in the 1890s when Semen Kanatchikov, having turned sixteen, was brought by his father to Moscow in a horse-drawn cart.[74] This future Bolshevik leader of the St. Petersburg metalworkers' union was turned over by his father to an acquaintance at the Gustav List factory who agreed to supervise the boy's apprenticeship while he mastered a trade.

Nearly all sales-clerical occupations demanded apprenticeship training. It was a common practice for store owners to acquire child-apprentices through the services of a middleman. As reported by A. Gudvan, a contemporary observer of sales-clerical workers:

These middlemen travel around to impoverished villages in Iaroslavl, Novgorod, and Pskov provinces during the winter months when food is scarce. They collect eight- to ten-year-old boys and send them to stores as apprentices without obtaining the consent of either the parents or the children.[75]

By the turn of the century, the training function of apprentices in commercial establishments had taken second place to the economic contribution of appren-

---

[72]Sher, *Istoriia*, p. 10.

[73]The 1900 Moscow city census provides a separate classification for apprentices in artisanal firms, but did not distinguish apprentices from other workers in factories except by age. The 1902 St. Petersburg city census does not distinguish between apprentices and other types of child labor.

[74]Kanatchikov, *Iz istorii*, p. 8. In his memoir, the St. Petersburg metalworker Buzinov recalls that his father intended to send his son to begin an apprenticeship at the Nevskii plant when the boy reached the age of sixteen and could work a full shift. Buzinov, *Za Nevskoi zastavoi*, p. 13.

[75]Gudvan, *Ocherki po istorii dvizheniia sluzhashchikh v Rossii*. Chast' 1: *Do revoliutsii 1905 goda* (Moscow, 1925), p. 125. The letter was originally published in *Novaia Rus'* in 1908. For a fuller English translation of Gudvan's study see Bonnell, ed., *The Russian Worker*, chap. 5.

tices as unpaid labor. This was also the case in the service sector, where cooks, waiters, barbers, and others entered the urban labor force at a young age, usually directly from the countryside, to begin an apprenticeship.[76]

Apprenticeship training for skilled craftsmen typically lasted four or five years.[77] Salesclerks spent three to four years as apprentices before entering the adult labor force,[78] while skilled factory workers spent even less. Kanatchikov, who trained as a metal patternmaker, served two years as an apprentice at the Gustav List factory in Moscow.[79] In the less skilled occupation of blacksmith's hammerer, a typical apprenticeship lasted for one year at the turn of the century.[80] Most factory workers required one to three years to master the basic skills of occupational specialties such as metalfitting, lathe operating, or smelting.

The effect of early and prolonged apprenticeship must have been profound, especially for those recruited directly from the countryside. Young and impressionable, these youths found themselves in an urban workshop, factory, or commercial establishment. Here they learned to submit to a status hierarchy, and at the same time to anticipate eventual promotion into the ranks of adult workers. They were subjected to arbitrary and often cruel treatment by the employer and other adults, but they also participated in workshop rituals and celebrations.[81] Drinking bouts represented a common feature of working-class life, and it was not long before young apprentices joined the revelry, a step that helped to integrate them into the adult community and provided their first experience of camaraderie with other workers. One such scene has been described by E. A. Oliunina, a contemporary observer of the apparel trades:

Apprenticeship is generally very hard on children. At the beginning they suffer enormously, particularly from the physical strain of having to do work well beyond the capacities of their years. They have to live in an environment where the level of morality is very low. Scenes of drunkenness and debauchery induce the boys to smoke and drink at an early age. For example, in one subcontracting shop which made men's clothes, a fourteen-year-old boy worked together with twelve adults. When I visited there at four o'clock on Tuesday afternoon, the workers were already half drunk. Some were lying

[76]On cooks, for example, see E. Ignatov, "Iz istorii obshchestva povarov Moskovskogo promyshlennogo raiona," *MIPDR*, 2:170–171; on waiters, see A. Kats, "Iz istorii Moskovskogo obshchestva vzaimopomoshchi ofitsiantov (1902–1916 gg.)," *MIPDR*, 1:1–56.

[77]Oliunina, *Portnovskii promysel*, p. 258; Sher, *Istoriia*, p. 57; Gruzdev, *Trud i bor'ba*, p. 27.

[78]Gudvan, *Ocherki*, pp. 131–132.

[79]Kanatchikov, *Iz istorii*, p. 42.

[80]Buzinov, *Za Nevskoi zastavoi*, p. 17.

[81]There are many contemporary descriptions of the cruel treatment of child apprentices. See, for example, Gordon, "K voprosu o polozhenii detei," and Gudvan, *Ocherki*, pp. 125–132. Shop rituals and celebrations are discussed further on in this chapter.

under the benches, others in the hallway. The boy was as drunk as the rest of them and lay there with a proud look on his face, dressed only in a pair of long underwear and a dirty, torn shirt. He had been taught to drink at the age of twelve and could now keep up with the adults.[82]

Their formative experiences in the urban workplace made a deep and lasting impression on workers whose rupture with the countryside took place when they were young. By the time they had reached their seventeenth or eighteenth birthday, these youths were often well adapted to the ways of the urban milieu and place of employment. Their early introduction to the workplace imparted to some of them an awareness, however fragile, of their position as urban workers—a self-image still comparatively rare in St. Petersburg and Moscow at the turn of the century. They began to acquire a new identification, considering themselves for the first time "a typesetter," "a tailor," "a metalfitter." Thus in the course of his two-year apprenticeship at Gustav List, Kanatchikov came to see himself in a new light as "a patternmaker," a highly skilled position that brought unaccustomed dignity and status to the boy who had so recently arrived from the countryside in a wooden cart.[83]

Early arrival in the urban workplace and the acquisition of a skill through apprenticeship training were events of decisive psychological importance for many workers, particularly in terms of the new self-image that individuals developed in an urban setting. In a labor force dominated by semiskilled and unskilled workers, many of them fresh from the countryside, the possession of a skill acquired through prolonged training gave workers a feeling of mastery, self-respect, and control over the work process.[84]

WORKERS' TIES TO THE COUNTRYSIDE

Skill was a major factor in shaping workers' self-images and the sense they had of their relation to the countryside. This relationship assumed a variety of forms

[82]Oliunina, *Portnovskii promysel*, p. 266. A portion of Oliunina's study appears in English translation in Bonnell, ed., *The Russian Worker*, chap. 4.

[83]Kanatchikov, *Iz istorii*, p. 40–43, 47. For an outstanding discussion of Kanatchikov's memoir and the psychological implications of his development into a skilled metalworker, see Reginald E. Zelnik, "Russian Bebels: An Introduction to the Memoirs of Semen Kanatchikov and Matvei Fisher," *Russian Review*, pt. 1, 35, no. 3 (July 1976); pt. 2, 35, no. 4 (October 1976).

[84]These issues are discussed further in the section "Life at the Workplace," below.

at the turn of the century. Generally speaking, there were three major—though fluid—categories: permanent urban workers with no ties whatsoever to the countryside, transitional workers with attenuated ties to the countryside, and semirural workers with ongoing ties to their native village.

Among permanent urban workers, some had been born into urban families, and others, beginning their lives in the countryside, had left for urban employment and subsequently ceased to have any connection with the village from which they had come. Although the data are sketchy, there is evidence that workers with high levels of occupational specialization and training were less likely to have continuing ties with the countryside than semiskilled or unskilled workers in the same industry or trade. By way of illustration, 65 percent of the highly skilled typesetters in Moscow no longer had any links with the village in 1907, whereas among lithographers and bindery workers, groups with a comparatively lower order of skill, only 24 percent and 28 percent respectively, no longer retained such ties.[85]

A survey conducted at the capital's Baltiiskii shipbuilding plant in December 1901 sheds further light on this problem.[86] The survey gathered information on the social origins of nearly four thousand workers (based on passport designations) employed in specific shops within the enterprise. In the plant as a whole, 80 percent of the workers were registered as "peasants" in their passports, but the proportion of peasant-workers in any given shop showed considerable variation, depending on the level of skill and expertise required of those employed there. Thus, only 50 percent of the workers in the highly demanding patternmaking shop were registered as peasants; the others belonged to the permanent urban population (*meshchane* or *remeslenniki*). In the steel foundry, by contrast, the general skill requirements were far lower than in patternmaking, and physical stamina counted for more than mental agility. Here peasant-workers constituted 89 percent of the labor force, with only 11 percent drawn from the ranks of *meshchane* or *remeslenniki*.[87]

But these data on social background do not disclose the full extent to which

[85]Svavitskii and Sher, *Ocherk*, pp. 8–9.

[86]A. Blek, "Usloviia truda na Peterburgskikh zavodakh po dannym 1901 g.," *Arkhiv istorii truda v Rossii*, Book 2 (Petrograd, 1921), pp. 65–85.

[87]Ibid., pp. 80, 82. The Russian term *meshchane* refers to a segment of the urban population, corresponding roughly to the petty bourgeoisie. The term *remeslenniki* (artisans) also refers to a legal category within the urban population. Not all cities had a separate legal category for *remeslenniki*, apart from the broader category of *meshchane*, but both St. Petersburg and Moscow used both classifications.

skilled workers at the Baltiiskii plant had relinquished all connections to the countryside. Within the ranks of peasant-workers there were many who had become permanent urban dwellers, having lost or severed their links with the village. In the enterprise as a whole, only two out of five peasant-workers retained land in the countryside in 1901. Of the remaining three-fifths, the report states that in many cases "their connection with the countryside is purely formal; they are future candidates for becoming *meshchane* and *remeslenniki*, that is, permanent city dwellers."[88] The survey offers no detailed information on this point, but we may infer from the plant-wide findings on landholding that as many as eight out of every ten workers in some highly skilled shops had permanent urban status or had relinquished all ties to their native village.

Urbanization had proceeded further among skilled segments of the St. Petersburg and Moscow labor force than among workers who were unskilled or semiskilled. A firsthand account of working-class life by P. Timofeev [P. Remezov]—one of the few available sources of its kind—illuminates the ways workers perceived their relations to the countryside. A metalworker in the capital, Timofeev first published his account in the journal *Russkoe bogatstvo* [*Russian Riches*], with installments appearing in 1903 and 1905.[89] Discussing the connection between skill and rural ties among metalworkers, Timofeev observed:

Once a worker starts earning thirty-five rubles a month and has almost become a skilled worker, he is no longer so willing to send money back to the village. I have often heard of disagreements between parents in the village and their children working at factories in the town. Often the disputes even end up in court, when a father refuses his son a passport for failing to send money back to the village. As for skilled workers, the majority probably feel that the village is nothing but a burden. At least, this was the opinion I personally heard from most of them. The only exceptions were those with such good land that they didn't have to send money home, and those who were the sons of prosperous village artisans and merchants. All the rest said that the village was more of a hindrance than a help.[90]

[88]Ibid., p. 80.

[89]P.T. [P. Timofeev], "Zavodskie budni: Iz zapisok rabochego," *Russkoe bogatstvo*, no. 8 (Aug. 1903), pp. 30–53; no. 9 (Sept. 1903), pp. 175–199. Further installments appeared in 1905. See P. Timofeev, "Ocherki zavodskoi zhizni," *Russkoe bogatstvo*, no. 9 (September 1905), and no. 10 (October 1905). These essays were subsequently published as a book under the title *Chem zhivet zavodskii rabochii* (St. Petersburg, 1906).

[90]Timofeev, *Chem zhivet*, p. 17. Selections from Timofeev's account are translated in Bonnell, ed., *The Russian Worker*, chap. 2.

The attitude of the unskilled metalworker toward the village, on the other hand, was quite different. According to Timofeev:

When he arrives in the city from the countryside and settles down at some factory or other, the unskilled [metal]worker almost always feels that he is in a suspended state. The first question he has to deal with is his relationship to the village. Of course, as long as his wife remains in the village it is impossible for him to cut all ties. But even when he has managed to bring his wife to live with him, his position is still not completely resolved. He knows that he is not a "skilled worker," that he can be thrown out at any time, and that it will be much more difficult for him to find a job again than it would be for a skilled worker. His awareness of all these things makes him unwilling to give up his ties to the village, where he can always find a crust of bread that will let him survive until the spring, when the factories start to pick up again.[91]

Many workers who retained their connection to the village did so as a form of social security. They held on to a house or a parcel of land, or sent money to relatives, in order to protect themselves against adversities that would deprive them of an urban livelihood. Without a pied-à-terre in the village, as Timofeev put it, "they would lose the last refuge during time of unemployment, once and for all."[92] After many decades in the city, it was not uncommon for a worker to return to the countryside in the event of illness, accident, unemployment, or old age.

Workers with these kinds of ties to the countryside often belonged to a large group of transitional elements in the labor force. They did not themselves engage in agricultural cultivation, and frequently their immediate family (spouse and usually children) resided in the city. Their involvement with rural life consisted in the possession of a house or a parcel of land (cultivated by family members or rented out) or monetary assistance to family members. A substantial number lived and worked in an urban center for ten, twenty, or even thirty years and returned only rarely to the village. For some of them, "their only connection with the village comes when they need to obtain a passport or when they have to pay taxes for land which is nominally theirs but is actually worked by other people."[93] Contact with the village had been attenuated but not yet severed, and many were, for all practical purposes, a part of the urban working class and viewed themselves as such.

[91]Ibid., pp. 12–13.
[92]Ibid., p. 14.
[93]Ibid., p. 17.

In contrast to transitional workers, semirural workers maintained close and continuing relations with their native village. These workers often owned a house or land in the countryside. Some returned seasonally to assist in cultivation, while others (mostly male) had a spouse and children in the countryside who looked to the urban wage earner for support.

At the beginning of the twentieth century, only a small percentage of the factory labor force in St. Petersburg and Moscow returned seasonally to their villages to participate in cultivation.[94] Annual migration to the countryside was far more common in some artisanal trades, where employment was seasonal. The off-season in the clothing trades, for example, coincided roughly with the agricultural cycle. Workshops began to taper off production in the spring and resumed again in September.[95] During these months, clothing workers faced the prospect of unemployment, and many chose to return to the countryside. In tailoring shops, more than half the workers surveyed in 1910–1911 reported active ties to their villages and annual visits to the countryside; about three out of five subcontracting shop workers can be described as semirural.[96]

Many semirural workers maintained contact with their village through immediate family members (spouse and children) who resided in the countryside rather than the city. Data collected in 1897 show that the percentage of St. Petersburg factory workers with families in the countryside varied inversely with the prevalence of skilled labor in a given industry. Thus, 87 percent of the capital's textile workers with families maintained their wives and children in the countryside, whereas the corresponding figures for the capital's printers was 67 percent, and 69 percent among the metalworkers. At the Baltiiskii shipbuilding plant, only 29 percent of the married workers had families in the countryside.[97]

Workers with families in the countryside did not always have regular or frequent contact with those they left behind. To be sure, many sent money to assist family members, but actual visits often took place at prolonged intervals. Timofeev has recounted the situation facing such workers in the capital's metalworking industry:

[94]In St. Petersburg, a mere 5 percent of the cotton workers were seasonal migrants in 1900, although 65 percent of them owned land. Surh, "Petersburg Workers in 1905," p. 10. For data on seasonal migration among Moscow workers, see Antonova, *Vliianie*, p. 201.

[95]Oliunina, *Portnovskii promysel*, pp. 202–203.

[96]Ibid., p. 175.

[97]*Istoriia rabochikh Leningrada 1703-fevral' 1917*, vol. 1 (Leningrad, 1972), p. 184, based on the 1897 national census, and Blek, "Usloviia truda," p. 77.

1. St. Petersburg printing shop at the turn of the century.

2. Apprentices, such as these in a St. Petersburg optical shop, could be found in many industries and occupations at the beginning of the twentieth century.

3. Two views of the machine shop, where metalfitters (above) and lathe operators (below) worked at the St. Petersburg Baltiiskii shipbuilding plant in the early 1900s.

4. Weaving room with male workers at Moscow's Prokhorovskaia Trekhgornaia textile mill after the turn of the century.

5. St. Petersburg bakers in the 1890s.

6. Tobacco workers in St. Petersburg in the early 1900s.

At the time I was very interested in workers' ties to the village, and so I immediately turned the conversation to that topic. Eleven of the eighteen men there were married, and all their wives lived in the village. Only one of them had been visited by his wife recently, and before that she hadn't seen her husband in four whole years. One of them had lived there [in St. Petersburg] for five years without seeing his wife.[98]

The problem of prolonged separation from wife and children plagued many different types of workers. The pressing and painful nature of the situation can be gauged from the demand put forward by Moscow bakers in 1905. In the bakers' first industry-wide strike in April 1905, workers insisted on the right to have their wives live with them in the employer's housing for two weeks each year at the latter's expense.[99]

Some semirural workers had years of experience in the urban labor force, and in these cases their social identity must have been confused and amorphous. A prolonged sojourn in the city differentiated them from peasants who had never experienced life in an urban factory or shop and who knew only the world of the village. But in the context of the urban working class, semirural workers also stood apart from others who had made a more complete break from the countryside and whose appearance, life style, and position in the skill hierarchy attested to their greater assimilation into the urban milieu.

PATTERNS OF STRATIFICATION AND STATUS DIFFERENTIATION

The command of a skilled occupation generally coincided with a cluster of other characteristics. As we have seen, skilled workers tended to enter the urban labor force at a young age and to remain there for a protracted period or indefinitely. Their ties with the countryside were often attenuated except in the case of seasonal trades. Skilled workers, most of them male, also displayed a relatively higher rate of literacy than did their unskilled and semiskilled counterparts.

According to the 1897 national census, 74 percent of all the male workers and 40 percent of the female workers in St. Petersburg were literate. In Moscow, 66 percent of workingmen were literate, and 25 percent of the women.[100] But

[98]Timofeev, *Chem zhivet*, p. 14.
[99]*Professional'noe dvizhenie Moskovskikh pishchevikov*, p. 27.
[100]*Chislennost' i sostav rabochikh v Rossii na osnovanii dannykh pervoi vseobshchei perepisi naseleniia Rossiiskoi Imperii 1897 g.*, vol. 2 (St. Petersburg, 1906), table 3, part 1, p. 174; table 3, part 2, p. 16.

literacy rates were higher than average among skilled substrata of the working population. The demonstration of basic literacy was a requirement for entry into apprenticeship in some artisanal trades. Apprentices in precious metalworking, most of them recruited from the countryside, had to show completion of rural primary school as a condition for entry into the trade, and as a result, literacy was virtually universal among these workers.[101]

A survey of Moscow printers in 1907 revealed that 81 percent of all the workers in this industry had completed primary school and another 11 percent had acquired literacy on their own.[102] In Moscow tailoring shops where skilled labor was concentrated, a survey in 1910–1911 disclosed that 90 percent of the workers were literate, compared with 66–75 percent in subcontracting shops. And whereas half the tailoring shop workers had completed primary school, only one-quarter of those in subcontracting shops had done so.[103]

Among St. Petersburg metalworkers in 1897, the literacy rate was 73 percent, compared with 44 percent among textile workers.[104] But in some metalworking plants the percentage was considerably higher than the average for this industry as a whole. Thus, the Erikson metalworking plant in the capital reported at the turn of the century that 85 percent of its labor force was literate.[105] In certain occupations, such as patternmaking, the "work was mentally challenging and literacy was an absolute requirement."[106]

The literacy rate among sales-clerical workers was also relatively high, as might be expected in occupations where the ability to handle figures and to read was often a requirement. Although data are available only for the Russian Empire as a whole, it is noteworthy that at the beginning of the twentieth century, 95 percent of the men in sales-clerical occupations, 86 percent of the women, and 90 percent of the children and juveniles were classified as literate.[107]

Apart from the greater prevalence of literacy among skilled workers, they were set apart from their unskilled or semiskilled counterparts by higher wages, a higher standard of living, and the respect they were accorded by other workers and even by management. At the upper reaches of the labor hierarchy, the

[101]Mamontov, "Dvizhenie rabochikh po obrabotke blagorodnykh metallov," *MIPDR*, 5:180–181.

[102]Svavistkii and Sher, *Ocherk*, p. 1.

[103]Oliunina, *Portnovskii promysel*, pp. 184–185.

[104]*Chislennost' i sostav*, vol. 2, table 3, part 2, pp. 16–18.

[105]Shuster, *Peterburgskie rabochie*, p. 52.

[106]Kanatchikov, *Iz istorii*, p. 18.

[107]Gudvan, *Ocherki*, p. 187.

"aristocrats" were distinguished by their appearance and demeanor. They have been described by a former tailor:

There were those who liked to dress well, who in the summer came to work on a bicycle, who always wore starched linens and who worked in their own smocks, who had fancy haircuts, attended theatres and dances and horseraces, were interested in sports, frequented clubs, and in general maintained a *bon ton*. These people were called "aristocrats" and would be nicknamed *barin*.[108]

The St. Petersburg metalworker Kanatchikov confirms the impression that this phenomenon extended across occupational lines:

The pattern shop was considered to be the "aristocratic" workshop [in the metalworking plant]. Most of the patternmakers were urban types—they dressed neatly, wore their trousers over their boots, wore their shirts "fantasia" style, tucked into their trousers, fastened their collars with a colored lace instead of a necktie, and on holidays some of them even wore bowler hats. They cut their hair "in the Polish style" or brush-cut. Their bearing was firm, conveying their consciousness of their own worth. . . . Most of them were family men and were related to various petty bourgeois strata. Some of them had put away savings "for a rainy day."[109]

"Aristocrats" were comparatively rare in the labor force. Far more numerous were the highly skilled and relatively well-off workers, including the majority of typesetters, tailors employed in custom tailoring shops, skilled metalworkers and woodworkers, and many others, whose life style and pretensions were not comparable to those of the "aristocrats," but who nevertheless stood apart from the mass of workers in their trade or industry. They attended clubs and theatrical performances, read newspapers, and even Russian classics, and had broader horizons and more contact with city life than most workers.[110] Many were like the metalfitter who "held his head higher, had stronger opinions, and was more quick-witted [than other workers]."[111] They shared the outlook of the typesetter who, standing at his type frame, felt himself to be on a higher level than other workers.[112]

Semipeasant workers, by contrast, lacked the fine skills, the high wages, and

---

[108]Gruzdev, *Trud i bor'ba*, p. 15. The term *barin* usually referred to a nobleman.

[109]Kanatchikov, *Iz istorii*, p. 18.

[110]E. O. Kabo, *Ocherki rabochego byta: Opyt monograficheskogo issledovaniia domashnego rabochego byta*, vol. 1 (Moscow, 1928), pp. 39ff., 86ff.

[111]Buzinov, *Za Nevskoi zastavoi*, p. 21.

[112]*ILS*, p. 11.

the cultural level of more urbanized workers. On the streets of St. Petersburg or Moscow, the very appearance of such workers testified to their position:

Workers with families in the countryside spend the smallest possible amount of their wages on food and clothing. They send everything they can back to their families. Tailoring shop workers and subcontract workers dress quite differently. The former, especially those working in the center of Moscow, wear suits, stylish boots, and different coats according to the season. The subcontract workers, on the other hand, wear quilted jackets and felt boots. In these workshops, one can find half-dressed workers wearing nothing but a calico shirt, often torn and dirty, and a pair of faded pants and long underwear. They work barefoot. When they go out, they cover themselves with a jacket.[113]

Prosperous and assimilated workers had a "haughty and condescending" attitude toward semipeasant workers and were repelled by their rural attire and their coarse ways.[114] Kanatchikov recalls that even in the highly skilled patternmaking shop at Gustav List where he served an apprenticeship, there was a small group of patternmaker peasants. Significantly, these semirural patternmakers "had never passed through a factory apprenticeship," that important socializing experience in the lives of so many workers. Their ties to the village were still strong, and "they wore high boots, traditional cotton-print blouses girdled with a sash, had their hair cut 'under a pot,' and wore beards that were rarely touched by a barber's hand. . . . They lived in crowded, dirty conditions and behaved stingily, denying themselves everything in order to accumulate more money for the village." Other patternmakers called them "grey devils" and frequently made fun of them.[115] Since many of the more urbanized patternmakers, such as Kanatchikov, were themselves erstwhile peasants, they may well have seen in these "grey devils" a too-fresh reminder of their own rural background, which they so carefully discarded but probably never forgot.

The workers themselves were clearly attuned to matters of status differentiation. Skilled workers in a factory setting, as we have observed, insisted upon their classification as *masterovye* rather than *rabochie*. The polite form of address—the Russian "vy" rather than "ty"—was also a sensitive issue for workers. Timofeev has described the ordeal of a metalfitter seeking employment in a large St. Petersburg plant around the turn of the century:

[113]Oliunina, *Portnovskii promysel*, p. 240.
[114]Gruzdev, *Trud i bor'ba*, p. 16.
[115]Kanatchikov, *Iz istorii*, pp. 18–19.

You find the foreman drinking tea in his office, which is located in the workshop itself. You walk up and stand outside the door respectfully. "Hey, you, what do you want?" he asks. His form of address will depend on your clothes. If you are well-dressed, he might address you politely.[116]

Workers were also self-conscious in matters of occupational specialization. Occupational designations, indicative of fine distinctions within larger categories, were widely utilized by workers to establish their place in the work hierarchy. Contemporary sources document the importance of these occupational designations in the workers' milieu. In textile mills, workers carefully distinguished among weavers, spinners, dyers, knitters, and other subspecialties, just as bakers considered themselves pastrymakers, *baranochniki,* breadbakers, or *kalachniki.*[117] In printing firms, the typesetter would seldom be confused with the lithographer or binder.

A survey conducted by the St. Petersburg union of metalworkers in January 1908 yielded a list of more than one hundred occupational categories used by workers to identify their place in the industry. These included not only metalfitters and lathe operators (the two largest occupational subgroups in the industry), but also such specialties as smelters, machinists, blacksmiths, milling-machine operators, and others.[118] Among these various subgroups there was a distinct occupational hierarchy within metalworking plants. The metalworker Aleksei Buzinov, a second-generation urban worker who apprenticed in the blacksmith shop at the Nevskii shipbuilding plant in the second half of the 1890s, recalled the sharp lines differentiating workers in the "hot" and "cold" shops within the plant:

The more I grew into the factory family, the clearer became to me its heterogeneity, even within the boundaries of one plant. Soon I began to realize that workers in the machine shop—the metalfitters and lathe operators—looked down on me. After this, the inferior position of workers in the "hot" shops—the smelting, rolling, and blacksmith shops— became obvious. . . . I was especially struck by the absence of equality among the

---

[116]Timofeev, *Chem zhivet,* p. 22.

[117]*Baranochniki* specialized in the baking of dry, bagel-shaped *baranki; kalachi,* or rolls made of white flour, were the specialty of the *kalachniki. Professional'nyi soiuz,* no. 14 (April 1, 1906), p. 12; M. Zaiats, ed., *Tekstili v gody pervoi revoliutsii (1905–1907 gg.): Materialy po istorii professional'nogo dvizheniia tekstil'shchikov tsentral'no-promyshlennogo raiona* (Moscow, 1925), pp. 41, 51.

[118]*Materialy ob ekonomicheskom polozhenii i professional'noi organizatsii Peterburgskikh rabochikh po metallu* (St. Petersburg, 1909), pp. 94–96.

workers. Now it seems a minor matter, something not even worth remembering. But at the time, it painfully wounded my pride. I didn't want to be worse than the others. I thought that if only I could master the skills of metalfitting and lathe operating, everything would fall into place.[119]

This attentiveness to occupational specialization was indicative of a widespread orientation among workers called *tsekhovshchina*, or craft identification. The word *tsekh* referred historically to the guilds formed by artisans, segregating them within each city into discrete corporate bodies based on a common trade. By the early twentieth century, however, the term had acquired broader connotations and was used by intelligentsia labor activists to describe the narrow bases of common identification among workers, premised on shared work characteristics in a shop within a larger factory, a type of enterprise, a district, or even a single firm. As Buzinov put it: "Each branch of industry and even each shop infects the workers with its professional or shop patriotism, which sings praise to its craft and spits on everything else."[120]

LIFE AT THE WORKPLACE

At the turn of the century, workers spent the better part of their waking hours at the place of employment. Working time varied considerably according to the industry or occupation, but it was not uncommon for workers (especially those in artisanal shops and sales firms) to spend as much as sixteen hours a day at the workplace, six or even seven days a week. Despite its centrality in the everyday life of workers, little is known about the place of employment and the conditions and social interactions there. Yet these circumstances had a profound effect on the outlook and attitudes of workers and their inclination to unite collectively.

In both Petersburg and Moscow factory industry, as noted earlier, there was a high concentration of labor per enterprise. This distinctive feature of Russia's economic development has obscured the fact that the country also had a sizable contingent of workers for whom the immediate work environment was a small workshop, a store, or a shop within a larger factory enterprise.

[119]Buzinov, *Za Nevskoi zastavoi*, p. 21. The Bolshevik activist V. Voitinskii draws attention to the contrasting character and composition of workers in "hot" and "cold" shops in his *Gody pobed i porazhenii*, Book 1, *1905-yi god* (Berlin, Petersburg, and Moscow, 1923), p. 114.

[120]Ibid., p. 20.

In artisanal trades the immediate work environment for most workers was the small shop. Contemporary descriptions emphasize the insulated, intense, and overcrowded environment in workshops where a small number of people worked and sometimes lived in close proximity.[121] Conditions in artisanal shops in the Moscow apparel trades have been described by Oliunina:

When entering a workshop, one is immediately struck by the long wide wooden planks alongside the window, the workbenches on which male tailors sit cross-legged. In tailoring shops, women workers do their sewing at tables. In subcontracting shops, however, all the workers sit on these benches, even the women. . . . In one typical shop run by the subcontractor K., there are thirty-two workers. There is not an inch of free space in the two rooms of the shop. All the space is taken by tables and chairs, and mannequins with dresses stand in the hallways. The constant hum and din puts the workers so on edge that swearing and coarse language are commonplace. In this atmosphere, twelve young girls are living and learning the trade.[122]

The immediate work environment in sales firms had much in common with the artisanal workshop, and salesclerks experienced many of the same depredations.[123] The typical store had no more than a dozen workers laboring in an intense and hectic atmosphere under the close scrutiny of the owner-employer.

In some industries, such as metalworking, large firms with hundreds or even thousands of workers were subdivided into a multitude of small workshops:

A large metalworking plant is like a world in miniature. Some factories contain up to two hundred different workshops. Large factories are usually broken up into several divisions, such as the metallurgical department, the foundry, the locomotive department, and the railroad car department. And if we take in turn any one department, say the railroad car department, it will contain a lumberyard, a carpentry shop, a painting shop, an upholstery shop, a roofing shop, a machine shop, a wheel shop, a tire shop, a forge, a foundry, a pattern shop, and so on. Working conditions are by no means the same in the different workshops.[124]

These workshops provided workers with their most significant daily experiences at the plant. Here they formed social networks with other workers, devel-

---

[121]For a nostalgic picture of life in Moscow artisanal shops, see Belousov's *Ushedshaia Moskva*. For a less benign recollection, see Maxim Gor'kii, *Detstvo*, in his *Sobranie sochinenii*, 30 vols. (Moscow, 1951), vol. 13. See also D. P. Nikol'skii, "O neobkhodimosti inspektsii dlia fabrichno-remeslennykh zavedenii," *Meditsinskaia beseda*, no. 9 (May 1904).

[122]Oliunina, *Portnovskii promysel*, pp. 247–249.

[123]Gudvan, *Ocherki*, pp. 122–177.

[124]Timofeev, *Chem zhivet*, pp. 4–5.

oped a sense of their place in the labor hierarchy, and in some cases gained a feeling of mastery and self-worth. This is not to say that the sheer size of a large metalworking plant, such as the St. Petersburg Putilov firm with twelve thousand workers, did not also make a profound impression on workers. Accounts by contemporaries convey a strong sense of appreciation for the awesome technological capability of these giant plants, which occupied such an important position in the economy of the city and the country as a whole.[125] But it was the workshop within the larger plant—with its small scale and, in many instances, relatively limited division of labor—that served as the real point of reference for workers who had completed an apprenticeship there, advanced through the ranks, and sometimes retained considerable control over the labor process. Maintaining its own traditions and a core of proud skilled workers of many years seniority, the workshop in a metalworking plant often supplied a close-knit atmosphere that had little in common with the work environment in other industries such as textiles.

Unlike the metalworking plant, which was compartmentalized into numerous small and discrete workshops, the textile mill was subdivided into large work units specializing in spinning, weaving, dyeing, and other facets of production. Many of the shops were organized on a massive scale to accommodate the long rows of machinery and the scores of workers required to tend the machines.[126]

The importance of the small shop as the immediate work environment for widely diverse groups was reinforced by a multitude of shop-level traditions and customs that fortified social relations among workers and their sense of camaraderie. Many of these practices centered around the intake of alcohol. "Blue Monday" was a widespread custom among male workers in artisanal workshops, commercial firms, and factory enterprises. Arriving at their jobs hung over from weekend drinking and carousing, they used Monday as an occasion for further alcoholic intake. " 'Blue Monday,' " recounted Oliunina, "is a custom

[125]Kanatchikov, describing his impressions of the Gustav List plant, a moderately large machine construction plant with eight hundred workers in 1897, has written, "As for me, I began to be gripped by the poetry of the large metal factory, with its mighty metallic roar, the puffing of its steam-driven machines, its columns of high pipes, its rising clouds of black smoke, which sullied the clear blue sky. . . . I had the feeling that I was merging with the factory, with its stern poetry of labor, a poetry that was growing dearer and closer to me than the quiet, peaceful, lazy poetry of our drowsy village life." Kanatchikov, *Iz istorii*, pp. 43–44.

[126]F. P. Pavlov, *Za desiat' let praktiki (Otryvki iz vospominanii, vpechatlenii i nabliudenii iz fabrichnoi zhizni)* (Moscow, 1901), pp. 2–5.

in most subcontracting shops that manufacture men's clothes. The whole work-shop gets drunk and work comes to a standstill. . . . 'Blue Monday' is a regular ritual. Even the owner himself is prone to alcoholic binges."[127]

Timofeev and Buzinov have both described similar practices taking place at the shop level of a metalworking plant.[128] Each new worker who entered the shop, moreover, underwent an initiation rite. In some factories, it was reported, "the new worker will not even be addressed by his real name [by other workers] but will be called 'Taras' " until he provided drinks for the whole shop. The appointment of a new shop foreman was accompanied by a ritual ceremony in which the workers expressed homage and the foreman reciprocated by buying drinks for all of them.[129]

There were other practices at the shop level of a metalworking plant that drew workers together. The periodic election of a *starosta,* or elder, to tend the shop icon represented one such event and another occasion for collective drinking. Workers also cooperated in collecting funds to assist fellow workers in time of adversity, and to purchase gifts for foremen and upper-management personnel. The latter practice had begun to lapse by 1905, however, when younger workers rejected the custom as demeaning and ridiculed those who persisted in it.[130]

On occasion, workers combined in opposition to the foreman, a key author-ity figure in many enterprises. Because of the foreman's discretionary power in assigning wage rates, he sometimes became an object of hatred and was sub-jected to a humiliating ritual punishment by workers (or even by apprentices with the tacit approval of their elders) who carried him from the shop in a wheelbarrow, with a dirty sack over his head. This practice has been noted among such diverse groups as metalworkers and bakers.[131] All of these customs served to unite workers and to create common bonds among them at the shop level.

It was a significant fact of working-class life at the turn of the century that some workers enjoyed considerably more control and autonomy in their lives than others, both at the workplace and outside it. One area of control involved

[127]Oliunina, *Portnovskii promysel,* p. 256.

[128]Timofeev, *Chem zhivet,* pp. 33–34; Buzinov, *Za Nevskoi zastavoi,* pp. 23–24.

[129]Timofeev, *Chem zhivet,* pp. 80–85. In addition to initiation rites, there were name-day celebra-tions, and celebrations on the occasion of marriages, the birth of children, and completion of apprenticeship.

[130]Ibid., pp. 80–85, 96–98.

[131]Ibid., pp. 98–99; *Listok bulochnikov i konditerov,* no. 8 (November 18, 1906), p. 6.

the labor process itself. The workers' autonomy in this area was often closely related to the extent of mechanization and the complexity of the division of labor. In artisanal enterprises and even within factories, many production processes still relied partially or exclusively on hand labor at the beginning of the twentieth century and involved only a limited division of labor. Workers in these situations were often able to exert more control over the labor process than others, such as mill operatives, for whom the pace of work was determined by a machine.

Prior to 1905, neither mechanization nor an elaborate division of labor had yet been introduced into most types of artisanal production. In the apparel trades, for example, manually operated sewing machines were in use, but electrically powered sewing and cutting machines were still quite rare. In 1900, electrically powered machines could be found only in some St. Petersburg firms manufacturing soldiers' uniforms, linens, and undergarments. Few electrically powered sewing machines were in operation in Moscow as late as 1910.[132] Even manually powered sewing machines were still comparatively rare at the beginning of the century, and it was common for ten seamstresses to share one or two machines as they needed them.

The division of labor in the clothing trades remained extremely limited on the eve of 1905. Apprentices were taught to complete an entire item from beginning to end and to specialize in the sewing of one particular type of garment (e.g., women's dresses, men's suits). Changes in the division of labor had not yet occurred in the clothing trades, and it was only in 1909, for example, that the Moscow firm Karl Lil' and Company, a manufacturer of soldiers' uniforms, introduced a complex division of labor involving seven to nine workers in the manufacture of a single portion of a garment.[133] Generally speaking, technical innovations in artisanal trades, such as electrical cutting and sewing machines in the apparel trades, typesetting machines in printing, and electrical kneading machines in baking, took place only after the 1905 revolution.[134]

Even in highly developed branches of industry there was considerable variation in mechanization and the division of labor. In large metalworking plants, the iron foundries with Bessemer or Martin furnaces were thoroughly mechanized and required an elaborate division of labor. As was noted by Timofeev, "the iron production process itself, by virtue of its uniformity and its demand for a

[132]Gruzdev, *Trud i bor'ba*, p. 4; Oliunina, *Portnovskii promysel*, pp. 45–46.

[133]Oliunina, *Portnovskii promysel*, p. 6.

[134]Sher, *Istoriia*, p. 10; *Professional'nyi vestnik*, no. 2 (January 20, 1907), p. 11; *Zhizn' pekarei*, no. 2(5) (May 10, 1914), p. 8.

complex division of labor, makes it easy for an unskilled worker to get used to a specific task."[135] Within the same enterprise, conditions in the machine or pattern shop presented a quite different picture. Here most of the work was performed by hand, relying on the skill of "factory artisans" who had mastered such crafts as metalfitting or patternmaking. Similarly, in printing firms, typesetting was still unmechanized at the turn of the century, with little division of labor. Elsewhere in the same firm, mechanical presses might be in operation, and in these shops an elaborate division of labor had already been introduced by 1905.

Workers with craft skills, whether they were employed in an artisanal shop or a workshop in a factory enterprise, often performed jobs that allowed considerable latitude for control over the labor process. In metalworking shops, a worker typically received an assignment from the foreman and a wage-rate for the job. From here on in, the individual was left to his own devices, a situation that engendered a certain amount of independence and self-sufficiency among skilled metalworkers. The textile mill hand, by contrast, seldom had an opportunity to experience autonomy or mastery on the job. The young woman who tended the self-acting spinning machines, "overseeing the frame [and] adjusting the torn thread while following the moving carriage,"[136] was scarcely in a position to feel the pride and self-sufficiency of a skilled worker who had completed a difficult assignment involving both discretion and specialized knowledge. These aspects of the work experience of skilled workers, in combination with other attributes, contributed to their readiness to combine collectively after the turn of the century for the purpose of exerting more extensive and meaningful control over other facets of the workplace as well.

LIFE OUTSIDE THE WORKPLACE

The labor process, however important, was not the only circumstance that shaped the way workers viewed themselves and life around them. Equally influential was the extent to which a worker could venture beyond the workplace into the city itself, to mix with other social groups and to participate in the cultural and recreational life of a large metropolis.

Some workers knew little of city life, for they were not permitted to leave the workplace at mealtimes or even at the end of the workday. In many artisanal and

[135]Timofeev, *Chem zhivet,* p. 11.
[136]Pavlov, *Za desiat' let,* p. 104.

commercial firms, workers remained confined to the shop during their laboring time, often for fourteen or sixteen hours at a stretch, taking all their meals in the workshop. Apprentices were the only ones who regularly left the premises to fetch tea or vodka for adult workers. Only in the more exclusive and better-paying shops did the employer provide a regular monetary subsidy for meals, enabling workers to eat in a local canteen or tavern.

In metalworking plants, by contrast, "the lunch whistle blows. You hurriedly hide your tools and leave the workshop with the other workers. They frisk you at the factory gates, and when nothing is found, they let you out into the street."[137] Workers fortunate enough to live in the vicinity of the plant returned home for their meal, while others went to a nearby canteen or tavern.

The right to depart at mealtimes represented only one aspect of a worker's control over nonworking time. More consequential still was the ability to live outside the premises of the workplace. At the turn of the century, there were still many segments of the St. Petersburg and Moscow labor force—mainly artisans, salesclerks, and service workers—for whom the workplace was both the location of employment and of lodging. In her study of Moscow apparel trades, Oliunina noted that living arrangements

usually depend on how closely [workers] are tied to the village, where many of them still have families. . . . A majority of tailoring shop workers rent rooms. However, those who still have ties to the village are more likely to live in the workshop or just rent a bed. Among subcontract workers, two-thirds of those with ties to the village sleep in the workshop or rent only a bed.[138]

Workers forced to live on the premises of the shop had to endure the continual surveillance of the employer, who, in many cases, controlled not only working hours but also their leisure time. In many small bakeries and candymaking shops, employers locked the doors at the end of the workday to prevent workers from departing.[139]

Not all artisanal workers and salesclerks lived at the workplace. The more prosperous workers rented accommodations in one of the working-class districts of St. Petersburg or Moscow. Several families often shared a single room, which sometimes also served as a workplace for a garret-master shoemaker or tailor. "Rented rooms," reported Oliunina, "are generally overcrowded and damp. There is constant noise and hubbub in such living quarters, and workers

[137]Timofeev, *Chem zhivet*, p. 31.
[138]Oliunina, *Portnovskii promysel*, p. 253.
[139]*Professional'noe dvizhenie Moskovskikh pishchevikov*, pp. 102, 147.

can never find the relaxation they need after a hard day's work. There is an obvious link between drunkenness and these kinds of living and working conditions."[140] Rented rooms were not always a physical improvement over conditions in the shops, but those who lived in such lodgings could extend their horizons and exert more control over their leisure time than their less fortunate counterparts confined to the workplace.

By the beginning of the twentieth century, the great majority of industrial workers in St. Petersburg and Moscow found housing outside the factory gates. In St. Petersburg, for example, only 10 percent of the factory labor force in 1897 lived in employer-provided housing, and those who did were generally unskilled or semiskilled workers in such industries as textiles or food processing.[141] There was often a close correlation between the type of lodging secured by a worker and the worker's level of skill, wages, and ties to the countryside. Housing was usually the largest single item in the worker's budget, and workers who supported a family in the village—many of them unskilled or semiskilled elements with relatively low wages—sought to minimize their housing costs by finding inexpensive lodging.[142] These workers frequently rented a cot or a corner of a room, or they joined an artel *(artel')*, a cooperative living arrangement, often involving workers from a certain village or rural district.[143] The members of an artel contributed a fixed sum to rent a room or an apartment together and to cover expenses for meals, often prepared by the wife of one of the workers.[144]

Regardless of the type or condition of the accommodations, workers who lived outside their place of employment enjoyed freedom in their leisure time which was seldom available to those obliged to live in a company dormitory or on the premises of the workshop or store. Living outside the workplace gave workers considerably more contact with city life and more opportunities for social interaction with other segments of the urban population and with workers from other firms and occupations. It enabled some of them—typically the more skilled, literate, and prosperous workers with shorter hours and more leisure

---

[140]Oliunina, *Portnovskii promysel*, p. 254. See also M. I. Pokrovskaia, *Po podvalam, cherdakam i uglovym kvartiram Peterburga* (St. Petersburg, 1903) for a discussion of contemporary workers' living quarters.

[141]Kir'ianov, *Zhiznennyi uroven'*, chap. 4; Kir'ianov, "Ekonomicheskoe polozhenie," pp. 169–172; *Professional'noe dvizhenie Moskovskikh pishchevikov*, p. 147.

[142]On workers' budgets, see S. N. Prokopovich, *Biudzhety Peterburgskikh rabochikh* (St. Petersburg, 1909); Kir'ianov, *Zhiznennyi uroven'*, pp. 199–212, 259–268.

[143]Johnson, *Peasant and Proletarian*, pp. 72–73, 91–92.

[144]For a vivid description of an artel in St. Petersburg, see Timofeev, *Chem zhivet*, pp. 15–16.

time—to take advantage of the cultural, recreational, and educational opportunities available in St. Petersburg and Moscow. This, in turn, helped to create
informal social networks that affected their disposition to participate in collective organizations with workers from other enterprises or industries.

During their leisure hours, many workers frequented the taverns and beer
halls that were a characteristic feature of working-class neighborhoods. In the
immediate vicinity of the St. Petersburg Putilov plant alone, more than fifty
drinking establishments were operating at the turn of the century. When workers
left the factory gates on payday (Saturday), there was hardly a free place in these
pubs.[145] On Sunday, a full or partial day of rest, many workers attended services
in the morning at the local Russian Orthodox church. Religious observance was
widespread among all segments of the laboring population, and some employers
even required church attendance as a condition of employment.[146] Few workers'
quarters lacked "a holy icon, blackened with age, [hanging] in the corner,"[147] and
an icon could be found in most places of employment.

Some workers, again typically the more skilled and prosperous elements,
sought self-improvement in their free time. Beginning in the 1860s, intellectuals
took an increasingly vigorous role in arranging educational activities for workers. Typical of these ventures were the Prechistenskie Workers' Courses, established by the Moscow branch of the Imperial Russian Technical Society in 1897.
Situated in a factory district of the city, the Prechistenskie courses attracted
workers from large plants and railway shops, and within a year of their establishment, three hundred workers were enrolled in courses.[148] With the advent of
Zubatov societies in Moscow in 1902–1903 and the Gapon Assembly in St.
Petersburg the following year, many workers were drawn to lectures and meetings.[149] The social dances organized by the Zubatov organizations also proved

[145]*Istoriia Putilovskogo zavoda 1801–1917* (Moscow, 1961), p. 66.

[146]Ibid., pp. 68–72; *Professional'noe dvizhenie Moskovskikh pishchevikov*, p. 147. An ethnographic
study conducted in the 1920s reported that 70 percent of the male workers and 85 percent of the
female workers who were interviewed had attended church prior to the 1917 revolution. Kabo,
Ocherki, p. 132. For a revealing account of one worker's attitude toward religion, see Kanatchikov,
Iz istorii, pp. 8, 11–14.

[147]Timofeev, *Chem zhivet*, p. 14. Timofeev is describing the interior of a workers' artel.

[148]*Istoriia Moskvy*, 5:249; *Sovremennoe khoziaistvo goroda Moskvy*, p. 75. The Prechistenskie courses
were organized on three levels: a lower school specializing in teaching basic skills and subjects; a
middle school, which offered more advanced and specialized courses; the higher school, which
provided lectures on history, literature, economics, and other subjects. Classes met in the evenings,
between 8 and 10 o'clock. The Moscow city government provided a subsidy to support the classes.
By 1910–1911, 1,700 workers were enrolled there.

[149]For a discussion of the Zubatov and Gapon movements, see below, chapter 2.

highly popular among the more skilled and better-paid workers.[150] But it was only in 1905 and afterward that broad strata of the St. Petersburg and Moscow laboring population found new and varied outlets for their leisure time, and gravitated in large and impressive numbers to the organizations brought into existence by the first great crisis in the autocratic system.

There were many lines of stratification within the urban working class at the beginning of the twentieth century, but none more important than the acquisition of skill in a labor force where unskilled and semiskilled workers predominated. Skill, to a greater extent than any other single factor, served to differentiate workers and to provide an important determinant of workers' attributes and life histories.

A key element in the formation of workers' social identities, the mastery of a skill often entailed early arrival at the urban workplace to serve an apprenticeship, prolonged or permanent residence in the city, and the attenuation or severance of ties to the village. Skilled workers generally attained higher wages, better working and living conditions, and more control over the labor process than unskilled or semiskilled strata of the labor in the same industry or occupation. They also tended to be male and to have a higher literacy rate than their unskilled or semiskilled counterparts. On the streets of St. Petersburg or Moscow, skilled workers were distinguished by their outward appearance, their demeanor, and their familiarity with city life. In a working population still dominated by semipeasant recruits who lacked skill and occupational specialization, the acquisition of a skilled trade and specialized knowledge frequently bestowed upon workers status and dignity denied to those beneath them in the labor hierarchy. These status gradations meant a great deal to the workers themselves, who valued highly their designation (for example, as *masterovye)* and respectful treatment by fellow workers and management (such as the form of address *vy)* to which they felt entitled.

Craft identification *(tsekhovshchina)* and more generally, occupational designations, provide further evidence of the workers' consciousness in matters relating to their placement in the urban labor force. Recognition and self-designation as a metalfitter or a ribbonweaver, a tailor or a baker, a salesclerk or a waiter, had important implications for workers, many of whom found themselves in a context quite different from the one where they had begun their lives. These new self-images were still sometimes confused and uncertain, but they were a signifi-

---

[150]*Professional'noe dvizhenie Moskovskikh pishchevikov,* p. 177.

cant aspect of workers' social identities and would provide an important basis of solidarity in collective organizations.

Experiences acquired at the workplace and outside it contributed further to the way workers came to view themselves and their relation to others. The immediate work environment—the location of a worker's daily experiences at the place of employment up to sixteen hours a day for six or even seven days a week—had a far-reaching effect on attitudes and social relationships. While it would be a mistake to disregard the particularities of the artisanal workshop, the sales firm, or the large factory, it is nonetheless significant that workers in these quite different situations sometimes encountered similar kinds of conditions and practices. Attention has been drawn to the relatively small scale of the immediate work environment, not only in artisanal workshops and many sales firms, but also in certain shops within large factories such as metalworking plants.

Notwithstanding Russia's technological advantage as a latecomer to industrialization, hand labor and a limited division of labor persisted in artisanal trades and even in some facets of factory produ on. While some aspects of production in industries such as metalworking and printing were already highly mechanized at the beginning of the twentieth century and involved an elaborate division of labor, others depended primarily or exclusively on the labor of highly skilled workers ("factory artisans"), who shared a number of common characteristics with their artisanal counterparts, namely, a reliance on hand labor to perform tasks requiring lengthy apprenticeship training, and a skilled work hierarchy. These "factory artisans," together with many artisanal workers, exerted significant control over the labor process itself, and this, in turn, reinforced their feelings of mastery, self-respect, and craft pride. The propinquity of skilled workers in certain work environments and the persistence of shop-level customs and traditions served to fortify common bonds and to build bases of solidarity among them that facilitated collective action.

Experiences acquired outside the workplace also contributed to the worker's outlook in subtle and complex ways. The disposition of leisure time, the opportunity to leave the workplace at mealtimes and after hours, the amount of leisure time available to partake of city life—all of these played a part in the gradual process by which some St. Petersburg and Moscow workers came to acquire a new social identity at the beginning of the twentieth century and to feel themselves part of a larger collectivity within urban society.

Chapter 2

The Foundations of the Organized Labor Movement Before 1905

> I found myself at several meetings whose characteristic feature was that they imbued all demands with a "search for justice," a general aspiration to put an end to the present impossible conditions. . . . And I thought that in all of these demands, workers were motivated not so much by considerations of a material character as by purely moral aspirations to settle everything "according to justice" and to force employers to atone for their past sins.
>
> *S. I. Somov on meetings of workers*
> *in the Gapon Assembly*[1]

On the eve of 1905, a variety of organizations in St. Petersburg and Moscow claimed a working-class membership. These organizations—some legal, others illegal—originated under widely different circumstances and pursued different goals. Included among them were artisanal guilds, mutual aid societies, government-sponsored labor associations, strike and factory committees, and radical political groups.

The importance of these organizations, for our purposes, lies in the foundation they provided for the labor movement that emerged in the course of 1905. The rapid and telescoped development of workers' associations during the revolution was facilitated, at least in part, by antecedent organizational experiences and models acquired by workers, particularly in the years after the turn of the century. Even under conditions of autocratic rule, which greatly inhibited the growth of voluntary associations, there were limited opportunities for collective organization and for the formation of a working-class leadership before 1905.

[1]S. I. Somov [I. M. Peskin], "Iz istorii sotsialdemokraticheskogo dvizheniia v Peterburge v 1905 godu (Lichnye vospominaniia)," *Byloe*, no. 4 (16) (April 1907), pp. 34–35.

ARTISANAL GUILDS AND MUTUAL AID SOCIETIES

The oldest legal associations among Petersburg and Moscow workers were artisanal guilds and mutual aid societies. Originating in the eighteenth and nineteenth centuries, respectively, these organizations were still active at the beginning of the twentieth century. But whereas in Western Europe, guilds and mutual aid societies provided significant collective experiences for workers before and during the introduction of a factory system,[2] in Russia these organizations did not play a comparable role.

From the outset, Russia's guilds differed fundamentally from their counterparts in Western Europe by virtue of two characteristics: they lacked the status of closed corporations and the exclusive authority over production and distribution.[3] Their activities, moreover, were determined by state regulation, and they functioned under direct government supervision. When industrialization began in the second half of the nineteenth century, guilds were permitted to remain juridically intact, but by 1900 most handicraft production was carried on outside their jurisdiction. Guild artisans remained quiescent in the face of this development, for their position and status had not suffered a deterioration. On the contrary, by the turn of the century, guild journeymen constituted an "aristocratic" elite in the workshops of St. Petersburg and Moscow.

A total of 52,075 artisans were registered in guilds in St. Petersburg in 1900, and 51,581 in Moscow.[4] They were subdivided into three categories: master craftsmen, journeymen, and apprentices. The former group, consisting mainly of workshop owners (10,275 in St. Petersburg and 27,174 in Moscow), cannot be

[2]There is a vast literature dealing with this question in various Western European countries. See especially E. P. Thompson, *The Making of the English Working Class* (New York, 1964); William G. Sewell, *Work and Revolution in France: The Language of Labor from the Old Regime to 1848* (Cambridge, England, 1980); P. H. Noyes, *Organization and Revolution: Working-Class Associations in the German Revolutions of 1848-1849* (Princeton, N.J., 1966).

[3]Reginald E. Zelnik, *Labor and Society in Tsarist Russia: The Factory Workers of St. Petersburg, 1855-1870* (Stanford, Calif., 1971), pp. 11–17; K. A. Pazhitnov, *Problema remeslennykh tsekhov v zakonodatel'stve russkogo absoliutizma* (Moscow, 1952), chap. 3. The first laws regulating artisanal trades were promulgated in 1721 during the reign of Peter the Great. In accordance with these regulations, guilds *(tsekhi)* on the German model were officially established in Russia. More than a half century later, in 1785, new regulations were drawn up setting the conditions for entering and practicing an urban handicraft. These Artisanal Statutes *(Remeslennoe polozhenie)* became the basis for all subsequent legislation concerning urban handicrafts.

[4]*Remeslenniki i remeslennoe upravlenie v Rossii* (Petrograd, 1916), p. 32.

considered part of the working population.[5] There were 41,800 journeymen and apprentices in the capital and 24,407 in Moscow, 28 percent and 16 percent of the total artisanal labor force in each city, respectively.

Guild artisans (journeymen and apprentices) were frequently second- or third-generation craftsmen or the offspring of skilled factory workers or urban working-class families. They formed a highly skilled elite within the workshops,[6] enjoying privileged status, high wages, and special treatment by employers. In the words of a contemporary baker, the *diplomnye*—as guild journeymen were called— "liked to hear sweet words such as 'monsieur,' and guild traditions were strong among them."[7]

Although they were part of the "aristocracy" within artisanal shops, often performing some sort of supervisory functions, guild journeymen could not anticipate upward mobility into the ranks of workshop owners. In contrast to an earlier time, most guild journeymen at the beginning of the twentieth century remained wage earners for the duration of their working lives.

The local Boards of Artisanal Trades, which administered guild affairs, were under the domination of workshop owners. The boards adopted a lax attitude toward the enforcement of labor protective regulations in the Artisanal Statutes, confining their activities to registration and certification.[8] Guild journeymen and apprentices who stood to benefit from these regulations were excluded from the local Boards and from direct participation in guild administration.

Guilds no longer exercised a direct influence over the lives of most artisanal workers in St. Petersburg and Moscow on the eve of 1905, but the traditions of craft pride, rooted originally in the guilds and perpetuated by them, continued to have widespread appeal even among nonguild artisans. The Boards of Artisanal Trades, moreover, served as the only legally constituted authority in artisanal

---

[5]Ibid. Some of the masters registered in the guilds were not engaged in handicraft production; they belonged, instead, to the legal category of *remeslennik* (artisan), a designation entitling them to urban residence. According to regulations enacted at an earlier time, individuals in this category were required to belong to a guild. On this point, see Pazhitnov, *Problema remeslennykh tsekhov*, pp. 134–135.

[6]For certification as a journeyman or master, the Artisanal Statutes required submission of sample workmanship to the local Board of Artisanal Trades, to be judged by a special craft certification board. Tsentral'nyi gosudarstvennyi istoricheskii arkhiv (TsGIA), f. 23, op. 7, d. 470, pp. 68, 72–3 for a description of this procedure in operation.

[7]*Zhizn' pekarei*, no. 2(5) (May 10, 1914), p. 7.

[8]*Vpered*, no. 4 (May 20, 1906), p. 3.

trades, a circumstance of some importance when workers turned their attention to collective organization in the spring and summer of 1905.[9]

Apart from the guilds, the earliest legal associations among St. Petersburg and Moscow workers were mutual aid societies established in the nineteenth century among artisans, sales-clerical employees, skilled service workers, and some factory groups. On the whole, the movement to form mutual aid societies in St. Petersburg and Moscow was exceedingly feeble, testimony to the government's highly restrictive and intrusive policies and to the inhospitable environment for voluntary association in Tsarist Russia.

The first and most consistently enthusiastic participants in mutual aid societies were printers and sales-clerical employees, whose skill, literacy, and urbanization rendered them exceptionally well suited to the tasks of collective organization. Printers, in fact, formed the first mutual aid societies in Russia, beginning in Warsaw in 1814, and then in Riga and Odessa in 1816.[10] In the capital, German printers were the first to establish a mutual aid society (1838), followed sixteen years later by Russian printers (1854).[11] Sales-clerical groups, who were second only to the printers in the friendly society movement, formed a mutual aid organization in 1865.[12] Moscovites were considerably slower to establish associations for mutual benefit, and right up to the 1905 revolution the friendly society movement in Moscow was far weaker than in the capital. Here, too, salesclerks and printers were the first to organize—the clerks in 1863, the printers in 1869.[13]

---

[9]See below, chapter 3.

[10]S. N. Prokopovich, *K rabochemu voprosu v Rossii* (St. Petersburg, 1905), p. 8; *Istoriia Leningradskogo soiuza rabochikh poligraficheskogo proizvodstva*. Book 1: *1904-1907* (henceforth *ILS*) (Leningrad, 1925), p. 7. For additional material on the development of mutual aid societies see V. V. Sviatlovskii, "Iz istorii kass i obshchestv vzaimopomoshchi rabochikh," *Arkhiv istorii truda v Rossii*, Book 4 (Petrograd, 1922), pp. 32–46, and O. Rozenfel'd, *Istoriia professional'nogo dvizheniia v Rossii: Sinkhronisticheskie tablitsy*, 3rd ed. (Moscow, 1924), pp. 7–14.

[11]*ILS*, p. 7; Prokopovich, *K rabochemu voprosu*, pp. 8–9; V. Grinevich, *Professional'noe dvizhenie rabochikh v Rossii* (St. Petersburg, 1908), p. 10.

[12]Maks Gordon, ed., *Iz istorii professional'nogo dvizheniia sluzhashchikh v Peterburge: Pervyi etap (1904-1919)* (Leningrad, 1925), pp. 9–10.

[13]A. M. Gudvan, *Ocherki po istorii dvizheniia sluzhashchikh v Rossii*, chast' 1: *Do revoliutsii 1905 goda* (Moscow, 1925), pp. 63–69; Prokopovich, *K rabochemu voprosu*, p. 22; V. V. Sher, *Istoriia professional'nogo dvizheniia rabochikh pechatnogo dela v Moskve* (Moscow, 1911), pp. 73–75. In 1863, the government changed the procedure for securing legalization of a mutual aid society. Whereas formerly the Tsar's personal approval had been required, henceforth the Minister of Internal Affairs was authorized to grant legal status.

In the decades that followed, a small number of other mutual benefit associations were established by Petersburg and Moscow artisans, sales-clerical workers, and skilled service groups, nearly all of them originating in the 1860s or in the period between 1889 and 1904.[14] Most of these organizations involved both employers and workers, and in some cases, the membership included supervisory personnel and even government officials, clergy, and others.[15] Friendly societies also arose among some factory groups in the nineteenth century, mostly in the metalworking industry. They were usually founded at individual enterprises and operated as joint ventures, depending on worker and employer contributions to subsidize benefits. A mutual aid society at the Petersburg Imperial China and Glass factory was established in 1860, followed by another at the Aleksandrovskii Railroad and Machine Plant in 1861.[16]

Metalworkers at the Nevskii Shipbuilding and Machine Plant in the capital attempted to form a mutual aid society for all metalworkers in the city during the 1880s, but the organizers were arrested and the project failed to materialize.[17] In

[14]In addition to mutual aid societies formed by Petersburg printers—including the organization of typesetters (1866), the burial society of printers (1899), and seven other societies established in individual printing firms between 1894 and 1904—several other societies were formed in St. Petersburg between 1862 and 1902 by German artisans (1862), gardeners (1864), Russian artisans (1867), salesclerks (1885), gold-silversmiths (1892), fabric cutters (1896), barbers (1899), waiters (1902), pharmacists (1902), accountants and bookkeepers (1904). In Moscow, societies were formed by artisans (1875), pharmacists (1885), commercial employees (1889), engravers and operators of roller printers in textile factories (1898–1899), waiters (1902). This list is not exhaustive, and no research on this important subject has been undertaken either by Soviet or by Western scholars. The above list was compiled from the following sources: Prokopovich, *K rabochemu voprosu*, pp. 8–9, 18–19; Grinevich, *Professional'noe dvizhenie*, p. 10; Gudvan, *Ocherki*, p. 70; *ILS*, p. 87; S. M. Gruzdev, "Iz istorii professional'nogo dvizheniia 1905 g. v Peterburge," in *Materialy po istorii professional'nogo dvizheniia v Peterburge za 1905-1907 gg.: Sbornik* (henceforth *MIPDP*) (Leningrad, 1926), pp. 43–44; *Biulleten' Muzeia sodeistviia trudu*, republished in *Obshcheprofessional'nye organy 1905-1907 gg.*, vyp. 1 (Moscow, 1926), pp. 97, 110, n. 30; S. M. Gruzdev, *Trud i bor'ba shveinikov v Petrograde 1905-1916 gg.* (Leningrad, 1929), pp. 42–43.

[15]The Petersburg mutual aid society of salesclerks (1865), for example, included among its members leading government officials such as K. P. Pobedonostsev and D. F. Trepov; the Grand Duke Sergei Aleksandrovich was a member of the Moscow mutual aid society of salesclerks. Gudvan, *Ocherki*, p. 73. In some societies formed in artisanal trades, such as the Petersburg mutual aid society of fabric cutters (1896), the membership consisted largely of workshop owners. Gruzdev, *Trud i bor'ba*, p. 43.

[16]F. A. Bulkin, *Na zare profdvizheniia: Istoriia Peterburgskogo soiuza metallistov 1906-1914 gg.* (Moscow and Leningrad, 1924), p. 91; Prokopovich, *K rabochemu voprosu*, pp. 36, 125.

[17]Bulkin, *Na zare*, pp. 92–93; V. Tsytsarin, "Vospominaniia metallista," *Vestnik truda*, no. 12 (61) (December 1925), p. 34.

1899, however, the Mutual Aid Society of Workers in Engineering Plants attained legal status in the capital.[18] By the beginning of the twentieth century, a small number of friendly societies existed in state-operated metalworking plants in or near St. Petersburg (including the Baltiiskii, Obukhov, Izhorskii, and Sestroretskii plants), at Moscow's Gustav List metalworking plant, and elsewhere.[19] In addition, several illegal mutual benefit funds became established at the end of the nineteenth century in the Vasil'evskii Island and Aleksandro-Nevskaia districts of the capital.[20]

The steep entry fees and monthly dues charged by most mutual aid societies restricted the number of working-class members,[21] and those who joined tended to be highly skilled and well paid. Few mutual aid societies had more than 1,000 members, and most had considerably fewer. On the eve of 1905, for example, the mutual aid society of Petersburg printers had a mere three hundred members, and only 910 typesetters belonged to the capital's mutual aid society of typesetters. The Petersburg Mutual Aid Society of Workers in Engineering Plants attracted only several hundred members.[22] The Moscow Mutual Aid Society of Salesclerks, with 2,726 members at the turn of the century, represented an exception to this pattern, as did the Petersburg Burial Society of Workers in the Printing Trades, with 2,000 members.[23] In subscription as well as initiative, printers and sales-clerical workers outpaced other groups in the friendly society movement, although even here the record is uneven. Moscow printers, in contrast to their counterparts in the capital, achieved a maximum membership of

[18]Bulkin, *Na zare*, pp. 92–93; P. Vasil'ev, "Ushakovshchina," *Trud v Rossii*, no. 1 (1925), pp. 143–144

[19]Bulkin, *Na zare*, p. 91; Jeremiah Schneiderman, *Sergei Zubatov and Revolutionary Marxism: The Struggle for the Working Class in Tsarist Russia* (Ithaca, 1976), p. 95; Prokopovich, *K rabochemu voprosu*, pp. 38–39.

[20]Bulkin, *Na zare*, p. 96. Some illegal mutual aid funds were also organized by Social Democrats to assist the families of workers who had been discharged or arrested for political activities. See Allan K. Wildman, *The Making of a Workers' Revolution: Russian Social Democracy, 1891–1903* (Chicago, 1967), pp. 94–100, for a discussion of the origin and role of these funds in St. Petersburg and elsewhere in the 1890s.

[21]*ILS*, p. 88, reports that monthly dues of 1 ruble to 1 ruble 25 kopecks was typical for mutual aid societies among Petersburg printers. A survey of the Moscow Mutual Aid Society of Printers conducted in 1907 revealed that 65 percent of the members earned more than forty rubles per month, and another 12 percent earned thirty-five to forty rubles, at a time when the average monthly wage in the printing trades was 34 rubles 70 kopecks. V. A. Svavitskii and V. Sher, *Ocherk polozheniia rabochikh pechatnogo dela v Moskve* (St. Petersburg, 1909), table 5.

[22]*ILS*, p. 87; P. Severianin, "Soiuz rabochikh pechatnogo dela," *Bez zaglaviia*, no. 14 (April 23, 1906), p. 53; Bulkin, *Na zare*, p. 93.

[23]Gudvan, *Ocherki*, p. 70; *ILS*, p. 87.

460 in the mutual aid society of printers, about 4 percent of the workers in the city's printing trades.[24]

The principal function of mutual aid societies was to provide material benefits to members in the event of illness or accident. Many societies, however, went beyond these basic tasks and offered assistance to widows and orphans of deceased members, burial costs, medical treatment for members and their families, unemployment benefits, assistance in finding employment, grants to individuals entering military service, pensions to those with a work-related disability, and legal aid in matters relating especially to labor regulations.[25] Mutual aid societies did not generally concern themselves with such matters as the terms and conditions of labor. Considering the prominent role of employers in many mutual aid organizations, it is understandable why they so seldom directed their attention to these issues. Yet there were a few instances when such matters were addressed. In March 1900 the Mutual Aid Society of Petersburg Typesetters raised the issue of Sunday rest.[26] Two years later, the same organization initiated its own journal, *Naborshchik* [Typesetter], which dealt with a wide range of problems in the printing trades and even took the initiative in proposing modest reforms to benefit printing workers.[27] At the all-Russian congresses of mutual aid societies of sales-clerical employees, held in 1896 and 1898, issues relating to labor-management problems were on the agenda.[28] The first gatherings of their kind, these congresses brought together representatives of mutual aid organizations from throughout the Empire.

On the whole, mutual aid societies appear not to have provided workers with opportunities for participation in administration. In most societies, employers and managerial personnel controlled the affairs of the association and were elected to key offices. At best, workers held token positions on the governing board.[29] Nevertheless, mere membership in a mutual aid society represented an important experience for workers, accustoming them to the procedures and benefits of a voluntary association. The impact of these experiences can be

[24]Sher, *Istoriia*, pp. 77–78.

[25]Prokopovich, *K rabochemu voprosu*, pp. 8, 9, 22; Sher, *Istoriia*, pp. 81–82; *ILS*, pp. 88–89.

[26]*ILS*, p. 100.

[27]*ILS*, pp. 52, 101; S. Nikitin, "Ocherki po istorii professional'noi pechati v Rossii: Pechat' 1905 goda," in *Materialy po istorii professional'nogo dvizheniia v Rossii*, (henceforth *MIPDR),* 5 vols. (Moscow, 1924–1927), vol. 2, pp. 147–148; Severianin, "Soiuz rabochikh pechatnogo dela," pp. 53–54. *Naborshchik,* which was renamed *Naborshchik i pechatnyi mir* in 1905, continued publication until 1916.

[28]Gudvan, *Ocherki*, pp. 96–119. The congresses were held in Nizhni-Novgorod (1896) and Moscow (1898) with government authorization.

[29]Bulkin, *Na zare*, p. 91.

discerned, for example, among the Petersburg printers. Eleven mutual aid societies existed among printers in the capital on the eve of 1905. With a combined membership of three to five thousand workers, these mutual aid societies attracted the participation of 16 to 27 percent of the labor force in the capital's printing and binding trades.[30] Typesetters were especially enthusiastic about mutual assistance, and within this highly skilled group, consisting primarily of "factory artisans," one out of every four or five workers belonged to the Mutual Aid Society of Typesetters alone on the eve of 1905.[31] In addition, some typesetters belonged to one of the other ten mutual aid societies in the capital. The involvement of Petersburg typesetters, and printing workers more generally, in mutual aid societies gave them a familiarity with collective organization and a preexisting network of contacts that facilitated their rapid progress toward trade unionism in 1905.[32]

Apart from the capital's printers, the mutual aid society movement in Petersburg and Moscow was confined to a small group of workers, usually the most prosperous and highly skilled within their industry or occupation. Thus, the mutual aid societies, like the artisanal guilds, did not directly touch the lives of most workers. But this does not mean that these organizations were without influence over the bulk of the labor force which stood outside their ranks. Just as the guilds served to fortify craft allegiances and parochialism even among nonguild members, so the mutual aid societies left their imprint on workers who were unable or unwilling to join them. Mutual aid societies demonstrated the benefits of collective self-help as a means of defense against the depredations of the industrial age, an idea with wide appeal among workers who lacked government or employer assistance in the face of illness, accident, or other adversity. At the first opportunity to create mass-membership organizations in 1905–1907, workers made the provision of mutual aid a paramount task.

THE ZUBATOV EXPERIMENT IN MOSCOW

In the decade preceding the revolution, Petersburg and Moscow workers intermittently engaged in strikes that sometimes acquired massive dimensions. Such

[30]*ILS*, p. 87; Severianin, "Soiuz rabochikh pechatnogo dela," p. 53. Severianin places membership in mutual aid societies at four to five thousand Petersburg printers.

[31]*ILS*, pp. 11, 87. In addition to mutual aid societies, Petersburg printers also formed a music and drama circle in February 1904, and they organized artels in the same year. *ILS*, pp. 90, 92.

[32]See below, chapter 3.

was the situation in the Petersburg textile industry in 1896–1897, in the capital's metalworking industry in 1901, and in the Moscow printing trades in 1903.[33] Work stoppages and the endeavor to organize collectively went hand in hand as workers searched for means of coordination and unity in labor-management conflicts. Reacting to these incidents of unrest, tsarist authorities attempted to devise new methods for reconciling the workers' demand for collective organization with the government's insistence on maintaining social control. The Zubatov and Gapon experiments in police-supervised labor association exemplify the interplay between workers' aspirations and government policy.

The Zubatov experiment, which was launched in Moscow in 1901, produced the first mass-based legal workers' organization in this city and laid the groundwork for the subsequent development of trade unions during the revolution.[34] In contrast to mutual aid societies, the Zubatov associations reached a larger and more heterogeneous group of workers and performed a variety of functions extending far beyond the provision of mutual assistance.

Sergei Zubatov, chief of the Moscow Okhrana from 1896 to 1902 and an energetic and committed monarchist, conceived and implemented the new government strategy for labor. His audacious and imaginative project had no precedent, either in Russia or in Western Europe. It rested on two key assumptions. First, Zubatov believed that the interests of workers and employers could be reconciled if the government intervened as a "supraclass arbiter" to ensure that workers received fair treatment at the workplace.[35] Zubatov's second premise was that workers would remain peaceful and politically loyal to the autocratic system once they had a legal means of achieving material improvement at the workplace and civil equality in the society at large.[36]

Whereas formerly the government had relied primarily, although not exclusively, on repression and punitive measures to contain labor unrest, Zubatov counseled a policy of active government involvement in industrial relations. A close observer of Western European labor movements and well versed in the works of Eduard Bernstein, Werner Sombart, and Beatrice and Sidney Webb, Zubatov was confident that workers would proceed along a reformist rather

[33]Strikes are discussed further in the sections "Factory Organization" and "Illegal Unions and Parties on the Eve of 1905" below.

[34]For a comprehensive discussion of the Zubatov experiment in Moscow and elsewhere in Russia, see Schneiderman, *Sergei Zubatov*.

[35]Schneiderman, *Sergei Zubatov*, p. 57. A valuable discussion of the Zubatovshchina can be found in Solomon M. Schwarz, *The Russian Revolution of 1905: The Workers' Movement and the Formation of Bolshevism and Menshevism* (Chicago, 1967), pp. 267–300.

[36]Schneiderman, *Sergei Zubatov*, p. 80.

than a revolutionary path if the government enforced existing labor legislation and permitted the factory masses to organize collectively, under close police supervision, for purposes of material improvement.[37] Under these conditions, he asserted, workers would reject the appeals of radical intellectuals, remain loyal to the autocratic system, and content themselves with incremental gains achieved by peaceful and lawful means.

Zubatov was not alone in the belief that some form of Western European trade unionism should be permitted to develop legally on Russian soil, albeit with special provisions to ensure government control. His views were shared by such diverse elements as the conservative journalist Lev Tikhomirov of the monarchist newspaper *Moskovskie vedomosti*,[38] and I. Kh. Ozerov, a reform-minded Moscow University professor.[39] Zubatov could not have implemented his project, moreover, without securing powerful support in government circles. Among the initial adherents to his plan were the Moscow Chief of Police, the Governor of Moscow Province, and many officials in the Ministry of Internal Affairs.

In the form originally conceived by Zubatov, the experiment functioned in Moscow for only about one year. Created under the legal rubric of mutual aid associations, the societies soon became involved in labor-management conflicts. By mid-1902 opposition from industrialists and some government ministries, notably the Ministry of Finance, forced Zubatov to modify the activities of the societies to emphasize religious indoctrination instead of industrial relations.[40] With Zubatov's transfer to another post in St. Petersburg in August 1902, the experiment suffered a severe setback, although some of the societies remained active well into 1905.[41]

---

[37]Ibid., pp. 80, 96.

[38]Schneiderman, *Sergei Zubatov*, pp. 161–162, 267. The conservative press in the capital, however, was less sympathetic to the project. Ibid., pp. 176–177. Schwarz, *The Russian Revolution*, p. 267.

[39]Ozerov's views were set forth in a memorandum to the Moscow Chief of Police on January 23, 1902. In the memorandum, Ozerov extolled the virtues of Western European trade unions and urged that they be introduced into Russia, where they would attract "the most cultivated, the uppermost layer, so to speak, in the workers' aristocracy," comprising, he believed, about 10 or 15 percent of the Petersburg labor force. Ozerov confidently assured the Chief of Police that once workers had acquired a legal right to establish trade unions and engage in collective work stoppages, they would moderate their demands and demonstrate political loyalty to the autocratic system. TsGIA, f. 1405, op. 539, d. 329, p. 406. Ozerov subsequently presented these views in his *Politika po rabochemu voprosu v Rossii za poslednie gody* (Moscow, 1906). See also Schneiderman, *Sergei Zubatov*, p. 164.

[40]Schneiderman, *Sergei Zubatov*, pp. 137, 140.

[41]For accounts of Zubatov's decline and dismissal, see ibid., pp. 350–351; Schwarz, *The Russian*

In all, ten Zubatov groups operated in Moscow between 1901 and 1905. Both factory and artisanal workers participated in the movement, and their initial enthusiastic response testifies to the widespread aspiration for collective organization in the years preceding the revolution. Skilled metalworkers and weavers formed the largest and most active societies, but Zubatov organizations also arose among carpenters, buttonmakers, box- and cartonmakers, candymakers, tobacco workers, perfumers, printers, and shoemakers.[42]

Skilled, literate, and experienced workers, some of them former Social Democrats, were recruited by Zubatov to lead the movement.[43] The composition of the rank and file, on the other hand, was highly diverse. Two of the most active groups—the metalworkers and the weavers—belonged to the relatively skilled strata of the labor force, but some recruits to the Zubatov societies appear to have been unskilled or semiskilled. There were also a number of female members.[44] In contrast to the earlier mutual aid societies, Zubatov societies often excluded foremen, assistant foremen, and clerical personnel, although government officials (e.g., police officers and Factory Inspectors), employers, and clergymen were permitted to belong.[45]

Actual membership in the Zubatov societies remained confined to a small number of workers. The tobacco workers' and candymakers' organizations, for example, each attracted only about two hundred members, a mere fraction of the labor force in these industries.[46] But the outreach of the movement was far

---

Revolution, p. 271; A. Kats and Iu. Milonov, eds., *1905:Professional'noe dvizhenie* (Moscow and Leningrad, 1926), pp. 5–6.

[42]Schneiderman, *Sergei Zubatov*, pp. 100–105, 145–146; *Professional'noe dvizhenie Moskovskikh pishchevikov v gody pervoi revoliutsii*, sbornik 1 (Moscow, 1927), pp. 149–151; F. Bogdanov-Evdokimov, "Zubatovshchina v Moskve," *Vestnik truda*, no. 9 (November 1923), p. 237.

[43]Schneiderman, *Sergei Zubatov*, pp. 81, 103; Kats and Milonov, eds., *1905*, p. 3. *Professional'noe dvizhenie Moskovskikh pishchevikov*, pp. 150, 171, notes that the leaders of the Zubatov society among candymakers were, for the most part, *starshie mastera* (master craftsmen with seniority).

[44]Schneiderman, *Sergei Zubatov*, p. 140; *Professional'noe dvizhenie Moskovskikh pishchevikov*, p. 171, notes that the rank and file attracted to the Zubatov society of candymakers were "simple unskilled candymakers."

[45]The Zubatov society of candymakers included, as consultative members, the Governor-General of Moscow Province, the Grand Duke Sergei Aleksandrovich, the Moscow Metropolitan, and the Chief of Police. *Professional'noe dvizhenie Moskovskikh pishchevikov*, p. 150. Kats and Milonov, eds., *1905*, p. 6.

[46]*Professional'noe dvizhenie Moskovskikh pishchevikov*, pp. 150, 184, reports that the society of tobacco workers had 150–200 members out of 3,000 employed in this industry; the candymakers' society attracted 200 members out of more than 3,000 workers employed in the industry. Labor force data are based on *Perepis' Moskvy 1902 g.*, chast' 1, vyp. 2 (Moscow, 1906), pp. 128–129, 150–151.

greater than can be gauged from membership figures alone. Through lectures and meetings, many thousands of Moscow workers came into contact with Zubatov organizations. At the height of the movement, meetings with one thousand workers were not uncommon, and even after the shift from socio-economic to religious and moral themes, lectures were attended by five to seven hundred people.[47]

Zubatov societies furnished the first legal forum in Moscow for the open discussion of problems concerning factory life. Eager to "speak about the inadequacies in our factories," as one former Zubatovist candymaker put it, workers flocked to Zubatov meetings, and for days afterward they discussed themes that had been raised at the lectures.[48] Under cover of these gatherings, radical party organizers sometimes established contact with workers. A Social Democratic group at the Dukat tobacco factory, for example, got started under the auspices of the Zubatov society in this industry.[49]

The Zubatov movement also performed an educative function, providing workers with valuable information about Western European labor movements, labor legislation, and the still unfamiliar practices of collective bargaining and the collective labor contract. A former tobacco worker has described the effect produced by his contacts with the Zubatov society:

When we now recall the speeches of Krasivskii about the conditions of Western European workers, about the organization of trade unions and so on, it is impossible not to recognize that these speeches despite their tendentiousness, had quite an effect on our young and feverish minds, and the thought was taking form in our minds concerning the necessity for struggle to attain an improvement in our condition.[50]

Zubatov societies not only imparted useful information to workers; they also furnished an unprecedented opportunity to seek workplace improvement through legal channels. In early 1902 Zubatov assigned a police officer to receive petitions and complaints from workers concerning workplace conditions and to provide legal consultation regarding their rights. The Moscow courts were subsequently besieged by workers' suits against factory owners.[51]

---

[47]Schneiderman, *Sergei Zubatov*, pp. 137, 140.

[48]*Professional'noe dvizhenie Moskovskikh pishchevikov*, p. 173.

[49]Ibid., pp. 98, 150.

[50]Ibid., p. 184. For similar statements, see pp. 150, 169. A worker at the Gujon mill has described the electrifying effect of Krasivskii on weavers who crowded into a tavern to hear him speak. Tsentral'nyi gosudarstvennyi arkhiv Oktiabr'skoi revoliutsii (henceforth TsGAOR), f. 6860, d. 431, p. 53.

[51]Schneiderman, *Sergei Zubatov*, pp. 143–144. The Moscow Chief of Police, D. F. Trepov, also received workers' petitions describing abuses and malpractices in their factories. Ibid., p. 142.

In one notable case, involving the Gujon and Mussi silk mills in 1902, the Zubatov weavers' organization initiated a work stoppage that spread to fifteen hundred weavers in Moscow mills. The demands put forth in this strike included employer recognition of workers' collective bargaining agents and the introduction of a closed shop—issues that were still comparatively rare in labor-management conflicts before 1905.

The conflict at the Gujon and Mussi mills, waged against an employer who subsequently headed the Moscow Society of Factory Owners, exemplifies the contradictory and problematic nature of Zubatov's experiment.[52] An intransigent employer such as Gujon placed the police in the untenable position of encouraging and supporting a militant mass movement among workers, a situation that produced alarm and indignation among industrialists and many government officials. At least in the short run, legal labor associations failed to validate the founder's prediction that they would eliminate labor unrest and fortify social stability in urban Russian society. Accordingly, this phase of the Zubatov experiment soon came to an end, but it gave Moscow workers their first glimpse of collective struggle conducted under the auspices of a legal workers' organization.[53]

Years later, a candymaker recalled his first introduction to the Zubatov movement in 1904 when he was fourteen years old and already employed at the Savel'ev candy factory:

I asked one candymaker who had been a member of the union:
What is this union for?
He answered:
To fight the factory owners.
Then I asked:
And why are they closing it down?
He answered:
It doesn't matter that they are closing it. We'll organize a new union, stronger, more powerful. When we are all in the union, you won't have to come to the factory before the rest of us to start up the burners.[54]

The Zubatovshchina contributed to the future development of Moscow's organized labor movement by training an indigenous group of working-class leaders, some of whom later put this experience into the service of trade unions. Future organizers of the unions of printers, tobacco workers, candymakers, and

---

[52]An account of this incident can be found in Schneiderman, *Sergei Zubatov*, chap. 5.

[53]For an assessment of the role of the Zubatov experiment by employers, see Kats and Milonov, eds., *1905*, p. 150.

[54]*MIPDR*, 3:328.

metalworkers acquired formative experiences in Zubatov societies.[55] The Zubatovshchina also provided an organizational model, based on a pyramidal three-tiered structure (enterprise, district, and citywide), that was later replicated by trade unions. Representatives from each Zubatov society participated in a citywide "workers' council," prefiguring the formation of the Central Bureau of Trade Unions in the fall of 1905.[56]

With its transparent police involvement, the Zubatov movement became an object of relentless vilification by Social Democrats and other radical groups. Most early liberal supporters of the experiment had deserted it by mid-1902 amid disclosures of police provocation and manipulation of the societies' affairs. The label "Zubatovets" became a term of opprobrium in many circles, a virtual synonym for "provocateur." Disheartened and disillusioned by their experience, some workers became suspicious of trade union type of organizations, which they associated with the Zubatov experiment. But the influence of the Zubatovshchina was not always negative, particularly among predominantly unskilled groups such as tobacco workers and candymakers.[57] By demonstrating the benefits of organized struggle, the Zubatov movement equipped these workers to recognize and respond to the opportunity for independent trade unionism when it arose during the 1905 revolution. As Fedor Bulkin [F. A. Semenov], a future organizer of the Petersburg metalworkers' union, observed:

The Zubatovshchina played . . . a great role in the workers' movement, facilitating the unification of workers, the development of class consciousness among them, giving [them] the possibility for organized struggle with employers and demonstrating to workers their strength.[58]

THE GAPON AND USHAKOV ORGANIZATIONS IN ST. PETERSBURG

Following his transfer to St. Petersburg in mid-1902, Zubatov attempted to organize workers in the capital. These efforts did not meet with success, and a

---

[55]See below, chapter 3.

[56]On the organizational structure of the Zubatov movement, see Kats and Milonov, eds., *1905*, pp. 3–4; Bogdanov-Evdokimov, "Zubatovshchina v Moskve," p. 237; Schwarz, *The Russian Revolution*, pp. 277–278.

[57]In this connection, Schneiderman writes, "The Moscow Zubatovshchina gave the confectioners, perfumers, and tobacco and cigarette workers . . . the rudiments of organizational unity and experience in economic agitation." Schneiderman, *Sergei Zubatov*, p. 184. The first strike ever conducted by Moscow candymakers was organized under Zubatov auspices. *Professional'noe dvizhenie Moskovskikh pishchevikov*, pp. 170–171.

[58]Bulkin, *Na zare*, p. 102.

year later Zubatov was dismissed from his post. But the Zubatov experiment provided fertile soil for yet another government-sponsored labor association in St. Petersburg: the Assembly of Russian Factory and Mill Workers under the direction of Father Georgii Gapon.[59] Like the Zubatov movement, the Gapon Assembly grew out of the government's cooptative strategy for labor. By permitting workers to organize for mutual benefit and self-improvement under the watchful eye of the authorities, government supporters of the project—again concentrated in the powerful Ministry of Internal Affairs—hoped to deflect workers' energies into peaceful, politically loyal channels.

Gapon's activities in the capital got under way in mid-1903 with the establishment of a tearoom-reading room for workers in the Vyborgskaia district. More than a year later, in May 1904, the Assembly had only 170 dues-paying members. It was only in the second half of 1904, with the general upsurge in political activity in the country generated by the Russo-Japanese War and a modest liberalization of government policy, that Gapon's Assembly began to attract a mass following. By the beginning of January 1905, the Assembly had grown to encompass eleven district groups in St. Petersburg with an estimated total of 9,000 members, 1,000 of them women.[60]

The statutes legalizing the Gapon Assembly restricted membership to male and female workers of Russian origin and Christian faith.[61] Both factory and artisanal groups participated in the Assembly, just as they had in the Moscow Zubatov societies, and the organization was subdivided along both district and occupational lines. The three major occupational subdivisions consisted of metalworkers, weavers, and lithographers, but there were also sections formed by shoemakers, tailors, watchmakers, and others. The sections served as centers for the discussion and formulation of economic demands, and appear to have functioned as proto-trade-union organizations.[62]

[59]The government approved the charter of the Assembly on February 15, 1904. V. Ia. Laverychev, *Tsarizm i rabochii vopros v Rossii 1861–1917 gg.* (Moscow, 1972), p. 166.

[60]W. Sablinsky, *The Road to Bloody Sunday: Father Gapon and the St. Petersburg Massacre of 1905* (Princeton, 1976), p. 106. For a discussion of the general atmosphere in the capital during the second half of 1904 and its effect on the Gapon Assembly, see Gerald Dennis Surh, "Petersburg Workers in 1905: Strikes, Workplace Democracy, and the Revolution," Ph.D. dissertation, University of California, Berkeley, 1979, pp. 167–169; Kats and Milonov, eds., *1905*, p. 9.

[61]Sablinsky, *The Road to Bloody Sunday*, p. 139, notes that in practice, these provisions were not observed at the end of 1904. The text of the Assembly statutes is reprinted in part in Kats and Milonov, eds., *1905*, pp. 90–95.

[62]V. V. Sviatlovskii, *Professional'noe dvizhenie v Rossii* (St. Petersburg, 1907), p. 92; P. Dorovatovskii and V. Zlotin, "Khronika," in *MIPDP*, p. 210; Bulkin, *Na zare*, p. 103. The section of lithographers had 150 members but never met. The other sections did hold meetings.

The social composition of the Gapon organization is a matter of considerable importance in light of the subsequent participation of Assembly members in 1905 factory committees, trade unions, and the Soviet of Workers' Deputies. Soviet historians have located the bases of support for the Assembly among the least skilled and most "backward" elements of the labor force, but the evidence does not entirely support this view.[63] There were, to be sure, unskilled and semiskilled workers who joined the organization, particularly in November and December 1904, when a large increase in membership took place.[64] But the largest enterprise-level groups affiliated with the Assembly were located in major metalworking firms such as the Putilov, Nevskii, and Siemens-Halske plants.[65] Gapon supporters at Putilov have been described by a former Assembly member as "very solid and well-read workers, among the highly skilled" in the plant.[66] A contemporary Menshevik, S. I. Somov [I. M. Peskin], who became involved with the Assembly at the end of 1904, observed that at the Putilov plant, "in contrast to the Social Democrats, the Gapon movement attracted the most experienced workers and at the head of [the movement] stood the old factory worker-aristocrats, who were comparatively well paid, sometimes even owned their own little houses near the plant and were firmly entrenched in the factory."[67] The Siemens-Halske plant, which had a large Gapon group, was notable for the predominance of highly skilled, well-paid workers.[68]

Among printing workers, another predominantly skilled group, the response to the Gapon Assembly was mixed. Although the journal *Naborshchik* published the charter of the Gapon Assembly, typesetters proved unenthusiastic. They already had their own mutual aid organizations and were not attracted to the Assembly. The situation was quite different, however, among lithographers, binders, and other groups in the printing trades. The lithographers formed a separate section in the Assembly, and a number of lithographers were prominent in district branches of the organization.[69]

[63]*Istoriia rabochikh Leningrada, 1703-fevral' 1917*, vol. 1 (Leningrad, 1963), p. 262. In making this assertion, Soviet historians are following Lenin's pronouncements. See V. I. Lenin, *Sochineniia*, 55 vols., 5th ed. (Moscow, 1958–1965), vol. 9, p. 217, cited in Laverychev, *Tsarizm*, pp. 166–167.

[64]N. S. Trusova et al., eds., *Nachalo pervoi russkoi revoliutsii: Ianvar'-mart 1905 goda* (Moscow, 1955), p. 9; S. I. Somov, "Iz istorii," *Byloe*, no. 4, p. 49.

[65]Sablinsky, *The Road to Bloody Sunday*, pp. 144, 164–165; F. Semenov-Bulkin, "Smesovshchina," *Trud v Rossii*, no. 1 (1925), p. 159; Somov, "Iz istorii," *Byloe*, no. 4, pp. 46–47.

[66]P. F. Kudelli and G. L. Shidlovskii, eds., *1905: Vospominaniia chlenov SPB soveta rabochikh deputatov* (Leningrad, 1926), p. 34. This statement is taken from the memoir of A. P. Serebrovskii.

[67]Somov, "Iz istorii," *Byloe*, no. 4, p. 46.

[68]Semenov-Bulkin, "Smesovshchina," p. 159.

[69]*ILS*, p. 105.

To a greater extent than Zubatov, Gapon discouraged the involvement of intellectuals and cultivated an indigenous working-class leadership capable of autonomous activity and self-management. The Assembly served as a training ground for activists, who proceeded from the ranks of older, experienced, skilled, literate workers.[70] The metalworker P. I. Kropin and the printer G. S. Usanov typify these Gaponist leaders at the district level.

P. I. Kropin was thirty-seven years old and a metalfitter at the Putilov plant when he joined the Narvskaia district group of the Assembly in July 1904.[71] Born in a village in Vologda province, he had completed rural school and arrived in the capital at the age of eleven. Two years later he entered an apprenticeship in a metalfitting shop, where he remained for six years, eventually joining the Putilov plant in 1898. A literate, skilled, and experienced worker with seniority, Kropin became the president of a district branch of the Assembly and served on the conflict commission created to settle disagreements between Assembly members and employers. In February 1905, Kropin was elected to the Shidlovskii Commission and, later that year, to the Petersburg Soviet.

G. S. Usanov, also in his thirties when he became active in the Assembly, was a second-generation worker and a lithographer by profession.[72] In the 1890s, he took part in Social Democratic circles among lithography workers that were organized by A. Karelin, a highly skilled chromolithographer and subsequently a leading figure in the Gapon movement.[73] Usanov served as the secretary of the Vasil'evskii Island branch of the Assembly, elected to this position because, according to his biographer, he was "highly literate and a very active and conscious worker."[74] In 1905, Usanov turned to trade union work and became the secretary of the Petersburg lithographers' union and a member of the union's directing board. He was also a deputy from the Markus lithographic firm to the Petersburg Soviet.

In contrast to the Zubatov societies in Moscow, the Gapon Assembly did not seek involvement in labor-management conflicts. For most of its brief existence, the Assembly emphasized "self-help, self-improvement and self-rule [mixed]

---

[70]Sablinsky, *The Road to Bloody Sunday*, pp. 98–99; Surh, "Petersburg Workers," pp. 118–122, 129–132; Kudelli and Shidlovskii, eds., *1905*, pp. 141–142, 171–174, 179–181, 186–188, 201, 207–208, 213–215.

[71]This account is taken from Kudelli and Shidlovskii, eds., *1905*, pp. 179–180.

[72]Ibid., pp. 213–214.

[73]For a summary of Karelin's career, see ibid., pp. 173–174, and Sablinsky, *The Road to Bloody Sunday*, p. 76 and passim.

[74]Kudelli and Shidlovskii, eds., *1905*, p. 213.

with temperance and a certain degree of religiousness."[75] This approach coincided with Gapon's belief that workers could better their lives by dint of their
own efforts. He did not have a coherent ideology to impart to his followers, and
whereas Zubatov converted worker-activists to his brand of economism, Gapon
himself became a partial convert to the more radical views of Social Democratic
activists who figured prominently in the inner circle of the Assembly.[76]

Nevertheless, the Gaponovshchina, like the Zubatov experiment that preceded it, acquainted workers with open broad-based collective activity and gave
them their first practical experience in erecting and administering a legal labor
association. The Gapon headquarters in local city districts served as centers for
day-to-day workings of the organization. Within the structure of the Assembly,
these district groups became the link between rank-and-file members and the
leadership group, a situation that anticipated the role of district soviets in
November 1905.[77]

At the district branches of the Assembly, workers gathered for meetings and
discussions, and it was here, on the eve of January 9, that rousing speeches were
delivered to thousands of eager listeners—not only by Gapon organizers, but
also by some Social Democrats.[78] These encounters fortified and deepened the
workers' feelings of injustice concerning their position in the workplace and
society at large, and helped to legitimate new claims, described by the Menshevik organizer Somov:

I found myself at several meetings [of workers in the Gapon Assembly] whose characteristic feature was that they imbued all demands with a "search for justice," a general
aspiration to put an end to the present impossible conditions. . . . And I thought that in
all of these demands, workers were motivated not so much by considerations of a
material character as by purely moral aspirations to settle everything "according to
justice" and to force employers to atone for their past sins.[79]

The atmosphere of moral indignation within the Assembly remained intense
during the final weeks preceding the fateful journey to the Winter Palace on
January 9, 1905. Although the Gapon movement did not emphasize industrial
relations and sought to avoid confrontations with employers, the demise of the

---

[75]Surh, "Petersburg Workers," pp. 178–179.

[76]Ibid., pp. 148–160; Sablinsky, *The Road to Bloody Sunday*, pp. 102–105, 125–128; Schwarz, *The Russian Revolution*, pp. 281–284.

[77]The organization of the Petersburg Soviet is discussed below in chapter 4.

[78]Somov, "Iz istorii," *Byloe*, no. 4, pp. 33–34.

[79]Ibid., pp. 34–35.

organization—as well as its peak influence among workers—was the result of a workplace dispute at the Putilov plant in December 1904. An unsympathetic foreman who belonged to a rival labor organization, the Mutual Aid Society of Workers in the Machine Industry, dismissed four leading Gaponists from the plant's woodworking shop, thereby precipitating the crisis. Gapon's response to the incident was intensified by the challenge it presented to the continuation and reputation of his organization.[80]

The Mutual Aid Society of Workers in the Machine Industry, like the Gapon Assembly, was a government-sponsored organization. Founded under Zubatov auspices in the spring of 1903,[81] the Mutual Aid Society of Workers in the Machine Industry briefly attracted the participation of Gapon himself, though he soon left to found the Assembly. The Society did not succeed in recruiting members until the following year, when it came under the leadership of M. A. Ushakov. A foundryman by occupation, Ushakov had acquired organizational experience in the Gapon Assembly and through a stint as a factory elder at the government paper and printing factory, Ekspeditsiia zagotovleniia gosudarstven-nykh bumag.[82] He was the only genuine worker to direct a legal labor organization in St. Petersburg or Moscow during this period.

Ushakov envisioned a labor movement whose conciliatory approach toward employers and allegiance to the autocratic system would achieve material improvements for workers. Under his leadership, the society attracted a small following, mainly among skilled and better-paid metalworkers and low-level managerial personnel.[83] By the end of 1904, the bulk of the membership was drawn from the Ekspeditsiia factory and the Putilov plant, where Ushakov's organization began to compete with Gapon's Assembly.

In late December and early January, the conflict escalated far more swiftly than anyone, including Gapon himself, had anticipated. The Assembly, by then encompassing some nine thousand members and many more sympathizers, mobilized around the case of the Putilov Gaponists who had been dismissed from their jobs and seized the opportunity to formulate a list of grievances. These were soon embodied in a petition prepared by the leadership of the Assembly for presentation to the Tsar.

The petition, which was widely circulated and discussed on the eve of Bloody Sunday, deplored the refusal of the Putilov management to negotiate over the

[80]This point is persuasively argued by Surh, "Petersburg Workers," pp. 166–173.

[81]The charter of the Society was legally approved on March 8, 1904. Laverychev, *Tsarizm*, p. 165.

[82]Vasil'ev, "Ushakovshchina," p. 144; Sablinsky, *The Road to Bloody Sunday*, p. 88.

[83]Sablinsky, *The Road to Bloody Sunday*, p. 146.

issue of the dismissal. To correct this situation, the petition called for the "mutual participation [of workers] in determining the rates for our work and in the settlement of grievances that might arise between us and the lower managerial staff."[84] Other points in the petition included the following demands:

- Permanent elected worker committees are to be established in factories and plants, and are to participate with management in the consideration of worker grievances. Workers must not be discharged without the consent of these committees.

- Freedom of cooperative associations and workers' trade unions is to be allowed without delay.

- Labor's freedom of struggle against capital is to be allowed without delay.

- Participation of representatives of the working classes in the drafting of a bill to provide state insurance for workers is to be put into effect without delay.[85]

Two aspects of the petition are especially noteworthy. First, the petition linked economic improvement to the broader issue of constitutional reform. The legal right to organize trade unions and to conduct strikes was put forth by the Assembly as a fundamental condition "to eliminate the oppression of labor by capital."

Second, the petition called for the institutionalization of worker representation at the enterprise level. As we shall see shortly, the demand for permanent factory committees had already found expression during a strike of Petersburg metalworkers in the spring of 1901. The concept of permanent factory-level worker representatives was also embodied—albeit in a highly circumscribed form—in the June 10, 1903, law on factory elders.[86] But the Assembly petition went beyond the 1903 law and extended the functions of the factory committee to include the direct participation of workers in matters relating to dismissal. The petition provided many Petersburg workers with their first exposure to concepts such as trade unionism and permanent factory-level grievance committees. The inclusion of these demands in the Gapon petition lent them an aura of respectability that facilitated their rapid acceptance by widely diverse segments of the laboring population.

---

[84]The text of the petition is reprinted in N. S. Trusova et al., eds., *Nachalo pervoi russkoi revoliutsii,* pp. 30–33; an English translation can be found in Sablinsky, *The Road to Bloody Sunday,* pp. 347–348. For a discussion of the petition, see Surh, "Petersburg Workers," pp. 224–225, and Sablinsky, *The Road to Bloody Sunday,* pp. 184–192. This translation and the one that follows are my own.

[85]N. S. Trusova et al., eds., *Nachalo pervoi russkoi revoliutsii,* p. 32.

[86]See the section "Factory Organization" below.

Judging from their positive response to Gapon's proposal for a petition of redress to the Tsar, many workers still believed that the state would intervene to rectify injustices and to provide greater equity in relations between labor and management. The Gapon Assembly, together with the earlier Zubatov experiment, served to reinforce the traditional view among Russia's lower classes that autocratic power could function as an arbiter and dispenser of justice. It took the events of Bloody Sunday and the ensuing developments of the revolution to shatter, once and for all, the workers' faith in the benevolent paternalism of the Tsar.

FACTORY ORGANIZATIONS

In the years preceding the outbreak of the 1905 revolution, some Petersburg and Moscow workers acquired formative experiences in collective association through their participation in factory and shop-level organizations. The individual enterprise was the locus for several different kinds of associational activity, both legal and illegal. Mutual aid societies were sometimes established within a single enterprise. Informal organizations existed on the shop level of many factories for the purpose of maintaining the shop icon or performing limited mutual assistance functions.[87] Shop organizations such as icon funds gave workers rudimentary experience in electing a leader—or elder—who collected funds, purchased icon oil, or dispensed monetary assistance to needy workers.[88]

Before 1905, some workers also formed factory committees. Composed of delegates elected by shops within a large firm, the factory committee usually arose in the context of an industrial dispute for purposes of coordination and representation vis-à-vis management. Factory committees of this kind existed intermittently during the closing decades of the nineteenth century, but nearly all of them proved transitory, disappearing at the conclusion of the conflict. It was only in the years immediately preceding the revolution that workers sought to introduce factory committees as a permanent feature of industrial life.[89] This

[87]The importance of the icon funds *(lampadnye kassy)* as precursors of 1905 workers' organizations is noted by P. Kolokol'nikov, *MIPDR*, 2:20, and by Somov, "Iz istorii," *Byloe*, no. 5 (17) (May 1907), p. 175.

[88]For a description of the election of a shop elder to maintain the icon, see P. Timofeev, *Chem zhivet zavodskii rabochii* (St. Petersburg, 1906), pp. 80–84.

[89]A brief discussion of pre-1905 factory committees can be found in A. Pankratova, *Fabzavkomy Rossii v bor'be za sotsialisticheskuiu fabriku* (Moscow, 1923) and E. Lerner, ed., *Fabzavkomy i profsoiuzy: Sbornik statei*, 2d ed. (Moscow, 1925).

demand, as we have seen, was incorporated into the Gapon petition on the eve of January 9, 1905.

The capital's metalworkers were among the first to call for permanent factory committees. In the spring of 1901, a work stoppage began at the state-operated Obukhov metalworking plant, a large enterprise with more than four thousand workers, and then spread to many other firms in the capital. Led by radical workers at Obukhov and elsewhere, the strike put forth a series of demands that included the establishment of permanent worker deputies at the enterprise level and their recognition by plant management.[90] The Obukhov administration accepted this demand, permitting workers to elect representatives from each shop and granting them immunity from retaliation and the right to hold meetings with plant workers and among themselves. A similar concession was made at the privately owned Nevskii Shipbuilding and Machine Plant, but the reform was never implemented, because the workers' representatives elected during the strike were arrested when the conflict ended.[91]

In response to the 1901 strikes in the Petersburg metalworking industry, the Ministry of Finance set in motion a legislative project designed to legalize workers' representatives. By the end of 1901, the Ministry had drawn up a draft proposal for a law on factory elders, and in 1902, on orders from the Minister of Internal Affairs, D. S. Sipiagin, the project was turned over to a special commission headed by Prince Obolenskii.[92]

Arguing on behalf of its proposed legislation, the Ministry of Finance contended that the difficulties faced by employers and the government in the labor sphere were caused by a failure to learn "the true wishes and needs of workers." Factory elders, the Ministry asserted, would facilitate communication with the workers, thereby eliminating disruptions and turmoil in industrial relations. The Ministry argued that the institution of elders already existed in the "popular culture generally and in factories in particular," and would not represent an innovation in factory life. Workers already elected elders in some enterprises to supervise factory cafeterias, asserted a ministry report, and "if instead of the present secret meetings [of workers] there were open and controlled meetings, then this would only be beneficial" and would eliminate "all kinds of agitation and frightful things."[93]

---

[90]Surh, "Petersburg Workers," p. 92.

[91]V. Tsytsarin, "Vospominaniia metallista," p. 34.

[92]TsGIA, f. 150, op. 1, d. 481, p. 23, from a report of the Ministry of Finance dated March 14, 1903.

[93]TsGIA, f. 150, op. 1, d. 481, p. 21.

Although the Ministry of Finance and the Ministry of Internal Affairs—frequent adversaries in matters of labor policy—endorsed the proposed project, not all government officials were enthusiastic about the legislation. When the project reached the State Council, a minority report opposed the introduction of factory elders:

If prior to the present time, as demonstrated by the Ministry of Internal Affairs, social-political agitation among workers has enjoyed relatively little success, then this can be explained primarily by the fact that it has come into contact with an unorganized mass. . . . Elders are incapable of preventing misunderstandings between factory owners and workers; on the contrary, they are likely to promote the rapid proliferation of such misunderstandings and lay the groundwork for extremely undesirable organizations of workers through which destructive teachings will penetrate the popular masses.[94]

Industrialists in St. Petersburg and Moscow lobbied hard against the proposed law, putting their case before government officials in the spring of 1903. Thirty-six leading industrialists in the capital, led by S. P. Glezmer—the head of the Petersburg Society to Assist the Development and Improvement of Factory Industry[95]—submitted a report to the Ministry of Finance asserting that

the question of the representation of workers stands in contradiction to the basic conditions of industrial life. The employer hires an individual worker, not a union of workers . . . and therefore [the employer] is not obliged to recognize representatives of workers and is not obliged to standardize his relations with workers, apart from the norms established by law.[96]

The Moscow textile magnate A. I. Morozov stated in a letter to the Minister of Finance on May 9, 1903, that the proposed legislation was highly risky and "might produce serious consequences, not only for native industry and commerce, but also for the government."[97] Another industrialist from the Moscow region went further still, claiming that the factory elders would become "an

---

[94]Prokopovich, *K rabochemu voprosu,* pp. 120–121.

[95]The Society was established by Petersburg industrialists in 1893, but did not obtain legal status until January 29, 1897, when it was officially recognized by the Ministry of Finance. TsGIA, f. 150, op. 1, d. 54, p. 9.

[96]Laverychev, *Tsarizm,* pp. 163–164; TsGIA, f. 150, op. 1, d. 481, p. 16. The petition referred to here was directed not only against the proposed law on factory elders but also against a law on insurance and pensions for workers that was promulgated on June 2, 1903.

[97]TsGIA, f. 150, op. 1, d. 481, p. 23.

agent for continually raising new demands for concessions from the [factory] administration."[98]

The law on the "Establishment of Elders in Industrial Enterprises," promulgated on June 10, 1903, represented a partial concession to the industrialists.[99] In approving the legislation, the State Council majority noted that "workers, lacking the right to act collectively, have been deprived of the possibility of a legal means to express their general needs."[100] But the law that was adopted made it exceedingly difficult for workers to overcome this deprivation. While permitting workers legally to elect representatives for the first time, it placed the initiation and implementation of the law exclusively in the hands of factory management. Introduction of the reform was thus left to the discretion of individual employers, who also retained the right to choose the elders from candidates elected by workers. Elders were permitted to hold meetings, both among themselves and with other workers, but only at a time and place approved in advance by the factory administration. The function of the elder was to serve as a conduit between workers and employers. The law specified that the elder was

to inform the administration of the enterprise . . . of the needs and wishes of the workers who elected him or of individual workers in the shop on matters relating to the fulfillment of the conditions of employment as well as the condition of workers in a given industry or trade. Regulations of the factory administration and directorate will be transmitted through the elder, who will also elucidate declarations of the administration.[101]

Despite the modest and restrictive character of the law of June 10, 1903, few employers cooperated with its provisions and permitted the introduction of factory elders into their firms. By early 1905, only thirty to forty enterprises in all of Russia had implemented the law, and many of these were relatively small-scale, employing fewer than five hundred workers.[102]

There is little evidence concerning workers' reactions to the new legislation. Most of them were probably unaware of its existence, although Moscow printers made the implementation of the law a key demand in a strike during the

[98]Ibid., p. 100.

[99]*Polnoe sobranie zakonov Rossiiskoi imperii s 1649 goda* (St. Petersburg, 1830–1916), sbornik 3, tom 23, 1903, pp. 734–735. The law is discussed in Laverychev, *Tsarizm*, pp. 163–165; Prokopovich, *K rabochemu voprosu*, pp. 120–123; K. A. Pazhitnov, *Polozhenie rabochego klassa v Rossii* (St. Petersburg, 1906), pp. 159–161.

[100]Prokopovich, *K rabochemu voprosu*, p. 120.

[101]*Polnoe sobranoe zakonov*, sbornik 3, tom 23, 1903, p. 733. Article 3.

[102]Prokopovich, *K rabochemu voprosu*, p. 122; Laverychev, *Tsarizm*, p. 165.

fall of 1903. For those who knew of the law, it must have given additional support and legitimacy to claims for organized worker representation at the enterprise level. Social Democrats, despite their critical reception of the law, adopted a resolution at the Second Congress of the Russian Social Democratic Workers' Party (RSDRP) in the summer of 1903, calling upon workers to utilize the law for organizational and agitational purposes.[103] In some firms where the law was put into effect, Social Democratic workers were elected to the position of elder.[104]

ILLEGAL UNIONS AND PARTIES ON THE EVE OF 1905

The struggle to achieve permanent factory representation shifted to Moscow in September 1903, when an industry-wide strike erupted among printing workers. Like the Petersburg metalworkers who had raised this demand two years earlier, the printers included a high proportion of skilled, literate, and urbanized elements. The printers' strike began at the city's largest firms and spread within a matter of days throughout most of the industry. At its peak, the work stoppage involved 80 percent of the workers and 60 percent of the enterprises in the Moscow printing trades.[105]

The solidarity of Moscow printing workers in the September 1903 strike was made possible by preliminary organizational efforts carried out over a period of months. The initial meeting to plan for the strike took place in late April, followed by a series of gatherings held at Moscow taverns and in the woods, where grievances and tactics were discussed, as well as Western European trade unions.[106] The organizers were particularly impressed by the example of the

[103]*Vtoroi s"ezd R.S.D.R.P., iiul'-avgust 1903 goda: Protokoly* (Moscow, 1959), pp. 410, 433. This resolution was introduced at the final meeting of the congress on August 10, 1903, by Iu. Martov. In a subsequent article in the Social Democratic organ *Iskra* [The Spark], Lenin asserted that the introduction of reforms such as the June 10, 1903, law on factory elders signified the imminence of a revolution. Ibid., p. 799.

[104]Kats and Milonov, eds., *1905*, p. 15.

[105]*Rabochee dvizhenie v Rossii v 1901–1904 gg.: Sbornik dokumentov* (Leningrad, 1975), pp. 178–181; N. Chistov, "Moskovskie pechatniki v revoliutsii 1905 goda," *Katorga i ssylka*, no. 73 (1931), p. 135, reprints a government report stating that 5,500 printers from fifty printing firms were on strike. In the following discussion, I have benefited from an unpublished seminar paper by Mark David Steinberg, "Moscow Printing Workers: The September Strikes of 1903 and 1905," University of California, Berkeley, Spring 1980.

[106]A. Borshchevskii, S. Reshetov, and N. Chistov, eds., *Moskovskie pechatniki v 1905 godu* (Moscow, 1925), p. 139–141, 143.

Moscow weavers, who had mounted an impressive campaign against their employers in 1902 under the direction of the Zubatov society. The typesetters went so far as to attend a meeting of the Zubatov society of metalworkers sometime during the spring, but they came away wary of police involvement and did not seek further links with the Zubatov movement.[107]

Some of the typesetters urged that contact be established with sympathizers among the radical intelligentsia, but others opposed these efforts on the grounds that they could conduct their own affairs and did not require the intervention of intellectuals, who would attempt to take over the leadership. More generally, a fear of political involvement, "of getting mixed up with the police, of falling into prison," inhibited workers from seeking the assistance of radical intellectuals.[108] Although one meeting with an SD intelligentsia organizer did take place, party activists remained peripheral to the printers' movement until the strike was under way.[109]

In July 1903 the typesetters proclaimed an illegal trade union—the Union of Typographical Workers for the Struggle to Improve Conditions of Labor—open to all workers in the city's printing trades.[110] Prior to the conclusion of the September strike, the union appears to have existed in little more than name only, despite the fact that a charter was drawn up and adopted. The strike committee, serving as a temporary directing board for the union, formulated a list of demands and directed the work stoppage that began on September 9.

The strike demands touched on a variety of issues, including wages, hours, and working conditions, medical assistance and insurance, polite address by employers, and the election of elders in accordance with the law of June 10, 1903.[111] The introduction of elders would have legalized and institutionalized the shop deputies that had already been elected in many firms during the strike.[112] Within a few days after the work stoppage had begun, employers made concessions and agreed to raise wages, shorten the working time, and permit the election of elders.[113] It is uncertain, however, to what extent committees of elders actually were elected in the city's printing firms. In the Sytin firm, the largest

---

[107]Ibid., pp. 144–146.

[108]Ibid., p. 146.

[109]Ibid., pp. 147–148.

[110]The union took as its motto, "In Unity, Strength; in Thrift, Independence." Borshchevskii et al., eds., *Moskovskie pechatniki*, p. 17; Steinberg, "Moscow Printing Workers," pp. 29–31.

[111]*Rabochee dvizhenie v Rossii v 1901–1904 gg.*, p. 359, n. 2.

[112]Steinberg, "Moscow Printing Workers," pp. 34–35.

[113]Sher, *Istoriia*, pp. 124–125; 161–162.

printing establishment in Moscow, workers again demanded the introduction of factory elders in January 1905.[114]

In the aftermath of the strike, the printers' union maintained an underground existence and continued to publish *Vestnik soiuza* [The Union Herald], an illegal journal that had first appeared in the summer of 1903. In December the union adopted the program of the Russian Social Democratic Workers' Party.[115] Contact with SD party organizers had intensified in the course of the strike, and most of the workers who retained their ties with the union had been drawn into the party orbit. But membership in the union was exceedingly small and probably did not include more than a few dozen committed Social Democrats who remained isolated from the mass of printing workers until the outbreak of the revolution.[116]

Another organization of printers also existed on the eve of 1905. Following the conclusion of the strike, a Zubatovist Society of Typographical Workers was formed in Moscow.[117] Operating openly and legally, the Society held weekly meetings that drew fifty to three hundred printers, and organized social dances, cultural outings, and a consumer cooperative.[118] By late 1904, however, this Zubatov society was on the wane, and it was only the outbreak of the revolution that prolonged its existence for a few more months.

The fate of the illegal Moscow printers' union, which became virtually indistinguishable from a party cell, exemplifies the more general dilemma facing radical political groups on the eve of the revolution. Whereas Social Democrats had made inroads among workers during the 1890s, most of these accomplishments were lost after the turn of the century.[119] Severe police persecution led to the repeated dissolution of party underground circles, while intraparty squabbles and domination by the intelligentsia had alienated many SD workers, driving some of them into the arms of the Zubatov and Gapon organizations. The exodus from SD groups was, in part, a manifestation of the strong aspiration among workers for open, mass-based, legal forms of collective association and

[114]Ibid., p. 154.

[115]Ibid., p. 114. The union declined, however, to establish formal organizational ties with the party, declaring this to be premature.

[116]Ibid., p. 148.

[117]Sher, *Istoriia*, pp. 127–128.

[118]Ibid., Schneiderman, *Sergei Zubatov*, p. 189.

[119]Wildman, *The Making of a Workers' Revolution*, chaps. 2 and 3; Richard Pipes, *Social Democracy and the St. Petersburg Labor Movement, 1885–1897* (Cambridge, Mass., 1963).

for independence from the tutelage of radical intellectuals.[120] The observations of an SD woman weaver in late 1904, recounted by Somov, sum up the situation in the capital and elsewhere:

She openly told me that, in her opinion, the best workers don't come to us and will not come to us; that the results of our [SD] work have been so insignificant that no intelligent person would be willing to risk arrest and abandonment of his family to hunger and cold, even someone inclined to self-sacrifice . . . [that] it is better to go to the Gapon organization, [because] thousands of people go there, people believe in it and have hopes for it.[121]

According to Somov, most of the worker SDs in the capital at the time were "extremely young, having just completed an apprenticeship [and] enjoying no influence whatever in their factory milieu."[122] Party groups, moreover, were in disarray. The Second Party Congress of the RSDRP had brought into the open the deep and irreparable differences between the two factions of Russian Social Democracy, the Bolsheviks and the Mensheviks.[123] In late 1904 Mensheviks in the capital had withdrawn from the Bolshevik-dominated Petersburg Committee to form their own organization, the Petersburg Group.

The issues that divided the Bolshevik and Menshevik factions, a subject discussed further on,[124] had profound implications for future strategy and tactics in the workers' movement. But on the eve of 1905, these conflicts were scarcely discernible or intelligible to most workers, few of whom could even distinguish between Social Democrats and Socialist Revolutionaries, the other, even less influential, radical party that attempted to win converts in the workers' milieu.

The contingent of Social Democratic and Socialist Revolutionary worker-activists was pitifully small in the years immediately preceding the revolution. Somov observed that in late 1904 the strongest SD organizations in St. Petersburg were situated in the Narvskaia, Peterburgskaia, and Vasil'evskii Island districts. In the Narvskaia district there were six or seven circles of SD workers

[120]Wildman, *The Making of a Workers' Revolution*, chaps. 4 and 8, especially pp. 89–90, 115–117, 251–253.

[121]Somov, "Iz istorii," *Byloe*, no. 4, p. 26.

[122]Ibid., pp. 26–27.

[123]These intraparty ideological and organizational divisions have been extensively discussed in Abraham Ascher, *Pavel Axelrod and the Development of Menshevism* (Cambridge, Mass., 1972), chaps. 5 and 6; Leopold Haimson, *The Russian Marxists and the Origins of Bolshevism* (Cambridge, Mass., 1955); Schwarz, *The Russian Revolution*, pp. 1–74; Leonard Schapiro, *The Communist Party of the Soviet Union* (New York, 1971), pp. 19–54; Wildman, *The Making of a Workers' Revolution*, chap. 8.

[124]See below, chapter 4.

recruited from the nearby Putilov plant and other metalworking firms. Each circle had no more than five or six worker participants, or at most a total of thirty-five workers in a district that employed some thirty thousand. In the entire Aleksandro-Nevskaia district, there were only three SD circles: one involving workers from the nearby Obukhov plant, another recruiting from the Nevskii Shipbuilding and Machine Plant, and a third that attracted workers from the Thornton and Nauman factories.[125]

Though worker participation in SD and SR groups was confined to a handful of individuals, these small and isolated groups could nonetheless be found in surprisingly diverse industries and occupations on the eve of 1905. Indeed, there was scarcely a segment of the Petersburg or Moscow labor force that did not harbor a few committed and politically active workers when the revolution began. They could be found not only in metalworking and printing, but also in many artisanal trades, sales-clerical occupations, and various branches of factory industry.[126]

Among Moscow bakers, for example, the first SD group was formed during the 1890s. Whereas the baking industry was predominantly an artisanal trade, the SD group arose at the large Filippov firm, which employed more than 350 bakers. The SD bakers' circle succeeded in making contact with radical students before it suffered devastating arrests in early 1902. Nevertheless, another small group had emerged by mid-1904. In addition to an organizing center of eight workers, this group established contact with SD bakers at a number of individual firms. Around the turn of the century, Socialist Revolutionaries also began a small circle among Moscow bakers. Notwithstanding the bakers' close ties to the countryside, this pro-peasant party had even fewer recruits than the Social Democrats.[127]

Similar SD and SR circles existed in Moscow candymaking, tobacco processing, metalworking, textiles, printing, and other industries here and in the capital on the eve of 1905.[128] But the severe limitations on open activity, coupled with the absence of a free press and the right of assembly, doomed these radical groups to isolation from the great majority of workers, who, in most cases, did not even know of their existence. It was only in the weeks preceding the Gapon demonstration at the Winter Palace that a handful of socialist workers began to

---

[125]Somov, "Iz istorii," *Byloe*, no. 4, pp. 25–26. The following account of party strength in the capital is derived from this source.

[126]*ILS*, p. 114; Gordon, *Iz istorii professional'nogo dvizheniia sluzhashchikh*, pp. 12–13.

[127]*Professional'noe dvizhenie Moskovskikh pishchevikov*, pp. 104–105.

[128]Ibid., pp. 150–151, 185, 198.

speak up for the first time, and they were not always well received.[129] The mood of workers in the capital has been described by Aleksei Buzinov, a metalworker in the blacksmith shop at the Nevskii plant:

I, together with the majority of our workers, continued to believe that the Tsar would provide justice and defend us against [our] enemies. Our faith in him had not yet been shaken. And workers took to heart everything that touched on this faith. Each effort to destroy it encountered unanimous resistance. When people began to talk about the planned procession to present the petition at the Tsar's palace, this faith flared up like a bright flame, concentrating in itself all the hopes of the workers for a better lot and for justice, about which the Tsar did not yet know and had to be told. Anyone who allowed himself to doubt this, even if he was your work partner or friend, became for all of us a blood enemy.[130]

These attitudes were prevalent among workers in both cities on the eve of 1905, and they presented a formidable obstacle to radical activists seeking to increase their influence among the rank and file. An event of great magnitude would be required to challenge the workers' faith in the Tsar and to make them receptive to the ideas and tactics of the radical left.

In comparison with Western European societies of an earlier period, Imperial Russia lacked a rich and varied tradition of voluntary association among lower-class groups prior to 1905. The guilds, mutual aid societies, *compagnonnages*, and other forms of association that had predated and accompanied the transition from an agrarian to an industrial economy in Western Europe developed only weakly, or not at all, in the harsh and repressive atmosphere of autocratic rule. The tsarist government, ever fearful of popular disorders, discouraged autonomous activity among nearly all social groups, particularly the urban lower classes.

Yet the half-decade preceding the outbreak of the First Russian Revolution was not without opportunities for collective organization (both legal and illegal), and these activities, however circumscribed, helped to lay the foundation for the workers' movement that arose so swiftly and impressively during 1905. Mutual aid societies, despite their limited membership, demonstrated the benefits of cooperative ventures and created an organizational network among groups such as the Petersburg printers. Through the Zubatov and Gapon movements, some

[129]Aleksei Buzinov, *Za Nevskoi zastavoi: Zapiski rabochego* (Moscow and Leningrad, 1930), pp. 29–32, recounts several incidents like this one, which took place at the Nevskii plant on the eve of the demonstration of January 9, 1905.

[130]Ibid., p. 32.

workers had their first exposure to a legal, mass-based labor organization. Factory and strike committees, arising out of workplace disputes, taught workers the necessity for collective association and representation vis-à-vis management. Even the guilds, though peripheral to working-class life on the eve of 1905, helped to fortify the craft allegiances that provided important bases of solidarity among workers during the revolution.

The social profile of workers who joined these pre-1905 organizations cannot always be established with certainty, but two patterns nevertheless emerge. First, there was considerable diversity in the types of workers who participated in voluntary associations, and they included factory, artisanal, sales-clerical, and service groups. Second, skilled workers—most of them male, literate, and urbanized—tended to predominate in the leadership of these organizations and, in some cases, among the rank and file as well. A working-class leadership was in the making before 1905 and a generation of worker-activists acquired formative experiences through their participation in these organizations.

Although skilled workers often predominated in pre-1905 organizations, some unskilled factory groups were involved as well. The Moscow candymakers and tobacco workers, and the rubber workers in the capital, were among those drawn into the Zubatov and Gapon movements. These groups acquired familiarity with the tasks and benefits of collective association during their brief encounter with a government-sponsored organization, a circumstance that subsequently assisted them to mobilize effectively during the revolution.

Before 1905 some workers conducted a struggle for workplace improvements under the auspices of a legal organization. In this respect, the Zubatov societies and Gapon Assembly can be considered important precursors of the trade unions and factory committees established during the revolution. Through these pre-1905 organizations, workers came into contact with new concepts derived from Western European labor movements, such as collective bargaining, the collective labor contract, industry-wide settlements, and the institutionalization of grievance procedures. Workers also initiated new claims on employers and the state, including demands for the right to establish permanent factory committees, legal trade unions, and the right to strike.

In sum, Petersburg and Moscow workers did not confront 1905 as a *tabula rasa*, entirely lacking prior organizational experiences and models to guide them in the task of erecting the first independent labor associations during the revolution. Many of the issues that first made an appearance in the years from 1900 to 1904 would become the focus for workers' activities in the new era that was about to begin.

Part Two

The Organization of Labor in the 1905 Revolution

Chapter 3

The Formation of Workers' Organizations in the 1905 Revolution

> I paid dearly for Bloody Sunday. On that day I was born
> again—no longer an all-forgiving and all-forgetting
> child but an embittered man ready to go into battle and
> win.

> *Aleksei Buzinov[1]*

On Sunday, January 9, 1905, workers proceeded peacefully toward the Winter Palace under the banners of the Gapon Assembly, carrying icons and a petition to the Tsar. Without warning, government troops opened fire, killing and wounding scores of workers. The outcome of the demonstration and the subsequent spread of massive popular unrest took most contemporaries by surprise, and yet signs of growing dissatisfaction could already be discerned in Russian society on the eve of 1905. A protracted economic recession and the disastrous Russo-Japanese War provided the background for the first stirrings of oppositional activity, not only among workers, but among educated groups in the cities and the countryside.

In the workers' districts of St. Petersburg, hundreds of new members joined the Gapon Assembly in November and December 1904, soon to be mobilized around a dispute at the Putilov plant and a still broader campaign for workplace improvements. An economic crisis dating from the turn of the century exacerbated chronic problems of inadequate wages and long hours, and created massive unemployment in some industries. Growing inflation further intensified

---

[1]Aleksei Buzinov, *Za Nevskoi zastavoi: Zapiski rabochego* (Moscow and Leningrad, 1930), p. 40.

106

the plight of workers, eroding their earning power and forcing them in the direction of confrontations with employers.[2]

There were also indications of mounting discontent in educated Russian society. The unpopular Russo-Japanese War, exposing the ineptness of government troops, accentuated the need for political reform and modernization of the country's military and industrial capacity. During the Banquet Campaign in late 1904 intellectuals, liberal members of the gentry, and industrialists spoke out against the antiquated autocratic system and its interference with the country's progress.[3]

The events of January 9 had a dramatic effect on Russian society. Within days, massive protest demonstrations were under way throughout the Empire, and in both St. Petersburg and Moscow workers took to the streets in large numbers. So profound was the impression of the massacre that many workers, as though overnight, grew disillusioned with the Tsar. The workers' faith in tsarist paternalism was severely shaken by Bloody Sunday, setting the stage for far-reaching changes in their attitudes during the months that followed.[4]

The first wave of protest demonstrations had scarcely subsided when workers turned their attention to workplace grievances. During January and February, strikes spread to factories and shops, where workers advanced demands against employers for improved wages, hours, and working conditions. In many cases they called for an eight-hour workday—a substantial reduction over current

[2]B. P. Orlov, *Poligraficheskaia promyshlennost' Moskvy: Ocherk razvitiia do 1917 goda* (Moscow, 1953), chaps. 7, 8; S. Gruzdev, "Iz istorii professional'nogo dvizheniia 1905 g. v Peterburge," in *Materialy po istorii professional'nogo dvizheniia v Peterburge za 1905-1907 gg.: Sbornik* (henceforth *MIPDP*) (Leningrad, 1926), especially pp. 29–35, for data on wages and cost increases for key commodities.

[3]Terrence Emmons, "Russia's Banquet Campaign," *California Slavic Studies* 10 (1977), pp. 45–86; S. I. Somov, "Iz istorii sotsialdemokraticheskogo dvizheniia v Peterburge v 1905 godu (Lichnye vospominaniia)," *Byloe,* no. 4 (16) (April 1907), pp. 29–30; E. D. Chermenskii, *Burzhuaziia i tsarizm v pervoi russkoi revoliutsii* (Moscow, 1970), chap. 1.

[4]S. Nikitin, "Moskovskoe stachechnoe dvizhenie v 1905–1907 gg.," in Iu. Milonov, ed., *Moskovskoe professional'noe dvizhenie v gody pervoi revoliutsii* (Moscow, [1925]), p. 47; *Istoriia rabochikh Leningrada 1703-fevral' 1917,* vol. 1 (Leningrad, 1972), pp. 269–273. On the workers' disillusionment, see Walter Sablinsky, *The Road to Bloody Sunday: Father Gapon and the St. Petersburg Massacre of 1905* (Princeton, N.J., 1976), chap. 10; Gerald Dennis Surh, "Petersburg Workers in 1905: Strikes, Workplace Democracy, and the Revolution," Ph.D. dissertation, University of California, Berkeley, 1979, pp. 228–232; Somov, "Iz istorii," no. 4, pp. 41–43; and especially Aleksei Buzinov, *Za Nevskoi zastavoi,* pp. 33–42, who presents a vivid personal account of his reaction to the events.

norms that often extended to eleven hours or even longer.[5] At the same time, striking workers also put forward demands for fundamental reforms in the conduct of industrial relations.

These demands centered around two interconnected issues that would repeatedly emerge in 1905 and afterward: employer recognition of the workers' right to elect permanent representatives at the enterprise level and the right to participate in decisions concerning hiring, firing, and wage rates. As discussed in the preceding chapter, workers had raised both of these demands before the outbreak of the revolution. In the Petersburg metalworkers' strike in 1901 and the Moscow printers' strike of 1903, workers had demanded the right to elect representatives in each firm. The Gapon petition carried to the Winter Palace also included demands for representation and participation in key decisions of factory life, and in the weeks preceding the January 9 demonstration, workers at some individual Petersburg plants had already presented these demands directly to factory management.[6]

Considering the widespread dissemination of the Gapon petition, it is not surprising that many of the same issues appear again during the January-February strikes in the capital.[7] But even in Moscow these demands were put forward by workers during the same period, and here, too, workers called for the introduction of permanent representatives at the enterprise level with a right to participate in such decisions as hiring, firing, and the determination of wage rates. On January 15, for example, workers at the Kerting Brothers' metalworking firm in Moscow demanded that

each section in the plant must have an elected commission that would review the reasons for dismissing [workers], and at the time of hiring, would set a wage and also involve itself as a mediator between both sides and see to it that the foreman doesn't say, "I don't need him. I'll find another worker."[8]

[5]Nikitin, "Moskovskoe stachechnoe dvizhenie," in Milonov, ed., *Moskovskoe professional'noe dvizhenie*, pp. 50–53; U. A. Shuster, *Peterburgskie rabochie v 1905-1907 gg.* (Leningrad, 1976), pp. 96–112; Surh, "Petersburg Workers," pp. 217–286.

[6]For example, on January 8, workers at the Sampsonievskii mill demanded the election of representatives to confer with management over workplace disputes. Similar demands were put forward by typesetters in the capital on the eve of January 9. Tsentral'nyi gosudarstvennyi istoricheskii arkhiv (TsGIA), f. 150, op. 1, d. 755, p. 230.

[7]For evidence on this point see TsGIA, f. 150, op. 1, d. 755, pp. 174, 226, 227, 229, 230, 234, 275; f. 150, op. 1, d. 646, p. 117.

[8]Tsentral'nyi gosudarstvennyi arkhiv Oktiabr'skoi revoliutsii (TsGAOR), f. 6860, ed. kh. 27, 1905, pp. 105–106.

Throughout January and February this basic demand was submitted to employers at many Moscow and Petersburg metalworking and textile factories, as well as Moscow railroad workshops, together with claims for higher wages, shorter hours, better working conditions, and more occasionally, the right to meet on factory premises, employer guarantees of the deputies' immunity from dismissal, and the participation of factory deputies in levying fines.[9] In addition, some workers began to demand the introduction of formal arbitration procedures in workplace disputes. At the Bari metalworking plant in Moscow on January 12, six hundred workers adopted twenty-two demands for presentation to the factory administration. Among them was a provision for the establishment of a board composed of an equal number of worker and employer representatives and a mutually acceptable arbitrator.[10] The board was to have authority over matters relating to the hiring and firing of workers and foremen, the fixing of wage rates for piecework, the operation of the plant cafeteria, sanitation and safety, and the training of apprentices in the workplace.[11]

Out of these demands for representation in January and February 1905 came the first workers' organizations of the revolution: factory committees. As a focus for the workers' initial organizational efforts in 1905, the factory committee was a logical and natural choice. The earlier strike committees had familiarized workers with this type of structure, and it was comparatively easy to organize on the enterprise level where workers were concentrated and where social networks were already in existence. Within larger firms, the shop usually served as the basic unit for the selection of worker representatives. The shop provided the immediate work environment in large factories, and it was here that workers developed a variety of social ties and gained experience in electing "elders" for icon funds and other purposes.

In contrast to prerevolutionary strike committees, which were almost always transitory, the goal of the factory committee movement was to establish *perma-*

---

[9]Ibid., pp. 56, 74, 86, 90, 127, 135–136; TsGIA, f. 275, op. 12, d. 328, pp. 89–90, 108; Z. Shchap, *Moskovskie metallisty v professional'nom dvizhenii: Ocherki po istorii Moskovskogo soiuza metallistov* (Moscow, 1927), p. 33. In the petition, workers used the term *treteiskii sud* or arbitration board.

[10]Arbitration had been part of Russian civil law for centuries, and prior to the revised Civil Code of 1864 it was binding or nonbinding in accordance with the wishes of the litigants. After the legal reforms of 1864, only nonbinding arbitration remained in the Civil Code, but in practice it was seldom utilized. I. Gessen, "Treteiskii sud," in *Entsiklopedicheskii slovar'*, vol. 33a (St. Petersburg, 1901), pp. 772–773.

[11]TsGAOR, f. 6860, ed. kh. 27, 1905, p. 79. A slightly different version of the petition appears in Shchap, *Moskovskie metallisty*, p. 33. Similar demands were advanced by workers at the Gustav List metalworking plant and elsewhere. TsGAOR, f. 6860, ed. kh. 27, 1905, p. 74.

nent organs, recognized by employers and serving as the workers' collective representative in negotiations between labor and management. The concept of collective representation was still new to many workers in early 1905, but would soon become a major issue in the growing labor movement.[12]

Although both St. Petersburg and Moscow workers demanded the recognition of factory committees during the January-February strikes, workers in the capital proved more successful in achieving implementation. Not until the fall of 1905 did the factory committee movement gain momentum in Moscow, spreading to a broader spectrum of industrial groups than had earlier been involved in the capital. The rapid development of factory committees in St. Petersburg during the first stages of the revolution was, in part, a consequence of elections to the Shidlovskii Commission.

THE FACTORY COMMITTEE MOVEMENT AND THE
SHIDLOVSKII COMMISSION

In the wake of the catastrophic events of January 9, V. N. Kokovtsov, the Minister of Finance, proposed to the Tsar that the government demonstrate its good intentions and impartiality toward workers by initiating new ameliorative labor legislation.[13] On January 13, the government proclaimed its intention to undertake such a review. Soon plans were under way for a full-scale reconsideration of labor legislation, including measures to shorten the work day, eliminate criminal penalties for strikes, remove the obstacles to workers' organizations, and institute medical assistance for workers.[14] Two committees were subsequently authorized by the State Council: the Kokovtsov Commission to consider labor legislation affecting workers in the Empire as a whole, and the Shidlovskii Commission to investigate labor problems in the capital.

The Shidlovskii Commission, announced by the government on January 30, was to include not only state officials but also elected representatives of both workers and employers.[15] For the first time in the country's history, the government authorized free elections to be held by workers—both men and women—employed in factories with a labor force of one hundred or more. The election

---

[12]See below, chapters 4 and 7.
[13]*Rabochii vopros v komissii V. N. Kokovtsova v 1905 g.* (n.p., 1926), pp. iii-v.
[14]Ibid., p. vi.
[15]TsGIA, f. 150, op. 1, d. 485, p. 1.

was to be held in two stages, beginning at the enterprise level. Workers were permitted to choose one elector *(vyborshchik)* for every five hundred workers in a large enterprise; those employed in firms with one hundred to five hundred workers were entitled to one elector.[16]

The government did not specify the procedures for choosing electors, and workers could determine the selection processes, provided that those elected were male workers, at least twenty-five years of age, and employed in the firm for a minimum of one year prior to the election. Following this first stage of the election, electors were to assemble on a citywide basis in sections corresponding to branches of industry.[17] Each section was entitled to elect a certain number of deputies to participate in the commission, based on the total size of the labor force in that branch.[18]

The workers' response to the announcement of the Shidlovskii Commission exemplifies the complex and contradictory tendencies within the capital's factory population at the beginning of 1905. Despite the widespread disillusionment produced by Bloody Sunday, some workers had not yet fully relinquished their hopes of obtaining government recognition of their demands. Recalling that prior to January 9 government authorities had countenanced the activities of the Gapon Assembly and even lent it support, these workers greeted the announcement of the Shidlovskii Commission as an auspicious event. As the metalworker Fedor Bulkin observed, "The workers' interest in the commission was extremely great. It seemed to them that the government had seriously decided to satisfy the basic needs of workers."[19] Another contemporary, the Menshevik D. Kol'tsov [B. A. Ginzburg], noted that "workers see in the [Shidlovskii Commission] an answer to their petition" carried to the Tsar on January 9,[20] a petition that had included a provision for worker participation in the drafting of insurance legislation.

[16]V. I. Nevskii, "Vybor v komissiiu senatora Shidlovskogo (1905 g.)," *Arkhiv istorii truda v Rossii,* Book 3 (1922); Solomon Schwarz, *The Russian Revolution of 1905: The Workers' Movement and the Formation of Bolshevism and Menshevism* (Chicago, 1967), pp. 87–88; TsGIA, f. 150, op. 1, d. 485, p. 1.

[17]The nine branches were textiles, paper and printing, woodworking, metalworking, minerals, processing of animal products, food processing, chemicals, and explosives.

[18]Details of the procedure can be found in Nevskii, "Vybor v komissiiu," p. 82.

[19]F. A. Bulkin, *Na zare profdvizheniia: Istoriia Peterburgskogo soiuza metallistov 1906-1914 gg.* (Moscow and Leningrad, 1924), p. 110. Similar statements can be found in Somov, "Iz istorii," *Byloe,* no. 4, p. 45.

[20]D. Kol'tsov, "Rabochie v 1905-1907 gg.," in *Obshchestvennoe dvizhenie v Rossii v nachale XX veka,* ed. Martov et al., vol. 2, pt. 1 (St. Petersburg, 1909), p. 196.

Not all workers shared this enthusiasm. Some metalworkers viewed the commission with suspicion and recommended a boycott of the elections, a position advocated in certain Social Democratic circles.[21] The extent of these sentiments can be judged by the fact that only 57 percent of the metalworkers employed in firms where elections were held chose to take part in the first stage of the electoral process. At some enterprises, such as the Novyi Arsenal (1,000 workers), Feniks (385 workers), and Aleksandrovskii (2,000 workers) plants, workers boycotted the election entirely.[22]

Following the announcement of the commission, many workers seized the opportunity to forward petitions to Senator Shidlovskii. The petition from workers at the government-operated Baltiiskii shipbuilding plant was typical of many others adopted by workers in the first half of February. The Baltiiskii petition demanded the personal inviolability of the deputies elected to the commission, the presence of members of the press at the commission's deliberations, and the immediate reopening of district branches of the Gapon Assembly.[23] In putting forward the latter demand, workers were calling for legal restoration of their local groups, but without the restrictions and government complicity of the earlier Gapon organization.

Some Petersburg workers refused to join in these demands. According to the Menshevik activist S. I. Somov, there were many workers whose "faith in the commission was enormous."[24] Somov has described the mood at the Russian-American Rubber Factory, where eight thousand workers were employed, most of them unskilled. Here the workers spoke in detail about their miseries, which should be brought to the attention of "his honor, Senator Shidlovskii, by the deputy-petitioners, and they genuinely hoped that now, at last, through the Senator, workers' misfortunes would be known where they should be. In a word, the mood was highly optimistic, and above all, they insisted on not making harsh and broad demands and not allowing into their midst seditionaries who could once again draw the workers onto the path of unrighteousness."[25]

Intelligentsia activists played an important part in helping workers to formu-

---

[21]Schwarz, *The Russian Revolution,* pp. 95–112.

[22]Bulkin, *Na zare,* p. 111; V. Tsytsarin, "Vospominaniia metallista," *Vestnik truda,* no. 12 (61) (December 1925), p. 36, for a discussion of the debate that took place at the Nevskii metalworking plant.

[23]Kol'tsov, "Rabochie v 1905–1907 gg.," in *Obshchestvennoe dvizhenie,* ed. Martov et al., p. 197; Schwarz, *The Russian Revolution,* pp. 90–91; Surh, "Petersburg Workers," pp. 295–296.

[24]Somov, "Iz istorii," *Byloe,* no. 4, p. 50.

[25]Ibid.

late petitions to Senator Shidlovskii. The liberal lawyer Georgii Nosar', who later would serve as chairman of the Petersburg Soviet of Workers' Deputies, made his debut in the Petersburg labor movement during these weeks, and he was present when the electors assembled to choose deputies on February 16–17.[26] At these meetings, the electors endorsed a series of demands directed to Shidlovskii, many of them already circulated in the preelection petitions. The electors agreed to refrain from choosing deputies until these demands had been satisfied. When, on February 18, Senator Shidlovskii declared his inability to meet the demands, this brief but important episode came to an end.

Elections to the Shidlovskii Commission had far-reaching consequences for the future of the organized labor movement in the capital. For most workers, elections to the commission provided the first opportunity to elect representatives on the shop and enterprise levels. A total of 417 workers served as electors, 188 of them from metalworking plants alone.[27] Many were respected, articulate, and civic-minded workers, the future leaders of factory committees, trade unions, and deputies to the Petersburg Soviets.

Although the evidence is far from complete, it appears that skilled, experienced, literate workers predominated among the electors.[28] At the Putilov plant, for example, the electors were the "most *intelligentnye* workers."[29] The leader among them was a metalfitter in his early forties, highly intellectual and well read, and an outstanding speaker.[30] At the Rechkin railroad car construction plant, with four thousand workers, a thirty-year-old electrician played a leading role. He did not have intellectual interests, but was an exceptionally active and energetic worker with some experience in the Gapon movement. Workers at the Russian-American Rubber Factory elected "the most experienced and oldest workers."[31] Among those chosen at the Nevskii plant was V. Tsytsarin, a highly

---

[26]Schwarz, *The Russian Revolution*, p. 92. G. S. Nosar' is frequently referred to in the literature as Khrustalev-Nosar' because he assumed the identity of a textile worker, P. Khrustalev, an elector to the Shidlovskii Commission from the Chesher textile mill, in order to gain admission to the deliberations.

[27]I am basing these figures on Surh, "Petersburg Workers," p. 312 and n. 42, who draws on an authoritative archival source; published contemporary accounts provide somewhat lower figures. Kol'tsov, "Rabochie 1905–1907 gg.," in *Obshchestvennoe dvizhenie*, ed. Martov et al., p. 198, n. 1, states that there was a total of 372 electors to the commission. This figure is also accepted by Schwarz, *The Russian Revolution*, p. 95.

[28]For a discussion of this issue, see Surh, "Petersburg Workers," pp. 313–325.

[29]TsGAOR, f. 6860, ed. kh. 51, 1905, p. 5.

[30]Somov, "Iz istorii," *Byloe*, no. 4, pp. 47–48, for a description of this Putilov leader.

[31]Ibid., pp. 48–50.

educated Social Democratic worker who subsequently participated in the plant's factory committee and helped to establish the Petersburg metalworkers' union.[32]

Some of the electors had formerly been active in the Gapon Assembly. Estimates of their strength vary. The Social Democratic press reported that 20 percent of the electors were Social Democrats, 40 percent were "politically radicalized" workers, and 30–35 percent were "economist," a designation that may have applied to former Gaponists. Another report placed the number of Gaponists at 180, or 43 percent, of the electors.[33]

It is, of course, difficult to ascertain the effect of prior participation in the Gapon Assembly on an individual workers' outlook a month after Bloody Sunday. What it meant to have been a Gaponist once the revolution got under way remains a problem for further investigation. There can be no doubt, however, that some Assembly activists had established a reputation among their fellows as articulate, capable organizers and spokesmen. Given the chance to elect representatives to a government commission, workers selected individuals who had already demonstrated their talents and earned the confidence of their fellow workers. The former elector from the Nevskii metalworking plant, Tsytsarin, reflected many years later that "it is curious that not a single Gaponist was among those elected [at the Nevskii plant]," an indication that, more often than not, Gapon's followers were chosen as electors.[34]

The Shidlovskii electors also included a number of Social Democratic workers. The figure of 20 percent, reported by the SD press, may have been an exaggeration, but a contingent of SD workers was nevertheless present when the electors assembled in mid-February. At the time the election campaign began, the Social Democrats commanded very little influence in the capital. SD groups were small and isolated and the working-class members were often young and inexperienced.[35] Reliable figures on party membership are lacking, but it is likely that party circles in St. Petersburg had no more than a few hundred working-class members in February when the elections were held. Yet party membership in and of itself does not reveal the extent of Social Democratic support among Petersburg workers at the beginning of 1905. As noted by the Menshevik organizer Viktor Grinevich [M. G. Kogan], there was also a group of "conscious, cultivated, and educated workers," who had once belonged to the party

[32]Tsytsarin, "Vospominaniia," p. 36.

[33]Schwarz, *The Russian Revolution,* p. 113; Kol'tsov, "Rabochie v 1905–1907 gg.," in *Obshchestvennoe dvizhenie,* ed. Martov et al., p. 198, n. 1.

[34]Tsytsarin, "Vospominaniia," p. 35.

[35]See above, chapter 2.

and had left it angrily, but still "proudly call[ed] themselves Social Democrats."[36] Some of these nonparty "SD" workers—more educated and articulate and politically sophisticated than their fellows—may very well have been among the electors to the Shidlovskii Commission.

The elections to the commission represented a turning point in SD party fortunes in the capital, providing Mensheviks and Bolsheviks with their first opportunity to utilize a legal channel for agitation. Both SD factions viewed the announcement of the commission with misgivings, but neither could realistically hope to deter workers from participating in the election. As would often happen in the months to follow, Mensheviks and Bolsheviks yielded to workers' preference. They proposed a boycott of the second stage of the election in the event that the government failed to meet the conditions set forth by the electors, a tactic that struck a responsive chord in a majority of the worker-electors.[37]

If some workers were willing to use the election as an opportunity to press their political demands, they were no less eager to take advantage of the election process as a means of forming factory-level organizations. They did this by adding an extra stage to the commission's electoral process. Elections held at the shop level created a group of shop delegates to serve on the factory committee.[38] At the Putilov Plant, when workers gathered in their workshops to choose deputies during the first week in February, a report in the local press noted that it was uncertain whether workers were electing representatives for a factory committee or for the Shidlovskii Commission.[39] This ambiguity in the February elections was characteristic of other Petersburg firms as well.[40]

---

[36]Unpublished letter by V. Grinevich, Hoover Institution on War, Revolution and Peace, Nicolaevsky Collection, No. 190, Box 5, Document 58 (henceforth Letter from St. Petersburg), p. 3. The letter, which is undated, was probably written in early September 1905, but Grinevich's observation can be applied as well to the early months of the revolution and is supported by similar statements by another Menshevik activist in the capital, Somov. See Somov, "Iz istorii," *Byloe*, no. 4, pp. 22 ff.

[37]Bolshevik and Menshevik policies toward the commission are discussed in Schwarz, *The Russian Revolution*, pp. 95–128.

[38]Attention is drawn to the importance of this fourth stage of the electoral process at the shop level by Nevskii, "Vybor v komissiiu," p. 85.

[39]TsGAOR, f. 6860, ed. kh. 51, pp. 2, 5. This observation was made in the pages of the newspaper *Birzhevye vedomosti*, February 5 (18) and 7 (20), 1905, p. 2. At the Putilov plant, each worker was given a list of all those employed in that shop. The individual was then asked to write the name of a preferred elector and an alternate candidate and to place the ballot in a wooden box.

[40]Tsytsarin, "Vospominaniia," p. 36. On this point, see also Somov, "Iz istorii," *Byloe*, no. 4, p. 46, and Schwarz, *The Russian Revolution*, p. 89.

The factory committee movement in the capital gained strong reinforcement and legitimation from the Shidlovskii elections. During February committees were established in a number of large enterprises, including the Putilov, Nobel', Nevskii, and Aleksandrovskii metalworking plants, the goverment-operated Obukhov and Baltiiskii plants, the Beier copper-smelting works, the Rechkin railroad car construction plant, the Okhtensk, Pal', Maxwell, and Thornton textile mills, and elsewhere.[41]

The case of the Nevskii plant illustrates the remarkable progress of some factory committees. An election held at the Nevskii plant on February 1 served the dual purpose of electing representatives to the commission and creating a factory committee.[42] In March, the plant administration agreed to recognize the worker deputies, but only under the terms of the 1903 law on factory elders.[43] It is interesting to note that workers seldom formulated their demand for factory representation in terms of the establishment of elders, although the elders constituted the only hitherto legal form of representation at the factory level.[44] The demand for factory elders may have seemed to them an invocation of the unsatisfactory 1903 law which had authorized the election of elders only on employer initiative and under conditions that deprived workers of final authority over the selection process. Employers, rather than workers, were usually the ones to invoke the 1903 law during the revolution, often in order to provide legal sanction for factory committees that had already been elected by workers, as was the case at the Nevskii plant.

On employer initiative, a second election was held by Nevskii workers on March 20, ostensibly in accordance with the 1903 law. But here as elsewhere, workers refused to abide by the restrictive provisions of this legislation, and they renewed their mandate for the twelve electors previously chosen in early February. From that time on, the Council of Elders at the Nevskii plant "acquired great significance in factory life," according to a former participant.[45] By November,

[41]E. I Shalaeva and I. P. Leiberov, "Profsoiuzy Peterburga v 1905 godu," *Voprosy istorii,* no. 10 (October 1955), pp. 19–20; P. Kolokol'nikov, "Otryvki iz vospominanii," in *Materialy po istorii professional'nogo dvizeniia v Rossii* (henceforth *MIPDR),* vol. 2 (Moscow, 1924), p. 214; Tsytsarin, "Vospominaniia," p. 35; TsGAOR, f. 6860, ed. kh. 27, 1905, pp. 156, 208.

[42]Tsytsarin, "Vospominaniia," pp. 35–37. See also Buzinov, *Za Nevskoi zastavoi,* pp. 44, 51.

[43]For a discussion of this law, see chapter 2 above.

[44]By way of exception to this general pattern, the demand for factory elders was advanced by some textile groups in the capital. N. S. Trusova et al., eds., *Nachalo pervoi russkoi revoliutsii: Ianvar'- mart 1905 goda* (Moscow, 1955), p. 171.

[45]Tsytsarin, "Vospominaniia," pp. 36–37.

the council was operating with a monthly budget of ten thousand rubles.[46] These funds, collected through the deduction of a fixed percentage from workers' wages, were far in excess of the sums available to most other workers' organizations at the time. The council took charge of the factory cafeteria and store, collected funds for striking Putilov workers, and performed some mutual aid activities.[47]

In the area of labor-management relations, however, the Nevskii Council of Elders did not succeed in extending its functions beyond those originally set forth by the 1903 law on factory elders. The council remained little more than an intermediary between labor and management, transmitting information from the factory administration and forwarding workers' complaints.[48] At no point did the council actually participate in hiring or firing or the setting of wage rates. Thus, although factory committees at some enterprises won the respect and confidence of fellow workers, who "turned to them at every step for all kinds of information and advice, sensing in the elected representatives their defenders,"[49] these committees were unable to make inroads into traditional employer prerogatives. This situation reflected the strong opposition of industrialists.

EMPLOYER AND STATE POLICIES TOWARD FACTORY COMMITTEES

The workers' demands for employer recognition of enterprise-level worker deputies and their participation in key aspects of factory life brought a swift response from industrialists. When the demand for factory representation first appeared in the Gapon petition on the eve of Bloody Sunday, the Petersburg Society to Assist the Development and Improvement of Factory Industry—an employer organization established in 1893[50]—adopted a set of principles to

---

[46]*Obshcheprofessional'nye organy 1905–1907 gg.* Vypusk 1: *Moskovskie zhurnaly 1905 goda* (Moscow, 1926), p. 105, n. 19.

[47]Ibid.

[48]Tsytsarin, "Vospominaniia," p. 37.

[49]P. F. Kudelli and G. L. Shidlovskii, eds., *1905: Vospominaniia chlenov SPB soveta rabochikh deputatov* (Leningrad, 1926), p. 39. For similar observations on the workers' response to factory representatives, see Kolokol'nikov, "Otryvki," *MIPDR*, 2:215.

[50]Established by Petersburg industrialists in 1893, the Society did not obtain legal status until January 29, 1897, when it was officially authorized by the Ministry of Finance. TsGIA, f. 150, op. 1, d. 54, p. 9.

guide member-industrialists in responding to workers' claims. On January 6 the Society declared that worker deputies should not be allowed to participate in setting wage rates or in settling conflicts between the factory administration and individual workers.[51] In addition, the capital's leading industrialists gave notice that wages and hours would remain unchanged and that they would refuse to recognize workers' declarations when nonworkers had participated in their formulation, a reference to the role of the Assembly in assisting workers to draw up lists of grievances.

Although labor unrest compelled many employers to yield to workers' demands for improved wages and hours during the January-February strikes, and even to sanction councils of elders, industrialists remained intractable on the issue of employer prerogatives in the months that followed. On February 11, 1905, S. P. Glezmer, President of the Petersburg Society, circulated a memorandum among member-industrialists calling for opposition to any encroachments on their traditional prerogatives. In this report, Glezmer set forth the view that the participation of workers in the direction of the factory was "absolutely impermissible to any degree and in any respect." Although in principle, he stated, it was desirable for workers to have the right to meet and discuss their affairs, as well as the right to declare their needs collectively, "it is hardly timely [to promote such rights] given the low level of personal development among workers and the incompatibility [of these rights] with the degree of civil freedom among other members of society." He added that working people showed "immaturity and ignorance," a low level of literacy, and persistent ties to the countryside.[52]

Finally, Glezmer counseled against permitting the introduction of workers' organizations in Russia, "whatever form these organizations take." He predicted that such organizations would lead to the workers' "complete and general unification on the basis of common interests and for the defense of their demands by every means at their disposal." There would be no way to limit this elemental force once it began, and the ultimate consequence would be the unification of Russian workers with "international workers' organizations."[53]

In Moscow, as well, industrialists adopted a firm line of resistance to workers' demands for factory committees during the early months of the revolution. At a

[51]M. S. Balabanov, *Ot 1905 k 1917 godu: Massovoe rabochee dvizhenie* (Moscow and Leningrad, 1927), p. 31.

[52]For the text of this memorandum, see TsGIA, f. 150, op. 1, d. 484, p. 3, and f. 150, op. 1, d. 500, pp. 3–4. It is discussed in Chermenskii, *Burzhuaziia i tsarizm*, pp. 53–54.

[53]TsGIA, f. 150, op. 1, d. 484, p. 3.

meeting of representatives of Russian industry held in Moscow on March 10–11, Moscow industrialists were instrumental in introducing a resolution barring workers from participating in setting wage rates, determining dismissals, or regulating the internal factory order. The resolution further objected to the establishment of joint worker-employer commissions. Petersburg industrialists endorsed the resolution, and 116 major employers in the capital subsequently signified their adherence to its provisions.[54] The leading industrialists in St. Petersburg and Moscow thus took a stand at the very outset of the revolution in opposition to enterprise-level councils, a position they soon extended to another important labor organization—the trade union.

There was only one major exception to this pattern. Printing firm owners, both in the capital and in Moscow, maintained a far more conciliatory approach to workers' organizations than employers in other major branches of industry. Thus, the employers in Petersburg printing trades agreed almost immediately after Bloody Sunday to conduct negotiations with representatives of the typesetters over industry-wide terms for the employment of labor.[55]

In contrast to most industrialists, officials in some government circles were prepared to grant new and far-reaching legal status to workers' organizations, both in individual enterprises and on an industry-wide basis.[56] The Kokovtsov Commission, created almost simultaneously with the Shidlovskii Commission at the end of January, signaled a shift in the government strategy toward labor, marking the ascendancy of the Ministry of Finance in opposition to the Ministry of Internal Affairs, the sponsor of earlier experiments in government-directed labor organizations. Calling for reduced government intervention in labor-management relations, the Minister of Finance, Kokovtsov, advocated the resolution of industrial conflicts in a relatively autonomous sphere of social action by legal workers' and employers' associations.[57]

Under the aegis of the Kokovtsov Commission, a legislative proposal was

---

[54]S. E. Sef, *Burzhuaziia v 1905 godu* (Moscow and Leningrad, 1926), pp. 24–27. Most of the 116 St. Petersburg signatories belonged to the 142-member St. Petersburg Society to Assist the Development and Improvement of Factory Industry.

[55]P. Severianin, "Soiuz rabochikh pechatnogo dela," *Bez zaglaviia*, no. 14 (April 23, 1906), pp. 55–56; *Istoriia Leningradskogo soiuza rabochikh poligraficheskogo proizvodstva*, Book 1: *1904–1907* (henceforth *ILS*), (Leningrad, 1925) p. 108; P. V. Vasil'ev-Severianin, "Tarifnaia bor'ba soiuza rabochikh pechatnogo dela v 1905–1907 godakh," *MIPDP*, p. 159.

[56]For a discussion of government policy toward workers' organizations in 1905 by a Western scholar, see Jacob Walkin, "The Attitude of the Tsarist Government Toward the Labor Problem," *American Slavic and East European Review* 13, no. 2 (April 1954), especially pp. 180–183.

[57]*Rabochii vopros v komissii V. N. Kokovtsova*, pp. 1–34.

prepared in the spring of 1905 to legalize three types of industrial organization: "workers' associations" *(rabochie tovarishchestva)* formed on the enterprise level; trade unions established by workers in a common occupation or industry but employed in different firms; and employers' associations.[58] Drawn up by F. V. Fomin, earlier a participant in the drafting of the 1903 law on factory elders, the proposed legislation sanctioned the very factory committees that the workers persistently sought to introduce from January onward in the face of employer opposition.

The factory associations envisioned in this draft legislation were to be accorded broad authority, not only to discuss labor problems but also to "search for measures to improve conditions and to *defend* the interests of the members."[59] The proposal further specified that workers' deputies elected at the shop level were to serve as intermediaries between workers and the factory administration, although individuals could still deal directly with management, bypassing their elected representatives.[60] Other significant provisions of the proposal included the right to free elections, the right of representatives to assemble at will, and most important of all, the right of workers to initiate such associations without employer approval.[61]

This, indeed, was a very permissive and forward-looking proposal, indicative of the thinking of some of the most liberal-minded elements in the government of the time. In addition to factory committees, the Fomin draft provided for the legalization of trade unions—a remarkable step, considering that the trade unions had barely been initiated in the spring of 1905. Finally, the Kokovtsov Commission went even further by drafting legislation which granted workers the right to strike.[62] Thus, the demands originally set forth in the Gapon petition of

[58]The full text of the draft legislation can be found in ibid., pp. 133–139. It is republished in partial form in A. Kats and Iu. Milonov, eds., *1905: Professional'noe dvizhenie* (Moscow and Leningrad, 1926), pp. 319–321, and in V. Sviatlovskii, *Istoriia professional'nogo dvizheniia v Rossii ot vozniknoveniia rabochego klassa do kontsa 1917 g.* (Leningrad, 1925), p. 84.

[59]*Rabochii vopros v komissii V. N. Kokovtsova*, pp. 133–134, Article 2. Italics mine.

[60]Ibid., pp. 134–135, Article 8 and note.

[61]Ibid., pp. 134–136, Articles 3, 5, and 16. There were, however, some conditions placed on each of these rights. The police had to be notified of a meeting three days in advance; electors had to be at least twenty-five years of age; meetings could be held on factory premises only with employer consent. There was no provision for the deputies' immunity from retribution by employers.

[62]*Rabochii vopros v komissii V. N. Kokovtsova*, pp. 141–281. This law was promulgated on December 2, 1905, but with severe restrictions on the types of work stoppages that were legally permissible. For a discussion of the law on strikes, see I. I. Shelymagin, *Zakonodatel'stvo o fabrichno-zavodskom trude v Rossii 1900-1917* (Moscow, 1952), pp. 172–183. The text of the law appears on pp. 274–279 of *Rabochii vopros v komissii V. N. Kokovstova*.

January 9, calling for permanent factory committees, trade unions, and the right to strike, all received recognition in internal governmental deliberations conducted in the course of the revolution.

In the summer of 1905, the Fomin proposal was turned over to V. I. Timiriazev, soon to be appointed the head of the newly created Ministry of Trade and Industry. Under Timiriazev's direction, the section of the draft dealing with factory associations was deleted, while provisions for trade unions and employer organizations remained virtually intact. The legislation did not reach the State Council until early 1906, however, and when it was enacted on March 4, 1906, it had been greatly modified and circumscribed.[63] For if some government officials were willing to make these concessions to workers—itself a matter of considerable importance—there were even stronger elements within the government that resisted fundamental changes in the policy toward labor.

Whereas workers repeatedly sought legal opportunities and sanction for their collective endeavors—issues raised in the Gapon petition, in the Shidlovskii petitions, and on many occasions afterward—the government withheld this authorization until October, when a general strike brought the economy to a halt and compelled the Tsar to issue the October Manifesto. By mid-October, however, the workers had grown increasingly disillusioned with the prospects for government recognition of their rights. As government authority declined in the face of a growing anti-autocratic coalition in the cities, workers more and more often took steps to erect organizations without legal sanction.

In the summer and fall of 1905, Moscow workers gave new momentum to the factory committee movement. Industry-wide strike councils composed of factory representatives were formed in August and September, beginning with the ribbonweavers and spreading to the printers, carpenters, tobacco workers, and others.[64] Meeting on October 4, representatives of Moscow trades and industries—the forerunners of the Moscow Soviet—called for the establishment of factory committees.[65] During the weeks that followed, this demand was reiterated by many different groups of striking workers, and by the time the barricades went up in early December, a majority of Moscow factories had elected committees, with or without employer consent.[66]

[63]See below, chapter 5.

[64]Kolokol'nikov, "Otryvki," *MIPDR*, 2:227.

[65]*Obshcheprofessional'nye organy 1905–1907 gg.*, pp. 16–18, 103–104, n. 16. This is a republication of the *Biulleten' Muzeia sodeistviia truda*, no. 1 (November 16, 1905).

[66]Ibid., pp. 41, 46, 76; Kol'tsev, "Rabochie v 1905–1907 gg.," in *Obshchestvennoe dvizhenie*, ed. Martov et al., p. 229; K. Dmitriev [P. N. Kolokol'nikov], *Professional'nye soiuzy v Moskve* ([St. Petersburg], 190[6]), p. 10.

By then, a new phase in the evolution of workers' organizations had already begun in both cities. Independent trade unions and citywide soviets, an expression of the same persistent urge for unity and solidarity that gave rise to the factory committee movement, rapidly surpassed all other forms of collective association as the most important focus of workers' energies in the closing months of 1905.

The shift to more broadly based forms of organization was dictated by the logic of the labor and revolutionary movements that rapidly unfolded in the second half of 1905. As workers soon recognized, a successful campaign could seldom be waged by one firm alone, acting in isolation. Only in the giant metalworking firms, employing many thousands of workers, did such isolated labor struggles have a chance of succeeding, and it was here that the factory committee movement reached its apogee during 1905. Most workers came to understand that workplace improvements and the rights of workers in society could best be achieved through the coordinated struggle of many firms, acting together. This, in turn, necessitated new forms of organization that transcended the individual enterprise, embracing an entire industry or trade or even the city as a whole. Trade unions and soviets, as workers discovered, were admirably suited to this task.

THE EMERGENCE OF TRADE UNIONS

The formation of trade unions—organizations still unfamiliar to many workers at the beginning of the revolution—got under way in the spring of 1905.[67] These early efforts, continuing in the summer of 1905, remained relatively circumscribed until October, when the union movement gained momentum. In November forty-two unions were established in the capital and forty-one in Moscow. Unionizing efforts declined sharply in December, but by the end of 1905, workers had proclaimed a total of seventy-four unions in St. Petersburg and ninety-one in Moscow (table 8).[68] In addition, three Zubatov societies and the illegal 1903 printers' union continued to function in Moscow during all or part of the year, and an illegal 1902 knitters' union continued its activities in St. Petersburg.

[67]Grinevich, Letter from St. Petersburg, p. 11.
[68]A complete list of trade unions in St. Petersburg and Moscow during 1905 appears below, in Appendix I.

Table 8

Union Formation in St. Petersburg and Moscow, 1905

	Jan.	Feb.	March	April	May	June	July	Aug.	Sept.	Oct.	Nov.	Dec.	N.D.	TOTAL
St. Petersburg	1	2	4	2	0	0	5	0	2	12	42	3	1	74
Moscow	0	3	5	1	5	0	4	3	3	20	41	6	0	91

Source: See Appendix I for a complete list of unions and the sources used to compile this list.

Note: In most cases it is possible to identify only the date of the first general union meeting. This meeting, particularly in the fall of 1905, was frequently an occasion for reaching a collective decision to found a union, although in some instances an initiative group took the opportunity to win approval for union statutes prepared in advance. Where the initiation date of a union is known—and often this date preceded by weeks or months the actual founding of a union at a general meeting—it is shown above. In all other cases, the date of the first general (founding) meeting is indicated. The initiation and founding dates for individual unions are shown below in Appendix I. Omitted from this table are the three Zubatov societies that continued to function in Moscow during 1905, the 1903 Moscow printers' union, and the 1902 Petersburg knitters' union. Included are the Moscow mutual aid societies of waiters and of technicians, which began to function as trade unions during 1905. The table shows the month in which this transformation took place.

The pace of unionization in 1905 was directly correlated with political conditions. In contrast to party circles, which could be conducted clandestinely by a small number of people, trade unions, to be effective, required a mass membership and opportunities for open assembly and freedom of speech and the press. A modicum of civil liberties was the indispensable precondition for an organized labor movement in Russia. Prior to September, however, workers were seldom able to obtain permission for public meetings, and clandestine gatherings were vulnerable to the police and the fearsome Cossack troops.[69]

Conditions were quite different for white-collar and professional groups during the spring and summer. Unlike the workers, they assembled openly and were soon successful in establishing collective associations. In May, many of these groups confederated into the Union of Unions, an umbrella organization under liberal influence.[70] The Union of Unions encompassed a wide range of professional associations among lawyers, doctors, professors, railway employees, engineers, bookkeepers and accountants, and others. These organizational activities helped to stimulate workers to form their own organizations.

September was a turning point for the organized labor movement and more generally, for the course of revolutionary events. A strong resurgence of the strike movement took place, particularly in Moscow, where the printers conducted an impressive work stoppage that set the stage for a general strike initiated by Moscow railroad workers a few weeks later. Sensing a growing threat of popular unrest, the authorities pursued a belated strategy of accommodation and liberalization. In early August, the government proclaimed its intention to establish a national assembly—the State Duma—with limited consultative powers, and at the end of the month, a government decree restored autonomy to the universities for the first time since 1884.

Following the decree on university autonomy, students seized control of these institutions and opened their doors to workers' meetings, the first to be held on a mass scale and without police interference since the elections to the Shidlovskii Commission in February.[71] Thousands of workers passed through

---

[69]Grinevich, Letter from St. Petersburg, pp. 11–12. For further discussion of these early gatherings, see the section below, "Routes to Unionization."

[70]S. D. Kirpichnikov, "L. I. Lutugin i soiuz soiuzov," *Byloe*, no. 6 (34) (1925), pp. 138–140; Paul Miliukov, *Political Memoirs 1905–1917*, ed. Arthur P. Mendel (Ann Arbor, Michigan, 1967), p. 29.

[71]A vivid description of these events is provided by Voitinskii, *Gody pobed i porazhenii*, Book I: *1905-yi goda* (Berlin, Petersburg, and Moscow, 1923), pp. 41–110. At the time, Voitinskii was a university student who had recently joined the ranks of the Bolsheviks and was actively engaged in agitation on the faction's behalf.

the university halls in these weeks, attentively absorbing lectures by Social Democratic and Socialist Revolutionary speakers on such topics as the trade union movement in the West, the eight-hour workday, the convening of a Constituent Assembly, the programs of the socialist parties, and current affairs.[72]

With the onset of the general strike in October, the number of public gatherings increased, and on October 12 the government issued a temporary law permitting meetings to be held without prior authorization of the police.[73] Five days later, the October Manifesto promised a full range of civil liberties, including freedom of press, association, assembly, and a national representative institution—the State Duma—with greater authority than had been envisioned in the proclamation of August 6, 1905. During the ensuing "days of freedom"—as contemporaries described the period between the Manifesto of October 17 and the Moscow uprising that began on December 7—the trade union movement rapidly expanded in St. Petersburg and Moscow. Not only were dozens of unions inaugurated during these weeks, but more than eighty trade union meetings were held in the capital, and over two hundred in Moscow.[74] Legal trade union and radical newspapers began publication in both cities, and the newly established Central Bureaus of Trade Unions openly functioned as coordinating and informational organs of the growing labor movement.[75]

These weeks also witnessed the formation of the Soviet of Workers' Deputies in St. Petersburg and, more belatedly, in Moscow.[76] The Petersburg Soviet met for the first time on October 13, amid the general strike. The Moscow Soviet did not convene until November 21. The earlier formation of the Soviet in the capital not only enabled this historically unprecedented organization to attain a

---

[72]Ibid., p. 60.

[73]*Polnoe sobranie zakonov Rossiiskoi imperii s 1649 goda* (St. Petersburg, 1830–1916), sbornik 3, tom 25, 1905, pp. 735–737.

[74]V. Grinevich, "Ocherk razvitiia professional'nogo dvizheniia v S.-Peterburge," *Obrazovanie* 15, no. 9 (September 1906), pp. 236; Laura Engelstein, *Moscow, 1905: Working-Class Organization and Political Conflict* (Stanford, 1982), p. 150, asserts that four hundred officially authorized public meetings were held in Moscow between October 17 and December 8. More than one half of them were concerned with trade union affairs.

[75]For a complete listing of the St. Petersburg and Moscow trade union press in 1905, see Ia. S. Roginskii, *Russkaia profsoiuznaia periodicheskaia pechat' 1905-1907 gg: Bibliographicheskii ukazatel'* (Moscow, 1957). On this subject see also S. Nikitin, "Ocherki po istorii professional'noi pechati v Rossii: Pechat' 1905 goda," in *MIPDR*, 2:141–158. On the Central Bureaus of Trade Unions, see S. P. Tiurin, *Moskovskoe tsentral'noe biuro professional'nykh soiuzov* (Moscow, 1913); *MIPDR*, 4:5–142; and chapter 4 below.

[76]The soviets are discussed below in chapter 4.

fuller development than its Moscow counterpart, but it also affected the progress of the trade union movement. In the capital, the relatively early establishment of the Soviet diverted attention away from the formation of trade unions, whereas in Moscow, the belated establishment of the Soviet permitted the trade union movement to develop without any distraction during October and most of November.

Artisanal and sales-clerical workers were the first to organize trade unions in both cities. The factory committee movement had not touched these workers, who for the most part were employed in a multitude of small and dispersed enterprises. With the exception of the semi-artisanal printers, they had taken little part in the January-February strikes, and only in the spring and summer did they begin to conduct work stoppages against employers—in some cases, such as the Moscow bakers in April, with a high degree of solidarity and coordination.[77]

Printers, tailors, clerks and bookkeepers, woodworkers, pharmacists, shoemakers, and watchmakers initiated trade unions in St. Petersburg during the first half of 1905.[78] In Moscow, bakers, pursemakers, salesclerks, pharmacists, municipal employees, railroad workers, and barbers took the first steps to form unions in the early months of the revolution. Some of these groups turned to the local police for permission to hold public meetings, but these requests were usually denied.[79] Nevertheless, the authorities in both cities occasionally made some exceptions. The Moscow bakers met openly in March, and the Petersburg printers held a union meeting in August, attended by the government inspector of printing firms in the capital.[80]

When watchmakers and tailors in the capital approached the local police for permission to organize a union, they were directed to the local Board of Artisanal Trades, although few of the workers were likely to have been guild members. The Board was not, however, sympathetic to the workers' proposal.[81]

[77]*Professional'noe dvizhenie Moskovskikh pishchevikov v gody pervoi revoliutsii*, sbornik 1 (Moscow, 1927), pp. 104–107.

[78]For accounts of these early unionizing efforts, see *Professional'nyi soiuz*, no. 3 (December 25, 1905), p. 5; Grinevich, "Ocherk," *Obrazovanie* 15, no. 8 (August 1906), pp. 216–226; Gruzdev, "Iz istorii," *MIPDP*, pp. 39–53.

[79]*Novaia zhizn'*, no. 1 (October 21, 1905), p. 4.

[80]*Professional'noe dvizhenie Moskovskikh pishchevikov*, pp. 105–106; Severianin, "Soiuz rabochikh pechatnogo dela," *Bez zaglaviia*, no. 14 (April 1906), pp. 58–59; Grinevich, Letter from St. Petersburg, p. 12, provides an eyewitness description of the printers' meeting.

[81]Following this incident, other artisans, such as shoemakers, decided not to petition the employer-dominated board for permission to unionize. Grinevich, "Ocherk," *Obrazovanie* 15, no. 8, pp. 219–221; *Novaia zhizn'*, no. 1 (October 21, 1905), p. 4.

These early efforts to unionize did not reach fruition until the fall. Basic civil liberties, the sine qua non of the union movement, were not granted until October 17, and it was only then that workers found it possible to form trade unions on a new and unprecedented scale.

ROUTES TO UNIONIZATION

Trade unions arose in different ways during 1905, but nearly all of them owed their beginnings to the turbulent strike movement that spread to many industries and occupations in the course of the revolution, reaching a high point in October and November. Strikes provided the impetus for collective association, and it was in the context of confrontations with employers that workers often took their first steps to proclaim a trade union.

There were several routes to unionization, depending in part on the extent of organizational experience predating the revolution. Familiarity with a prior organization and the availability of working-class or intelligentsia leaders greatly assisted the unionizing activities of some groups. Few of the pre-1905 associations developed directly into trade unions, however. One exception was the Moscow Society of Waiters and Other Tavern and Hotel Personnel. This mutual aid society, dating from 1902, had become a thriving organization with more than twelve hundred members by the beginning of 1905. It was not until the spring and summer of 1905 that Moscow waiters were drawn into the strike movement. During October and November they organized a major work stoppage and, despite concerted opposition from some members, began to transform the society into a trade union.[82]

Struggles took place in several other mutual aid organizations over the future direction of the organization, but in most cases, the pro-union faction did not succeed. In November 1905 a group of radical workers, led by the Menshevik printer Nikolai Chistov, sought unsuccessfully to instigate a change in the character and activities of the Moscow Mutual Aid Fund of Typo-Lithographical Workers (founded in 1869). They attempted to rewrite the charter of the society to include assistance to unemployed and striking workers, but failed to secure

[82]*Obshcheprofessional'nye organy 1905-1907 gg.,* p. 110, n. 30; Dmitriev [Kolokol'nikov], *Professional'nye soiuzy,* p. 8; A. Kats, "Iz istorii Moskovskogo Obshchestva vzaimopomoshchi ofitsiantov (1902-1916 gg.)," *MIPDR,* 1:43-49. Only in September 1906 did the Society adopt a new charter corresponding to its new activities as a trade union.

majority support within the society.[83] A similar conflict arose in the Moscow Society of Commercial Employees (1889), and here too the trade union advocates were defeated.[84]

Although few unions arose directly out of preexisting organizations, many were founded by worker-activists who had acquired training and experience in a prerevolutionary organization such as a Zubatov society, the Gapon Assembly, or one of the underground political parties. The worker-organizers in the Moscow unions of printers, tobacco workers, and candymakers, and the incipient organization of metalworkers, came out of the Zubatov movement.[85] Gaponists were heavily influential in the establishment of the St. Petersburg unions of bronze smelters and lithographers, and A. E. Karelin, a central figure in the Assembly, served on the directing board of the lithographers' union. Gaponists also played a part in helping to organize woodworkers and office clerks in the capital.[86] Ushakov, who directed the government-sponsored Mutual Aid Society of Workers in the Machine Industry before the revolution, founded two new labor associations, with government support: the Central Workers' Union and the Union of Women Workers.[87]

Workers who participated in Social Democratic and Socialist Revolutionary circles before 1905 sometimes organized and led the new trade unions. Members of the 1903 Moscow printers' union provided the leadership among

[83]V. V. Sher, *Istoriia professional'nogo dvizheniia rabochikh pechatnogo dela v Moskve* (Moscow, 1911), pp. 96–97. When this incident took place, Chistov was serving as secretary to the Moscow Union of Workers in the Printing Trades.

[84]*Obshcheprofessional'nye organy 1905–1907 gg.*, p. 97, n. 7. Apart from the Moscow waiters' union, the Moscow union of technicians had continuity with an earlier mutual aid society.

[85]The Zubatovist printer A. S. Borshchevskii was a leader in the printers' union established in October 1905, and served as a deputy to the Moscow Soviet. A. Borshchevskii, S. Reshetov, and N. Chistov, eds., *Moskovskie pechatniki v 1905 godu* (Moscow, 1925), pp. 122–124. F. Bodganov-Evdokimov and Alekseev, two former Zubatovists, founded the Moscow union of tobacco workers in 1905. Bodganov-Evdokimov became a Social Democrat and attended the Fourth Congress of the RSDRP in Stockholm in 1906 as a Moscow delegate. Kats and Milonov, eds., *1905*, p. 6. The former Zubatovist candymaker, Petrov, helped to organize the candymakers' union and was elected to the union's directing board in 1906. *Professional'noe dvizhenie Moskovskikh pishchevikov*, pp. 157, 169–170. Several leaders of the Moscow metalworkers' union, which became established in 1906, had been members of the earlier Zubatov society. TsGAOR, f. 6860, d. 431, p. 101.

[86]Kudelli and Shidlovskii, eds., *1905*, pp. 102–107, 136–138, 150–155, 180–181, 185–188, 203–207, 211, 213–215; *ILS*, pp. 252–253.

[87]P. Vasil'ev, "Ushakovshchina," *Trud v Rossii*, no. 1 (1925), pp. 146–147. It is noteworthy that Ushakov was also elected as a deputy to the Shidlovskii Commission from the state printing firm, Ekspeditsiia zagotovleniia gosudarstvennykh bumag.

Moscow printers in 1905. The Menshevik worker Chistov, "who had been politically shaped by underground propaganda circles [before 1905]," was a founder of the new nonparty union among printers in October.[88]

Similarly, the pre-1905 circles of SD bakers in Moscow organized the city's first industry-wide strike in April, which laid the groundwork for a trade union in the baking industry. When the union finally became established in November, six of the eight members of the 1904 SD circle were elected to the union directing board, and they held all but one of the major offices in the new organization. An SR circle had also been active among the bakers before the revolution, and one of its members, M. E. Lazerev, was elected vice-president of the new union.[89]

Members of the pre-1905 SD circle in the Moscow candymaking industry organized a major strike of candymakers in May and June 1905, and they went on to found the union in November. Six of the fifteen members of this union's directing board in May 1906 had been participants in the illegal SD group of candymakers before the revolution, including three out of four members of the union directing board.[90] Among Moscow tobacco workers, I. Ia. Tikhomirov, a Zubatov follower who joined an SD circle in 1904, was active in founding the union, together with several other former Zubatovists. Tikhomirov was elected the first president of the tobacco workers' union.[91] Worker-radicals from pre-revolutionary circles also became active in the Petersburg unions of textile workers, woodworkers and lithographers (together with Gaponists) and the incipient metalworkers' union.[92]

Strike committees and industry-wide councils also served as the nuclei of trade unions. The typesetters in the capital were the first to make the transition from a strike committee to a trade union. Following Bloody Sunday, the typesetters intensified their campaign for an industry-wide *tarif,* an agreement with employers to improve and standardize wage rates throughout the city's printing trades.[93] The typesetters were unable to reach an agreement with employers, and

---

[88]P. A. Garvi, *Revoliutsionnye siluety,* Inter-University Project on the History of the Menshevik Movement (New York, 1962), p. 28.

[89]*Professional'noe dvizhenie Moskovskikh pishchevikov,* pp. 104, 112.

[90]Ibid., pp. 150–151, 157, 170.

[91]Ibid., p. 201. On Tikhomirov, see above, chapter 2.

[92]Kudelli and Shidlovskii, eds., *1905,* pp. 48–52, 99–101, 165–166, 173–174, 186–188, 203–207, 213–215.

[93]Vasil'ev-Severianin, "Tarifnaia bor'ba soiuza rabochikh pechatnogo dela v 1905–1907 godakh," *MIPDP,* p. 159; *ILS,* p. 108. According to Vasil'ev-Severianin, the term *tarif*—borrowed from French and German labor practices—was first used by Russian printing workers in 1884. A

they finally resorted to a strike, which failed, however, when other workers in the printing industry remained on their jobs. This defeat taught strike organizers the importance of solidarity, and they went on to found a trade union uniting all workers in the printing trades. In June printers' representatives assembled to approve a draft of the union charter, and two months later it was formally adopted at a founding meeting.

Like the typesetters, Moscow's highly skilled ribbonweavers made the transition from an industry-wide strike council to a trade union. In August the ribbonweavers organized a major strike, directed by an interfactory strike council under Menshevik leadership and modeled on an earlier council created in May by striking textile workers in Ivanovo-Voznesensk, a textile village in the Central Industrial Region.[94] The ribbonweavers' council, and others established in the fall by striking Moscow printers, tobacco workers, carpenters, and gold- and silversmiths, led directly to the formation of trade unions.[95] Similarly, the Moscow union of teapackers arose out of an industry-wide strike and consumer boycott that began in October to protest the dismissal of factory committee deputies at the Vysotskii firm.[96]

Factory committees elected earlier in the year were also sometimes the initiators of trade unions. In the Petersburg metalworking industry, for example, the Council of Elders at the Nevskii plant led the way in attempting to establish a trade union in the summer of 1905. Factory committees at other major metalworking plants in the capital also took steps toward unionization during the "days of freedom," but for reasons discussed below, none of these efforts reached fruition before the end of the year.

Intelligentsia activists frequently participated in the initial stages of union formation, and they usually did so at the request of workers who sought

---

discussion of the origins and use of this term can be found in A. Iakovlev, "K voprosu o tarifnykh soglasheniiakh," *Professional'nyi vestnik,* no. 9 (June 21, 1907), p. 4.

[94]Beginning with Podvoiskii, *Pervyi sovet rabochikh deputatov (Ivanovo-Voznesenskii—1905 g.)* (Moscow, 1925), Soviet historians have called the *sobranie upolnomochennykh* formed in Ivanovo-Voznesensk a *sovet deputatov* (soviet of deputies). In fact, the first industry-wide strike council to be designated by contemporaries as a *sovet* was probably the one established by Moscow ribbonweavers in August 1905. On this controversy, see Schwarz, *The Russian Revolution,* Appendix II, pp. 335–338.

[95]Ibid., p. 341; Kolokol'nikov, "Otryvki," *MIPDR,* 2:227–228; Iu. K. Milonov and M. Rakovskii, *Istoriia Moskovskogo professional'nogo soiuza rabochikh derevoobdelochnikov,* vypusk 1 (Moscow, 1928), p. 92; N. S. Mamontov, "Zoloto-serebrianniki v 1905," *MIPDR,* 5:184.

[96]*Istoriia odnogo soiuza* (Moscow, 1907), pp. 7–8; *Professional'noe dvizhenie Moskovskikh pishchevikov,* pp. 44–46; Kolokol'nikov, "Otryvki," *MIPDR,* 2:226.

assistance in the complex and unfamiliar task of creating a trade union. The Menshevik Grinevich, a bookkeeper by profession and an SD organizer since the 1890s, arrived in the capital in June 1905 to carry on party work in the capital's City District.[97] Almost immediately Grinevich was approached by a group of shoemakers eager to form a union but at a loss to know how to proceed. In July Grinevich met secretly in the woods with more than one hundred shoemakers, many of them of non-Russian origin.[98] He lectured them about Western European labor movements and advised them on how to set up their own organization. Reporting on this and other encounters with Petersburg workers, Grinevich observed in the early fall that the "widespread aspiration of workers to form trade unions" coincided with a "shocking ignorance of trade unions and their tasks, among both organized and unorganized workers."[99]

This "shocking ignorance" is not difficult to understand, for workers had little opportunity before 1905 to become acquainted with the concept and tasks of trade unions. Some information on Western European labor movements had reached workers through the Zubatov societies in Moscow and the Gapon Assembly in the capital. Workers also had before them the spectacle of professional and white-collar groups currently engaged in a lively effort to form collective organizations. Newspapers that enjoyed popularity among workers, such as *Syn Otechestva* [Son of the Fatherland], carried extensive coverage of these professional unions, and this in turn prompted workers to initiate their own associations.[100] But when it came to implementation, workers often turned for models and practical assistance to intelligentsia activists.

Intellectuals made two major contributions to the incipient union movement. At meetings and lectures, and in the labor and radical press, they acquainted

[97]For a summary of Grinevich's background and career, see P. Kolokol'nikov and S. Rapoport, eds., *1905-1907 gg. v professional'nom dvizhenii: I i II Vserossiiskie konferentsii professional'nykh soiuzov* (Moscow, 1925), pp. 420–421; V. Grinevich, "Ocherki," *Obrazovanie* 15, no. 9, pp. 221–226; idem, Letter from St. Petersburg, pp. 10–16.

[98]Grinevich, Letter from St. Petersburg, p. 11; idem, "Ocherk," *Obrazovanie*, 15, no. 8, p. 221. There is evidence that workers of non-Russian origin may have been involved in the formation of several different unions in the capital. Grinevich reported that Finns, Estonians, and Jews were active among the shoemakers. Kolokol'nikov noted that Finnish, Estonian, and Latvian metalworkers employed at the Lessner and Erikson plants in the Vyborg district were eager for unionization. Kolokol'nikov, "Otryvki," *MIPDR*, 2:223. Tailors of non-Russian origin also participated in the effort to unionize the Petersburg apparel trades. *Obshcheprofessional'nye organy 1905-1907 gg.*, p. 115, n. 58; *Professional'nyi soiuz*, no. 3 (December 25, 1905), p. 5.

[99]Grinevich, Letter from St. Petersburg, p. 17; idem, "Ocherk," *Obrazovanie* 15, no. 8, p. 221.

[100]Grinevich, Letter from St. Petersburg, p. 17.

workers with the history, theory, and practice of Western European trade unions. No founding meeting was complete without a lecture on the subject, and no issue of the newly established trade union press failed to address the topic.[101] Numerous translations of Western European books and pamphlets on trade unionism appeared during 1905, greatly enlarging the available literature, which at the time included only a few works dating from the turn of the century.[102] In the eyes of some intelligentsia organizers, their activities during the revolution were aimed at nothing less than "transport[ing] trade unions of the European type onto our soil."[103]

Second, intellectuals supplied valuable assistance in erecting and sustaining trade unions. Their services proved especially vital in facilitating the organization of unskilled groups such as cabmen, household servants, building superintendents and doormen, and many others.[104] But even among predominantly skilled groups, such as printers, metalworkers, and tailors, intelligentsia activists performed a no less vital function in assisting workers to form trade unions.[105]

---

[101]For numerous examples, see the *Biulleten' muzeia sodeistviia truda*, the informational organ of the Moscow Central Bureau of Trade Unions, republished in *Obshcheprofessional'nye organy 1905–1907 gg.*, and *Professional'nyi soiuz*, the organ of the St. Petersburg Central Bureau of Trade Unions.

[102]These translations included P. Lafarg [Paul LaFargue], *Professional'noe dvizhenie v Germanii* (Moscow, 1905); V. Zombart [Werner von Sombart], *Rabochii vopros* (St. Petersburg, 1905); K. Kautskii [Karl Kautsky], *Vozniknovenie rabochego klassa* (St. Petersburg, 1905); B. Shenlank, *Soiuzy podmaster'ev vo Frantsii* (Moscow, 1905); K. Kautskii, *Professional'noe dvizhenie i politicheskaia partiia proletariata* (St. Petersburg, 1905); M. Shippel', *Professional'nye soiuzy* (Rostov-na-Donu, 1905). In addition, a number of books by Russian authors appeared on the subject of Western European trade unions, including A. Kedrov, *Rabochie soiuzy v zapadnoi Evrope* (Moscow, 1905); Iu. Lavrinovich, *Rabochie soiuzy* (St. Petersburg, 1905). These works were regularly commended to working-class readers in the pages of the newly established legal labor press. See, for example, *Biulleten' Muzeia sodeistviia truda*, no. 1 (November 16, 1905).

[103]A. Evdokimov, "Iz vospominanii tred-iunionista," *MIPDR*, 5:124.

[104]The Menshevik A. A. Isaev helped to organize Petersburg cabmen. *Obshcheprofessional'nye organy 1905–1907 gg.*, p. 117, n. 70. Intelligentsia women in the League for Women's Equality assisted in organizing Moscow household servants. Ibid., pp. 42, 112, n. 38. The liberal university professor V. Sviatlovskii assisted gardeners in the capital to form a union. *Professional'nyi soiuz*, no. 2 (December 4, 1905), p. 3. Social Democratic intelligentsia activists participated in the unionization of building superintendents and doormen. *Novaia zhizn'*, no. 9 (November 10, 1905), p. 5. Numerous other instances of intelligentsia involvement in the incipient labor movement could be cited.

[105]The Menshevik intelligentsia activists Grinevich and Somov assisted the St. Petersburg printers to unionize. Grinevich, Letter from St. Petersburg, p. 12. Intelligentsia organizers were active among metalworkers in both cities. See the section "Craft Unionism and Factory Patriotism" below. The SD intelligentsia activists E. A. Oliunina and K. M. Kolokol'nikova helped to organize the Moscow tailors' union.

From September on, intelligentsia activists began to assume an increasingly active role as initiators of trade unions. Under the auspices of the newly created Central Bureaus of Trade Unions, they provided regular consultations for prospective union groups. "During reception hours," recollected a former Moscow intelligentsia labor organizer, Pavel Kolokol'nikov, "there was a crowd at the Central Bureau. They came for information and advice, for help in establishing an organization, and for speakers to attend meetings."[106] Intellectuals furnished legal assistance for the incipient union movement and provided the editorial staff and know-how required to publish the first trade union newspapers.[107]

After helping to found trade unions, intellectuals often remained in key positions. Grinevich, for example, was elected to the directing board of the Petersburg printers' union in mid-August. Initially, some printers opposed him, fearing that Grinevich, a member of the Petersburg Menshevik group, would "speak too much about politics and would bring about the destruction of the union."[108] But in this case as in others, workers became reconciled to the presence of intelligentsia activists whose knowledge of European labor and willingness to take part in union work made them extremely valuable to the nascent organizations.

Trade unions furnished one of the most important arenas for interaction between intelligentsia activists and workers during the revolution. The lawyers, students, writers, university professors, and others who participated in the burgeoning labor movement brought a wide range of political outlooks and party associations. Within their ranks could be found Social Democrats (Bolsheviks, Mensheviks, and nonfaction SDs), Socialist Revolutionaries, syndicalists, and liberals. Although a legacy of suspicion and even antagonism existed between workers and intellectuals on the eve of 1905,[109] a small but diligent group of intelligentsia activists made deep inroads into the workers' milieu during the revolution through the medium of the trade unions, exerting far-reaching influence over the direction of the labor movement.

[106]Dmitriev [Kolokol'nikov], *Professional'nye soiuzy*, p. 6. For other reports on the activities of the Central Bureaus, see *Professional'nyi soiuz*, no. 1 (November 27, 1905), pp. 3–4; S. P. Tiurin, *Moskovskoe tsentral'noe biuro professional'nykh soiuzov* (Moscow, 1923), p. 21.

[107]*Obshcheprofessional'nye organy 1905-1907 gg.*, p. 129, n. 117, for an account of the legal assistance offered by the Bureaus. The Petersburg Central Bureau of Trade Unions published *Professional'nyi soiuz*, and the Moscow Central Bureau published the *Biulleten' muzeia sodeistviia truda*. In addition, there were many publications issued by individual unions. Roginskii, *Russkaia profsoiuzaia periodicheskaia pechat'*.

[108]Grinevich, Letter from St. Petersburg, p. 13.

[109]Allan K. Wildman, *The Making of a Workers' Revolution: Russian Social Democracy, 1891-1903* (Chicago, 1967).

THE SIZE AND COMPOSITION OF TRADE UNIONS

Workers in all sectors of the urban economy took steps to create trade unions during 1905. Those employed in the manufacturing sector formed the largest number of unions (forty-one in both St. Petersburg and Moscow), followed by sales-clerical, service, and other workers (table 9). In each sector, moreover, trade unions attracted workers who had never before been involved in any kind of organization. Groups that in Western Europe were traditionally the last and most difficult to organize took part in the trade union movement, including house-hold servants, cabmen, bath attendants, superintendents and doormen, chimney sweeps, window washers, gardeners, floor polishers, and cooks. More than any other single indicator, the unionization of these workers testifies to the broad impact of the revolutionary upheavals and the widely felt need for collective association among all segments of the laboring population.

Of the seventy-four Petersburg unions and the ninety-one in Moscow, few were fully formed organizations by the end of 1905. The majority arose during the "days of freedom" and scarcely managed to take the first important steps to proclaim their existence. Most succeeded in holding a public meeting, drafting a founding charter *(ustav)*, and electing a directing board *(pravlenie)*. Only a small number were sufficiently developed to recruit members and collect dues.

Membership data are available for only twelve Petersburg unions, which had a combined total of 12,000 members; twenty-three Moscow unions for which data are available attracted nearly 25,000 members into their ranks.[110] These figures are incomplete, but they provide an accurate picture of the relatively more developed state of the trade unions in Moscow and the still limited development of the organized labor movement as a whole.

Even relatively well-established organizations did not yet draw a clear distinction between members and nonmembers, however. Both participated in decisions taken at public meetings, and enterprise-level deputies to unions were often elected by all workers, not just those whose names were inscribed on union rolls.[111] The atmosphere during these tumultuous weeks, with the frenzy of organizational activities and mass meetings, precluded a strict differentiation between members and nonmembers.

[110]These figures are based on my own data on union membership, collected from a wide variety of contemporary sources. My finding for Moscow agrees with contemporary estimates. *Vtoraia konferentsiia professional'nykh soiuzov: Doklady i protokoly* (St. Petersburg, 1906), p. 46. I have not located any contemporary estimates of the total union membership in St. Petersburg.

[111]On this point, see Sher, *Istoriia*, p. 193.

Table 9
Sectoral Composition of Trade Unions Formed
in St. Petersburg and Moscow in 1905

| | MANUFACTURING | | SALES-CLERICAL | |
	Number of Unions	Percent of Total Unions	Number of Unions	Percent of Total Unions
St. Petersburg	41	55	8	11
Moscow	41	45	21	23

| | CONSTRUCTION* | | TRANSPORTATION | |
	Number of Unions	Percent of Total Unions	Number of Unions	Percent of Total Unions
St. Petersburg	3	4	2	3
Moscow	6	7	4	4

| | COMMUNICATIONS | | SERVICE | |
	Number of Unions	Percent of Total Unions	Number of Unions	Percent of Total Unions
St. Petersburg	1	1	11	15
Moscow	2	2	9	10

| | MUNICIPAL | | MISCELLANEOUS | |
	Number of Unions	Percent of Total Unions	Number of Unions	Percent of Total Unions
St. Petersburg	4	5	4	5
Moscow	5	5	3	3

| | TOTAL | |
	Number of Unions	Percent of Total Unions
St. Petersburg	74	100
Moscow	91	100

Source: See Appendix I.
*Unions with both skilled and unskilled construction workers are included here.

Membership data, therefore, provide only the slightest indicator of the massive worker response to the union movement. Since most of these organizations were still in the process of formation, attendance at union-sponsored meetings, rather than actual membership, offers a more accurate picture of the workers' enthusiasm for the prospect of unionization. Attendance at these meetings was sometimes remarkable. On October 19, for example, 800 Moscow printers met under union auspices. Three thousand Moscow tailors attended a union meeting on November 27, and in another hall, 900 Moscow teapackers gathered on the same day.[112] In the capital, as well, union-sponsored meetings drew large crowds: 3,000 tailors on October 30, 2,000 salesclerks on November 6, 600 shoemakers on November 13, and 2,000 waiters in late November.[113] These attendance figures—never again matched prior to February 1917—testify to the enthusiasm for collective association during the revolution and the tolerant political atmosphere in the aftermath of the October Manifesto.

Only a small proportion of the workers who attended these meetings entered their names on union rolls. Many were wary of invitations to join an organization that operated semilegally and might invite unpleasant repercussions from employers or government authorities. For others, the concept of a trade union was still unfamiliar, and there was a great deal of uncertainty and confusion about the character and role of these organizations.

Some individual unions nevertheless struck a responsive chord among a large and impressive number of workers who paid the entry fee (usually 50 kopecks) to join the organization. Printers were among the most avid recruits to trade unions, and their union attracted more than 3,000 members in the capital and 4,000 in Moscow, or about 19 percent and 32 percent, respectively, of the printers in each city.[114] The Moscow bakers, with over 1,700 members (18

[112]Ibid., p. 185; E. A. Oliunina, *Portnovskii promysel v Moskve i v derevniakh Moskovskoi i Riazanskoi gubernii. Materialy k istorii domashnei promyshlennosti v Rossii* (Moscow, 1914), p. 290. Other large meetings in Moscow included 1,500 household servants on November 1, 900 teapackers on November 13, and 500 employees in meat and fish stores on November 28. *Obshcheprofessional'nye organy 1905–1907 gg.*, pp. 40–42; *Bor'ba*, no. 2 (November 29, 1905), p. 3.

[113]Grinevich, "Ocherk," *Obrazovanie* 15, no. 9, p. 236; *Novaia zhizn'*, no. 11 (November 12, 1905), p. 4, and no. 9 (November 10, 1905), p. 5.

[114]The capital's printers' union reported a membership of 3,339 in December 1905. *Professional'nyi vestnik*, no. 3 (February 10, 1907), p. 7. The Moscow printers' union reported 4,000 members by the end of 1905. *Obshcheprofessional'nye organy 1905–1907 gg.*, p. 70. This figure was reported in *Materialy po professional'nomu dvizheniiu rabochikh*, no. 1 (1906), the organ of the Moscow Central Bureau of Trade Unions. The Petersburg figures do not include members of the lithographers' union, which would have increased the total union membership in this industry still further. The proportion of unionized workers here and below is based on the total number of

percent of the labor force), ranked among the more successful unions in the city, while the Petersburg bakers' union attracted over 800 members (12 percent of the labor force).[115]

Among factory groups, food processing workers, such as Moscow tea-packers, tobacco workers, and candymakers, also proved eager for unionization. The Moscow teapackers' union, following an effective strike and consumer boycott in October-November, drew a membership of 2,000 workers, or two-thirds of the labor force in this industry.[116] The Moscow tobacco workers' union, with 1,000 members, claimed 30 percent of the industry's labor force, while the Moscow candymakers' union, with 800 members, represented 23 percent of the labor force.[117] Both of the latter groups had earlier been involved in Zubatov societies. The Petersburg Union of Salesclerks, with about 3,000 members, attracted 5 percent of the city's salesclerks.[118] Other unions with an aggregate membership of more than 500 included Moscow sales-clerical workers, tailors, carpenters, waiters, clerks and bookkeepers, and ribbonweavers, and the Petersburg textile workers, tailors, and woodworkers.[119]

Some unions stood at the very fringes of the workers' movement by virtue of their mixed composition and the presence within them of a substantial proportion of professional and white-collar elements. The most important of these unions—the All-Russian Union of Railroad Employees and Workers—occupied an ambiguous position in relation to the workers' movement, notwithstanding its role in precipitating the general strike in October 1905. The All-Russian Union of Railroad Employees and Workers, one of two unions to develop on a national scale,[120] coalesced in Moscow in the spring of 1905, when

---

workers in a particular occupation or industry as given in the 1902 Moscow city census and the 1900 St. Petersburg census. *Perepis' Moskvy 1902 g.*, chast' 1, vyp. 2 (Moscow, 1902), pp. 117–159; *S.-Peterburg po perepisi 15 dekabria 1900 g.*, vyp. 2 (St. Petersburg, 1903), pp. 1–137.

[115]*Obshcheprofessional'nye organy 1905–1907 gg.*, p. 70. R. G. Ramazov, "Sozdanie profsoiuzov Peterburgskogo proletariata i ikh deiatel'nost' v pervoi russkoi revoliutsii," candidate dissertation, Higher School on Trade Unions, Moscow, 1975. In early January 1906, this union reported a rise in membership to 1,170. *Professional'nyi soiuz*, no. 6–7 (January 21, 1906), p. 10.

[116]*Obshcheprofessional'nye organy 1905–1907 gg.*, p. 40; Tiurin, *Moskovskoe tsentral'noe biuro*, p. 12; labor force data for teapackers are from *Professional'noe dvizhenie Moskovskikh pishchevikov*, p. 3.

[117]Tiurin, *Moskovskoe tsentral'noe biuro*, p. 12.

[118]Ibid.; P. Dorovatovskii and V. Zlotin, "Khronika rabochego i professional'nogo dvizheniia v Peterburge v 1905 g.," *MIPDP*, p. 223.

[119]See table 10 in chapter 4 for a list of unions with 500 or more members.

[120]The other union operating on a national scale in 1905 was the All-Russian Union of Postal and Telegraph Employees.

other professional and white-collar groups were moving to form collective associations. Predominantly a white-collar and professional association, the Moscow branch of the railroad union included only a small contingent of blue-collar members. The mixed composition and the politically liberal outlook of the national organization did not appeal to most manual workers employed in railroad shops and on the lines. A branch of the All-Russian Union also functioned briefly in the capital in the late summer and fall, but here, too, it recruited only a small contingent of blue-collar workers.[121]

ARTISANAL WORKERS AND THE TRADE UNIONS

Within the manufacturing sector, many of the workers who joined the organized labor movement belonged to the ranks of skilled labor, and a considerable proportion of them were employed in artisanal workshops or as "factory artisans." Three criteria, it will be recalled, distinguished these groups: they performed work that relied mainly on hand labor, and had, concomitantly, a limited division of labor; the tasks of the trade required considerable skill acquired by means of lengthy apprenticeship training; and the labor force was stratified hierarchically, with a subdivision into apprentices, journeymen, and master craftsmen. Some of them, such as typesetters, qualify as "factory artisans" because they were mainly employed in firms classified under the contemporary rubric as "factory enterprises." Most, however, could be found in industries and trades where the bulk of the labor force was employed in very small shops, despite the presence in some cases (e.g., woodworking, tailoring, and baking) of one or two relatively large-scale establishments.

Although the exact composition of union membership cannot always be ascertained, it appears that about one-quarter of the 1905 unions in Moscow and slightly more than one-fifth in St. Petersburg were composed primarily or exclusively of artisanal workers (excluding "factory artisans").[122] The unionizing zeal of artisanal groups can be gauged from the proliferation of unions in key

[121]For discussions of these unions, see Walter Sablinsky, "The All-Russian Railroad Union and the Beginning of the General Strike in October 1905," in *Revolution and Politics in Russia: Essays in Memory of B. I. Nicolaevsky*, ed. Alexander and Janet Rabinowitch with Ladis K. D. Kristof (Bloomington, Ind., 1972); Henry Frederick Reichman, "Russian Railwaymen and the Revolution of 1905," Ph.D. dissertation, University of California, Berkeley, 1977; I. M. Pushkareva, *Zheleznodorozhniki Rossii v burzhuazno-demokraticheskikh revoliutsiiakh* (Moscow, 1975).

[122]See Appendix I for a list of artisanal unions.

trades. Within the apparel and leather trades, eight different unions were formed both in St. Petersburg and in Moscow, involving tailors, shoemakers, purse-makers, glovemakers, corsetmakers, harness- and saddlemakers, and others. Among specialized workers in nonferrous metals, three unions arose in the capital and four in Moscow, drawing the participation of coppersmiths, jewelers, tinsmiths, bronze smelters, and gold thread makers. In the construction trades, carpenters, plumbers, stucco molders, marble workers, and others established separate unions.

Artisanal workers in both St. Petersburg and Moscow were also among the first to organize trade unions in 1905. In the capital, shoemakers, watchmakers, tailors, woodworkers, and printers began to unionize before October, as did bakers, pursemakers, printers, joiners, and jewelers in Moscow. Grinevich, who represented the St. Petersburg Mensheviks in the predominantly artisanal City District of the capital in June and July, reported that "what forced me to become a 'specialist' [on trade unions] was that, as an organizer in the City District, I had dealings with artisans who, from my first visit to this artisanal neighborhood, began speaking about trade unions."[123]

Not only did artisanal groups gravitate to the union movement earlier than most other workers; their organizations were among the most fully developed in the city: the first to publish union newspapers, to provide monetary benefits for members, to assume leadership in labor-management struggles throughout the entire industry, and to participate in the soviets.[124] How can the artisans' excep-tional propensity for unionization be explained?

Together with other skilled strata of the labor force, artisanal workers had three common characteristics that were important facilitators of labor activism in 1905: a relatively high level of literacy, early arrival and prolonged residence in an urban center, and the acquisition of a specialized skill through prolonged apprenticeship training. Skilled literate workers who had entered the urban labor force at a young age and spent many years there were exceptionally well equipped to participate in the formation of trade unions. The ability to read, however elementary, facilitated an encounter with new ideas and enabled work-

---

[123]Grinevich, Letter from St. Petersburg, p. 11.

[124]For further discussion, see below, chapter 4. By way of illustration, the Petersburg tailors' union was one of the first to publish a trade union journal in the capital and to provide medical assistance for members. *Obshcheprofessional'nye organy 1905–1907 gg.*, p. 115, n. 58, observes that "in general, from the first steps of its life, the union [of Petersburg tailors] was distinguished by its organization and initiative." Similarly, the Petersburg union of gold- and silversmiths, which grew out of a strike committee, "became one of the strongest unions in Petersburg." Ibid., p. 117, note 73.

ers to participate in the complicated tasks of creating and sustaining a union. Permanent or long-term urban residence enabled workers to develop a new social identity distinct from the peasantry from which many had come. Their skill gave them a sense of dignity and status and created bases of solidarity among them.

Apart from these characteristics, several other circumstances affected the artisans' disposition to participate in the burgeoning union movement. Writing in the 1920s, S. Ainzaft noted the importance of trade unions for workers dispersed in many small firms:

The process of production itself did not organize them: it did not assemble them into a large mass and it did not unite them. In view of the fact that a small number of workers or employees were employed in separate enterprises, workers in these enterprises were not in a position to conduct the struggle independently. This led, on the one hand, to the fact that the scope of their strike movement was much weaker than among workers in large industrial enterprises; on the other hand, it led to the fact that they attempted to create all-city organizations to direct the economic struggle.[125]

The distribution of artisanal workers in numerous establishments, according to Ainzaft, forced them to seek a means of coordinating their strike movement on a citywide basis. This, indeed, accurately describes the circumstances that led to the formation of trade unions among certain artisanal groups, such as the Moscow gold- and silversmiths and others. But in some of the most important artisanal trades, the impetus for unionization came not from workers dispersed in small firms but rather from those concentrated in the very largest ones.

The movement for unionization among Moscow bakers, for example, began in the large Filippov bakery with nearly 400 workers.[126] When the Moscow tailors held the founding meeting of their union in early November 1905, most of the new union recruits worked at the Mandl' and Lamanovaia workshops, the largest in the Moscow tailoring trades with about 200 workers on the premises. Members of the Petersburg tailors' union also came from the largest workshops in the capital's garment industry.[127] Similarly, unionization among Moscow carpenters began at the Shmidt woodworking factory, a firm which employed

[125]S. Ainzaft, "Professional'noe dvizhenie v 1905 godu," in *Moskovskoe professional'noe dvizhenie,* ed. Milonov, p. 160.

[126]A. Kats and Iu. Milonov, eds., *1905,* p. 51; Iu. K. Milonov, *Kak voznikli professional'nye soiuzy v Rossii,* 2d ed. (Moscow, 1929), p. 121.

[127]Kolokol'nikov, "Otryvki," *MIPDR,* 3:226; *Obshcheprofessional'nye organy 1905–1907 gg.,* p. 113, n. 45; p. 115, n. 58.

250 workers, in an industry where most workers could be found in small shops.[128]

These cases indicate that while dispersion among a multitude of small workshops induced some artisanal groups to unionize, the largest and most active artisanal unions arose first among workers employed in relatively large firms in industries where small firms predominated. No doubt there were structural advantages that enabled the larger groups to mobilize for the purpose of union formation. Not only did these workers enjoy a stronger sense of their collective potential than their counterparts in small shops, but they were also far more likely to have been exposed to the proselytizing efforts of political and labor organizers. Most of these unions arose through the efforts of an initiative group, often composed of Social Democrats or Socialist Revolutionaries, and involving intelligentsia activists. These radical groups, many of them predating the revolution, became established primarily in larger firms, where party activists tended to focus their energy and attention in the hope of reaching a substantial contingent of workers.

Despite their large scale, however, these firms were either unmechanized or only partially mechanized in 1905, and the division of labor was still quite limited. Yet the workers employed there had one distinctive characteristic: compared with most other workers in their industry, they had relatively high levels of skill.[129] Tailors at the Mandl' and Lamanovaia firms, for example, have been described as "the most highly qualified and well-paid" workers in the industry.[130] A similar situation prevailed among carpenters at the Shmidt woodworking factory.[131] But if these workers had relatively higher skills than others in their trade, they did not belong to the "aristocratic" elite, a group that generally remained aloof from labor struggles in 1905. Instead, the workers employed at the Mandl' and Shmidt firms, and other enterprises of this type, were part of a broader stratum of skilled groups that could be found in virtually all industries and trades.

The deteriorating position of artisans in the urban economy also led some groups to seek unionization. An economic recession dating from the turn of the century had particularly adverse effects on the partially artisanal printing industry. Unemployment mounted in the printing trades from 1903 on, and by the

[128]Ibid., pp. 17, 104.
[129]See chapter 1.
[130]Kolokol'nikov, "Otryvki," *MIPDR,* 3:226.
[131]*Obshcheprofessional'nye organy 1905–1907 gg.,* pp. 17, 104.

spring of 1905, one out of six typesetters in the capital was out of work.[132] This circumstance undoubtedly contributed to the typesetters' solidarity in the January-February campaign to introduce a *tarif* into the city's printing industry, an effort that resulted in the early formation of a trade union.

Like their counterparts in Western Europe at an earlier time, some artisanal groups were experiencing an actual or threatened decline following the introduction of the factory system. Subcontracting arrangements had made deep inroads into the large apparel and shoemaking trades, causing a severe deterioration in wages, hours, and working conditions for many workers and posing a threat to the position of others. In the Moscow garment industry, where subcontracting shops had rapidly proliferated, tailors were acutely aware of the dangers that subcontracting presented to their livelihood. Thus, at the founding meeting of Moscow tailors in early November 1905, attended by more than one thousand workers, the first speaker rose to call for an end to subcontracting as "the primary task of the union." The meeting later endorsed a series of demands that included the abolition of all subcontracting shops and putting-out work in the industry.[133]

In an effort to halt the deterioration in their condition, some Russian artisanal and skilled groups behaved much the same way as their counterparts in Western Europe at an earlier period: they attempted to control and restrict entry into the trade. Considering the incompleteness of guild authority in Russia historically, it is particularly interesting to observe that in 1905 various artisanal groups sought to utilize trade unions to limit access to their trade. The Moscow printers' union drew up regulations in November 1905 placing control over the number of apprentices in the hands of worker-representatives.[134] The charter of the Petersburg bakers' union demanded the right of the union's directing board to participate with employers in determining the number of apprentices in each firm.[135] Moscow carpenters and skilled ribbonweavers demanded that workers, rather than employers, control entry into apprenticeship. Moscow jewelers attempted to exclude women from membership and, more generally, from employment in the trade.[136] The same provision was adopted by the unions of waiters in both cities.[137]

---

[132]Orlov, *Poligraficheskaia promyshlennost'*, p. 215. One thousand out of a total of about six thousand typesetters were unemployed in the spring of 1905.

[133]*Professional'nyi soiuz*, no. 1 (November 27, 1905), p. 5; Oliunina, *Portnovskii promysel*, p. 290.

[134]Dmitriev [Kolokol'nikov]. *Professional'nyi soiuz*, p. 25; Sher, *Istoriia*, pp. 204–209.

[135]*Professional'nyi soiuz*, no. 2 (December 4, 1905), p. 12.

[136]*Novaia zhizn'*, no. 26 (December 1, 1905), p. 4.

[137]*Obshcheprofessional'nye organy 1905-1907 gg.*, p. 100, n. 30.

In sum, a variety of circumstances contributed to the rapid and impressive mobilization of artisanal workers. Dispersion in small shops impelled some striking artisans to unite collectively in trade unions; concentration in large (though unmechanized) firms accelerated the unionization of others. An actual or threatened decline in economic position also helped to mobilize key artisanal groups. Above all, however, the artisans' disposition to participate in the incipient labor movement was affected by the prevalence among them of relatively high levels of skill and literacy, and their prolonged urban residency. These characteristics account in large measure for the pattern of collective organization not only among artisans but among workers in virtually all sectors of the urban economy.

Time and again, skilled workers took the initiative to organize trade unions. In major factory industries such as textiles, workers who unionized belonged to skilled subgroups, including ribbonweavers, engravers, dyers, and machine embroiderers. Among sales-clerical groups, bookkeepers and clerks formed unions, as did skilled workers in the construction trades.[138] In all sectors of the urban economy, except for service, skilled workers predominated in the trade union movement. And in the "days of freedom," when workers had an unprecedented opportunity to fashion independent organizations for the first time, they created trade unions in accordance with their conceptions of commonality. Significantly, a large majority of these trade unions belonged to the craft rather than the industrial variety.

CRAFT UNIONISM AND FACTORY PATRIOTISM

Throughout 1905, workers repeatedly organized trade unions along craft rather than industrial lines. The tendency of workers in artisanal trades to divide themselves in accordance with narrow occupational categories resulted in a multiplicity of small craft unions in apparel, leatherworking, printing, construction, metalworking, and other trades. Some unions, moreover, formed special sections for occupational subgroups. The Petersburg bakers' union, for example, had more than a dozen separate sections for occupational subgroups, such as bread bakers, pastrymakers, *pirog*-makers, *prianik*-makers, and others. The Moscow tailors' union adopted a similar organizational arrangement.[139]

---

[138]The stucco molders, a highly skilled craft group, predominated in the Petersburg construction workers union. Gruzdev, "Iz istorii," *MIPDP,* p. 34.

[139]*Professional'nyi soiuz,* no. 2 (December 4, 1905), p. 12; *Bor'ba,* no. 9 (December 7 [20], 1905), p. 4.

But this trend was not confined to artisanal groups alone. There were four specialized craft unions in the Moscow textile industry. Efforts to found the Moscow Union of Workers in the Textile Industry did not succeed until the following year, but in 1905 the organizers envisioned an industrial type of union that was subdivided into eight separate sections to accommodate specialized textile groups.[140] The Petersburg Union of Office Clerks and Bookkeepers had six sections for specialized subgroups.[141] A number of unions that formally adopted an industrial principle of organization were actually little more than confederations of semiautonomous craft groups. Such was the case, for example, in the Moscow Union of Industrial Construction Workers.[142] The Union of Sales-Clerical Employees in Moscow ("In Unity, Strength") consisted of many small unionized groups (e.g., clerks in hardware stores, stationery stores, and groceries) which agreed to confederate into a larger organization.[143]

Craft consciousness, or *tsekhovschina,* was also a unifying element among skilled subgroups in a factory setting. Technicians, electricians, and other skilled groups employed in factories formed craft unions during the revolution. The Petersburg Union of Draftsmen, for example, attracted 3,225 members from eight different metalworking plants in the capital, including the Baltiiskii plant (62 union members), the Putilov plant (40 members), the Obukhov plant (40 members), the Novyi Admiralteiskii plant (37 members), and others.[144]

Intelligentsia labor organizers, particularly the Social Democrats, were highly critical of this tendency, and they waged a vigorous campaign to induce workers to form unions on an industrial model. Unable to dissuade workers from combining along narrow occupational lines, they pressed hard for industrial unions that accorded specialized subgroups semiautonomous rights within the larger organization.[145] In some cases, intelligentsia activists were instrumental in

---

[140]*Obshcheprofessional'nye organy 1905-1907 gg.,* p. 78.

[141]*Novaia zhizn',* no. 25 (November 30, 1905), p. 3.

[142]*Obshcheprofessional'nye organy 1905-1907 gg.,* pp. 91, 113, note 44. Carpenters, stucco molders, house painters, marble workers, and plumbing and heating workers each formed separate sections in the Moscow construction workers' union.

[143]See below, Appendix I.

[144]*Professional'nyi soiuz,* no. 6 (January 21, 1906), p. 13.

[145]*Vtoraia konferentsiia,* p. 46. This issue was discussed, for example, by the Moscow Central Bureau of Trade Unions. A compromise solution proposed by P. N. Kolokol'nikov was adopted recommending that specialized subgroups form sections within larger unions. These subgroups were to be accorded considerable autonomy within the organization, including the right to declare strikes. A summary of the debate over this issue in the Central Bureau on November 17 can be found in *Obshcheprofessional'nye organy 1905-1907 gg.,* p. 108, n. 27.

bringing about a merger of separate craft unions into a single association. Thus, in late November the Moscow jewelers and gold-silversmiths joined their unions, and watchmakers and jewelers in the capital contemplated unification.[146] But *tsekhovshchina* could not easily be surmounted, and despite the pressure of intelligentsia organizers, workers persisted in establishing trade unions along craft lines.

A related phenomenon can be described as "factory patriotism,"[147] or allegiance to a particular enterprise. A long tradition of factory patriotism existed among workers employed in large plants. Rooted most strongly among a core group of older skilled workers with many years' seniority, factory patriotism manifested itself in the custom of self-identification as Putilovtsy, Obukhovtsy, or Semiannikovtsy (as workers at the Nevskii Shipbuilding and Machine Plant, once owned by Semiannikov, still preferred to call themselves).[148] A similar trend can be discerned among Moscow metalworkers in well-established firms such as Gustav List and elsewhere.

The factory committee movement in early 1905 strengthened and extended these sentiments of factory patriotism among workers, who could now derive genuine satisfaction from organizational accomplishments within their enterprise.[149] Some of these factory committees (or councils of elders) registered a very impressive record of accomplishments. One of the most impressive, the Nevskii Council of Elders in St. Petersburg, also took steps to initiate the formation of a metalworkers' union. The failure of this effort was partly connected to the strength of factory patriotism.

The first discussions of unionization in the Petersburg metalworking industry took place in the spring of 1905, when Sergei Prokopovich, an erstwhile Social Democrat and advocate of "economism" who had joined forces with the liberal Union of Liberation, made contact with a liberationist worker on the Nevskii Council of Elders. Prokopovich's project was modeled after the Union of Unions, which had been established among white-collar and professional groups in May. He envisioned factory-based unions, operating independently and joined together in a loose industry-wide confederation.[150] His proposal had no

[146]Mamontov, "Zoloto-serebrianniki," *MIPDR*, 5:184.

[147]This term is used in *Materialy ob ekonomicheskom polozhenii i professional'noi organizatsii Peter-burgskikh rabochikh po metallu* (St. Petersburg, 1909), p. 28.

[148]On this point, see Aleksei Buzinov, *Za Nevskoi zastavoi*, pp. 20–21, 61–62.

[149]*Materialy ob ekonomicheskom polozhenii*, p. 28.

[150]*Obshcheprofessional'nye organy 1905–1907 gg.*, p. 105, note 19; Kats and Milonov, eds., *1905*, p. 38.

immediate practical effect, and another effort, undertaken in May by a Menshevik organizer, Iu. Larin, also failed to produce results.[151]

In July the Nevskii Council of Elders held a meeting in the plant cafeteria to discuss plans for forming a union.[152] The participants included factory committee members from other major plants, such as the Putilov, Obukhov, and Aleksandrovskii firms, and representatives of the local Mensheviks and Socialist Revolutionaries. The instigators of the meeting were intelligentsia activists who had just begun to unite into the Petersburg Central Bureau of Trade Unions. Grinevich has described the meeting:

It seems that the idea of creating a union had developed among them earlier and they gladly appeared at our invitation. Their charter was carefully worked out, but it had the character of charters of mutual aid funds, and not of a militant trade union. After long and heated arguments, they agreed in principle to our changes. One more meeting was to be held to work out the final draft.[153]

The final version of the charter, which was subsequently approved by an initiative group and published in the labor press, provided for an industrial union of Petersburg metalworkers, focusing primarily on labor-management struggle.[154] But unionizing efforts, begun in July, were interrupted in October by the general strike and the formation of the Petersburg Soviet. The Nevskii Council became involved in the campaign for an eight-hour workday during November, thereby diverting attention away from unionization.[155] In mid-November, factory committees at several other Petersburg metalworking firms, including the Odner and Beier, Lessner, Obukhov, Westinghouse, and Artur Koppel' plants, began their own union projects. Sometimes workers succeeded in drafting a charter; others took the first steps toward preparing statutes for the proposed organization.[156]

[151]*Obshcheprofessional'nye organy 1905-1907 gg.*, p. 105, n. 19.

[152]For an account of this meeting by a Menshevik participant, see Grinevich, "Ocherk," *Obrazovanie* 15, no. 8, pp. 225-226; idem, Letter from St. Petersburg, pp. 14-16, provides by far the most detailed and candid account of this event; Kolokol'nikov, "Otryvki," *MIPDR*, 2:218; Bulkin, *Na zare*, p. 128; *Obshcheprofessional'nye organy 1905-1907 gg.*, p. 105, n. 19.

[153]Grinevich, Letter from St. Petersburg, pp. 14-15.

[154]*Obshcheprofessional'nye organy 1905-1907 gg.*, pp. 20, 105, n. 19.

[155]Buzinov, *Za Nevskoi zastavoi*, pp. 62, 81-89.

[156]Ibid., pp. 54, 117; *Nasha zhizn'* (November 15, 1905), p. 4; *Novaia zhizn'*, no. 19 (November 23, 1905), p. 4; and no. 20 (November 24, 1905), p. 3. The leader of unionizing efforts at the Odner and Beier plant, A. O. Iatsynevich, a nonfaction SD worker, subsequently became the first president of the Union of Metalworkers in the capital, a position he occupied until 1910. For a discussion of Iatsynevich, see Kolokol'nikov, "Otryvki," *MIPDR*, 4:277; and below, chapter 5.

The metalworkers' failure to form a citywide trade union in the capital in 1905 can be attributed to several circumstances. Some workers were disillusioned by the earlier experiments in government-sponsored labor association and hesitated to become involved in new organizational ventures.[157] But more important, progress toward unionization was arrested by the centripetal pull of the large, self-contained, and internally well-organized plants that predominated in this industry. It was not the case, as Soviet historians have contended, that metalworkers were so preoccupied by political struggles that they had little time or energy to devote to the formation of trade unions, an organization focusing on workplace struggles for economic improvement. The fact is that the metalworkers were very much involved with workplace struggles in the course of 1905, and they created for this purpose the highly effective institution of the factory committee.

Factory committee members in large Petersburg metalworking plants—often highly respected and influential in their milieu—may have been less than enthusiastic about prospects for forming an industry-wide union that would have superseded the factory committee, diluting or even eliminating their position and authority. The draft charter prepared by the Nevskii Council of Elders in July 1905, with its plan for factory-based unions, points to a preference among some plant leaders for organizations centered at the enterprise level.

The evidence on this question is fragmentary, and available sources do not permit generalizations about the attitudes of factory committee members who might have carried through the project for an industry-wide trade union in 1905. Their role in the formation of trade unions must have been further minimized by the fact that many of them were concurrently serving as deputies to the Petersburg Soviet.[158] Thus, a variety of circumstances conjoined to retard the emergence of a Petersburg metalworkers' union during the revolution. But such efforts were not delayed for long. Only a few months later, in early 1906, metalworkers finally organized a union which rapidly developed into one of the largest labor associations in the capital. Significantly, however, only a small number of recruits to the newly created union were employed in large metalworking plants where factory committees remained active. In these plants, factory committees led to the further strengthening of factory patriotism to the detriment of the union cause.

Moscow metalworkers also failed to form a union in 1905. The circumstances delaying unionization in this city were quite different from those in the

---

[157]Bulkin, *Na zare*, p. 120.
[158]On this point, see below, chapter 4.

capital. Some metalworkers initially avoided unionizing projects because they feared a repetition of earlier Zubatov experiments.[159] But above all, political disputes among radical parties, rather than factory patriotism, delayed the formation of a union. By October there were factory committees in many Moscow metalworking firms, and on October 29, representatives of these plants assembled for the purpose of uniting various factory committees into one trade union organizaion.[160] Nearly a month later, on November 24, seventy representatives of the city's metalworking firms attended a second meeting, which agreed to organize a union on the federative principle. Instead of uniting individual factory-based unions, however, Moscow metalworkers decided to confederate separate sections based on common occupational specializations.[161] Thus, a strong craft orientation among Moscow metalworkers was combined with an attempt to form a union along industrial lines.

At the founding meeting of the union on December 4, held at the Polytechnical Museum, a conflict arose over the issue of the union's political affiliation.[162] Social Democrats present at the meeting, most of them Bolsheviks, argued that because economic struggle was inextricably linked to political struggle, the union should affiliate formally with the RSDRP. They refused to approve the version of the charter presented to the meeting, and demanded, among other changes, deletion of the point which stated that the union was fighting for the goal of a democratic republic. As a consequence of these disputes, no agreement was reached on the charter, and the next scheduled meeting failed to take place because of the outbreak of the December uprising. The Moscow metalworkers did not succeed in founding a trade union until April 1906. The political conflict that delayed the formation of a Moscow metalworkers' union was part of a broader pattern of politicization within the incipient labor organizations. As the

[159]G. Matveev, "Moskovskii soiuz rabochikh-metallistov," *MIPDR*, 2:251. A small group of Zubatovist metalworkers kept this organization in operation through much of 1905. It appears, however, to have had very limited influence.

[160]Z. Shchap, *Moskovskie metallisty v professional'nom dvizhenii: Ocherki po istorii Moskovskogo soiuza metallistov* (Moscow, 1927), p. 52. Factory committees existed at many Moscow metalworking plants, including Bromlei, Dobrova-Nabgol'ts, Gopper, Gakental', Banaker, Grachev, Zotov, Mytishchenskii. Milonov, *Kak voznikli*, p. 111; Shchap, *Moskovskie metallisty*, p. 49. An earlier attempt to organize Moscow metalworkers was undertaken in September by the Menshevik activist I. A. Isuv, but it failed to produce results. *Obshcheprofessional'nye organy 1905-1907 gg.*, p. 104, n. 16.

[161]These sections were to unite metalfitters, lathe operators, bronze workers, copper workers, gold gilders, and tinsmiths. *Bor'ba*, no. 1 (November 27 [December 10], 1905), p. 4.

[162]TsGAOR, f. 6860, ed. kh. 27, 1905, p. 27; Shchap, *Moskovskie metallisty*, pp. 51–52.

union movement developed in the fall of 1905, political parties and groups took an increasingly active role in it, a subject examined in chapter 4.

_____

The eagerness for organization was one of the most distinctive features of workers' collective behavior in the 1905 revolution. From the very outset, workers took steps to form associations for the purpose of conducting a more effective, coordinated struggle for common purposes. These efforts began with the creation of factory committees on the enterprise level, and by the end of 1905 had led to the formation of scores of trade unions in both St. Petersburg and Moscow, as well as the establishment of Soviets of Workers' Deputies.

The factory committee movement, which began in the early weeks of the revolution, called for two major reforms in factory life: employer recognition of the workers' right to organize and to represent themselves collectively in industrial relations, and the involvement of workers in key decisions of factory life, including hiring, firing, and the setting of wage rates. In advancing these claims at the very inception of the revolution, workers issued a bold and audacious challenge to employers. Not only did the workers insist on the institutionalization of industrial conflict—itself a significant departure from previous labor practices—they also asserted their rights in areas where employer prerogatives were most firmly entrenched.

The factory committee movement set the stage for workers' demands pertaining to participation and control not only at the workplace but also in the society at large. These explicitly political claims were already evident, to some extent, in labor conflicts during the initial revolutionary period. But they acquired centrality in the workers' movement only during the fall of 1905 under the impact of a broadening revolutionary upheaval and the increasing involvement of political parties in the workers' milieu.

If the factory committee movement anticipated in crucial respects the aspirations and activities of workers later manifested in the trade unions, so the response of employers and government authorities to the formation of enterprise-level organizations foreshadowed their subsequent policies and conduct toward organized labor. Industrial employers, who also took steps to establish collective organizations in 1905, initially rejected workers' attempts to modify traditional procedures and relations at the workplace, and they recognized factory committees only in the face of formidable pressure from workers.

Government authorities responded to the growing threat of popular unrest by initiating consideration of new labor policies, including a recognition of the workers' right to organize legally on enterprise- and industry-wide bases. But no legislation was forthcoming on workers' combinations or, indeed, on other key issues of concern to workers—such as the right to strike—prior to the issuance of the October Manifesto. The government's failure to take action in these critical areas served to deepen and extend the workers' disillusionment with the authorities and to dispel any lingering hopes for paternalistic intervention on their behalf. Instead, workers increasingly came to believe that they could achieve an improvement in their condition only by dint of their own efforts, through struggles waged collectively under the auspices of strong, independent, legal, mass-based labor organizations.

Although highly diverse groups from all sectors of the urban economy took part in the formation of trade unions, skilled workers stood in the forefront of the union movement during 1905. These groups proved singularly well equipped to unite collectively. In a working class where unskilled and semi-skilled elements predominated, skilled workers were characterized by early entry into and a prolonged sojourn in the urban labor force, relatively high levels of literacy, and the attainment of specialized occupational training and skills that imparted to them special status and a clearly defined social identity. These factors helped to facilitate their participation in the burgeoning labor movement, and, not surprisingly, they played an exceptionally active role in all organizational activities in the course of 1905, including the factory committees, the Shidlovskii Commission, the trade unions, and as we shall see shortly, the soviets as well.

Within the ranks of skilled labor, attention has been drawn to the propensity for unionization among artisanal workers. I have argued that apart from the characteristics that artisans had in common with other skilled groups, workers in some trades faced deleterious economic trends, such as the spread of sub-contracting arrangements, which intensified their desire to defend themselves through collective activity. These artisans sought to halt the deterioriation in conditions by combining collectively to control and restrict access to their trade—a solution pursued by many Western European artisans at earlier periods. Artisans in a single large firm amid many smaller ones often led the way in forming trade unions. But the size of enterprise per se was not a determinant of unionization, since workers in small dispersed firms also unionized with consid-erable enthusiasm in the course of 1905. Nor was the extent of mechanization a factor, since both large and small firms in artisanal trades still relied almost entirely on hand labor at the time of the revolution.

The craft orientation of many skilled workers, *tsekhovshchina,* and the related phenomenon of factory patriotism, were important features of the incipient labor movement in tsarist Russia. Here, as in Western Europe in an earlier period, the first manifestations of labor activism were accompanied by a strong sense of craft pride and exclusiveness. The widespread evidence of craft consciousness among Russian workers is especially significant, for in contrast to Western Europe, artisanal traditions were weakly established in Russia, and guilds had failed to attain the importance and influence they displayed in urban centers elsewhere. How, then, can we account for the importance of *tsekhovshchina* in 1905?

The answer lies precisely in the circumstances that might have been expected to distinguish Russia from the rest of Europe. Since the country lacked a substantial core of urban-born workers with established traditions and organizations, the workers who flocked to the city could not turn to ongoing institutions or adapt to existing bases of social solidarity. For workers who had arrived in the city at a young age to acquire a particular skill, the primary and most logical source of identification in the bewildering and unfamiliar atmosphere of the big city was a common position in the work hierarchy or employment in a specialized occupation or type of enterprise. The skilled workers' strong identification with others sharing common work characteristics, exemplified by the formation of craft-based trade unions in 1905, was thus partially an outcome of the accelerated pace of economic development taking place in Russia, particularly in urban centers that offered little in the way of preestablished bases of social solidarity to which these workers might have turned.

Among skilled segments of the labor force in all sectors of the urban economy, craft consciousness proved to be a strong unifying factor during 1905. But by the fall of that year, a growing number of workers came to see themselves as part of a larger social group in urban Russian society: the working class, whose boundaries transcended the narrow confines of craft identification. Under Russian conditions craft consciousness, with its discrete and localized allegiances, was not incompatible with an awareness of belonging to a larger collectivity, such as a citywide labor movement or, indeed, the working class as a whole.

Images of craft and class coexisted among Petersburg and Moscow workers in 1905 and formed bases for collective action. This synchronous evolution of craft and class consciousness, so central to the dynamic of the workers' movement during the revolution, was closely connected to another development: the growing involvement of radical, for the most part Social Democratic, activists in the workers' milieu. It is to this development that we must now turn.

Chapter 4

The Politics of Organized Labor in the 1905 Revolution

> With the help of the union, after we have developed
> self-consciousness and raised our legal, intellectual, and
> material level, *we shall be transformed into free citizens.*
> Not as pathetic and dispersed cowards, but as brave
> men, proud of our solidarity, fully armed with justice
> and truth, we shall present our demands before those
> insatiable sharks who are our employers.
>
> *President of the Petersburg Union*
> *of Watchmakers, November 27,*
> *1905[1]*

When the movement to form trade unions gradually got under way in the second half of 1905, liberals, Socialist Revolutionaries, syndicalists, and representatives of the two factions of Russian Social Democracy—the Mensheviks and the Bolsheviks—gravitated to the incipient organizations. They all hoped to put their ideological imprint on the labor movement and to gain support among the rank and file of the Petersburg and Moscow working class. Faced with the complex and unfamiliar tasks of founding and maintaining a trade union, the workers themselves often sought the assistance of intellectuals. The attraction was mutual, therefore, and each group, albeit for different reasons, sought to establish contact with the other. These encounters multiplied in the fall of 1905, when the proliferation of labor organizations provided a major new channel for sustained interaction between rank-and-file workers and their radical mentors.

SOCIAL DEMOCRATIC POLICIES TOWARD THE TRADE UNIONS

Despite their eventual ascendancy in the 1905 trade unions, Social Democrats were initially uncertain how to respond to the union movement. In the early

[1]Quoted in V. V. Sviatlovskii, *Professional'noe dvizhenie v Rossii* (St. Petersburg, 1907), p. 107. Italics in the original.

months of the revolution, most Social Democrats, including Mensheviks, Bolsheviks, and nonfaction SDs, remained aloof from the incipient trade unions. Somov, still serving as a Menshevik organizer in the capital during this period, observed that prior to May, party members "completely ignored the organized [labor] movement that was getting under way among workers on economic grounds."[2] Only in the late spring did some SD activists begin to respond to the workers' growing interest in trade unions. But even as late as September, Grinevich reported in private correspondence that there were "phrase-mongers" in the capital's Menshevik faction who "scream about Zubatovism, about opportunism," and still preferred underground party circles to trade-union work.[3] According to Kolokol'nikov, many Mensheviks feared that trade unions would "fall into one-sided activity and forget about the general interests of the working class."[4] The reluctance to encourage trade unions was even more deeply rooted among the Bolsheviks, and many members of this faction viewed the advent of trade unions as evidence that the party had failed to revolutionize the workers.[5]

These attitudes in SD circles stemmed in part from the vexing problem of relations between the party and trade unions. Prior to 1905 this issue had not arisen in such a concrete and pressing form. Now, however, workers were eagerly taking the first steps to create unions, and in some cases calling on party organizers, the so-called *praktiki,* to provide assistance. Confronted by the immediate practical task of establishing a suitable relationship between the underground party and the more broadly based trade union movement that was taking shape, some Social Democrats advocated formal organizational ties between unions and the party.

The Bolsheviks were the first to organize a party-affiliated union. Following the formation of the All-Russian Union of Railroad Employees and Workers in April, the Bolsheviks attempted to establish a competing railroad union under direct party auspices, the Union of Railroad Employees of the Moscow Junction. The union, which was little more than a party group, consisted mainly of white-collar workers and failed to develop into a lively, well-subscribed organization.[6]

---

[2]S. I. Somov [I. M. Peskin], "Iz istorii sotsialdemokraticheskogo dvizheniia v Peterburge v 1905 godu (Lichnye vospominaniia)," *Byloe,* no. 5 (17) (May 1907), p. 175.

[3]V. Grinevich in an unpublished letter, written in September 1905. Nikolaevsky Collection, No. 109, Box 5, Document 58, p. 9 (cited henceforth as Letter from St. Petersburg).

[4]A. Kats and Iu. Milonov, eds., *1905: Professional'noe dvizhenie* (Moscow and Leningrad, 1926), p. 360. The statement was made by P. Kolokol'nikov on November 16.

[5]Kats and Milonov, editors, *1905,* p. 339. This statement appears in an article by M. Borisov, published by the Bolshevik newspaper *Proletarii* on October 4, 1905.

[6]Henry Frederick Reichman, "Russian Railwaymen and the Revolution of 1905," Ph.D. dissertation, University of California, Berkeley, 1977, p. 341; Walter Sablinsky, "The All-Russian Railroad

In June the Moscow Mensheviks tried their hand at implementing a similar union policy, also without success. The Menshevik faction, up to that time, had no clear guidelines regarding union-party relations. A resolution adopted at the All-Russian Conference of Mensheviks in April 1905 had left that matter ambiguous, calling only for "constant links between party organizations and trade unions."[7]

When Pavel Kolokol'nikov arrived in Moscow in late June, therefore, he set about organizing trade unions with close formal party ties. Kolokol'nikov, the son of a Moscow factory owner, had joined SD circles in the 1890s.[8] During the early months of the revolution, he served as a Menshevik organizer in the capital.[9] Following his arrival in Moscow, Kolokol'nikov assisted dairy clerks to form a Union of Employees in the Sale of Foodstuffs, and under his leadership they adopted the entire program-minimum of the Russian Social Democratic Workers' Party, including the party's political as well as economic demands. Some three hundred dairy clerks joined the union, which "bore a party stamp and differed little from a regular party cell."[10] Other clerks were frightened away by the political character of the organization, however, and it soon ceased to recruit new members.[11]

Kolokol'nikov next turned his attention to the illegal Moscow union of printers. Dating from the printers' strike of 1903, this illegal union had a small, predominantly Social Democratic membership.[12] Although it had earlier

Union and the Beginning of the General Strike in October 1905," in *Revolution and Politics in Russia: Essays in Memory of B. I. Nicolaevsky*, ed. Alexander and Janet Rabinowitch with Ladis K. D. Kristof (Bloomington, Ind., 1972), pp. 116–122; I. M. Pushkareva, *Zheleznodorozhniki Rossii v burzhuazno-demokraticheskikh revoliutsiiakh* (Moscow, 1975), pp. 109, 125–127.

[7]Kats and Milonov, eds., *1905*, pp. 354–355.

[8]The Menshevik P. A. Garvi has left a vivid account of Kolokol'nikov, his background, personal characteristics, and career. P. A. Garvi, *Revoliutsionnye siluety* (Inter-University Project on the History of the Menshevik Movement, New York, 1962), pp. 1–7. Biographical information on Kolokol'nikov can also be found in P. Kolokol'nikov and S. Rapoport, eds., *1905–1907 gg. v professional'nom dvizhenii: I i II Vserossiiskie konferentsii professional'nykh soiuzov* (Moscow, 1925), pp. 422–423.

[9]A personal account of these activities can be found in P. Kolokol'nikov "Otryvki iz vospominanii: 1905–1907 gg.," *Materialy po istorii professional'nogo dvizheniia v Rossii* (henceforth *MIPDR*), 5 vols. (Moscow, 1924–1927), vol. 2, pp. 213, 221–224, 226–233; vol. 3, pp. 223–231.

[10]*MIPDR*, 2:225. The dairy clerks' first unsuccessful effort at unionization had taken place in 1904. *Obshcheprofessional'nye organy 1905–1907 gg.*, vypusk I: *Moskovskie zhurnaly 1905 g.* (Moscow, 1926), p. 97, n. 7 (15).

[11]K. Dmitriev [P. Kolokol'nikov], *Professional'nye soiuzy v Moskve* ([St. Petersburg], 190[6]), p. 5.

[12]The illegal printers' union had four hundred members in July 1905. *Obshcheprofessional'nye organy 1905–1907 gg.*, p. 96, n. 7.

adopted the program-minimum of the RSDRP, the union had not established formal affiliation with the party. In July 1905, Kolokol'nikov met with three of the leaders of the illegal printers' union who would soon become key figures in the citywide workers' movement: the intelligentsia activists I. Kruglov [A. S. Orlov] and Vasilii Sher, and the printer Nikolai Chistov.[13] Following this meeting, the union decided to affiliate formally with the Moscow Menshevik group. As in the case of the dairy clerks, the decision proved detrimental to recruitment, and although the small illegal union remained highly influential, it failed to recruit additional members. In October, members of the Social Democratic union helped to establish a new nonparty printers' union, which absorbed the predecessor organization.

The cases of the Moscow food clerks and printers show that in the spring and summer of 1905, some Mensheviks adopted a policy of partisan unions, an approach they subsequently criticized and abandoned. Not all Menshevik labor organizers shared the enthusiasm for party-affiliated unions, however. In the capital, for example, Grinevich called instead for trade union independence from all political parties. After he arrived in St. Petersburg in June, Grinevich quickly became the leading Menshevik labor organizer there.[14] He appreciated the great potential presented by trade unions as "an arena in which Russian Social Democrats can undertake broad and fruitful work," but steadfastly opposed formal union-party ties.[15]

Menshevik participation in the trade union movement gathered momentum in September. By then, Kolokol'nikov had abandoned his effort to establish party-affiliated unions, and had accepted instead the concept of parallel organizations—unions and parties—with different but equally important tasks to perform in the workers' movement and united by a Social Democratic perspective.[16] Mensheviks were far less suspicious than the Bolsheviks of worker inde-

---

[13]Kolokol'nikov, "Otryvki," *MIPDR*, 2:225. For biographical information on these three important trade unionists, see Garvi, *Revoliutsionnye siluety*, pp. 23–29. Orlov and Sher were intelligentsia activists from the Moscow Menshevik group. Chistov was a leading representative of the Moscow Social Democratic worker intelligentsia. He, too, had close ties with the local Menshevik organization.

[14]Grinevich was not, however, the first Menshevik union organizer in the capital. Apart from Kolokol'nikov's activities noted above, S. I. Somov and P. Strel'skii [V. S. Lavrov] were also involved in union formation during the spring of 1905. Grinevich, Letter from St. Petersburg, pp. 10–11; *Obshcheprofessional'nye organy 1905–1907 gg.*, p. 105, n. 19; Kats and Milonov, eds., *1905*, p. 38; S. I. Somov, "Iz istorii, *Byloe*, no. 5, pp. 175.

[15]Grinevich, Letter from St. Petersburg, p. 10.

[16]On the philosophical and ideological underpinnings of Menshevism in this period, see Solomon M. Schwarz, *The Russian Revolution of 1905: The Workers' Movement and the Formation of Bolshevism*

pendence and self-management, and more confident that workers, left to their own devices, would naturally develop revolutionary consciousness and gravitate into the orbit of Social Democracy. Drawing heavily on Western European labor movements to guide them, the Mensheviks viewed trade unions as performing an indispensable part in preparing workers for their future tasks in the transition from capitalism to socialism.

In making the shift to nonparty unions, Moscow Mensheviks were responding in large measure to the workers' reluctance to join organizations formally identified with an illegal underground political party. Here was one instance, and others would follow, when party activists altered their stand to accord more closely with the preferences of the workers. In the fall, Menshevik *praktiki* in both cities turned much of their energy and attention to the unions, assisting unionizing groups to draw up founding charters for trade unions that maintained autonomy from the party while adopting the party's economic program-minimum, including demands for an eight-hour workday, a forty-two hour workweek, and the abolition of overtime and night work.[17]

The Bolsheviks proved far more reluctant than the Mensheviks to come to terms with the trade union movement. Within this faction, Lenin's powerful indictment of trade unionism had left an indelible impression. As early as 1895, Lenin had foreseen the possibility that unions would eventually become established in Russia, and in 1900 he published a translation of the Webbs' famous study of English trade unionism.[18] Two years later, he made his own definitive statement on trade unions in *What Is To Be Done?*[19] Responding to the so-called

---

and Menshevism (Chicago, 1967), and Abraham Ascher, *Pavel Axelrod and the Development of Menshevism* (Cambridge, Mass., 1972).

[17] The economic program-minimum of the RSDRP was drawn up and approved at the Second Party Congress in 1903. It included sixteen points, the first four of them as shown above. Other provisions related to child and female labor, government insurance, factory inspection, sanitary conditions, criminal responsibility for delinquent employers, joint employer-worker industrial courts (*promyslovye sudy*), and labor exchanges to assist the unemployed. *Rossiiskaia kommunisticheskaia partiia (bol'shevikov) v rezoliutsiiakh ee s"ezdov i konferentsii (1898-1921 gg.)* (Moscow, 1922), pp. 15–19. For an English translation of the 1903 program, see Sidney Harcave, *The Russian Revolution of 1905* (London, 1970), pp. 263–268. The Menshevik model charter was prepared by S. P. Tiurin, an intelligentsia activist, for the Moscow teapackers' union. It was subsequently utilized by both Moscow and Petersburg unions in which Mensheviks were active.

[18] *Teoriia i praktika angliiskogo tred-iunionizma (Industrial Democracy)*, 2 vols. (St. Petersburg, 1900–1901), trans. V. I. Lenin. The Lenin translation was reissued in the 1920s: *Teoriia i praktika angliiskogo tred-iunionizma: v perevode s angliiskogo Vladimira Il'ina (V. Ul'ianova-Lenina)* (Moscow, 1925).

[19] V. I. Lenin, *Selected Works,* 3 vols. (New York, 1967), vol. 1, pp. 97–256; V. I. Lenin, *Sochineniia,* 3d ed., 30 vols. (Moscow, 1928–1937), vol. 4, pp. 358–507.

"economists"—a group of Social Democrats led by S. N. Prokopovich and E. D. Kuskova, advocating the primacy of economic over political struggles—Lenin attacked trade unions as vehicles for the "ideological enslavement [of workers] . . . by the bourgeoisie." Unions, he asserted, would divert workers from their revolutionary tasks to the quest for petty economic improvements unless the organizations were subordinated to party leadership and utilized as instruments of revolutionary struggle.[20]

Saddled with this inauspicious legacy, Bolsheviks found it difficult to respond positively to the workers' aspirations for unionization. At the Third Party Congress of the RSDRP, unilaterally convened by Lenin in April 1905 and not attended by Mensheviks, the question of trade unions did not even occupy a formal place on the agenda. A congress resolution called upon party organizations to

utilize all legal or illegal workers' societies, unions, and other organizations to insure that Social Democracy's influence predominates in them and to transform them insofar as possible into bases of support for the future open Social Democratic workers' party in Russia.[21]

Nothing more was heard on the subject for several months. During the summer, the Bolshevik newspaper *Proletarii* carried several articles about trade unionism that did little to dispel the widespread antagonism toward unions in Bolshevik circles. In late September a leading member of the Moscow Bolshevik Committee contended that unions were antithetical to the revolutionary movement and should not be encouraged, an outlook that was shared by many other Bolsheviks at the time.[22]

When in October and November scores of trade unions emerged in St. Petersburg and Moscow, the Bolsheviks could scarcely afford to ignore this new channel for reaching a mass audience. Nor could they tolerate the growing influence of Mensheviks and other political organizers among the workers, who were beginning to join trade unions in considerable numbers. Starting in the second half of October, the Bolsheviks took an increasingly active part in the unions, but they continued to advocate a policy of formal union affiliation with the RSDRP. This approach had already been utilized unsuccessfully in Moscow by both factions, and the Bolsheviks were the only ones to advocate it in the fall.

Reports of union debates over the issue of union-party relations are fragmen-

---

[20]Lenin, *Selected Works,* vol. 1, p. 130.

[21]Kats and Milonov, eds., *1905,* p. 328; Schwarz, *The Russian Revolution,* p. 154. The final resolution adopted by the congress was written by Lenin and P. P. Rumiantsev.

[22]Kolokol'nikov, "Otryvki," *MIPDR,* 2:231.

tary, but in each case the contending viewpoints were presented by party activists, and intellectuals did most of the talking. At a meeting of Moscow
carpenters on October 25, a Bolshevik spokesman presented a draft charter
which called for the subordination of the union to the Moscow (Bolshevik)
Committee on all political matters and required the union to turn over 10
percent of its revenues to the party organization. Mensheviks at the meeting
argued against a partisan union, declaring that the adoption of the Bolshevik
charter would discourage most carpenters from joining the organization. They
drew this conclusion from their own earlier experiences with the unions of food
clerks and printers. In the end, however, the meeting voted to accept the
Bolshevik charter, and an all-Bolshevik directing board was elected to manage
union affairs.[23]

Similar debates took place in other Moscow unions, including the gold- and
silversmiths, bakers, tailors, gold threadmakers, and metalfitters in the construction trades.[24] But only a few adopted the Bolshevik model charter: the Moscow
gold- and silversmiths, workers in metal rolling shops, technicians, bakers,
candymakers, and carpenters.[25] Of these unions, the bakers commanded the
largest and most effective organization. With 1,770 members, it ranked as the
fourth largest union in the city by the end of the year. The bakers' decision to
accept party affiliation reflected the Bolsheviks' energetic leadership in this trade,
beginning with a successful industry-wide strike in April. Since the Bolsheviks
had initiated the union, they evidently elicited the confidence and support of
many rank-and-file workers.[26] Although firm evidence is lacking, similar circumstances may have accounted for the Bolshevik victory among Moscow carpenters, technicians, candymakers, gold- and silversmiths, and workers in metal
rolling shops.

The most dramatic confrontation over the issue of union-party relations took
place at a Moscow theatre on November 16.[27] Fifteen hundred workers attended
this gathering, which had been organized by the newly formed Central Bureau of
Trade Unions. The principal speakers represented the two factions of Social
Democracy.

[23]Iu. K. Milonov and M. Rakovskii, *Istoriia Moskovskogo professional'nogo soiuza rabochikh derevoobdelochnikov*, vypusk 1 (Moscow, 1928), p. 101.

[24]N. S. Mamontov, "Dvizhenie rabochikh po obrabotke blagorodnykh metallov v Moskve," *MIPDR*, 5:196–197; *Obshcheprofessional'nye organy 1905–1907 gg.*, p. 102, n. 12.

[25]Dmitriev, *Professional'nye soiuzy*, p. 35.

[26]*Obshcheprofessional'nye organy 1905–1907 gg.*, p. 97, n. 7 (10), pp. 106–107, n. 22.

[27]Ibid., pp. 35–37.

Kolokol'nikov spoke on behalf of the Menshevik position, arguing that "the task of trade unions is to improve the conditions of labor within the framework of the capitalist system."[28] This goal, he asserted, could only be achieved if unions attracted the broadest possible membership. Unions with formal affiliation to a political party, Kolkol'nikov concluded, would discourage the mass of workers from participation, and these unions would remain restricted to a few hundred members. Pointing to the experience of the Moscow dairy clerks and to the history of labor unions in Western Europe, Kolokol'nikov emphasized the limitations on union development imposed by a party label.

While rejecting formal organizational ties, Kolokol'nikov was not prepared to see the trade unions operate outside of party influence. "We must strive," he concluded, "for the political actions of unions to coincide with those of the [SD] party." Unions, moreover, should take an active role in political life and "struggle for freedom, for the right to unionize and to strike."[29] Parties and unions were thus envisioned as proceeding in tandem, with close but formal cooperation. This, in essence, had become the Menshevik position regarding trade unions, a position maintained by the faction in the years to come.

The Bolshevik speaker, Stanislav Vol'skii [A. V. Sokolov], presented a very different view of union-party relations. Kolokol'nikov's proposal, he claimed, was "appropriate abroad, but we live in Russia."[30] Unions, in his view, ought to be political organizations closely united with the RSDRP through a common program and common leadership of the party. Another Bolshevik speaker put the matter more succinctly: "In their political activities, trade unions must proceed under the workers' banner, under the banner of Social Democracy."[31] Marat [V. L. Shantser], a member of the Bolshevik Committee, echoed Lenin's pronouncement in *What Is To Be Done?* when he noted that

the working class should now be particularly fearful of the liberal parties, which are attempting to attract workers to themselves for a struggle on behalf of bourgeois interests. Workers at this time should place themselves under the banner of the Social Democratic party. We should fear nonparty organizations; this is an open door for liberals to control workers.[32]

[28]Ibid., p. 35.
[29]Ibid., p. 36.
[30]Ibid.
[31]Ibid., p. 37.
[32]Ibid.

Socialist Revolutionaries did not make a formal presentation at the November 16 meeting, but they participated in the discussion. A spokesman asserted that his party generally concurred with Social Democrats on the question of workers. On the subject of labor organization, he asserted, the Socialist Revolutionaries opposed the branding of unions with a particular party stamp.[33]

Spectators in the hall, according to Kolokol'nikov, favored the Bolshevik position.[34] But the audience response on this occasion can scarcely be considered characteristic of the labor movement in the city as a whole. Even during the turbulent closing weeks of the revolution, when the mood of many workers was more intensely political than ever before, the Bolshevik policy on union-party relations had limited appeal among workers. Despite their growing radicalism and receptivity to Social Democratic ideas, most of the workers drawn to the union movement voted to support the principle of independent trade unions, without formal affiliation to any party or group.

SOCIAL DEMOCRATIC SUPPORT IN THE TRADE UNIONS

If workers sought to avoid formal ties with the RSDRP, they were scarcely averse to recognition of the party's economic program-minimum or to the leadership of Social Democrats in their organizations. Social Democrats, regardless of factional affiliation, made inroads into the union movement during the final months of 1905. Information on the composition of the leadership or the type of the founding charter is available for only about 20 percent of the Petersburg unions and 40 percent in Moscow, samples that are too small to provide a reliable picture of the union movement as a whole. Nevertheless, in each city, two out of three unions with an identifiable political orientation were under Social Democratic influence. The party's position can be further judged from the fact that all of the Petersburg and Moscow unions with more than five hundred members were either fully or partially under the leadership of Social Democrats (table 10).

The Bolsheviks secured the adoption of their charter in only a few Moscow unions, but they were influential in a number of others, including the Moscow unions of waiters, bookstore clerks, railroad workers, and office clerks and

---

[33]Ibid.
[34]Kolokol'nikov, "Otryvki," *MIPDR*, 4:14.

Table 10

Political Orientation of the Leadership of Petersburg and Moscow Unions with More Than Five Hundred Members, 1905

Union	Peak Membership	Political Orientation
St. Petersburg:		
1. Printers	3,339	Social Democrat (Menshevik, Bolshevik, and nonfactional), Liberationist
2. Salesclerks	3,000	Social Democrat (Bolshevik)
3. Woodworkers	866	Social Democrat (Menshevik)
4. Bakers and confectioners	856	Social Democrat (nonfactional)
5. Tailors and furriers	751	Social Democrat (Menshevik and Bolshevik), Socialist Revolutionary
6. Textile workers	725	Social Democrat (Menshevik)
Moscow:		
1. Printers	4,000	Social Democrat (Menshevik)
2. Sales-clerical employees	2,500	Social Democrat (Menshevik)
3. Teapackers	2,000	Social Democrat (Menshevik)
4. Bakers	1,770	Social Democrat (Bolshevik)
5. Carpenters	1,200	Social Democrat (Bolshevik)
6. Tailors	1,200	Social Democrat (Menshevik)
7. Tobacco workers	1,000	Social Democrat (Menshevik)
8. Waiters	1,000	Social Democrat (Bolshevik)
9. Office clerks and bookkeepers	950	Kadet, Social Democrat (Bolshevik)
10. Ribbonweavers	800	Social Democrat (Menshevik)

Sources: *Istoriia Leningradskogo soiuza rabochikh poligraficheskikh proizvodstva* (Leningrad, 1925), pp. 134, 145–147, 424, 438; P. F. Kudelli and G. L. Shidlovskii, eds., *1905: Vospominaniia chlenov SPB soveta rabochikh deputatov* (Leningrad, 1926), passim; S. M. Gruzdev, *Trud i bor'ba shveinikov v Petrograde 1905-1916 gg.* (Leningrad, 1929), pp. 101–104; Grinevich, Letter from St. Petersburg, pp. 12–13; *Obshcheprofessional'nye organy 1905-1907 gg.*, pp. 97, 104–107, 110, 113–117; A. Belin, *Professional'noe dvizhenie torgovykh sluzhashchikh v Rossii* (Moscow, 1906), p. 14; R. G. Ramazov, "Sozdanie profsoiuzov Peterburgskogo proletariata a ikh deiatel'nost' v pervoi russkoi revoliutsii," candidate dissertation (Higher School on Trade Unions), Moscow, 1975, pp. 75–76, 107; *Profes-sional'nyi vestnik*, no. 3 (February 10, 1907), p. 7; *Professional'nyi soiuz*, no. 3 (December 25, 1905), p. 6; *Tkach*, no. 1 (June 11, 1906), p. 5; Kats and Milonov, eds., *1905*, pp. 41–55; Milonov, *Kak vozniki*, pp. 115–116, 120, 142; Kolokol'nikov, "Otryvki," *MIPDR*, 3:225, 228.

bookkeepers, the Petersburg union of salesclerks, and to a lesser extent, the Petersburg unions of printers and tailors.[35] The faction also drew support from metalworkers in both cities and from the Moscow tram workers, although neither group succeeded in unionizing before the end of the year.

The Mensheviks, who proved to be more active and enthusiastic union organizers than the Bolsheviks, made greater inroads into the organized labor movement. Judging by union charters and the composition of the leadership, there were at least twelve unions fully or partially under this faction's influence in Moscow and four in the capital. Among them were the printers' unions in both cities, as well as the Moscow unions of tobacco workers, teapackers, ribbon-weavers, tailors, sales-clerical employees, foodstore clerks, Brest railroad shop workers, workers in toy and umbrella factories, lower-level employees in the Moscow City Administration, and church artists; and the Petersburg unions of textile workers, woodworkers, and tailors. The Mensheviks also attracted a following among some Petersburg metalworkers, but they had few contacts in large Moscow metalworking plants.[36] Apart from the unions that can be associated with one or the other SD faction, an additional five or six unions in each city were led by nonfaction Social Democrats.

Many of the trade unions under Social Democratic influence were artisanal. Of the Petersburg and Moscow unions known to be under SD leadership or to have adopted an SD (Menshevik or Bolshevik) model charter, about 40 percent involved artisanal groups. Three of the six largest Petersburg unions (woodworkers, bakers, and tailors) with SD leadership were artisanal in character, as were three of the ten largest unions with SD leadership in Moscow (bakers, carpenters, and tailors). In the semi-artisanal Moscow ribbonweaver's union and the printers' unions in both cities, Social Democrats were also influential.

Artisanal workers, such as Moscow bakers, carpenters, and gold- and silver-smiths, were among the handful of unionized groups that endorsed the Bolshevik concept of party-affiliated unions. Clearly, contemporary Bolsheviks did not

[35]This information and what follows has been assembled from the trade union press. See also Kolokol'nikov, "Otryvki," *MIPDR,* 4:14; Iu. K. Milonov, *Kak voznikli professional'nye soiuzy v Rossii,* 2d ed. (Moscow, 1929), pp. 72, 120, 217, 220; Kats and Milonov, eds., *1905,* p. 50; *Obshcheprofessional'nye organy,* p. 105. Milonov claims that the Bolsheviks were also dominant in the Moscow unions of postal and telegraph employees and household servants *(Kak voznikli,* pp. 217, 220), but I have found no evidence to confirm this.

[36]Nicolaevsky Collection, Letter from Iu. Larin, No. 91, p. 1.

restrict their organizational efforts to groups that conformed to a narrow definition of the "working class," that is, workers employed only in large-scale,
technologically developed branches of industry such as metalworking. Bolshevik *praktiki* accorded great importance to organizational efforts among metalworkers, and they achieved growing influence in this industry during 1905. But
ideological presuppositions did not prevent the Bolsheviks from seeking support
wherever they could find it, even if this meant investing their energy to win
recruits among artisans, sales-clerical workers, and other nonfactory groups.

The willingness of Moscow bakers, carpenters, and gold- and silversmiths to
adopt the Bolshevik approach to union-party relations foreshadowed the enthusiastic following that this faction elicited among other artisanal groups in the
years to come. But the Bolsheviks were not alone in attracting the support of
artisanal workers in 1905. The Mensheviks were also influential in a number of
artisanal unions. Considering the workers' confusion and lack of comprehension
of factional differences, the striking fact is that Social Democrats of all varieties
(Bolshevik, Menshevik, and nonfaction) did extremely well in artisanal unions
during the revolution.

The Social Democrats' success in a wide variety of unions, not only in
artisanal trades but also among factory workers, sales-clerical employees, and
others, can be ascribed, in large measure, to the highly politicized atmosphere
after the October general strike. The October Manifesto gave workers a strong
sense of their own power, and they joined in the general euphoria over the Tsar's
capitulation. But there were also expressions of cynicism and sentiments that
the reforms did not go far enough and would not be honored by the authorities
in good faith.[37] Already disillusioned with their past beliefs and open to new
ideas, the workers were more receptive than ever before to the appeals of radical groups. Social Democrats were the principal beneficiaries of the workers'
mood.

The presence of energetic and articulate organizers gave the Social Democrats a decided advantage over their competitors in reaching workers during
these turbulent weeks. To be sure, there were serious organizational weaknesses
in the local committees of both SD factions. Throughout 1905 the coterie of
full-time SD *praktiki* always fell short of the needs and ambitions of the local

[37]V. S. Voitinskii, *Gody pobed i porazhenii*, Book 1: *1905-yi god* (Berlin, Petersburg, and Moscow,
1923), pp. 169–193; Aleksei Buzinov, *Za Nevskoi zastavoi: Zapiski rabochego* (Moscow and
Leningrad, 1930), p. 80.

groups. But the Social Democrats were nevertheless better organized than the other parties and groups active in the workers' milieu.

Social Democratic activists in the unions included both workers and intellectuals. Socialist worker-activists elicited a good deal of respect and attention from their fellow workers during 1905,[38] and those who became involved in the trade unions represented a great asset to the party and helped to enhance its appeal among the rank and file. Nikolai Chistov, an SD printer and union leader in Moscow, exemplifies this type. A Moscovite, Chistov served as the first president of the printers' union established in October (having earlier been active in the Menshevik-dominated predecessor union), and he chaired the first meeting of the Moscow Soviet in November. Another Menshevik organizer, Petr Garvi, has described Chistov's position in the Moscow labor movement:

Of course, the ideological leaders of the [Moscow] union of printers were the party intellectuals, Sher and Orlov [Kruglov]. But it was "Kirillich" [Chistov] who was the soul of the union, its moral and organizational core; he was the one whom workers believed and trusted. Kirillich was a Menshevik, one of the first representatives of the Social Democratic workers' intelligentsia, those who had been politically shaped by underground propaganda circles [before 1905], but whose true potential was realized only in the arena of the open workers' movement.[39]

Some of the most avid union leaders in 1905 belonged not to the working class but to the intelligentsia, including students, professionals, and others. Workers actively sought the assistance of intelligentsia sympathizers and called upon them to provide valuable services to the incipient labor movement. For their part, many of the intellectuals in the unions were tirelessly devoted to the labor cause, and they helped to spread the party's influence in the union movement.[40]

LIBERALS, SOCIALIST REVOLUTIONARIES, AND SYNDICALISTS IN
THE TRADE UNIONS

Although Social Democrats came to occupy a preeminent place in the organized labor movement, they were not the only political activists to become involved in

---

[38]Buzinov, *Za Nevskoi zastavoi*, pp. 44, 48, 49.
[39]Garvi, *Revoliutsionnye siluety*, pp. 28–29.
[40]See chapter 3, "Routes to Unionization," for further discussion of this point.

the trade unions. Liberals occupying the left wing of the Union of Liberation also took an active part in the unions. Early in 1905, liberals helped to organize the Petersburg printers' union, and in the spring they approached metalworkers at the Nevskii plant with a proposal for a workers' counterpart to the Union of Unions.[41]

All told, however, liberals recruited only a small following among unionized workers in St. Petersburg and Moscow. Their greatest influence was concentrated among low- and middle-level white-collar sales-clerical employees and others, such as railroad employees and some service groups standing at the margins of the workers' movement. They also won the support of a small but active group in the Petersburg printers' and textile unions.[42]

Liberals failed to exert a significant ideological or tactical influence over the growing number of blue-collar workers who participated in the trade unions. The liberal philosophy—a blend of "economism," class collaboration, and political reform—did not appeal to most blue-collar workers during 1905. Moreover, the liberals lacked a group of dedicated grass-roots organizers needed to penetrate extensively into the workers' milieu.

Nevertheless, a small but energetic group of liberal intellectuals presided over the birth of the union movement and helped to establish some of its key organs. Vladimir Sviatlovskii, for example, a liberal assistant professor at Petersburg University, became a leading figure in the capital's union movement during the fall.[43] He was among the early participants in the Petersburg Central Bureau of Trade Unions, and an editor of the Bureau's trade union organ *Professional'nyi soiuz.*

Georgii Nosar' [Khrustal'ev-Nosar'], a liberal lawyer whose organizational activities began at the time of elections to the Shidlovskii Commission in February, served as a legal consultant to a number of unions in the capital and

---

[41]Kolokol'nikov and Rapoport, eds., *1905-1907 gg.*, pp. 168–169; Schwarz, *The Russian Revolution,* Appendix 7. See above, chapter 3. On the Union of Liberation, see Shmuel Galai, *The Liberation Movement in Russia 1900-1905* (Cambridge, England, 1973).

[42]*Obshcheprofessional'nye organy 1905-1907 gg.*, p. 99, n. 8, on the role of Liberationists in the important Petersburg printers' union. Liberationists were also active in the following unions: Petersburg office clerks and bookkeepers; Moscow postal and telegraph employees, lower-level employees in the Moscow city administration, pharmacists, hired workers in trade and industry, office clerks and bookkeepers, waiters, window washers, and the All-Russian Union of Railroad Employees and Workers.

[43]A summary of Sviatlovskii's career appears in Kolokol'nikov and Rapoport, eds., *1905-1907 gg.*, pp. 421–422.

helped them draw up founding charters.[44] He represented the union of printers in the Soviet of Workers' Deputies, and was later elected chairman. Nosar' also represented the St. Petersburg textile workers' union at the First All-Russian Conference of Trade Unions held in Moscow in October 1905.[45]

Andrei Evdokimov [pseud. A. Belin], a liberal sympathizer, became a key figure in the Moscow union movement in the fall of 1905. Evdokimov's involvement in the labor movement had begun in the 1890s when, as a Social Democrat, he helped to organize a "Union of Workers of Russian Manchester" in Ivanovo-Voznesensk, a textile village in the Central Industrial Region.[46] After that project failed, he moved to Kharkhov in 1900 and became active in the mutual aid society movement. His "economist" views soon drew him to the left Liberationists, a position he still occupied in 1905 when he became the chief promoter of the idea of an all-Russian conference of mutual aid societies. In this connection, Evdokimov traveled throughout the country, eventually settling in Moscow, where he took a leading role in the trade union movement and in the Moscow Central Bureau of Trade Unions. Evdokimov, alone among the intelligentsia activists in Moscow, brought to the incipient labor movement a background of practical experience and knowledge of workers' organizations acquired through his earlier efforts in Ivanovo-Voznesensk and Kharkhov.[47]

Nikolai Murav'ev, another liberal, was elected president of the Moscow Museum for Assistance to Labor in mid-March 1905. The Museum dated from 1901, when it was founded as a branch of the Imperial Russian Technical Society. It participated briefly in the Zubatov experiment,[48] withdrawing soon after disclosures of police involvement. The Museum provided cultural, educational, and legal services for workers, and under the direction of Murav'ev and a committee that included Social Democrats and Socialist Revolutionaries, it functioned as a center for the organized labor movement in 1905, hosting the

[44]See above, chapter 3. On the involvement of Nosar' in the labor movement, see Kolokol'nikov and Rapoport, eds., *1905–1907 gg.*, pp. 169–170; *Obshcheprofessional'nye organy 1905–1907 gg.*, p. 99.

[45]Kolokol'nikov and Rapoport, eds., *1905–1907 gg.*, pp. 161–172. Also attending the conference was Prokopovich, another leading Petersburg liberal.

[46]Ibid., pp. 123–125.

[47]For an assessment of Evdokimov's contribution, see V. Sher, "Tsentral'noe biuro," *MIPDR*, 4:47.

[48]For a history of the Museum for Assistance to Labor, see Kolokol'nikov and Rapoport, eds., *1905–1907 gg.*, pp. 156ff.; *Obshcheprofessional'nye organy 1905–1907 gg.*, pp. 93–94; Tsentral'nyi gosudarstvennyi arkhiv Oktiabr'skoi revoliutsii (henceforth TsGAOR), DP IV, f. 102, d. 236, prod. I, 1908, p. 175.

first meetings of the Central Bureau of Trade Unions and the Moscow Soviet of Workers' Deputies.

Socialist Revolutionaries also took steps to gain a foothold in the burgeoning trade union movement. A draft program published in May 1904 stated the party's support for the "organization of trade unions among workers" and called for the "progressively increasing participation of unions in the determination of internal regulations for industrial establishments."[49] With its pro-peasant collectivist ideology, the SR party attracted its strongest following among unionizing workers with close continuing ties to the countryside, such as the *bashmak* shoemakers, chimneysweeps, parquetry workers, and beer-hall employees in Moscow and the dockworkers in the capital. SRs were also influential in the All-Russian Union of Railroad Employees and Workers, the Union of Workers in the Workshops of the Kazan Railroad, and the Union of Postal and Telegraph Employees.[50]

One of the two major parties of the socialist left, SRs (together with the SDs) were accorded formal representation in the Central Bureau of Trade Unions and the Soviets of Workers' Deputies. Like the liberals, however, they suffered from a scarcity of party cadres in St. Petersburg and Moscow, and they were not in a position to compete with the Social Democrats in the day-to-day affairs of the union movement. But if the Socialist Revolutionaries were unable to establish widespread influence over the trade unions, they were nevertheless a presence to be reckoned with, and they presented the Social Democrats with their major political adversaries in the organized labor movement.

A small group of syndicalists could also be found in the 1905 trade unions. Although they did not constitute a cohesive or organized party, individuals with a syndicalist orientation left their imprint on several unions, including the All-Russian Union of Railroad Employees and Workers.[51] Syndicalism also had an appeal among some Social Democratic labor activists in the capital, such as

---

[49]Harcave, *The Russian Revolution of 1905*, p. 271.

[50]*Professional'noe dvizhenie Moskovskikh pishchevikov v gody pervoi revoliutsii*, sbornik 1 (Moscow, 1927), p. 106; Walter Sablinsky, "The All-Russian Railroad Union and the Beginning of the General Strike in October 1905," in *Revolution and Politics in Russia*, ed. Rabinowitch with Kristof, p. 120; K. V. Bazilevich, *Ocherki po istorii professional'nogo dvizheniia rabotnikov sviazi: 1905-1906 gg.* (Moscow, 1925), p. 211; Kolokol'nikov, "Otryvki," *MIPDR*, 3:227. For an account of the party's activities in 1905, see P. P. Maslov, "Narodnicheskie partii," in *Obshchestvennoe dvizhenie v Rossii v nachale XX veka*, ed. L. Martov, P. Maslov, and A. Potresov (St. Petersburg, 1914), vol. 3, book 5, pp. 107–112.

[51]*Obshcheprofessional'nye organy 1905-1907 gg.*, p. 114, n. 5.

Somov.[52] Evdokimov, a Liberationist during most of 1905, moved to a syndicalist position late in the year, and in 1906 he became a leading advocate of syndicalism in the Moscow labor movement.

THE SPREAD OF SOCIAL DEMOCRATIC IDEAS

From mid-October to mid-December, more than eighty trade union meetings were held in St. Petersburg, and more than two hundred in Moscow. These meetings, which sometimes attracted hundreds or even thousands of workers,[53] represented the most significant form of public assembly during the "days of freedom." Radical activists reached more workers at these gatherings than through any other channel available in 1905. The meetings had an electrifying atmosphere. Packed tightly into a crowded theatre or auditorium, the workers' mood was tense and expectant. Many of them were witnessing for the first time an assemblage of fellow workers from firms throughout the city, and this spectacle, together with the unprecedented opportunity to create their own independent organization, gave them a sense of collective solidarity, determination, and strength. The speakers generally included worker-organizers of the union, a Social Democrat or some other political activist, and rank-and-file workers who rose to expose the misery and oppression in their daily lives. These speeches were frequently interrupted by applause and shouts of approval from the audience, and it was not uncommon for workers to join in the singing of the Marseillaise at the close of the meeting.

Social Democrats who participated in these meetings emphasized several themes. One important point concerned the nature of class conflicts in Russian society. The idea of class struggle was especially important in shaping workers' attitudes during 1905 because it went to the very core of official ideology, which stressed the mutual compatibility of workers' and employers' interests and the possibility of their reconciliation within the framework of the tsarist state. A

[52]Ibid., p. 109, n. 28. Other Petersburg Mensheviks inclined toward syndicalism included V. Akimov [V. P. Makhnovets] and Markov [P. F. Teplov]. This group sought to strengthen worker autonomy and independence from party organs, and to make the Central Bureau of Trade Unions a leadership center for the workers' movement. Akimov was the author of a declaration, published on November 26, 1905, "in which the idea of a Social-Democratic Party based on trade unions received its definitive formulation." Schwarz, *The Russian Revolution*, p. 322. See Appendix 8 of Schwarz's book for a discussion of his views on trade unions.

[53]See above, chapter 3, p. 136.

Social Democrat, speaking to a union meeting of three thousand Petersburg tailors on October 30, proclaimed that

society is divided into different classes, and these classes are divided, in turn, into still smaller groups. In opposition to the workers, there are not small groups but an entire class of capitalist-exploiters. In order to struggle against the capitalists, workers must organize in two ways: politically, in a political party . . . and economically, in trade unions.[54]

Social Democrats were particularly adamant in their advocacy of proletarian class solidarity, and they fought hard against the workers' repeated inclination to unify along narrow craft lines. The appeal to class unity coincided with developments actually under way in the workers' movement, where the first major class-based organization—the Soviets of Workers' Deputies—had just emerged.[55] But Social Democrats not only stressed the solidarity of all Russian workers against their class enemies, employers and the state; they also emphasized the still novel idea that the workers' localized struggles, as one SD speaker put it, were part of the "great political class struggle of the international proletariat for its ideals."[56]

Another common theme in the speeches of Social Democrats was the close interconnection between economic and political struggles. "The very history of struggle in recent days," declared one SD speaker at a meeting of the Petersburg union of draftsmen in mid-November, "clearly demonstrates that until the proletariat presents political demands, it cannot achieve anything from its economic program."[57] Workers could readily understand that workplace improvements depended on the prior attainment of political and civil rights. After all, their participation in the trade unions was plainly contingent on basic civil liberties, such as freedom of assembly, which had only weeks earlier been proclaimed by the October Manifesto.

The eventual goal of socialism was mentioned in these weeks, but it must have appeared to workers as a remote prospect of uncertain nature. It was not socialism but a democratic republic and full civil liberties that offered a more immediate and comprehensible alternative to the existing arrangements in tsarist Russia, and these ideas were frequently mentioned at union meetings, both by workers and by their radical mentors.

The workers' needs as *citizens*—their entitlement to basic freedoms as well as

[54]*Novaia zhizn'*, no. 6 (November 2, 1905), p. 3.
[55]See the section "Trade Unions and the Soviets of Workers' Deputies," below.
[56]*Obshcheprofessional'nye organy 1905–1907 gg.*, p. 40.
[57]Ibid., p. 56.

to the special rights of labor—can be considered one of the most important ideas disseminated through the incipient trade union movement during the revolution. It was emphasized not only by Social Democrats, but by liberals and Socialist Revolutionaries as well. Social Democrats imparted to workers the idea that these goals could only be reached by an overthrow of the existing autocratic system and the introduction into Russia of a fully democratic government, with a constituent assembly and a complete array of civil rights and freedoms. Mensheviks and Bolsheviks were not, however, in full accord over the means of achieving this revolutionary transformation. The Bolsheviks' preoccupation with an armed uprising of workers against the autocracy found little support in Menshevik circles. On the whole, the latter group tended to stress the importance of building a mass labor movement capable of carrying through a "bourgeois revolution" in conjunction with other antiautocratic groups in Russian society.[58]

Not all workers who attended union meetings were comfortable with revolutionary exhortations. A speaker who called for the overthrow of the monarchy at a meeting of the union of Moscow food store employees was challenged with cries from the audience: "That's not necessary!" "Enough!" Others were reported to have signified their support for the speaker by applauding. And at a meeting of Petersburg shoemakers on December 6, an appeal to join in a general strike against the government met with exclamations from some workers: "We don't need any politics!"[59] A speaker from the floor at a large meeting of Petersburg tailors in October called upon fellow workers to concentrate on organizing for economic improvement and to avoid political involvement.[60]

The extent of such sentiments is difficult to judge, but there can be no doubt that demands for civil liberties and for a constitutional system of government had the support of a great many workers during the final months of 1905. At union meetings and in union resolutions, workers asserted their moral and legal entitlement to full equality and citizenship. Thus, at a meeting of Petersburg watchmakers, attended by several hundred workers on November 27, the union president proclaimed:

---

[58]For a discussion of Bolshevik and Menshevik policies see John L. H. Keep, *The Rise of Social Democracy in Russia* (Oxford, 1963), chaps. 6 and 7. V. Voitinskii, *Gody pobed* provides an insider's view of factional politics in the capital in the fall of 1905.

[59]*Bor'ba*, no. 2 (November 29 [December 12], 1905), p. 3; *Peterburgskii sapozhnik*, no. 1 (March 28, 1906), p. 3.

[60]*Professional'nyi soiuz*, no. 1 (November 27, 1905), p. 6.

The union represents something grandiose for the working people and something threatening for the owners because the union signifies organized economic struggle with capitalist exploitation. With the help of the union, after we have developed self-consciousness and raised our legal, intellectual, and material level, *we shall be transformed into free citizens.* Not as pathetic and dispersed cowards, but as brave men, proud of our solidarity, fully armed with justice and truth, we shall present our demands before those insatiable sharks who are our employers. The failure of our strike demonstrates even more powerfully the very necessity for and the very significance of the union.[61]

Similarly, the founding group of Petersburg tavern employees declared on November 9:

Our condition is difficult and demeaning. At the present time all the laboring classes of Russia are united in defense of their rights. The toilers of all Russia are struggling to obtain satisfaction of their basic economic needs and their *needs as citizens.*[62]

Toward the end of 1905, workers were thus increasingly preoccupied with issues concerning political and civil rights, as well as the special rights of labor to unionize and to strike. A heightened awareness of these questions was due, in part, to the workers' exposure to Social Democratic ideas through the trade unions. But contact between Social Democrats and workers was not confined only to these organizations. In mid-October another development of great consequence took place: the formation of the Petersburg Soviet.

TRADE UNIONS AND THE SOVIETS OF WORKERS' DEPUTIES

With the spread and intensification of labor unrest in September, the problem of coordination in the workers' movement had become acute. Prior to October, when a general Strike Committee was established in Moscow, no citywide organs existed in either St. Petersburg or Moscow to provide leadership and direction for the workers' movement.[63] Two approaches to citywide organization were debated in labor circles on the eve of the general strike. One approach called for the creation of a citywide organ in which the individual enterprise

---

[61]Sviatlovskii, *Professional'noe dvizhenie,* pp. 107–108. Italics in the original.

[62]*Obshcheprofessional'nye organy 1905–1907 gg.,* p. 51. Italics mine.

[63]For an account of the formation of the Moscow Strike Committee, see Laura Engelstein, *Moscow, 1905: Working-Class Organization and Political Conflict* (Stanford, Calif., 1982), pp. 115–116.

would serve as the basic unit of representation in assemblies operating on the district and city levels. A second model was based on trade and industrial units. Industry-wide strike councils had already made an appearance in Moscow in September, and a number of trade unions were already in existence. These alternatives were debated by Moscow Social Democrats at a meeting on October 2:[64]

There was no objection to the suggestion to bring together deputies from individual factories as representatives in a general soviet. Disagreements arose only over the form of that unification. Some proposed the path followed by the typographers, that is, unification initially of each profession, and then sending representatives of these soviets of each profession to a general soviet. Others, recognizing the necessity for organization by profession, stood at the same time for a general soviet consisting of representatives of different plants and factories.[65]

The final resolution adopted at the October 2 meeting called on each professional group to decide individually the best means of representation.

A similar uncertainty characterized the genesis of the Petersburg Soviet. Here the Mensheviks issued a proclamation on October 13—the very day on which the Soviet was set in motion—that betrays the same ambiguity over the type of organizational principle underlying this organization:

We propose that each plant, each factory, and *each profession* elect deputies on the basis of one for every five hundred people. The meeting of deputies at each factory or plant will constitute a factory committee. The meeting of deputies of all factories and plants will constitute a general Petersburg workers' committee.[66]

Two concepts emphasizing, respectively, representation at the enterprise level, and representation based on an entire industry, trade, or occupation, thus provided alternative models for a citywide workers' institution in the fall of 1905.

[64]*Obshcheprofessional'nye organy 1905-1907 gg.*, pp. 16–18 and 103, n. 16. The meeting included representatives of the Moscow printers, carpenters, ribbon weavers, metal-, textile, and tobacco workers, and a number of leading Menshevik *praktiki*. Further meetings of the pre-soviet took place on October 4 and October 15. Nonparty activists participated in the October 15 meeting, including some Zubatovists. Kolokol'nikov, "Otryvki," *MIPDR*, 3:217.

[65]*Obshcheprofessional'nye organy 1905-1907 gg.*, p. 18. This statement is taken from the report of the meeting held on October 2, 1905.

[66]N. I. Sidorov, ed., *1905 god v Peterburge*, vyp. 2: *Sovet rabochikh deputatov: Sbornik materialov* (Leningrad, 1925), p. 6. Italics mine. Voitinskii, *Gody pobed*, p. 143, notes that the principle of electing one deputy for every five hundred workers was modeled after the Shidlovskii Commission election.

Each approach rested on a previously established form of worker organization: the factory committee or the trade union. As it turned out, representatives both from factory committees and from trade unions, as well as newly elected delegates, took their seats in the soviets, which brought workers together, for the first time, on a broad class basis.

Unionized printers, meeting on October 13, were among the first groups in the capital to elect deputies to the St. Petersburg Soviet.[67] Three thousand printers, holding a union meeting that evening, greeted the news of the Soviet with great enthusiasm:

One had only to be at the meeting of the union of printers on October 13 in the university cafeteria to be convinced of the hopefulness and jubilation with which workers received the idea of organizing a "workers' parliament." Illuminated by the mysteriously flickering candles, the crowd, three thousand strong, listened with bated breath to the speeches of familiar orators, and with thunderous applause they welcomed the orators' oaths to give up their lives for the workers' cause. In turn, the workers promised to support their leaders as one man.[68]

Two days later, representatives of five unions—printers, watchmakers and jewelers, office clerks, salesclerks, and technicians[69]—had already taken their places in the Soviet. At its peak, the St. Petersburg Soviet had 562 deputies (voting and consultative). Among them was a large and influential contingent of trade unionists.

According to Nosar', the Liberationist lawyer who became Chairman of the Soviet on November 15, sixteen Petersburg unions were represented in the assembly: printers, lithographers, salesclerks, office clerks, pharmacists, technicians, watchmakers and jewelers, tailors, shoemakers, electricians, newspaper deliverers, dock-, wood-, tobacco, railroad, and postal-telegraph workers.[70] All of these unions were accorded full voting rights, with the exception of the unions of railroad and postal-telegraph workers, which had a consultative voice only.

At least four other unions, not mentioned by Nosar', sent representatives to

[67]Kudelli and Shidlovskii, eds., *1905: Vospominaniia,* pp. 53–57.

[68]Grinevich, "Ocherk razvitiia professional'nogo dvizheniia v S.-Peterburge," *Obrazovanie* 15, no. 9 (September 1906), p. 233.

[69]Georgii S. Nosar', "Istoriia soveta rabochikh deputatov (do 26-go noiabria 1905 g.)," in *Istoriia soveta rabochikh deputatov g. S.-Peterburga* (St. Petersburg, 1906), pp. 66, 71. The unions of watchmakers and jewelers were not formally united, but they cooperated to send deputies to the Soviet.

[70]Ibid., pp. 146–147, n. 1.

the Soviet: draftsmen, gardeners, cooks, and binders. Each of these unions had one deputy, except the union of cooks, which had two.[71] Thus, in addition to the sixty-three union deputies whose presence in the Soviet is noted by Nosar', there were at least five others, bringing the union contingent to sixty-eight (representing twenty different unions) out of a total of 562 deputies, or twelve percent.

In fact, however, the presence of trade unionists was even greater than these figures indicate, because some deputies elected from their place of employment were concurrently involved in trade union activity. The exact number of these individuals cannot be ascertained on the basis of available evidence. Yet there is reason to believe that as many as one out of five deputies may have been simultaneously involved in the union movement.[72]

Some of the union delegations were quite large. The union of printers sent fifteen representatives, for example, and ten deputies participated from the union of salesclerks.[73] Considering the influence of Social Democrats in the organized labor movement, it is not surprising to find Social Democrats within the union delegations. Four of the fifteen printers' union deputies were Social Democrats, together with five of the eleven deputies from the union of salesclerks, two of the deputies elected by the unions of watchmakers and jewelers, and others.[74]

The importance of trade unions in the Petersburg Soviet can be further judged by the composition of the Soviet Executive Committee. The Soviet's first Executive Committee, elected on November 17, had thirty-one members: twenty-two workers' deputies and nine representatives of political parties. Eight of the twenty-two workers' deputies represented trade unions (printers, office clerks, salesclerks, and pharmacists). A second Executive Committee with fifty members was elected on November 19. It included twenty-eight workers' deputies from district soviets within the city, nine representatives of political parties,

---

[71]*Novaia zhizn'*, no. 16 (November 18, 1905), p. 4 (draftsmen); no. 9 (November 10, 1905), p. 5 (gardeners); no. 26 (December 1, 1905), p. 4 (cooks); no. 19 (November 23, 1905), p. 4 (binders).

[72]This statement is based on a sample of 113 deputies to the Soviet for whom biographical information is available in Kudelli and Shidlovskii, eds., *1905: Vospominaniia*. Of these deputies, 29, or 26 percent, were concurrently involved in trade-union work during 1905. Of these 29, 18 formally represented their trade union in the Soviet, while 11 others were factory representatives who were actively engaged in the union movement. Based on this sample of 113 deputies, therefore, nearly 1 out of 10 deputies took part in the union movement but did not formally represent their union in the Soviet.

[73]On the printers' union delegation, see Kudelli and Shidlovskii, eds., *1905: Vospominaniia*, pp. 53–57; the size of the delegation from the union of salesclerks is reported in *Novaia zhizn'*, no. 20 (November 24, 1905), p. 3.

[74]Nosar', "Istoriia," in *Istoriia soveta*, p. 72.

and thirteen trade-union deputies (representing the unions of printers, office clerks, salesclerks, pharmacists, railroad and postal-telegraph workers).[75] Thus, nearly one-third of the worker-members of the November 19 Executive Committee (thirteen out of forty-one) were from the trade unions.

Factory committees also provided an important basis for representation in the Petersburg Soviet. Whereas some enterprises held new elections to choose deputies to the Soviet, in other cases members of a preestablished factory committee were reassigned, as it were, to the new "workers' parliament." At the Rechkin wagonworks, for example, members of the factory committee took their seats in the Soviet. By mid-October, however, one factory committee member had changed his place of employment. Nevertheless, his former coworkers sought him out with a request to represent them in the Soviet. New elections, they explained, would not be held at the Rechkin plant.[76]

In enterprises where no factory committee or Council of Elders had yet been formed, workers proceeded to elect deputies to the Soviet. These elections were often conducted in the manner originally set forth at the time of the Shidlovskii Commission in February.[77] Thus, the Petersburg Soviet arose partly on the foundations earlier erected by the factory committee movement and the Shidlovskii Commission elections. As was noted by Nosar':

The authoritative influence of the soviets of deputies on the electorate can be traced to the Shidlovskii Commission [elections]. It is interesting to note that many of the electors to the Shidlovskii Commission were deputies to the Soviet.[78]

The Moscow Soviet of Workers' Deputies did not convene until November 21, although preliminary discussions were already under way at meetings held on October 2, 4, and 15.[79] Arising late in the year and convening on only a few occasions (November 21, 27, December 4, 6), the progress of the Moscow Soviet differed in important respects from its counterpart in the capital.[80] As a general citywide assembly of workers, the Moscow Soviet failed to acquire the

[75]Ibid., pp. 153–154. Included among the party representatives were delegates from the local Menshevik and Bolshevik organizations and the Central Committee and Organizational Committee of the RSDRP. Evgenii, "Peterburgskii Sovet," *Otkliki sovremennosti*, p. 7.

[76]Kudelli and Shidlovskii, eds., *1905: Vospominaniia*, p. 40.

[77]Ibid., p. 43.

[78]Nosar', "Istoriia," in *Istoriia soveta*, p. 48.

[79]*Obshcheprofessional'nye organy 1905–1907 gg.*, pp. 16–18, 103, n. 16.

[80]For a general history of the Moscow Soviet, see Oskar Anweiler, *The Soviets: The Russian Workers, Peasants, and Soldiers Councils*, trans. Ruth Hein (New York, 1974), and Engelstein, *Moscow, 1905*.

influence or significance of the Petersburg Soviet. Here the district soviets were more important and more lively than those in the capital, and it was in the district organizations that the Moscow Soviet achieved its fullest, albeit brief, development.

In Moscow, as in the capital, local Mensheviks initiated the formation of the Soviet. It was delayed, however, by opposition from the Moscow Bolshevik Committee.[81] Considerably stronger than the local Menshevik Group, the Moscow Bolsheviks hesitated to endorse a new workers' assembly that might easily elude party control and succumb to the "spontaneity" of the masses. One particularly troublesome issue centered around the role that trade unions were to play in the Soviet.

The belated formation of the Moscow Soviet enabled the trade union movement to make rapid advances. Whereas only a handful of unions functioned in the capital when the Soviet was announced there on October 13, more than eighty unions had been created in Moscow by late November, some of them with an impressive membership. And although the Bolshevik party organization in Moscow was stronger than the Menshevik Group, the Mensheviks had acquired greater influence than the Bolsheviks in the trade unions.

In light of this development, Moscow Bolsheviks opposed the representation of trade unions in the Soviet along the lines already adopted in the capital. The reasons for Bolshevik resistance have been recounted by M. I. Vasil'ev-Iuzhin:

The Bolsheviks, at least Moscow [Bolsheviks], were not able to muster sufficient force for work in the trade unions. Naturally, we, the Bolsheviks, reacted with a certain caution to the representation of trade unions in the Soviet of Workers' Deputies; we feared the dominance of the Mensheviks in the soviets.[82]

Bolshevik objections resulted in the adoption of a compromise resolution that permitted the larger trade unions to elect deputies to the Soviet in addition to deputies already chosen in enterprise-level elections. Unions with more than five hundred members could send one deputy; unions with fewer than five hundred were entitled to send a deputy following a special review of their request.[83] A small number of unions took advantage of this provision, and among the 204 members of the Moscow Soviet were representatives of eight unions: printers, tailors, glovemakers, shoemakers, metalfitters in construction

---

[81]Schwarz, *The Russian Revolution*, pp. 339–354; Engelstein, *Moscow, 1905*, chap. 7; Kolokol'nikov, "Otryvki," *MIPDR*, 3:221.

[82]M. I. Vasil'ev-Iuzhin, *Moskovskii sovet rabochikh deputatov v 1905 g.* (Moscow, 1925), pp. 41–42.

[83]Ibid.

trades, engineers, commercial employees, and pharmacists.[84] As in the capital, the union of postal-telegraph employees was granted a consultative voice.

The Executive Committee of the Moscow Soviet, like its Petersburg counterpart, included leading trade union activists, although in contrast to procedures in the capital, trade unions were not directly represented in the executive organ. Here, each district soviet was entitled to two representatives, who were joined by two representatives from each of the major political groups: the Mensheviks, Bolsheviks, and Socialist Revolutionaries. Among the leaders of the Executive Committee of the Moscow Soviet were Kruglov and Chistov of the printers' union, and the Menshevik union organizers, Kolokol'nikov and Isuv.[85] Kolokol'nikov chaired the sessions of the Executive Committee.[86] Chistov, the president of the Moscow printers' union, chaired the opening session of the Soviet, and Kruglov, another leader of this union, chaired the second meeting.

Trade unions were not only involved in both the Petersburg and Moscow Soviets; they also provided a critical base of support for these organizations. The reasons for this have been described by Grinevich, who took a leading part in both the Petersburg Soviet and the trade union movement:

It must not be forgotten that the Soviet of Workers' Deputies, unceasingly expanding in the revolutionary atmosphere and broadening its functions, required some kind of organizational apparatus. It could not create its own on such short notice, and the Social Democratic party, as noted earlier, was not designed for such a broad sphere of activity. There remained only the trade unions. Although the preceding period had been difficult for them, they [the unions] had nonetheless succeeded in accomplishing something in the area of strengthening their organizations. Some of them already had their own headquarters and their own funds. At the head of the unions there already stood a group of individuals who were *known* to the mass of workers and who knew them, and there already existed *organizational discipline*. All of this was made available to the Soviet of Workers' Deputies.[87]

The printers' union, above all others, occupied a central place in the Petersburg Soviet. When the Soviet emerged in mid-October, the union of printers was well established and the most influential union in the capital, with a mem-

---

[84]*Obshcheprofessional'nye organy 1905–1907 gg.*, p. 121, n. 91; Kats and Milonov, eds., *1905*, pp. 315–316; S. Ainzaft, "Iz istorii professional'nogo dvizheniia Moskovskikh kozhevnikov v 1905–1907 gg.," *MIPDR*, 4:307.

[85]*Obshcheprofessional'nye organy 1905–1907 gg.*, p. 121, n. 91.

[86]Kolokol'nikov, "Otryvki," *MIPDR*, 3:221.

[87]Grinevich, "Ocherk," *Obrazovanie* 15, no. 9, pp. 232–233. Italics in the original.

bership of three thousand or about one out of five Petersburg printers. Meetings of the Soviet's Executive Committee took place at the union's headquarters, and the union arranged for publication of the Soviet's newspaper, *Izvestiia Soveta rabochikh deputatov,* which had a press run of thirty thousand by November 7. When, on October 20, the Soviet adopted a resolution inaugurating a campaign against government censorship, this important effort was undertaken jointly with the printers' union.[88]

In late October, the Petersburg Soviet launched a struggle to introduce an eight-hour workday. This campaign, which was taken up by metalworkers and other groups in the capital, became a major focus for the Soviet's activities during the month of November. At the same time, the Soviet urged workers to form unions, and in mid-November it endorsed a plan for an all-Russian congress of workers' organizations.[89] To some extent, the Soviet itself performed the functions of a trade union organization, a situation noted by Nosar':

Serving the working masses on the basis of everyday needs, the Soviet replaced trade union organizations. The Soviet was at one and the same time a trade confederation of all Petersburg workers and a central bureau of trade unions. The Soviet not only called upon the working masses to organize militant trade unions. The Soviet itself organized them.[90]

The Petersburg Soviet remained active until December 3, when the government arrested the Executive Committee and several hundred deputies. It was reconstituted almost immediately, but the second Soviet never really functioned, and on December 19 it was abandoned.

The Moscow Soviet, by contrast, existed for only a few weeks; its final session was held on December 6. During this brief period it could do little more than attempt to control and direct the strike movement. On the day of its formation, November 21, the Soviet issued a proclamation calling on workers to conduct strikes only when conditions in a given firm were significantly worse than in comparable enterprises, or when an employer violated rights that a factory committee had already won, such as the right to assemble in the factory.[91] The latter point illustrates the importance workers attached to the institution of factory representation, which had only recently been introduced into many Moscow firms. In its November 21 proclamation, the Soviet also called upon workers to concentrate on the building of trade unions.[92]

---

[88]Sidorov, ed., *1905 god v Peterburge,* p. 14.
[89]Anweiler, *The Soviets,* p. 55.
[90]Nosar', "Istoriia," in *Istoriia soveta,* p. 148.
[91]Vasil'ev-Iuzhin, *Moskovskii sovet,* pp. 36–37.
[92]Engelstein, *Moscow, 1905,* p. 168.

Following the formation of the Moscow Soviet, a number of unions in the city—including the large printers' union—adopted resolutions subordinating their actions to the decisions of the Soviet.[93] And with the announcement of a general strike on December 6, many unions declared their solidarity with the Soviet and participated in the insurrection. Among the most active unions during the uprising were the organizations of printers, tailors, shoemakers, bakers, pursemakers, and salesclerks.[94] Armed militia *(druzhiny)* were formed under the auspices of some unions, such as the bakers and printers.[95] The bakers' union, which by December included nearly one-fifth of the labor force in this trade, instructed bakery workers to comply with orders from the Soviet to prepare only black bread during the strike.[96] Writing about the Moscow Soviet, a former activist observed:

It is completely clear that the unions not only participated in the elections to the [Moscow] Soviet of Workers' Deputies, but were the periphery on which the Soviet relied in its actions. When the Soviet of Workers' Deputies began to prepare for the forthcoming general strike, which was to turn into an armed uprising, many unions began to collect money for purchasing arms; some unions began to organize military detachments.[97]

Trade unions and the soviets were thus closely interconnected in 1905. The unions furnished an organizational foundation for the soviets and participated in major campaigns and mass actions directed by these assemblies. The Petersburg Soviet ventured into the area of labor-management relations and even performed some proto-union functions. In both cities, the soviets encouraged the formation of trade unions, and trade unions, in turn, gave support to the soviets. A sharp distinction cannot be drawn, therefore, between the soviets and the trade unions, ascribing militant political activities to the former while relegating the latter to purely economic struggles. In reality, the leadership and the activities of trade unions and the soviets overlapped, and these two organizations cooperated on more than one occasion in the closing weeks of the revolution.

Trade unionists participated in the soviets, where they were accorded formal

[93]Kolokol'nikov and Rapoport, eds., *1905-1907 gg.*, p. 271.

[94]Dmitriev [Kolokol'nikov], *Professional'nye soiuzy*, p. 36.

[95]*Professional'noe dvizhenie Moskovskikh pishchevikov*, p. 113; V. Sher, "Moskovskie pechatniki," in *Moskovskie pechatniki v 1905 godu*, ed. A. Borshchevskii, S. Reshetov, and N. Chistov, (Moscow, 1925), pp. 72–85.

[96]*Professional'noe dvizhenie Moskovskikh pishchevikov*, p. 113.

[97]S. Ainzaft, "Professional'noe dvizhenie v 1905 godu," in *Moskovskoe professional'noe dvizhenie v gody pervoi revoliutsii*, ed. Iu. Milonov (Moscow, [1925]), p. 211.

representation and figured prominently in the leadership. Their presence in these assemblies illustrates the simultaneous development during the revolution of craft consciousness and class consciousness. Groups that were actively involved in the formation of craft unions, such as the printers, or who manifested a strong sense of factory patriotism, such as the metalworkers, also took part in the soviet, a class-based association which spoke on behalf of all workers in the city. The worker-deputies to both the St. Petersburg and the Moscow Soviet, moreover, were drawn from the same stratum of skilled labor that gravitated to trade unions and to factory committees. Whereas in one organizational context these workers displayed discrete and localized allegiances, in another they identified with the working class as a broader entity. Thus, in contrast to many Western European countries in the nineteenth century, where craft and class consciousness developed sequentially among workers, these phenomena appeared concurrently in Russia during 1905. This was yet another case of the telescoping of developments so characteristic of all aspects of the Russian labor movement.

The simultaneous emergence of craft and class consciousness was the result of the unique conjuncture of events during 1905. The first independent mass-based labor organizations in St. Petersburg and Moscow arose in the midst of a major revolutionary upheaval that sharpened and intensified social and political conflicts, accentuating the workers' awareness of their common plight in Russian society. Whereas the urge to unite in factory committees and trade unions was rooted in a strong disposition toward localism and craft particularism, experiences acquired in the process of struggle during the revolution generated among workers a class conception of solidarity. Progress in this direction was greatly accelerated by the extensive penetration of radical activists—many of them intellectuals—into the workers' milieu.

THE CENTRAL BUREAUS OF TRADE UNIONS

The Central Bureaus of Trade Unions, created in the summer and fall of 1905, provided intelligentsia organizers with another important vehicle for transmitting their influence to the fledgling labor movement. The Central Bureaus, like the soviets, were conceived as class-based associations. Uniting all of the city's organized workers, the Central Bureaus further extended the contact between political activists and unionizing groups during the final weeks of the revolution.

Many circumstances contributed to the formation of the Central Bureaus. The increased tempo of the union movement made it urgent to create some kind of informational and coordinating center for widely dispersed groups of unionizing workers. Intelligentsia activists familiar with Western European labor movements, moreover, were eager to implant a unifying organ in Russian soil.[98]

The Bureaus began to take form in the early fall. The initiative came from Evdokimov, who at the time represented the Kharkov Society for Mutual Assistance to Workers Engaged in Artisanal Labor. Established in 1898, the Kharkov Society conceived the idea of convening an all-Russian congress of mutual aid societies in 1902, but it was not until 1905 that conditions were propitious for carrying out the project. As a preliminary organizational step, Evdokimov held meetings of trade unionists in the capital in the summer and fall and in Moscow on September 24 and October 1. These gatherings, attended by a small group of leading labor activists in each city, many of them intelligentsia organizers, laid the groundwork for the Central Bureaus.

On October 6–7, trade unionists from Moscow, St. Petersburg, and several other cities met in Moscow for the First All-Russian Conference of Trade Unions.[99] No more than one-half of the thirty-two participants were actual workers, some of them representing unions-in-formation or merely an initiative group. The remainder were intelligentsia activists who had become involved in the growing labor movement.[100] Two major decisions came out of the conference. First, there was agreement on a plan to prepare for a national congress of workers' organizations in December 1905. A second resolution called for the establishment of central bureaus of trade unions in each city. Circumstances intervened in December 1905 to delay the congress, however, and subsequent obstacles prevented it from taking place in the years that followed. A second all-Russian conference of trade unions was held in February 1906, but a full-scale national congress of trade unions had to await the February Revolution. By contrast, the Central Bureaus began to function in the final months of 1905, and they remained on the labor scene during the ensuing decade.

Like the soviets, the Central Bureaus of Trade Unions relied upon a mixed basis for representation. Whereas trade and industrial organizations provided the backbone for the Bureaus, there were also representatives of factory committees,

[98]V. Grinevich, *Professional'noe dvizhenie rabochikh v Rossii* (St. Petersburg, 1908), pp. 51–52.

[99]A comprehensive report on these meetings can be found in Kolokol'nikov and Rapoport, eds., *1905–1907 gg.*, pp. 179–182. Some accounts consider the Moscow meetings of September 24 and October 1 part of the First All-Russian Conference.

[100]Ibid., pp. 161–172. The participants included V. V. Sher, P. N. Kolokol'nikov, I. Kruglov, N. I. Chistov, I. A. Isuv, M. G. Lunts, Stanislav Vol'skii, I. A. Gornostaev, A. A. Evdokimov, S. N. Prokopovich, G. S. Nosar', and others.

particularly from the metalworking industry, where enterprise-level organizations were exceptionally strong and trade unions had not yet been established. The Bureau in each city consisted of representatives from "proletarian unions," a term that was broadly applied to encompass such groups as office clerks and bookkeepers, municipal workers, and pharmacists. In the capital city, where only unions with fifty or more members were eligible for representation in the Central Bureau, a total of thirty-five organizations participated between November 9 and the end of December 1905.[101] The Moscow Central Bureau had no comparable membership requirement, and here forty-two workers' associations were represented.[102]

The Central Bureaus in both cities made important contributions to the organized labor movement in the final months of the revolution. Above all, they provided practical guidance and assistance to unionizing groups. Each Bureau held daily consultation hours open to all workers seeking guidance in establishing a union.[103] In some cases, such as the metal and textile workers in both cities, the Central Bureau helped to initiate the formation of a union. The Bureaus furnished legal assistance and published the first general trade-union newspapers.[104]

Intelligentsia activists figured prominently in the Central Bureaus. Menshevik *praktiki* dominated these organizations in both cities, but there were also representatives of the Bolshevik faction, the Socialist Revolutionaries, and the Union of Liberation. The leadership included Somov, Grinevich, Riazanov, and Sviatlovskii in the capital, and Kolokol'nikov and Evdokimov in Moscow.[105] Labor leaders with syndicalist leanings, such as Somov and Evdokimov, advocated a leadership role for the Bureaus, envisioning them as a directing force in the workers' movement.[106] But the majority rejected this proposal, designating

---

[101]See Kats and Milonov, eds., *1905*, p. 290, for a list of unions and factory committee representatives in the Petersburg Central Bureau of Trade Unions.

[102]See *Obshcheprofessional'nye organy 1905-1907 gg.*, pp. 66–67, for a list of participating organizations in the Moscow Central Bureau of Trade Unions.

[103]Dmitriev [Kolokol'nikov], *Professional'nyi soiuz*, p. 6. For other reports on the activities of the Central Bureaus, see *Professional'nyi soiuz*, no. 1 (November 27, 1905), pp. 3–4; S. P. Tiurin, *Moskovskoe tsentral'noe biuro professional'nykh soiuzov* (Moscow, 1913), p. 21.

[104]*Obshcheprofessional'nye organy 1905-1907 gg.*, p. 129, n. 117, for an account of the legal assistance offered by the Central Bureaus. The Petersburg Bureau published *Professional'nyi soiuz*, and the Moscow Bureau published the *Biulleten' muzeia sodeistviia trudu*.

[105]Kats and Milonov, eds., *1905*, p. 291; *Obshcheprofessional'nye organy 1905-1907 gg.*, p. 101, n. 11.

[106]*Novaia zhizn'*, no. 18 (November 20, 1905), p. 3; *Obshcheprofessional'nye organy 1905-1907 gg.*, p. 95, n. 5; *Vtoraia konferentsiia professional'nykh soiuzov: Doklady i protokoly* (St. Petersburg, 1906), p. 50.

the Bureaus as consultative and coordinating organs, a position advocated by both factions of the RSDRP.

Although the Central Bureaus refrained from taking a leadership role, they did attempt to guide trade unions in resolving key issues relating to union-party relations, craft versus industrial unionism, labor-management conflicts, and the provision of mutual aid.[107] They endorsed a policy of union neutrality and organizational independence from political parties; they propagated the idea of industrial unionism among workers whose repeated inclination was for a craft-based union; they helped to disseminate new methods and concepts in the area of labor-management relations, and they discouraged unions from engaging in mutual-aid activities apart from strike and unemployment funds.[108] In all of these areas, the Central Bureaus helped to shape the direction of the incipient labor movement and to spread the influence of left-wing political parties and groups.

TRADE UNIONS AND LABOR-MANAGEMENT RELATIONS

Radical activists helped to politicize the incipient trade union movement and to broaden the workers' class perspective. These efforts enjoyed considerable success because they proceeded within the larger context of a revolutionary situation. But trade unions were, above all, designed to assist workers in their struggle for improved conditions at the workplace. Many workers had only a vague and confused conception of the character and functions of the newly established unions, and they flocked to union meetings "to pour out their grief, to lighten their spirit from the weight of an accumulation, over decades, of oppression and lack of rights."[109]

Notwithstanding the heightened political atmosphere in October, November, and early December, workers never lost sight of their grievances and miseries at the place of employment, and at union meetings they rose to express these sentiments:

Alongside calls for an armed uprising, alongside brilliant speeches on the bright future of socialism, you could hear the simple and naive speeches of the tailor-waistcoatmaker who saw a solution [to his plight] in a fifty-kopeck increase in the [piecework] wage for each waistcoat. And this was not the naiveté of the individual tailor-waistcoatmaker. It must not be forgotten that tens of thousands of workers attended meetings, and until

[107]Grinevich, *Professional'noe dvizhenie*, p. 55.
[108]On the latter point, see Grinevich, "Ocherk," *Obrazovanie* 15, no. 8, p. 225.
[109]Kats and Milonov, eds., *1905*, p. 193.

that time, the majority of them still had never heard a free revolutionary word. And if they responded rapturously to speeches about political freedom, about the victory of socialism, it was because the mass of workers *felt* in [these ideas] something new, bright. But speeches about the economic oppression of capital, about the frightful conditions of labor, were for them much more accessible and comprehensible.[110]

The trade unions provided a new public forum where workers could find comfort by sharing their anger and frustrations. The unions were no less important, however, in shaping workers' attitudes toward employers and in popularizing new conceptions of labor-management relations.

The appearance of collective labor associations—beginning with the factory committees in early 1905 and culminating in the formation of unions—altered the terms and relations of struggle between workers and employers. Confronted by the new collective associations among workers, employers proceeded to establish their own associations to meet the challenge of organized labor. The Kokovtsov Commission, which became active in February, accelerated employers' efforts to present effective and unified opposition to the far-reaching legislative changes contemplated in government circles.[111]

By the end of the year, industrialists in both cities had taken steps to create new organizations whose principal purpose was to deal more effectively with labor problems. The Society of Factory Owners in the Central Industrial Region was established in October 1905. Foundations for a similar organization were laid in the capital in the second half of 1905, but the Petersburg Society of Factory Owners was not formally founded until early 1906. Printing firm owners also established associations: the Petersburg Society of Printing Firm Owners (October) and the Moscow Society of Owners of Typographical-Lithographical Firms (November).[112]

The framework for labor-management relations was fundamentally transformed in the course of 1905 by the advent of collective associations among both parties to industrial disputes. At the same time, workers attempted to introduce new methods and procedures for handling labor-management relations. Some of these ideas had already been raised earlier in the year by the factory committee movement, and some even predated the revolution. During the closing months of 1905, trade unions became the major vehicle for developing and disseminating innovative concepts to settle workplace conflicts and to achieve improved contractual terms for workers.

[110]*Vtoraia konferentsiia professional'nykh soiuzov,* p. 38–39. Italics in the original.
[111]V. Ia. Laverychev, *Tsarizm i rabochii vopros v Rossii 1861–1917 gg.* (Moscow, 1972), p. 198.
[112]See below, chapter 7.

7. Factory Committee at the Baltiiskii shipbuilding plant in St. Petersburg in 1905.

8. Participants in the First All-Russian Conference of Trade Unions held in Moscow on September 24 (date shown in photo is a misprint) and October 1, 6, and 7, 1905: (1) N. K. Murav'ev; (2) N. I. Chistov; (3) V. V. Sher; (4) Nechaev; (5) M. G. Gordeev; (6) S. I. Bychkov; (7) V. M. Akimov; (8) K. V. Parfinenko; (9) P. N. Kolokol'nikov; (10) M. G. Lunts; (11) A. A. Evdokimov; (12) I. Z. Zheludkov; (13) S. N. Prokopovich; (14) G. S. Khrustalev- Nosar'; (15) V. I. Shimborskii; (16) A. A. Iavorskii; (17) N. N. Kuznetzov.

9. Participants in the Second All-Russian Conference of Trade Unions held in Moscow, February 24–28, 1906: (1) V. Grinevich; (2) A. A. Evdokimov; (3) A. Litvak-Gel'fand; (4) P. N. Kolokol'nikov; (5) D. B. Riazanov; (6) V. V. Sviatlovskii; (7) A. S. Orlov [Kruglov]; (8) V. Grosser; (9) A. Bovshovskii; (10) A. A. Belozerov; (11) F. I. Ozol; (12) V. M. Turbin; (13) G. I. Lur'e.

10. Aleksandr Osipovich Iatsynevich, a metalfitter at the Odner plant, served as president of the St. Petersburg metalworkers' union from 1906 to 1910.

11. V. P. Nogin, the leading Bolshevik union organizer in Moscow in 1906–1907.

Demands for permanent factory and shop committees and their control over key decisions of factory life were included in numerous union charters and other union documents during the fall of 1905, evidence of the continuing importance workers attached to these issues.[113] The statutes of the Petersburg textile workers' union illustrate the contemporary formulation of this demand, calling for "the introduction of a commission elected by the workers themselves to establish the daily wage in different shops" and "the establishment in each shop of a separate commission, composed of workers, to *control* hiring and firing."[114]

Similar provisions were incorporated into the charter of the Moscow tobacco workers' union, which demanded

employer recognition of [workers'] deputies, without whose agreement no one can be fired or hired, and whose participation is required for setting all wage rates, conditions of employment and rules of internal [factory] order.[115]

Whereas earlier in the year the demand for worker involvement in key decisions of factory life had been put forward mainly by metal and textile workers in the two cities, during the fall it was adopted by a wide variety of groups. The most elaborate proposal for factory deputies was drawn up by the Moscow printers' union. The union's "Regulations on Factory Deputies," prepared in early November for submission to the newly founded organization of printing firm owners, set forth a detailed system of factory representation.[116] According to the conditions set forth in the Regulations, any worker eighteen years or older was eligible to serve as a deputy or to participate in the election. The term of service was one year, and employers were enjoined from firing deputies before the expiration of their term.

Deputies were to perform a variety of functions in the individual enterprise. Most important, they were authorized to handle *all* relations between workers and the administration, and to exert control over decisions concerning hiring

[113]For examples, see *Obshcheprofessional'nye organy 1905–1907 gg.*, pp. 45, 46, 47, 54, 55, 87, 91, concerning such varied groups as Moscow marbleworkers, Petersburg glassmakers, railroad, metal-, and woodworkers.

[114]*Professional'nyi soiuz*, no. 2 (December 4, 1905), p. 5. These points are numbers 3 and 15, respectively, in the union charter. Italics mine.

[115]*Obshcheprofessional'nye organy 1905–1907 gg.*, p. 25. Similar provisions appear in charters drawn up by Petersburg workers. See, for example, the charter prepared by metalworkers under the leadership of the Nevskii plant Council of Elders, Ibid., pp. 20–21.

[116]Ibid., pp. 83–84; V. V. Sher, *Istoriia professional'nogo dvizheniia rabochikh pechatnogo dela v Moskve* (Moscow, 1911), pp. 198–211. According to the provisions of the Regulations, there was to be one deputy for every fifty workers and one deputy in enterprises with fewer than fifty workers.

and firing. Apart from those provisions, which were already commonplace in the factory committee movement, the printers' union added several new ones, such as the deputies' right to determine the number of apprentices admitted to each shop and enterprise. This demand, as noted in chapter 3, was put forward by other unions of artisanal or highly skilled workers in 1905, and can be considered part of an attempt to halt the deterioration of skill requirements and to protect the exclusiveness of their trades.

Two other provisions in the Regulations gave factory deputies the responsibility for "maintaining internal order in the factory and for all the misdeeds of their comrades" and "for the unwavering fulfillment of all factory rules, regulations, prior agreements, both on the part of the administration and on the part of the workers."[117] Deputies were charged not only with representing workers collectively and supervising hiring, firing, and the engagement of apprentices; they were also expected to act as an enforcement agency to ensure worker compliance with the rules of internal factory order in such matters as lateness, thefts, and drunkenness.

It was indicative of the still underdeveloped state of the organized labor movement in 1905 that the printers' Regulations failed to specify the relationship between factory deputies and the trade union. Apart from a general provision requiring deputies to serve as a liaison between workers at the enterprise level and other labor organizations,[118] the Regulations did not address this issue. One year later, unions would devote considerable attention to this problem, but in 1905 the nascent organizations did not yet draw a clear line of authority between factory deputies, with their proto-union functions, and the trade union itself.

As early as January 1905, workers had called for another innovative measure in labor-management relations: the resolution of conflicts by means of a board of arbitration *(treteiskii sud)* or a joint worker-employer conciliation board *(primiritel'naia kamara)*. Originally the demand had been formulated mainly by metalworkers, but by the end of 1905 it was incorporated into the union charters of highly diverse unionizing groups. Petersburg unions of gold-silversmiths, draftsmen, rubber workers, gardeners, and textile workers included it in their founding statutes, as did the Moscow printers, office clerks and accountants, sales-clerical workers, municipal workers, and metalfitters in construction

---

[117]*Obshcheprofessional'nye organy 1905-1907 gg.*, pp. 83–84, points 9–13, 15, 19 in the Regulations.
[118]Ibid., pp. 83–84, point 19.

trades.[119] Still other unions in both cities raised this demand in strikes or in their programs.[120]

The concepts of arbitration and conciliation boards were almost certainly unfamiliar to most workers at the beginning of 1905. Such boards were mentioned in the 1903 Social Democratic party program, and in the program of the Union of Liberation adopted in March 1905.[121] The spread of the idea to broad and variegated segments of the Petersburg and Moscow working class by the end of 1905 took place mainly through the medium of the trade unions. Intelligentsia activists in the unions popularized the idea, which appealed to workers who were eager to find ways of increasing their own participation in workplace decisions.

Workers envisioned arbitration and conciliation boards as functioning only on the enterprise level. With a few notable exceptions, such as the Petersburg printers, they did not yet conceive of the application of these institutions to the resolution of disputes involving workers in an entire industry, occupation, or trade. Thus, the Petersburg textile workers' union charter called for "the establishment of boards with an equal number of workers and representatives of the [factory] administration to settle disputes."[122]

In a few cases, these procedures were actually put into practice by workers and employers. A dispute in Petersburg binderies was submitted in late November to a conciliation board composed of an equal number of representatives of employers and the Petersburg union of printers.[123] Arbitration was utilized by the Moscow union of bookstore clerks to settle a conflict that arose at the Putilov bookstore.[124]

Implicit in union proposals for permanent factory deputies and for arbitration and conciliation boards was the notion that workers should deal with their employers not as individuals but as a collectivity. For most workers this was a

---

[119]Ibid., pp. 19, 20, 22, 54, 55, 87, 91; *Professional'nyi soiuz,* no. 2 (December 4, 1905), pp. 5, 7, 8.

[120]Unions where this issue was raised in a context other than the founding charter were the Petersburg tailors, waiters, and tavern employees; the Moscow unions of waiters, beer-hall employees, and bakers. *Obshcheprofessional'nye organy 1905–1907 gg.,* pp. 50, 51, 38, 39; *Professional'nyi soiuz,* no. 2 (December 4, 1905), pp. 11, 12.

[121]Sidney Harcave, *The Russian Revolution of 1905,* pp. 267, 278. On arbitration, see above chapter 3, note 10.

[122]*Professional'nyi soiuz,* no. 2 (December 4, 1905), p. 5; see *Obshcheprofessional'nye organy 1905–1907 gg.,* pp. 20–22, for other examples.

[123]*Novaia zhizn',* no. 27 (December 2, 1905), p. 3.

[124]*Obshcheprofessional'nye organy 1905–1907 gg.,* p. 111, n. 36.

new concept in 1905. Collective bargaining did not yet exist in St. Petersburg or Moscow before the revolution, although on a few occasions—such as the weavers' strike at the Moscow Gujon and Mussi mills in 1902—demands for collective bargaining had already been advanced.[125] But collective bargaining remained an impossibility in Russia as long as workers' organizations had neither legal status nor recognition from employers. The trade unions that arose in 1905 helped to popularize among workers the still-unfamiliar concepts of collective bargaining and the collective labor contract.

The Petersburg typesetters were the first to engage in collective bargaining and to demand an industry-wide collective contract, the so-called *tarif,* standardizing wage rates throughout the capital's printing trades. This campaign, initiated by workers even before January 9, preceded the formation of the union. Employers conducted negotiations with the typesetters, but a settlement was never reached.[126] In addition, the unions of the Moscow printers, electricians, and beerhall employees attempted to engage in collective bargaining with employers during 1905.[127] These efforts seldom succeeded, however, and when they did, employers repudiated the agreement after December.

A number of unions also demanded that employers accord workers "polite treatment."[128] This issue, which had first arisen at the outset of the revolution as part of the factory committee movement, was a key element in the workers' struggle to attain the position and respect to which they felt they were entitled. It was one aspect of a broader struggle waged by workers in 1905 to upgrade their status and to achieve respectability at the workplace and in the society at large.

The revolution of 1905 inaugurated a new era in labor-management relations. Henceforth, workers raised claims not only for improved wages, hours, and working conditions, but also for collective representation, collective bargaining, and the institutionalization of grievance procedures. Although the workers' accomplishments in the latter areas were still modest at the end of 1905, they had the satisfaction of achieving employer recognition of their representatives in many factory enterprises. "Factory and mill owners had reconciled themselves to

---

[125]See above, chapter 2.

[126]Vasil'ev-Severianin, "Tarifnaia bor'ba," *MIPDP,* pp. 157–160.

[127]*Obshcheprofessional'nye organy 1905-1907 gg.,* p. 121, n. 91; Dmitriev [Kolokol'nikov], *Professional'nye soiuzy,* p. 24.

[128]These demands were put forward by many groups of organized workers, including the Moscow unions of sales-clerical workers, beer-hall employees, household servants, and metalfitters in construction, as well as the Petersburg union of tavern employees. *Obshcheprofessional'nye organy 1905-1907 gg.,* pp. 19, 39–40, 45–47, 51–52; *Professional'nyi soiuz,* no. 2 (December 4, 1905), p. 11.

factory representation," as Kolokol'nikov put it, "but they attempted to narrow its functions."[129] Employer recognition of trade unions, an issue with more far-reaching implications, did not become a major point of contention in industrial relations until 1906–1907.

Employers reluctantly recognized factory committees, but they were far less amenable to demands for the institutionalization of grievance procedures. Notwithstanding some statements to the contrary,[130] industrialists in the major branches of industry—with the notable exception of printing firm owners—refused to cooperate with workers during 1905 in setting up arbitration or conciliation boards, and they emphatically rejected demands for worker control over hiring, firing, apprenticeship, and wage rates.

Workers proved more successful in their endeavor to achieve material improvements. Impressive gains in wages and hours were registered by groups that had never before mounted a coordinated struggle, such as the Moscow bakers.[131] At the end of the year, many workers were laboring for shorter hours at higher wages than at the outset of the revolution. In the important Petersburg metalworking industry, the workday in many plants was reduced to ten hours (many had formerly had an eleven or eleven-and-one-half-hour workday), and some state-operated firms even instituted a nine-hour workday.[132] Nominal wages also increased for metalworkers in the capital by an average of 27 percent.[133] Tangible gains were made by many different groups in the Petersburg and Moscow labor force, giving them a growing appreciation of "their role and their proportional weight, as a mass, in the economic life of the country."[134]

In the course of 1905, Petersburg and Moscow workers acquired a new sense of their collective strength and began to develop new ways of viewing themselves and their relationship to employers and the state. The events of Bloody

---

[129]Kolokol'nikov, "Otryvki," *MIPDR*, 3:223.

[130]For example, Petersburg industrialists in the metalworking industry declared a willingness during 1905 "to take measures to resolve conflicts peacefully by agreement or arbitration," and to establish conciliation boards to work out standard wage rates and conditions of labor. These statements appear in the draft charter drawn up by industrialists for an organization of employers in the metalworking industry. TsGIA, f. 150, op. 1, d. 3, pp. 18, 50.

[131]*Professional'noe dvizhenie Moskovskikh pishchevikov*, pp. 105–107.

[132]Buzinov, *Za Nevskoi zastavoi*, p. 65; Gerald Dennis Surh, "Petersburg Workers in 1905: Strikes, Workplace Democracy, and the Revolution," Ph.D. dissertation, University of California, Berkeley, 1979, pp. 23–24.

[133]F. A. Bulkin, *Na zare profdvizheniia* (Moscow and Leningrad, 1924), pp. 113–114.

[134]Buzinov, *Za Nevskoi zastavoi*, p. 65.

Sunday and the government's failure to enact labor reforms prior to October induced many—perhaps most—workers to relinquish their faith in the beneficent paternalism of the Tsar. The break with paternalism was critical because it led workers to focus instead on their own collective efforts to win improvements in their lives. Whereas a petition to the Tsar mobilized workers in early January, over the ensuing ten months workers increasingly turned their energy and attention to the creation of independent labor organizations—factory committees, trade unions, and soviets.

Skilled workers were exceptionally active in every form of labor association during the revolution. Above all, their disposition for labor activism was connected to their placement in the urban work force and to their individual attributes. Skilled workers in Petersburg and Moscow were generally literate and urbanized, and they had acquired a social identity as urban "workers" and a sense of their relative status and self-worth, attributes that equipped them—psychologically and otherwise—to participate in the burgeoning labor movement.

Skilled workers were inclined to find sources of solidarity with others sharing an occupational specialization or, in some cases, employment in a particular firm. Craft consciousness—*tsekhovshchina*—and factory patriotism provided the two most important bases for unification in labor organizations during 1905. Craft allegiances were widespread, not only among artisanal workers, where this mentality might be expected, but also among other groups in all sectors of the urban economy.

A distinctive feature of 1905, however, was the simultaneous emergence of class consciousness and craft consciousness, whereas in Western Europe they developed sequentially. The Soviets of Workers' Deputies and the Central Bureaus of Trade Unions were both class-based institutions, and they elicited support from many of the same groups that displayed a strong propensity for craft unionism and factory patriotism.

The synchronous development of craft and class consciousness was not the only instance of a telescoping of stages in 1905. A similar pattern can be discerned in workers' claims at the workplace and in society at large. In the area of labor-management relations, workers advanced demands for collective representation and the institutionalization of procedures for resolving workplace disputes. These demands, typical of incipient labor movements in Western Europe, were combined in 1905 with far-reaching claims for worker control over key decisions of factory life. In the political sphere as well, workers' demands for citizenship and civil liberties coincided during the revolution with a radical vision of the workers' role in political life which found expression in the soviets—the exclusively working-class assemblies that functioned briefly in the closing weeks of the revolution.

How can we explain the appearance of this bold and audacious vision of worker control? These claims were shaped by a complex combination of circumstances, some of them predating the revolution and others concurrent with it. At the outset of 1905, workers raised the issue of control at the workplace. It took both the spread of a broadly based antiautocratic movement and the extensive penetration of radical activists in the workers' milieu to extend this vision beyond the confines of the factory or workshop to the society and polity as a whole. Underlying this demand was a diametric reversal of the position to which workers felt themselves consigned in tsarist Russia. Their painful and degrading situation, their lack of participatory power and elementary rights, became transformed into its opposite image. Reacting against the hardships and depredations to which they are subjected, workers sought extensive new powers at the workplace, which would have reversed past inequities and stripped employers of some of their most basic prerogatives.

I have emphasized the involvement of radical activists—particularly Social Democrats—in the trade unions and their extensive contact with rank-and-file workers through the medium of these organizations. To a greater extent than any other party or group, the Social Democrats succeeded in utilizing the unions as a means of exposing workers to an alternative ideology and conveying to them new ideas and concepts of organization.

In their contacts with workers at union meetings and elsewhere, Social Democrats emphasized the themes of proletarian solidarity and class struggle. The dissemination of these ideas gave shape to the vague and often amorphous inclinations of workers, providing for the first time a specific set of guidelines for defining social and political relationships and goals. By all accounts, the workers involved in trade unions and the soviets received these ideas with eagerness and often with approbation, although it took years for the full effects of these important encounters to make themselves felt in the workers' movement.

The interaction between workers and their radical mentors was more complex and more reciprocal than historians have generally portrayed. Workers had their own conceptions and priorities, and in some areas they led the way for Social Democratic activists and forced party *praktiki* to make significant tactical adjustments. The factory committee movement at the beginning of 1905 arose mainly on the initiative of the workers themselves, as did some of the earliest trade unions among printers, tailors, shoemakers, and others. Radical activists, at least initially, were drawn to the trade unions because these organizations had become important to the workers they sought to reach. Social Democrats and other intelligentsia labor organizers helped to shape the direction of the incipient union movement, but they could not overcome—at least at this stage—the workers' repeated preference for craft unionism, a situation that would persist in the years that followed.

There was considerable diversity in workers' attitudes and aspirations at the end of this revolutionary year as there had been at the beginning. The conventional dichotomies between class and craft consciousness, or political and economic demands, cannot do justice to the complex combination of issues and perspectives in the workers' movement. Nor is it possible to classify the workers' outlook as exclusively "revolutionary" or "reformist" during these months. As we have seen, many metalworkers called for an overthrow of the autocratic system, but they were also the first and most persistent advocates of institutionalized methods for dealing with labor-management relations. Whereas in one context workers demanded fundamental and far-reaching political changes, in another they sought improvements through a modification of the existing arrangements. It is significant that both of these aspects of the workers' movement emerged during the revolutionary upheavals of 1905, and that they were conflated precisely at a time of major social unrest. These quite different but complementary aspects of the workers' mentality would remain important in the organized labor movement during the years to come.

For workers whose lives were touched by the organizations that emerged in 1905—and many thousands were directly affected—the experience was often transformative. Never before did they have an opportunity to create their own autonomous labor associations for the purpose of defending and asserting their rights. This experience made a profound impression, giving workers a feeling of pride and dignity and a sense of their own power, which was heightened, no doubt, by employer concessions in industrial disputes and the Tsar's partial capitulation on October 17. Even the severe wave of government repression that followed the abortive Moscow insurrection in December did not erase the new awareness among workers that they could, through their own collective efforts, bring about real changes in their lives. In the spring of 1906, workers resumed these efforts in the new era of legal labor organization.

Part Three

The Era of Legal Labor Organization, 1906–1911

Chapter 5

The Emergence of a Legal Trade Union Movement, 1906–1907

> Without a trade union, we are tobacco dust and nothing
> more. With a union we are strong; with it, we will
> struggle for a better, happier destiny.
>
> Golos tabachnika [*Voice of the*
> *Tobacco Worker*][1]

On March 4, 1906, the government issued the "Temporary Regulations on Unions and Societies," legalizing trade unions and employers' associations for the first time.[2] Over the next fifteen months, until the Stolypin "coup d'état" of June 3, 1907, trade unions developed with exceptional rapidity in St. Petersburg and Moscow. Two important circumstances affected their progress. First, notwithstanding the stern measures adopted in the wake of the December uprising, the government did not fully reconstitute its former powers until mid-1907. During the intervening months, the regime's coercive apparatus and interventionist policies remained markedly attenuated, and even the increasingly severe

---

[1] *Golos tabachnika,* no. 1 (December 21, 1906), p. 2.

[2] The law of March 4, 1906, abrogated earlier criminal statutes outlawing worker combinations. The law of July 1, 1874, established penalties for the illegal association of workers, adding this to the list of proscribed activities already specified in earlier statutes of 1866 and 1868. *Polnoe sobranie zakonov Rossiiskoi imperii s 1649 goda* (St. Petersburg, 1830–1916), sobranie 2, vol. 49:1 (1874). A subsequent law of March 22, 1903, established criminal penalties for attempting to form trade unions or participating in them. I. I. Shelymagin, *Zakonodatel'stvo o fabrichno-zavodskom trude v Rossii 1900–1917* (Moscow, 1952), p. 183.

194

policies imposed from late 1906 on did not prevent most unions from actively conducting their affairs.

A second major circumstance affecting trade unions was the relative weakness of employer associations, which were not yet in a position to erect the formidable obstacles to organized labor they later imposed. Reacting sharply to the rapid and impressive organizational achievement of workers, employers also formed collective associations under the terms of the March 1906 law. But employers were sometimes disunited, and they did not always succeed in mounting coordinated opposition to labor. During this fifteen-month period, the two adversaries in labor management relations stood on a more nearly equal footing than at any other time in the tsarist era. Neither employers nor government authorities were in a position to deploy their customary resistance to the workers' movement—a situation that afforded labor a temporary opportunity to achieve substantial gains through organized struggle.

Although these conditions existed only briefly, they created important new historical possibilities in tsarist Russia. For the first and last time under the *ancien régime*, the political climate made it possible for organized workers to introduce new methods for handling workplace disputes. In a country where labor-management conflicts had become a major threat to social stability, the creation of a mass legal labor movement opened up alternative solutions to industrial conflict—solutions that might have taken Russia along a path similar to that of Imperial Germany after 1890, when legal trade unions gained recognition and secured incremental improvements that helped to reconcile workers to nonrevolutionary methods of struggle. Trade unions, above all, illustrate the potential for a peaceful resolution of labor problems in tsarist Russia during 1906–1907 and the obstacles that made this impossible.

THE LAW OF MARCH 4, 1906

The fragile antiautocratic alliance that extracted constitutional reforms in October 1905 collapsed on the Moscow barricades in December, when the government suppressed the insurrection, and with it the soviets, trade unions, mass meetings, strikes, and demonstrations that had animated the country during the "days of freedom." By January 1906 the workers' movement had fallen into disarray.

Petersburg and Moscow workers marked time during the early months of 1906, still hoping for a resurgence of the revolutionary momentum that had been abruptly interrupted in December. But their mood had changed. No longer as militant and audacious as in the weeks following the October Manifesto, workers were profoundly sobered by the spectacle of the Moscow defeat and the ensuing wave of government and employer retribution.[3]

The sudden deterioration in political conditions might have been less traumatic, however, had it not been for another development that affected the lives of many Petersburg and Moscow workers. Unemployment, partly a consequence of the growing economic recession, was rapidly becoming a major problem in 1906. The demobilization of troops from the Russo-Japanese War further exacerbated the situation, returning many workers to a labor market that was sharply contracting.

Employers took advantage of these conditions to purge their firms of "those worthless and undesirable elements who interfere with the peaceful and normal conduct of work."[4] In the Moscow printing industry, mere possession of a union card cost many workers their jobs.[5] By the end of January, the resulting layoffs and dismissals had already acquired massive dimensions. Twelve hundred workers out of 6,000 were dismissed from Moscow's Prokhorovskaia Trekhgornaia textile mill; an estimated 1,500 Moscow printers were out of work, together with 800 carpenters and many others. In the capital, mass dismissals occurred in nearly all the major metalworking plants and soon spread to other industries. The number of unemployed workers in St. Petersburg had reached 39,000 in late January.[6]

Workers were at first quiescent in the face of economic crisis and political repression. Widespread arrests had removed many worker-activists from factories and shops; others had fled to the countryside or joined the growing unem-

---

[3]Between the end of December 1905 and the end of January 1906, over 1,700 individuals were arrested in St. Petersburg. For a description of conditions in the capital during this period, see *Istoriia rabochikh Leningrada: 1703-fevral' 1917*, vol. 1 (Leningrad, 1972), pp. 303–305. On Moscow, see A. M. Nikitin, "Moskovskie soiuzy v 1906 godu," in *Moskovskoe professional'noe dvizhenie v gody pervoi revoliutsii*, ed. Iu. Milonov (Moscow, [1925]).

[4]From instructions issued by the administration of the Baltiiskii plant in St. Petersburg to foremen in early 1906, cited in *Materialy ob ekonomicheskom polozhenii i professional'noi organizatsii Peterburgskikh rabochikh po metallu* (St. Petersburg, 1909), pp. 124–125.

[5]V. Sher, *Istoriia professional'nogo dvizheniia rabochikh pechatnogo dela v Moskve* (Moscow, 1911), p. 230.

[6]*Obshcheprofessional'nye organy 1905-1907 gg.*, vyp. I: *Moskovskie zhurnaly 1905 goda* (Moscow, 1926), p. 74, which republished the contemporary trade union journals, *Biulleten' Muzeia sodeistviia trudu* (1905) and *Materialy po professional'nomu dvizheniiu rabochikh* (1906), organs of the Moscow Central Bureau of Trade Unions.

ployment lines. Deprived of leadership, strike and factory committees quickly collapsed. Beyond the shop floor or workshop, the situation was equally discouraging. The citywide soviets had been thoroughly and permanently dispersed by the authorities. Of the fledgling trade unions, only a handful continued to function in the harsh climate of January 1906.

Some workers vented their anger and frustration against the unions. Crowds of jobless workers gathered at the headquarters of the Moscow printers' union, demanding "bread and money":

The majority [of the workers] conducted themselves peacefully, but some of the less conscious unemployed workers were in a defiant mood. They accused the union of everything. They believed that the December strike had been instigated by the union. They openly accused the directing board of embezzlement and provocation, threatened to go to the secret police, threatened death.[7]

Even the leadership of this union became demoralized by the turn of events, and one founding member, M. A. Volkov, "threw up his hands and thought that all was destroyed."[8]

By mid-February, however, the mood in labor circles had already begun to shift. Many of the unions that had been decimated in December were slowly reemerging, setting up headquarters, and recruiting members. One contemporary activist observed:

No one believes in the strength and duration of the reaction, in the possibility of its prolongation. A temporary lull, a breathing space before new social and popular forces arise—this is the view all around. Enthusiasm and energy have not forsaken our "unionized" proletarian movement.[9]

It was against this background that the new law on trade unions was promulgated on March 4, 1906. The first draft of a legislative proposal on trade unions, as we have already seen, was completed many months earlier, in May 1905. Prepared under the auspices of the Kokovtsov Commission and drafted by F. V. Fomin, an official at the Central Bureau of Factory Affairs,[10] the original version

[7]Sher, *Istoriia*, p. 231, quoted from a report in the contemporary union newspaper, *Pechatnik*.
[8]Ibid.
[9]V. Portugalov, "Nasha 'konstitutsiia' i professional'noe dvizhenie rabochikh," *Bez zaglaviia*, no. 4 (February 12, 1906), p. 151.
[10]Unknown to fellow labor activists, the liberal Petersburg university professor, V. Sviatlovskii, assisted in drafting the legislation. *Materialy po istorii professional'nogo dvizheniia v Rossii* (henceforth *MIPDR*) 5 vols., (Moscow, 1924–1927), vol. 4, p. 26.

of the law had provided for the legalization of trade unions whose function was to "defend" workers' economic interests and improve the conditions of labor. Permissible union activities had explicitly included the collection of funds for striking workers and thus, by implication, union involvement in strikes. Under the terms of Fomin's proposal, unions were subject to the legal jurisdiction of the court system and could lawfully confederate with other unions for common purposes.[11]

Fomin's proposal on trade unions remained virtually intact until it reached the State Council in late 1905. A majority on the State Council opposed most of the provisions of Fomin's draft, and despite some opposition within the Council itself, adopted a revised version, which was enacted on March 4, 1906.[12] Since the legislation was promulgated prior to the convocation of the First State Duma (the representative assembly created by the October Manifesto), it retained provisional status during the next eleven years, until it was swept away by the February Revolution.[13]

The final version of the law departed in crucial respects from previous drafts. Instead of the earlier broad authorization to "defend" workers' interests, trade unions now had permission only to "seek means of eliminating, by means of agreements or by submitting to arbitration [*treteiskoe razbiratel'stvo*] the misunderstandings that arise over conditions in labor contracts between employers and employees." The law remained silent on the matter of strike funds, although certain categories of economic strikes by nongovernment workers had already been legalized on December 2, 1905.[14]

[11]*Rabochii vopros v komissii V. N. Kokovtsova v 1905 g.* (n.p., 1926), pp. 133–139.

[12]*Polnoe sobranoe zakonov Rossiiskoi imperii,* sobranie 3, vol. 26:1 (1906), pp. 201–207. For the full text of the law and subsequent elucidations, see *Zakon 4-go marta 1906 goda o soiuzakh i obshchestvakh s posleduiushchimi k nemu raz'iasneniiami Pravitel'stvuiushchago senata i Ministerstva vnutrennikh del* (St. Petersburg, 1906). V. Sviatlovskii, *Professional'noe dvizhenie v Rossii* (St. Petersburg, 1907), provides an account of the State Council deliberations on the law.

[13]According to a government manifesto of February 20, 1906, the reformed legislative structure consisted of two chambers, the State Duma and the State Council. No law could be passed without approval of both houses and the sanction of the Tsar. Since the First State Duma had not yet convened in March, the new legislation regarding workers' and employers' associations was deemed to be "temporary."

[14]The issue of union-sponsored strike funds was finally resolved in a report from the Ministry of Internal Affairs to the State Senate, following consultations with the Ministries of Finance and Trade and Industry. The report, dated November 30, 1907, declared that such funds were legal with respect to strikes authorized by the law of December 2, 1905. Tsentral'nyi gosudarstvennyi arkhiv Oktiabr'skoi revoliutsii (TsGAOR), DP IV, d. 119, ch. 43, 1908, pp. 13–15. In practice, however, unions were frequently deprived of legal status for any involvement in strikes. For a list of unions closed on these grounds, see TsGAOR, DP IV, f. 236, 1908, p. 116.

The March 4 law also explicitly sanctioned the following union activities:

- To elucidate the wage scales and other conditions of labor in various branches of industry and trade;

- To provide material benefits to members;

- To establish funds for funerals, dowries, mutual aid, and the like;

- To establish libraries, trade schools, reading rooms, and to offer courses;

- To provide members with the opportunity to obtain necessities and work tools at a good price;

- To assist in the search for work or workers;

- To furnish legal aid for members.[15]

The 1906 law created new administrative organs, the Bureaus on Unions, responsible for union registration in each province. In addition, eight cities were authorized to create their own bureaus (St. Petersburg, Moscow, Odessa, Kronshtadt, Nikolaev, Kerch, Sevastopol, Rostov-na-Donu) which operated independently of the provincial bureau. Headed by the provincial governor or the city chief of police, these bureaus were composed of members of the courts and local government.[16] At the time of registration, each union was required to submit a charter specifying the goal, composition, leadership, conditions of membership, and other facts about the proposed organization. Within one month of receiving the charter, the bureau was required to grant or deny registration. Subsequent jurisdiction over the unions' legal status remained in the hands of the bureau, with a right of appeal only to the state Senate. Thus, in contrast to the earlier version of the law, trade unions were placed under the jurisdiction of a special bureau and not under the regular court system, a

---

[15]*Zakon*, Part II, Article 2, pp. 15–16.

[16]The St. Petersburg Special City Bureau on Unions had the following members in late 1906: the St. Petersburg chief of police, the St. Petersburg province marshal of the nobility, the director of the St. Petersburg Treasury, the procurator of the St. Petersburg district court, a representative of the Ministry of Internal Affairs, the president of the Petersburg province *zemstvo* governing board, the St. Petersburg City mayor, the president of the St. Petersburg City Duma, a member of the St. Petersburg City Duma, and the senior factory inspector. This, however, was only the formal composition of the bureau, and most of these individuals did not attend personally but sent representatives. At a meeting of the bureau held on August 21, 1907, for example, there were only three members present. Leningradskii gosudarstvennyi istoricheskii arkhiv (LGIA), f. 287, opis' 1, d. 16, p. 23.

circumstance that exposed these organizations to administrative arbitrariness.

The law explicitly forbade unions to engage in political activities or to pursue goals that threatened the government or the social order.[17] They were also prohibited from forming confederations of unions, and this prohibition prevented regional or national unification of organized labor. The law did, however, authorize the formation of union branch organizations, and in the Moscow region some unions took advantage of the provision to create a regional network within a given industry.

Despite all of these limitations, the March 4 law represented a significant advance over the only previous legislation that had explicitly authorized workers' organizations, the law of June 10, 1903, on factory elders.[18] In contrast to this earlier law, which placed the initiative for factory elders in the hands of employers, the March 4 law gave workers the right to initiate trade unions and to conduct their own affairs. And apart from the stipulation that workers of both sexes might belong to unions as long as they were employed in a state or private enterprise, the March 4 law did not attempt to dictate the requirements for union membership or participation in union affairs.

Though modest and circumscribed compared with the version drawn up by Fomin in 1905, the 1906 law on trade unions and employer associations marked the beginning of a new phase in government policy toward the labor movement. The State Council itself commented on the historic significance of the law at the time of promulgation:

The issuance of the present code will *signify a transition from a system which has regulated the employers' treatment of workers and engaged in administrative tutelage over them, to a system which enables both the employers and the workers* to conduct autonomous and, at the same time, legal activity within the framework of professional organizations, whose main goal is to coordinate and reconcile *conflicting* interests between industrial employers and their employees.[19]

The text of the law had already appeared in the press when the Second All-Russian Conference on Trade Unions convened in St. Petersburg at the end of February 1906. Delegates from ten factory centers (including three from Moscow—Andreev, Zakharov [Kolokol'nikov], Kruglov—and three from St. Petersburg—Grinevich, Riazanov, Sviatlovskii) debated the impending legisla-

[17]*Zakon*, Part I, Articles 6 and 13, Part II, Article 13, pp. 6, 8, 17.
[18]See above, chapter 3.
[19]Sviatlovskii, *Professional'noe dvizhenie*, p. 360. Italics in the original.

tion and its implications for the labor movement.[20] Speaking for a small minority of the delegates, Zel'tser [B. Grosser], a Bundist from Warsaw, opposed all compliance with the laws on the grounds that acquiescence would dampen the revolutionary mood of the masses. A somewhat larger minority at the conference also opposed compliance, but for different reasons. Riazanov, a nonfaction Social Democrat from St. Petersburg, argued that genuine legal status for trade unions could not be achieved under the prevailing political system in Russia. Since fundamental civil and political freedom did not yet exist, he stated, "unions would be committing suicide if they were to register in the absence of basic laws."

The Menshevik representative of the Moscow printers' union, Kruglov, presented the resolution that secured majority support at the conference. Asserting that the "broad and open" activity of unions was "extremely important," the resolution recommended that unions comply with the registration procedures in those localities where union work would otherwise be obstructed. Noncompliance was considered preferable where unions could continue to function illegally.

This position coincided with the outlook of many labor activists in Moscow, who were chastened by the events following the December insurrection and were therefore inclined to accept the laws' provisions as a disagreeable but necessary condition for resuming effective activity. Soon after the promulgation of the law, the Menshevik-dominated Moscow Central Bureau of Trade Unions issued the following resolution urging workers to register under the new regulations:

The Moscow Bureau of Representatives of Trade Unions, recognizing that the temporary law of March 4 on unions completely fails to provide necessary freedom for the activity of trade unions but, on the contrary, strives to suppress the trade union movement . . . [nevertheless] believes that trade unions can use the temporary laws for the development of the proletarian struggle and without altering their character and the directions of their activity, [unions] can declare their existence to the administration in accordance with the second section of the laws of March 4.[21]

---

[20]The protocols of the Second All-Russian Conference on Trade Unions were subsequently published: *Vtoraia konferentsiia professional'nykh soiuzov: Doklady i protokoly* (St. Petersburg, 1906). For a list of participants, see p. 23. For a personal reminiscence of the Second Conference, see P. Kolokol'nikov, "Otryvki iz vospominanii," *MIPDR*, 4:270–273. The following account of the debate at the conference over compliance with the new law is reconstructed from the protocols, *Vtoraia konferentsiia*, pp. 144–163.

[21]S. Tiurin, *Moskovskoe tsentral'noe biuro professional'nykh soiuzov* (Moscow, 1913), pp. 33–34.

Even in St. Petersburg, where labor activists felt less keenly the impact of the December debacle and were more disposed, at least initially, to resist compliance with the registration procedures, the position adopted at the Second Conference of Trade Unions served as the basis for conducting union affairs in the new era of legal labor organization.[22] Despite widespread reservations about the law in labor and political circles,[23] it provided a tremendous impetus for collective association, and workers were not long in turning this opportunity to their own advantage.

THE PROLIFERATION OF TRADE UNIONS

During the fifteen months that elapsed between the promulgation of the March 1906 law and the Stolypin "coup d'état" of June 1907, seventy-two unions acquired legal status in St. Petersburg, and sixty-five in Moscow. Not all of these unions involved separate groups, however, because some unions were forced to reregister when they lost their legal status (see Appendix II). There were thirteen instances of repeat registrations in the capital and one in Moscow during this period. In addition to legal trade unions, a number of unionized groups functioned illegally. Seventeen unregistered unions existed in St. Petersburg, and eleven in Moscow. These unions either had failed to secure registration or, more rarely, had refused to comply with the law's registration procedures. The total number of unionized groups, legal and illegal, excluding repeat registrations, was 76 in the capital and 75 in Moscow (table 11).

In the country as a whole, 904 unions were registered between March 1906 and December 1907. Of these, 104 subsequently lost their legal status. Ninety-four unions functioned illegally, a figure that includes organizations deprived of legal status and others that failed to register.[24]

The legalization of unions proceeded more gradually and more episodically

[22]The vote in the Petersburg Central Bureau of Trade Unions on compliance with the law took place in March. At the conclusion of the first meeting, the vote was ten in favor of compliance, twenty-one opposed. At a second meeting, ten favored compliance, seventeen were opposed, and two favored illegal unions. U. A. Shuster, *Peterburgskie rabochie v 1905–1907 gg.* (Leningrad, 1976), p. 250.

[23]Both the liberal Kadet party and the Socialist Revolutionary party introduced into the First State Duma alternative legislative proposals on trade unions, but neither was enacted into law. See *Vestnik pechatnikov*, no. 9 (June 24, 1906), p. 2, for the Kadet proposal, and *Delo naroda*, no. 4 (May 4, 1906), p. 2, for the SR proposal.

[24]*Svod otchetov professional'nykh obshchestv za 1906–1907 gg.* (St. Petersburg, 1911), p. 22. Gudvan presents a summary of varying estimates of union registration in the country as a whole in "K

Table 11
Petersburg and Moscow Unions,
March 1906–May 1907

	Total Unions Registered under March 4 Law	Repeat Registrations out of Total Registered	Total Registered Unions (excluding repeats)
St. Petersburg	72	13	59
Moscow	65	1	64
	Unregistered Unions	Total Unions, Legal and Illegal (excluding repeats)	
St. Petersburg	17	76	
Moscow	11	75	

Sources: See Appendix II for a complete list of unions and the sources used to compile this list.

in St. Petersburg than in Moscow, where workers hastened to apply for registration and fifty-two unions obtained legal status in the first six months of the law's implementation. In St. Petersburg, by contrast, there were two periods of intensive unionization in the summer of 1906 and the spring of 1907 (table 12).

The high points of union registration in St. Petersburg coincided with major political events: the sessions of the First and the Second State Dumas (April 27-July 9, 1906, and February 20-June 3, 1907, respectively). The Duma sessions accelerated union registration in two ways. The new representative assemblies, with their contingents of labor deputies and the bold stance toward the authorities, generated enthusiasm among workers for collective organization. Local officials, facing public scrutiny and possible public disorder during the sessions, adopted a more lenient attitude toward the labor movement and more readily approved applications for registration. Overall, however, Petersburg trade unionists encountered harsher local policies than their Moscow counterparts, a circumstance that helps to account for the protracted period from September 1906 to February 1907 when only seven new trade unions succeeded in registering in the capital.

Membership data are available for only forty-two Petersburg unions. At their

voprosu," *MIPDR*, 2:162. Data published in the *Svod otchetov* were collected under the auspices of the Ministry of Trade and Industry.

Table 12

Petersburg and Moscow Unions
Registered under the March 4, 1906, Law
from March 1906 to June 1907

	March–May 1906	June–August 1906	September–November 1906	December 1906–February 1907	March–May 1907	Total
St. Petersburg	9	30	2	5	26	72
Moscow	25	27	12	1	0	65

Source: See Appendix II.

peak, these unions reported a combined nominal membership of 55,000 workers. Comparable data for Moscow reveal a combined peak nominal membership of 52,000 for forty-four unions.[25]

Two attempts were made in this period to ascertain the total number of workers enrolled in trade unions in the Russian Empire. Membership data collected by the Ministry of Trade and Industry in the spring of 1907, covering only 273 registered unions, show a total of 106,462 nominal members.[26] The Organizational Commission for the convocation of a nationwide congress of trade unions assembled data from 653 unions whose total nominal membership was 246,547.[27] Both figures are far from complete, and it is likely that the total number of unionized workers exceeded 300,000 in the country as a whole.[28] Petersburg and Moscow trade unions, with a combined total of 107,000 nominal members in unions for which data are available, thus accounted for approximately one-third of all the unionized workers in Russia in 1906–1907.

Within each city, unionized workers constituted a small but significant minority of the total labor force and, of course, a larger proportion of those

---

[25]In the following discussion of membership, I have calculated aggregate membership using the peak figure available for each union in the period between March 1906 and June 1907. Included in this calculation are both registered and unregistered unions, but no unionized group is counted more than once. A survey conducted by the Organizational Commission for an All-Russian Trade Union Congress in the spring of 1907 reported a total of 51,782 nominal trade union members in Petersburg and 48,051 in Moscow. *Portnoi,* no. 7–8 (October 13, 1907), p. 8.

[26]*Svod otchetov,* p. 2.

[27]Gudvan, "K voprosu," *MIPDR,* 2:165.

[28]Gudvan performs this calculation, ibid., p. 167.

employed in industries and occupations represented by unions. Combining the total number of workers in all sectors of the urban economy, we find that roughly 9 percent of the total labor force in the capital and 10 percent in Moscow had joined a trade union in this period.[29] Considering the short period of union recruitment—barely one year when membership data were collected—this compares favorably with Germany, where unions had been functioning openly and legally since 1890 and where 22 percent of the industrial labor force belonged to a union in 1907.[30]

The figures on citywide union membership are not without interest, but they fail to indicate the full strength of trade unions during these months. More telling are the data showing the number and percentage of unionized workers in specific industries, occupations, and trades. When we assess the union movement from this perspective, we find that among certain segments of the Petersburg and Moscow labor force, unions made astonishing gains in a brief period (see tables 13, 14, 15).

Among the most impressive organizations in each city were those formed in the printing industry. At its peak, the Petersburg printers' union attracted 12,000 members (66 percent of the labor force); its Moscow counterpart drew 8,000 members (65 percent). The bakers' unions also attracted a large membership of about 4,000 workers in each city, accounting for 63 percent of the industry's labor force in St. Petersburg and 42 percent in Moscow. Other food-processing industries also had a high rate of recruitment. Two-thirds of the Moscow tea-packers and nearly one-half of the Moscow candymakers joined a union in this period, as did one-third of the Petersburg candymakers. Additional unions with a successful recruitment record include the Petersburg dyers (38 percent), precious metalworkers (32 percent), and marble and granite workers (29 percent), and the Moscow perfume workers (65 percent), plumbers and heaters (62 percent), photographical workers (45 percent), wallpaper workers (43 percent), and others (tables 14 and 15).

Nearly 11,000 workers joined the Petersburg metalworkers' union (13 percent) and nearly 5,000 metalworkers (14 percent) joined the union in Moscow.

---

[29]The labor force data used as the basis for this calculation are drawn from the 1900 Petersburg municipal census and the 1902 Moscow municipal census. As shown above in chapter 1, table 6, there was a total of 641,656 workers in St. Petersburg and 537,522 in Moscow in all sectors of the urban economy, according to these censuses. No comparable labor force data are available for 1907.

[30]Barrington Moore, Jr., *Injustice: The Social Bases of Obedience and Revolt* (White Plains, N.Y., 1978), pp. 175, 182.

Table 13

Petersburg and Moscow Unions with One Thousand or More Nominal Members at Peak Membership, 1906–1907

ST. PETERSBURG

Union	Peak membership	Date of membership
1. Printers*	12,000	January 1907
2. Metalworkers*	10,700	January 1907
3. Bakers	4,140	March 1907
4. Textile workers*	4,000	January 1907
5. Construction workers	3,730	February 1907
6. Salesclerks*	2,688	January 1907
7. Office clerks and bookkeepers	2,000	February 1907
8. Woodworkers*	1,965	March 1907
9. Tailors*	1,514	January 1907
10. Shoemakers	1,200	July 1906
11. Gold-silversmiths*	1,110	January 1907
12. Furnace workers	1,100	November 1906

MOSCOW

Union	Peak membership	Date of membership
1. Printers*	8,000	September 1906
2. Metalworkers*	4,725	March 1907
3. Bakers	4,000	June 1906
4. Tailors	3,415	May 1907
5. City employees	2,800	March 1907
6. Waiters	2,618	March 1907
7. Textile workers	2,382	March 1907
8. Teapackers*	2,000	March 1907
9. Candymakers	1,626	August 1906
10. Office clerks and bookkeepers	1,500	September 1906
11. Woodworkers	1,500	March 1907
12. Dyers	1,400	March 1907
13. Railroad workers*	1,311	March 1907
14. Workers in precious metals*	1,296	March 1907
15. Tobacco workers	1,218	March 1907
16. Construction workers	1,200	March 1907
17. Plumbers	1,154	March 1907

Source: These data were collected from a wide variety of sources. A complete list of unions and nominal membership where available can be found in Appendix II. In this table, "peak membership" refers to the highest level of union recruitment, and "date of membership" refers to the time period when the union reached peak recorded membership.

*These unions were functioning illegally at the time these membership levels were reached, but all of them succeeded in registering at some point in 1906–1907, with the exception of the Moscow Union of Railroad Workers.

The rate of recruitment in this industry was adversely affected by the high rate of unemployment among metalworkers during 1906 and 1907, which was more severe and widespread than in most other industries at the time.[31] The Petersburg metalworkers' union, moreover, was forced to operate illegally for nine of these fifteen months, a circumstance that interfered with recruitment. All factors considered, the metalworkers' unions—with about one out of seven workers in their ranks—elicited a positive response from the workers in this industry.

A survey conducted by the Organizational Commission for an All-Russian Congress of Trade Unions in the spring of 1907, covering 653 of the 904 legal unions in the country, reveals that 8.6 percent of the workers belonged to a union in industries and occupations where organizations were established. These data are based on the 1897 census, however, and the labor force in some industries had increased in the intervening decade, thus reducing the proportion of organized workers. The printers' unions drew the highest percentage of the labor force in the country as a whole, followed at a great distance by the unions of leather- and metalworkers, and workers in commerce and service, food, and textile industries (table 16).

All of the foregoing figures apply to nominal rather than regular dues-paying membership. In the former category were those who placed their names on union rolls, having paid the initial entry fee. But not all of these workers continued to pay monthly dues on a regular basis, and unions frequently dropped delinquent dues-payers from the membership rolls after four or five months of nonpayment. Workers described as nominal members included all who formally joined a union, regardless of the length of time they continued to make regular dues payments.

The custom of monthly dues payment had not yet become established among Russia's organized workers, and dues-paying members almost invariably constituted a minority of those inscribed on the membership rolls. In a handful of large and flourishing Petersburg unions, such as printers, metalworkers, tea-packers, and bakers, a considerable proportion of the membership, ranging from 31 to 63 percent, made regular dues payments. But in most cases, only one out of six or even fewer members paid dues regularly.[32]

[31]By the end of 1907, more than one-third of the capital's metalworkers were out of work. F. A. Bulkin, *Na zare profdvizheniia* (Moscow and Leningrad, 1924), p. 159.

[32]Detailed data on dues-paying membership in Petersburg and Moscow unions, based on the Organizational Commission survey, were published in *Professional'nyi vestnik*, no. 6 (May 3, 1907), and *Professional*, no. 3–4 (May 17, 1907). These data are reprinted in Sviatlovskii, *Professional'noe dvizhenie*, pp. 190–191, 198–199.

Table 14
Percentage of Unionized Workers in Selected Petersburg Industries and Occupations, 1906–1907

Union	Total Workers (1900–1902)	Total Union Members	Percent Unionized
1. Printers and binders	18,048	12,000	66
2. Bakers and pastry makers	6,606	4,140	63
3. Dyers	655	251	38
4. Candymakers	2,880	998	35
5. Precious metalworkers	3,509	1,110	32
6. Marble and granite workers	1,306	374	29
7. Blacksmiths	1,758	300	17
8. Leatherworkers	5,452	771	14
9. Metalworkers	80,834	10,700	13
10. Construction (excluding plumbers and marble and granite workers)	31,405	3,730	12
11. Textile workers	36,716	4,000	11
12. Woodworkers	24,146	1,965	8
13. Plumbers	2,469	200	8
14. Shoemakers	17,131	1,200	7
15. Tobacco workers	7,318	500	7
16. Tailors and furriers	45,839	1,420	3

Source: Formidable difficulties stand in the way of calculating the total number of workers in a given occupation or industry, since census categories and other data collections did not always define occupational groups in the same way that workers did when they formed trade unions. In some instances the boundaries of the union itself are unclear, and it is difficult to decide precisely which occupational groups were included in the organization. Labor force data are taken from *S.-Peterburg po perepisi 15 dekabria 1900 g.*, vyp. 2 (St. Petersburg, 1903), pp. 38–137, and sources noted above in Tables 1 and 2.

Table 15

Percentage of Unionized Workers in Selected
Moscow Industries and Occupations,
1906–1907

Union	Total Workers (1902)	Total Union Members	Percent Unionized
1. Teapackers	3,000	2,000	67
2. Perfume workers	1,068	692	65
3. Printers and binders	12,384	8,000	65
4. Plumbers and heaters	1,845	1,154	62
5. Candymakers	3,451	1,626	47
6. Photographical workers	264	119	45
7. Workers in wallpaper production	808	350	43
8. Bakers and pastry makers	9,475	4,000	42
9. Button- and hookmakers	1,075	400	37
10. Tobacco workers	3,396	1,218	36
11. Ribbonweavers	1,439	367	26
12. Precious metalworkers	6,554	1,296	20
13. Metalworkers	32,647	4,725	14
14. Leather workers	5,665	627	11
15. Tailors	33,647	3,415	10
16. Woodworkers	17,443	1,500	9
17. Floorpolishers	1,770	150	8
18. Textile workers (excluding weavers, knitters, and ribbonweavers)	52,779	2,382	5
19. Shoemakers	14,429	500	3

Sources: Labor force data for Moscow present difficulties similar to those for Petersburg statistics. The total number of workers in each industry or occupation is based on the 1902 city census. *Perepis' Moskvy 1902 g.*, chast' 1, vyp. 2 (Moscow, 1906), pp. 117–159. Data on the teapackers are from *Professional'noe dvizenie Moskovskikh pishchevikov v gody pervoi revoliutsii*, sbornik 1 (Moscow, 1927), p. 3. The labor force figure for tailors includes only those categories of garment workers recruited by the union of tailors.

PATTERNS OF UNIONIZATION: SKILL

The legal labor movement attracted workers in all sectors of the urban economy. Manufacturing workers (both factory and artisanal) formed the largest proportion of unions in each city (63 percent in St. Petersburg and 55 percent in Moscow), followed by sales-clerical, service, transportation, and construction workers (table 17).

In the Russian Empire as a whole, factory and artisanal workers also predominated in legal trade unions. The exact proportion of the former group cannot be ascertained, however, because government statistics failed to provide a separate accounting of unions involving factory workers. Furthermore, the Ministry of Trade and Industry classified as "artisanal" only workers actually registered in a guild. Since most workers engaged in artisanal occupations were no longer guild members by 1906,[33] the Ministry's data considerably underestimate the role of artisanal workers in the trade union movement. The proportion of unionized sales-clerical workers in the country (25 percent) is higher than in either St. Petersburg or Moscow, possibly because the Ministry data include some organizations more nearly resembling professional associations than trade unions (table 18).

Trade unions were established by a wide variety of working-class groups in 1906–1907. Factory workers in both St. Petersburg and Moscow became more active in the union movement than they had been in 1905, and for the first time, metalworkers succeeded in forming citywide organizations. Artisanal workers remained enthusiastic participants in the organized labor movement, accounting for about one-third of the total number of unions in each city, if we include skilled construction workers but exclude "factory artisans." Sales-clerical workers also maintained a strong interest in the unions, and groups such as household servants, window washers, gardeners, floor polishers, chimneysweeps, and coachmen—usually the last to organize in any labor movement—established legal unions in this period.

Notwithstanding the heterogeneity of unionized groups in 1906–1907, there were certain patterns in union membership that help to explain why some workers were more readily disposed to join the organized labor movement than others. As in 1905, the one circumstance, above all, that facilitated unionization was the command of a specialized skill. The role of skilled labor in the union movement can be discerned from table 19, which subdivides unions into two

[33]See above, chapter 2.

Table 16

*Occupational Breakdown of Unions in the
Russian Empire in 1907*

Occupation	Number of Unions	Number of Members	Labor Force in 1897	Percent Unionized
1. Printing	72	28,654	52,175	54.9
2. Leatherworking	85	12,066	74,270	16.2
3. Metalworking	81	54,173	370,933	14.6
4. Commerce and service	101	32,475	255,588	12.7
5. Food	78	24,848	265,640	9.3
6. Textiles	25	37,214	530,138	7.0
7. Woodworking	38	9,927	181,836	5.5
8. Apparel	59	14,322	326,470	4.4
9. Construction	43	12,396	345,724	3.6
10. Mining	6	3,467	206,376	1.7
11. Other manufacturing	65	17,005	243,386	7.0
Total	653	246,547	2,852,536	8.6

Source: *Professional'nyi vestnik*, no. 8 (May 30, 1907), pp. 8–9; no. 9 (June 21, 1907), p. 11. Membership data are corrected for numerical errors in Grinevich, *Professional'noe dvizhenie*, p. 278, and further corrected by Gudvan, "K voprosu," *MIPDR*, 2:165. Labor force data originally reported in *Professional'nyi vestnik* are incorrect. The data shown above are from *Chislennost' i sostav*, vol. 2, pp. viii-ix.

categories: those involving mainly skilled workers, and those whose membership was drawn primarily from semiskilled or unskilled strata of the labor force. The first category includes such groups as the tailors, bakers, plumbers, wood-workers, printers, and salesclerks. Metalworkers have also been included in this category, since a large proportion of union members in this industry consisted of the skilled workers, a subject to be discussed shortly. Among semiskilled and unskilled unionized groups were textile workers, candymakers, teapackers, to-bacco workers, laundresses, floorpolishers, coachmen, and others. On the basis of this survey, we find that about three out of four unions in each city involved workers who were entirely or predominantly skilled.

Membership data drawn from specific unions further attest to the importance of skill in facilitating participation. The most comprehensive and detailed survey of union membership in this period was conducted by the Petersburg metal-

Table 17

Sectoral Composition of Trade Unions in St. Petersburg and Moscow, 1906–1907

UNIONS FORMED BY:

	MANUFACTURING WORKERS		SALES-CLERICAL WORKERS		SERVICE WORKERS		CONSTRUCTION WORKERS		TRANSPORTATION WORKERS		MISCELLANEOUS WORKERS		Total number of Unions
	Aggregate number of Unions	% of Total	Aggregate number of Unions	% of Total	Aggregate number of Unions	% of Total	Aggregate number of Unions	% of Total	Aggregate number of Unions	% of Total	Aggregate number of Unions	% of Total	
St. Petersburg	48	63%	9	12%	7	9%	3	4%	5	7%	4	5%	76
Moscow	41	55%	14	19%	10	13%	5	7%	4	5%	1	1%	75

Source: This table lists each unionized group only once. For a complete list of the unions classified here, see Appendix II.

workers' union. Of the 9,338 workers belonging to this union in January 1908, 8,459 were included in the survey, which was based on the registration forms of union members, most of whom had joined the organization prior to September 1907.[34]

The two largest occupational groups in the Petersburg metalworkers' union were metalfitters (2,594 members) and lathe operators (1,425 members), both highly skilled trades. Together, these two groups accounted for nearly one-half of the union's membership. A total of 116 different occupational specializations were represented in the union, but only 16 percent of the members can be considered unskilled. The remainder range from highly skilled to semiskilled, with the bulk of the membership falling into the former category.[35] Bulkin, a metalworker and union organizer in the capital, has summed up the characteristics of the membership:

The more complex the production process and the more highly skilled the labor in a certain branch of production, the higher the percentage of organized workers there. In machine tool manufacture, electrical engineering, and instrument making, that is, precisely the location of the most highly qualified labor force, the workers' aristocracy, the percentage of organized workers ranged from 24 to 26 percent of the labor force employed in those branches. And, on the contrary, in nailmaking, in the iron and copper foundries, that is, where the majority are not highly qualified but merely unskilled workers, the percentage of organized workers falls to 7 or even to 3 percent of the total number of workers in these branches.[36]

Membership in the Moscow metalworkers' union followed a similar pattern. In February 1907, fifty-two occupational specialties were represented in the union. Metalfitters made up 32 percent of the membership, lathe operators 17 percent, and smelters 16 percent. These three skilled trades accounted for nearly two-thirds of the membership, while the remaining 49 occupational groups accounted for one-third of the total.[37]

In both cities, metal patternmakers showed a strong inclination to unionize. In Moscow, where patternmakers formed a section within the metalworkers' union, 120 patternmakers out of about 500 in the city (or about 24 percent) were union members.[38] Similarly, the Petersburg patternmakers' union drew 300

[34]*Materialy ob ekonomicheskom polozhenii,* pp. 71 ff. F. A. Bulkin, *Na zare,* pp. 310–311.

[35]*Materialy ob ekonomicheskom polozhenii,* pp. 94–96.

[36]Bulkin, *Na zare,* p. 307.

[37]*Pervaia konferentsiia professional'nykh soiuzov rabochikh po metallu Moskovskogo promyshlennoga raiona* (Moscow, 1907), p. 8.

[38]Ibid., p. 14.

Table 18

Unions in the Russian Empire, 1906–1907

	Number of Registered Unions	Percent of Total Registered Unions	Number Denied Registration
Workers in manufacturing, mining, and other industries	489	54.1	94
Artisanal workers	129	14.3	19
Sales-clerical employees	227	25.1	48
Others	59	6.5	13
Total	904	100.0	174

Source: *Svod otchetov*, p. 22.

members, which must have represented a comparable or even higher percentage of the craftsmen in this highly skilled trade.[39] Evidence drawn from other trade unions supports the impression that unionization was often directly correlated with skill. In the Petersburg printers' union, the highly skilled typesetters constituted the largest single category of members in 1907, accounting for 24 percent of the total. Unionized typesetters comprised about two-thirds of the typesetters in the industry as a whole. By contrast, unskilled workers in the printing trades furnished only 3 percent of the union membership.[40]

Detailed breakdowns of membership are not available for other unions, but certain trends emerge nevertheless. In the textile industry, the Moscow ribbon-weavers first unionized in 1905 and then attempted unsuccessfully to register in 1906. Ribbonweavers belonged to one of the most skilled subgroups in this industry. There were 367 members of the union in 1907, out of about 1,400 in the city, or 26 percent of the total.[41] The Moscow tailors' union drew most of its

[39]G. Gol'dberg, *K istorii professional'nogo dvizheniia v Rossii: Sostoianie soiuzov nakanune Vtoroi Gosudarstvennoi Dumy* (St. Petersburg, 1907), p. 11.

[40]V. A. Svavitskii and V. Sher, *Ocherk polozheniia rabochikh pechatnogo dela v Moskve (Po dannym ankety, proizvedennoi obshchestvom rabochikh graficheskikh iskusstv v 1907 godu)* (St. Petersburg, 1909), table 7. These figures are based on a survey of printing workers, a majority of them (80 percent) union members, conducted in March 1907. Of the 6,500 nominal members of the union, 3,246 replied to the questionnaire.

[41]M. Zaiats, *Tekstili v gody pervoi revoliutsii (1905-1907 gg.): Materialy po istorii professional'nogo dvizheniia tekstil'shchikov tsentral'no-promyshlennogo raiona* (Moscow, 1925), pp. 24, 50. Labor force data are based on the 1902 municipal census, *Perepis' Moskvy 1902 g.*, pp. 124–125, 146–147.

Table 19

Composition of Petersburg and Moscow
Unions by Skill, 1906–1907

UNION COMPOSITION:	PREDOMINANTLY SKILLED WORKERS		PREDOMINANTLY SEMISKILLED AND UNSKILLED WORKERS		
	Number of unions	Percentage of total unions	Number of unions	Percentage of total unions	Total number of unions
St. Petersburg	59	78	17	22	76
Moscow	56	75	19	25	75

Source: In classifying unionized groups, I took into account whether the majority of workers in a given industry or occupation required apprenticeship training (one to five years) to master the skills of their trade. Where such apprenticeship was obligatory and widespread, I classified the workers as "predominantly skilled." Decisions concerning classification were also based on information about the composition of the membership. But in most cases, these data are not available.

following from workers in tailoring shops *(masterskie khoziaev)* rather than sub-contracting shops *(masterskie khoziaichikov)*.[42] The latter, operating on a modified putting-out basis for large wholesale-retail enterprises, generally produced lower-quality garments than tailoring shops situated on the actual premises of a firm. The level of skill required of workers in subcontracting shops was correspondingly inferior to that of tailoring shops, where most union members were employed. Among salesclerks, a disparate group that included highly qualified bookstore sales personnel and semiliterate clerks in retail food stores, the more skilled strata showed a greater propensity for organization.

Since skill and wages were closely correlated, it is not surprising to find that union members often had earnings that were higher than the average in a given industry. In 1906 the average monthly wage for a unionized metalworker in St. Petersburg was 46 rubles 60 kopecks, while that of nonmembers was 36 rubles 90 kopecks.[43] The highly skilled tailoring shop workers, who constituted the bulk of the membership in the Moscow tailors' union, earned an average of 37 rubles 20 kopecks per month, compared with 23 rubles 10 kopecks for sub-contracting shop tailors.[44] In the Moscow printers' union nearly one-quarter of

[42]E. A. Oliunina, *Portnovskii promysel v Moskve i v derevniakh Moskovskoi i Riazanskoi gubernii: Materialy k istorii domashnei promyshlennosti v Rossii* (Moscow, 1914), p. 302.

[43]*Materialy ob ekonomicheskom polozhenii*, p. 109.

[44]Oliunina, *Portnovskii promysel*, p. 204. These data apply to the years 1910–1911, but the ratio of earnings of members and nonmembers was little different three years earlier.

Table 20
Percentage of Women Members in Selected
Moscow Unions, February 1907

Union	Women as a Percent of Total Union Membership	Women as a Percent of the Labor Force in 1902
Tobacco workers	44	60
Perfume workers	34	33
Button- and hookmakers	17	39
Bookstore employees	15	11
Tailors	13	66
Teapackers	10	n.d.
Low-level city employees	8	n.d.
Photographical workers	6	5
Textile workers	4	44
Employees in wholesale and retail pharmaceutical stores	4	13
Candymakers	3	53
Railroad workers	3	6
Printers and binders	1.5	6
Shoemakers	0.8	10
Metalworkers	0.5	2
Technicians	0.4	n.d.
Barbers	0.3	3
Pursemakers	0.3	n.d.
Bakers	none	1
Workers in the glass and crystal industry	none	15
Workers in precious metals	none	2
Waiters and tavern employees	none	5
Floorpolishers	none	2
Plumbers and heaters	none	0.1
Woodworkers	none	2
Hatmakers	none	28
Construction workers	none	0.8
Metalfitters in the construction industry	none	n.d.

Table 20 (Continued)

Union	Women as a Percent of Total Union Membership	Women as a Percent of the Labor Force in 1902
Electrical workers	none	0.5
Workers in the leather industry	none	6
Workers in wallpaper production	none	6

Source: *Perepis' Moskvy 1902 g.*, pp. 117–173. The figure for female members of the metal-workers' union is taken from *Materialy ob ekonomicheskom polozhenii*, p. 78. All others are from Milonov, ed., *Moskovskoe professional'noe dvizhenie*, pp. 382–387.

the membership was drawn from the ranks of typesetters—the industry's second-highest-paid group, with an average monthly wage of 43 rubles 9 kopecks in an industry where the monthly average for all printing workers was 34 rubles 70 kopecks.[45] Moscow ribbonweavers earned an average of 35 rubles a month, whereas most workers in the city's textile industry earned only a little more than half that amount.[46]

Even in industries and occupations where the bulk of the labor force was unskilled or semiskilled, a relative command of skill appears to have facilitated unionization. Data on the sexual composition of union membership indirectly support this conclusion. Skill and gender were often connected: women performed the unskilled and semiskilled jobs, while men generally held the more qualified positions. A predominance of male union recruits, particularly in industries with many female workers, suggests a corollary, namely, that skilled (male) workers were more inclined to join the organization than those (female) who were unskilled or semiskilled.

Data on female membership in trade unions indicate that women were generally underrepresented in comparison with male workers. The Moscow textile industry employed more than 26,000 women, over two-fifths of the labor force, but the union attracted a mere 100 female workers into its ranks (4 percent of the union's total membership).[47] A similar situation prevailed in the Petersburg and Moscow tailors' unions. There were only 27 women among the 1,420 members of the Petersburg tailors' union (2 percent), and 322 women out of 2,483 members of the Moscow union (13 percent), although about two-thirds

[45]Svavitskii and Sher, *Ocherk*, table 5; Sher, *Istoriia*, p. 35.
[46]Zaiats, *Tekstili*, p. 50.
[47]*Perepis' Moskvy*, pp. 146–147; Milonov, ed., *Moskovskoe professional'noe dvizhenie*, p. 386.

of the labor force in each city's garment industry was female.[48] Table 20 shows the percentage of women members in selected Moscow unions, according to a survey conducted by the Moscow Bureau of Trade Unions in February 1907.[49]

In only three Moscow unions (perfume, bookstore, and photographic workers) did female members approximate their representation in the labor force. The tobacco workers' union had the largest percentage of female members in the city, but their participation in the union was still well below the proportion of female workers in the industry as a whole. Insofar as women participated in trade unions, their presence was usually connected to special circumstances. As we shall see shortly, changes in the production process, prior exposure to a labor association, or the presence of an energetic leadership group could, on occasion, draw workers into the union movement who were not otherwise disposed to join.

Workers who joined trade unions were often literate. The ability to read gave workers access to new sources of information, widened their horizons, and equipped them to deal with the tasks presented by a labor association. In some of the largest and most active unions, not only were most of the members literate, but many had even completed primary-school education.[50]

Described by contemporaries as a magnet for "the most intellectual and organized stratum of the proletariat," the Petersburg metalworkers' union drew a high proportion of literate workers. Ninety-two percent of the union members were literate, compared with 73 percent in the city's metalworking industry as a whole.[51] Many of them had completed the city or district primary school. Among Moscow printing workers, 96 percent of the union members were literate in 1907, compared with 92 percent in the industry as a whole. Literacy was universal among unionized typesetters in Moscow, and 93 percent had been graduated from primary school.[52]

In Moscow tailoring shops, about 90 percent of the labor force was literate,

[48]V. V. Sviatlovskii, *Istoriia professional'nogo dvizheniia v Rossii ot vozniknoveniia rabochego klassa do kontsa 1917 g.* (Leningrad, 1925), p. 102.

[49]I have been unable to locate comparable data for Petersburg unions in either published or unpublished sources. Inexplicably, it would appear that the survey conducted in the capital did not include this question on the questionnaire.

[50]According to a contemporary study of the effects of literacy on workers, the ability to read had greater significance for the employment prospects of men than of women. Moreover, literacy was indispensable for most skilled workers, who "must exercise greater resourcefulness in [their] work." G. V. Zilin, "Shkola i fabrika," *Zavety*, no. 4 (April 1913), p. 43.

[51]*Materialy ob ekonomicheskom polozhenii*, pp. 90–91; Shuster, *Peterburgskie rabochie*, p. 52.

[52]Svavitskii and Sher, *Ocherk*, table 2.

and 50 percent had completed primary school. In subcontracting shops, by contrast, 66 to 75 percent of the workers could claim basic literacy, and only one-quarter had completed primary school.[53] Since unionized tailors came from tailoring rather than subcontracting shops, there is reason to believe that union members were on the whole more literate and educated than other workers in the Moscow garment industry.

Organized workers were seldom new recruits to the urban labor force, and most had prolonged experience living and working in an urban center. Skilled workers, as we have seen, nearly always served an apprenticeship, lasting up to five years depending on the trade. Apprenticeship training in factory industries generally began when an individual reached the age of sixteen, but in artisanal trades and sales-clerical occupations it was not uncommon to begin an apprenticeship between the ages of twelve and fourteen. Thus, by the time they reached their twenties, skilled workers had usually spent a number of years in an urban work environment.[54]

A prolonged experience of living and working in an urban center fortified the individual's self-image as a "worker," as distinct from the peasantry out of which many had come. The awareness of oneself as a "worker" was still comparatively rare in Russia, and most industries and occupations depended upon the rural population to furnish a steady stream of new recruits to the urban labor force. The self-image as a "worker" proved indispensable to the union movement, since a common identification with other workers was a basic prerequisite for engaging in a sustained struggle to achieve collective improvement. Individuals who regarded their sojourn in the city as a brief interlude in an essentially rural existence were far less likely to join an organization such as a trade union than those who perceived themselves as a more or less permanent part of the urban population.

The age structure of union membership sheds light on the length of time workers had lived and worked in a city. These data do not, of course, indicate the proportion of union members born in the city, but they do show that in two quite different unions, a majority of the workers had spent a protracted period in the city by the time they joined a labor organization.

In the Petersburg metalworkers' union, 72 percent of the members were twenty-five years or older (table 21). Many of these workers had probably lived and worked in an urban center for nearly a decade by the time they reached the

[53]Oliunina, *Portnovskii promysel*, pp. 184–185.
[54]See above, chapter 1.

Table 21
Age Distribution, Petersburg Metalworkers' Union,
September 1907

Age	Number of Members		Percent of Membership
Under 17 years	61		
		624	10
17–19 years	563		
20–24	1,130		18
25–29	1,515		
30–34	1,301	3,625	57
35–39	809		
40–44	477		
45–49	272	855	14
50–54	106		
55–59	51		
60–64	16	80	1
65 and over	13		
Total	6,314		100

Source: *Materialy ob ekonomicheskom polozhenii,* p. 79. I have rounded off the percentages to the nearest tenth. In addition to prolonged urban residence, unionized metalworkers in the capital tended to have a relatively stable pattern of employment. One-half of the union's members had spent more than five years in a single firm; 40 percent were employed in the same enterprise for five or more years, and 10 percent for ten to twenty years. Ibid., p. 82.

age of twenty-five—a relatively long period of city living. A survey of workers who belonged to the Moscow metalworkers' union (table 22) shows a somewhat different pattern of age distribution. Here, a far larger percentage of the membership included in the survey belonged to the youthful cohort of workers between the ages of sixteen and twenty (28 percent in Moscow compared with only 10 percent in the capital). Nevertheless, 44 percent of the Moscow members ranged from ages twenty-six to forty, and another 8 percent were over forty years of age. Thus, slightly over one-half of the members of the Moscow metalworkers' union who participated in the survey were twenty-six years of age or older, and had probably already spent a considerable period living and

Table 22

Age Distribution, Moscow Metalworkers' Union,
January 1907

Age	Number of Members	Percent of Membership	
Under 16 years	5	0.25 ⎫	
			28
16–20 years	495	28 ⎬	
21–25	353	20	20
26–30	406	23 ⎫	
31–35	212	12 ⎬	44
36–40	159	9 ⎭	
41–45	88	5 ⎫	
46–50	35	2 ⎬	8
51–55	9	0.5	
56–60	5	0.25 ⎭	
Total	1,767		100

Source: *Pervaia konferentsiia,* p. 103. The table is based on a survey of 1,767 members of the union out of a total of 4,725.

working in an urban center. We do not know how many workers in the sample were born in the city, but at least some members (especially those in the younger age brackets) must have been second-generation workers or have come from urban families.

In the Petersburg tailors' union, three-quarters of the membership fell between the ages of twenty and thirty-nine (table 23). Considering that apprenticeship training in the tailoring trades generally began three or four years earlier than in metalworking, a typical twenty-year-old tailor had already lived and worked in a city for seven or eight years or even longer.

In sum, union members were often skilled and literate and had prolonged urban living and working experience. They were generally male and earned wages that were higher than average in a given industry or occupation. These attributes were particularly prevalent among artisanal workers, "factory artisans," and those employed in sales-clerical occupations.

Table 23
Age Distribution, Petersburg Tailors' Union,
November 1906

Age	Number of Members	Percent of Membership
17–19	178	13
20–39	1,069	75
40–59	119	8
60+	10	1
Unknown	45	3
Total	1,421	100

Source: *Listok dlia rabochikh portnykh, portnikh i skorniakov,* no. 18 (November 18, 1906), p. 6. Of the union members who responded to this particular survey, 1,323 were male and 97 female.

PATTERNS OF UNIONIZATION: THE WORKPLACE

One of the striking features of the union movement in 1906–1907 is the strong showing made by workers employed in small (fifty workers or fewer) and medium-sized (fifty-one to five hundred workers) firms. U. A. Shuster offers an interesting explanation for the high degree of solidarity among workers in small firms:

In small enterprises, where everyone knows one another well, where any violation of comradely social rules leaves its mark on the entire group, and where the character of internal life [in the enterprise] depends on the quality of the collectivity as a whole (especially in enterprises with self-imposed rules), workers zealously maintain their own code of ethics.[55]

Shuster suggests that group pressure for conformity and cooperation in small firms was considerably greater than in large ones, a circumstance that facilitated collective organization. He also notes that there was greater stability in the labor force in small firms, and that labor turnover had a less disruptive effect on the work force in a small enterprise than in large ones. A 10-percent labor turnover in a firm with one thousand workers brought one hundred new workers into the enterprise, a significant alteration in the character of the work force. In a small firm with forty to fifty workers, by contrast, the addition of four or five new

[55]Shuster, *Peterburgskie rabochie,* p. 255.

workers had little impact and the group could easily isolate such a small number. Employers in small firms, moreover, were not in a position to declare massive lockouts or to fire a substantial proportion of their labor force, a frequent occurrence in large firms during these years.[56] We may add to these observations that workers dispersed in numerous small firms had an especially compelling need for coordination and organization in order to win concessions from employers.

Even in industries with a high concentration of labor per enterprise, workers in small- and medium-sized firms displayed a higher *propensity* for unionization than those employed in large-scale enterprises. The very smallest metalworking firms in the capital—those with fewer than fifty workers (employing only 3 percent of the industry's labor force)—had a higher proportion of unionized workers (15 percent) than firms with over one thousand workers (10 percent). Since the union made virtually no effort to recruit workers in small enterprises, focusing instead on large- and medium-sized firms, the workers in small metalworking shops who joined the organization had to seek it out on their own. The self-motivation and initiative of workers in small firms earned them a reputation as "the most conscious, active elements [of the union], who stood on the very highest level of development."[57] Within the union, however, workers from large firms predominated, providing nearly one-half the total union members compared with only 3 percent from very small firms. The highest rate of recruitment in the capital's metalworking industry occurred in medium-sized firms (fifty-one to five hundred workers) where about one out of five workers joined the union. These firms supplied about one-third of the total union members (table 24).

In the Moscow metalworkers' union, the recruitment rate in small firms (eleven to fifty workers) was 44 percent. In firms with more than five hundred workers, by contrast, only 10 percent of the labor force had joined union ranks by December 1906. The propensity for unionization was substantially higher in small firms than in very large ones. Workers in medium-sized firms also proved eager to unionize and they accounted for the bulk of the union membership (59 percent) (table 25).

But even large metalworking plants with more than five hundred workers were subdivided into numerous small workshops—a machine shop, a pattern shop, a foundry, and so on. The skilled metalfitters and lathe operators who provided numerous recruits for the metalworkers' unions in both cities generally

---

[56]Ibid., p. 254.
[57]*Materialy ob ekonomicheskom polozhenii*, p. 91.

Table 24

Membership in the Petersburg Metalworkers' Union by Size of Firm, September 1907

	PETERSBURG METALWORKING INDUSTRY			PETERSBURG METALWORKERS' UNION		
Size of Enterprise	Number of Enterprises	Number of Workers	Workers as % of Total	Number of Members	Members as % of Workers in these Enterprises	Members as % of Total Union Membership
Over 1,000 workers	13	41,835	62	4,159	10	48
501–1,000	15	11,069	17	1,619	15	19
201–500	20	6,355	9	1,404	22	16
51–200	56	5,910	9	1,229	21	14
50 and under	78	2,071	3	307	15	3
Total	182	67,240	100	8,718	13	100

Source: *Materialy ob ekonomicheskom polozhenii*, p. 77.

Table 25

Membership in the Moscow Metalworkers' Union by Size of Firm, December 1906

Size of Enterprise	Number of Enterprises with Union Members	Total Number of Workers Employed in these Enterprises	Number of Members	Members as % of Workers in these Enterprises	Members as % of Total Union Membership
501–3,000 workers	3	4,030	412	10	24
201–500	7	2,400	546	23	32
101–200	8	1,288	412	32	24
51–100	4	297	51	17	3
11–50	20	635	282	44	17
Total	42	8,650	1,703	20	100

Source: *Pervaia konferentsiia*, p. 6. This table is based on a survey of 1,703 union members (out of 4,725) conducted in December 1906, when the union had been in existence only about eight months. Union members who participated in the survey were employed in forty-two different firms employing a total of 8,650 workers (out of roughly 33,000 in this industry in the city as a whole). In contrast to the foregoing table for the Petersburg metalworkers' union, this table discloses the proportion of unionized workers only in relation to the total labor force in firms where unionized workers were employed, rather than in relation to all firms in the industry.

had a relatively small-scale *immediate* work environment within large plants. In the machine shop, for example, the fitters and lathe operators were likely to know each other, to participate in shop-floor rituals and to share social ties. Thus, in assessing the connection between the size of an enterprise and the propensity to unionize, we must keep in mind that even in very large-scale firms, such as those in metalworking, many skilled workers confronted a small-scale work environment at the shop level.

In some industries, changes taking place in the organization of production and the character of the labor force also affected the workers' disposition to unionize. The proliferation of subcontracting shops in the apparel and shoemaking trades led to an actual or threatened deterioration in the conditions of many workers. This circumstance hastened unionization among tailors and shoemakers in 1905, a situation that continued into 1906–1907. Following the legalization of the Petersburg and Moscow unions of tailors, these workers persistently called for the abolition of subcontracting in the apparel trades.[58]

Workers in artisanal trades were not the only ones whose disposition to unionize was fortified by adverse developments at the point of production. The Moscow tobacco workers' union attracted more than one-third (36 percent) of the industry's workers into its ranks, and in contrast to most organizations, 44 percent of the members were female. In this industry, machinery had begun to replace hand labor at the end of the nineteenth century. The continued mechanization of production, with its threat to jobs and wage rates, contributed to the solidarity of the tobacco workers.

A somewhat different circumstance affected the Moscow candymaking industry, where the union drew 47 percent of the industry's workers. This was an industry in which unskilled adult women constituted 53 percent of the labor force in 1902. Beginning in 1905, employers systematically replaced male workers with women, who were deemed to be more passive (the industry had witnessed several large strikes in 1905), and who generally earned lower wages than their male counterparts.[59] Largely in response to this crisis in employment, male workers joined the union in impressive numbers. Significantly, only 3 percent of the union members were female (see table 20). In addition, both tobacco workers and candymakers had acquired, by 1906, considerable prior

[58] *Portnoi*, no. 5–6 (July 14, 1907), p. 3; Oliunina, *Portnovskii promysel*, p. 290; *Ekho*, no. 4 (June 25, 1906). This demand was also adopted by the all-Russian conference of tailors' unions in August 1906.

[59] *Professional'noe dvizhenie Moskovskikh pishchevikov v gody pervoi revoliutsii*, sbornik 1 (Moscow, 1927), pp. 76, 131–132.

exposure to collective organization—before 1905 through contact with the Zubatov societies, and in trade unions during the revolution.

OTHER FACTORS AFFECTING UNIONIZATION

The bakers provide a further illustration of the circumstances that sometimes facilitated unionization. Baking was a relatively low-status occupation, despite the fact that extensive apprenticeship training was required to master the trade. Except for a minority of highly skilled worker "aristocrats" in the baking industry, most bakers lacked the literacy level and sophistication found among other strata of the artisanal population, such as the tailors. Almost exclusively male and recruited from the countryside, the bakers retained a semipeasant character after long years of employment in the city. In large measure this was a consequence of the insular conditions in small bakeries, where employers frequently confined workers to the premises even during nonworking hours.[60]

The industry was in a state of flux at the beginning of the twentieth century because of the growth of large bakeries, such as the Filippov firm. These large establishments placed competitive pressure on small bakeries, which were forced to lower production costs in order to survive.[61] The resulting degeneration of conditions in smaller bakeries helped to mobilize workers in the years 1906–1907. It was this circumstance, among others, that explains why the bakers' union in the capital attracted nearly two-thirds, and the Moscow bakers' union over two-fifths, of the industry's labor force into their ranks by early 1907.

In the Petersburg baking industry, a major strike waged under union auspices in June 1906 also accelerated recruitment. The union, which was already well established in late 1905, claimed more than 1,300 members in April 1906. During June it conducted a successful strike in the capital's baking industry, and in that month the flow of new members increased from 382 in May to 1,346 in June, bringing the total union membership in mid-1906 to 3,065, or nearly half the workers in Petersburg bakeries.[62]

The presence of energetic and effective leaders in this industry further assisted

[60]*Professional'nyi vestnik*, no. 2 (January 20, 1907), p. 11; *Zhizn' pekarei*, no. 2 (5) (May 10, 1914), p. 8.

[61]*Professional'noe dvizhenie Moskovskikh pishchevikov*, pp. 102, 105, 112, 116.

[62]*Listok bulochnikov i konditerov*, no. 10 (January 28, 1907), p. 9; *Professional'nyi vestnik*, no. 2 (January 20, 1907), p. 13.

union recruitment. The Social Democratic and Socialist Revolutionary bakers who had received their formative experience in radical circles before 1905 continued to furnish many of the leaders of the Moscow bakers' union. In 1905 they helped to create the union, and in the following year they were elected to union offices.[63] Salesclerks in bakeries, generally better educated and informed than the bakers, supplied organizational skills and leadership that were in short supply. Thus, the bakery salesclerk Smirnov was one of the founders of the Moscow bakers' union and became its first president in 1906.[64]

A core group of able and active labor leaders often proved decisive in the establishment and growth of a trade union. As in 1905, labor leaders during this period frequently belonged not to the working class but to the intelligentsia, many of them closely associated with a political party or group (the Social Democrats, Socialist Revolutionaries, Kadets, and syndicalists). Organizers such as Grinevich, Kolokol'nikov, Sher, and Kruglov remained prominent figures in the unions during 1906–1907. They were joined by many others, including students, lawyers, and party activists, who dedicated their time and energy to the union movement. Intelligentsia activists possessed the skills, the know-how, and the free time required to conduct union affairs, and they exerted a powerful influence over these organizations. Under their tutelage, a new generation of worker activists emerged that would carry on union activity in the years to follow.

The presence of intelligentsia activists was especially critical in occupations such as floorpolishing, chimneysweeping, and cab driving, where the bulk of the labor force was unskilled and ill-equipped to handle the complex tasks of establishing and sustaining a union.[65] Nearly every union represented in the Petersburg Central Bureau of Trade Unions had one intelligentsia organizer active in its affairs.[66] Lawyers, in particular, played an important part in the union movement. Beginning in 1905, they organized a legal aid committee under the auspices of the Central Bureau of Trade Unions, and in 1906–1907 they assisted in drawing up charters under the new law and providing legal defense for the unions.[67]

---

[63]*Professional'noe dvizhenie Moskovskikh pishchevikov*, pp. 105, 112, 116.

[64]Ibid.

[65]Kolokol'nikov, "Otryvki," *MIPDR*, 4:269–270; Sviatlovskii, *Istoriia*, p. 108; F. I. Andronov, "Iz istorii professional'nogo dvizheniia izvozchikov v Peterburge," *Krasnaia letopis'*, no. 1 (12) (1925), pp. 111–113.

[66]Kolokol'nikov, "Otryvki," *MIPDR*, 4:269–270.

[67]TsGAOR, DPOO, f. 111, opis' 5, d. 263, 1909, pp. 112–113.

As the trade union movement developed, a growing number of working-class leaders acquired prominence. Many had already become active in 1905, and continued to serve as union officers over the next three or four years. Regrettably, little is known about the life histories of the workers who became labor leaders in this period. One such worker was Aleksandr Iatsynevich, a metalfitter elected president of the Petersburg metalworkers' union in 1906. Five years earlier, in 1901, Iatsynevich first became involved in Social Democratic activities while he was employed at the Obukhov plant. In 1903 he was arrested for his underground work and exiled to Tver. Returning to the capital in 1904, he found a job at the Odner plant, and in January 1905 he joined the Gapon march to the Winter Palace, where he was wounded in the mêlée. Kolokol'nikov first encountered Iatsynevich in early 1905, and later described him as "a good organizer, with a clear practical mind and a restrained, perhaps even somewhat cold character."[68] In the fall of that year, Iatsynevich took part in efforts to form a Petersburg metalworkers' union, and in the following spring he was one of the founding members. Elected to the first union directing board, Iatsynevich served as treasurer and then as president, a position he retained until 1910.

Another worker activist in the Petersburg metalworkers' union was Roman Malinovskii, a lathe operator, who rose to fame on the eve of World War I as a Social Democratic deputy to the Fourth State Duma.[69] In 1907 Malinovskii was elected secretary of the metalworkers' union. Recalling Malinovskii's activities in the union, Bulkin observed that "no one knew better than [Malinovskii] how to inspire and direct the young worker, or to give him general knowledge and instruction on how to draw new elements into the union, how to interest rank-and-file members in the life and work of the union."[70]

Iatsynevich and Malinovskii belonged to a new generation of labor activists. Many of them had earlier experiences with SD or SR circles, the Zubatov or Gapon organizations, or even a mutual aid society. During 1905 they often took the lead in forming strike committees, factory committees, and trade unions, and in the following year they carried forward the effort to build a mass-based labor movement. Their activities will be examined further on, but suffice it to note that their enthusiasm for the union cause was a decisive factor in the rapid growth of trade unions during these months.

---

[68]Kolokol'nikov, "Otryvki," *MIPDR*, 4:277.

[69]On Malinovskii's career, see Ralph Carter Elwood, *Roman Malinovsky: A Life Without a Cause* (Newtonville, Mass., 1977), and below, chapter 10.

[70]Bulkin, *Na zare*, p. 199.

CRAFT UNIONISM AND DISTRICT PATRIOTISM

During the first phase of union formation in 1905, craft unions far outnumbered those organized along industrial lines. Industrial unionism gained new adherents among workers in 1906–1907, but there was still considerable support for craft-based organizations. About two-thirds of the legal organizations in each city were organized on a craft basis during this period. Artisanal workers established about one-third of all the unions in St. Petersburg and Moscow, and with the exception of the woodworkers and some skilled construction trades, they formed craft unions. But craft unions also emerged among a variety of factory, service, and sales-clerical groups, such as metal patternmakers, tinsmiths, waiters, and salesclerks. The prevalence of craft unions reflected the persistence among workers of *tsekhovshchina*. "Shop cliquishness," as one labor organizer put it,[71] remained a force to be reckoned with.

The years 1906–1907 witnessed the growing involvement of factory workers in the organized labor movement and the formation of new industrial unions. These industrial organizations sometimes attracted a large membership and overall, more workers belonged to industrial than to craft unions in this period. In the Petersburg metalworking industry, for example, the union of metalworkers—an industrial organization—boasted a peak membership of about 10,700 workers, whereas the various craft unions in metalworking (blacksmiths, patternmakers, workers in gold, silver, and bronze, and others) attracted a combined total of only about 2,500 workers. But some unions ostensibly organized on an industrial principle—such as the woodworkers' and construction workers' unions—were little more than confederations of semiautonomous craft groups. Among the Moscow woodworkers, union organizers complained about the "craft aspirations" of various specialized subgroups within the industry, such as parquet-floor workers, toy makers, umbrella makers, and icon makers. All of these groups tried to establish separate craft unions, but eventually consented to become incorporated as sections within the larger industrial union of woodworkers.[72]

A former organizer of the Moscow metalworkers' union has described the

[71]Kolokol'nikov, "Otryvki," *MIPDR*, 4:275.

[72]Bulkin, *Na zare*, pp. 286–287. Iu. K. Milonov and M. Rakovskii, *Istoriia Moskovskogo professional'nogo soiuza rabochikh derevoobdelochnikov*, vyp. 1 (Moscow 1928), p. 156. Similarly, among Moscow textile workers, the hand printers formed a separate section within the larger union. Zaiats, *Tekstili*, p. 180. On the construction workers, see T. V. Sapronov, ed., *Iubileinyi sbornik: Po istorii dvizheniia stroitel'nykh rabochikh Moskvy* (Moscow, 1922).

resistance to industrial unionism in 1906, when this union was in the process of formation:

The directing board wasted a great deal of time and energy discussing how to organize the union: on industrial or occupational lines. Among the members there was a rather strong inclination to construct the union according to occupation. Thus, for example, the patternmakers pointed out that they should join the union of woodworkers— "there, after all, they can better appreciate our work and more correctly assess our labor." The tinsmiths also wanted to form their own union, as did the mechanics. I recall that we repeatedly pointed out to them that this would create difficulties for conducting a strike. Workers in a single enterprise would belong to different unions, and on this account the conduct of a strike and the provision of assistance to strikers would have to be implemented simultaneously by several unions, which would be very complicated. Finally it was decided to construct a union along industrial lines, with the provision that occupational groups such as patternmakers, tinsmiths, mechanics, and electricians would be separated into special sections within the union, with their own directing board and their own union fund.[73]

By the end of 1906, however, there were only two sections within the Moscow metalworkers' union: tinsmiths and patternmakers. Although each section met to discuss special problems and needs, the patternmakers voted in late October not to establish a separate directing board and treasury for their section but to subordinate themselves to the larger organization. Not all patternmakers supported this decision, but a majority prevailed.[74]

Whereas the Moscow metalworkers' union accommodated most specialized groups by forming autonomous sections within the larger union, Petersburg tinsmiths, blacksmiths, patternmakers, and several other groups resisted incorporation and maintained separate craft unions in 1906–1907. "Even the metalworkers' union," noted one contemporary account, "did not succeed in upholding entirely consistently the principle of industrial organization," because about 5 percent of the union members consisted of metalworkers employed in firms other than metalworking, for example, in textiles or printing. In accordance with the principles of industrial unionism, these workers should have belonged to the textile or printers' union, but their identity as metalworkers led

[73]Matveev, "Moskovskii soiuz rabochikh-metallistov," *MIPDR*, 2:253. Moscow tinsmiths also organized a separate union. It is significant that metalworkers employed in other industries, such as textiles, made a point of joining the metalworkers' union. This violation of the principle of industrial unionism was criticized in the contemporary labor press. *Stanok*, no. 2 (March 11, 1908), p. 6.

[74]Z. Shchap, *Moskovskie metallisty v professional'nom dvizhenii. Ocherki po istorii Moskovskogo soiuza metallistov* (Moscow, 1927), pp. 99–100.

them to make common cause with others of the same occupational specialization.[75]

A shared occupational specialization provided the basis for solidarity in many of the trade unions established in 1906–1907. But this was not the only kind of particularistic allegiance that drew workers together during these months. "Factory patriotism" had been an important unifying factor in 1905, and some factory committees, especially in metalworking, remained active following the revolution.[76] In 1906–1907, "district patriotism" also became a force in the labor movement.

District patriotism, or allegiance to a specific city district, was especially pronounced in the capital because of the high degree of labor concentration and social homogeneity in certain neighborhoods.[77] In the spring of 1906, the trade union press reported that efforts were under way in three city districts—the Vasilevskii Island, Nevskaia, and Narvskaia districts—to form general unions incorporating workers of various occupations.[78] These efforts did not succeed, but an organization with a district focus was legally registered in April 1907: the Narvskii Union of Tailors.

One attempt at using district allegiance as the basis for unionization enjoyed brief success in 1906. V. I. Smesov, a metal draftsman and former Social Democrat who had served as an informant for the Okhrana since 1904, began to organize a general union in the capital in January 1906. He went so far as to prepare a charter for the "St. Petersburg General Professional Workers' Union," and was received by an official from the Ministry of Internal Affairs. But for unknown reasons, this project failed to materialize.[79]

In the summer of 1906, Smesov tried his hand at a more modest project involving workers in the Vasilevskii Island district. The union, which attracted mainly metalworkers from the Siemens-Halske, Baltiiskii, and Trubochnii plants,

---

[75]*Bez zaglaviia*, no. 10 (March 26, 1906), p. 418; *Materialy ob ekonomicheskom polozhenii*, pp. 72–73.

[76]TsGAOR, f. 6860, d. 30, 1907, p. 11; *Materialy ob ekonomicheskom polozhenii*, pp. 53–54.

[77]K. Dmitriev [P. Kolokol'nikov], *Iz praktiki professional'nogo dvizheniia v Rossii* (Odessa, 1907), p. 97; Bulkin, *Na zare*, p. 288.

[78]*Listok dlia rabochikh portnykh, portnikh i skorniakov*, no. 6 (April 15, 1906), p. 3.

[79]LGIA, f. 560, opis 26, d. 586, pp. 6–8. The Smesov union charter specified that the basic tasks of the organization were "to organize workers to defend their legal and professional interests, to improve the intellectual and moral level of workers, and to give material assistance to members." Membership was open to all workers, regardless of sex, religion, or nationality. Dues were high—50 kopecks per month—and the union attracted mainly the very prosperous, highly skilled segments of the labor force. The charter is dated January 23, 1906, and signed by Smesov.

was not recognized by the Central Bureau of Trade Unions, but it managed to establish "rather deep roots" in the district and to interfere with recruitment by the Petersburg metalworkers' union. The metalworkers' union even entered into negotiations with Smesov to incorporate his organization as a section of the union, but Smesov demanded too much autonomy, and the negotiations collapsed. On April 15, 1907, after Smesov had left the organization, the remaining members decided to merge with the metalworkers' union.[80] The apparent success of the Smesov venture, however brief, was indicative of the vitality of district allegiances in the capital.

The legal labor movement that emerged following the March 4 law attracted thousands of Petersburg and Moscow workers from all sectors of the urban economy. About one-tenth of the total labor force in each city joined a trade union between March 1906 and June 1907, and in some industries and occupations as many as two out of three workers became organized in these months. This was an impressive record in so short a time, comparing favorably with union movements elsewhere. Never before had so many Petersburg and Moscow workers directly participated in a collective labor association. Their responsiveness to the new legal trade unions was partly an outcome of experiences acquired during the preceding revolutionary year, which had taught workers the necessity for organization. But the aspiration to unite collectively had even deeper roots, extending back to the years preceding the revolution when some workers had taken their first steps to find bases of solidarity with others in illegal groups, government-sponsored organizations, and mutual aid societies.

The workers who joined trade unions in 1906 and early 1907 were employed in widely diverse industries, occupations, and trades. Trade unions arose not only among printers and metalworkers, but also among household servants, chimneysweeps, and cabmen, groups that had already been drawn into the organized labor movement during the revolutionary upheavals of 1905. Notwithstanding the diversity of the trade unions, however, certain workers were more likely than others to join a labor organization. I have argued that the acquisition of a specialized skill was the single most distinctive common characteristic among unionized workers in this period, continuing the pattern already discerned in 1905 and earlier. Skilled workers were generally more literate and more ur-

---

[80]Kolokol'nikov, "Otryvki," *MIPDR,* 4:287. For additional material on Smesov, see P. Vasil'ev, "Ushakovshchina," *Trud v Rossii,* no. 1 (1925), pp. 151–152; F. Semenov-Bulkin, "Smesovshchina," *Trud v Rossii,* no. 1 (1925), pp. 153–170.

banized than others in their industry or occupation, and they had a clearer conception of themselves as "workers" and a stronger sense of their status and self-worth. Skilled workers provided the backbone for the union movement in 1906–1907 and furnished many of its recruits.

Nevertheless, there were notable exceptions to this pattern, and some predominantly unskilled groups also formed well-subscribed and lively unions in this period. Several circumstances help to explain why these groups were able to unionize successfully. In certain cases, the impetus for unionization came from a deterioration in workplace conditions and employment opportunities; in others, energetic union organizers or a victorious union-directed strike induced workers to add their names to union rolls. Workers with prior experience in collective organization dating back to the Zubatov societies and other pre-1905 associations often responded positively to the union movement in 1906–1907.

Factory groups, such as the metalworkers, became a major force in the union movement during this period, and their involvement was accompanied by the spread of industrial unions. Craft and industrial unions, which tended to emerge sequentially in Western Europe at an earlier time, thus developed simultaneously in Russia during 1906–1907. But notwithstanding the growth of industrial unions, craft unionism remained a widespread form of labor organization. In 1906–1907 craft consciousness was a powerful unifying factor, not only among artisanal workers but among many others as well.

Craft unionism was only one of several manifestations of narrow parochial allegiances in this period. Apart from factory patriotism—a waning but still significant phenomenon in 1906–1907—some workers showed a strong disposition to unite on the basis of their ties to a city district. District patriotism, which can be traced back to the highly successful local branches of the Gapon Assembly before the revolution, received further reinforcement from the creation, of district soviets during the fall of 1905 and the growth of large decentralized unions the following year.

Thousands of workers put their names on union rolls during the fifteen months between March 1906 and June 1907, joining for the first time labor organizations that functioned openly and legally in tsarist Russia. But the act of becoming a union member was merely the first, albeit important, step for workers who joined the organized labor movement. To be effective, trade unions needed the steady support of the membership and a solid organizational and administrative infrastructure. Their creation was one of the most pressing tasks facing trade unionists in the new era of legal labor association.

Chapter 6

The Organization and Ideology of Trade Unions, 1906–1907

> What can the trade union give to the workers and what can they expect from it? The union can give them new methods of professional struggle for workers' interests, methods that have been developed through the practice of European trade unions.
>
> *First Conference of Metalworkers' Unions, February 1907*[1]

The swift collapse of trade unions in December 1905 impressed upon labor leaders the critical importance of creating institutional structures and a membership base capable of withstanding future adversities.[2] Yet it was no simple matter to build a workers' organization in a country where individuals had so little prior experience with independent voluntary associations. Apart from a small number of mutual aid societies, transitory strike committees, and the short-lived government-sponsored labor associations, workers had little opportunity for self-management prior to 1905. Even such activities as the election of an "elder" on the shop floor were traditionally conducted under the direct supervision of the factory administration.

It was not until 1905 that workers established their first independent, mass-

---

[1] *Pervaia konferentsiia professional'nykh soiuzov rabochikh po metallu Moskovskogo promyshlennogo raiona* (Moscow, 1907), p. 34.

[2] When the Second All-Russian Conference of Trade Unions convened in February 1906, the first topic on the agenda for discussion was "Organizational Questions of the Trade Union Movement." *Vtoraia konferentsiia professional'nykh soiuzov: Doklady i protokoly* (St. Petersburg, 1906), pp. 15–16.

based organizations—factory committees, soviets, and trade unions. Most of these associations, hastily improvised in the midst of a revolutionary upheaval, did not survive the government's counteroffensive in December, and they provided a scant foundation for subsequent organizational endeavors in the era of legal trade unionism inaugurated by the law of March 4, 1906.

The effort to build a legal labor movement in St. Petersburg and Moscow took place under conditions that had no analog in Russia's history. The year 1906 and the first half of 1907 represented a transitional period, when the forces of revolution, though subsiding, were still quite palpable, and the forces of reaction had not yet succeeded in fully reconstituting their former powers. The regime's coercive apparatus and interventionist policies toward labor remained markedly attenuated prior to June 1907, and the fear of provoking popular disorders served to moderate government conduct toward workers and to create an environment for organized labor that was more hospitable than at any other time in the tsarist era, except in the "days of freedom" during October and November 1905.

Unions were thus in a position between March 1906 and June 1907 to take advantage of the newly established principle of legal authorization for collective labor associations, and even to transcend some of the limitations and restrictions of the March 1906 law. The Menshevik trade unionist Sher has described the situation in which unions operated during these months:

It is extremely difficult now to convey the conditions of work in the [St. Petersburg] trade union movement in 1906–1907. These conditions involved a curious web of contradictions between the law [of March 4, 1906] and reality. The forces of the revolution were still too imposing and real in this period for the limitations of the law on unions promulgated on March 4, 1906, to have been realized. Without exaggeration, it can be said that the law of March 4 began to be implemented by the government only after the dissolution of the Second [State] Duma [in June 1907]. Until that time, we succeeded in expanding significantly the limits of the law.[3]

But despite the relatively tolerant atmosphere in 1906 and early 1907, there were complex and disparate tendencies. On the one hand, as Sher observes, the limitations of the March 4 law were sometimes surmounted by unions in bold and audacious ways. Yet trade unionists were also subjected to intermittent harassment and intimidation, and most important, the government had the power to withhold or to rescind the legal status of an organization. In the capital,

[3]V. Sher, "Stranichka iz vospominanii," *Materialy po istorii professional'nogo dvizheniia v Rossii* (henceforth *MIPDR*), 5 vols. (Moscow, 1924–1927), vol. 4, p. 68.

to a greater extent than in Moscow, local officials exercised this power on a number of occasions.

Trade unionists—both the leadership and the rank and file—were, on the whole, eager to establish and maintain the legal status of their organizations. Many intelligentsia radicals shared Grinevich's view that "one of the greatest achievements of the October days was the opportunity for the open existence of workers' organizations which are directing the economic struggle of the proletariat."[4] Convinced that unions provided a training ground for the Russian working class, these intelligentsia activists—many of them members of the Menshevik faction—placed tremendous importance on maintaining and strengthening labor's legal rights. Only under such conditions, they argued, would it be possible to build mass-membership organizations capable of equipping workers for their future tasks as agents of social change and social reconstruction.

Rank-and-file members were also concerned about preserving the legal status of their organizations. They feared the potential hazards of membership in an illegal union, and the experiences of the preceding year had taught them that legal status was indispensable for the growth and activities of trade unions. Without it, unions were barred from holding general membership meetings, a circumstance that obstructed recruitment. Employers, moreover, usually refused to enter into negotiations with representatives of an illegal organization. Under conditions such as these, trade unionists did their best to acquire and retain legal status, or, if forced to relinquish it, to reregister on the earliest possible occasion.

UNION DEMOCRACY AND PROBLEMS OF INTERNAL
ORGANIZATION

The trade union movement that developed in 1906–1907 provided many workers with their first opportunity to participate in or even to observe a voluntary association organized along democratic lines. In introducing both the theory and the practice of union democracy to the rank and file, intelligentsia activists drew heavily on the example of Western European labor movements for guidance and models.

A reliance on Western models was entirely logical, since many trade unionists (including Mensheviks, liberals, syndicalists, and even some Socialist Revolu-

[4]V. Grinevich, writing in *Professional'nyi vestnik*, no. 14 (September 29, 1907), p. 1.

tionaries) took it for granted that Russian workers were proceeding along the same well-trodden path as had their Western European counterparts at an earlier period. "As soon as the Russian workers' movement emerged from the underground," wrote Grinevich in 1906, "it followed the form of organization that had been tested in Western Europe—the trade union."[5] The organized labor movement in Germany, he observed, provided the most relevant example for Russian trade unionists. But contemporaries did not confine their interest to Germany alone; they sought instruction in virtually all of the more advanced industrialized countries of Europe and, to a lesser extent, North America.

Numerous books, pamphlets, articles, and translations on the subject of Western European unions appeared in these years, many of them written by intellectuals who were themselves active in the labor movement.[6] Mensheviks and liberals, in particular, devoted considerable time and energy to educating workers about contemporary and historical aspects of trade unionism in the West. They arranged lectures on the subject, and as editors of many union newspapers, they saw to it that not an issue appeared without a column devoted to labor movements abroad. Only a handful of Russian workers had any personal contact with Western European labor unions. They learned about labor movements abroad through the energetic efforts of intellectuals who were "the ideologists for the unions and the bearers of Western European experience."[7]

One issue stressed by many intelligentsia activists was the importance of establishing democratic organs and procedures within the unions. Most of the unions formed in 1905 had been organized on the principle of direct democracy. The general membership meeting proclaimed the founding of the union, approved its charter, elected a directing board (typically consisting of ten to fifteen voting members), and served as the paramount decision-making body. Following legalization, many unions continued to rely on the general meeting as the

[5]V. Grinevich [M. G. Kogan], Introduction to P. Umbreit, *Znachenie i zadachi tsentral'nykh biuro professional'nykh soiuzov* (St. Petersburg, 1906), p. 4.

[6]See, for example, S. I. Somov, *Professional'nye soiuzy i sotsialdemokraticheskaia partiia* (St. Petersburg, 1907); V. Sviatlovskii, *Sovremennoe zakonodatel'stvo o professional'nykh rabochikh soiuzakh. Frantsiia. Bel'giia. Angliia. Avstraliia. Germaniia. Rossiia.* (St. Petersburg, 1907); idem, *Professional'nye rabochie soiuzy na zapade* (St. Petersburg, 1907). Among the many translations of Western European works on the subject were Umbreit, *Znachenie;* F. Gardins, *Professional'nye soiuzy v rabochem dvizhenii* (Moscow, 1906). The contemporary press carried many articles on the subject as well.

[7]F. A. Bulkin [F. Semenov], *Na zare profdvizheniia: Istoriia Peterburgskogo soiuza metallistov 1906-1914 gg.* (Moscow and Leningrad, 1924), p. 201.

final arbiter in union affairs. But it soon became apparent that this arrangement, spontaneously generated during the preceding year, was ill suited to a period of consolidation rather than revolutionary mobilization.

By the late spring of 1906, unions had begun to raise publicly some of the problems presented by this form of direct democracy. A report by the Petersburg shoemakers' union described the dilemma facing many labor organizations at the time. General meetings, the shoemakers declared, had grown so large as to be unsuited for real discussion of important questions. Union leaders were complaining that they encountered serious obstacles in conveying the nuances of complex issues to rank-and-file members, who sometimes displayed what was described as a "low level of consciousness." Members, moreover, were said to have an exceedingly passive disposition at these meetings—they simply "listened, remained silent, and voted, often in ways that were approved by the directing board."[8]

Although some union meetings occasionally drew hundreds or even thousands of workers, complaints about low levels of attendance and poor participation appeared more and more often in the labor press during the second half of 1906. The Moscow metalworkers' union reported in December 1906, for example, that "the general membership meeting has outlived its usefulness as a decision-making organ." The meetings, it was observed, were attended by only about one-quarter of the union's membership, and consequently these gatherings did not have legal force, because so few were in attendance.[9] Compared with 1905, the meetings themselves had lost most of their revolutionary élan, and instead of rousing speeches, there were uninspired reports on the practical aspects of day-to-day union affairs. For workers who remembered the emotion-filled gatherings of the preceding year, the more routinized meetings of 1906 seemed dull and lifeless events.

The decline in attendance and the apathetic disposition of many workers at membership meetings was indicative of a larger and persistent problem facing the trade unions. Workers had demonstrated a capacity for intensive activity during the revolutionary months of 1905, but they were not yet accustomed to the methodical and routine kinds of activity required for a sustained organizational effort. As Kolokol'nikov observed in 1907:

[8]*Peterburgskii sapozhnik,* no. 2 (May 21, 1906), p. 1.
[9]*Listok professional'nogo obshchestva rabochikh po obrabotke metallov.* Supplement to *Rabochii soiuz,* no. 9 (December 1, 1906), p. 1.

In our unions we have the same picture as in Western Europe, only here the colors are even more exaggerated. The habit of social activity among us is so little developed, the everyday manifestation of workers' initiative is so weak, the link between rank-and-file members and the union is so feeble, that their participation in the life [of the union] is even more haphazard, and their relationship to union affairs is even more indifferent [than in Western Europe].[10]

The trade unions of 1906–1907 confronted the problem of surmounting a long legacy of lower-class apathy and inexperience in self-management. It fell to the first generation of union organizers to devise structures and procedures that would bring rank-and-file members into regular and sustained contact with the organization, thereby implanting the "habits of social activity" that had received so little nurture in the past.

By mid-1906 it was already apparent that the general meeting was unsatisfactory, both as a locus for decision-making power and as a means of drawing workers into union afairs. Worker attendance and participation were far from encouraging, and the authorities made it difficult to schedule frequent meetings. Under these circumstances, trade unionists adopted a different approach, involving an alternative model of decision making, based on the principle of representation.[11]

During the summer of 1906, many unions began to establish citywide delegate councils—variously termed *sovety delegatov* or *sovety vybornykh*—whose members were elected at the enterprise level. The directing board of the Petersburg textile workers' union decided in July 1906 to create a delegate council with one representative for every forty or fifty members.[12] The First All-Russian Conference of Tailors held on August 25–27, 1906, resolved that "the directing board [of the union] should be responsible to the general meeting, but [in order to maintain] links between the directing board and the masses, it is recommended that delegate councils be elected by workshops to conduct agitation on behalf of the union and to collect dues." The Petersburg construction workers' union adopted a modified version of the delegate system. Instead of electing union delegates at the place of employment as was customary in other unions,

[10]K. Dmitriev [P. Kolokol'nikov] in *V pomoshch' rabochemu: Sbornik statei (o professional'nom i kooperativnom dvizhenii)*, vyp. 1 [Moscow, 1907], p. 18.

[11]K. Dmitriev [P. Kolokol'nikov], *Iz praktiki professional'nogo dvizheniia v Rossii* (Odessa, 1907), pp. 75–77.

[12]*Tkach*, no. 5 (August 19, 1906), p. 4. Similarly, in the Petersburg metalworkers' union, members in large firms elected one delegate per fifty members, while those in small firms elected one per twenty-five members. Bulkin, *Na zare*, pp. 290–291.

here union members assembled by residential district to elect representatives.[13]

Delegate councils were not an entirely new phenomenon in 1906. They had already made an appearance in the Petersburg printers' union and in several Moscow unions during 1905, in response to the need for improved communication and coordination among widely dispersed union members.[14] The widespread introduction of delegate councils in 1906 may have been facilitated by their similarity to the organizing principle of the Soviets of Workers' Deputies. Citywide soviets were based on a delegate system, but whereas all workers were theoretically entitled to participate in elections to the soviet, only unionized workers in a single industry or occupation elected delegates to the citywide union council. The concept of delegate councils may also have been borrowed from Western labor movements, where such councils had long been in operation.

During 1906–1907 delegate councils frequently assumed the functions formerly vested in the general membership meeting.[15] Henceforth, the highest executive organ of the union, the directing board, was elected by a two-stage procedure: rank-and-file members first elected delegates at the enterprise level, who in turn elected the board. This form of indirect election was already familiar to Petersburg and Moscow workers, for the Executive Committee of the Soviet of Workers' Deputies had been elected by delegates originally chosen in factories and shops.

The shift in decision-making power from the general membership meeting to the delegate council was accompanied by a good deal of discussion and debate. Intelligentsia union leaders were divided over the issue. Some, such as Kolokol'nikov, defended the inherently democratic nature of the arrangement by analogy to the election of a Ministry by the English Parliament.[16] But when the issue was debated in the Petersburg metalworkers' union, Grinevich objected to the indirect form of election as "insufficiently democratic."[17] In the Petersburg union of electrical workers, where the matter was considered in June 1906, some members argued that the delegate system was inherently undemocratic because

[13]V. Sviatlovskii, *Professional'noe dvizhenie v Rossii* (St. Petersburg, 1907), p. 292; Dmitriev, *Iz praktiki*, p. 79.

[14]*Istoriia odnogo soiuza* (Moscow, 1907), p. 15, for a discussion of this arrangement among Moscow teapackers in 1905.

[15]Dmitriev [Kolokol'nikov], *Iz praktiki*, p. 89, for an enumeration of the functions assumed by the delegate councils.

[16]Ibid., pp. 90–91.

[17]Kolokol'nikov, "Otryvki," *MIPDR*, 4:278.

workers in small firms would not have an opportunity to elect their own delegates. In the end, however, this union and many others adopted the delegate system.[18]

Delegate councils assumed final authority over the resolution of various practical, financial, and policy issues. Some council meetings were conducted with considerable orderliness and attention to procedural matters. In the Moscow printers' union, "everything was permeated with such sedateness and respectability," a former worker recalled, "that it seemed as if you were attending some kind of a *zemstvo* assembly and not a workers' meeting."[19]

In other unions, however, worker-delegates had difficulty accustoming themselves to formalities and procedures. A Moscow teapacker urged his fellow delegates to restrain themselves at council meetings, to speak only in turn, to present reports expeditiously, and finally, to elect a chairman to conduct meetings.[20] But even where council meetings were disorganized and unruly, the citywide gatherings provided the occasion for an exchange of views, and decisions were nearly always reached by majority vote.

Individual delegates soon came to perform a variety of vital functions in the union. The detailed instructions for delegates drawn up by the Petersburg metalworkers' union in February 1907 specified that the delegate was expected to collect membership dues, distribute the union newspaper, circulate union questionnaires, hold meetings on the shop level, and serve as a conduit between the members and the union directing board. Obviously a great deal depended on the vigor and competence of those elected to this position.[21] In turn, worker-delegates acquired valuable training and experience in handling union affairs. Union executive officers and dedicated core members of the organization frequently proceeded from delegate ranks.

In the larger unions the delegate system did not prove entirely successful, either as a forum for decision making or as a means of drawing the rank and file into union affairs. The number of delegates in some councils—reaching two hundred in the Petersburg metalworkers' union—made it difficult to engage in

---

[18]*Ekho*, no. 2 (June 23, 1906), p. 4.

[19]G. Matveev, "Moskovskii soiuz rabochikh-metallistov v 1906–1907 gg. (po lichnym vospominaniiam)," *MIPDR*, 2:251. The *zemstvos* were organs of rural self-government introduced in 1864 and dominated by the local nobility.

[20]*Istoriia odnogo soiuza*, p. 34.

[21]The delegate's functions are described in Bulkin, *Na zare*, p. 291; Shchap, *Moskovskie metallisty v professional'nom dvizhenii: Ocherki po istorii Moskovskogo soiuza metallistov* (Moscow, 1927), p. 68; *Zhizn' pechatnika*, no. 8 (July 20, 1907), p. 11.

genuine discussion and debate.[22] Individual delegates, moreover, could not easily perform the many duties that now rested on their shoulders, and contact with union members at the shop level became attenuated.

But there were other problems as well. The Petersburg printers' union published a revealing account in mid-1907 of the misconduct of some union delegates. The article called attention to incidents of embezzlement of union dues and noted that many delegates came to union meetings drunk. In response to this situation, the directing board no longer scheduled delegate meetings immediately after payday. Some delegates, according to the report, behaved badly on the job and earned the disrespect of fellow workers. The misconduct of even two or three delegates, the article concluded, discredited the whole organization.[23]

The Moscow metalworkers' union encountered a different problem. Here, it was noted in December 1906, delegates had difficulty meeting on a citywide basis because they were so dispersed among numerous enterprises. Some trade unionists proposed district branches to overcome this difficulty.[24] Influential labor leaders, such as Kolokol'nikov, enthusiastically endorsed the concept of district-level groups in the expectation that these local union organs would bridge the gap between the leadership and the rank and file:

Thanks to the [district-level] groups, the union begins to acquire flesh and blood in the eyes of the rank-and-file membership, ceasing to be an abstraction which exists in some never-never land; and the moral and material bond between the members and the union grows stronger while the union's influence over the masses broadens and deepens.[25]

During 1906 many unions—including the metalworkers, printers, shoemakers, and tailors in both cities—formed district-level groups that soon became the most lively and vigorous centers for union activity.[26] District patriotism, as we have seen, was an important element in the allegiance of some workers, and it is not surprising, therefore, that district groups proved so successful in mobilizing their participation. To a greater extent than citywide leaders,

[22]Bulkin, *Na zare*, pp. 290–291.

[23]*Zhizn' pechatnika*, no. 8 (July 20, 1907), pp. 11–12.

[24]*Listok professional'nogo obshchestva rabochikh po obrabotke metallov*, p. 1.

[25]Dmitriev, *Iz praktiki*, p. 94.

[26]Bulkin, *Na zare*, p. 88; *Listok professional'nogo obshchestva rabochikh po obrabotke metallov*, p. 1; *Golos pechatnika*, no. 5 (September 16, 1906), p. 12; *Ekho*, no. 3 (June 24, 1906), p. 3; *Istoriia Leningradskogo soiuza rabochikh poligraficheskogo proizvodstva*, Book 1: *1904–1907 gg.* (henceforth *ILS*) (Leningrad, 1925), p. 294.

district officers were in a position to maintain personal relations with workers in the vicinity and to respond more promptly to problems requiring union intervention.

But district organizations presented their own problems, for they tended to undermine the central leadership of the directing board, especially when they had substantial monetary resources at their disposal. The Moscow metalworkers' union, for example, assigned 50 percent of the monthly membership dues to district groups.[27] The district organizations began to exert their autonomy from the union center, and in some unions the tension between centralization and localism became a matter of heated controversy.

The Petersburg metalworkers' union came to grips with this dilemma in early 1907. Since July 1906 the union had functioned illegally. During this time local government officials had done little to interfere with the district-level groups, though they prevented the citywide organization from regaining legal status. As a result, the authority and autonomy of district groups had increased steadily at the expense of the central leadership.

The controversy over the role of district union groups generated considerable disagreement within union ranks. Following an acrimonious debate at a meeting of the citywide organization of metalworkers in February 1907, the membership voted to downgrade the district groups and to make the delegate council the main decision-making body in the union.[28] But when the union finally regained legal status in May 1907, the Petersburg Chief of Police prohibited the establishment of a delegate council.[29] Obliged to assemble clandestinely, the council could not assume the full range of functions and powers ascribed to it in the resolutions of February 1907, and district groups retained considerable de facto authority over the conduct of union affairs.

Whereas district patriotism remained an important factor in the labor movement during this period, factory patriotism was on the decline, and served as a basis for unification mainly in the metalworking industry. In both St. Petersburg and Moscow, factory-level committees continued to exist independently of the union in some large metalworking plants during 1906–1907. These committees,

---

[27]*Listok professional'nogo obshchestva rabochikh po obrabotke metallov*, p. 1; Kolokol'nikov, "Otryvki," *MIPDR*, 4:278, cites this as a key problem in the Petersburg metalworkers' union as well.

[28]Bulkin, *Na zare*, pp. 187–188. According to Bulkin, there were protracted discussions of this question at five separate union meetings held during February, April, and May 1907. The opposition to centralization was centered in the Nevskaia district of the capital, where district loyalties were particularly strong.

[29]*Tsentral'nyi gosudarstvennyi istoricheskii arkhiv* (TsGIA), f. 1284, opis' 187, d. 202, pp. 1, 2, 8, 9.

which originated during 1905, had assumed many of the functions of trade unions.[30] Since only a small proportion of the metalworkers in major firms were unionized, union influence remained circumscribed when it came to the election of a factory committee.[31] The metalworkers' unions in both cities regarded these committees not so much as competitors as incipient forms of organization, still rooted in localistic tendencies, which would gradually be absorbed into the union framework. The unions instructed their members to join factory committees and to propagate the virtues of industry-wide rather than factory-level forms of organization.[32] At this historical juncture, factory committees did not occupy an antagonistic position vis-à-vis the unions, as would later be the case in 1917.

Apart from the issues of decision making and the distribution of authority, trade unions had to come to grips with the tasks of day-to-day administration. At the union center, these responsibilities were vested in four officers—the president, vice-president, secretary, and treasurer—who owed final accountability to the delegate council (which usually elected them) or, more rarely, to the general meeting. Given the formative state of the unions, the lack of an established administrative infrastructure, and the impediments to regular union meetings, the executive officers shouldered an enormous burden in the conduct of union affairs. To compound matters, workers were inexperienced and ill-equipped to handle these responsibilities. As one trade unionist recalled: "I had been in the union for only a year when I had to assume the leadership of the huge [Petersburg] shoemakers' union, which had over two thousand people."[33]

The most problematical union office was that of the treasurer. A union's reputation for integrity and reliability in monetary matters was crucial for the survival and growth of the organization, and substantial sums of money flowed in and out of union coffers. The Petersburg tailors' union had a total income from dues of nearly 3,000 rubles between November 1905 and October 1906, while expenditures amounted to nearly half that sum.[34] But this was very modest compared with the Petersburg printers' union, which had an income of 26,000 rubles in 1906 and expenditures amounting to 29,000.[35] The Moscow printers'

[30]*Pervaia konferentsiia*, pp. 33–34.

[31]See above, chapter 5, tables 24 and 25.

[32]Bulkin, *Na zare*, pp. 291–293. Even in those instances when union members were elected to factory committees, they did not succeed in controlling these committees and sometimes failed to maintain close communication with the union.

[33]*MIPDR*, 4:10.

[34]*Listok dlia rabochikh portnykh, portnikh i skorniakov*, no. 18 (November 19, 1906), p. 6.

[35]*ILS*, pp. 378–379, 382–383. The source of deficit funds is not known.

union alone took in nearly 10,000 rubles in the three months between May and August 1906 and expended 4,000.[36] With cash flows of such dimension, it is little wonder that union members expressed concern over the disposition of their hard-earned membership dues.[37]

On the whole, workers were predisposed to take a wary and even cynical view of those who handled communal funds. This attitude is scarcely surprising in a society rife with corruption at all levels, but some workers had personal experiences that deepened their distrust. Factory workers, for example, were familiar with the shop-floor elder whose job was to tend the icon, using funds contributed by all the workers. The sums of money collected were minimal, but workers commonly believed that the elder diverted part of the funds to personal use.[38]

These negative attitudes were reinforced by occasional but widely discussed incidents involving the actual embezzlement of union funds. In the spring of 1906, for example, the president and the treasurer of the Moscow sausage workers' union stole some two hundred rubles from the union treasury, and a year later, an official of the Moscow candymakers' union absconded with strike funds of the organization. The Petersburg printers' union, as was noted earlier, reported incidents of embezzlement by union delegates.[39] Employers who were hostile to the unions sometimes exploited these incidents to alarm workers and provoke mistrust in the organization.

Unions took deliberate measures to ensure and to demonstrate their financial integrity. Virtually every union elected an auditing committee to maintain steady surveillance over all union financial transactions. The auditing committee reported regularly to the membership, both at meetings and in the union press. Unions further attempted to ensure fiscal responsibility by providing remuneration for the treasurer and, in some cases, for the union secretary as well. A paid union bureaucracy barely began to take form in these months, and few unions

---

[36]Sher, *Istoriia professional'nogo dvizheniia rabochikh pechatnogo dela v Moskve* (Moscow, 1911), p. 243. The income of the Moscow metalworkers' union in 1906 was 600–700 rubles per month, while the Petersburg metalworkers' union reported a monthly income of 1,500–2,000 rubles per month in 1906. *Pervaia konferentsiia*, p. 105.

[37]Unions faced the additional problem of locating a secure place for their funds. They were reluctant to use the banks for fear of confiscation by the government. In many cases, unions turned to a prominent and sympathetic member of the intelligentsia who agreed to retain union funds in his personal possession. Kolokol'nikov, "Otryvki," *MIPDR*, 5:130; ibid., 4:34.

[38]Timofeev, *Chem zhivet zavodskii rabochii* (St. Petersburg, 1906), pp. 80–84.

[39]*Professional'noe dvizhenie Moskovskikh pishchevikov v gody pervoi revoliutsii*, sbornik 1 (Moscow, 1927), pp. 87, 162; *Zhizn' pechatnika*, no. 8 (July 20, 1907), p. 11.

could afford more than one, or at best two, positions. The most extensive bureaucratic infrastructure was created by the Moscow printers' union, which had six paid employees. The secretary and the treasurer of the union each received fifty rubles a month, far more than the average printing worker was in a position to earn. In addition, the union employed a cashier (forty rubles a month), a director of the employment bureau (thirty rubles), a messenger (twenty rubles), and a watchman (fifteen rubles). The secretary to the editorial board of the printers' union newspaper also received a regular salary.[40]

In a number of unions, intelligentsia activists served as union officers, often taking over the position of secretary or treasurer, jobs requiring skill and expertise. These intellectuals, who held important elected positions in the unions, included prominent party figures as well as numerous students and others who made common cause with the attempt to establish labor unions on Russian soil.[41] As in 1905, many of these intelligentsia activists were Social Democrats, and in the new era of legal labor organization they continued to dominate the ideological and organizational centers of the unions.

SOCIAL DEMOCRATS AND TRADE UNIONS

In both Menshevik and Bolshevik circles, the general policy toward trade unions adopted in 1905 still guided party *praktiki* in the new era of legal labor organization. When the Fourth (Unification) Congress of the Russian Social Democratic Workers' Party met in Stockholm in April 1906, the Menshevik majority adopted a resolution instructing party members to assist in the formation of nonparty unions, utilizing for this purpose the law of March 4, 1906. Noting that "a widespread aspiration toward trade-union organization can be observed among the Russian proletariat," the resolution called on party activists to take an active role in the unions and "constantly to strengthen among [trade union] members their class solidarity and class consciousness." The unions and the

[40]Sher, *Istoriia*, p. 301. These data apply to the period between September 1906 and June 1907. The Moscow metalworkers' union employed two paid workers at monthly salaries of twenty-five and thirty-five rubles respectively. The Petersburg metalworkers' union had only one paid employee, who received a monthly salary of fifty rubles. *Pervaia konferentsiia*, pp. 104–105.

[41]For example, a student Volzhin was the first paid secretary of the Petersburg metalworkers' union. Kolokol'nikov, "Otryvki," *MIPDR*, 4:276. Bulkin states that the bookkeepers for the Petersburg metalworkers' union were also intelligentsia activists. Bulkin, *Na zare*, pp. 201, 202.

party, it declared, should be linked only "organically, in struggle and agitation."[42]

Menshevik organizers in St. Petersburg and Moscow, many of them already established figures in the labor movement since 1905, advocated the formation and strengthening of independent trade unions that "resembled the standard type of Western European union."[43] In looking to Western Europe for models, the Mensheviks did not abandon the strategic goal of revolution. But they recognized the waning of popular momentum in the cities following the abortive December uprising, and were determined to take advantage of the limited achievements produced by the 1905 upheavals. In this connection, Mensheviks stressed the tactical importance of utilizing to the fullest extent all legal opportunities available to workers, including not only the trade unions but also the State Duma. These activities, they believed, would provide workers with valuable experiences in self-administration, raising their consciousness and generating working-class leaders for future struggles.[44]

The Bolshevik position, like that of the Mensheviks, underwent little modification in the immediate aftermath of 1905. The Bolsheviks continued to advocate formal organizational ties between trade unions and the party, and union recognition of the party "as a leader in all political actions."[45] Lenin's draft resolution on trade unions prepared for the Fourth Congress of the RSDRP advised unions, whenever possible, to join the party directly, "though by no means excluding from membership their nonparty members."[46] These resolutions were not formally presented to the Fourth Congress, where the Menshevik majority was certain to have rejected them.

One year later, in May 1907, the Bolshevik-dominated Fifth Congress of the

[42]*Kommunisticheskaia partiia Sovetskogo Soiuza v rezoliutsiiakh i resheniiakh s"ezdov, konferentsii i plenumov TsK*, Part 1: *1898-1924* (Moscow, 1954), p. 131.

[43]Sher, *Istoriia*, p. 294.

[44]For the outlook of two leading Menshevik activists on the unions during this period, see Dmitriev, *Iz praktiki*, and V. Grinevich, *Professional'noe dvizhenie rabochikh v Rossii* (St. Petersburg, 1908).

[45]From a resolution passed by the Moscow Committee on March 2, 1906. G. M. Derenkovskii et al., eds., *Vtoroi period revoliutsii: 1906-1907 gody* (Moscow, 1957), Book 1, p. 297.

[46]Lenin's resolution stated, ". . . the party must strive in every way it can to educate workers who are members of trade unions in the spirit of a broad understanding of the class struggle and of the proletariat's socialist tasks, so as to gain . . . de facto leadership in such unions and . . . enable these unions under certain conditions to join the party directly—though by no means excluding from membership their nonparty members." Solomon M. Schwarz, *The Russian Revolution of 1905: The Workers' Movement and the Formation of Bolshevism and Menshevism* (Chicago, 1967), p. 165.

RSDRP, held in London, passed a new resolution on trade unions that reversed the position adopted at the Fourth Congress in 1906. The Fifth Congress resolved that party workers in trade unions should adopt as one of their principal tasks "the recognition by trade unions of the ideological leadership of the Social Democratic party as well as the establishment of organizational ties with it [the party]."[47]

During 1906–1907, the Bolsheviks began to play a more vigorous role in the unions than they had in 1905. In Moscow the individual largely responsible for this activity was the textile worker Viktor Nogin, who joined the RSDRP in 1898 and was elected to the Central Committee in 1907. Nogin made an energetic effort to strengthen Bolshevik leadership in the trade unions, and his efforts received encouragement and support from Lenin, who visited Moscow twice in the first half of 1906. On his second visit in March, Lenin met with party workers in Zamoskvorech'e, a district with many metalworking factories. He stressed the importance of involvement in nonpartisan organizations as a concominant to regular party work, and urged party workers to conduct propaganda in the unions.[48]

Despite the activities of Nogin and others, the Bolsheviks took many months to improve their standing within the union movement. Only two of the twenty-two delegates to the Second All-Russian Conference of Trade Unions in February 1906 were Bolsheviks, and there were none in the three-member delegation from Moscow. But in Moscow, to a greater extent than in the capital, the Bolsheviks had a strong party group, and by the spring of 1907 the Bolsheviks had made inroads into the organized labor movement, achieving a majority on the SD-dominated Central Bureau of Trade Unions and taking control of its newspaper, *Professional*.[49]

Though the Bolsheviks extended their influence in the trade-union movement, they did not win converts to their position on formal union-party relations. In this period of legal opportunity, the establishment of formal ties to a political party appealed to very few organized workers. The handful of unions in Moscow that had adopted the Bolshevik model charter in 1905 began to encounter serious difficulties even before the March 1906 law was officially promulgated. By the end of February, the leadership of the Moscow bakers' union was

[47]Grinevich, *Professional'noe dvizhenie*, p. 240.
[48]*Istoriia Moskvy*, 6 vols. (Moscow, 1952–1959), vol. 5, p. 188.
[49]*Professional* was under the editorial control of three leading Bolshevik trade unionists in Moscow beginning in April 1907: V. P. Nogin, M. G. Lunts, and A. Shestakov. Iu. Milonov, ed., *Moskovskoe professional'noe dvizhenie v gody pervoi revoliutsii* (Moscow, [1925]), p. 356.

embroiled in divisive ideological controversies, and rank-and-file members began to leave the organization because they feared its ties with an illegal underground party. When the bakers' union applied for registration under the new law, it adopted a nonpartisan position that terminated its formal relationship with the RSDRP. A similar situation developed in the Moscow carpenters' union.[50]

In 1906–1907 few unions endorsed formal union-party ties. It was an exception, therefore, when the First All-Russian Conference of Leatherworkers in March 1907 resolved that unions should not only be Social Democratic in spirit but have organizational links to the party as well.[51] Most of the unions rejected this position, though they identified in a general way with the cause of socialism. In the terminology of contemporary labor leaders, it was said that the unions "stood for the point of view of the contemporary workers' movement," a phrase that connoted a socialist orientation without formal ties to a party organization, an arrangement that contemporaries associated with the German trade union movement.[52]

The opposition to formal union-party ties was shared by other political groups active in the organized labor movement—the Socialist Revolutionaries, the syndicalists, and the Kadets. An SR resolution in the spring of 1906 urged party members to establish legal nonparty unions under the terms of the March 1906 law.[53] The syndicalists did not adopt a formal stand on the issue until early 1907, but in practice they consistently advocated trade-union independence from all outside political groups.[54] A Kadet resolution approved at the party congress in Helsinki in 1906 called for unions of a "nonparty character."[55]

A rejection of formal union-party ties did not, however, signify a dissolution

---

[50]A. Belin [A. A. Evdokimov], "Zametki o professional'nom dvizhenii rabochikh (Pis'mo iz Moskvy)," *Bez zaglaviia*, no. 6 (Feb. 26, 1906), p. 241.

[51]*Kozhevennik*, no. 3 (August 9, 1907), p. 4.

[52]*MIPDR*, 4:16.

[53]*Delo naroda*, no. 4 (May 6, 1906), p. 2. The Socialist Revolutionary legislative proposal for a revised law on trade unions, prepared in the spring of 1907, authorized unions to "defend, strengthen, and develop [workers'] economic and social-political interests." *Professional'noe dvizhenie*, no. 1 (May 1, 1907), p. 1.

[54]P. Vasil'ev, "Sindikalistskie i drugie gruppy v professional'nom dvizhenii v 1905–1907 gg.," *Materialy po istorii professional'nogo dvizheniia v Peterburge za 1905-1907 gg.: Sbornik* (henceforth *MIPDP*) (Leningrad, 1926), pp. 192–207.

[55]Grinevich, *Professional'noe dvizenie*, p. 231. The Kadet party also drew up a proposal for a new law on trade unions, which was debated by the First State Duma in June 1906 but was not adopted. *Vestnik pechatnikov*, no. 9 (June 24, 1906), p. 2.

of the extensive informal network of association between radical political parties and the trade unions. As in 1905, trade unions attracted many radical activists, both workers and intellectuals, into their ranks. The labor press, meetings, and other union channels helped to educate workers politically and to expose them to the ideologies of the radical left. To be sure, political allegiances were still in a formative state of development, and many workers had only the most rudimentary conception of competing political ideologies and tactics. But the trade unions became a locus for politically-minded workers and served to politicize others who had joined union ranks.

The most comprehensive information on the political allegiances of trade unionists appears in a report prepared by the Petersburg Okhrana in September 1909.[56] Regrettably, the report does not specify the source of this information or the details surrounding its collection. The report contains information on the dominant political orientation of thirty-four union directing boards, together with the number of SD sympathizers within each union. It may have been gathered by Social Democrats in the unions or, more likely, by the Organizational Commission for an All-Russian Congress of Trade Unions, which initiated a broad survey of trade unions and their membership in the spring of 1907. Portions of the latter survey published in the contemporary labor press conform in nearly every detail to the Okhrana report, including the order (apparently random) in which unions are listed and their nominal membership. Where the two differ, however, is that published sources do not include information on political orientation, an omission that can be explained by the reluctance of trade unionists to disclose information that would have alarmed the authorities and provoked repression.

According to the Okhrana report, Social Democrats predominated on the directing boards of more than one-half (eighteen) of the thirty-four unions surveyed (table 26). Nearly one-quarter of the boards were dominated by Socialist Revolutionaries, and in seven others, the board members had no dominant political allegiance. Corroborating evidence on the political composition of these union boards is extremely limited, but the available information confirms the Okhrana report. Two Socialist Revolutionaries sat on the board of the Petersburg metalworkers' union in the spring of 1907, and the remainder were Social Democrats, mostly Mensheviks. Twelve of the fifteen board members in the Petersburg tailors' union were Social Democrats in April 1906. Social Democrats

[56]*Tsentral'nyi gosudarstvennyi arkhiv Oktiabr'skoi revoliutsii* (TsGAOR), DPOO f. 111, op. 5, d. 263, pp. 121–122.

Table 26

Political Orientation of Trade Unionists in St. Petersburg, Spring 1907

Union	Dominant Political Orientation of the Directing Board	Number of Nominal Union Members	Number and Percent of Social Democrat Sympathizers	
Printers	Social Democrat	9,388	2,116	(23)
Metalworkers	Social Democrat	10,700	4,011	(37)
Bakers	Social Democrat	3,713	1,019	(27)
Gold-silversmiths	Socialist Revolutionary	1,100	306	(28)
Textile	Socialist Revolutionary	4,000	1,125	(28)
Tailors	Social Democrat	1,514	412	(27)
Lithographers	Socialist Revolutionary	566	417	(74)
Salesclerks	Social Democrat	2,688	1,277	(48)
Construction workers	Social Democrat	3,730	633	(17)
Woodworkers	Social Democrat	1,714	1,024	(58)
Knitters	Social Democrat	85	79	(93)
Glassmakers	Social Democrat	97	37	(38)
Cardboard workers	Social Democrat	120	43	(36)
Dyers	Social Democrat	225	n.d.	n.d.
Blacksmiths	Socialist Revolutionary	220	132	(60)
Low-level medical personnel	Nonparty	500	22	(4)

Occupation	Party			
Wallpaper workers	Nonparty	240	39	(16)
Paper workers	Social Democrat	287	162	(56)
Barbers	Nonparty	102	13	(13)
Leather workers	Social Democrat	771	635	(82)
Photographic workers	Social Democrat	200	77	(39)
Cooks	Nonparty	400	132	(33)
Watchmakers	Socialist Revolutionary	202	62	(31)
Shoemakers	Social Democrat	1,100	615	(56)
Tallow and soap workers	Nonparty	120	32	(27)
Technicians	Social Democrat	85	76	(89)
Candymakers	Socialist Revolutionary	794	112	(14)
Pharmacists	Nonparty	30	11	(37)
Office clerks and bookkeepers	Social Democrat	2,000	737	(37)
Draftsmen	Social Democrat	252	137	(54)
Tobacco workers	Socialist Revolutionary	450	209	(46)
Carriage makers	Nonparty	163	19	(12)
Marble workers	Socialist Revolutionary	374	122	(33)
Cabmen	Socialist Revolutionary	123	n.d.	n.d.
Total		48,053	15,843	(33)

Sources: TsGAOR, DPOO f. 111, op. 5, d. 263, pp. 121–122.

also predominated on the board of the Petersburg shoemakers' union.[57]

Comparable survey data for Moscow have not been located, but scattered evidence indicates that apart from a handful of unions under Socialist Revolutionary, syndicalist, or Kadet influence, most Moscow unions were "entirely or predominantly under SD influence."[58] Mensheviks found their strongest support in the Moscow printers' union, while the Bolsheviks exerted their greatest influence over the union of textile workers. In the Moscow metalworkers' union, where the two factions struggled for hegemony, 80 percent of the union delegates in 1907 were Social Democrats, whereas only 8 percent were Socialist Revolutionaries.[59] Even in the Moscow union of sales-clerical personnel, where the liberal Kadets mounted a concerted campaign to win support, a 1907 survey of enfranchised salesclerks revealed that while 57 percent supported the Kadets, 38 percent considered themselves Social Democrats.[60]

The influence of Socialist Revolutionaries was confined to two or three Moscow unions, including the union of clerks in meat, fish, and vegetable markets. Syndicalism, which gained adherents under the leadership of A. A. Evdokimov, was influential among plumbers, construction workers, and metalfitters in construction trades.

The dominant political orientation of union directing boards cannot, however, be directly correlated with political attitudes among the union rank and file. As disclosed by the Okhrana report, there was sometimes a discrepancy between the political allegiances of the leadership and the membership—evidence that party lines were not sharply etched and that effective leadership qualities as well as craft or localistic affinities were occasionally as important as party preferences in determining the workers' choice of leaders.

Little is known about the political allegiances of rank-and-file union members. The Okhrana report provides information only on SD sympathizers and excludes workers who supported other political parties and groups. According to the report, three out of four unions surveyed had a substantial contingent of SD sympathizers, amounting to 25 percent or more of the union's total membership. In four small unions (leatherworkers, technicians, knitters, and lithographers), the percentage of SDs was so high that the union resembled a party

[57]Kolokol'nikov, "Otryvki," *MIPDR*, 5:146; S. M. Gruzdev, *Trud i bor'ba shveinikov v Petrograde 1905-1916 gg.* (Leningrad, 1929), p. 54; *Professional'noe dvizhenie*, no. 1 (May 1, 1907), p. 20.

[58]A. M. Nikitin, "Moskovskie soiuzy v 1906 godu," in *Moskovskoe professional'noe dvizhenie*, ed. Milonov, p. 275.

[59]*Nash put'*, no. 6 (August 31, 1913), p. 2.

[60]*Zhizn' prikazchika*, no. 3, p. 6, cited in Grinevich, *Professional'noe dvizhenie*, p. 232.

organization (table 26). But in the absence of further information on the method of data collection, we cannot be certain how to interpret these figures or what, in fact, it really meant to be an SD sympathizer in the spring of 1907.

The unions also included a contingent of actual party members among the leadership, some of them joining a union on instructions from their local party organization.[61] "It would be difficult to draw the line between purely trade-union and political work," observed the former secretary of the Moscow tobacco workers' union, "because those individuals who directed the trade-union organizations were [SD] party people."[62] There were also party members among the rank and file. The Petersburg printers' union reported that two hundred of its members belonged to the RSDRP in mid-1906,[63] but few other unions had such a large number.

Notwithstanding their presence within the unions, radical activists did not *control* union affairs behind the scenes—the situation commonly depicted by contemporary police reports on the labor movement.[64] The major unions were already too large to be easily manipulated, and most unions encouraged the rank and file to participate in decision making. But party activists in the labor movement nevertheless exerted far-reaching *influence* over union policies, actions, and ideology, all the while contending with diverse and contradictory sentiments among the rank and file. As one former activist put it in the 1920s: "I would say that [at that time] no party exercised [over the unions] what we now mean by 'party leadership' in a narrow sense of the words."[65]

TRADE UNIONS AND MUTUAL ASSISTANCE

The interplay between Social Democratic activists—many of them intellectuals—and the union rank and file was highly complex in this period. As in 1905, radical activists performed an important ideological and practical role in the unions, and they often provided knowledge and skills beyond the reach of

[61]The Menshevik Kibrik reported that he was sent by the Moscow Menshevik group in the spring of 1906 to work in the city's printers' union. *MIPDR*, 4:52. Similarly, Kolokol'nikov was instructed by the Petersburg Mensheviks to become involved in the capital's union movement. Kolokol'nikov, "Otryvki," *MIPDR*, 4:266.

[62]Bogdanov-Evdokimov in *MIPDR*, 4:62.

[63]*Ekho*, no. 1 (June 29, 1906), p. 3.

[64]See below, chapter 7.

[65]Ozol, in *MIPDR*, 4:9.

most workers, at least in the early months of the legal labor movement. Workers continued to rely on the assistance of these intelligentsia organizers, and relations between them were generally harmonious.[66] Yet there were also tensions between the two groups, and these came to the surface over specific issues, when the ideological position of SD activists did not coincide with the needs and demands of union members. Union sponsorship of mutual aid programs was one issue that brought this tension into the open.

Mutual aid programs occupied a central place in union activities during 1906–1907, absorbing as much as one-half of the typical union budget and a great deal of energy and effort. Nearly all trade unionists supported the provision of material aid to workers engaged in union-directed strikes. Where they disagreed was over the issue of union-sponsored funds for such purposes as unemployment, sickness benefits, and funeral expenses. Social Democrats argued that union involvement in these mutual aid programs would divert energy and resources away from the demanding tasks of labor-management struggle. Others took the position that while strike funds strengthened the "front line of struggle," mutual aid funds were indispensible because they fortified the rear.[67]

Bulkin has described the circumstances that led to the introduction of mutual aid programs in the Petersburg metalworkers' union, a union noted for the high proportion of politically active workers. At the time of the union's establishment in the spring of 1906, the union leadership—most of them Social Democrats—considered mutual aid

not only of secondary importance, but even dangerous, capable of drawing the union from the correct path of class struggle into the quagmire of trade unionism. However, the economic situation soon forced the leaders of the union to take another view of the matter: the strike struggle was unlikely to produce real results in the short term. Therefore, it was impossible not to undertake by other means efforts to assist, even a little, in easing the oppressive material conditions of union members and [thereby] teaching them to appreciate the union as an organization which [was] valuable to them, and capable of giving them aid and support in a time of need.[68]

---

[66]For a discussion of the interaction between the workers and intelligentsia activists in the Petersburg metalworkers' union, see Bulkin, *Na zare*, pp. 200–202. According to Bulkin, Roman Malinovskii was the only worker-trade-union leader in this organization with an antagonistic attitude toward intelligentsia labor activists.

[67]*Golos pechatnika*, no. 12 (November 16, 1906). For a contemporary critique of union-sponsored mutual aid funds, apart from strike funds and unemployment assistance, see Grinevich, *Professional'noe dvizhenie*, p. 117, and "K voprosu o vzaimopomoshchi v professional'nykh soiuzakh," *Professional'nyi vestnik*, no. 6, 1907, pp. 4–5.

[68]Bulkin, *Na zare*, p. 347.

Rank-and-file trade unionists did not, on the whole, share the reservations of their leaders. In fact, many workers failed to draw a clear distinction between the functions of a labor union and those of a mutual aid society. There existed, moreover, a pressing need for such assistance that was not satisfied either by voluntary associations or by the state. Mutual aid societies before 1905 generally attracted only a small proportion of the labor force, usually the more prosperous workers who could afford the steep entry fees and monthly membership dues. Government-sponsored programs for illness and accident insurance were available only to a relatively small number of workers employed in state-owned enterprises. But even for those in state-owned factories, there was no provision for unemployment insurance, and in this and other areas the unions offered a valuable source of support in times of adversity.

It is little wonder, then, that the prospect of receiving material assistance attracted many workers to the trade unions. Petersburg metalworkers, the victims of massive unemployment, frequently "entered the union in the hope of generous benefits," while an economic recession in the Moscow printing industry in early 1906 led workers to demand bread and money from the union.[69] Similar expectations motivated other groups of organized workers as well. A member of the Moscow tobacco workers' union observed in the spring of 1907 that

only a small core of organized [workers] see the union as a means of struggle against exploitation; the majority look upon the union as a useful institution which gives shelter to all unfortunates, those who have been thrown out of the factory or for some other reason have lost their income, are sick or maimed.[70]

Petersburg textile workers were said to join the union "only when they had need of it, in the event of illness or unemployment."[71]

These attitudes were fostered by the unions themselves. An article in the Petersburg trade union newspaper *Golos tabachnika* [Voice of the Tobacco Worker], summoned workers to join the union, promising a variety of tangible

---

[69]Ibid., p. 303; *Materialy ob ekonomicheskom polozhenii i professional'noi organizatsii Peterburgskikh rabochikh po metallu* (St. Petersburg, 1909), p. 83; Sher, *Istoriia*, p. 231.

[70]*Professional*, no. 1 (April 4, 1907), p. 13.

[71]*Tekstil'noe delo*, no. 1 (November 25, 1907), p. 1. When members of the Moscow tailors' union discussed whether the organization should provide material benefits for illness, a majority of the members supported such mutual aid activities. E. A. Oliunina, *Portnovskii promysel v Moskve i v derevniakh Moskovskoi i Riazanskoi gubernii: Materialy k istorii domashnei promyshlennosti v Rossii* (Moscow, 1914), p. 296.

benefits, including funds for striking workers, financial assistance in the event of illness, support for travel and funerals, and even assistance in finding employment.[72]

The anticipation of receiving material assistance induced many workers to join a union and to commit a portion of their meagre resources to the organization. But when such assistance was not forthcoming, workers remained aloof and hesitated to make common cause with the organization. The Petersburg union of leatherworkers attracted fewer than eight hundred members because, in the opinion of the organizers, workers "perceive[d] no benefit whatsoever for themselves from the union and therefore consider[ed] it unnecessary to pay thirty kopecks [membership dues] for nothing."[73]

A similar situation was reported among Moscow metalworkers. Only 177 out of more than 6,000 workers at the Kolomenskii machine construction plant on the outskirts of Moscow had joined the union by early 1907. The dismal recruitment record was attributed to an unemployment assistance program organized by the plant director's wife. The availability of this monetary assistance made many workers feel that they had no need for the trade union, whose mutual aid program, instituted on the urging of the membership, was administered haphazardly and could not adequately meet workers' needs at a time of massive unemployment.[74]

A survey of Petersburg unions conducted in March 1907 shows the expenditure of union funds for various kinds of mutual aid and services (table 27). Altogether, mutual aid absorbed nearly one-half of these union budgets. Excluding aid to striking workers and those arrested or exiled, one-quarter of the union funds were utilized for such matters as unemployment assistance, dormitories, and loans. The needs and demands of rank-and-file workers had prevailed over the objections of their radical mentors.

The amount of support received by individual workers from these union programs was, however, exceedingly meagre. The Petersburg metalworkers' union provided unemployed metalworkers with 1 ruble 35 kopecks per week for a maximum of four weeks, at a time when the typical skilled metalworker earned 2 rubles 60 kopecks per day.[75] The Moscow printers' union distributed 15

[72]*Golos tabachnika,* no. 1 (December 21, 1906), p. 2.

[73]*Rabochii po kozhe,* no. 1 (December 30, 1906), p. 3.

[74]Matveev, "Moskovskii soiuz," *MIPDR,* 2:265–266, for a copy of the Moscow metalworkers' union instructions on the distribution of mutual aid; *Pervaia konferentsiia,* p. 17, for an account of the events at the Kolomenskii plant.

[75]Bulkin, *Na zare,* p. 383. At the Putilov and Nevskii plants in 1906, skilled workers earned an average of 2 rubles 32–65 kopecks per day; unskilled workers at these plants earned an average of 1 ruble 32–90 kopecks per day. Ibid., p. 384.

Table 27

*Expenditure of Funds in Petersburg Unions
for Mutual Aid, Spring 1907*

Type of Expenditure	Amount in Rubles	% of Total Union Expenditure
Striking workers	13,005	18.2
Arrested workers	1,913	2.7
Exiled workers	1,169	1.6
Other unions and organizations	2,073	2.9
Emergency grants	175	0.2
Free grants	345	0.5
Loans to members	5,208	7.3
Unemployed workers	6,717	9.4
Funeral expenses	66	0.1
Dormitories and lodging	3,029	4.2
Medical assistance	22	0.0
Total	33,722	47.1

Source: Sviatlovskii, *Professional'noe dvizhenie,* pp. 201–202. Errors in Sviatlovskii's computation of percentages have been corrected.

kopecks per day to single unemployed men and 25 kopecks to those who were married, with a 5-kopeck supplement per child.[76] This was a small sum, considering that the average wage in the Moscow printing industry was 34 rubles 70 kopecks per month.[77] Some unionized workers expressed dissatisfaction with these modest unemployment benefits,[78] but even a small supplement was gratefully received by workers who had never before had an alternative source of support available to them in time of need.

[76]Sher, *Istoriia,* p. 248. These data apply to the printers' union that functioned until August 1906, when it was closed by the police. The successor union gave 25 kopecks to all unemployed workers. Ibid., p. 349.

[77]A. Svavitskii and V. Sher, *Ocherk polozheniia rabochikh pechatnogo dela v Moskve* (St. Petersburg, 1909), table 5.

[78]*Professional,* no. 2 (April 11, 1907), p. 4, carried a complaint concerning the inadequacy of unemployment assistance provided by the Moscow metalworkers' union. The union replied that it had no more to give and that the government should step in to provide support.

Workers also looked to the trade unions for cultural, educational, and even social activities, and in this area the attitudes of the rank and file and their radical mentors more nearly coincided. Many radical activists, especially the Mensheviks, believed that the future tasks of the Russian working class required a substantial upgrading of the general cultural and intellectual level, and they shared Grinevich's view that

> without a rise in the cultural-intellectual level of the working masses, trade-union struggle in Russia will be doomed to spontaneous and perhaps frequently heroic outbursts, but it will never be able to take the form of a continuous gradual process of achieving serious improvement in the conditions of labor. This conception has penetrated deeply into the consciousness not only of the union leaders, but also the broad strata of union members.[79]

Enthusiasm for self-improvement was indeed prevalent among the rank and file, particularly the skilled, literate, and relatively well paid workers who predominated in many unions. The support for union-sponsored cultural and educational activities among Petersburg metalworkers has been described by Bulkin:

> Although the majority of workers approached the union with a purely utilitarian yardstick, valued it as a source of direct benefit, and complained about each kopeck that was spent, in their opinion, on nonunion matters, we never once encountered any protest whatsoever or any expression of dissatisfaction concerning expenditures on cultural-educational work. On the contrary, at general meetings there was always someone who criticized the directing board for too little attention to the cultural needs of the membership, for failing to arrange lectures, for not extending the library, and so on.[80]

The budget for the Petersburg metalworkers' union testifies to the support these activities elicited among the rank and file. Unions in the capital expended an average of 11.6 percent of the budget on lectures, concerts, meetings, the trade-union press, libraries, reading rooms, and various union publications. The metalworkers' union, by contrast, expended 20 percent.[81]

The newspaper was generally the most costly item among cultural and

[79]Grinevich, *Professional'noe dvizhenie*, p. 136.
[80]Bulkin, *Na zare*, p. 323.
[81]Sviatlovskii, *Professional'noe dvizhenie*, p. 201; Bulkin, *Na zare*, p. 192.

educational programs, consuming roughly one-tenth of the total union budget.[82] Fifty-two different union newspapers made an appearance in the capital, and fifteen in Moscow.[83] Published biweekly or monthly in press runs of two to three thousand copies, these union newspapers performed multiple functions, helping to educate workers, fortify the feelings of solidarity, supply information on a variety of subjects, and ensure regular channels of communication between the leadership and the rank and file. The organ of the Petersburg metalworkers' union, *Rabochii po metallu* [The Metalworker], "appeared regularly and was widely distributed in factories by the factory [union] delegates."[84] During the protracted period of this union's illegal status, the newspaper provided a major source of support for the organization.

These newspapers were lively and interesting, calculated to elicit the workers' attention. Apart from articles on contemporary political and economic topics, they contained several standard features. Almost invariably, there was a report on trade unionism or labor conflicts in Western Europe and in other parts of the Russian Empire, usually prepared by an intelligentsia activist. A special section also carried information about conditions in individual factories or shops. Frequently these reports were sent in by the workers themselves, and they conveyed feelings of indignation and rage against employers, which must have struck a responsive chord among readers. Some of the newspapers also published short stories and poems by workers. With the exception of the printers' union newspapers, most of these publications were written in a clear, simple language that made them accessible to a literate worker.

Other union-sponsored educational and cultural activities included the establishment of libraries and reading rooms. Fourteen union libraries were already in operation in the capital by early 1907.[85] The largest library, founded by the Petersburg printers' union, contained two thousand volumes.[86] The capital's metalworkers' union boasted a library with five hundred books in its collection.[87] Many Moscow unions also maintained libraries in this period, including the unions of printers, metalworkers, bakers, and salesclerks in colonial and grain

---

[82]Sviatlovskii, *Professional'noe dvizhenie*, p. 201; Sher, *Istoriia*, pp. 243, 295.

[83]For a complete list of the trade union newspapers that appeared in 1906–1907, see Ia. S. Roginskii, *Russkaia profsoiuznaia periodicheskaia pechat' 1905–1907 gg.: Bibliograficheskii ukazatel'* (Moscow, 1957), pp. 62–64.

[84]Kolokol'nikov, "Otryvki," *MIPDR*, 5:131.

[85]Grinevich, *Professional'noe dvizhenie*, p. 137.

[86]*ILS*, p. 25.

[87]Bulkin, *Na zare*, p. 341.

stores. Apparently the latter organization concentrated all of its effort and resources on this type of activity, establishing not only a library but also a cafeteria and a boardinghouse for unemployed salesclerks.[88]

Unions arranged lectures and access to cultural events, such as theatrical and musical performances. In general, such activities remained circumscribed during these months when unions focused their attention on more pressing problems. Nevertheless, the Petersburg tailors' union reported in June 1906 that three lectures had been held under union auspices during recent weeks, on such topics as the trade union movement, labor legislation, and political parties in the Duma. Each lecture was attended by 200–250 tailors.[89]

Unions not only provided modest cultural and educational programs, they also served as centers for congregation and fellowship among workers. Except for the ubiquitous tavern, there were few opportunties for workers to gather informally outside the factory or shop. From the turn of the century onward, workers had flocked to the lectures, evening courses, and social dances sponsored by the Zubatov and Gapon societies and the Moscow Society for Popular Enlightenment. But it was only with the advent of trade unions that workers sought and found sustained contact and fellowship with others in the setting of an independent organization. Union-sponsored activities brought dispersed workers together for the first time in what must have been for many an important personal experience as well as an occasion for solidarity and even pride.

TRADE UNION IDEOLOGY

In a short period of months, unions succeeded in devising formal structures as well as administrative means to cope with the increasing volume and complexity of union business. But these efforts at organization building could proceed only to the extent that unions attracted a solid core of committed members. As it was, however, unions witnessed sharp fluctuations in membership, and only a minority of those who joined the unions continued to pay their dues for a sustained period. Some exceptions to this pattern could be found in larger unions, where the proportion of regular dues-paying members was often considerably higher than in smaller ones. But even here, membership turnover plagued such relatively solid unions as the Moscow printers, where the "organizational work [of recruit-

[88]*Zhizn' prikazchika*, no. 13 (March 10, 1907), p. 12.
[89]*Ekho*, no. 3 (June 24, 1906), p. 3.

ment] had a broad impact but did not penetrate deeply."[90] On the whole, unions faced a serious problem caused by delinquent dues payment and high turnover rates and the resulting uncertainties, material and otherwise, to which they were subjected by the inconstancy of their members.

The creation and enlargement of a core of dedicated trade unionists thus represented a fundamental component of the organizational tasks confronting unions. Central to these efforts was the endeavor to change the way in which workers thought about themselves, their society, and the role of trade unions. The impressive range of union activities and accomplishments brought many new members into these organizations and sustained the support of some of them. But workers had to develop an ideological commitment as well, that is, a set of beliefs that would ensure an abiding association with the trade union movement. As one labor organizer observed in June 1906, unions remained vulnerable to government repression and might again be subjected to the crushing blows administered in December 1905. Unification and centralization of the unions provided the only protection against such an outcome, and this in turn could only be achieved by developing to the fullest extent the consciousness of union members.[91]

Union leaders expended considerable energy and resources to reach workers and deepen their understanding and devotion to the union cause, using for this purpose public and private meetings, lectures, pamphlets, books and perhaps most important of all, the large legal trade union press. The press, as we have seen, occupied an important place in union affairs, and it was here that many intelligentsia activists put their talents and resources at the disposal of the union movement. Three major themes dominated the trade union press in 1906–1907: proletarian solidarity, the irreconcilability of class interests, and the necessity for collective and institutionalized solutions to labor problems. These ideas, time and again repeated by activists at union meetings and conferences, constituted, broadly speaking, the ideology of trade unionism in this period. The formulation of these ideas reflects the extensive ideological influence of Social Democrats over the trade unions.

The notion of proletarian solidarity was the most basic ideological concept underlying the union movement. Unions disseminated a broad internationalist conception of the proletariat, with an emphasis on the essential unity of all workers regardless of occupational specialization or geographical dispersion.

[90]Sher, *Istoriia*, p. 260.
[91]*Ekho*, no. 8 (June 30, 1906), p. 3.

"The interests of hired workers everywhere are the same," proclaimed *Chasovshchik* [The Watchmaker], "because everywhere these workers are subjected to the same capitalist oppression."[92]

A related theme emphasized the irreconcilability of class interests. Not only did all workers share the same interests, but these interests were in fundamental conflict with other classes. "Between labor and capital there is an eternal battle," declared *Tekstil'noe delo* [Textile Affairs], the organ of the Petersburg textile workers' union. "The interests of the employer and the interests of workers are opposed, like fire and water, like day and night."[93] The Moscow railroad workers' union newspaper commented in October 1906: "Every trade union, if it is truly a union of working people, must possess a class perspective, that is, view the interests of labor and capital as irreconcilable."[94]

Unions taught workers that their suffering and depredations arose not from accidental causes or the actions of individuals but rather from fundamental socioeconomic arrangements in capitalist Russia. *Konfetchik* [Candymaker], published by the capital's candymakers' union, proclaimed in late 1906:

We work in a capitalist epoch in which we are paid just enough to keep us alive. The greater part of what we produce goes into the fat pocket of our capitalists. We are people, just like the capitalists, but they do not consider us people. They view us as things or cattle.[95]

Anticapitalist sentiments were not, of course, unfamiliar to workers. As early as 1903, the organizers of the Zubatov movement were sufficiently concerned about the spread of anticapitalist sentiments to emphasize the compatibility of workers' and employers' interests. In 1906–1907 the unions accelerated the spread of anticapitalist attitudes by inculcating the notion that workers' difficulties were rooted in the systemic nature of capitalist society. "Every feature of modern capitalist society depends on the economic factors which govern a given society," declared *Golos prikazchika* [Voice of the Salesclerk] in May 1906. "The struggle to survive, [the struggle] of the strong over the weak, is especially clear in commerce."[96]

Another central theme emphasized by trade unions concerned the necessity for collective representation, collective bargaining, and institutionalized meth-

[92]*Chasovshchik*, no. 1 (February 13, 1907), p. 1.
[93]*Tekstil'noe delo*, no. 1 (November 25, 1907), p. 1.
[94]*Zheleznodorozhnaia zhizn'*, no. 1–2 (October 1, 1906), p. 15.
[95]*Konfetchik*, no. 1 (November 23, 1906), p. 1.
[96]*Golos prikazchika*, no. 4 (May 7, 1906), p. 7.

ods for dealing with labor problems.[97] Union efforts to popularize and to implement these procedures will be discussed at length in chapter 7. Suffice it to note that they provided a major preoccupation for these organizations in 1906–1907, continuing a trend that had begun in 1905.

Trade union ideology in 1906–1907 corresponded to a genuine dualism in the political situation during these months. The revolutionary atmosphere in the country was still quite tangible, and the memory of the preceding year was still vivid, but the urban popular movement had lost its momentum and workers now faced a situation conducive to a new kind of struggle—one that was open, mass based, and legal. The strategic goal of revolution remained alive, and unions reminded workers of the "importance of political freedom in the economic struggle."[98] Yet conditions in the aftermath of 1905 made it possible to adopt tactics designed to win immediate improvements through collective and institutionalized methods of struggle, and trade unions encouraged these activities. Commenting on the widespread campaign to achieve collective agreements, the St. Petersburg union newspaper *Professional'nyi vestnik* [The Union Herald] asserted in June 1907 that "such agreements do not change the economic problems of society, but [they enable] workers to improve their immediate conditions and limit the power of industrialists."[99]

Most workers had not forgotten the remarkable events of 1905, but they were nonetheless eager to take advantage of the opportunities in 1906 to achieve "a better, happier destiny" through organized labor struggle.[100] The textile workers' newspaper in the capital echoed a common theme in August 1906 when it declared that illegal actions by government authorities (in this case an illegal search of union headquarters) "should not slow our work. Only through trade unions can we fight capital. Remember that in Germany, France, and other European countries, trade unions survive and grow despite repressions and reaction."[101]

---

[97]See, for example, the draft resolutions for a general trade union conference in the Moscow Industrial Region, published in *Professional*, no. 5 (May 30, 1907), pp. 1–24; resolutions of the First All-Russian Conference of Tailors, August 1906, cited in Sviatlovskii, *Professional'noe dvizhenie*, p. 274, note 2; *Protokoly pervoi vserossiiskoi konferentsii soiuzov rabochikh pechatnogo dela* (St. Petersburg, 1907), pp. 13–16, 75–105.

[98]*Golos prikazchika*, no. 9 (June 18, 1906), pp. 5–6. See also *Professional'nyi vestnik*, no. 1 (May 1, 1907), p. 1.

[99]*Professional'nyi vestnik*, no. 9 (June 21, 1907), p. 5.

[100]*Golos tabachnika*, no. 1 (December 21, 1906), p. 2.

[101]*Tkach*, no. 4 (August 5, 1906), p. 1.

CONSOLIDATION OF THE TRADE UNION MOVEMENT

No facet of union activity more clearly illustrates the "curious web of contradictions" facing trade unions in this period than the efforts to achieve regional and national consolidation. The unification of the trade unions, it will be recalled, got under way in the summer of 1905, resulting in the creation of the Petersburg and the Moscow Central Bureau of Trade Unions and the First All-Russian Conference of Trade Unions. The Bureaus and the conference, which were viewed as preliminary steps toward the convocation of a congress of unions, marked the beginning of a national network for organized labor.

The Central Bureaus played a leading role in the labor movements of both cities during the closing months of the 1905 revolution. With the promulgation of the March 1906 law, however, the future of the Bureaus, which had existed without official permission, was called into question. The new law explicitly outlawed federations of unions, as well as the formation of organizations involving more than one industry or occupational group.[102] Ostensibly, the prohibition applied equally to workers and employers. But it soon became clear that industrialists were in practice exempted from the law's prohibition of multiindustrial combinations. The powerful Society of Factory Owners in both St. Petersburg and Moscow obtained legal registration under the law in 1906, a situation that evoked considerable cynicism and resentment in labor circles.[103]

Notwithstanding the March 1906 law, the citywide bureaus of trade unions, though technically illegal, remained active during 1906–1907, and more important still, they functioned openly and publicly, with virtually no attempt at concealment and little interference from the authorities. Their activities testify to the remarkably tolerant atmosphere in St. Petersburg and Moscow prior to June 1907. As one former trade unionist recalled, "It could not be said that even after the publication of the [March 1906] law, the existence of the Central Bureau became very difficult. [State] power was too disorganized to mount a general offensive against the trade union movement."[104]

---

[102]*Zakon 4-go marta 1906 goda o soiuzakh i obshchestvakh s posleduiushchimi k nemu raz'iasneniiami Pravitel'stvuiushchego senata i Ministerstva vnutrennikh del* (St. Petersburg, 1906), Part II, Articles 6, 7, p. 16.

[103]Grinevich, *Professional'noe dvizhenie*, p. 251. A writer in the labor press commented that there were really two laws on combinations: "Complete freedom of action for the capitalist, complete arbitrariness in relation to the workers—that is the policy of the government." *Professional*, no. 2 (April 11, 1907), pp. 5–6.

[104]MIPDR, 4:8.

Modeled after their German counterparts,[105] the Petersburg and Moscow Bureaus drew up a formal charter, maintained an independent budget based on dues contributions by member unions, and published a citywide trade union newspaper that was openly circulated with detailed accounts of the Bureaus' proceedings. In each city, the Bureau assisted in the formation and registration of new unions, adjudicated interunion disputes, facilitated the collection and distribution of strike funds, arranged legal, medical, and other services for member unions, and furnished tactical and political leadership.[106]

The Petersburg Bureau permitted each qualified union to send three voting representatives, one of whom was typically an intelligentsia activist. In Moscow the Bureau consisted of two voting representatives from each union, but this provision was more laxly enforced than in St. Petersburg, where the Bureau attained a high degree of procedural regularity. Both the Petersburg and the Moscow Bureau also included in their charters a provision for party representatives to attend Bureau meetings with a consultative vote. Some Social Democratic labor activists, such as Riazanov in St. Petersburg, had opposed this provision, but the Second All-Russian Conference of Trade Unions, meeting in late February 1906, nevertheless endorsed the concept of party participation, and it was subsequently implemented by both Bureaus.[107]

Social Democrats virtually controlled the Moscow Bureau, and only one non-Social-Democrat, the syndicalist A. A. Evdokimov, became centrally involved. The Petersburg Bureau, by contrast, had more political diversity and included Socialist Revolutionaries and syndicalists, as well as many Social Democrats. But here, too, Social Democrats—particularly the Menshevik Grinevich and the nonfaction Social Democrat Riazanov—played a leading role. The Bureaus, in fact, took on a dual function. They served all trade unions by providing a number of important services as well as citywide coordination; at the same time they functioned as political centers for the unions. Meetings were

[105]Grinevich introduction to Umbreit, *Znachenie*, p. 4.

[106]The Central Bureaus of Trade Unions are an important but neglected aspect of the labor movement in this period, and they deserve far more extended discussion than is possible here. The major sources on this subject, from which the following discussion is drawn, include S. P. Tiurin, *Moskovskoe tsentral'noe biuro professional'nykh soiuzov* (Moscow, 1913); P. Kolokol'nikov and S. Rapoport, eds., *1905-1907 gg. v professional'nom dvizhenii: I i II Vserossiiskie konferentsii professional'nykh soiuzov* (Moscow, 1925); Iu. Milonov, ed., *Moskovskoe professional'noe dvizhenie*, pp. 277–282, 329–339; Sviatlovskii, *Professional'noe dvizhenie*, pp. 117–134; Grinevich, *Professional'noe dvizhenie rabochikh v Rossii*, pp. 51–77; "K istorii tsentral'nykh biuro: Vechera vospominanii," *MIPDR*, 4:5–140; ibid., 4:200–208.

[107]*MIPDR*, 4:31.

attended by the leading party activists, who used the Bureau as a forum for debate and policy formulation on key trade union issues. Not infrequently, the contending policies under discussion represented the positions put forward by each of the two factions of Russian Social Democracy, and the disputes within the Bureaus became extensions of the intraparty struggle.

A perceptive observer of the labor scene, the Menshevik Sher, has described the relationship between the Central Bureau of Trade Unions and the Social Democratic party:

In the course of the winter of 1906–1907, the [St. Petersburg] Central Bureau was rather active. In comparison with Moscow, the Petersburg Central Bureau to a great extent deserved to be called the ideological center of the trade union movement. . . . The ideological leadership of the [Petersburg] Central Bureau stemmed from party directives. This is why, in those cases when the directives of different parties and factions coincided, the position of the Central Bureau was simple and clear. Such was the case, for example, when it was a matter of assessing some deviation of a given union from the general line of the trade union movement. But there were other questions on which the Central Bureau did not give clear answers, bound as it was by its nonpartisan status as a representative of the entire union movement.[108]

The intertwining of party and union issues in the Central Bureaus occurred on a number of critical occasions during 1906–1907. One such occasion was the debate over worker participation in elections to the First State Duma and the ensuing controversy over the Bureau's disposition toward the Duma's Workers' Group. Another controversy centered around the creation of a program to aid the unemployed. In both St. Petersburg and Moscow, the Bureau considered two competing plans, formulated by the Mensheviks and the Bolsheviks respectively, and the outcome of the debates was, to a large extent, indicative of the alignment of political forces within each Bureau.[109]

The attempt to unify the labor movement on a citywide basis was part of a larger vision of the regional, national, and even international consolidation of trade unions. As one trade union newspaper put it in August 1906: "From the factory *kassa* it is necessary to move to a union; from a citywide union to a national union, and then to the international struggle of all workers."[110]

[108]*MIPDR*, 4:72.

[109]See, for example, the controversy over the creation of a program to aid unemployed workers in the Moscow Bureau of Trade Unions. Milonov, ed., *Moskovskoe professional'noe dvizhenie*, pp. 334–336.

[110]*Tkach*, no. 4 (August 5, 1906), p. 3.

On the regional level, some unions took advantage of the March 1906 law to establish subsidiary branches in other cities and towns. This practice became widespread in Moscow when provincial governors in the surrounding Moscow Industrial Region refused to register trade unions. Consequently, a number of unions, including the tailors, metalworkers, textile workers, and printers, set up headquarters in the city of Moscow and then opened branch offices in the adjacent provinces.[111] The drawback in this arrangement was that closure of the main union office entailed, according to law, the closure of all subsidiary branches.

Labor leaders also attempted to build bridges among the various local organizations through the convocation of regional and national trade union conferences. The Second All-Russian Conference of Trade Unions, as we have seen, took place in February 1906 with eighteen voting delegates from ten factory centers.[112] Following the Second Conference, trade unionists formed an Organizational Commission to proceed with plans for a trade union congress which, however, failed to convene before the Stolypin "coup d'état" of June 3, 1907. The Organizational Commission served as an interim coordinating body on a national level, and one of its major accomplishments was to gather statistical information from unions throughout Imperial Russia.[113] Nearly all of the participants at the Second All-Russian Conference and members of the Organizational Commission were intelligentsia political activists, mostly Social Democrats.[114]

Six major trade union conferences were also held in this period:

1. The Third Congress of Mutual Aid Societies of Employees in Private Businesses, June 1906.[115]

2. The First All-Russian Conference of Tailors, August 1906.

---

[111]*Zakon*, Part II, Article 5, p. 16. The Moscow tailors' union, for example, had ten subsidiary branches in Kostroma, Kaluga, Vladimir, Ivanovo-Voznesensk, Iaroslavl', Orekhovo-Zuevo, Kolomna, Kokhma, Kovrov, and Riazan'. Oliunina, *Portnovskii promysel*, p. 300. The Moscow metalworkers' union had twelve branches in Serpukhov, Tver, and elsewhere in the Central Industrial Region. Milonov, ed., *Moskovskoe professional'noe dvizhenie*, p. 266.

[112]For the protocols of the conference, see *Vtoraia konferentsiia*.

[113]The results of this survey appeared in *Professional'nyi vestnik*, no. 6 (April 3, 1907), and no. 8 (April 30, 1907). They are reprinted in Grinevich, *Professional'noe dvizhenie*, pp. 284–285.

[114]For a list of participants in the Second All-Russian Conference, see *Vtoraia konferentsiia*, p. 23. A list of members of the Organizational Commission can be found in Kolokol'nikov, "Otryvki," *MIPDR*, 5:135.

[115]This congress functioned as an all-Russian gathering of sales-clerical unions. Sviatlovskii, *Professional'noe dvizhenie*, pp. 32, 298, 310–312.

3. The First All-Russian Conference of Teapackers, January 1907.

4. The First All-Russian Conference of Construction Workers, February 1907.

5. The First Conference of Metalworkers in the Moscow Industrial Region, February 1907.[116]

6. The First All-Russian Conference of Workers in the Printing Industry, April 1907.

In addition, a regional conference of unions of technicians was held in St. Petersburg in April 1907, while in the Moscow Industrial Region, conferences were convened by the unions of sales-clerical workers in March 1907, the unions of tailors in April 1907, and the unions of textile workers in February and again in July 1907.[117]

In September 1906 the Moscow Central Bureau, with Menshevik backing, launched a plan to hold a conference of trade unions in the Moscow Industrial Region, including representatives of all workers' organizations: strike and factory committees, cultural organizations, mutual aid societies, cooperatives, and trade unions. The Menshevik plan was devised under the influence of a project for a general workers' congress advocated by Pavel Axelrod,[118] and it acquired considerable support in Menshevik circles during 1906.

Axelrod conceived of the congress as a means of achieving a unified mass workers' movement animated by the principles of Social Democracy. But his plan encountered strenuous opposition from the Bolsheviks, who contended that it would divert leadership of the workers' movement into nonparty channels and expose the masses to bourgeois influence. Bolsheviks presented these arguments to the Moscow Central Bureau of Trade Unions, where the Menshevik plan for a regional conference was put to a vote in March 1907. By a vote of thirteen to eleven, the Bolshevik proposal was accepted, limiting the conference

[116]Although this conference was officially a meeting of unionized metalworkers in the Central Industrial Region, it attracted representatives from metalworkers' unions in other cities, including St. Petersburg.

[117]Several conferences subsequently published protocols of the proceedings. See *Pervaia konferentsiia* (metalworkers), *Protokoly pervoi vserossiiskoi konferentsii* (printers), *Pervaia oblastnaia konferentsiia professional'nykh soiuzov rabochikh po obrabotke voloknistykh veshchestv Moskovskogo promyshlennogo raiona* (Moscow, 1907) (textile workers).

[118]On Axelrod's plan, see Abraham Ascher, *Pavel Axelrod and the Development of Menshevism* (Cambridge, Mass., 1972), pp. 254–258.

to trade unions only.[119] As it turned out, however, a change in the political atmosphere three months later prevented the conference from taking place.

Social Democratic activists and sympathizers were often in a majority at the conferences that convened in these months. Of the seventy-two voting delegates (fifty-seven of them were actual workers) attending the first All-Russian Conference of Printers, forty-eight were SD party members, another five were SD sympathizers, and one was an SR party member. The other participants included Zionist Socialists (4), Bundists (1), and nonparty people (6).[120] Similarly, at the First All-Russian Conference of Metalworkers, twenty-six of the twenty-nine delegates were Social Democrats.[121]

Agendas for regional and national conferences display a striking uniformity.[122] Broadly speaking, these gatherings addressed issues relating to the structure and activities of unions, especially the question of labor-management relations in the new era of trade unionism. Invariably, the conferences passed resolutions declaring the urgency for centralized leadership and coordinated action among workers on regional and national levels. The regional conference of textile workers, for example, resolved to "create a Central Bureau which would direct the economic struggle of workers in the region."[123] Similarly, the all-Russian conference of printers recommended that efforts be undertaken to create regional organizations as a step toward eventual consolidation on the national level.[124]

The activities of the Central Bureaus and the regional and national conferences were evidence of the spread of class consciousness among organized workers and their growing awareness of themselves as part of a movement that transcended narrow occupational lines and parochial allegiances. Social Democrats, particularly intellectuals, played an important part in promoting these activities designed to strengthen the workers' sense of proletarian unity. But if union members supported efforts to build regional and national organizations,

---

[119]Tiurin, *Moskovskoe tsentral'noe biuro*, pp. 124–125; Stulin, "Moskovskoe professional'noe dvizhenie," in *Moskovskoe professional'noe dvizhenie*, ed. Milonov, pp. 341–342.

[120]Grinevich, *Professional'noe dvizhenie*, p. 244, n. 2.

[121]*Pervaia konferentsiia*, p. 101. The 26 Social Democrats were as follows: 11 Mensheviks, 5 Bolsheviks, 10 nonfaction. Of the 29 delegates at the conference, 19 were workers.

[122]Apart from the protocols of conferences cited above, additional material on various conferences can be found as follows: Sviatlovskii, *Professional'noe dvizhenie*, pp. 290–291 on the conference of tailors; *Istoriia odnogo soiuza* on the conference of teapackers; *Professional*, no. 3–4 (May 17, 1907), p. 15, on the regional conference of textile workers.

[123]Milonov, ed., *Moskovskoe professional'noe dvizhenie*, p. 310.

[124]Sher, *Istoriia*, p. 390.

they did not easily relinquish their bases of solidarity rooted in a common occupation, enterprise, or city district. Multiple images of collective identity continued to evolve along parallel lines during this period, just as they had in 1905. Craft and class consciousness were two dimensions of the workers' aspiration to unite in the common defense of their rights.

The consolidation of the organized labor movement on citywide, regional, and national levels produced an atmosphere of optimism in some labor circles. "All of this created among printers," Sher reported, "a conviction that the [government] administration, if it would not [legally] permit an all-Russian organization [of printers], would not persecute those who participated in it."[125] This optimism was soon dispelled by the "stern reality" of the Stolypin era, but for a brief period some workers came to believe in the prospect of a mass labor movement that would eventually attain national dimensions.

Trade unionists thus made significant progress in building mass-based associations in 1906 and early 1907. Under the tutelage of their radical mentors, they took steps to lay the foundations for democratically organized labor unions and to develop a trade union ideology with a socialist perspective. Through the establishment of the first national network among labor organizations, the union movement helped to fortify the workers' class awareness and their aspiration for national unification.

Continuing the trend already established in 1905, trade unions remained closely connected to political parties and radical intellectuals. Social Democrats, above all, extended and deepened their position in the unions, drawing substantial support from skilled workers, including many artisanal groups. Socialist Revolutionaries, syndicalists, and the liberal Kadets also attracted a small following among unionized workers.

To a greater extent than any other party or group, the Mensheviks exerted far-reaching influence over trade union development in this period. They introduced Western European practices and institutions and helped to train a generation of worker-activists that rose through union ranks. The unions themselves were a magnet for politically minded workers who had passed through the crucible of 1905 and were receptive to the tactical and ideological appeals of their socialist mentors. Yet the relationship between these two groups—unionized workers and intelligentsia radicals—was mutually influential, and the outlook and priorities of each group left an imprint on the other.

[125]Ibid., p. 389.

The intense organizational efforts of trade unionists following the March 1906 law yielded some impressive accomplishments. Notwithstanding the lack of opportunities for voluntary association before 1905, workers managed to erect trade unions with exceptional rapidity and determination. This organizational activity was intended, not as an end in itself, but as the means to a goal. Quite simply, unions held out the promise that workers could attain a better life through sustained collective organization. In their endeavor to realize this promise, trade unionists made their boldest and most innovative efforts in 1906–1907, and realized some of their greatest achievements.

Chapter 7

Trade Unions, Employers, and the State, 1906–1907

> The working class must rely only on its own strength
> and not expect anything from above. It is essential to
> work only in one direction: to strengthen organizations,
> to increase their readiness for battle, to fight unceasingly
> for better conditions of life. The government, in league
> with capital, does not *yield* anything voluntarily. They
> only know how to *take*.
>
> Professional, *April 1907*[1]

The political and juridical conditions in tsarist Russia during 1906 and the first half of 1907 made it possible for trade unions to grow rapidly and to carry out a variety of activities on behalf of their membership. Above all, the unions sought to assist workers in attaining collective improvement and protection against the depredations of industrial life. The definition and performance of these functions was at the very core of union development in this period, bringing these organizations into direct contact with their principal antagonists: the tsarist government and employers.

TRADE UNIONS AND THE STATE

Government circles were deeply divided over the approach to industrial relations that had been embodied, albeit hesitantly and incompletely, in the law of March 4, 1906. The law itself represented a triumph of the policies advocated by the

[1]*Professional,* no. 2 (April 11, 1907), p. 5. Italics are in the original.

274

Ministry of Finance and promoted, from October 1905 on, by the newly established Ministry of Trade and Industry. This approach called for a minimum of government intervention in workplace disputes and the creation, instead, of a new legal framework enabling labor and management to work out their differences in a relatively autonomous sphere of social action. In the view of M. M. Fedorov, the Minister of Trade and Industry, the law

represented a shift from detailed regulation of relations between industrialists and workers and administrative tutelage over them, to a new path which opened for workers and their employers the possibility for free autonomous action through the medium of professional societies.[2]

Envisioning a fundamental reorientation of state policy in the area of labor-management relations, a Ministry report declared that whereas the government had formerly focused exclusively on the maintenance of order and tranquility among workers, now it pursued a different objective: to place both sides in industrial disputes in a position where neither had predominance over the other, and to ensure an improvement of workers' conditions through appropriate state action. The laws of December 2, 1905, and March 4, 1906, the Ministry observed, provided the foundation for this new and laudable approach to industrial relations.[3]

Weakened by political instability and fearful of renewed political disorders, the government briefly adopted the strategy toward labor advocated by the Ministry of Trade and Industry. But its acceptance of this approach was at most halfhearted, and the law of March 1906, as well as its subsequent implementation, failed to live up to the far bolder vision of its promoters in some government circles.

The labor policies advocated by the Ministry of Trade and Industry encountered their strongest and most relentless opposition from the Ministry of Internal Affairs and its subsidiary organs, the Department of Police and the Okhrana. Headed by the formidable Petr Stolypin from April 1906 until his assassination in September 1911, the Ministry of Internal Affairs advocated strict limitations on the activities of legal workers' organizations, close surveillance to ensure their compliance, and government intervention in the relations between workers and

---

[2]Cited in V. Ia. Laverychev, *Tsarizm i rabochii vopros v Rossii 1861–1917 gg.* (Moscow, 1972), p. 203. The Ministry of Trade and Industry was established on October 27, 1905.

[3]Tsentral'nyi gosudarstvennyi istoricheskii arkhiv (TsGIA), f. 560, op. 26, d. 585, p. 2. The law of December 2, 1905, had authorized certain types of economic strikes for the first time. Details of the March 4, 1906 law are discussed above in chapter 5.

employers. The Ministry's view of the trade union movement, which was reflected in its activities during 1906–1907, was set forth in a report prepared in early 1908 by Blazhchuk, a Ministry official assigned the task of reviewing the implementation of the March 1906 law during the first several years following its enactment.[4]

The Blazhchuk report began with the assertion that the March 1906 law provided "a full, almost uncontrolled opportunity for association in legal unions." Following the enactment of the new regulations, it continued, "administrative authority . . . turned out to be powerless in contending with the aspiration for association," and radical political parties took advantage of the trade unions for unlawful purposes:

The revolutionary parties, striving to destroy the existing state and social system, [and] having failed in their criminal aspirations during the troubled times, blame their failure on the fact that the popular masses were not involved in the struggle with the government in 1905 and 1906. At that time, in the absence of a law permitting associations, there was no opportunity to unite and arm the proletariat against the government. Now such a law exists, and in the event of new unrest, the revolutionary parties are recommending that [the March 1906 law] be used to increase the forces hostile to the government.[5]

Blazhchuk was not alone in calling attention to the penetration of trade unions by radical activists. This view was shared by other law-enforcement authorities and those, such as provincial governors, charged with administration of the new law. A memorandum from the Okhrana to the Petersburg Chief of Police warned on December 13, 1906, that the local RSDRP organization was using trade unions for "propagandistic goals."[6] In a lengthy report on trade unions, the Governor of Moscow Province stated that one-half of the legal unions established in this region during 1906 "pursue antigovernment political goals and provide a convenient opportunity for interaction among politically like-minded people, and sometimes even serve as a place where evil plans are hatched and where weapons and illegal literature are stored."[7]

The cause of this dangerous situation, according to Blazhchuk and others,

---

[4]TsGIA, f. 23, op. 17, d. 652, 1907, pp. 15–22; Tsentral'nyi gosudarstvennyi arkhiv Oktiabr'skoi revoliutsii (TsGAOR), DPOO, f. 102, op. 00, d. 1000, ch. 14, t. 1, 1905, pp. 225–227.

[5]TsGAOR, DPOO, f. 102, op. 00, d. 1000, ch. 14, t. 1, 1905, p. 225.

[6]Leningradskii gosudarstvennyi istoricheskii arkhiv (LGIA), f. 287, op. 1, d. 16, p. 9.

[7]M. Balabanov, "Pravitel'stvo i professional'nye soiuzy v 1905–1907 gg.," in *Materialy po istorii professional'nogo dvizheniia v Peterburge 1905–1907 gg.* (henceforth *MIPDP*) (Leningrad, 1926), p. 75.

was the March 1906 law, "which does not give government authorities the means of putting an end to the activities of the revolutionary mass [within the unions]."[8] In a similar vein, the Petersburg Chief of Police concluded that the law granted too much autonomy and scope for the trade unions,[9] while the Governor of Moscow Province recommended major modification of the law in order to "limit the range of [union] activity, the composition of the membership, and the geographical area where a union may operate."[10]

Notwithstanding the defects and dangers thought to be inherent in the March 1906 law, neither Blazhchuk, the Department of Police, nor the provincial governors proposed to abolish the legal position of trade unions altogether. Such action, Blazhchuk asserted, "was unthinkable" for three major reasons.[11] First, the experience of Western Europe had demonstrated that "the aspiration arises from fundamental vital needs which cannot be satisfied by governments acting to regulate by law the mutual relations between labor and capital." Secondly, the employers themselves accepted legal workers' organizations as "necessary in the interests of the orderly development of industry and trade." Finally, the report cited the declaration of the State Council, affirming that "in Russia, the time has come for legal recognition of the right of the working masses to form associations."

A memorandum prepared by the Department of Police in late 1907 or early 1908 also reached the conclusion that "a law on professional societies is inevitable,"[12] and cited two reasons for permitting labor organizations to operate legally. Most important, the memorandum asserted, such organizations eased the task of surveillance over the workers. Trade unions were also credited with performing a positive function because under their influence "workers were sobering up from the revolutionary hangover [of 1905] and beginning to develop a consciousness of their purely professional needs."[13]

The ideal, in the Ministry's view, was to design a legal framework that would exclude radical intellectuals from the labor movement and ensure that the

---

[8]TsGAOR, DPOO, f. 102, op. 00, d. 1000, ch. 14, t. 1, 1905, p. 225.

[9]Balabanov, "Pravitel'stvo," *MIPDP*, p. 76.

[10]Upon receiving the governor's report, Tsar Nicholas II declared the proposal for amendment of the March 1906 law to be a "very important matter." Ibid, p. 75. See below, chapter 9, for a discussion of the legislative review that was subsequently undertaken.

[11]TsGAOR, DPOO, f. 102, op. 00, d. 1000, ch. 14, t. 1, 1906, p. 226.

[12]Balabanov, "Pravitel'stvo," *MIPDP*, p. 78.

[13]Ibid., p. 79. His report was prepared by two officials from the Department of Police on orders from the Ministry of Internal Affairs.

"ultimate and sole goal [of the unions was the] complete and equitable agreement of workers' and employers' interests."[14] Some government officials thus anticipated an eventual reconciliation between labor and capital, a notion that even the 1905 revolution had not succeeded in dispelling. To accomplish this, the Blazhchuk report recommended a drastically revised law that would have greatly augmented the power of the Ministry of Internal Affairs and its subsidiaries over the organized labor movement. Henceforth, unions would adopt a charter prepared by the Ministry, elect officers approved by the Ministry, and confine all activities to mutual aid and cooperation with employers.

These views influenced the attitude of the Ministry of Internal Affairs toward the implementation of the March 1906 law. On matters relating to the registration of unions, officials in this Ministry adopted a wary and critical approach that contrasted sharply with the position of the Ministry of Trade and Industry. Interministerial differences are illustrated by the case of the Moscow ribbon-weavers' union, a lively and well-subscribed organization formed in the fall of 1905. The ribbonweavers' union was one of the first groups in Moscow to apply for registration under the terms of the new law. When the union's application came before the Moscow Bureau on Trade Unions on April 11, 1906, a majority voted to grant the union legal status. But two members were opposed, one of them the powerful Moscow Chief of Police, who declared that the union had impermissible political goals because its charter proposed to promote "the education of workers and the development of their ability to participate in the so-called 'liberation struggle.' "[15]

The Chief of Police, in accordance with the law's provisions, appealed the Bureau's ruling to the Ministry of Internal Affairs, which in turn consulted the Ministry of Trade and Industry and the Ministry of Justice. On June 9, 1906, Privy Councillor Shtoff of the Ministry of Trade and Industry stated his agreement with the majority on the Moscow Bureau of Trade Unions. Asserting that the union's charter did not include any statements that violated the March 1906 law, Shtoff noted that even the union's provision for using half its revenue to support a strike fund could not be considered sufficient grounds for denying registration in light of the December 2, 1905, law legalizing certain categories of strikes.[16]

The opinion of the Ministry of Trade and Industry contrasted sharply with

[14]TsGAOR, DPOO, f. 102, op. 00, d. 1000, ch. 14, t. 1, 1905, p. 226.
[15]TsGIA, f. 1284, op. 187, d. 298, 1906, p. 1.
[16]Ibid., p. 3.

that of the Ministry of Justice. Responding on October 28, 1906, the Ministry of Justice asserted that the charter submitted by the Moscow union of ribbon-weavers violated the law because it stated that workers would join together to "struggle" for improved conditions. "Struggle," according to this Ministry, remained outside the permissible range of union activities.[17]

Finally, the Ministry of Internal Affairs filed its report, reviewing the arguments for and against the registration of the Moscow union of ribbonweavers. Taking issue with the opinion of the Ministry of Trade and Industry, the report asserted that the union's charter included political objectives of an unspecified nature and that "the establishment of a union whose goal is to develop in its members the ability to carry on the 'liberation struggle' constitutes a threat to destroy the security of society and state order."[18] On November 14, 1906, the Senate ruled that the union's application for registration should be denied. Despite several subsequent efforts, this union never achieved legal status.

The Ministry of Internal Affairs also took steps to increase police surveillance and control over the unions. These efforts were considerably hampered prior to June 1907, however, by unstable political conditions and apprehensiveness about provoking new unrest in the cities while rebellion was still in progress in the countryside.

The first major circular issued by the Ministry of Internal Affairs to the police and provincial governors was dated May 10, 1907. In it, the Ministry asserted that unions had fallen under the influence of Social Democratic groups seeking to "propagandize the 'unconscious' workers, not only for the purpose of attracting them into underground organizations, but also to acquire ready cadres of armed militia in anticipation of an uprising in the event of the dissolution of the Second State Duma."[19] The circular further warned that "as a result of the especially intense activity of Social Democrats, trade unions are already acquiring the fully defined character of Social Democratic organizations and are therefore highly dangerous for the state system." The success of the Social Democrats in the unions, it continued, had attracted other revolutionary parties to the labor movement, where they, too, attempted to transform the unions into "social political organizations with platforms that closely resemble party programs." Local authorities were advised to devote "the closest and most serious

---

[17]Ibid., p. 8.
[18]Ibid., p. 10.
[19]Balabanov, "Pravitel'stvo," *MIPDP,* p. 65.

attention" to the unions and to prosecute them when they deviated from the law.[20]

A subsequent circular from the Ministry dated July 27, 1907, reiterated these warnings and declared that the link between unions and revolutionary organizations was growing "closer and closer." On this occasion, provincial governors were requested to supply extensive information on both legal and illegal unions in their province and to maintain special surveillance over trade union publications.[21]

The powerful Ministry of Internal Affairs, with the Department of Police and the Okhrana under its jurisdiction, did not restrict itself to memoranda, circulars, and cases received on appeal from the Bureaus on Trade Unions. Unions required permission from the local chief of police to hold general membership meetings, and this became one important means of controlling and obstructing union activities.[22] On several occasions, all trade union meetings were prohibited. This occurred in Moscow in February 1906 at the time of elections to the First State Duma and again in St. Petersburg during elections to the Second State Duma.[23] In some instances, the police authorized a union meeting, only to withdraw permission at the last minute, throwing the union into disarray. On May 7, 1906, for example, general meetings of the Petersburg unions of construction workers, tailors, and knitters were forbidden at the last minute.[24] Law enforcement authorities also subjected the unions to searches, confiscations, and more rarely, the arrest of officers and members.

Despite incidents of harassment, the authorities exercised greater moderation in their dealings with the unions than they had before 1905 or would again after June 1907. Even unions without legal standing carried on their activities with a good deal of freedom. Thus, the Petersburg metalworkers' union functioned for ten months without legal status (July 1906 to May 1907), but as one member recalled: "Illegal existence was in essence a semilegal existence; [the authorities]

---

[20]Ibid.

[21]TsGAOR, DPOO, f. 192, op. 5, d. 1000, ch. 14, t. 3, p. 6; DP IV f. 102, op. 99, d. 100, ch. 2, p. 79. Subsequent circulars were issued by the Ministry of Internal Affairs on September 21, 1907, and October 14, 1907.

[22]According to the March 1906 law, meetings of the union board did not require prior authorization from the local chief of police. But permission was necessary to hold general membership meetings.

[23]*Professional'nyi soiuz*, no. 11 (February 26, 1906), p. 1; LGIA, f. 287, op. 1, d. 16, p. 9; TsGIA, f. 150, op. 1, d. 659, pp. 1–4.

[24]*Volna*, no. 12 (May 9, 1906), p. 7.

knew about the [illegal Petersburg metalworkers'] union and about its secret activity, but tolerated it." The police "looked through their fingers" at unions that functioned illegally.[25]

Government intervention in relations between labor and management also remained relatively limited until the fall of 1907. To be sure, worker representatives were sometimes arrested on the request of employers,[26] and the cossacks were mobilized during a citywide work stoppage of Petersburg bakers in June 1906. But the overall picture is one of governmental restraint in the face of extensive union involvement in the strike movement and union efforts to conclude collective agreements with employers.

EMPLOYERS AND TRADE UNIONS

The revolution of 1905 led employers to establish a new type of collective organization. Whereas employers had previously united for the primary purpose of promoting industrial interests in government circles, now they were drawn together by their opposition to the growing workers' movement. As one employer in the Moscow tailoring industry put it, "They will push us to the wall if we don't organize."[27] By mid-1907, there were eighteen employers' societies in St. Petersburg and seventeen in Moscow (Appendix III). All of the Moscow societies obtained registration under the provisions of the March 1906 law; ten employer groups in the capital were also registered, while no information has been located on the remaining eight. In the Russian Empire as a whole, there were 120 employer organizations at the end of 1907.[28]

These associations fall into two types. One, exemplified by the St. Petersburg Society of Factory Owners (Obshchestvo zavodchikov i fabrikantov) and its counterpart in the Central Industrial Region, brought together representatives of large-scale enterprises in many different branches of industry. The second united

[25]*Materialy ob ekonomicheskom polozhenii i professional'noi organizatsii Peterburgskikh rabochikh po metallu* (St. Petersburg, 1909), p. 32.

[26]An illustration of this is the case of the Petersburg printing firm Ulia, where the worker representative was arrested by the police when he arrived for negotiations with the employer. *Golos*, no. 10 (June 2 [15], 1906), p. 3.

[27]*Listok dlia rabochikh portnykh, portnikh i skorniakov*, no. 5–6 (March 24, 1907), p. 3.

[28]*Rabochee dvizhenie: Biulleten': Obshchestvo zavodchikov i fabrikantov*, no. 6 (January 1908), p. 7.

employers within a single industry, occupation, or type of enterprise. Such associations arose in artisanal or semiartisanal trades (e.g., printing, tailoring, sausagemaking, bread baking, or jewelrymaking) and among owners of sales and service establishments (e.g., taverns, dairy stores, or bathhouses).

The St. Petersburg- and Moscow-based Societies of Factory Owners were the largest and most powerful entrepreneurial associations in tsarist Russia by 1907. The Petersburg Society of Factory Owners grew out of the Society to Assist the Development and Improvement of Factory Industry, an organization founded in the 1890s to strengthen the industrialists' influence on state policy making.[29] In 1905, industrialists in the capital took steps to transform the Society into an organization capable of resisting the workers' "unreasonable aspirations."[30]

Soon after the enactment of the March 1906 law, S. P. Glezmer, the Chairman of the Society to Assist the Development and Improvement of Factory Industry, proposed to fellow industrialists that they reorganize the association in conformity with the new circumstances and the new legislation. In a letter dated March 24, 1906, Glezmer observed that the current charter of the Society "no longer corresponds to the activities of the organization," activities that were now directed primarily toward a "grave struggle with the strike movement."[31]

Just as the workers borrowed extensively from their Western European counterparts, so industrialists turned to the example of Western Europe for guidance in the new phase of labor relations inaugurated by the 1905 revolution. Employers directed their attention primarily to Germany, where at the end of the 1880s employers had also formed associations (*Arbeitgeberverbände*) in reaction to the incipient trade union movement.[32] But Russian industrialists not only modeled their own organizations after those in Germany; they also adopted from Western Europe new techniques for coping with labor unrest, such as blacklists, lockouts, and antistrike funds. Some of these techniques had already made an appearance

---

[29]The Society to Assist the Development and Improvement of Factory Industry was established by Petersburg industrialists in 1893, but did not obtain legal status until January 29, 1897, when it was officially authorized by the Ministry of Finance. TsGIA, f. 150, op. 1, d. 54, p. 9.

[30]TsGIA, f. 150, op. 1, d. 3, p. 1.

[31]Ibid., p. 75.

[32]A. Ermanskii, "Soiuzy rabotodatelei," *Sovremennyi mir,* Book 12 (December 1909), pp. 26–27. Ermanskii notes that the Petersburg Society of Factory Owners published a Russian translation on German employer organizations: V. V. Groman, *Organizatsiia rabotodatelei v Germanii,* with a forward by the Society. He further states that industrialists from St. Petersburg, Moscow, and elsewhere in Russia turned to the central employers' organization in Germany in 1906 for counsel. Ibid., p. 29.

in Russia in 1905 and earlier, but they were utilized in a systematic way for the first time in these years.[33]

The charter for the Petersburg Society of Factory Owners was submitted to the capital's Chief of Police on June 20, 1906, and on September 5, 1906, the Society attained legal status under the law of March 1906.[34] A conglomerate organization that included employers from seven different branches of industry,[35] the Society violated the law's prohibition against combinations involving more than one industrial or occupational group. But this violation evidently presented no obstacle to registration. In fact, it was not until June 1911 that the Petersburg Chief of Police called the Society's attention to eight separate violations of the March 1906 law in the Society's charter. The matter was quickly settled, however, when the Minister of Internal Affairs notified the zealous police chief that the government was thoroughly satisfied with the Society in its present form, and even had occasion to rely upon it in times of unrest.[36]

The Society of Factory Owners in the Central Industrial Region, another multiindustrial employer association, was registered on August 19, 1906. It, too, arose in response to the massive labor disturbances during 1905. A Commission on the Labor Question, formed under the aegis of the Moscow Stock Exchange Committee in January 1905, led the way in establishing the Society of Factory Owners.[37] As in St. Petersburg, only large-scale industrialists were admitted to the organization.[38] The Moscow-based Society extended its jurisdiction to no fewer than nine provinces of the Central Region,[39] and was dominated by textile manufacturers, the region's leading employer.

[33]According to F. A. Bulkin [F. Semenov], *Na zare profdvizheniia: Istoriia Peterburgskogo soiuza metallistov 1906–1914 gg.* (Moscow and Leningrad, 1924), pp. 167–168, the blacklist was first used by the Society of Factory Owners in August 1906 when it recommended that workers fired for their participation in five strikes in metalworking plants be denied employment at other industries.

[34]The Society forwarded a special request to the Ministry of Internal Affairs on August 22, 1906, urging expeditious registration of the organization in light of the "dangerous manifestations of the workers' movement at the present time and the necessity for counteracting these. . . ." LGIA, f. 287, op. 1, d. 12a, p. 47.

[35]See below, table 29.

[36]LGIA, f. 287, op. 1, d. 12a, pp. 98, 101, 106.

[37]TsGIA, f. 150, op. 1, d. 646, pp. 117, 161–162; f. 150, op. 1, d. 484, pp. 40, 66.

[38]Membership in the Moscow-based Society of Factory Owners was restricted to employers in the city of Moscow employing one hundred or more workers and to employers in Moscow Province employing three hundred or more workers. TsGIA, f. 150, op. 1, d. 661, p. 4.

[39]The nine provinces encompassed by the Society of Factory Owners in the Moscow Industrial Region included Moscow, Vladimir, Kostroma, Nizhni-Novgorod, Riazan, Smolensk, Tver, Tula, and Iaroslavl.

By contrast, employers in the metalworking industry constituted the largest single group within the Petersburg Society (table 28). The Revolution of 1905, with its massive upheavals among metalworkers, brought many of these industrialists into the organization for the first time.[40] By 1907 nearly all the major privately owned metalworking plants in the capital were represented in the Society, which then included 171 firms in seven branches of industry, with a combined labor force of 110,365 workers.

By virtue of its location and industrial importance, the Petersburg Society of Factory Owners emerged as the country's leading exponent of entrepreneurial ideology and policy in this period. The charter of the organization stated that its goal was to "create peaceful relations between employers and workers."[41] To this end, the Society declared a readiness to seek the resolution of workplace conflicts by means of arbitration and conciliation boards, to work out standard wage rates and other conditions of labor, and finally, to appeal to the government for new industrial legislation. It further asserted a willingness to recognize the just requests of workers while opposing "unfair aspirations and claims of the workers and their organizations."[42]

Notwithstanding these declarations, however, the Society adopted an antagonistic and uncooperative approach to labor organizations and to workers' demands for the negotiation or mediation of labor-management disputes. In February 1905, when trade unions had barely made an appearance in the capital, Glezmer was already warning of the deleterious consequences that would ensue from the establishment of workers' organizations.[43] On August 11, 1906, the Society resolved that "unfortunately it is impossible to come to an agreement with trade unions for one simple reason: at the present moment they do not exist. What we have now are thoroughly political workers' organizations, existing under a legal cover but promulgating terror and anarchy."[44] In July 1907, on the tenth anniversary of its founding, the Society again set forth its views:

The existing unions do not constitute real unions of workers, since only an insignificant number of workers participate in them. [Union] organizers, who in a majority of cases are

[40]TsGIA, f. 150, op. 1, d. 3, pp. 1, 6–7, 18, 50a, on the efforts of industrialists in the Petersburg metalworking industry to organize collectively in 1905.

[41]TsGIA, f. 150, op. 1, d. 3, pp. 85–95.

[42]Ibid.

[43]TsGIA, f. 150, op. 1, d. 484, p. 3; f. 150, op. 1, d. 500, p. 304.

[44]M.S. Balabanov, *Ot 1905 k 1907 godu: Massovoe rabochee dvizhenie* (Moscow and Leningrad, 1927), p. 44. Balabanov's quotation is drawn from the protocols of the August 11, 1906, meeting of the Society.

Table 28

Membership in the St. Petersburg Society of
Factory Owners, 1898, 1906, 1907

	NO. OF FIRMS REPRESENTED			NO. OF WORKERS EMPLOYED IN MEMBER FIRMS		
	1897	1906	1907	1897	1906	1907
Textiles	35	37	35	27,760	29,150	29,216
Metals	22	66	72	9,840	52,510	53,603
Paper	9	11	11	3,240	4,270	3,308
Wood	5	9	10	575	880	1,097
Food	4	12	13	2,190	6,330	7,093
Leather	5	6	5	1,160	3,600	3,512
Technical-chemical	18	26	25	9,770	12,600	12,536
Total	98	167	171	54,535	109,340	110,365

Source: Ermanskii, "Soiuz rabotodatelei," p. 45.

people alien [to the industry], attempt to assume the role of [workers'] representatives, to create representative organs in a way similar to the "Soviet of Workers' Deputies." They also try to establish communication with industrial employers, but this type of intercourse cannot be considered appropriate until it becomes known who are the members of the union and who is responsible for their actions.[45]

Faithful to these pronouncements, members of the Petersburg Society remained opposed to union recognition and virtually all forms of collective bargaining.[46]

Employer groups also arose in artisanal trades such as tailoring, jewelrymaking, and baking; in factory industries such as candymaking and brickmaking; and among merchants and owners of commercial establishments (see Appendix III). The most important of these organizations was established in the printing trades. Before 1905 some printing firm owners already belonged to the Russian Society of Specialists in the Printing Trades, founded in St. Petersburg in 1899. The Society included not only employers but also writers and even some highly

[45] TsGIA, f. 150, op. 1, d. 661, p. 4.
[46] The Society drew up "general directives" for dealing with strikes in the spring of 1907. Included in these directives was a provision enjoining members from entering into agreements with trade unions. *Rabochee dvizhenie: Biulleten'*, no. 1 (1907), p. 5.

skilled technical experts.[47] By mid-1906, two organizations composed exclusively of employers had arisen in the capital in response to the printers' unionizing activities. The Society of Printing Firm Owners was registered on October 31, 1906, and the Union of St. Petersburg Owners of Typographical Firms obtained legal status on December 5, 1906.[48]

Similarly, in the Moscow printing industry, a branch of the Russian Society of Specialists in the Printing Trades was established in 1900. It played a role during the September 1903 strikes and again in September 1905, but was supplanted on November 10, 1905, by the Moscow Society of Owners of Typographical-Lithographical Firms, which was officially registered in December 1906. This Society consisted entirely of employers and was designed primarily to counteract the growing strength of organized labor.[49]

The Petersburg and Moscow organizations of printing firm owners came into existence on the initiative of some of the largest employers in the printing trades, a pattern that was duplicated in other industries as well.[50] But the owners of relatively large-scale enterprises were not the only ones to join these associations, and many small firms were also represented within their ranks. At the time of its founding in late 1905, the Moscow Society of Owners of Typographical-Lithographical firms had forty-nine member firms; twenty-one of them employed fewer than fifty workers.[51] By 1907, the representation of small firms in the organization had begun to decline as a consequence of the domination of the largest firms over policy matters. The group then had thirty-two member

[47]P. V. Vasil'ev-Severianin, "Tarifnaia bor'ba soiuza rabochikh pechatnogo dela v 1905–1907 godakh," in *MIPDP*, p. 164.

[48]Ermanskii, "Soiuz rabotodatelei," p. 30. The Society of Printing Firm Owners met for the first time on October 23, 1905. At the founding meeting, two hundred printing firms were represented. *Istoriia Leningradskogo soiuza rabochikh poligraficheskogo proizvodstva*, Book 1: *1904-1907 gg.* (henceforth *ILS*) (Leningrad, 1925), p. 219.

[49]V. V. Sher, *Istoriia professional'nogo dvizheniia rabochikh pechatnogo dela v Moskve* (Moscow, 1911), pp. 98–99, 106–107, 200.

[50]The Petersburg Society of Printing Firm Owners was established by owners of twenty-five of the capital's largest printing establishments. *ILS*, p. 373. Similarly, the owners of large firms led the way in establishing the Moscow Society of Owners of Typographical-Lithographical Firms and the Moscow Society of Owners of Tailoring Shops. Sher, *Istoriia*, p. 200; E. A. Oliunina, *Portnovskii promysel v Moskve i v derevniakh Moskovskoi i Riazanskoi gubernii: Materialy k istorii domashnei promyshlennosti v Rossii* (Moscow, 1914), p. 297. A notable exception to this pattern was the Petersburg Society of Bakery Owners, which did not include the bakery industry's largest employer in the capital, the Filippov firm. TsGAOR, DP IV, d. 999, t. 2, 1905, p. 68.

[51]Sher, *Istoriia*, p. 200.

firms, with a combined labor force of six thousand workers (approximately one-half the industry's workers, based on 1902 census data).

Single-industry employer associations were seldom in a position to mount the kind of concerted resistance to workers' demands achieved by the Societies of Factory Owners. To be sure, they resorted to blacklists and lockouts, and instituted antistrike funds amounting sometimes to thousands of rubles.[52] Heavy fines were imposed on member firms that unilaterally granted concessions to workers without securing the prior approval of the organization. But these employer groups were weakened by internal divisions and did not easily reach a consensus, vacillating between a militant approach to industrial conflicts which relied upon lockouts, blacklists, and antistrike funds, and a conciliatory approach based on negotiation of a collective contract.

Owners of large and small firms often found it hard to agree on tactics. The Moscow Society of Owners of Tailoring Shops split along these lines during a labor conflict in the fall of 1906,[53] as did the organization of printing firm owners in both cities on several different occasions, a subject discussed below. In some trades, employer ranks were further weakened by cleavages between Russian and non-Russian employers. The Petersburg Union of Bakery Owners, for example, was internally divided between Russian and German employers during a labor conflict in June 1906.[54]

The interaction between workers and employers thus proceeded in 1906–1907 within a new and increasingly organized framework. But there was still considerable unevenness in the extent to which employers achieved solidarity within their organizations, and in some industries and trades, owners of small firms remained outside employer associations or had not yet organized at all. These were the circumstances that confronted trade unions as they attempted to introduce important reforms in the conduct of labor-management relations.

TRADE UNION POLICIES TOWARD LABOR-MANAGEMENT RELATIONS

In the era of legal labor organization inaugurated by the March 1906 law, trade unions advocated two major innovations in the area of industrial relations: the

[52]The Moscow organization of printing firm owners collected an antistrike fund amounting to ten thousand rubles. *Listok rabochikh po obrabotke dereva,* no. 6 (November 1907), p. 11.

[53]Oliunina, *Portnovskii promysel,* p. 293.

[54]B. Ivanov, *Professional'noe dvizhenie rabochikh khlebo-pekarno-konditerskogo proizvodstva Petrograda i gubernii (s 1903–1907 g.)* (Moscow, 1920), p. 43.

introduction of collective representation and the collective contract, and the institutionalization of procedures for dealing with grievances and workplace disputes. The workers' quest for greater control over key decisions of factory life, so important to labor protests during 1905, remained an intrinsic part of the claims they put forward in 1906–1907. Workers continued to demand control over such matters as hiring, firing, and wage rates, but now these demands were incorporated into a broader struggle for union recognition, collective bargaining and the collective contract.

The concept of a collective agreement was still a novelty for many workers, and trade unionists devoted considerable attention to the subject, publishing articles on the historical background and significance of such agreements. Union conferences in this period drew up resolutions declaring that "unions should attempt in every way possible to conclude agreements, not between individual workers and employers, but between unions and individual employers or [employer] groups."[55] For practical reasons, trade unionists restricted their efforts to industry-wide contracts covering workers in a single city but they envisioned a time when such contracts would extend to an entire region or even to the Empire as a whole.[56] They designated this comprehensive contract a *tarif,* a term borrowed from the German and French labor movements.[57]

Collective bargaining and collective labor contracts were achieved in 1906–1907 in many different industries and occupations. The Petersburg bakers, for example, reached an industry-wide contract with employers in June 1906; in the same month, the Moscow union of printers concluded a preliminary agreement with the Society of Printing Firm Owners. A year later, the Petersburg printers'

[55]This resolution was drawn up in connection with the conference of trade unionists planned in the Moscow industrial region in the spring of 1907. *Professional,* no. 5 (May 30, 1907), p. 17. For a similar resolution by the First All-Russian Conference of Teapackers, see *Istoriia odnogo soiuza* (Moscow, 1907), p. 48. The Moscow Society of Factory Owners reported that in July 1907 one of the principal demands of factory workers in the Moscow region was for employer recognition of trade unions as representatives in labor-management negotiations. *Rabochee dvizhenie: Biulleten',* no. 2 (1907), p. 3.

[56]See, for example, the discussion of this matter at the First All-Russian Conference of Printers in April 1907. *Protokoly pervoi vserossiiskoi konferentsii soiuzov rabochikh pechatnogo dela* (St. Petersburg, 1907), pp. 75–104. The significance of the comprehensive collective contract is also discussed in A. Iakovlev, "K voprosu o tarifnykh soglasheniiakh," *Professional'nyi vestnik,* no. 9 (June 21, 1907), p. 4. See also *Pechatnoe delo,* no. 6 (November 29, 1906), pp. 11–13, and no. 8 (December 16, 1906), pp. 5–7.

[57]Vasil'ev-Severianin, "Tarifnaia bor'ba," *MIPDP,* p. 159. An extended discussion of German usage and practice can be found in Iakovlev, "K voprosu," *Professional'nyi vestnik,* no. 9 (June 21, 1907), p. 4.

union signed a similar agreement with the organization of employers and embarked upon extended negotiations over a comprehensive collective contract for the city's printing industry as a whole. Trade unions in metalworking, textiles, woodworking, printing, shoemaking, jewelrymaking, and other industries and occupations also represented workers in collective bargaining with individual employers, and in some cases a collective agreement was concluded.[58]

Trade unions also waged a campaign to create institutional channels for resolving workplace disputes. The March 1906 law had explicitly authorized the use of arbitration as a means of settling "misunderstandings" between workers and employers. An arbitration board *(treteiskii sud)* included representatives of the two parties to the dispute and a mutually acceptable arbitrator who rendered a judgment concerning the conflicting claims of the two sides and proposed the terms of a settlement.[59]

In the view of many trade unionists, arbitration boards were best suited for the resolution of conflicts arising after a collective contract had already been negotiated. Basic contract issues, they believed, were far too important to relegate to the decision of a neutral arbitrator, and ought to be negotiated directly by worker and employer representatives.[60] The labor press carried explanatory articles on the subject of arbitration, drawing extensively on examples from Western Europe,[61] and trade unionists attempted to use such boards in a variety of labor disputes that arose during these months. Arbitration boards actually functioned by mutual consent of workers and employers in widely publicized labor disputes involving the Petersburg and Moscow printers, the Petersburg bakers and textile workers, and others.[62]

[58]Collective bargaining was conducted by the unions of Moscow metalworkers (G. Matveev, "Moskovskii soiuz rabochikh-metallistov v 1906–1907 gg. [Po lichnym vospominaniiam]" *MIPDR*, 2:61); Petersburg textile workers *(Vpered,* no. 10 [June 16, 1906], p. 31); Petersburg woodworkers *(Listok rabochikh po obrabotke dereva,* no. 6 [November 1907], p. 8); Petersburg printers *(Zhizn' pechatnika,* no. 7 [July 13, 1907], pp. 13–14); Petersburg shoemakers *(Peterburgskii sapozhnik,* no. 2 [May 21, 1906], p. 1, and *Vol'na,* no. 5 [April 29, 1906], p. 3); Petersburg gold- and silversmiths *(Vestnik zolotoserebrianikov i bronzovshchikov,* no. 8 [May 23, 1907], p. 5).

[59]On the history of arbitration boards in Russia, see I. Gessen, "Treteiskii sud," in *Entsiklopedicheskii slovar',* vol. 33a (St. Petersburg, 1901), pp. 772–773.

[60]For a survey of union attitudes on this issue, see V. Grinevich, *Professional'noe dvizhenie rabochikh v Rossii* (St. Petersburg, 1908), pp. 181–184; *Protokoly,* p. 101.

[61]See, for example, *Pechatnik,* no. 6 (June 4, 1906), pp. 12–13, no. 7 (July 9, 1906), pp. 7–9, no. 8 (July 23, 1906), pp. 13–14.

[62]The cases of the printers and bakers are discussed below. On the textile workers, see V. Sviatlovskii, *Istoriia professional'nogo dvizheniia v Rossii ot vozniknoveniia rabochego klassa do kontsa 1917 g.* (Leningrad, 1925), p. 157.

The conciliation board *(primiritel'naia kamera)*, by contrast, was considered by many trade unionists an acceptable method both for reaching a negotiated settlement with employers and for resolving grievances and matters of interpretation arising on the basis of an existing contract.[63] The conciliation board generally consisted of an equal number of representatives from both parties to the dispute; in some instances a neutral mediator was also invited to participate. Such boards helped to resolve a number of industrial disputes during these months.[64]

Trade unionists also advocated the election of representatives *(upolnomochennye)* within each enterprise to serve as intermediaries between workers and management. This proposal did not, of course, originate in the trade unions. Since the turn of the century, as we have seen, workers had intermittently demanded some form of representation at the shop and enterprise levels, and in 1905 they spontaneously elected factory committees. In industries such as metalworking, some of these committees continued to function in 1906 and early 1907, although they did not always have employer recognition.[65]

The demand for permanent worker representatives at the shop level was frequently present in union-directed strikes, such as the one conducted under union auspices at the Soldatov teapacking firm in Moscow in the fall of 1906. Here workers demanded employer recognition of elected deputies to negotiate with management over labor conflicts—a demand to which the employer consented following a three-week strike.[66] The Petersburg and Moscow printers' unions, as we shall see shortly, actually negotiated a detailed agreement regulat-

[63]A. Sashin, "O primiritel'nykh kamerakh," *Professional*, no. 2 (April 11, 1907), pp. 10–100.

[64]This procedure was utilized by Petersburg book clerks, furnace loaders, printers, and others. Grinevich, *Professional'noe dvizhenie*, pp. 180–181; *Delo naroda*, no. 9 (May 12 [25], 1906), p. 3. Toward the end of 1907, the Petersburg metalworkers' union attempted unsuccessfully to obtain employer cooperation in instituting conciliation boards.

[65]Some factory committees still functioned in this period. The elders at the Dobrovy and Nabgol'ts metalworking plant in St. Petersburg represented workers in presenting a series of demands to the management in February 1907. The administration refused to discuss these demands with them, claiming that it would first have to consult with the Society of Factory Owners. TsGAOR, f. 6860, d. 30, 1907, p. 11.

[66]*Professional'noe dvizhenie Moskovskikh pishchevikov v gody pervoi revoliutsii*, sbornik 1 (Moscow, 1927), pp. 72–73. Similar demands had been made by other teapacking firms in June 1906. Other unions presenting this demand included the woodworkers, bakers, shoemakers, and numerous factory groups. The Moscow Society of Factory Owners reported that this was one of the principal demands made by workers in the period May 31-July 1, 1907. *Rabochee dvizhenie: Biulleten'*, no. 1 (1907), p. 2.

ing the role of worker representatives in the day-to-day operation of a factory or shop.

These union proposals in the area of labor-management relations encountered little principled opposition among the rank and file. Despite the workers' very limited previous experience with institutions of this type, their deep-rooted mistrust for employers, and their still-fresh memories of the preceding revolutionary year, widely diverse groups—including printers, bakers, metal and textile workers, shoemakers, and salesclerks—actively endeavored to implement what one metalworker described as "the new methods that have been developed through the practice of European trade unions."[67]

Labor leaders were careful to point out that this approach would not eliminate the "enormous struggle" between labor and capital, but would merely avoid petty conflicts that diminished the workers' strength as they prepared for the "decisive struggle with capital."[68] But in contrast to such issues as union-party ties or mutual aid, union tactics and strategy in labor-management relations did not generate heated controversy and debate within these organizations. Writing in 1908, Grinevich commented on the workers' receptivity to union efforts in this area:

Thanks to Western European experience, trade union activists [in Russia] did not treat the above-mentioned institutions with the kind of prejudice that their counterparts in Western Europe had to make an effort to overcome. We know that arbitration and conciliation boards and industry-wide collective contracts have been viewed as institutions undermining class struggle and contrary to its principles. This had been the case in Germany for a long time and is true of France even now. Fortunately for us, we have had an opportunity to take into account the practice of the Western European trade union movement and to see for ourselves that within a specified framework all of these institutions, far from contradicting the principles of class struggle, contribute to the success of the labor movement.[69]

A similar statement was made by a delegate to the First All-Russian Conference of Printers' Unions, who observed that the negotiation of a "collective agreement is a procedure which takes into account the strength of both sides, and such an agreement is not, therefore, a cessation of the class struggle, but a continuation of it. The struggle between organized labor and organized capital is

---

[67]*Pervaia konferentsiia professional'nykh soiuzov rabochikh po metallu Moskovskogo promyshlennogo raiona* (Moscow, 1907), p. 34.

[68]Sashin, "O primiritel'nykh kamerakh," *Professional,* no. 2 (April 11, 1907), p. 11.

[69]Grinevich, *Professional'noe dvizhenie,* p. 180.

the highest form of class struggle and is undoubtedly strengthening the development of class consciousness among workers."[70]

In these months, some organized groups actually achieved significant, albeit short-lived, reforms in the conduct of labor-management relations. The record of accomplishments was uneven, however. In large-scale industries such as metalworking and textiles, the Societies of Factory Owners blocked most union efforts to obtain recognition and to bargain collectively on behalf of workers. The unions themselves failed to attract a majority of the labor force into their ranks, and in the metalworking industry workers were adversely affected by widespread unemployment resulting from a deterioration in market conditions. In contrast to employers, workers in many large-scale factory industries were poorly organized and unable to mount disciplined strikes to win their demands.

Only forty-five conflicts took place in the capital's beleaguered metalworking industry between June 1906 and December 1907; fourteen of them were resolved without a work stoppage. The Petersburg union of metalworkers, with ten thousand members (about one-seventh of the labor force) by July 1906, actively directed two-thirds of the strikes in 1906 (11 out of 17 strikes) and one-third (5 out of 14) in 1907. Most of the strikes took place in small or medium-sized enterprises whose owners did not belong to the Society. And only in the smallest firms (with fewer than 101 workers) did the workers win full or partial satisfaction of their demands.[71]

The metalworkers' unions, both in the capital and in Moscow, attempted to obtain employer recognition. At the Siemens-Halske plant in the capital, for example, striking workers in April 1906 requested the union to negotiate on its behalf. Union representatives presented the plant owner with a proposal to establish a conciliation board composed of an equal number of worker and employer representatives. The employer, a member of the Society, refused to cooperate with the union after the Society instructed him "to ignore completely the [workers'] proposal and in general to refrain from any communication with the workers' union without informing the Society first."[72]

Similar incidents took place in Moscow when the metalworkers' union sought to engage in collective bargaining.[73] A former activist in this union recalled that

[70]*Protokoly,* p. 104.
[71]Bulkin, *Na zare,* pp. 376–381.
[72]Balabanov, *Ot 1905,* p. 44.
[73]*Pervaia konferentsiia,* p. 5.

the directing board at the time was engaged in a major effort to achieve employer recognition of the union. We even tried to enter into negotiations with the Society of Factory Owners. . . . As far as the management of individual factories was concerned, many of them, in effect, recognized factory deputies, and as a rule during strikes, the union directing board negotiated with them directly. For example, I remember that at the List, Tryndin, Til'mans, Shmulevich, and Livshits plants, we were able to institute [this kind of procedure] only after a major struggle with the owners. The point is that at those enterprises, the union conducted a broad offensive against employers. While conducting these strikes, the union provided considerable [material] assistance to the strikers.[74]

The metalworkers' unions in St. Petersburg and Moscow succeeded in gaining the recognition and cooperation of employers mainly in small and medium-sized firms that were not represented in the Societies of Factory Owners. In these cases, where the employer did not belong to an organization and the union could coordinate an effective struggle, workers introduced collective representation and collective bargaining into the metalworking industry for the first time.

The capital's textile workers encountered similar obstacles in their effort to negotiate with employers. Workers at the Nikol'skaia mill struck in May 1907.[75] Three representatives of the Petersburg union of textile workers appeared at the mill soon afterward with a proposal to turn the dispute over to an arbitration board, but the factory administration replied that such action required prior permission of the Society of Factory Owners. The union then appealed directly to the Society. On April 27 a woman from the union, identifying herself as the temporary executive secretary, appeared at Society headquarters. She stated that the union had existed legally for more than one year and was growing rapidly, with one out of ten textile workers in the capital already in the union and two hundred members at the Nikol'skaia mill alone. She proposed to settle the dispute at the Nikol'skaia mill by means of arbitration and invited the Society to enter into regular relations with the union. There was a strong possibility of additional strikes in this industry during the coming months, she asserted, and "the manufacturers must decide whether it is desirable to contend with a spontaneous mass of workers or with an organized union. If the manufacturers prefer the latter," she concluded, "then they must recognize the organization of workers and assist in its development."[76] The Textile Section of the Society rejected

[74]Matveev, "Moskovskii soiuz rabochikh-metallistov," *MIPDR*, 2:261.

[75]The following account was reported in the proceedings of the Textile Section of the Petersburg Society. TsGIA, f. 150, op. 1, d. 69, p. 256.

[76]Ibid.

the union proposal for mediation of the Nikol'skaia conflict, however, and refused to establish relations with the union, leaving open a vague possibility of future contact.[77]

The Societies of Factory Owners remained opposed to all actions that implicitly or explicitly amounted to union recognition. As one commentator put it in the labor press:

Employers do not want to have anything to do with the trade unions as such. They know that to agree to participate in conciliation boards on an equal basis with labor unions . . . they are taking a step toward recognition of labor unions as an equal party. They can only speak about [conciliation boards] in programs and charters. But to put their words into effect—God forbid![78]

In sum, industrialists belonging to the Petersburg Society declined to recognize trade unions or any other workers' representatives; they rejected collective bargaining and, notwithstanding the provision of their own charter, refused to participate in arbitration or conciliation boards. Despite their greater economic independence from the state and their relatively liberal political outlook, large-scale Moscow industrialists adopted the same position and were unresponsive to workers' demands.

LABOR-MANAGEMENT RELATIONS IN THE MOSCOW
PRINTING TRADES

A different constellation of circumstances characterized labor-management relations in industries and trades that stood outside the powerful Societies of Factory Owners. Three cases, involving the Moscow printers and the printers and bakers in the capital, illustrate the progress made by some unions in securing employer recognition and negotiating citywide labor contracts. In these trades, there were large and well-subscribed unions; economic conditions proved favorable to the workers, and the labor market was expanding; and employers did not achieve coordinated opposition to labor.

The Moscow union of printing workers had suffered extensive disruption in

[77]Ibid.; Balabanov, *Ot 1905*, p. 45.

[78]This statement, which appeared in *Professional'nyi vestnik*, no. 20 (April 2, 1908), p. 6, referred to the unwillingness of employers to participate in conciliation boards established to reach a settlement in industrial accidents.

Table 29
Labor Disputes in the Moscow Printing
Industry, May 1-July 1, 1906

DISPOSITION OF CONFLICTS RESOLVED PEACEFULLY	
Concessions by employers	12
Intervention by union	4
Conciliation board	12
Total conflicts	28
STRIKES	
Defensive	5
Offensive	46
With union approval	47
Without union approval	4
Total strikes	51
RESULTS OF STRIKES	
Victory for workers	39
Compromise	8
Defeat for workers	—
Result unknown	4

Source: Sher, *Istoriia*, p. 255.

the aftermath of the December uprising, but the organization rapidly revived in the spring of 1906 and promptly applied for registration under the new law. By the beginning of May, the union had become the largest and most stable labor association in the city, and a mere two months later it obtained the cooperation of employers in the negotiation of a citywide collective agreement. The prelude to this important event was a major strike movement conducted under union auspices in the spring of 1906.

The Moscow printers' union took part in forty-seven of the fifty-one strikes in the city's printing industry between May 1 and July 1, 1906 (table 29). The great majority ended with a complete or partial victory for the printers. Another twenty-eight conflicts were resolved without recourse to a strike, and sixteen of these were settled either by direct negotiation with union representatives or by a conciliation board.

Faced with widespread labor unrest in the spring of 1906, the Moscow Society of Printing Firm Owners adopted a dualistic policy, calling alternately for lockouts and for negotiation. In late April the Society first approached the union with a proposal to create a conciliation board to adjudicate disputes. The union accepted the idea in principle, but insisted on reaching a prior agreement over some general issues. On May 25 representatives of the union and the employer association met for the first time to discuss these preconditions. The union made four demands: the introduction of permanent worker representation in each enterprise, union approval of all hiring, the rehiring of workers' deputies fired since December 7, 1905, and permission to hold workers' meetings on the shop floor. The employer representatives agreed to review the cases of fired deputies and accepted the other three demands.[79]

On the following day this preliminary agreement was brought before a plenary session of the Society of Printing Firm Owners, which rejected the concessions made by their representatives and voted instead to declare a lockout of striking workers. But the implementation of this resolution was thwarted by a cleavage within the organization. Owners of small and medium-sized printing establishments refused to cooperate in declaring a lockout because they could not sustain the financial loss it would have entailed.[80]

Weakened by internal disunity, the Society of Printing Firm Owners decided to renew talks with the union. On June 6, it reached an agreement with the union which contained two major provisions. First, employers accepted all four of the conditions noted above. Second, both parties agreed to begin negotiations for a comprehensive contract to cover all branches of the Moscow printing trades. While negotiations were in progress, conflicts were referred to a conciliation board composed of an equal number of worker and employer representatives. The union, for its part, agreed not to declare any strikes until the negotiations had been completed; employers consented not to worsen the conditions of work during this interim period.[81]

The negotiations soon got under way and continued for another month and a half. Before the talks ended in late July, the joint commission had reached an agreement on the establishment of workers' representatives at the shop level. The "Regulations on Workers' Representatives in Printing Firms"[82] were

[79]*Pechatnik*, no. 3 (May 14, 1906), p. 10; no. 5 (May 28, 1906), p. 3; Sher, *Istoriia*, p. 263.

[80]Sher, *Istoriia*, pp. 264–265; *Pechatnik*, no. 6 (June 4, 1906), pp. 2, 5–7; *Pechatnik*, no. 7 (July 9, 1906), p. 2.

[81]Sher, *Istoriia*, pp. 265–267; *Pechatnik*, no. 7 (July 9, 1906), p. 7.

[82]The text of the Regulations appears in *Pechatnik*, no. 8 (July 23, 1906), p. 7.

intended as one portion of a more extensive contract agreement governing the terms and conditions of labor in the Moscow printing trades. The comprehensive contract never reached completion, but the Regulations were eventually approved by both parties to the negotiations.[83]

The Regulations provided for employer recognition of workers' representatives to be elected at the shop level. Although they were not granted control over internal factory conditions, the representatives were authorized to supervise the implementation of the *tarif* and to serve as intermediaries between individual workers and employers. Serious disputes arising during the duration of the contract were to be referred to a conciliation board composed of an equal number of worker and employer representatives. The Regulations placed the election of representatives entirely in the hands of the workers themselves, and all workers, regardless of sex or duration of employment, were eligible to serve.[84]

The printers' union, meanwhile, drew up Instructions governing the election of the workers' representatives authorized by the Regulations. The Instructions stipulated that representatives had to be union members. The proposals formulated by the Moscow Union of Printers in 1905 had permitted shop representatives to act independently of the union because they represented all workers in a given firm and not merely union members, whereas the Instructions made factory delegates subordinate to the trade union, although all workers in a given firm still participated in the election. The Instructions also gave the union the authority to issue instructions to the representatives and to remove them from office prior to the expiration of the six-month term.[85] This change in policy was indicative of the growing strength and confidence of the union, which had a substantial membership and was gaining respect for its effective conduct of the strike movement.

In early 1907 the Society of Printing Firm Owners violated the provision of the June agreement which had enjoined member firms from altering the prevailing wage rates, hours, and conditions of work. Following a strike, the dispute was turned over to an arbitration board, which ruled against the employers.[86] The terms of the June agreement were reinstated and the two sides continued their negotiations for a comprehensive contract until June 12, 1907, when the

[83]Sher, *Istoriia*, p. 267.
[84]*Pechatnik*, no. 8 (July 23, 1906), p. 7.
[85]Sher, *Istoriia*, pp. 269–270.
[86]*Pechatnoe delo*, no. 16 (February 17, 1907), p. 1; no. 17 (February 19, 1907), pp. 4–5; no. 18 (February 28, 1907), p. 3; no. 19 (March 10, 1907), pp. 3–4; no. 20 (March 16, 1907), pp. 7–8; no. 21 (March 30, 1907), p. 1.

union lost its legal status. By then the atmosphere in the country had changed. Deprived of a collective organization that functioned openly and legally, the printers found themselves without adequate defenses and could no longer withstand employer measures to worsen labor conditions.

LABOR-MANAGEMENT RELATIONS IN THE PETERSBURG
PRINTING TRADES

As in Moscow, the campaign for a citywide contract in the Petersburg printing industry grew out of a vigorous strike movement conducted under union auspices in the spring of 1906. The high point of these strikes was a work stoppage at the large publishing house of the newspaper *Dvadtsatyi vek* [Twentieth Century]. A union-directed campaign for a six-day workweek had succeeded in many of the capital's printing firms, when A. A. Suvorin, the owner of *Dvadtsatyi vek*, refused to concede. The union not only struck but declared a consumer boycott of the firm, a method of struggle that had been utilized in another major dispute involving the Moscow teapackers during 1905.[87]

The printers' boycott of *Dvadtsatyi vek* proved enormously successful, drawing the support of the democratic intelligentsia in St. Petersburg and readers throughout the country.[88] Suvorin refused to recognize the union, calling it an "unknown organization."[89] The boycott severely curtailed the circulation of *Dvadtsatyi vek*, however, and after two weeks he sent the union a proposal to submit the conflict to an arbitration board. At the end of May, the arbitration board convened. Union representatives included the Menshevik Fedor Dan and Viktor Chernov, a leader in the Socialist Revolutionary party. Grinevich presented evidence on behalf of the union. On July 4, 1906, a decision was rendered in favor of the workers. Suvorin at first complied with the ruling, and the printers' union gained a major victory.[90] But in November 1906 he rescinded the

[87]*Vestnik pechatnikov,* no. 3 (May 9, 1906), pp. 2–3; *Delo naroda,* no. 1 (May 3 [16], 1906), p. 3; P. Kolokol'nikov, "Otryvki iz vospominanii," *MIPDR,* 4:281; Grinevich, *Professional'noe dvizhenie,* pp. 176–177.

[88]*Volna,* no. 14 (May 11, 1906), p. 4; Grinevich, *Professional'noe dvizhenie,* p. 176; Kolokol'nikov, "Otryvki," *MIPDR,* 4:281.

[89]*Delo naroda,* no. 2 (May 4 [17], 1906), p. 2; *Vestnik pechatnikov,* no. 3 (May 9, 1906), p. 2.

[90]*Vestnik pechatnikov,* no. 1 (February 2, 1907), p. 1 and addendum; no. 6 (May 2, 1906), pp. 4–5; no. 7 (June 6, 1906), pp. 4–5; no. 11 (July 7, 1906), pp. 3–6; no. 12 (July 15, 1906), pp. 6–7; no. 13 (July 31, 1906), pp. 4–5.

concessions made in June and restored Sunday work in the firm.[91] The well-publicized victory of the printers' union in mid-1906 nevertheless gave momentum to the campaign for a comprehensive citywide contract, which the union had already announced on June 2.

The announcement of the *tarif* project generated a great deal of enthusiasm in union ranks. "Now we move from words to action," wrote one trade unionist in the printers' newspaper; "now, comrades, we stand before the main fortress that we will have to seize."[92] The union organized special sections by occupational subgroup to consider detailed provisions for a draft proposal, and a *Tarif* Commission was elected by the union as a whole to oversee the project. These efforts had barely begun when the government intervened to close the union on July 21, 1906, in retaliation for the union's involvement in demonstrations following the dissolution of the First State Duma. The police also arrested the leadership, including all the members of the *Tarif* Commission.[93] Undeterred by these events, the union immediately issued a statement reaffirming its commitment to the campaign for a collective contract. Activities barely slackened in the months that followed, despite the illegal status of the organization and its inability to reregister until the spring of 1907.

Owners took advantage of the union's illegal status. As one printing firm owner put it: "Now that your union no longer exists, you will work under the earlier conditions."[94] Beginning in August 1906, many employers attempted to lower wages and lengthen the work time in printing firms. The workers responded by going on strike, and with the assistance of the union they were often successful in maintaining the concessions that had been made in 1905 and the first half of 1906. In some of these conflicts, the now illegal union was recognized by employers as a collective bargaining agent in direct negotiations or in arbitration proceedings.[95]

No longer content to hold the line against employers who rescinded earlier concessions, many printers were eager to mount an "offensive" struggle to extract further improvements. Union approval was a matter of importance to striking workers, for without the prior consent of the organization, participants in work stoppages were ineligible for union strike funds. On December 31, 1906, under pressure from the rank and file, the union leadership resolved to

[91]Kolokol'nikov, "Otryvki," *MIPDR*, 4:281–282.
[92]*Vestnik pechatnikov*, no. 8 (June 11, 1906), p. 1.
[93]*Protokoly*, p. 76.
[94]*ILS*, p. 295. This incident occurred on August 3, 1906, at the Iablonskii printing firm.
[95]*ILS*, pp. 298–299, 316.

support strikes to achieve improved wages, hours, and working conditions. Between January and March 1907 about one hundred strikes took place, many of them in small and medium-sized firms.

Union leaders concentrated on waging a series of strikes at individual printing firms rather than mounting a struggle across a broad front, as a way of strengthening the workers' position in forthcoming negotiations for a comprehensive contract.[96] The tactic of "partisan struggle," as it was called, proved effective because workers in other firms cooperated in imposing a secondary boycott and refused to process printing orders that would ordinarily have been handled by the firm engaged in a labor dispute. The union actively directed many of these strikes and provided monetary support.

The printing industry was in an expansionist phase and employers with many new orders to fill were reluctant to become entangled in labor disputes. Anxious to avoid a strike, many individual employers disregarded the regulations of the Society and made concessions to the workers' demands. Some of the largest firms, such as the Kirkhner printing house and the Soikin typographical firm, strongly urged the employer association to begin negotiations for a collective agreement.

It was not until after the union regained legal status in mid-April, however, that negotiations finally got under way. The first joint meeting between union and employer representatives was held on May 24, and by June 4, 1907, a preliminary agreement had been concluded between the union and employers, outlining the basic features of a contract whose detailed provisions were to be worked out in future discussions.[97] The preliminary agreement specified that the contract would cover all aspects of the printing industry and would provide an increase in the average wage of printing workers, to be effective from the date of the final contract agreement. Employers consented not to alter the terms of employment in their firms during the period of negotiation, and workers agreed not to present any new demands to individual employers. Disagreements arising between labor and management prior to the conclusion of the *tarif* negotiations were referred to a conciliation board.

Seeking approval for this preliminary agreement from the rank and file, union leaders characterized it as "an armed peace" between labor and management.

---

[96]*Protokoly,* p. 100; *Vestnik pechatnikov,* no. 1 (February 2, 1907), p. 1; no. 2 (February 10, 1907), p. 11.

[97]The text of this agreement, entitled "Conditions for Conciliation Concluded by the Society of Employers and the Union of Printers," appeared in *Zhizn' pechatnikov,* no. 4 (June 9, 1907), p. 11. It is reprinted in *ILS,* pp. 374–375.

According to contemporary reports, "there [was] scarcely any principled opposition [within union ranks] to a citywide agreement."[98] Since the negotiations required cooperation from employers, union leaders took care to point out the benefits of a contract for them as well, noting that it would lower the illness and accident rate, raise the cultural level, and improve labor productivity.[99] The union newspaper further commended the agreement as a means of placing labor-management conflicts "in a new, more organized framework. For the employers, this is beneficial because the constant threat of a strike, the uneven distribution of orders, makes it almost impossible to run the enterprise properly."[100]

Employers cooperated with the union for a variety of reasons in the summer of 1907. The reluctance to tolerate a continuation of "partisan" strikes certainly influenced many printing firm owners to enter contract negotiations. For others, the paramount consideration may have been the restoration of internal order within their firms. Some may also have been affected by public opinion. Unlike many sectors of industry, employers in the printing industry were sensitive to the general public that purchased their newspapers, journals, books, and other printed matter. The sympathetic response to the boycott of *Dvadtsatyi vek* had not been forgotten, and the owners of printing firms were eager to maintain a positive image with the reading public.

The union entered into negotiations for a citywide contract with a detailed proposal already in hand. The first part specified the hours and wage rates for printers and apprentices, including provisions for an eight-hour day throughout the entire industry, an average wage increase of 25–30 percent, Sunday rest, overtime pay, and new regulations for apprentices. The second section of the union's proposal dealt with hygienic conditions in workshops, employer-supported illness and accident insurance, working conditions, worker representation on the shop floor, and union control over hiring. The last two provisions were undoubtedly the most controversial elements of the union's proposal and they testify to the continuing importance of the issue of worker control—an issue that encroached directly on traditional employer prerogatives. It is therefore a matter of great significance that the agreement worked out by union and employer representatives in the summer of 1907 included both of these union demands.

The joint commission drew up "Rules of Internal Order in Petersburg Print-

[98]*Zhizn' pechatnika*, no. 4 (June 9, 1907), p. 2.
[99]Vasil'ev-Severianin, "Tarifnaia bor'ba," *MIPDP*, p. 169.
[100]*Zhizn' pechatnika*, no. 4 (June 9, 1907), p. 2.

ing Firms" that provided for the election of permanent worker delegates at the shop level.[101] All male and female workers could participate in the election for a shop floor delegate if they had been employed by the firm for at least two weeks. Only apprentices were excluded. Employers agreed to compensate delegates by paying them an additional one hour's wage for each working day.

The principal function of the shop floor delegates was "to oversee the precise fulfillment of the rules of internal order and of the collective agreement"[102] and to serve as intermediaries in all matters between workers and management. Henceforth, communications concerning dissatisfactions or disagreements over internal shop rules and regulations were to be processed by the delegates. If the dispute could not be settled within three days, it was referred either to informal negotiation by the trade union and employer association or to a conciliation board.[103] The implementation of this arrangement would have altered authority relations at the workplace. Henceforth, the relationship between workers and employers would have been mediated by the delegates, who acted with the support of the entire trade union organization behind them.

The relationship between shop floor delegates and the trade union remained somewhat vague in the agreement. In contrast to the similar project prepared by the Moscow printers' union a year earlier, the Petersburg delegates were not required to be members of the union or to subordinate themselves to the authority of the union.[104] Nor were there provisions, as in the Moscow agreement, to give the union jurisdiction over the dismissal of delegates or to assign the delegates any specifically union-related functions.[105] The agreement did, however, grant the union one important prerogative: new workers could be hired only from a list of those registered in the union's hiring hall. Although it was not a requirement that workers be union members, this provision accorded the union control over the pool of prospective applicants.[106]

In the course of the summer of 1907, the joint union-employer commission

[101]*Zhizn' pechatnika*, no. 12 (September 14, 1907). The text of the agreement was published as an addition to this issue, with no pagination.

[102]Provision 28 of the "Rules of Internal Order," ibid.

[103]Provision 30 of the "Rules of Internal Order," ibid.

[104]Provision 29 of the "Rules of Internal Order," ibid.

[105]Provision 31 of the "Rules of Internal Order" only states that if a delegate does not obey the rules of internal order, he or she can be fired.

[106]*Zhizn' pechatnika*, no. 9 (August 11, 1907), p. 5, reprinted this section of the agreement entitled "The Employment of Workers." Points 2 and 3 of this portion of the agreement concern union prerogatives in hiring. A similar provision was included in the Moscow Regulations of July 1906.

continued to prepare a contract agreement. The completed portions, apart from the one on shop floor delegates, concerned wages, overtime work, the hiring and firing of workers, medical care, sanitary conditions, apprenticeship, and time off.[107] Employers made concessions on a number of issues, granting Sunday rest, an eight-hour night shift, and a holiday on May Day. For their part, union negotiators agreed to a variety of internal factory rules whose infraction would lead to dismissal. The union leadership did not, in principle, oppose the inclusion of rules governing lateness, theft, drunkenness, and violent or insulting conduct on the part of workers. The First All-Russian Conference of Printers, held in April 1907, had declared that responsible conduct on the part of workers was indispensable for the exercise of autonomy at the workplace. As one conference speaker put it, "autonomy demands discipline from the workers themselves."[108] The agreement accorded worker-delegates unprecedented authority over the maintenance of internal factory rules and established a grievance procedure to handle contested cases.[109]

The negotiations continued until mid-October 1907, when, after several months of intermittent harassment, the union was declared illegal. The political atmosphere in the country had deteriorated following the declaration of a revised electoral law on June 3, 1907, the so-called Stolypin coup d'état, and many Petersburg unions had already been suppressed. The official notification to the Petersburg printers' union alleged that the organization had engaged in several impermissible activities, including the publication of a newspaper and the establishment of a citywide delegate council.[110] But all of these activities had been going on for several years, and the real reason for government action in mid-October lay elsewhere.

At the time of the union's closure, employers' and workers' representatives were nearing the completion of the negotiations, and government authorities viewed the imminent conclusion of a citywide contract with trepidation. A collective agreement of this scope, negotiated by a trade union and an employer association, had no precedent in the capital, and it would have signaled an impressive victory for the labor movement. Apart from substantial material improvements that the contract would have given workers, it recognized the union as the sole representative of printing workers and granted the union

[107]Ibid., pp. 5–6.
[108]*Protokoly*, p. 83.
[109]*Zhizn' pechatnika*, no. 9 (August 11, 1907), p. 6.
[110]*ILS*, p. 396.

important prerogatives, such as control over hiring. A proclamation by the Petersburg Chief of Police indicates that the contract was indeed a key factor in the decision to close the union:

The Union of Workers in the Printing Trade is closed by order of the St. Petersburg Bureau on Unions and therefore all of its activities are now illegal. Consequently, it is forbidden for employers of printing firms as well as for all printing workers to enter into any kind of relations with the union.[111]

Progress toward the first citywide collective agreement negotiated by a union and an employer association thus came to a halt in the fall of 1907 as a result of government intervention. Fearful of autonomous social activity, especially among lower-class groups, the Ministry of Internal Affairs and its allies in other government circles took advantage of conditions after June 1907 to curtail the trade unions and their attempts to introduce collective institutionalized methods of handling industrial disputes. The printers' union presented a particularly alarming spectacle from the point of view of this Ministry, and was singled out in the Blazhchuk report of early 1908 as "the most harmful . . . and most dangerous" labor association because of its high level of organizational development and its leadership role in the union movement as a whole.[112]

The suppression of the union was a sharp blow to many printers who aspired to see their organization "function like a Western European labor union."[113] Nevertheless, the accomplishments of the union in 1906–1907 had been impressive, and this gave substance to their hopes of eventually establishing a Western European type of union on Russian soil, a vision that remained alive among a core group of printer trade unionists during the next half decade of government repression.

LABOR-MANAGEMENT RELATIONS IN THE PETERSBURG BAKING INDUSTRY

The second most impressive labor conflict in the capital during 1906–1907 took place in the baking industry. Petersburg bakers had formed a union in October 1905, but the organization collapsed in December and did not revive until the

---

[111]*ILS*, p. 398.
[112]TsGAOR, DPOO, f. 102, op. 00, d. 1000, ch. 14, t. 1, 1905, p. 275.
[113]*Zhizn' pechatnika*, no. 10 (August 21, 1907), p. 2.

following spring. The bakers soon applied for registration under the new law, and although legal status was not conferred until July 14, 1906, the union commenced open activities immediately following the submission of a charter to the Petersburg Bureau on Trade Unions.[114]

At a general union meeting held on April 23, 1906, bakers decided to prepare for a major confrontation with employers. Their first step was to call upon all bakery workers to elect representatives to a citywide delegate council or strike committee.[115] Three weeks later, 150 delegates—including both union members and nonmembers—gathered to adopt a set of demands and to prepare a strike strategy. The demands, the same as those formulated in the fall of 1905, included a ten-hour work day, a wage increase, Sunday rest, yearly holidays including May Day, the abolition of fines, substitution of a cash payment for employer-provided room and board, the reform of apprenticeship regulations, and the creation of a permanent arbitration board to settle disputes.[116]

The union led the strike, and on the eve of the actual work stoppage many workers joined its ranks. Eight hundred new members were registered by the union between May 15 and June 1, bringing the total number of members to about two thousand when the strike began on June 3, or about 30 percent of the capital's bakers.[117]

The strike proved an immediate success, spreading throughout the city and even to some outlying districts. On the first day, the strike committee decided to provide monetary support for all strikers, regardless of union membership, a measure deemed essential to deter strike-breaking. Bakers were allocated twenty kopecks for each day of the work stoppage, and although this was a small sum even by bakers' standards, the strike fund lifted morale and fortified the workers' determination. Petersburg bakers displayed extraordinary solidarity during the eleven-day work stoppage.[118]

The subsequent progress of the strike illustrates the complex interaction in

---

[114]*Listok bulochnikov i konditerov*, no. 4–5 (July 8, 1906), p. 12; *Professional'noe dvizhenie*, no. 1 (May 1, 1907), p. 18, provides a history of the Petersburg bakers' union from its founding in 1905.

[115]Ivanov, *Professional'noe dvizhenie*, p. 34.

[116]*Listok bulochnikov i konditerov*, no. 3 (June 3, 1906), pp. 1–2.

[117]In early May 1906, the bakers' union had 1,370 members. Ibid., no. 2 (May 6, 1906), p. 7. The influx of 800 members between mid-May and early June was reported in ibid., no. 4–5 (July 8, 1906), p. 12.

[118]Ibid., no. 4–5 (July 8, 1906), pp. 12–16. The union expended a total of 2,488 rubles on strike support: 929 from the union's treasury, 560 from the St. Petersburg Council for the Unemployed, 500 from "sympathizers," and the remainder from other unions and workers.

this period among the workers, led by the union-dominated strike committee, employers, and government authorities. Having attempted unsuccessfully to negotiate individually with their workers, employers agreed to meet with members of the strike committee and accepted the workers' demand that negotiations be handled by an arbitration board. Soon after, however, the local police arrested several members of the union directing board for giving financial aid to strikers in violation of the March 1906 law. On June 5 cossacks were brought in to break up a meeting of three thousand bakers.[119]

Not all authorities took this harsh approach to the strike. Representatives of the Petersburg City Duma called upon the strike committee and the employers to meet together on June 12, with a mediator appointed by the city. Employers and workers agreed to this, but negotiations collapsed when the employers walked out over a dispute concerning the length of the workday.[120]

Two days later, the strike committee received a proposal from twenty-eight of the largest bakeries in the capital to resume negotiations. Another arbitration board was established, this time chaired by Professor Iavein, a man with socialist sympathies. An agreement was immediately reached for a comprehensive collective contract. Workers secured major improvements, including a 10–20 percent wage increase, an eleven-hour workday, Sunday rest, various holidays including May Day, provision of an individual bed, knife, fork, and spoon for each worker, workbooks, weekly pay, amnesty for strikers, and reform of the apprentice regulations. A permanent employer-worker board was created to resolve future disputes.[121]

Twenty-five of the largest bakery owners in the capital signed this agreement, including the city's largest employer, Filippov, whose signature headed the list.[122] Many smaller firms agreed to the terms of the contract in the days that followed. The victory of the bakery workers had a profound effect on other labor groups, especially unionized workers in artisanal and semiartisanal occupations. Summing up the reaction to the bakers' achievement, the newspaper of the Moscow tailors' union observed on June 24:

One often hears that it is harder for artisanal workers to conduct a struggle than for factory workers, since artisanal workers work in groups of two or three in tiny work-

[119]Ibid., pp. 1–14, for the account that follows. Ivanov, *Professional'noe dvizhenie*, p. 39.

[120]Ivanov, *Professional'noe dvizhenie*, p. 39. The workers demanded a ten-hour workday, while the employers were only willing to grant a twelve-hour workday.

[121]The workbooks at issue here were already required in factory enterprises. Ivanov, *Professional'noe dvizhenie*, pp. 45–46; *Listok bulochnikov i konditerov*, no. 4–5 (July 8, 1906), p. 6.

[122]*Listok bulochnikov i konditerov*, no. 4–5 (July 8, 1906), p. 6, for a list of signatories.

shops, dispersed all over the city. The brilliant strike of bakers and pastry shop workers in St. Petersburg shows that these obstacles can be overcome through planned and persistent organization.[123]

Indeed, it was not long before other artisanal workers took steps to emulate the Petersburg bakers. In the ensuing months, the Moscow bakers, as well as the tailors, woodworkers, gold- and silversmiths, shoemakers, and other artisanal groups in St. Petersburg and Moscow mounted major struggles against employers.

The subsequent evolution of labor-management relations in the capital's baking industry followed the course already discerned in the printing trades. At the end of July 1906, in the aftermath of the dissolution of the First State Duma, the Petersburg Bureau on Trade Unions withdrew the legal standing of the bakers' union that had been conferred only a few weeks earlier. Commenting on this development, the union's newspaper editorialized that "although the union never advanced strictly political objectives, it was nevertheless perceived [by the authorities] as dangerous."[124] Like the Petersburg printers' union that also lost its registration around this time, the bakers' union did not succeed in reregistering until the following summer (August 28, 1907).

Despite the protracted period of illegality, the collective agreement concluded by workers and employers on June 14, 1906, remained in effect. But as the months passed, employers gradually attempted to restore precontract conditions in their bakeries.[125] Conflicts with employers grew increasingly acute during the early months of 1907. By now the owners of bakery firms had formed an organization that obtained registration under the March 1906 law. On April 19, 1907, this newly established organization disavowed the earlier collective agreement and declared a lockout of workers who would not voluntarily agree to repudiate the 1906 contract and accept lower wages. The workers responded by proclaiming a general strike. At this point, the union claimed the membership of 4,140 bakery workers or 63 percent of the industry's labor force,[126] a recruitment record exceeded only by the capital's printers' union.

The union-directed work stoppage was widespread and disciplined, and soon employers agreed to restore the 1906 contract provisions in their firms.[127] It was only after the Stolypin "coup d'état" of June 1907 that employers began to

[123]*Listok dlia rabochikh portnykh, portnikh i skorniakov,* no. 11 (June 24, 1906), p. 2.

[124]*Listok bulochnikov i konditerov,* no. 6 (August 10, 1906), p. 1.

[125]Ibid., no. 9 (December 22, 1906), p. 7.

[126]*Professional'nyi vestnik,* no. 6 (April 3, 1907), p. 8; see above, table 14.

[127]*Professional'noe dvizhenie,* no. 1 (May 1, 1907), p. 19.

rescind these terms and restore the conditions that had existed prior to June 1906. By then, government repression had severely undermined the union, and in July 1908 its membership had declined to only about 600 workers.[128]

Both the bakers' and the printers' union were uncommonly strong and attracted a large base of worker support amounting, at their peak, to about two-thirds of the labor force. Under union leadership, workers waged a disciplined campaign for a collective agreement. Economic conditions, moreover, placed the workers in an advantageous position to sustain strikes. Employers were, on the whole, less united than the workers, and their organizations suffered from internal divisions. Faced with a concerted strike movement, employers—sometimes led by the owners of the largest firms—capitulated to workers' demands for union representation and a collective agreement. The government, rather than employers, represented the major obstacle to a continuation of these efforts. State intervention remained relatively limited prior to mid-1907, notwithstanding intermittent incidents of harassment and intimidation. With the shift in government policy toward labor in June 1907, trade unions were targeted for suppression, and organized workers lost the large and well-disciplined base of support they needed to extract employer concessions.

In the metalworking and textile industries, by contrast, powerful employer associations effectively resisted the trade union movement. Metal and textile workers, like the printers and bakers, sought to introduce collective bargaining and institutionalized methods of resolving conflict. But they lacked the means to compel employer cooperation. The strength of organized employers far surpassed that of the workers, whose position was further undermined, in the case of the metalworkers, by severe unemployment. Union success in these industries was confined mainly to small and medium-sized firms not represented in the Societies of Factory Owners.

TRADE UNIONS AND ELECTORAL POLITICS

Despite their attention to labor-management relations, organized workers never lost sight of political struggles, and in 1906, after some hesitation, they turned their attention to electoral politics, utilizing the newly established State Duma—a national representative assembly created by the October Manifesto—to pro-

[128]*Novaia rus'*, no. 26 (September 10, 1908), p. 4; TsGAOR, DPOO, f. 111, op. 5, d. 263, pp. 121–122.

mote the interests of labor. When elections to the State Duma first got under way in early 1906, most trade unions had not yet succeeded in reconstituting an organization and rebuilding their membership. There was widespread skepticism concerning the Duma in labor circles and little enthusiasm for the forthcoming election. Many workers, particularly those who had been highly active in the events of the preceding year, were not yet able to envision the Duma as an institution that would accord them any advantage in their struggle for a better life.

Within the ranks of Russian Social Democracy, Mensheviks and Bolsheviks did not agree over the correct tactic to take in the Duma election. The Mensheviks urged participation in the first stage of the three-tiered electoral process whereby factory workers elected representatives at the enterprise level. According to the election law of December 11, 1905, these enterprise-level election meetings were placed entirely in the hands of the workers themselves, without the involvement of the factory administration.[129] In the Menshevik view, this provided a valuable opportunity for political discussion and agitation. Nevertheless, the Mensheviks urged workers to boycott the second stage of the election, when the electors assembled to choose the Duma deputies from the workers' curiae.

The Bolsheviks, by contrast, favored a boycott of the entire election. They were convinced that the revolution had faltered but not yet failed, and that the popular movement would soon regain its momentum. Participation in the Duma election, the Bolsheviks argued, would merely divert workers from their revolutionary tasks and encourage parliamentary illusions.[130]

Trade union organizations—many of them under the leadership of Social Democrats—adopted a passive or even negative approach to the election. The

[129]The election law of December 11, 1905, provided for the election of deputies from workers' curiae in nine industrial centers in the Russian Empire, including St. Petersburg and Moscow. Elections in the workers' curiae commenced at the enterprise level with the selection of a delegate *(upolnomochennyi)* in firms with no fewer than fifty workers. One delegate was to be elected for every firm with fifty to one thousand workers, and another delegate for each additional thousand workers per firm. The delegates then assembled to choose electors *(vybornye)*. Finally, these electors participated in electoral assemblies along with electors from other curiae to choose the Duma deputies. According to the December 11, 1905, law, male workers were entitled to participate in the first stage of the election. The workers themselves were permitted to decide whether a plurality or a majority was required to elect a delegate, and whether voting would take place by ballot, a show of hands, or some other method.

[130]The Bolshevik position was described by D. B. Riazanov during an evening of recollections, *MIPDR,* 4:30.

Petersburg and the Moscow Central Bureau of Trade Unions, both dominated by Mensheviks, did little more than issue a resolution urging eligible workers to enter their names on the electoral list entitling them to vote.[131] The printers' union in the capital called for a boycott of the election, and this appeal evidently struck a responsive chord, for only printers in state-owned firms and in a handful of private printing houses actually participated in the first stage of the election.[132]

The boycott extended to widely diverse segments of the labor force. In the Moscow baking industry, the election of delegates was completed only at the large Filippov firm. The administration gathered all the Filippov workers in a dormitory room to vote on delegates, but they refused to cooperate. Several days later, the administration assembled a smaller group of older, more reliable workers and juveniles—a total of only one hundred out of five hundred workers employed at the Filippov firm—who carried out the election under the supervision of their superiors.[133] Not all workers boycotted the election, however. The Moscow candyworkers were generally enthusiastic about the campaign and willingly participated in the election.[134]

Despite the boycott, some workers were elected as deputies to the First Duma. One such deputy was I. Savel'ev, a typesetter employed at the newspaper *Russkie vedomosti* [Russian Gazette] and a member of the Moscow printers' union.[135] Elected with assistance from the Kadet party,[136] Savel'ev was initially criticized by the printers' newspaper, which asserted that Savel'ev "[did] not have the right to speak for all the workers in view of the fact that a negligible and hardly-conscious *(malosoznatel'naia)* group of people participated in the election to the Duma."[137]

This condemnation was echoed by the Moscow union of tailors, which issued the following statement on May 11, 1906:

---

[131]*Professional'nyi soiuz*, no. 6–7 (January 21, 1906), p. 1; Grinevich, *Professional'noe dvizhenie*, pp. 219–220.

[132]*ILS*, pp. 260–261, reports that only a small number of printers participated in the first stage of the election. For example, at the Trenke printing firm, 27 of the 90 workers participated; at the Senatskii firm, 160 out of 400; at the Efron firm, 53 out of 160; at the Suvorin firm, 73 out of 400. Boycott sentiment was also strong among Petersburg metalworkers. Bulkin, *Na zare*, p. 413.

[133]*Bulochnik*, no. 3 (March 12, 1906), p. 41.

[134]*Professional'noe dvizhenie Moskovskikh pishchevikov*, p. 155.

[135]Sher, *Istoriia*, pp. 282–283.

[136]*ILS*, p. 260.

[137]Sher, *Istoriia*, p. 283.

The State Duma, which was elected under impossible conditions and not by all the people, cannot be the spokesman for the will and needs of the people if it continues its activity as it has up to this time. If the State Duma sincerely wants to act in the name of the people, it must listen attentively to the voice of the people and immediately fulfill their demands; [it must] ignore the basic laws of an obsolete system, ignore the State Council and all the obstacles which the government places before it. The State Duma must immediately abolish the law of March 4 on trade unions, it must bring to trial all the guilty rulers who drown Russia in a sea of blood, and it should create conditions for the convocation of a constituent assembly on the basis of a general election law.[138]

Following the convocation of the Duma, trade unions gradually changed their assessment of worker participation. The Moscow printers' union led the way with an editorial in its newspaper, *Pechatnik* [The Printer], expressing the hope that Savel'ev, who stood politically between the Mensheviks and the Kadets, would not "break his ties with the workers." Subsequently, the printers' journal congratulated the workers' deputies for their activities on behalf of workers' interests. Finally, *Pechatnik* conveyed its "fervent comradely greetings to Savel'ev, and through him to the entire workers' faction in the Duma."[139]

Once the First Duma was actually in session, trade unions in both cities altered their stance toward the worker deputies. This change was summed up by a resolution of the Petersburg Central Bureau:

Of course, the Duma is powerless, but it can provide us with a great service if we succeed in turning it into a forum for disseminating loud and brave words in defense of the working class, and together with it, the entire laboring population.[140]

Very soon, the SD-affiliated Workers' Group and the more broadly based Labor Group within the Duma established contact with union representatives.[141] Members of the Workers' Group received complaints from trade unionists

---

[138]Iu. Milonov, ed., *Moskovskoe professional'noe dvizhenie v gody pervoi revoliutsii* (Moscow, [1925]), p. 260.

[139]Sher, *Istoriia*, pp. 283–284.

[140]Grinevich, *Professional'noe dvizhenie*, p. 221.

[141]Unlike the Workers' Group, the Labor Group included Socialist Revolutionaries, Social Democrats, and other representatives of left-wing parties. A typical example of contact between deputies and unions, reported in *Volna*, no. 19 (May 17, 1906), p. 4, involved Deputy Sedel'nikov's attendance at a meeting of the Petersburg union of cabmen, where he presented a report on Labor Group activities.

concerning police violations of union rights.[142] The capital's printers' union turned to the Labor Group in April for assistance during the boycott of the newspaper *Dvadtsatyi vek*.[143]

The First Duma was short-lived, lasting only from April 27 to July 9, when the government proclaimed its dissolution. Workers did not immediately respond to this announcement, although plans for a general protest and a new Soviet of Workers' Deputies were discussed in St. Petersburg following July 9.[144] An uprising of Kronstadt and Sveaborg sailors finally precipitated a strike on July 21 in St. Petersburg which spread to Moscow three days later. The printers' union in the capital took a central role in planning the strike, and most printing houses shut down during the protest.[145] In Moscow, representatives from the unions of printers, shoemakers, gold- and silversmiths, tailors, and construction and textile workers participated in a planning session for the strike on July 23.[146] Virtually all printing firms joined the strike in Moscow as well. In each city, there were about eighty thousand strikers, including many artisanal, sales-clerical, and construction workers.[147] Although metalworkers joined the strike in Moscow,[148] their participation in the capital was limited to declarations of support. The strike and the abortive attempt to revive the Soviets of Workers' Deputies lasted only a few days and brought severe police retribution. In both cities, many unions lost their legal status, including the unions of Petersburg and Moscow printers, Petersburg metalworkers, bakers, and others.

By the time the election to the Second Duma got under way in the winter of 1906–1907, trade unionists and political activists had completely revised their position. Whereas formerly Social Democrats and labor leaders had discouraged participation in the election, at least beyond the first stage, now they advocated full and active involvement in the electoral process. And although some had earlier feared that the Duma would instill false illusions of parliamentarianism among the workers, now they argued that the Duma could be used to raise the level of workers' consciousness. The newspaper of the Petersburg metalworkers' union declared:

[142]Grinevich, *Professional'noe dvizhenie*, p. 221.

[143]*ILS*, p. 267.

[144]Derenkovskii, "Vseobshchaia stachka i sovety rabochikh deputatov v iiule 1906 g.," *Istoricheskie zapiski*, vol. 77 (1965), pp. 115–122.

[145]*ILS*, p. 288.

[146]Derenkovskii, "Vseobshchaia stachka," p. 131.

[147]*ILS*, p. 287.

[148]Derenkovskii, "Vseobshchaia stachka," p. 145.

The election struggle can be a good school for the workers' practical experience and political education if politically conscious comrades use [the election] to explain to the broad masses of working people who are their true friends and enemies.[149]

Defending the unions' involvement in electoral politics against wary rank-and-file members, the organ of the Moscow Central Bureau of Trade Unions, *Rabochii soiuz* [Workers' Union], observed in late 1906:

In the great majority of cases, our unions trace their origins to the memorable October days. And this close link between our trade union movement and the workers' general political struggle never allowed our unions to confine themselves exclusively to economic struggle but [instead] to take an active part in the political life of the proletariat.[150]

The Menshevik Garvi, who was active in the Petersburg metalworkers' union, noted in December 1906 that "there is not a single union which has a negative attitude toward the Duma elections."[151] Garvi called upon trade unionists, following the example of their counterparts in Germany and Austria, to participate in electoral politics "hand in hand" with the party of the working class. Although unions were committed to political neutrality, he asserted, "neutrality has nothing in common with political indifference, and the independence of trade unions does not exclude their support of a specific party in an election and generally, in a political campaign."[152] Trade unionists were thus exhorted not only to participate in the election but also to endorse the candidates of Russian Social Democracy.

But few unions were prepared to go beyond a general endorsement of the "socialist parties" by specifying their support for SD or SR candidates. The Petersburg unions of shoemakers and tobacco workers, which openly endorsed candidates of the RSDRP, were something of an exception.[153] The Petersburg Central Bureau of Trade Unions set the general tone when it urged that "representatives of the socialist parties be given every assistance in explaining their program."[154] Many unions simply recommended that workers vote for candidates who supported a four-point program with demands for an eight-hour

---

[149]Bulkin, *Na zare*, p. 414.

[150]Quoted from *Rabochii soiuz*, no. 5, in Iu. Ch. [Garvi], "Professional'nye soiuzy i vybory v Gos. Dumu," *Otkliki*, vyp. 1 (December 17, 1906), p. 52.

[151]Ibid., p. 49.

[152]Ibid., pp. 55–56.

[153]Sviatlovskii, *Professional'noe dvizhenie v Rossii* (St. Petersburg, 1907), p. 316; *Golos tabachnika*, no. 1 (December 21, 1906), p. 3; *Krasil'shchik*, no. 1 (February 2, 1907), p. 3.

[154]Grinevich, *Professional'noe dvizhenie*, p. 245.

workday, a comprehensive legislative program to protect labor, unlimited freedom of assembly, association, the press, strikes, and conscience, and a full
popular representative body, elected on the basis of a general, equal, and direct
secret ballot.[155]

Some unions even raised the possibility of entering their own candidates in
the electoral contest. The printers were the first to venture this suggestion, but
the idea was rejected on the grounds that Duma deputies should represent the
working class as a whole and not merely those workers who belonged to a
particular trade union.[156]

A number of unions attempted to take an active role in the campaign. The
Petersburg metalworkers' union admonished its members, "Let not one vote
among the members of our union go in vain."[157] The union newspaper carried
legal advice concerning registration procedures, and canvassers were dispatched
by the union to workers' quarters to ensure the maximum registration of those
who were eligible to vote in the city curia. Election literature and lists of socialist
party candidates were circulated through union channels.[158]

Once the Second Duma was in session, trade unionists took a growing
interest in its proceedings.[159] Through the small but active faction of Social
Democratic deputies in the assembly, trade unionists attempted to draw public
attention to incidents of administrative repression and harassment. Members of
the faction introduced a proposal calling for a Duma inquiry into the illegal
persecution of unions by the Petersburg Chief of Police.[160] Social Democratic
deputies attended union meetings in the capital, and union representatives were
invited to assist in the preparation of new draft legislation on strikes.[161] Accord-

[155] *Vestnik zolotoserebrianikov i bronzovshchikov*, no. 1 (December 23, 1906), p. 2; *Rabochii po kozhe*,
no. 1 (December 30, 1906), p. 1.

[156] Sviatlovskii, *Professional'noe dvizhenie*, pp. 318–319; Grinevich, *Professional'noe dvizhenie*, p.
245. The issue was also debated by the Petersburg unions of salesclerks and bookkeepers and by the
Nevskii group of the Petersburg metalworkers' union. This subject is discussed by Garvi in
"Professional'nye soiuzy," *Otkliki*, vyp. 1 (December 17, 1906), p. 54.

[157] Bulkin, *Na zare*, p. 415.

[158] Ibid.

[159] For a fascinating analysis of the popular vote in the Petersburg workers' curia in this election,
based on survey research, see Andrei Mikhailov, "Vybory vo vtoruiu Dumu v Peterburgskoi
rabochei kurii," *Otzvuki* (August 1907), pp. 41–51, and "Ianvarskie vybory po rabochei kurii v
gorode Peterburge," *Otkliki*, no. 2 (April 1907), pp. 65–78. The survey revealed that 47 percent of
the workers' vote was cast for SD candidates and 36 percent for SR candidates. Social Democrats
won their strongest vote (61–66 percent) in firms with 50–500 workers.

[160] Bulkin, *Na zare*, p. 415; Grinevich, *Professional'noe dvizhenie*, p. 225.

[161] *Professional'nyi vestnik*, no. 8 (May 30, 1907), p. 10.

ing to Kolokol'nikov, the SD faction in the Second Duma became the "political center" of the workers' movement in the capital during the spring of 1907.[162]

By June 1907, when the Second Duma was prorogued and a new electoral law announced, trade unionists had become extensively involved in the affairs of the SD Duma faction. Social Democrats, who by now fully supported participation in the Duma, repeatedly reminded workers that they could never achieve full recognition and protection of their rights under the tsarist autocracy. A major transformation—the long-awaited "bourgeois revolution"—would be necessary to accomplish this. But in the interim there were many compelling reasons for taking an active part in Russia's new representative assembly. The example of Western European trade union involvement in electoral politics, as well as their own brief experience, led many organized workers to view the Duma as an important forum for labor and a valuable opportunity to defend their rights publicly.

In summation, the years 1906–1907 witnessed several developments in the outlook and activities of Petersburg and Moscow trade unionists. As the urban revolution subsided, trade unionists turned their attention to the new legal opportunities that had been won in the upheavals of 1905. They directed their energy and resources toward two major objectives. First, they sought to attain immediate tangible improvements. These efforts assumed a variety of forms: the struggle to improve workplace conditions and to institutionalize labor-management relations, as well as the introduction of mutual aid programs and services.

At the same time, trade unionists attempted to ensure the continuation and improvement of political and juridical conditions that were necessary for the survival and development of the organized labor movement. Endeavoring to defend labor's legal rights and to publicize the workers' cause, trade unionists extended their activities into a number of areas, including the establishment of a legal labor press and participation in electoral politics.

These activities were part of an attempt by organized workers to enter into the realm of civil and political life from which they had hitherto been excluded. Following the model of Western European labor movements, Russian trade unionists demanded employer recognition of the union's right to represent workers collectively and to play a permanent role in matters relating to job rights, grievance procedures, and working conditions at the shop level. Venturing into electoral politics for the first time, trade unionists took steps to place the

[162]*MIPDR*, 5:132.

collective strength of organized workers in the service of political candidates and to lobby for workers' interests through labor deputies in the Duma.

This strategy corresponded to the new constellation of circumstances confronting the organized labor movement in 1906 and the first half of 1907— circumstances that made it possible for trade unionists to register significant, albeit short-lived, accomplishments in their endeavor to establish Western European type trade unions on Russian soil. These efforts acquire further historical importance in view of the size, composition, and diversity of the unions. Roughly one-tenth of the labor force in each city joined a trade union in this period, and the percentage of unionized workers was considerably higher in some industries and occupations. Union membership extended to widely diverse segments of the laboring population, but many of those drawn to the unions had a level of skill, literacy, and urban living and working experience that was relatively higher than others in a given industry and trade.

Unionized men and women were generally the most articulate and politically-minded elements in the labor force, and it was a matter of great significance that they endorsed and supported union policies designed to introduce collective institutionalized methods of handling industrial disputes and, more generally, sought to improve the conditions of labor by working within the framework of newly created or established institutions. Many unionized (and some non-unionized) workers displayed an exceptional degree of discipline and self-organization in pursuing these objectives.

There was, to be sure, a duality in union ideology and practice during this period. In the immediate aftermath of 1905, revolutionary sentiments remained strong among many labor leaders and rank-and-file union members, especially those with ties to the Social Democratic and Socialist Revolutionary parties. They continued to believe that only an overthrow of the autocracy and the establishment of a democratic constitutional system would ensure, once and for all, a political and juridical climate in which workers could fully defend their rights. Incidents of intermittent government harassment and persecution served as a constant reminder that the legal rights of labor were far from secure under the prevailing system. But the longer-term strategic goal of revolution still harbored by many trade unionists did not prevent them from utilizing the new legal channels and the opportunities for open mass organization that became available in this period. These two strands in union ideology—a reformist approach to industrial relations and a commitment to revolutionary change— coexisted during 1906 and early 1907, reflecting the peculiar combination of circumstances that confronted labor.

Contrary to conventional Soviet and Western interpretations portraying these months as the disappointing last act of a revolution manqué, we have seen that organized workers attempted to implement a bold new vision of industrial relations. To an extent previously unacknowledged in the literature, some trade unionists briefly succeeded in realizing this vision. Urban workers eventually succumbed to the rising tide of counterrevolution, but for a brief time they waged a remarkable campaign to assert and defend their rights, using the new legal opportunities created by the 1905 revolution.

The evolution of the organized labor movement in 1906 and early 1907 sheds light on what one scholar has called "suppressed historical alternatives,"[163] enabling us to discern the conditions that briefly facilitated and then interrupted the progress toward a restructuring of industrial relations. Progress was possible, as we have seen, because neither the government nor employers presented a monolithic policy toward labor. In the wake of the 1905 upheavals, the tsarist government sanctioned a brief and halfhearted experiment in the implementation of this approach, making possible not only the emergence of a mass-based trade union movement but also a new group of employer organizations designed to counteract the growing strength of organized labor. The direction of labor-management relations in any given industry or occupation depended to a considerable extent on the relative organizational capacity of these two antagonists, as well as on the general economic conditions affecting the labor market. Thus, industrial progress was most impressive among those partially nonfactory groups, such as bakers and printers, where the workers' level of organization and solidarity surpassed that of employers, and where the labor market was either stable or expanding.

In the final analysis, a shift in state policy and, concomitantly, a deterioration in the country's political climate brought to a close this important era in Russian labor history. The Stolypin "coup d'état" of June 3, 1907—revising the Duma election law to ensure a more politically conservative assembly—signaled the ascendancy of an approach toward labor advocated by the Ministry of Internal Affairs. This approach, calling for a combination of repression and government tutelage over the labor movement, testifies to the deep and chronic anxiety in some government circles over the issues of social autonomy and instability. The preoccupation with these issues, which had shaped state policy toward labor since the onset of industrialization, can be attributed to the government's in-

---

[163]Barrington Moore, Jr., *Injustice: The Social Bases of Obedience and Revolt* (White Plains, N.Y., 1978), chapter 11.

creasingly attenuated social base and its failure to integrate new entrepreneurial elements, not to speak of the growing working class, into the political life of the country prior to 1905.

Paradoxically, the success of the organized labor movement contributed directly to its demise. Government officials were alarmed by the spectacle of trade unions that made such rapid advances in recruiting a substantial membership, erecting an organizational infrastructure, mounting a campaign to achieve workplace improvements, and even participating in electoral politics under the banner of the socialist parties. Collective organizations capable of such progress in fifteen months might indeed pose a threat to the delicate and precarious balance of forces in Russian society.

The events of mid-1907 brought to an end this phase in the development of mass-based legal trade unions. Never again in the tsarist period would unions enjoy such a favorable constellation of circumstances as they did between March 1906 and June 1907. It is not possible to predict what might have happened had the unions been permitted to grow and function over a longer term with some modicum of success. Perhaps under different conditions these organizations would have performed the same function as many of their Western European counterparts, gradually facilitating the integration of workers into the existing system. It is conceivable that in Russia as well, unions would have given workers a stake in the institutions and social organizations that had enabled them slowly but perceptively to improve their lives. But circumstances did not permit Russian unions to continue their efforts to achieve collective improvements for the working class, and after June 1907 a dramatic shift in the political climate compelled trade unionists to turn their attention instead to a struggle for survival in the face of growing counterrevolution.

Chapter 8

Workers' Organizations in the Years of Repression, 1907–1911

> Our task is to carry on the struggle for as broad a legal
> existence as possible. For a mass organization to exist
> and to function underground is almost impossible—that
> is what the experience of recent years has taught us.
>
> Golos zhizni *[Voice of Life]*[1]

The "coup d'état" of June 3, 1907, inaugurated a government campaign to destroy the trade unions. Noting the change in political atmosphere, employers hastened to suppress the unions and to withdraw many of the concessions granted to workers during the preceding two years. The crisis facing the trade unions was further intensified by a severe deterioration in the economy. Between 1907 and late 1909, the country experienced a major recession that resulted in widespread unemployment in virtually all branches of industry. By the end of 1907, 25 to 30 percent of the metalworkers in the Moscow region and 36 percent in the capital were out of work.[2] A contraction in the textile industry acquired crisis proportions in 1908, while severe cutbacks put thousands of printers, tailors, leatherworkers, and others out of work.[3] It was not until the

[1]*Golos zhizni*, no. 3 (September 22, 1910), p. 1.

[2]*Istoriia Moskvy*, 6 vols. (Moscow, 1952–1959), vol. 5, p. 222; F. A. Bulkin, *Na zare profdvizhenie: Istoriia Peterburgskogo soiuza metallistov 1906–1914 gg.* (Moscow and Leningrad), p. 159.

[3]*Tekstil'noe delo*, no. 1 (November 25, 1907), p. 7; Tsentral'nyi gosudarstvennyi arkhiv Oktiabr'skoi revoliutsii (TsGAOR), DPOO, f. 102, g. 17, ch. 29, 1908, p. 6; *Kozhevnik*, no. 3 (September 25, 1909), p. 5. Out of 13–14,000 Petersburg printers, 2,500 were unemployed in early 1908.

winter of 1909–1910 that the economic situation began to improve.

Not only did the labor market contract sharply in many industries and trades, but the composition of the work force changed as well. Following the 1905 revolution, employers in widely diverse sectors of the economy began to substitute women for male workers, further exacerbating the unemployment situation. A report by the senior factory inspector for Moscow province in 1909 describes the situation:

One encounters factories [in the textile industry] which in principle have decided to replace male labor with female labor and which are replacing fired workers with women. This process is also spreading in some other industries—sugar, tobacco, watchmaking, ropemaking, glass, cement and brick factories; the sphere to which it is spreading is continually widening, affecting branches of industry where formerly male labor was exclusively employed. The reasons for such a phenomenon have already been explained in former reports: women are a more peaceful and moderate element in factories, and above all—they are a significantly cheaper labor force than men.[4]

Although unions had made rapid advances over the preceding fifteen months, this proved too short a time to build sturdy organizations capable of withstanding the impact of repression and economic crisis. Disheartened and dismayed, union organizers attributed this misfortune "not only to external repression, but also to internal [factors]—the indifference and apathy among the broad masses."[5] Complaints of the workers' "indifferent attitude" filled the pages of the labor press in these years, and some observers noted that demoralization turned workers to "alcoholism, boulevard literature and boulevard newspapers."[6]

Systematic persecution, economic distress, and the accompanying demoralization from mid-1907 to 1912, sharply depleted union ranks. Nevertheless, the preceding two and a half years had left an imprint on the workers' movement

---

[4]A. G. Rashin, *Formirovanie rabochego klassa Rossii: Istoriko-ekonomicheskie ocherki* (Moscow, 1958), p. 226, cited from *Svod otchetov fabrichnykh inspektorov za 1909* (St. Petersburg, 1910), p. xiv.

[5]*Professional'nyi vestnik*, no. 20 (April 2, 1908), p. 91.

[6]*Nadezhda*, no. 2 (September 26, 1908), p. 10. Similar sentiments were reiterated in other union newspapers. See, for example, *Nash golos*, no. 1 (March 14, 1908), p. 1. The boulevard newspapers referred to here were the so-called "kopeck" newspapers that catered to a mass urban audience. The first was the Petersburg *Gazeta kopeika*, which began publication in June 1908; the *Moskovskaia gazeta kopeika* appeared in April 1909. Both were an immediate success, and within ten months the Petersburg edition had a circulation of 150,000. Jeffrey Brooks, "Readers and Reading at the End of the Tsarist Era," in *Literature and Society in Imperial Russia, 1800–1914*, ed. William Mills Todd III (Stanford, Calif., 1978), p. 146.

that could not be entirely erased, even during the period of Prime Minister Stolypin's harsh regime. Trade unions declined, but they did not vanish. Some organized workers turned their attention to other legal opportunities for collective association, such as clubs, cultural societies, consumer cooperatives, and production artels. Among a small but influential group of workers, the aspiration for organization remained intact during these years of repression and disappointment.

THE DECLINE OF TRADE UNIONS

One year after the Stolypin "coup d'état," the number of Petersburg unions had declined from seventy-six to thirty-seven, and the combined nominal union membership had dropped by 40 percent to 22,000 (9,356 dues-paying members).[7] Among the unions still active in the capital on July 1, 1908, only the metalworkers succeeded in maintaining a substantial membership. The printers' and bakers' unions, formerly large and flourishing organizations, were scarcely recognizable (table 30).

By the fall of 1909, a slight revival had taken place. The total number of functioning unions had declined to twenty-five,[8] but some of them, notably the printers and leatherworkers, showed an increase in membership over the preceding year (table 30). Only the Petersburg metalworkers' union registered a decline. Altogether, forty-six different groups in St. Petersburg were active in the union movement at some time between mid-1907 and 1911.[9] The combined peak nominal membership for thirty-nine of these forty-six unions was 35,153, a considerable decline from the 55,000 in 1906 and early 1907.

The Moscow union movement fared even worse than its counterpart in the capital. The five major unions in the city (printers, metalworkers, textile workers, tailors, and teapackers) claimed only a handful of members in September 1907 compared with four months earlier (table 31). A survey of Moscow unions

[7]V. Fedorovich, "Professional'noe dvizhenie v Peterburge," *Novaia rus'*, no. 26 (September 10 [23], 1908), p. 4. The total number of dues-paying union members, 9,356, applies to all thirty-seven unions functioning in mid-1908 and is therefore somewhat higher than the total figures shown in table 30, which includes only the largest unions.

[8]Ibid., p. 4.

[9]A total of fifty unions existed in St. Petersburg between mid-1907 and early 1912; all but four of them were legally registered. Four were cases of repeat registration. For a complete list, see Appendix IV.

Table 30
Membership in Selected Trade Unions in St. Petersburg, July 1, 1908, and 1909

Union	Date of Registration	Nominal Membership July 1, 1908	Dues-paying Membership July 1, 1908	Nominal Membership 1909	Peak Nominal Membership, 1906–1907
Metalworkers	May 15, 1907	9,791	4,645	6,789	10,700
Printers	January 8, 1908	2,087	517	5,666	12,000
Bakers	August 28, 1907	n.d.	595	1,195	4,140
Woodworkers	May 15, 1907	1,300	422	1,699	1,965
Gold- and silversmiths	May 1, 1907	480	346	637	1,110
Leatherworkers	November 13, 1907	200	166	1,273	771
Candymakers	May 12, 1907	300	n.d.	825	998
Office clerks	April 17, 1907	565	100	n.d.	2,000
Tobacco workers	May 8, 1907	400	20	576	500
Textile workers	May 15, 1907	2,000	1,190	2,257	4,000
Tailors	October 20, 1908	n.d.	n.d.	1,019	1,514
Shoemakers	July 24, 1907	n.d.	n.d.	987	1,200
Total		17,123	8,001	22,923	40,898

Source: Fedorovich, "Professional'noe dvizhenie," p. 4; TsGAOR, DPOO, f. 111, opis' 5, d. 263, 1909.

conducted in June 1909 disclosed that only sixteen unions were functioning in the city.[10] The eight largest of these unions had a combined dues-paying membership of 1,231 (table 31), and the remaining unions were even smaller. A total of forty-seven different unions existed in Moscow at some point between mid-1907 and 1912.[11] Their combined peak nominal membership was only 12,433, or slightly more than one-third of the members in Petersburg unions during the same period.

The rapid and precipitous decline of unions in the country's two major urban centers was part of a broader pattern throughout the Empire. Although data on the number and size of unions in the country as a whole during the Stolypin years are not available, a Department of Police report in May 1910 noted that from 1907 to 1910 a total of 214 unions had been closed by the authorities—105 of them for allegedly violating the provisions of their charter and 109 for "revolutionary activity."[12] Since there were 904 legally registered unions in the country by December 1907, we may estimate that about one-quarter of them lost their legal standing over the next three years. Many others, though not directly closed down by the police, ceased activities because of the adverse political and economic circumstances and 401 were denied registration, another form of repression. Most of these groups had earlier been legally registered and, in some cases, had formerly established large and active organizations.[13]

PATTERNS OF UNIONIZATION

The overall sectoral composition of the union movement did not change significantly in the Stolypin period compared with earlier years. Manufacturing workers formed the largest number of unions, followed at a great distance by sales-clerical groups (table 32). Artisanal workers, including those in manufacturing and skilled construction trades, remained highly active in the union movement, forming fifteen unions, or one-third of the total number in each city.

As in earlier years, skilled workers predominated. The Petersburg printers' union reported a total membership of 1,510 workers in 1911. Of these, 58 percent (876 workers) were typesetters. The second largest group in the Petersburg union was also skilled—the lithographers—who constituted 16 percent

[10]*Vestnik truda,* no. 1 (November 28, 1909), pp. 5–7.
[11]See Appendix IV.
[12]TsGAOR, DP IV, d. 119, ch. 43, 1908, p. 73.
[13]*Nashe vremia,* no. 1 (April 3, 1911), p. 6.

Table 31
Dues-Paying Members in Selected Moscow
Unions, 1907–1909

Union	May 1907	September 1907	December 1908	June 1909
Printers	4,000	1,000	313	519
Metalworkers	2,000	200	n.d.	97
Textile workers	1,500	200	89	40
Precious metalworkers	n.d.	n.d.	62	22
Leatherworkers	n.d.	n.d.	14	111
Carpenters	n.d.	n.d.	51	25
Tailors	1,500	150	100	90
Salesclerks	n.d.	n.d.	392	327
Teapackers	1,000	250	n.d.	n.d.
Total	10,000	1,800	1,021	1,231

Sources: *Professional'nyi vestnik*, no. 2 (April 2, 1908), pp. 5, 9; *Vestnik truda*, no. 1 (November 28, 1909), pp. 5–7.

of the total membership.[14] A breakdown of the membership of the Moscow tailors' union in 1910 shows a similar pattern. More than three-quarters of the 354 members of this union were employed in workshops that produced men's clothing, shops that attracted the most highly skilled tailors in the trade.[15]

Skilled workers also provided the bulk of the membership in some factory-based unions such as the Petersburg metalworkers' union. Of the 1,005 metalworkers who joined this union between January and June 1908, 526 were metalfitters, 175 were lathe operators, 141 were smelters. Together they made up 84 percent of the new membership. Whereas in 1907, 16 percent of the union's total membership had been unskilled, in 1909 the proportion of unskilled workers declined to 10 percent, and in 1910 to a mere 5 percent of the total.[16]

Unionized workers often had considerable experience living and working in an urban center. Two-thirds of the workers who joined the Petersburg metalworkers' union in the first half of 1908, for example, were twenty-five years of age or older. The largest group, 44 percent of the new members, ranged from

[14]Tsentral'nyi gosudarstvennyi istoricheskii arkhiv (TsGIA), f. 23, opis' 29, d. 44, p. 5.
[15]*Vestnik portnykh*, no. 1 (June 6, 1911), p. 8.
[16]*Nadezhda*, no. 1 (July 31, 1908), p. 6; Bulkin, *Na zare*, p. 309.

twenty-five to thirty-four years of age; 19 percent were between the ages of thirty-five and forty-nine, and 2 percent were fifty or older.[17]

Despite the influx of women into many industries, the female contingent in the trade unions remained exceedingly small in the Stolypin period. The Petersburg printers' union in 1911 had 49 women members out of 1,510, or a mere 3 percent. The Moscow textile workers' union reported 63 women members in 1911 out of a total of 693 (9 percent).[18] Women constituted only 4 percent of the members of the Petersburg tailors' union in 1910, and the Moscow tailors' union attracted 29 women members in 1910 out of a total of 354 (8 percent).[19] The Petersburg textile workers' union represented something of an exception, therefore, when it reported that one-quarter of its membership was female in late 1908.[20] Women workers, nearly all of them unskilled or semiskilled, generally did not enter the unions in this period, despite efforts to draw them into union ranks.[21]

Industrial unionism continued to develop in these years, and a majority of unionized workers belonged to an organization formed on an industrial rather than a craft basis. Yet workers persisted in their inclination for craft unions, and many of the small unions were organized along craft lines. Twenty-seven out of forty-six Petersburg unions (59 percent) and thirty-five out of forty-seven in Moscow (74 percent) were of a craft variety, compared to about 66 percent in each city during 1906–1907.

The decrease in craft unionism in St. Petersburg was due to the amalgamation of specialized craft groups into unions organized on an industrial principle. By way of illustration, the patternmakers joined the woodworkers' union, the electrical workers joined the metalworkers' union, and the knitters joined the textile workers' union.[22] But even in these cases, occupational specialization remained a strong basis for unification within industrial unions. The textile workers' union, for example, permitted the seventy knitters who joined the organization to form

[17]*Nadezhda*, no. 1 (July 31, 1908), p. 6. TsGAOR, DPOO, f.102, d. 17, opis' 11, ch. 46, L. B. 1910, p. 22; f. 6835, opis' 4, d. 111, p. 16.

[18]TsGIA, f. 23, opis' 29, d. 44, p. 5; *Golos zhizni*, no. 5 (March 4, 1911), p. 4.

[19]*Vestnik portnykh*, no. 1 (June 6, 1911), p. 8.

[20]*Stanok tekstil'shchika*, no. 1 (November 18, 1908), p. 13.

[21]Special efforts to recruit women were made by a number of different unions, including the Petersburg tailors' union, the Moscow textile workers' union, and the Petersburg leatherworkers' union. *Golos portnogo*, no. 1–2 (May 10, 1910), p. 5; *Golos zhizni*, no. 5 (March 4, 1911), p. 4; *Kozhevnik*, no. 6 (April 6, 1911), p. 6.

[22]Fedorovich, "Professional'noe dvizhenie," *Novaia rus'*, no. 26, p. 4.

Table 32
Sectoral Composition of Trade Unions
in St. Petersburg and Moscow,
June 1907-December 1911

	St. Petersburg	Moscow
Unions Formed by Workers in:		
Manufacturing		
Number	33	27
Percent	72	57.5
Sales-Clerical		
Number	8	9
Percent	17	19
Service		
Number	1	6
Percent	2	13
Construction		
Number	3	3
Percent	7	6.5
Transportation		
Number	1	—
Percent	2	—
Municipal		
Number	—	1
Percent	—	2
Miscellaneous		
Number	—	1
Percent	—	2
Total		
Number	46	47
Percent	100	100

Sources: See Appendix IV.

a semiautonomous section and to meet separately to discuss their special needs.[23] This indicates that although some craft groups appreciated the benefits of joining a larger and potentially more powerful organization, craft allegiances had not disappeared. In Moscow the union movement did not display a similar trend toward amalgamation, and here the proportion of small craft unions actually increased (by 9 percent) over the preceding period.

A Petersburg Menshevik writing in 1910 distinguished three groups in the Petersburg working class: unskilled workers, whom he described as the "dark masses," an intermediary category of more skilled segments of the labor force, and finally, workers with a very high level of skill. Each group, he observed, had a different attitude toward trade unions and political parties.[24]

Unskilled workers, who often retained close ties to the countryside, generally regarded legal labor associations "with equanimity or animosity." Some had earlier participated in trade unions during the revolutionary and immediate postrevolutionary period, but now they had withdrawn. Eager for immediate material gains, they did not appreciate the "educational significance of these organizations," and were prone to alcoholism and card playing, habits which they had similarly indulged before 1905. Nevertheless, there was "some growth of consciousness" among these workers. They had begun to read newspapers and showed "a desire in one way or another to understand their economic and political situation, although often all of this, arising spontaneously, manifests itself in extremely ugly forms that combine revolutionary barricades with the pogrom politics of the Union of the Russian People."[25]

Workers in the intermediary category furnished the major base of support for trade unions in this period. These workers, more skilled and educated than the first group, were inclined to read newspapers regularly and to take a lively interest in social and political life. Often "socialist and democratic" in orientation, they had a deeper sense of class antagonism to the bourgeoisie than other workers. Most of them were far from being committed Social Democrats, however, and the Menshevik correspondent noted that they might easily fall

---

[23]*Stanok*, no. 1 (February 14, 1908), p. 16.

[24]TsGAOR, DPOO, d. 5, ch. 57, opis' 11, 1910, pp. 112–120. The identity of the correspondent is not disclosed in the police archive. The letter, dated September 29, 1910, was addressed to M. Valeri, Director, Cuisines Economiques, Geneva.

[25]The Union of the Russian People, an organization of extreme reactionaries, was founded in St. Petersburg in 1905 under the leadership of V. M. Purishkevich and A. I. Dubrovin.

under the influence of Socialist Revolutionaries, anarchists, syndicalists, or maximalists.[26]

Finally, there was a third group—the highly skilled workers who formed the worker-intelligentsia. Although they enthusiastically joined legal organizations and frequently provided the leadership for trade unions, they had a tendency toward careerism, manifested in their striving for a technical education, higher wages, and the material basis of a comfortable life. Some even sought to advance their own careers by holding positions as paid employees of the unions, thereby "satisfying their petty bourgeois vanity."

Despising the "dark masses" of unskilled workers on the one hand, they also had contempt for narrow SD party types on the other. In certain cases these worker-intellectuals used their high cultural level "to attain a clearer understanding of their class tasks, without losing class solidarity," and some of them joined party cells. But the majority were attracted to the "liquidators"—that is, to the advocates of purely legal forms of activity directed toward economic improvement, and they were inclined to look upon trade unions not as "militant organizations" but primarily as mutual aid societies. Left-wing liberals, the correspondent asserted, also enjoyed success among them.

WORKERS' CLUBS AND EDUCATIONAL SOCIETIES

With the decline of trade unions, workers turned their attention to a variety of other legal labor organizations. Clubs, educational and cultural societies, consumer cooperatives, and production artels proliferated in the harsh climate of the Stolypin period. The movement to form workers' clubs began in the capital in 1907 and gathered momentum during the following year. In 1909 there were twenty-one clubs and cultural societies in St. Petersburg, with a peak nominal combined membership of 6,830 (table 33). They included an evening school for workers and a women's mutual aid society, both founded in 1907. Nearly all of these organizations functioned legally, having obtained registration under the March 4, 1906, law.

Many of the Petersburg clubs were organized within the confines of a particular city district, evidence of the continuing importance of district patriotism as a

[26]The maximalists referred to here were an ultra-left-wing group within the Bolshevik faction formed in 1908. Otherwise known as the *otzovisty*, or recallists, for their extreme opposition to the participation of Social Democrats in the Third State Duma, they included A. A. Bogdanov, A. V. Lunacharskii, and several others.

12. Library of the St. Petersburg metalworkers' union, 1907.

13. Workers active in the St. Petersburg textile workers' union, 1907–1911.

14. Members of the directing board of the St. Petersburg Union of Men and Women in the Tailoring Trades on an excursion to Shuvalovo, a suburb of the city, in May 1911.

15. Four leading Moscow trade unionists who were informants for the Okhrana on the eve of the First World War: A. Poskrebukhin, union of sales employees; A. K. Marakushev, union of metalworkers; S. I. Sokolov, union of metalworkers; A. N. Nikolaev, union of printers.

Table 33
Workers' Clubs, Schools, and Cultural Societies
in St. Petersburg, 1907–1911

Organization	Date of Founding	Peak Nominal Membership	Political Orientation of Directing Board
1. "Enlightenment" Society	1907	560	Social Democrat
2. Educational Society of the Narvskaia District	n.d.	350	Social Democrat
3. Educational Society "Ray"	1907	365	n.d.
4. Baltiiskii Society "Science and Life"	1907	n.d.	n.d.
5. Educational Society of the Sampsonievskii Plant	1907	n.d.	Social Democrat
6. Educational Society of the Aleksandro-Nevskaia District	1907	550	n.d.
7. Educational Society "Light" of the Nevskaia Zastava	1907	250	Social Democrat
8. Nekrasov Educational Society	1907	410	n.d.
9. Educational Society of the Vyborgskaia District	n.d.	400	n.d.
10. Obukhov Society "Knowledge is Light"	1907	669	Social Democrat
11. The Second Educational Society of the Narvskaia District	1907	400	n.d.
12. Enlightenment Society "Science"	1907	250	n.d.
13. Educational Society of the Vasil'evskii Island District	1907	370	n.d.
14. "Source of Light and Knowledge" Society (Vasil'evskii Island)	1907	210	Social Democrat
15. Educational Society of the Moskovskaia Zastava	1908	450	Social Democrat
16. "Knowledge" Society	1909	226	n.d.

(continued on next page)

Table 33 (Continued)
Workers' Clubs, Schools, and Cultural Societies
in St. Petersburg, 1907–1911

Organization	Date of Founding	Peak Nominal Membership	Political Orientation of Directing Board
17. Educational Society of the Moskovskaia District	1909	n.d.	n.d.
18. "Knowledge is Strength" Society	1908	600	n.d.
19. Typographers' Musical, Dramatic, and Educational Circle	n.d.	n.d.	Social Democrat
20. Petersburg Workers' Evening School	1907	360	n.d.
21. Women's Mutual Aid Society	1907	400	n.d.
Total		6,830	

Sources: I. D. Levin, "Rabochie kluby v Peterburge (1907–1914 gg.)," *MIPDR*, vol. 3, p. 98; *Vozrozhdenie*, no. 5–6 (April 1909), p. 54; no. 9–12 (1909), p. 143; *Golos portnogo*, no. 5 (December 22, 1910), pp. 14, 16; Okhrana report dated March 1910, TsGAOR, DPOO, f. 102, d. 5, ch. 57, opis' 11, 1910, p. 17; TsGAOR, DPOO, f. 102, d. 1000, op. 00, ch. 14, 1905, t. 2, p. 106; TsGIA, f. 287, op. 1, d. 68a, p. 130; *Fabrichnyi stanok*, no. 5 (September 18, 1908), p. 8.

basis for collective association among workers. Three other clubs centered around specific enterprises: the large Obukhov and Baltiiskii metalworking plants and the Sampsonievskii (Nevskii) textile mill. The printers, who had an earlier history of cultural societies, established their own citywide club.

The movement to form workers' clubs spread to Moscow, but did not acquire the same importance there as in the capital. Nevertheless, a total of seven clubs and cultural societies functioned in Moscow in 1910 (table 34). Among these was a school for workers, the Prechistenskie Workers' Courses, founded in 1897 by the Cultural Commission on Technical Education of the Imperial Russian Technical Society. In 1908 the school attracted 1,500 workers to its courses.

Two of the Moscow clubs—the Khamovnicheskii District Society "Knowledge" and the First Society for Sensible Entertainment—applied for registration under the March 1906 law, but were refused legal status and attempted to function illegally. The Club for Popular Entertainment obtained registration in March 1909, but was closed by the police in April 1910 for "calling on workers

Table 34

Workers' Clubs, Schools, and Cultural
Societies in Moscow, 1910

	Organization	Date of Founding	Nominal Membership
1.	Khamovnicheskii District Society "Knowledge"	1910 (refused registration)	n.d.
2.	Club for Popular Entertainment	1909	1,000
3.	First Society for Sensible Entertainment	1910 (refused registration)	n.d.
4.	Moscow Club of Commercial and Industrial Employees	1908	624
5.	Waiters' Club	1907	n.d.
6.	Third Women's Club	1908	n.d.
7.	Prechistenskie Workers' Courses	1897	1,500
	Total		3,124

Sources: *Nash put'*, no. 3 (July 25, 1910), p. 6; TsGIA, f. 23, opis' 29, d. 40; p. 239; *Istoriia Moskvy*, 5:249.

to struggle against the government."[27] The other clubs were legally registered.

Clubs provided a legal opportunity for workers to congregate openly, hold meetings and lectures, operate a library, and conduct various educational, recreational, and cultural events. Some had an impressive record of activities. The Educational Society of the Moskovskaia Zastava in St. Petersburg, for example, conducted 37 lectures in a six-month period (1908–1909), attended by a total of 5,271 workers. It also maintained a library.[28] The Petersburg "Enlightenment" Society, which attracted many printers from the City District and the state-operated printing factory, held 354 lectures over a three-year period (1908–1910), attended by 19,834 workers. Some clubs, such as the Petersburg Enlightenment Society "Science," held evening classes for workers.[29] Entry and monthly dues in the clubs usually ranged from 20 to 25 kopeks, about one-half

[27]*Vozrozhdenie*, no. 9–10 (June 15, 1910), p. 94.

[28]*Vozrozhdenie*, no. 9–12 (1909), p. 142. The article cited here is by V. Miliutin, "Rabochee dvizhenie v Rossii."

[29]*Golos portnogo*, no. 5 (December 22, 1910), p. 14, and no. 6 (March 1, 1911), p. 13; *Vozrozhdenie*, no. 5–6 (April 1909), p. 55, article by S. Kanatchikov, "Kul'turno-prosvetitel'naia deiatel'nost' v Peterburgskikh professional'nykh soiuzakh."

that of trade unions, and many of the events sponsored by these organizations were held free of charge.

The memberships of clubs and trade unions frequently overlapped. A government ruling in mid-1907 barred unions from sponsoring concerts, social dances, and plays for their members,[30] thereby hastening the formation of clubs and inducing trade unionists to join them. The Moscow printers' and tailors' unions, for example, were instrumental in establishing the Club for Popular Entertainment.[31] In two Petersburg clubs, "Science and Life" and "Knowledge," 54 percent and 41 percent of the membership, respectively, was concurrently enrolled in a trade union in 1913–1914.[32] Contemporary accounts indicate that this pattern of dual membership was commonplace in the Stolypin period as well, extending into the ranks of club officers.[33]

The clubs attracted workers who were eager for self-improvement. In 1908 a contributor to the Petersburg metalworkers' union newspaper, *Nadezhda* [Hope], observed that workers joined clubs in the expectation that these organizations would

become the center of their entire intellectual life. They want systematic courses and lectures. From these courses, they expect, above all, assistance in working out their world view. A knowledge of natural, social, and economic sciences, a knowledge of the theory of the development of the world, of animals, and human beings can better than anything else facilitate the formation of a world view.[34]

In addition to lectures on scientific, social, and economic topics, some clubs held weekly readings of foreign and Russian literary works. These activities, observed the writer in *Nadezhda*, developed the workers' aesthetic and artistic taste and made them think about the "big questions of life."[35]

Clubs brought workers into close continuing contact with intellectuals, on whom they depended for lectures and other activities. So essential were the services of intelligentsia sympathizers that the clubs could not function during the summer months when most intellectuals departed from the city for their dachas in the countryside.[36] A Petersburg Menshevik writing in March 1908

[30]TsGAOR, DP IV, d. 119, ch. 43, 1908, p. 73.

[31]*Nash put'*, no. 3 (July 25, 1910), p. 6; TsGAOR, f. 102, d. 1000, opis' 00, ch. 14, t. 2, 1905, p. 112.

[32]*Severnaia rabochaia gazeta*, no. 16 (February 27, 1914), p. 5, and no. 59 (April 20, 1914), p. 4.

[33]*Vozrozhdenie*, no. 5–6 (1909), p. 55.

[34]*Nadezhda*, no. 2 (September 26, 1908), p. 8.

[35]Ibid.

[36]*Vozrozhdenie*, no. 5–6 (1909), p. 55.

observed that there was a general shortage of "Marxist" intellectuals to give lectures in the clubs. Out of necessity, some clubs were turning to the liberal Prokopovich, although "he is barely a Marxist." Soon it will be summer, he concluded, and intellectuals will go to their dachas, forcing the clubs to cease their activity—a situation that workers view with irony.[37]

Relations between workers and their intelligentsia mentors underwent some changes in this period. Fear, exhaustion, disillusionment, and other circumstances led to the withdrawal of former intelligentsia activists from workers' organizations. A Petersburg observer of the labor scene noted in February 1910 that recent widespread arrests had created a more acute shortage of intellectuals than ever before. Other former activists, he asserted, now hesitated to take part in labor organizations because "in their opinion workers are ungrateful swine."[38]

If some intellectuals believed that workers were ungrateful for the assistance they received, workers increasingly felt a need to assert their autonomy from the tutelage of intelligentsia mentors. Alongside complaints that "there are no teachers,"[39] workers also proclaimed that they could take matters into their own hands. Commenting on the newly established network of workers' clubs in the capital, a contributor to *Nadezhda* observed:

Workers have shown an aspiration for learning. They have understood that the need for education, like all the other fundamental necessities of the working class, can be fully satisfied only when the workers *themselves* take matters into their own hands and create *their own* workers' enlightenment institutions, which can provide them with unfalsified spiritual nourishment.[40]

Skilled, educated, and articulate worker-leaders felt capable for the first time of managing their own affairs in clubs, unions, and other legal labor organizations, and they were eager to assert their independence from the intellectuals who had so extensively dominated the labor movement in the years from 1905 to 1907. Nevertheless, try as they might, workers could not operate clubs and educational societies without the assistance of intellectuals who provided lectures, legal services, and access to cultural events. The tension between workers'

---

[37]TsGAOR, DPOO, f. 102, d. 17, 1908, p. 39. Intercepted private correspondence, dated March 13, 1908. Author unidentified.

[38]TsGAOR, DPOO, d. 5, ch. 57, op. 11, 1910, p. 8. Intercepted private correspondence from N. Boitsov, written February 13, 1910.

[39]*Golos portnogo*, no. 6 (March 1, 1911), p. 2.

[40]*Nadezhda*, no. 1 (July 31, 1908), p. 2. The article is entitled "O kul'turno-prosvetitel'noi deiatel'nosti" by V. L. Italics in the original.

aspirations for autonomy and their continuing reliance on intellectuals created a frustrating dilemma for workers and a situation of incipient conflict with their intelligentsia mentors.

Many of the intelligentsia organizers who remained involved in workers' organizations belonged to the ranks of Social Democracy, and there was a close interpenetration of the radical activists and club members and officers. A report prepared by the secret police in 1910 noted that club officers, particularly in district-based cultural societies, were often members of district party groups.[41] "At present," noted the police, "a majority of the members of subdistrict and district [SD party committees] are simultaneously members of the directing boards of clubs and educational societies."[42]

According to police sources, eight out of twenty-one Petersburg clubs and cultural societies were dominated by Social Democrats.[43] The "Enlightenment" Society was the Menshevik club center, whereas Bolshevik influence was strongest in the Vasil'evskii Island club, "Source of Light and Knowledge."[44] Social Democrats in the capital organized an illegal Interclub Commission to coordinate activities in these organizations; they also used the clubs as meeting places for the illegal Central Bureau of Trade Unions.[45] Under the leadership of the Interclub Commission, some clubs assisted in collecting funds for underground organizations.[46]

Frequent arrests had decimated the party underground, and party work was partially carried on under the legal cover of clubs and cultural societies. Party members resorted to various tricks to conduct party business under club auspices. Sometimes meetings of the club board began earlier than was officially announced, and by the time police arrived to keep an eye on the proceedings, party business had already been transacted. At other times the police were bribed or taken off to the buffet.[47]

CONSUMER COOPERATIVES AND PRODUCTION ARTELS

Consumer cooperatives provided another legal outlet for workers' efforts to organize collectively during the Stolypin period. Cooperatives grew very rapidly,

[41]TsGAOR, DPOO, f. 102, d. 17, ch. 57, opis' 11, 1910, p. 1.
[42]Ibid., p. 16b.
[43]TsGAOR, DPOO, f. 102, d. 5, ch. 57, opis' 11, 1910, p. 168.
[44]TsGIA, f. 287, opis' 1, d. 68a, p. 130.
[45]TsGAOR, DPOO, f. 102, d. 5, ch. 57, opis' 11, 1910, p. 16b.
[46]Ibid.
[47]TsGAOR, DPOO, f. 102, d. 17, ch. 57, opis' 11, 1910, p. 1.

and by 1909, 32 cooperatives had been established in Moscow with 17,808 members; 31 cooperatives existed in St. Petersburg.[48] Moscow cooperatives also formed a central coordinating organization, the Union of Consumer Cooperatives, which published its own journal. The great popularity of these organizations led one trade unionist to comment in April 1908: "If we ask ourselves in what domain there exists a more or less broad mass organization, we would have to answer: in the domain of cooperatives."[49]

The first major workers' consumer cooperative, Trudovoi soiuz (Labor Union), was founded in St. Petersburg in 1906 by syndicalists, against the opposition of local Social Democrats.[50] Only after cooperatives began attracting a mass membership did the Social Democrats reconsider their stance toward the cooperative movement. The debate over this issue became intense in the spring of 1907, when the formation of cooperatives gathered momentum.

Social Democrats were deeply divided over the cooperatives. The SD-dominated Organizational Committee, which was preparing draft resolutions for a forthcoming Moscow regional conference of trade unions, endorsed a resolution stating that cooperatives did not offer the workers a solution to their problems and that "for the struggle of the working class against capitalist exploitation, consumer societies cannot compare with trade union organizations of the working class." A minority within the Organizational Committee favored the establishment of workers' cooperatives, however, and called on cooperatives and trade unions to assist each other in their common tasks.[51]

The Moscow Regional Conference of Unions of Commercial Employees, held in April 1907, also debated the question of cooperatives. The Bolshevik intellectual I. I. Skvortsov-Stepanov opposed the creation of cooperatives, while the syndicalist trade unionist Evdokimov supported them. A moderate position was taken by the Moscow Menshevik trade unionist S. A. Regekampf, who became one of the Moscow Okhrana's most valuable informers in 1912. On his suggestion, the conference adopted a resolution declaring that trade unionists

---

[48]TsGAOR, DP IV, d. 121, t. 2, 1908, pp. 242–243, 228–262; *Biulleten'*, no. 9 (1909), p. 4. I have not been able to locate a general membership figure for the capital.

[49]*Professional'nyi vestnik*, no. 21 (April 2, 1908), p. 3.

[50]P. Kolokol'nikov, "Otryvki iz vospominanii," *Materialy po istorii professional'nogo dvizhenie v Rossii (MIPDR)*, 5 vols. (Moscow, 1924–1927), vol. 5, p. 148. On consumer cooperatives that predated this period, see Jeremiah Schneiderman, "The Tsarist Government and the Labor Movement, 1898–1903: The Zubatovshchina," Ph.D. dissertation, University of California, Berkeley, 1966, pp. 202–203; Robert Eugene Johnson, *Peasant and Proletarian* (New Brunswick, N.J., 1979), pp. 186–190.

[51]Iu. K. Milonov, ed., *Moskovskoe professional'noe dvizhenie v gody pervoi revoliutsii* (Moscow, [1925]), pp. 350–351.

should not take the initiative in establishing cooperative organizations but should join existing cooperatives for the purpose of linking them more closely with trade unions and using them in the interests of class struggle.[52]

The Bolshevik-dominated Fifth Congress of the RSDRP in May 1907 debated the issue of cooperatives, and in February 1908 the Central Committee organized a special commission on unions and cooperatives, whose members included the Moscow Bolshevik trade unionist Viktor Nogin and the St. Petersburg Menshevik M. Bragin [M. I. Broido].[53] The commission was assigned the task of coordinating the participation of Social Democrats in publications and conferences organized by trade unions and cooperatives.[54] It showed virtually no activity, however, perhaps because of intraparty conflicts.[55]

One of the most enthusiastic defenders of cooperatives was the Menshevik Bragin. Writing in *Professional'nyi vestnik* in April 1908, he asserted:

The current mass establishment of cooperatives has a notable political significance as one of the organizational forms of the broad strata of the people, as organizations which under the existing conditions can facilitate the growth of the political formation of the masses and the accumulation of concealed political forces; on the other hand, cooperatives in the right circumstances can significantly assist the growth of class struggle in the cities as well as the countryside.[56]

Many Social Democrats did not share Bragin's optimistic assessment of the cooperative movement. Some opponents argued that cooperatives represented a concession to capitalism and should be discouraged; others believed that cooperatives had no significance for the workers' movement at that particular historical juncture.[57]

Like clubs and cultural societies, cooperatives attracted trade unionists into their ranks. The contemporary labor organ, *Nash put'* [Our Path], described them as "conscious and active workers" who had earlier been involved in trade unions that no longer functioned.[58] Police records indicate that the directing boards of

---

[52]Martyn, "Moskovskie professional'nye soiuzy i kooperatsiia," *Professional'nyi vestnik*, no. 20 (April 2, 1908), p. 7.

[53]Kolokol'nikov, "Otryvki," *MIPDR*, 5:137.

[54]TsGAOR, f. 102, d. 5, ch. 84, 1908, p. 75.

[55]Kolokol'nikov, "Otryvki," *MIPDR*, 5:137.

[56]*Professional'nyi vestnik*, no. 20 (April 2, 1908), p. 3.

[57]P. Kolokol'nikov and S. Rapoport, eds., *1905–1907 gg. v professional'nom dvizhenii: I i II Vserossiiskie konferentsii professional'nykh soiuzov* (Moscow, 1925), pp. 712–713.

[58]*Nash put'*, no. 3 (July 25, 1910), p. 3.

cooperatives included workers who had previously been arrested for their participation in union activities.[59]

There were also a number of Social Democrats, Socialist Revolutionaries, and syndicalists active in the cooperative movement. Some of them took part in the First All-Russian Congress of Cooperatives, held in Moscow in April 1908. A leading participant was the trade unionist Roman Malinovskii, a Social Democratic representative from the St. Petersburg cooperative Truzhenik. The future Okhrana agent and Bolshevik Duma Deputy from Moscow made one of his first major public appearances at this congress, where he spoke in opposition to credit selling by cooperatives.[60]

The rise in workers' consumer cooperatives coincided with a proliferation of producers' cooperatives, or artels, based on the principle of collective ownership. Moscow workers in the construction industry were the first to form production artels in order to bypass the contractor by substituting collectively owned contracting organizations. By 1909 sixty-nine artels were functioning in the capital and forty in Moscow,[61] including organizations among tailors, candymakers, furriers, shoemakers, leatherworkers, pianomakers, carpenters, marble workers, engineers, and others.

Trade unionists sometimes became extensively involved in production artels. The board of the Moscow candymakers' union, for example, assumed the leadership of the candymakers' artel.[62] Members of the Moscow tailors' union were involved in the city's tailoring artel.[63] Artels frequently attracted young and idealistic workers, some of whom, such as Timofei Sapronov, later turned to trade unionism. A leading Moscow Social Democratic trade unionist from 1912 on, Sapronov received his first organizational experience in a construction workers' artel during 1910–1911.[64]

Cooperatives—both producers' and consumers'—played an important role

[59]TsGAOR, DP IV, d. 121, t. 2, 1908, pp. 242–243, 259–262.

[60]TsGAOR, f. 6963, opis' 4, d. 110, p. 15; M. S. Balabanov, *Istoriia rabochikh kooperatsii v Rossii (1864–1917)* (Kiev, 1923), p. 155.

[61]TsGAOR, DP IV, d. 121, t. 3, 1908, p. 255; *Professional'nyi vestnik*, no. 25 (August 18, 1909), p. 28; TsGAOR, DP IV, d. 121, t. 2, 1908, pp. 210, 215; *Professional'noe dvizhenie Moskovskikh pishchevikov v gody pervoi revoliutsii*, sbornik 1 (Moscow, 1927), p. 167. On artels of an earlier period, see Johnson, *Peasant and Proletarian*, pp. 91–92.

[62]*Professional'noe dvizhenie Moskovskikh pishchevikov*, p. 167.

[63]TsGAOR, DP IV, d. 121, t. 2, 1910, pp. 128–218.

[64]Sapronov, ed., *Iubileinnyi sbornik*, p. 63; Victoria E. Bonnell, Introduction to T. V. Sapronov, *Iz istorii rabochego dvizheniya (po lichnym vospominaniyam)* (Newtonville, Mass., 1976).

in perpetuating the cultural and educational work formerly conducted by trade unions. They maintained reading rooms, held lectures and excursions and offered their members tickets to cultural events. Thus, in addition to the economic advantages workers may have derived from their membership in these organizations, cooperatives and artels helped to raise the cultural level of the workers who participated in them.

SOCIAL DEMOCRATS AND THE TRADE UNIONS

The unions that survived the repression of the Stolypin years often had close ties with radical political parties. Eighteen of twenty-five Petersburg unions surveyed by the secret police in 1909 were said to be under Social Democratic influence, including those of the printers, metalworkers, bakers, gold- and silversmiths, tailors, salesclerks, shoemakers, and wood, construction, leather, and tobacco workers. Socialist Revolutionaries predominated in only seven unions: cabmen, candymakers, watchmakers, wallpaper workers, blacksmiths, lithographers, and textile workers.[65] A similar though less extensive pattern of SD influence over the unions was reported by the Moscow secret police, which claimed that one-third of the Moscow unions were under SD influence in November 1909.[66]

The intelligentsia-dominated Central Bureaus of Trade Unions, moreover, were almost exclusively controlled by Social Democrats. From April 1907 until his arrest in June 1908, Petr Smidovich, a Bolshevik, directed the Moscow Central Bureau. Following his arrest, the Bureau was taken over by two Menshevik students who carried on agitation in the spirit of Menshevik resolutions aimed, according to the police, at "the creation of nonparty and fully legal trade unions."[67] The Petersburg Central Bureau of Trade Unions was continuously dominated by Mensheviks throughout these years. The core group in the Central Bureau, arrested in January 1910, consisted of Kolokol'nikov, A. I. Ginzburg, B. I. Magidov, N. I. Andreev, and S. I. Kanatchikov.[68] Apart from the Bolshevik worker Kanatchikov, they all belonged to the Menshevik intelligentsia. In late

[65]TsGAOR, f. 111, opis' 5, d. 263, 1909, pp. 121-122.

[66]TsGAOR, DPOO, f. 102, d. 5, ch. 57, opis' 11, 1910, p. 46.

[67]TsGAOR, f. 6963, opis' 4, d. 110, p. 12. This report from the Moscow Okhrana is dated December 31, 1908.

[68]TsGAOR, f. 102, d. 5, ch. 57, opis' 11, 1910, p. 1.

1909 two Socialist Revolutionaries joined the capital's Central Bureau, which until then had been composed exclusively of Social Democrats.[69]

Bolsheviks, particularly in Moscow, had begun to take an energetic role in trade unions by early 1907. Largely through the efforts of Nogin, the faction increased its support in the city's union movement and dominated the Moscow Central Bureau of Trade Unions. In the immediate aftermath of the Stolypin "coup d'état," Nogin and other Moscow Bolsheviks misjudged the seriousness of the mounting government attack on the labor movement.

At the Second Regional Conference of Textile Workers' Unions in the Central Industrial Region in mid-June 1907, the Bolsheviks—who had a strong base of support in the Moscow textile workers' union—agitated for a general strike in the textile industry.[70] Despite growing evidence to the contrary, the Bolsheviks insisted that the revolutionary energy of the masses remained intact and that a catalyst, such as the proposed economic strike, would unleash the suppressed political opposition of the entire proletariat and restore the momentum of the revolution. Few textile workers even responded to the strike appeal, however, and only one small Moscow factory joined the strike. At the giant Prokhorovskaia Trekhgornaia mill, the management dissuaded workers from joining the strike by making a timely offer of a small wage increase.[71]

The strike called by Bolshevik-led textile unions proved a complete failure, and had disastrous consequences for the trade union movement of textile workers in the region. In Moscow, the police closed all three registered textile unions on July 24, 1907, in retribution for their participation in the strike.[72] Of the three, only the union of textile workers attempted to continue its activities illegally. But by September 1907 its membership had dropped from 1,500 to a mere 200 dues-paying members. A similar fate overtook other unions in this industry. Whereas 30,000 textile workers in the Moscow region were union members in the spring of 1907, only 5,000 or 6,000 remained by September 1907.[73]

---

[69]Ibid, p. 46.

[70]M. Zaiats, *Tekstili v gody revoliutsii (1905–1907 gg.)* (Moscow, 1925), pp. 72, 200. Other leading Bolsheviks at the conference included Terentii [Markovin], assigned by the Moscow Committee to work in textile unions; A. V. Shestakov, associated with the regional party committee; and K. D. Gandurin, a leading Bolshevik in the Ivanovo-Voznesensk party organization.

[71]Zaiats, *Tekstili*, p. 229.

[72]Milonov, ed., *Moskovskoe professional'noe dvizhenie*, p. 375.

[73]*Professional'nyi vestnik*, no. 20 (April 2, 1908), p. 9.

The dramatic failure of the textile strike, together with intensified persecution of the unions, prompted the Bolsheviks to undertake a review of their policies toward the labor movement. Meeting soon after the disastrous textile workers' strike, the Bolshevik-dominated Moscow Regional Conference of the RSDRP endorsed a resolution advocating the creation of illegal labor unions. The conference resolution noted the dim prospects for sustaining legal trade unions in the growing atmosphere of repression but disapproved of rechanneling trade union activities into other legal organizations, such as mutual aid societies:

Utilization of legal opportunities by organizing mutual aid societies and so forth not only does not satisfy to any degree this need [for organizations that would provide leadership for the economic struggle], but would lead to a degradation of the workers' movement, facilitating the development in the masses of a narrow corporate spirit and protecting the interests of the most prosperous stratum of the proletariat.[74]

The resolution recommended, instead, the creation of illegal underground trade unions.

The conference directives on illegal trade unionism did not receive unanimous approval, even within Bolshevik ranks. In the summer of 1907, Lenin was still advocating the full utilization of legal opportunities, including the mutual aid societies contemptuously dismissed by some Moscow party workers. There is evidence that he disapproved of the Moscow resolution, as did Nogin.[75]

During the summer and fall of 1907 a number of Moscow unions, recently liquidated by the police, attempted to carry on their activities illegally. But these illegal unions soon declined under the pressure of police harassment, and labor leaders began to have second thoughts about this strategy for the union movement. The leadership of the Moscow metalworkers' union, for example, made a sharp reversal in its assessment of the situation:

Following the second closing of the union of metalworkers, the directing board opposed all efforts again to obtain legalization. Union delegates supported this position at the regional meeting of metalworkers. Five months of illegal existence, which led to the almost complete disintegration of the organization, convinced members of the board of the incorrectness of the position they had taken, and at one of their last meetings they unanimously resolved to utilize all the possibilities of legal existence. In attempting to implement this decision they clashed with prejudices against legalization which became

[74]Kolokol'nikov, "Otryvki," *MIPDR*, 5:138.
[75]Kolokol'nikov and Rapoport, eds., *1905-1907 gg.*, p. 716; V. Nogin, "1906-1907 gg.," *Vestnik truda*, no. 3 (March 1924), pp. 233-235.

open opposition. But the board nevertheless intends to proceed along the path of legalization.[76]

Many trade unionists disavowed the policy of illegality. *Chelnok* [Shuttle], the newspaper of the Petersburg textile workers' union, commented in September 1907 that "to give up our belief [in legal trade unionism] and to start wandering in the slums of the underground would be absolutely foolish. This is a tactic for the fainthearted, and under no circumstances should we resort to it."[77] In a similar vein, an editorial in *Portnoi* [Tailor], the newspaper of the Petersburg tailors' union, observed in March 1908 that unions which thought they could continue to function illegally had come to see that they could not. "Unions need a broad open life," the editorial asserted; "they need conditions of political freedom." The Moscow union of tailors had attempted to exist illegally, it noted, but by November 1907 the union treasury was empty. The Petersburg union was unable to register for an entire year, and during that period of illegality it lost three-quarters of its members.[78] The Moscow union newspaper *Professional'nyi vestnik* [Union Herald] commented in April 1908 that unions attempting to exist illegally had ended in complete failure, including those of Moscow metal-workers, textile workers, printers, tailors, and others.[79]

Whereas the Menshevik *praktiki* in both cities remained committed to a legal trade union movement, the Bolsheviks continued to equivocate over the issue of legal workers' organizations. In the spring of 1908 Lenin revived the notion of party cells originally proposed by M. Borisov in October 1905.[80] The idea was for party activists to create Bolshevik groups within legal trade unions for the purpose of maximizing party influence and control over these organizations. At about the same time, the Bolshevik Regional Bureau in the Central Industrial Region notified party workers that they should attempt to strengthen Bolshevik influence in legal associations, particularly trade unions.[81]

These proposals had little practical effect, however, because Bolshevik party organizers harbored strong reservations about legal organizations, preferring

[76]*Professional'nyi vestnik*, no. 16 (November 29, 1907), p. 11.

[77]*Chelnok*, no. 1 (September 25, 1907), p. 2.

[78]*Portnoi*, no. 1–2 (March 12, 1908), p. 1.

[79]*Professional'nyi vestnik*, no. 20 (April 2, 1908), p. 9.

[80]V. I. Lenin, *Sochineniia*, 3rd ed., 30 vols. (Moscow, 1928–1937), vol. 12, p. 140. Lenin's article appeared in *Proletarii* on March 4, 1908. On Borisov's proposal, see *Proletarii*, October 4, 1905.

[81]TsGAOR, DPOO, f. 102, opis' 5, d. 1000, ch. 14, t. 3, 1905, pp. 3–4.

instead to devote their attention to underground work. Nogin has described Bolshevik attitudes toward legal trade unionism in this period:

Many of our comrades had a skeptical attitude toward trade unions, pointing out that the trade union movement is opportunistic and that we should have nothing to do with it. This was the point of view of the late comrade Shantser, and of Stanislav Vol'skii—a view shared by those who later became "recallists" *(otzovisty).*[82]

The dominant ethos in Bolshevik party circles, relegating those who engaged in legal activity to the ranks of "traitors and betrayers,"[83] was scarcely conducive to participation in the legal trade union movement. Most Bolsheviks withdrew from the unions and from other legal organizations, such as clubs and cultural societies. According to Bulkin, there were only two Bolshevik leaders active in the capital's legal labor organizations in 1909: Kanatchikov and Malinovskii.[84]

In mid-1909 Lenin summoned his followers to resume legal work:

Generally speaking, there must now be talk not only about what precise place "legal opportunities" occupy alongside other branches of party work, but about *how* to utilize available "legal opportunities" for the greatest benefit of the party. In the course of long years of underground work the party accumulated enormous experience concerning illegal work. The same cannot be said about another area—about the utilization of legal opportunities. Here the party, *in particular the Bolsheviks,* has not done enough. Utilization of this area requires that more attention, initiative and strength be applied than has been done up to this time. The utilization of legal opportunities must *teach* and teach as persistently as we learned from and are learning by means of illegal activity.[85]

Lenin's pronouncement brought Bolsheviks in both cities back into the legal trade union movement.[86] The "new Leninists," as one contemporary called them, were mostly young propagandists who reintroduced factional struggles into the trade unions and workers' clubs. They read party documents at meetings of union boards, alienating workers who feared that such actions would lead to government reprisals.[87] But if some Bolsheviks returned to legal organizations, there remained considerable opposition among Bolshevik *praktiki* to the new

[82]Nogin, "1906–1907 gg.," p. 235. On the *otzovisty,* see n. 26 above.

[83]Kolokol'nikov and Rapoport, eds., *1905-1907 gg.,* p. 716.

[84]Bulkin, *Na zare,* p. 419.

[85]"Izveshchenie o soveshchenii rasshirennoi redaktskii 'Proletariia,' " Lenin, *Sochineniia,* 14:95. Italics in the original.

[86]TsGAOR, DPOO, d. 5, ch. 57, opis' 11, 1910, p. 120.

[87]Ibid.

party directives, and it was not until after the Prague Conference in early 1912 that party workers launched a full-scale effort to enter legal labor associations and wrest control of them from the Mensheviks and to a lesser degree the Socialist Revolutionaries, who had been active in these organizations for the preceding half-decade.

Lenin's pronouncements on legal activity in mid-1909 followed by only a few months the first official Bolshevik attack on "liquidationism." This pejorative term, first used officially at the Fifth All-Russian Conference (Bolshevik) of the RSDRP in Paris in December 1908,[88] referred to the alleged Menshevik tendency to concentrate on legal activity at the expense of the party underground. As time went on, Lenin's use of the term acquired even broader meaning, and he accused the Mensheviks of "economism" and an abdication of revolutionary goals.[89]

The point of view known as "liquidationism" actually began as a "legalistic tendency"[90] among labor activists, who responded to the repressive Stolypin era by stressing the importance of preserving the few remaining opportunities for open, mass-based organizations. The preoccupation with legality was widespread among union leaders in this period, and it generated a highly circumspect attitude toward union activities. As the leadership of the Petersburg textile workers' union put it in September 1909, "It is necessary to observe caution in all kinds of trivial details so as to avoid accidentally providing a justification for the closing of the union, the arrest of its officers and members."[91]

By 1910, the legalist perspective had developed into a more comprehensive position. The "liquidators" now called for the abandonment of all underground party work and its replacement with activity in legal organizations, such as trade unions, clubs and schools, evening courses, and cooperatives.[92] In contrast to Lenin's allegations, however, the prononents of this approach represented a distinct minority within Menshevik ranks. But their visibility was enhanced by their prominent position in key unions and by the fact that a number of them were leading worker-activists. "Liquidators" were concentrated, above all, in the leadership of the large and influential Petersburg metalworkers' union, where they retained control until the spring of 1913. Their approach made them wary

[88]Abraham Ascher, *Pavel Axelrod and the Development of Menshevism* (Cambridge, Mass., 1972), pp. 277–278.

[89]Ibid.

[90]Bulkin, *Na zare*, p. 416.

[91]*Fabrichnyi stanok*, no. 5 (September 18, 1908), p. 6.

[92]TsGAOR, f. 102, d. 5, opis' 11, 1910, p. 107; Bulkin, *Na zare*, pp. 417ff.

of strikes that might jeopardize the union's legal status, and they concentrated their efforts instead on organizational matters, mutual aid programs, and institutionalized methods of resolving industrial disputes.

A meeting of Social Democratic activists—most of them Mensheviks—in St. Petersburg in September 1910 brought out sharply the division between the "liquidator" minority (no more than five or six out of sixty participants in the meeting supported this view) and the much larger contingent of Menshevik activists. The majority at the meeting called upon party cadres to "shift the center of gravity of all work" with the masses to legal organizations. At the same time, they resolved that "illegal organizations must be created consisting of only senior [party] workers who are experienced and have passed through the political school." Scattered in different unions and other organizations, these cadres should use the illegal party network to "retain their solidarity" and to act "according to an established plan."[93]

This position, combining legal and illegal forms of activity, characterized the mainstream of Menshevik thought.[94] While emphasizing the primacy of legal activity, these Mensheviks hoped to keep alive the party underground, utilizing it to direct the workers' movement. They attempted to tread a delicate line between the two forms of activity, stressing the virtues of legal, open, mass-based organizations on the one hand without relinquishing the illegal conspiratorial aspects of party work on the other. It is, of course, difficult to know how this and the "liquidationist" position were perceived by rank-and-file workers who participated in legal labor organizations. In practice—as opposed to theory—it must have been difficult for many of them to distinguish between the two Menshevik groups, both of whom advocated a cautious and legal policy to preserve and expand trade unions in the face of considerable adversity.

UNION ACTIVITIES IN THE STOLYPIN YEARS

The conditions facing trade unionists in this period led them to concentrate much of their energy and resources on sustaining their organizations. The largest

[93]TsGAOR, f. 102, d. 5, opis' 11, 1910, p. 107. This statement is taken from a police report of the meeting; its accuracy as a description of the Menshevik position is confirmed by Bulkin, *Na zare*, p. 420.

[94]Ascher, *Pavel Axelrod*, p. 279. See the formulation of this position by F. Dan in *Golos sotsialdemokrata*, 3, no. 19–20 (January-February 1910).

single expenditure in virtually all unions was for basic organizational needs, including the rental of union headquarters and meeting halls and the retention of a paid secretary. These expenditures generally consumed 60 percent or more of union funds.[95]

Mutual aid programs and services represented the second largest expenditure. In this period of widespread unemployment, most unions sought to provide some kind of unemployment benefits, however meagre and insufficient to meet the pressing situation. Union-sponsored mutual aid programs sometimes included assistance in the event of illness as well as unemployment, and there were modest outlays to support the occasional striking workers. Unions also continued their earlier efforts to offer legal and medical services. But on the whole, these material benefits remained very restricted in the years from mid-1907 to 1912. Membership in the unions declined precipitously, and members were frequently delinquent in monthly dues payments. Consequently, union budgets that had once reached thousands of rubles could now be counted in the hundreds. Few unions had a monthly income exceeding 200 rubles.[96]

Union-sponsored cultural and educational activities grew in importance during this period. Many unions maintained libraries, and some organized evening courses for workers.[97] Unable to obtain official permission to hold lectures, they collaborated with the clubs and cultural societies that appeared in these years. As in 1906 and early 1907, workers remained highly receptive to union-sponsored educational and cultural events, and there were complaints that some unions did not do enough in this area.[98]

The inability of unions to provide assistance and services discouraged workers from joining these organizations or maintaining regular dues payments, a situation that, in turn, further reduced union funds and the unions' capacity to sponsor various types of mutual aid. The resulting dilemma was described by the Moscow trade union newspaper, *Nash put'* [Our Path] in May 1910:

Many workers do not enter the unions, on the grounds that unions give nothing, that they don't provide help for their members in time of need. Membership dues are so small

[95]A survey of eight major Moscow unions in 1908–1909 disclosed that they spent 63.8 percent of their budget on organizational matters in 1908 and 68.6 percent in 1909. *Vestnik truda,* no. 1 (November 28, 1909), p. 6; Sher, *Istoriia,* p. 428; *Vestnik portnykh,* no. 1 (1911), p. 8.

[96]*Golos portnogo,* no. 6 (March 1, 1911), p. 2.

[97]Kanatchikov, "Kul'turno-prosvetitel'naia deiatel'nost'," *Vozrozhdenie,* no. 5–6 (1909), pp. 50–53.

[98]*Nash put',* no. 1 (May 30, 1910), p. 6. This complaint was made by members of the Moscow textile workers' union.

that it is impossible even to think about giving proper planned assistance. A vicious circle is the result. Workers don't join the unions, because unions give them nothing. Unions are unable to give anything because so few workers join the unions and, therefore, pay little into the union treasury.[99]

Unions also withdrew from labor-management disputes. After a number of unsuccessful strikes in the second half of 1907, the strike movement subsided, not to revive again until 1910. Throughout the Stolypin period, workers were in a weak position in industrial disputes. Employer associations remained intact, but labor unions suffered a sharp decline. Taking advantage of the disorganization of labor and the widespread unemployment, employers retracted concessions made in the preceding two and a half years. Thus, a mere two or three hours after it became known that the Petersburg printers' union would be closed by the police in mid-October 1907, the employers' association broke off negotiations that had been under way for several months over an industry-wide contract.[100] Soon afterwards, printing firm owners began to rescind many of the improvements earlier granted to workers.

There were only fourteen strikes in the entire Petersburg metalworking industry during 1908–1909. The union took an active part in nine of these strikes. Nearly all were defensive in character, arising in response to the withdrawal of concessions made during the preceding years. Only one of the fourteen conflicts ended with the full satisfaction of workers' demands; five others yielded partial satisfaction, and eight ended in total defeat.[101]

In labor-management disputes, union efforts to assist workers were hampered not only by employer resistance and union weakness, but also by severe government persecution and the fear of losing legal status. The situation in the Petersburg printing industry was typical in this respect. In late 1910, fifty workers at the Kan printing firm elected delegates on the shop level and approached the union for assistance.[102] The union board allocated strike funds and helped the workers to formulate their demands, which included an eight-hour workday, abolition of overtime work, polite treatment, recognition of workers' representatives elected at the shop level, and improvements in workplace conditions. When the employer refused to accept all of the workers' terms, the union

[99]Ibid., p. 2.

[100]*Trud pechatnika*, no. 1 (October 27, 1907), p. 2.

[101]Bulkin, *Na zare*, p. 392.

[102]The following account is drawn from secret police reports. TsGAOR, DP IV, d. 119, ch. 43, 1908, pp. 9–13; f. 6935, opis' 4, d. 97, pp. 2, 9.

called a strike. Unlike most factory owners, this one did not fight the union but agreed to negotiate a settlement.[103] After the settlement was reached, however, the owner asked the police to arrest the union agitators at the firm. On December 14, 1910, the police closed the union and rescinded its legal status. At the time of its closing the union had 5,666 members.

Following notification of its closure, the Petersburg printers' union contacted members of the Social Democratic faction in the Third State Duma, which called for an immediate inquiry.[104] Although the inquiry does not appear to have taken place, the incident was one of a number of instances in which trade unionists sought the assistance of workers' deputies in exposing government harassment and persecution. In April 1909, for example, thirty-one Duma deputies signed a declaration protesting the government's suppression of trade unions and its restrictions on their activities.[105]

Union efforts to make use of legal channels for redress—both at the workplace and in the society at large—was one of the notable features of this period. In 1908, three of the largest Petersburg unions—metalworkers, textile workers and woodworkers—coordinated a campaign to gain employer cooperation in establishing conciliation boards to settle disputes over workers' insurance claims arising on the basis of the insurance law of June 2, 1903.[106] The three unions jointly drafted a letter to 180 employers and seven insurance companies in St. Petersburg, urging them to institute conciliation boards for this purpose.

Only four employers responded to the unions' letter. Two agreed to establish conciliation boards, and two others refused. The workers' indignation at the outcome of the project was expressed by the newspaper of the Petersburg textile workers' union, *Stanok* [Loom]:

It was not long ago that factory owners bitterly complained that the Russian worker recognized only brute force, only the strike, the riot [*bunt*], physical destruction. Not long ago, they pointed out to us the example of foreign workers who settle many issues by peaceful means, through negotiations. Indeed, the ink has not yet dried with which they wrote about their unflagging intention "to accommodate the interests of the workers" and "to resolve by peaceful means the legitimate needs of the workers." In the Society of Factory Owners, during a discussion of this question, the following conclusion was

---

[103]Collective contracts were occasionally concluded with individual employers. See *Golos portnogo*, no. 3 (May 10, 1910), p. 11; Bulkin, *Na zare*, p. 295.

[104]*Golos portnogo*, no. 5 (December 22, 1910), p. 10.

[105]TsGIA, f. 1405, opis' 539, d. 509, pp. 1–3; TsGAOR, DP IV, d. 236, 1908, pp. 19ff.

[106]*Rabochee dvizhenie: Biulleten'*, no. 7 (1908), p. 6; *Professional'nyi vestnik*, no. 20 (April 2, 1908), p. 5; *Stanok*, no. 1 (February 14, 1908), p. 16, and no. 2 (March 11, 1908), p. 7.

reached: conciliation boards are not needed, because a decent worker always settles matters peacefully and only the scoundrels drag their cases into litigation. Well, well, gentlemen! Is it for you to talk about decency?![107]

The newspaper concluded that employers rejected the unions' proposal because "up to now [employers] have not recognized the unions and do not want to recognize them." Consequently, trade unionists were "forced to waste a lot of effort and strength and make many sacrifices to gain recognition of their organizations."[108]

Earlier efforts to establish factory and shop representatives also continued during the Stolypin period. Such committees as existed in 1905–1907 were usually disbanded in late 1907 and early 1908. This prompted trade unionists to resurrect the 1903 law on factory elders—a law they had earlier repudiated because of its restrictive provisions. Now, however, even the 1903 law became desirable as a means of preserving some kind of organizational network on the factory level, and a number of unions advocated its implementation. But employers refused to cooperate, and the campaign failed.[109]

In late 1911 the Petersburg metalworkers' union again attempted to utilize the law on factory elders. A union resolution adopted in December called on members to participate in the elections for elders and to vote only for union members.[110] This resolution provided the basis for a campaign conducted in the first half of 1912 to reintroduce factory elders into metalworking plants and to use them as a base for trade union activities.

<hr />

The organized labor movement suffered a severe setback after June 1907, when the relatively tolerant political atmosphere gave way to harsh government repression. Employers hastened to take advantage of the situation and to withdraw many of their earlier concessions. Prior to 1910, widespread unemployment further exacerbated the difficulties faced by the still young and vulnerable trade unions. Within one year of the Stolypin "coup d'état," the Petersburg and Moscow union movements had been sharply curtailed.

The precipitous decline of most trade unions did not, however, extinguish the aspiration for collective association. There remained a small but dedicated group of worker-activists in St. Petersburg and Moscow that carried on union affairs

---

[107]*Stanok*, no. 2 (March 11, 1908), pp. 7–8.
[108]Ibid.
[109]*Rabochee dvizhenie: Biulleten'*, no. 6 (December 1907-January 1908), p. 5.
[110]*Metallist*, no. 7 (December 30, 1911), p. 9.

despite the very considerable difficulties and risks this entailed. Some workers attempted to utilize other channels for legal organization, turning their attention to clubs and educational societies, consumer cooperatives, and production artels. These organizations, operating mainly under legal auspices, attracted workers eager for material and cultural improvement.

A working-class leadership emerged during these years, replacing to a considerable extent the intelligentsia activists who had earlier helped to lead many of the unions and other workers' organizations. The new generation of working-class leaders, drawn from the ranks of skilled and experienced workers, emphasized independence, self-reliance, and self-help. Following a brief experiment with illegal unions—centered mainly in Moscow—these labor leaders adopted a cautious approach to labor problems. And significantly, some of them—particularly in St. Petersburg—subscribed to the legalist and gradualist position that contemporaries called "liquidationism."

Despite the moderation shown by many union activists during the Stolypin years, ties between legal labor associations and the Social Democratic party grew closer than ever before. The Bolsheviks, as we have seen, withdrew from the organized labor movement after a brief and unsuccessful effort to establish illegal party-affiliated unions, and they did not return to the legal labor movement until the winter of 1909–1910. Even then, most Bolsheviks remained ambivalent and unenthusiastic about legal forms of activity. Consequently, the Mensheviks had a clear field in these organizations, encountering only slight competition from Socialist Revolutionaries, syndicalists, and the liberal Kadets. The Stolypin era marked the highpoint of Menshevik influence among organized workers.

Most Menshevik *praktiki* did not endorse the "liquidationist" position, calling instead for a combination of legal and illegal methods of struggle. Nevertheless, the Mensheviks conveyed to workers the importance of building an open, mass labor movement in Russia, a task that could only be accomplished by legal means. They urged workers to bide their time in the beleaguered trade unions and other legal labor organizations until conditions improved. A small core of committed workers accepted this view, but when the long-expected revival finally took place, it produced consequences few of them had expected.

Part Four

Organized Labor on the Eve of the First World War

Chapter 9

The Revival of the Organized Labor Movement, 1912–1914

> If a persecution is badly managed, tardily undertaken,
> laxly and falteringly applied, it almost always helps to
> further the triumph of a doctrine; whereas a pitiless and
> energetic persecution, which strikes at the opposing
> doctrine the moment it shows its head, is the very best
> tool for combatting it.
>
> *Gaetano Mosca,* The Ruling Class[1]

Even before the Lena massacre disrupted the country's fragile equilibrium in April 1912, a new era of social and political instability had begun. Toward the end of 1909, economic growth resumed after nearly a decade of stagnation. Expansion of the industrial economy first made itself felt in the consumer sector and then spread to heavy and capital goods industries. In both St. Petersburg and Moscow, this economic revival brought increased employment opportunities, and during the next several years, tens of thousands of workers joined the labor force.

Economic expansion and labor militance went hand in hand. When jobs were scarce and unemployment widespread, workers were reluctant to risk their jobs for the chance of some improvement in wages, hours, or working conditions. With an expanding labor market, however, workers once again began to demand redress of their grievances. Artisans, construction workers, and printers were among the first to feel the effects of the economic upturn, and they revived

[1]Gaetano Mosca, *The Ruling Class*, trans. Hannah D. Kahn (New York, 1939), p. 191.

the strike movement in 1910–1911, followed by textile and metalworkers.[2] The number of participants in strikes waged over economic demands more than doubled in 1911, compared with the preceding year.[3] For the most part, these strikes were offensive rather than defensive, as workers attempted to retrieve some of the improvements won in 1905–1907 and relinquished during the Stolypin years.[4] In 1911 workers won complete or partial victory in about half the strikes involving economic demands,[5] and these successes created an optimistic and militant mood on the eve of the Lena massacre.

Workers were not alone in showing new boldness and determination during these months. In educated urban Russian society, as well, there were signs of impatience with the autocratic policies forged by Prime Minister Stolypin, the architect of repression and rural reform.[6] An increasingly open and articulate opposition to the government was emerging among diverse groups that attempted to reclaim the rights granted by the October Manifesto of 1905 but retracted during the Stolypin years.

Following Stolypin's assassination in September 1911, government policy took a new turn. Faced with demands for reform and plagued by internal tensions and uncertainty, the authorities took the first hesitant steps toward relaxing their rigid controls and permitting greater freedom for autonomous social action. The event that accelerated this shift in official policy was the Lena massacre.

On April 4, 1912, workers peacefully assembled at the Lena gold mines in Siberia to present their demands to the mine authorities. Unexpectedly, soldiers opened fire on the petitioners, killing and wounding hundreds of workers.[7] News of the incident spread rapidly to European Russia, where workers responded with massive strikes and demonstrations on a scale reminiscent of the

---

[2] M. S. Balabanov, *Ot 1905 k 1917 godu: Massovoe rabochee dvizhenie* (Moscow and Leningrad, 1927), pp. 132–133, 143.

[3] The data are for the country as a whole. G. A. Arutiunov, *Rabochee dvizhenie v Rossii v periode novogo revoliutsionnogo pod"ema 1910–1914 gg.* (Moscow, 1975), p. 381.

[4] M. Balabanov, *Rabochee dvizhenie v Rossii v gody pod"ema 1912–1914 gg.* (Leningrad, 1927), pp. 19, 46.

[5] Balabanov, *Rabochee dvizhenie*, pp. 14, 46; Balabanov, *Ot 1905*, p. 193; Arutiunov, *Rabochee dvizhenie*, p. 382.

[6] Leopold Haimson, "The Problem of Social Stability in Urban Russia, 1905–1917," *Slavic Review*, pt. 1, 23, no. 4 (December 1964); pt. 2, 24, no. 1 (March 1965); V. Ia. Laverychev, *Tsarizm i rabochii vopros v Rossii (1861–1917 gg.)* (Moscow, 1972), chap. 5; V. Ia. Laverychev, *Po tu storonu barrikad (Iz istorii bor'by moskovskoi burzhuazii s revoliutsiei)* (Moscow, 1967), pp. 96–108.

[7] Balabanov, *Ot 1905*, pp. 165 ff.

1905 revolution. In the month following the Lena massacre, twice as many Russian workers participated in strikes as in the preceding four years combined.[8]

In St. Petersburg, 140,000 workers joined protest demonstrations.[9] The reaction was similar in Moscow, where more than 57,000 workers participated in strikes and demonstrations protesting the massacre during the last week of April alone.[10] Metal and printing workers predominated among the strikers in both cities, but many artisans and workers in communications, transportation, and sales-clerical occupations also joined the protests. Soon afterward, the annual May Day celebration, an event which had elicited only sporadic and small-scale observance during the previous four years, brought hundreds of thousands of workers into the streets of St. Petersburg and Moscow.[11] Under the impact of these events the strike movement over workplace demands acquired new momentum.[12]

With the acceleration of industrial conflicts during the second half of 1912, workers and employers found themselves on very unequal footing. Trade unions had been decimated during the Stolypin years, and only a handful of unions in each city survived the half-decade of harsh governmental policies toward labor. Employers, on the other hand, had continued to build their organizations throughout the Stolypin period. Even in the face of a strong resurgent strike movement, they were now able to mount coordinated and effective opposition. As the Moscow Society of Factory Owners observed:

The success of employers [during 1912] is due more than anything to their organizations, which step by step conducted the struggle with the workers' excessive demands. In all the most important industrial centers the onslaught of workers was met by the calm organized force of industrialists and was broken by force.[13]

Confronted by the formidable resistance of employer associations, workers attempted to revive their own collective organizations. Eight months after the

---

[8]Laverychev, *Po tu storonu*, p. 83.

[9]*Istoriia rabochikh Leningrada*, vol. 1 (Leningrad, 1972), p. 425. These protests occurred between April 14–22, 1912.

[10]Tsentral'nyi gosudarstvennyi arkhiv Oktiabr'skoi revoliutsii (TsGAOR), DP IV, f. 102, d. 4, ch. 2, opis' 121 (1912), pp. 12–16, 18, 20, 25.

[11]In St. Petersburg alone there were 200,000 demonstrators on May Day in 1912. *Istoriia rabochikh Leningrada*, p. 425. In Moscow, there were 38,000 May Day demonstrators. Balabanov, *Ot 1905*, p. 178. The participants in both cities included not only factory workers but artisanal and construction workers as well. Ibid.

[12]*Rabochee dvizhenie: Biulleten'*, no. 17 (1913), p. 7.

[13]Ibid., p. 15.

Lena massacre, in December 1912, a secret agent of the Moscow Okhrana who was active in labor circles reported that "in 1912 a significant revival in the sphere of 'legal opportunities' can be observed. Of the unions which ceased to exist, some are opening again and others are beginning to be strengthened by a new influx of members." He identified fifteen unions in Moscow, five recently established and the rest dating back to earlier years.[14]

By mid-1914 thirty-five different groups in Moscow were unionized. All but four of these unions had legal status; the metalworkers were forced to reregister their union following a loss of legal standing. The combined nominal membership in seventeen of these unions for which data are available was 16,434.[15] Compared with 1906–1907, when seventy-five separate unions existed in Moscow with a combined peak nominal membership of more than 52,000, the prewar unions in this city made a weak recovery.

The situation in St. Petersburg was scarcely better. Between April 1912 and July 1914, twenty-nine legal unions were active in this city, six of them cases of reregistration by groups that had lost their legal status. In addition, another fourteen unions either had been denied or had lost registration, or else were in the process of formation when the war intervened. A total of thirty-seven different groups unionized in the capital (including both legal and illegal unions, but excluding repeat registrations). Membership data are available for twenty of these unions, which attracted a combined peak nominal membership of 28,629 workers. In 1906–1907, by contrast, Petersburg workers had formed seventy-six different unions with a combined peak nominal membership of more than 55,000.

The feeble resurgence of trade unionism in Russia's two major cities was indicative of trends in the rest of the country. The data are incomplete, but it appears that there may have been as few as 63 unions functioning in Russia at the beginning of 1912. The number had increased to 188 by December 1913; 73 of these unions had a dues-paying membership of 34,266.[16] Nominal membership was, of course, considerably higher. But this was a poor showing compared with

[14]TsGAOR, DPOO, f. 102, d. 17, ch. 46, L. B. (1912), p. 14.

[15]For a complete list of unions in 1912–1914, see Appendix V. V. Sher, writing in early 1914, noted the existence of thirteen functioning unions in Moscow with 9,584 members. V. Sh-r [Sher], "Nashe professional'noe dvizhenie za dva poslednykh goda," *Bor'ba*, no. 1 (February 22, 1914), p. 22. Sher relied on information from the workers' press, but my own survey of this source turned up many more unions that at one time or another were active in the prewar period.

[16]Balabanov, *Rabochee dvizhenie*, pp. 50–51. Somewhat different figures can be found in Sher, "Nashe professional'noe dvizhenie," *Bor'ba*, no. 1, p. 21.

1906–1907, when more than 300,000 workers joined trade unions in the country as a whole.

The recruitment record of individual unions in St. Petersburg and Moscow during the prewar years further illustrates the difficulties that unions encountered in restoring a strong membership base. Metalworkers, printers, bakers, and textile workers in the capital formed unions with the largest aggregate membership in the prewar years, just as they had during the earlier period. Compared with 1906–1907, however, only the union of metalworkers retained a substantial following. With the exception of the workers in leather and cardboard factories, all other large Petersburg unions (five hundred or more nominal members) failed to reach their former recruitment levels. The printers' union, once a large and flourishing organization, attracted only one-third the membership of its predecessor in 1906–1907 (table 35).

The picture in Moscow was much the same. Here, the unions of printers, tailors, metalworkers, and bakers ranked as the four largest organizations in 1912–1914. But all four had suffered a substantial drop in recruitment compared with 1906–1907, and the printers' union drew only one-half the membership of the earlier period. Whereas the metalworkers' union in the capital attracted about the same number of members as in 1906–1907, its Moscow counterpart declined by 59 percent. Among the largest Moscow unions, only the cooks showed an aggregate increase in membership over the earlier period (table 35).

Fewer than 50 percent of the nominal union members regularly paid dues in 1912–1914, and sometimes the percentage fell as low as 30–40 percent, as in the case of the Petersburg union of salesclerks.[17] Unions excluded delinquent dues-payers after a fixed period of nonpayment (usually three months), and this created a frequent turnover in union membership. The Petersburg bakers' union, for example, excluded 350 members out of 1,200 for nonpayment in the fall of 1913.[18] But prewar figures for nonpayment of dues were not appreciably higher than those in the Stolypin period, and in some instances they were lower. In the Moscow tailors' union 52 percent of the membership was excluded for nonpayment in 1908, 44 percent in 1909, 39 percent in 1910, and 33 percent in 1913.[19]

---

[17]*Pravda*, no. 63 (207) (March 16, 1913), p. 4. Similar evidence can be found concerning other unions. On the Petersburg printers' union, see *Novoe pechatnoe delo*, no. 4 (April 11, 1913), p. 8; on Petersburg leatherworkers, see *Zhizn' kozhevnika*, no. 1 (May 1914), p. 7; on Petersburg textile workers, see *Severnaia pravda*, no. 30 (September 16, 1913), p. 3.

[18]*Pravda truda*, no. 20 (October 9, 1913), p. 3.

[19]*Vestnik portnykh*, no. 8 (March 31, 1914), p. 8.

Clearly, dues paying still had not become a habit among many union members. The irregularity of dues payment weakened the struggling labor unions by severely limiting union funds and hence the range of activities, services, and benefits which they could offer their membership. This, as we shall see shortly, had an adverse effect on union growth.

PATTERNS OF UNIONIZATION

The sectoral composition of Petersburg and Moscow trade unions in 1912–1914 follows the same general pattern as in earlier years. The bulk of the unions—roughly three-fifths in both cities—were formed by workers in the manufacturing sector (table 36). Sales-clerical workers represented the second largest unionizing group in St. Petersburg and Moscow, though they were far less active than their counterparts in manufacturing. Service, construction, transportation, and miscellaneous groups each accounted for a small number of unions in this period.

Ten Petersburg unions and twelve in Moscow (including three in skilled construction trades) were formed by artisanal workers. Artisans thus remained active in the union movement, as did "factory artisans" (for example, electricians, draftsmen, and mechanics). A total of eleven unions were formed by factory workers in the capital, and thirteen in Moscow, and many were composed entirely or predominantly of skilled workers, who continued to provide the backbone of the union movement. As in earlier years, these skilled groups tended to form craft unions or, alternatively, to create special sections within industrial organizations. About two-thirds of the unions in each city were of a craft variety, although the largest unions tended to be organized along industrial lines.

Only a small number of unskilled or semiskilled factory groups unionized in these years. Among them were workers in textiles, tobacco processing, teapacking, leather, glassmaking, boxmaking, and candymaking. Whereas in 1906–1907 some of these factory groups—for example, in food processing—had formed lively and well-subscribed organizations, in 1912–1914 they showed little enthusiasm for unionization. The low level of union participation by these factory workers was affected, at least partly, by changes that had taken place in the composition of the labor force.

Following the economic upturn in 1909–1910, thousands of jobs opened up in Petersburg and Moscow factories. By 1913 the number of factory workers in

Table 35

Petersburg and Moscow Unions with Five Hundred or More Nominal Members at Peak Membership,
1912–1914

ST. PETERSBURG

Union	Peak membership in 1912–1914	Peak membership in 1906–1907
1. Metalworkers	11,000	10,700
2. Printers	3,870	12,000
3. Bakers	1,700	4,140
4. Textile workers	1,500	4,000
5. Salesclerks in textiles	1,500	n.d.
6. Woodworkers	1,200	1,965
7. Tavern employees	1,075	—
8. Leatherworkers	1,000	771

MOSCOW

Union	Peak membership in 1912–1914	Peak membership in 1906–1907
1. Printers	4,000	8,000
2. Tailors	2,460	3,415
3. Metalworkers	1,960	4,725
4. Bakers	1,725	4,000
5. Cooks	1,061	483
6. Precious metalworkers	1,000	1,296
7. Candymakers	800	1,626
8. Sales employees	700	900

9. Accounting clerks	1,000	2,000
10. Tailors	973	1,514
11. Clerks in foodstuffs	800	n.d.
12. Workers in cardboard manufacture	514	120
13. Clerks in household goods	500	—

9. Waiters	627	2,618

Source: A complete list of unions and union membership in 1912–1914 appears in Appendix V below, together with a list of the sources used to compile these data. The Petersburg unions of tavern employees and clerks in household goods did not exist in 1906–1907.

Table 36

Sectoral Composition of Trade Unions in St. Petersburg and Moscow, 1912–1914

UNIONS FORMED BY:

	MANUFACTURING WORKERS		SALES-CLERICAL WORKERS		SERVICE WORKERS		CONSTRUCTION WORKERS	
	Aggregate number	% of Total	Aggregate number	% of Total	Aggregate number	% of Total	Aggregate number	% of Total
St. Petersburg	21	57	7	19	3	8	—	—
Moscow	22	63	6	17	3	8.5	3	8.5

	TRANSPORTATION WORKERS		MISCELLANEOUS WORKERS		TOTAL	
	Aggregate number	% of total	Aggregate number	% of total	Aggregate number	% of total
St. Petersburg	3	8	—	—	37	100
Moscow	—	—	1	3	35	100

Sources: See Appendix V below. These figures include both legal and illegal unions, but exclude repeat registrations.

the capital had increased by 44 percent (69,774 workers) since 1908; in Moscow the number had increased by 31 percent (37,900 workers) since 1906. The Petersburg metalworking industry experienced the largest increase (77 percent), followed by woodworking (56 percent), and rubber (54 percent). In Moscow, woodworking (96 percent), printing (62 percent), and metalworking (45 percent) had the largest proportional increases (tables 37 and 38).

Workers who joined the Petersburg and Moscow factory labor force by 1913 usually found employment in the very largest enterprises, that is, in firms with more than 1,000 workers. Out of nearly 70,000 workers entering Petersburg factories during this period, about 54,000 found employment in firms with more than 1,000 workers. By 1913 the labor force in very large firms had increased by 75 percent over 1908 (table 39).

In Moscow the largest aggregate increase also took place in firms with more than 1,000 workers, although here the extent of change was far less dramatic than in the capital (table 40). The very smallest firms (up to 50 workers) in both cities showed either a decline or a small increase in the size of the labor force by 1913. In these enterprises—and only those classified as "factories" are included in the data—the labor force was barely affected by the massive changes taking place in larger firms.

Who were the thousands of workers entering the Petersburg and Moscow labor force on the eve of the First World War? First, there were those who had previous experience in an urban factory but had lost their jobs during the years when production was curtailed. Unemployed workers either remained in the city trying to find work, often surviving precariously on odd jobs, or returned to their villages if this option was open to them. Many of them were unskilled. The St. Petersburg Labor Exchange (Birzha Truda), which served as a city-operated employment agency, reported that in 1910, 90 percent of the 94,000 workers seeking jobs through that organization were classified as unskilled.[20] With the expansion of employment opportunities in the prewar period, these workers frequently returned to the factory labor force. They were not fresh recruits to the industrial labor force, since they brought with them previous experience of factory employment.

Other jobs in the expanding industrial sector were filled by second-genera-tion urban workers—the sons and daughters of a growing group of permanent city dwellers who had severed their ties with the countryside. A third group newly employed in factories and plants consisted of peasants entering the urban

[20] Arutiunov, *Rabochee dvizhenie*, p. 44.

Table 37

Distribution of the Factory Labor Force in St. Petersburg by Branch of Industry in 1908 and 1913

Industry	Number of Workers		Aggregate Increase from 1908 to 1913	Percent Increase from 1908 to 1913
	1908	1913		
Metal and machine working	53,945	95,336	41,391	77
Mechanized woodworking	4,569	7,146	2,577	56
Rubber	7,157	11,000	3,843	54
Chemicals	6,789	9,685	2,896	43
Paper and printing	19,038	24,507	5,469	29
Textiles	33,972	42,965	8,993	26
Animal products (leather, soap, etc.)	6,794	8,325	1,531	23
Bricks, cement, glass	7,604	8,556	952	13
Food processing	18,284	20,406	2,122	12
Total	158,152	227,926	69,774	44

Source: E. E. Kruze, *Petersburgskie rabochie v 1912–1914 godakh* (Moscow and Leningrad, 1961), p. 69. These data are based on Factory Inspectorate reports which excluded workers in state-owned enterprises. About 30,000 metalworkers were employed in state-owned firms, and there were several thousand workers in the state-owned paper and printing firm.

Table 38

Distribution of the Factory Labor Force in Moscow
by Branch of Industry in 1906 and 1913

Industry	Number of Workers 1906	Number of Workers 1913	Aggregate Increase from 1906 to 1913	Percent Increase from 1906 to 1913
Wood	2,600	5,100	2,500	96
Printing	7,700	12,500	4,800	62
Metal and machine tool	21,200	30,800	9,600	45
Textiles	53,800	66,600	12,800	24
Food	16,600	19,700	3,100	19
Chemical	6,600	7,700	1,100	17
Animal products	5,200	5,000	−200	−4
Miscellaneous	7,700	11,900	4,200	55
Total	121,400	159,300	37,900	31

Sources: A. G. Rashin, *Formirovanie promyshlennogo proletariata v Rossii: Statistichesko-ekonomicheskie ocherki* (Moscow, 1958), p. 201, based on Factory Inspectorate data. A somewhat different set of figures is given by S. I. Antonova, *Vliianie stolypinskoi agrarnoi reformy na izmeneniia v sostave rabochego klassa* (Moscow, 1951), p. 167, based on *Statisticheskii ezhegodnik goroda Moskvy za 1911–1913*, vyp. 4 (Moscow, 1916).

Table 39
Concentration of Factory Workers in St. Petersburg, 1908 and 1913

ENTERPRISES WITH:

	15–50 workers	51–100 workers	101–500 workers	501–1,000 workers	Over 1,000 workers	Total workers
1908	12,084	8,555	35,295	30,705	71,513	158,152
1913	10,628	11,924	46,725	33,607	125,042	227,926
Aggregate change 1908–1913	−1,456	+3,369	+11,430	+2,902	+53,529	+69,774
Percent of change 1908–1913	−12	+39	+32	+9	+75	+44

Source: E. E. Kruze, *Peterburgskie rabochie v 1912-1914 godakh* (Moscow and Leningrad, 1961), p. 71. These data are from *Spisok fabrik i zavodov evropeiskoi Rossii* (St. Petersburg, 1912) and *Fabrichno-zavodskie predpriiatiia Rossiiskoi imperii*, 2d ed. (Petrograd, 1914). State-owned enterprises are excluded.

labor force for the first time. Some were attracted by the prospects of a better life in the city. Many others were pushed off the land by growing economic hardship in rural areas, a situation created by chronic overpopulation, land scarcity, and the Stolypin land reforms of 1906–1907. Placing a "wager on the strong," Stolypin provided a legal opportunity for peasants to break their ties with the commune *(mir)* and establish private farms. Although the actual impact of the reform was limited, in some areas the consolidation of land and its severance from the commune adversely affected poor and middle-income peasants. Disposing of their tiny parcels through sale to richer neighbors, they sank to the level of landless laborers. For these peasants, industrial employment offered a way out of their impoverished and hopeless existence in rural Russia.

The three groups of workers—returnees to the factory, second-generation workers, and new peasant recruits—joined the urban labor force beginning in 1910. Although it is impossible to determine the size of these three groups with any precision, new peasant recruits were undoubtedly the largest group. These peasants gravitated mainly to large-scale enterprises which had a high demand for unskilled labor.

Many of the new recruits to the urban labor force were female workers who found employment in industries such as textiles and food processing where large enterprises and unskilled labor predominated.[21] In the words of one historian: "The larger the factory, the more women it employed."[22] The percentage of women workers in the Petersburg textile industry increased from 57 percent in 1900 to 63 percent in 1910 and 68 percent in 1913.[23] Similarly, in the capital's food processing industry, the proportion of women workers increased from 33 percent in 1900 to 47 percent in 1913.[24] The expanding labor force of the prewar economy included, therefore, numerous peasants, many of them female and fresh from the countryside. Their presence affected the prospects for unionization in certain industries.

Industries with a large influx of unskilled female and peasant workers developed a correspondingly weak union movement in 1912–1914. The textile and food processing industries, with their large-scale enterprises and high proportion of unskilled female labor, illustrate this point. The Moscow textile workers' union, for example, reported 730 nominal members in the period between November 1913 and January 1914, and only 100 of them regularly paid dues. In early 1907 this union had a nominal membership of 2,382.[25] The once-lively factory unions in the food processing industry (excluding the predominantly artisanal bakers) underwent a similar decline in the prewar period. The low level of union participation among these workers in 1912–1914 can be attributed to the massive influx of new workers, who proved unreceptive to the union movement. The small contingent of skilled experienced workers (most of them male) in these industries found themselves isolated and incapable of advancing the union cause among thousands of uncomprehending peasants (most of them female) who were ill equipped to appreciate the virtues of collective organization.

The Petersburg metalworking industry, as we have seen, also witnessed a tremendous influx of new workers, but the metalworkers' union became a well-

---

[21]In 1910, 42 percent of the peasants who migrated to St. Petersburg were female. James H. Bater, *St. Petersburg: Industrialization and Change* (London, 1976), p. 307.

[22]Antonova, *Vliiania*, p. 177, writing about Moscow province, but the statement applies elsewhere as well.

[23] *S.-Peterburg po perepisi 15 dekabria 1900 g.*, vyp. 2 (St. Petersburg, 1903) pp. 58–61, 126–129; *Petrograd po perepisi 15 dekabria 1910 g.*, chast' 2, vyp. 1 (Petrograd, 1915), pp. 8–9. Data for 1913 are from Factory Inspectorate reports on Petersburg province, but 85 percent of the workers were in the city of St. Petersburg. Kruze, *Peterburgskie rabochie*, pp. 78–79.

[24]Kruze, *Peterburgskie rabochie*, p. 79.

[25]*Tekstil'nyi rabochii*, no. 2 (March 1914), p. 9.

Table 40

Concentration of Factory Workers in Moscow,
1910 and 1913

ENTERPRISES WITH:

	Up to 20 workers	21–50 workers	51–100 workers	101–500 workers	501–1,000 workers	Over 1,000 workers	Total workers
1910	2,066	10,052	15,422	42,412	22,307	45,441	137,700
1913	2,230	10,514	16,567	48,427	27,559	54,481	159,300
Aggregate change 1910–1913	+164	+462	+1,145	+6,015	+5,252	+9,040	+21,600
Percent of change 1910–1913	+8	+5	+7	+14	+24	+20	+16

Sources: Rashin, *Formirovanie*, p. 107, for data on 1910; Antonova, *Vliianie*, pp. 156, 167, for data on 1913. The discrepancy between the total number of factory workers in 1913 and the sum of the workers in each of the categories shown in this table was unavoidable because the aggregates in subcategories were calculated using percentages given by Antonova, which total 100.3.

subscribed and lively organization. Metalworking, in contrast to food processing and textiles, employed mostly male workers, a high proportion of them skilled.[26] Notwithstanding technological changes that took place in the metalworking industry over the preceding half-decade, bringing more unskilled and semi-skilled workers into the plants, many firms retained a large and solid core of skilled workers with apprenticeship training and long employment experience. Unionization could proceed in the metalworking industry despite an influx of new workers, because there remained a substantial group of responsive and experienced workers who were not easily submerged in a mass of raw recruits, and whose skill, literacy, and urbanization facilitated participation in a trade union.

Nevertheless, even in this industry, large metalworking plants that received a sudden and massive influx of new workers showed a correspondingly low level of unionization in the prewar years. In the entire Nevskii district, the location of such enormous firms as the Nevskii and Alexandrovskii plants, there were only 394 members of the Petersburg metalworkers' union in mid-1913, compared with 2,583 members in mid-1908 (nearly all employed in eight very large plants) and 3,500 in mid-1906. The Nevskii plant was one of a number of very large firms that had had an enormous labor turnover in the Stolypin period. An estimated 35–40 percent of the Nevskii workers were dismissed from the plant in 1907 and 1908.[27]

A worker-correspondent for the Bolshevik newspaper *Pravda* observed in late 1913 that the low proportion of unionized metalworkers in some districts could be explained by the fact that many of the metalworkers employed there were "directly from under a wooden plough." Since they had just arrived from the countryside, their wages were lower and their hours longer than those of other workers. These workers, he continued, were known for their obsequious-ness to management, and on Sunday they all drank. Such workers were unlikely to join a trade union.[28]

[26]*Istoriia rabochikh Leningrada*, vol. 1, p. 393; Arutiunov, *Rabochee dvizhenie*, p. 31. Only 3.3 percent of the labor force in the Petersburg metalworking industry was female in 1913.

[27]F. A. Bulkin, *Na zare profdvizheniia: Istoriia peterburgskogo soiuza metallistov 1906–1914 gg.* (Moscow and Leningrad, 1924), pp. 306, 390; *Pravda*, no. 127 (331) (June 5, 1913), p. 3; no. 136 (340) (June 15, 1913), p. 1; *Materialy ob ekonomicheskom polozhenii i professional'noi organizatsii Peterburgskikh rabochikh po metallu* (St. Petersburg, 1909), pp. 72 fn. 3, 74. *Pravda* states that membership in the Nevskii district was only 126 in mid-1913, but Bulkin is a more reliable source. Total membership in the union in June 1913 was 5,133.

[28]*Za pravdu*, no. 42 (November 23, 1913), p. 4.

Prewar unions drew their support primarily from workers in small rather than large enterprises. The Moscow candymakers' union reported that most of its eight hundred members were employed in small candymaking firms rather than in large enterprises, which predominated in this industry.[29] The Moscow printers' union attracted workers employed in very small firms, often with only six or eight employees.[30] The handful of large firms in the city, such as the Sytin printing house, furnished few union members. With nearly one thousand workers, Sytin had only twelve union members in the spring of 1914, and some of them failed to pay their membership dues.[31] A similar recruitment pattern was reported by the Petersburg printers' union, and in Moscow the bakers' union complained that the large Filippov firm had few union members, although formerly this large bakery was a strongpoint of the organization.[32]

Small firms in all branches of the economy were less affected than larger ones by changes in the labor force, a circumstance that helps to account for the pattern of unionization in the prewar years. Factory enterprises with fewer than fifty workers either contracted in size or increased very slightly by 1913, and in virtually all branches of the economy there was considerably more labor force continuity in small firms (fewer than fifty workers) than in large ones. But even a high turnover or accretion in the labor force of a small firm had different consequences than in a very large factory. As the Soviet historian Shuster has pointed out, a ten percent change in the work force of an enterprise with one thousand workers, bringing one hundred new employees into the firm, had a more disruptive effect on social networks and solidarity than a comparable 10 percent change in a firm with only forty or fifty workers.[33] An analysis of individual union members lends further support to the view that unionized workers in the prewar period were employed in enterprises least affected by changes in the composition of the labor force.

PROFILE OF UNION MEMBERS

Evidence on individual union members is extremely fragmentary for the years 1912–1914, but the data indicate that as in earlier periods, the workers who

[29]*Put pravdy*, no. 77 (May 4, 1914), p. 5.
[30]*Luch*, no. 123 (209) (May 30, 1913), p. 4.
[31]*Severnaia rabochaia gazeta*, no. 43 (March 30, 1914), p. 3.
[32]*Novoe pechatnoe delo*, no. 2 (January 18, 1913), p. 6; *Zhizn' pekarei*, no. 2 (June 29, 1913), p. 6.
[33]U. A. Shuster, *Peterburgskie rabochie v 1905–1907 gg.* (Leningrad, 1976), p. 254, and above, chapter 5.

joined trade unions generally had a high level of skill compared to others in that industry or trade. Skilled workers predominated, of course, in artisanal unions. But even within skilled trades, workers with high levels of competence and specialization were well represented in union ranks. Thus, in the Petersburg bakers' union in 1913, the relatively skilled and well-paid *baranochniki* made up one-half of the membership, whereas they constituted only one-fifth of the labor force in the city's baking industry as a whole. Similarly, the bulk of unionized tailors in Moscow were employed in tailoring shops rather than subcontracting firms.[34]

The skill distribution of members of the Petersburg metalworkers' union cannot be ascertained from sources currently available, but it appears that the union continued to attract skilled workers. Unskilled workers, by contrast, remained, for the most part, outside union ranks. In 1907 unskilled workers had made up 16 percent of the union membership; by 1909 their proportion had declined to 10 percent and in 1910 to only 5 percent of the total union membership.[35] Following a reduction in membership dues on the eve of the war, the proportion of unskilled workers in the union increased, although the exact percentage cannot be established on the basis of available sources. Data on the earnings of union members in 1914, however, show that 13 percent of the membership earned less than 30 rubles a month, which placed them in the unskilled category. Two-thirds of the members earned from 30 to 50 rubles a month at a time when the average monthly wage in this industry was 43 rubles.[36] Nearly one out of five members had earnings of more than 50 rubles a month, an income that indicates a high level of skill and occupational specialization.[37]

Women workers, who were nearly always unskilled, took a very limited part in the organized labor movement during 1912–1914. The proportion of women in the labor force had grown steadily since 1905, but female workers showed little interest in trade unions. The Petersburg tailors' union was typical of most other unions in industries with a high proportion of women workers. This union attracted 30 or 40 women tailors (4–5 percent of the total union membership in 1913), out of a total of 23,000 female workers employed in the industry.[38]

[34]*Pravda*, no. 129 (333) (June 7, 1913), p. 3; *Metallist*, no. 9 (33) (October 4, 1913), p. 9; *Vestnik portynkh*, no. 6–7 (January 2, 1913), p. 2. For a description of *baranochniki* see above chapter 1, n. 117.

[35] Bulkin, *Na zare*, p. 309.

[36] The average month's wage applies to the metalworking industry in St. Petersburg province in late 1913. *Svod otchetov fabrichnykh inspektorov za 1913 god* (Petrograd, 1914), p. 46.

[37]*Put' pravdy*, no. 1 (January 22, 1914), p. 3; these data are also cited in Bulkin, *Na zare*, p. 276.

[38]*Vestnik portnykh*, no. 5 (October 13, 1913), p. 8; the number of women in the Petersburg tailoring industry is based on 1909 data, cited in ibid, no. 4 (June 15, 1913), p. 8.

By the end of 1913, women constituted 14 percent of the membership of the Moscow tailors' union (289 adult women and 50 female apprentices). Compared with most other unions in industries with many female workers, this was a significant accomplishment and a slight increase over the percentage of women members in 1907 (13 percent). Yet women made up two-thirds of the labor force in the Moscow apparel trades, which employed about 67,000 workers. Thus, only a very few women made common cause with the union in these years.[39]

After launching an energetic campaign to draw women into the organization, the Petersburg textile workers' union reported 300 women members, or 20 percent of the total union membership. A substantial improvement over 1910, when 12 percent of the membership was female, the prewar recruitment record nevertheless failed to match the representation of women workers in this industry (63 percent). In 1913 the Petersburg textile workers' union elected three women to the seventeen-member union board.[40]

Union members in 1912–1914 sometimes had a long-standing association with a labor organization, dating back several years or more. The Petersburg woodworkers' union reported in 1912 that one-quarter of the membership (250 out of 1,000) had formerly belonged to the union in 1907.[41] Similarly, 40 percent of the members of the Moscow tailors' union (710 out of 1,775) in early 1914 had regularly paid dues since 1908.[42] The Petersburg metalworkers' union reported in January 1914 that 2,000 out of 9,000 members had belonged to the defunct predecessor organization, closed in March 1912. These metalworkers had continuous union membership for at least two years or longer by 1914.[43]

The age structure of union membership indicates that workers who joined labor unions had often spent many years living and working in an urban center.

[39] E. A. Oliunina, *Portnovskii promysel v Moskve i v derevniakh Moskovskoi i Riazanskoi gubernii* (Moscow, 1914), p. 309. Labor force data are for 1912. *Statisticheskii ezhegodnik goroda Moskvy i Moskovskoi gubernii za 1914–1925 gg.*, vyp. 2: *Statisticheskie dannye po gorodu Moskve* (Moscow, 1927), pp. 68–72.

[40] *Metallist*, no. 10 (30) (October 25, 1913), p. 8; Tsentral'nyi gosudarstvennyi istoricheskii arkhiv (TsGIA), f. 23, opis' 29, d. 44, p. 21; *Severnaia pravda*, no. 30 (September 6, 1913), p. 3. Labor force data are for 1910. *Petrograd po perepisi 15 dekabria 1910 g.*, p. 8.

[41] *Metallist*, no. 10 (34) (October 25, 1913), p. 8.

[42] *Vestnik portnykh*, no. 8 (March 31, 1914), p. 8. The predecessor union opened in February 1908 and was officially closed in October 1911, functioning illegally until reregistration was obtained in November 1912.

[43] V. Sh-r [Sher], "Nashe professional'noe dvizhenie za poslednie dva goda," *Bor'ba*, no. 2 (March 18, 1914), p. 13; *Pravda*, no. 27 (331) (June 5, 1913), p. 3.

The Moscow tailors' union, for example, reported in late 1913 that most of its members were between the ages of twenty-two and thirty-five.[44] Given the early entry into apprenticeship in the apparel trades, these workers already had considerable experience in the work force by the time they reached their early twenties. In the fall of 1913 the largest membership group in the Petersburg leatherworkers' union was aged twenty-five to thirty.[45]

Some unions, such as the Petersburg metalworkers, leatherworkers, and bakers, noted an influx of young workers into their ranks during the summer of 1913.[46] It is likely that these young union recruits were, for the most part, skilled, literate, second-generation workers. But no further details have been located concerning this important development, and Moscow sources make no mention of it in accounts of the city's labor organizations.

To sum up, skilled male workers joined trade unions between 1912 and 1914, just as they had in previous years. Most were probably literate and urbanized, although the educational background and residency patterns of union members cannot be documented on the basis of available sources. In some unions, moreover, a substantial minority of the members had earlier trade union experience. Overall, we may conclude that unskilled recent peasant recruits to the Petersburg and Moscow labor force did not gravitate to trade unions on the eve of the First World War.

THE GOVERNMENT AND ORGANIZED LABOR

If changes in the composition of the labor force inhibited the revival of trade unionism in many industries, then the policies and actions of the government and employers account for the overall failure of unions to recapture their earlier momentum and fulfill their promise as centers for collective struggle. The Lena protests had called into question the effectiveness of Stolypin's approach, which relied on full-scale repression to keep a lid on explosive conflicts in urban Russia. An Okhrana report candidly observed in 1913: "The Lena events were only the stimulus bringing into the open the muted dissatisfaction that had been ac-

[44] *Proletarskaia pravda*, no. 10 (December 18, 1913), p. 3.

[45]*Metallist*, no. 10 (34) (October 25, 1913), p. 8.

[46]*Severnaia pravda*, no. 6 (August 8, 1913), p. 4 on the leatherworkers' union; Bulkin, *Na zare*, p. 282 on the metalworkers' union; *Severnaia pravda*, no. 17 (August 22, 1913), p. 4, on bakers.

cumulating in the population during recent years."[47] Clearly, repression alone could not be considered a satisfactory long-term solution to the problem of social disorder in tsarist Russia. Confronted by a mounting strike movement in the prewar years, the government groped for appropriate measures to reduce popular dissatisfaction, restore tranquility, and fortify its authority.

In the fluid and disorderly atmosphere of the prewar period, no single approach commanded unequivocal government support, and interministerial controversy as well as general uncertainty characterized policy formulation in these years. The result was an ambiguous stance toward both labor and management, a situation which led St. Petersburg industrialists to observe in May 1912 that "at present, we cannot expect government support for manufacturers, because [the government] is vacillating."[48]

Vacillation was, in fact, the salient feature of the government approach to labor problems during the prewar period. Abandoning the repressive policies applied so relentlessly during the Stolypin years, the government permitted a limited restoration of trade unions, together with the labor and radical press. But the regime never ceased to view these manifestations of worker activity with apprehension, and its increased tolerance for autonomous organization coincided with recurrent attempts to maintain close supervision and control. The outcome of this policy was a combination of limited legal opportunities for labor and intermittent episodes of repression.

Several circumstances conjoined in the prewar years to moderate government policies toward labor. The strong resurgent strike movement that got under way in the spring of 1912 was profoundly disquieting to the authorities. But worker unrest would have presented less of a problem had it not been for the larger context of social discontent in which it occurred.[49] Mindful of the more and more open expression of dissatisfaction in educated Russian society, the government used its coercive power with greater restraint and circumspection in the prewar period than at any time since mid-1907. In June 1912 the Minister of Internal Affairs, A. A. Makarov, openly acknowledged that a change had taken place in state policy. Meeting with representatives of the Petersburg Society of Factory Owners who protested the appearance of the new legal Bolshevik

---

[47]TsGAOR, DPOO, f. 102, d. 341, 1913, p. 8, from a report of January 10, 1913 on Petersburg workers.

[48] Kruze, *Peterburgskie rabochie*, p. 99.

[49]Haimson, "The Problem of Social Stability."

newspaper, *Pravda*, Makarov replied that "it is no longer as in the past, when the Ministry had almost unlimited power in relation to the daily press."[50]

Government sensitivity to public opinion further intensified following elections to the Fourth State Duma in the fall of 1912. Among the Duma delegates was a small but highly articulate group of Social Democrats and a much larger contingent of reform-minded deputies. Left-wing deputies used the Duma to publicize the repression of legal labor organizations, and by July 1914 they had initiated six separate inquiries into government conduct.[51] These inquiries were a matter of concern to the government, and in June 1913 the Minister of Internal Affairs cautioned that the excessive repression of workers was "harmful, since it almost always serves as grounds for an inquiry in the State Duma which, drawing general attention and sympathy in certain social circles, strengthens the self-awareness of workers, gives moral support to the strikers, and often even produces a flow of material contributions for their benefit."[52]

Such cautionary sentiments, expressed in various government documents of this period, did not prevent the authorities from reacting harshly to the re-emergence of mass-based legal labor organizations, as in the case of the Moscow printers' union. Formerly the most successful labor association in Moscow, the printers' union had been closed by the police in 1910 and did not revive until the end of 1912. Its first attempt to obtain registration failed, but a revised version of the charter finally received approval in March 1913. Following legalization the union rapidly began to recruit members, but at the end of the first year the results were disappointing. Only about one-fifth of the city's printers had joined the union by the spring of 1914, compared with two-thirds of the printers in 1906–1907.[53] The recruitment record in 1913 was particularly disheartening for con-

[50] TsGIA, f. 150, opis' 1, d. 57, p. 147. This account is drawn from a report by the Petersburg Society of Factory Owners.

[51] In December 1912 a group of Duma deputies requested an investigation into two matters: the actions by the St. Petersburg Chief of Police in prohibiting unions from holding public meetings, and the difficulties encountered by St. Petersburg unions seeking legal registration. TsGIA, f. 1278, opis' 5, d. 856, 855. In November 1913 two more inquiries were initiated. Both were directed at the Ministry of Internal Affairs for its persecution of trade unionists and its refusal to allow workers to hold meetings concerning the insurance law. Ibid, d. 927, 929. Two more inquiries in January and June 1914 protested illegal acts of government officials against trade unions and the general persecution of unions. Ibid. d. 948, 1011.

[52] "Tsarizm v bor'be s rabochim dvizheniem," *Krasnyi arkhiv*, vol. 1 (74) (1936), p. 41.

[53] *Luch*, no. 50 (136) (March 1, 1913), p. 3; *Pravda*, no. 70 (274) (March 24, 1913), p. 5; *Nasha rabochaia gazeta*, no. 52 (July 4, 1914), p. 3.

temporaries because this was an industry with a long history of unionization and a high proportion of skilled, literate, and urbanized workers.

Government repression was largely responsible for the union's weakness. During the first year of its existence, one hundred members of the union were arrested, and forty of them sentenced to exile for offenses associated with their union work.[54] The police subjected an estimated one-fifth of the rank and file to some form of harassment because of participation in the union.[55] To make matters worse, two leading agents of the Moscow Okhrana infiltrated the union and obtained positions on the union's directing board. A. N. Nikolaev and V. M. Buksin both served in key positions and were two of the most active and enthusiastic union leaders. Their presence facilitated systematic police persecution of union members, and this, in turn, created an atmosphere of fear and suspicion within the organization, which reduced membership and interfered with activities.[56]

The Moscow printers' union retained its legal status throughout the prewar period, and despite incidents of repression, continued to hold monthly membership meetings with three to five hundred workers. But in the important area of collective bargaining, where the predecessor union of 1906–1907 had made notable advances, the union was too weak and disorganized by government persecution to secure agreements with employers between 1912 and 1914.

The government treated the Petersburg metalworkers' union in a similar manner. It was only after two unsuccessful efforts at reregistration that the union

---

[54] Persecution of the union began immediately after its founding when a member of the union's temporary directing board was arrested in March 1913; a month later the union's secretary and treasurer were arrested also. They were sentenced to eight months in prison and two years in Siberian exile for alleged revolutionary activities. *Novaia rabochaia gazeta*, no. 67 (October 26, 1913), p. 3. In September 1913, the president, vice-president, treasurer, and a member of the board were arrested. Replacements were found for these officers, but in November 1913 the secretary, the treasurer, and another member of the board were again arrested and exiled from Moscow. *Novaia rabochaia gazeta*, no. 83 (November 15, 1913), p. 3; Ibid., no. 107 (December 14, 1913), p. 3. On the night of December 20–21, 1913, the police raided a number of Moscow unions, including the printers. They arrested one member of the board and six rank-and-file members. *Novaia rabochaia gazeta*, no. 117 (December 29, 1913), p. 4. Several weeks later, on January 8, 1914, thirty-five members of the union were arrested, including the union's entire board with the exception of two members. *Proletarskaia pravda*, no. 8 (26) (January 11, 1914), p. 2; *Severnaia rabochaia gazeta*, no. 1 (January 31, 1914), p. 4. Then on March 7, 1914, the secretary and a member of the union were arrested.

[55] *Rabochaia pravda*, no. 109 (December 17, 1913), p. 3.

[56] See below, chapter 10.

obtained legal status in March 1913. As the Petersburg Chief of Police acknowledged in an internal government memorandum, registration was finally granted because the union charter conformed to the law, and the Bureau on Unions could find no grounds for refusing registration.[57] The harassment of union members began almost immediately. By early August 1913 one-third of the full and candidate members of the directing board had been arrested, and the police had confiscated the union membership books.[58] Even before the union meeting of August 25, 1913, which elected a large Bolshevik majority to the union directing board, the police had already initiated efforts to close the union.

The authorities were so alarmed by the union's rapid growth and its potential for conducting Social Democratic agitation among metalworkers that the Director of the Department of Police, S. P. Beletskii, recommended as early as August 7, 1913, that the union be closed.[59] On August 20 the Petersburg Chief of Police used his power under the March 1906 law to halt temporarily the union's activities pending a final decision by the Bureau on Unions, but his decision was eventually overturned by the Bureau, which "for the time being did not find sufficient grounds for closing this union."[60] The union was placed under strict police surveillance, and retained its legal status for another seven months. Subsequent arrests proved so extensive that by January 1914 a complete turnover had taken place in the union board.[61] The prewar history of the Petersburg union of metalworkers was thus marked by an initial struggle for registration followed by episodic police harassment and threats of suppression.

The government feared the trade union movement and its capacity to unite workers in collective action.[62] They also wanted to prevent Social Democrats

[57]TsGAOR, DPOO, f. 102, opis' 14, d. 17, ch. 57, 1913, p. 34. On earlier unsuccessful efforts to obtain registration, see *Pravda*, no. 49 (253) (February 28, 1913), p. 4; no. 50 (254) (March 1, 1913), p. 1.

[58]*Severnaia pravda*, no. 13 (August 17, 1913), pp. 3–4.

[59]TsGAOR, DPOO, f. 102, opis' 14, d. 17, ch. 57, 1913, pp. 15, 25. Bulkin, *Na zare*, pp. 273–275.

[60]TsGAOR, DPOO, f. 102, opis' 14, d. 17, ch. 57, 1913, p. 34.

[61]Bulkin, *Na zare*, p. 269. According to a report in *Proletarskaia pravda*, no. 15 (33) (January 19, 1914), p. 1, between April 21, 1913, and January 1, 1914, fourteen members of the board and six candidate members had been arrested, including one president of the union, one vice-president, two secretaries, and two assistant secretaries. The article enumerated other instances of harassment and administrative restrictions of union activity: of twelve requests for general and district meetings, only seven were approved and of these only four were held, because police persecution made the other meetings impossible. The union was subjected to numerous searches, and on one occasion everyone attending a meeting of the union's board was arrested and exiled.

[62] TsGAOR, DP IV, f. 102, opis' 122, d. 61, ch. 2, t. 2, p. 24, for a report by the Petersburg Okhrana, May 27, 1913.

from penetrating the unions and using them for their own purposes.[63] A secret circular of October 1912 from the Minister of Internal Affairs and the Director of the Department of Police, for example, asserted that trade unions provided "a base for the propaganda of [SD] ideas among the masses and their gradual [conversion to] revolution *(revoliutsionizirovaniia)*." The country's provincial governors were urged to keep unions under surveillance and to conduct "an energetic struggle" against their infiltration by political parties.[64]

Some government officials, centered in the Ministry of Internal Affairs and its subordinate organs, attributed these problems to the law of March 1906 that had legalized trade unions. In 1910 an interministerial commission was convened under the auspices of the Ministry of Internal Affairs to prepare a revised law. Representatives of the Petersburg Society of Factory Owners, on their own request, were invited to participate in the deliberations.[65] The commission's work made little headway during the Stolypin years when most legal labor unions were forced to curtail or discontinue their activities. Consequently, the revised legislative project did not reach the Council of Ministers until May 1914.

The revised legislative project, and the debates surrounding its preparation, illustrate government attitudes toward legal labor organizations on the eve of the First World War. The Blazhchuk report of 1908 was the first to set down a systematic alternative to the existing law of March 1906. The report, it will be recalled, had recognized the inevitability of trade unionism in Russia but proposed to eliminate radical influences and ensure that the "ultimate and sole goal [of the unions was the] complete and equitable agreement of workers' and employers' interests."[66] This reconciliation was to be accomplished by government intervention.

When the interministerial commission met to consider revisions, it faced several key issues. One of the most basic questions centered around the right of unions to defend the economic interests of their members. The March 1906 law had taken a cautious position on this question, granting unions only the right to "elucidate and reach agreement on economic interests." Over the years, unions had repeatedly claimed the right to strike as a fundamental part of their endeavor to protect and promote such interests if the strikes conformed to the requirements of the December 2, 1905 law. A Ministry of Internal Affairs report issued

    [63] See TsGAOR, DP IV, f. 102, opis' 122, d. 61, ch. 2, t. 2, p. 24; TsGIA, f. 1495, opis' 530, d. 1054, p. 10.

    [64] TsGAOR, DPOO, f. 102, opis' 5, d. 1000, ch. 14, t. 3, 1903, pp. 20a, 21, 22.

    [65] TsGIA, f. 150, opis' 1, d. 500, pp. 1, 7, 50.

    [66] TsGAOR, DPOO, f. 102, opis' 00, d. 1000, ch. 14, t. 1, 1905, p. 226.

on November 30, 1907, had concurred with this view,[67] but in practice the authorities tolerated union-directed strike activity and strike funds only very briefly in 1906 and early 1907. The commission was bound to consider this crucial point in its deliberations, and its final report recommended that unions be permitted to organize funds for strikes that "either occur under peaceful conditions or else take place in enterprises which have no social or governmental significance."[68] This stipulation would have effectively prevented unions from legal involvement in most strikes.

On the issue of collective bargaining, employers urged that a provision be incorporated into the new law permitting unions to represent only their membership in negotiations with employers. But the commission refused to include an explicit provision to this effect, claiming that such a limitation on union jurisdiction was in any case "taken for granted."[69] The commission's minimal attention to the jurisdictional question reflects the underdeveloped state of labor relations in tsarist Russia and the reluctance of government authorities to contemplate the full implications of union participation in the resolution of industrial conflicts.

The most striking aspect of the legislative project presented to the Council of Ministers in May 1914 was its obvious intention to extend and to institutionalize government control and surveillance over the trade unions. The proposed revisions would have dictated union membership requirements for the first time by prohibiting unemployed workers from belonging to unions, as well as those unable to show uninterrupted factory employment for one year. Union officers, moreover, had to be twenty-five years of age or older. But these provisions were less stringent than those recommended by the employers, who advocated the exclusion of all workers under the age of twenty from union membership on the grounds that they were "restless" and prone to troublesome behavior.[70] Another important new provision in the proposed law concerned union meetings. Whereas general membership meetings already required police permission and were invariably attended by a police officer, meetings of the union directing board had been exempt from police surveillance. The new law would have instituted police surveillance over all union gatherings.[71]

[67]TsGAOR, DP IV, d. 119, ch. 42, 1908, pp. 13–15.

[68]Laverychev, *Tsarizm*, p. 266.

[69]Balabanov, *Ot 1905*, pp. 221–222.

[70]TsGAOR, DPOO, f. 102, opis' 14, d. 17, 1913, p. 1; Balabanov, *Ot 1905*, pp. 222–223.

[71]It is noteworthy that the police attempted to impose surveillance over union board meetings, and the issue eventually became the subject of a Duma inquiry. *Pravda*, no. 40 (June 15, [28], 1912), p. 2.

The proposed revisions actually represented a compromise; some government officials advocated a far harsher and more restrictive version of the law.
Provincial governors, for example, recommended that unions be deprived of the
right to investigate labor conditions, resolve conflicts, or provide legal assistance
to members. They urged that unions be confined to the functions of mutual aid
and cultural societies, and several governors even proposed the complete abolition of unions on the grounds that it was too difficult to define "what exactly is a
trade union."[72]

The revised legislation was abandoned following the outbreak of the First
World War, when wartime mobilization and government repression virtually
extinguished the union movement. Nevertheless, it was indicative of governmental attitudes that this legislative proposal, completed in early 1914, sought to
extend police control and surveillance over the trade unions. Whereas in 1905–
1906 the government had supported, albeit briefly and halfheartedly, a legal
framework in which labor and management could work out their conflicts in a
relatively autonomous sphere of social action, by 1914 this strategy for labor no
longer received serious consideration in government deliberations.

Proposals for a comprehensive liberalization of the law on trade unions in the
prewar years issued not from government ministries but from political parties
represented in the Fourth State Duma. On December 3, 1912, thirty-four Duma
deputies introduced new legislation on trade unions, which had been drafted by
the liberal Kadet party as part of a broader set of legal reforms dealing with
freedom of conscience, assembly, the press, and sexual equality.[73]

In contrast to the government proposal, the Kadet project would have
permitted unions to engage in a wide range of activities (religious, educational,
political, economic) so long as they did not violate criminal laws or "good
mores." Union confederations were permissible, and the local courts, rather than
administrative boards, were authorized to determine a union's status. Had this
law been enacted, trade unions would have enjoyed extensive freedom to
organize and to act collectively, but the proposal became mired in bureaucratic
channels of the Duma, where it remained until the outbreak of the war.

In the prewar period, the Social Democratic Duma faction also introduced a

[72]TsGIA, f. 150, opis' 1, d. 500, p. 14.

[73]Gosudarstvennoi Dumy: Chetvertyi sozyv: Prilozheniia k stenograficheskim otchetam, vyp. 1: Sessiia
pervaia (St. Petersburg, 1913), no. 13, for text of the Kadet proposal. See also Gosudarstvennaia
Duma: Chetvertyi sozyv: Stenograficheskie otchety 1912-1913 gg.: Sessiia pervaia, chast' 1 (St. Petersburg, 1913), pp. 1554–1555, 1627–1652, 1777–1789. Ibid., Sessiia vtoraia 1913-1914 gg., (St.
Petersburg, 1914), p. 887.

legislative project "on the freedom of assembly, unions, and coalition." This proposal would have given full freedom to citizens wishing to form organizations "in defense of their economic, legal, and political interests." It, too, failed to reach the floor of the Duma before the summer of 1914.[74]

The tendency in government circles to augment rather than diminish official involvement in labor-management relations is illustrated by another project contemplated in the prewar years. During the summer of 1913, the St. Petersburg Chief of Police proposed that the government introduce conciliation courts *(primiritel'nye sudy)* to resolve industrial conflicts. The proposal would have resulted in the establishment of permanent courts composed of representatives of workers, employers, and the government.[75]

The idea appealed to N. A. Maklakov, who became the Minister of Internal Affairs in December 1913. He revised the proposal, however, to exclude both workers' and employers' representatives, recommending instead that the courts operate under the supervision of either the governor or the chief of police, with membership drawn from the local Factory Inspectorate and the local courts.[76] Maklakov envisioned courts that not merely resolved conflicts once they had arisen, but also intervened in relations between management and labor to prevent conflicts from arising in the first place. In addition to taking over functions formerly performed by the Factory Inspectorate, the court was "to enter into discussion of the conditions of factory life and take measures on its own initiative and within the limits of existing laws, in order to eliminate undesirable phenomena regardless of whether the interested parties requested it."[77] The Minister of Internal Affairs thus imagined a sweeping interventionist role for the government, whose representatives on the board would serve as the "authoritative source for a comprehensive and impartial elucidation of the circumstances that caused friction between the workers and the employers."[78]

The Council of Ministers subsequently expressed approval for conciliation courts to supplement the work of factory inspectors and the police in industrial conflicts.[79] In its opinion, "one of the most effective means of preventing strikes

---

[74]*Nashe pechatnoe delo,* no. 13 (June 21, 1914), pp. 7–8; *Novaia rabochaia gazeta,* no. 5 (123) (January 7, 1914), p. 2; no. 79 (November 10, 1913), p. 1, for text of the proposal.

[75]Laverychev, *Tsarizm,* p. 261.

[76] "Tsarizm v bor'be s rabochim dvizheniem v gody pod"ema," *Krasnyi arkhiv* 1 (74) (1936), pp. 51–52, 57; Balabanov, *Ot 1905,* pp. 224–225.

[77] "Tsarizm v bor'be," *Krasnyi arkhiv,* p. 55.

[78]Ibid.

[79]Ibid., pp. 57–63.

would be a more responsive attitude toward [worker] demands, as long as they are not exaggerated and are actually justified by the rising cost of living which is currently evident everywhere."[80] Unlike Maklakov's proposal, however, the version approved by the Council of Ministers restored the participation of labor and management representatives on the court while preserving the idea of extensive government involvement in labor-management disputes. Further elaboration of the project was left to an interministerial commission that was duly appointed under the auspices of the Minister of Trade and Industry.

Employers raised strong objections to the government proposal for permanent conciliation courts. At a meeting of the Petersburg Society of Factory Owners in April 1914, industrialists asserted that such courts would be a dangerous weapon against employers because "decisions of the boards, for political reasons, would obviously always be directed against the manufacturers."[81] The Society feared that employer interests would be sacrificed to the cause of maintaining industrial peace.

Notwithstanding this opposition, the interministerial commission proposed the establishment of nonbinding conciliation courts in its report of July 1914. To be composed of an equal number of employer and worker representatives, the courts were to operate under the direction of a government official "as [a party] standing outside the interests of the [two] sides and concerned only with the equitable settlement of conflict."[82] Worker representation on the courts was to be drawn from the insurance councils *(bol'nichnye kassy)* which had been created in connection with a new insurance law promulgated in June 1912. The commission decided to utilize the insurance councils for this purpose because new elections, it claimed, would almost certainly stir up unrest among workers and serve as an occasion for political agitation.[83] The outbreak of the First World War soon after the issuance of the commission's report brought a temporary halt to strikes, thereby removing the central justification for undertaking an experiment in government-sponsored conciliation courts.

In the years immediately preceding the First World War, the government gave little attention to legislative projects regulating employment conditions and the labor contract, except insofar as these were directly related to punitive measures against workers. The efforts by sales workers seeking legislation to regulate labor

[80]Ibid., p. 47.

[81]TsGIA, f. 150, opis' 1, d. 671, p. 2.

[82] "Bor'ba so stachechnym dvizheniem nakanune mirovoi voiny," *Krasnyi arkhiv* 3 (34) (1929), p. 121.

[83]Ibid., pp. 122–123.

time, and by artisanal workers demanding legislative action to repeal the anti-quated law of 1785 regulating craft occupations, failed to elicit government action. Legislative projects revising existing legislation on child and female labor did not proceed beyond the discussion stage.[84] The government did, however, enact a new insurance law for workers which provided accident and illness insurance for factory, transport, and mining workers through compulsory contributions made by employees and employers.[85] In the final version of the law, the insurance fund was placed in the hands of a council jointly administered by employers and elected worker-representatives. Despite elaborate precautionary measures by the government and industrialists, the councils soon provided a new legal arena for worker activity, and another opportunity for radical political groups seeking to reach the rank and file.

EMPLOYERS, TRADE UNIONS, AND INDUSTRIAL CONFLICTS

The development of trade unions in the prewar period was further affected by powerful employers' associations. The most important of these were the Societies of Factory Owners in St. Petersburg and Moscow. Established primarily for the purpose of coordinating labor policies, the Societies had maintained a low profile during the quiescent Stolypin years, only to reemerge in full strength in 1912.

The Petersburg Society of Factory Owners stated its position on trade unions, factory elders, and other forms of worker representation in a new convention adopted in May 1912. At the first meeting of the commission appointed to draw

[84]*Rabochee dvizhenie: Biulleten'*, no. 17 (January-June 1913), p. 47.

[85]The law of June 23, 1912, applied to factory, mine, and transport workers in mechanized firms with no fewer than twenty workers, and to nonmechanized firms with no fewer than thirty workers. Excluded from the insurance law were agricultural, sales-clerical, and construction workers, artisans, household servants, and workers in government enterprises. According to the provisions of the law, employers contributed two kopecks for every three kopecks contributed by a worker. Insurance coverage was extended to about 20 percent of the three million workers in European Russia and the Caucasus. Laverychev, *Tsarizm*, p. 241. For a discussion of events leading up to the adoption of the insurance law, see Ruth Amende Roosa, "Workers' Insurance Legislation and the Role of the Industrialists in the Period of the Third State Duma," *Russian Review* 34, no. 4 (October 1975). An earlier, more limited, insurance law had been promulgated on June 2, 1903. For a description of this law, see I. I. Shelymagin, *Zakonodatel'stvo o fabrichno-zavodskom trude v Rossii, 1900–1917* (Moscow, 1952), pp. 80 ff.

up a new convention, the industrialists resolved not to recognize trade unions or permit any permanent workers' representation or any "outside intervention or mediation" in relations between employers and their workers.[86] The final version of the convention included provisions that members of the Society

1. must not permit representation of workers by deputies, [factory] elders, etc.;

2. must not permit intervention or mediation on the part of trade unions, societies, and generally by organizations outside the factory; Note: When necessary, [it is permissible] to enter into negotiations only with one's own workers;

3. in particular, must not permit interference with
   a. the hiring and firing of workers,
   b. the establishment of wages and conditions of employment,
   c. matters of internal factory order.

The convention included a provision that enjoined employers from undertaking negotiations with workers following the declaration of a strike. Members who violated the agreement were subject to steep fines.[87]

The more liberal-minded Moscow industrialists, in contrast to their counterparts in the capital, declared a willingness to recognize trade unions and enter into negotiations with them. In early 1914 the Moscow Society stated that "our Society takes into consideration the inevitability of the organization of workers into large professional units whose activity under normal circumstances makes economic strike struggle more rational."[88] Yet in actual practice, Moscow industrialists rejected union efforts to achieve recognition and to conduct negotiations on behalf of workers. They even refused to accept the establishment of factory elders when, in 1912, workers demanded their introduction in accordance with the 1903 law.

Workers in large-scale factory enterprises were not the only ones in the prewar period to encounter well-organized and effective resistance from employers. In the fall of 1912, employers in the Moscow apparel trades turned to the tailoring section of the Mutual Aid Society of Artisans. Using the Society as an organizational base, the leading tailoring shop employers drew up a joint agreement to

[86]TsGIA, f. 150, opis' 1, d. 505, p. 11.
[87]TsGIA, f. 150, opis' 1, d. 78, pp. 27, 13, 18.
[88]*Rabochenie dvizhenie: Biulleten'*, no. 18 (July-December 1913), p. 29.

undertake a variety of measures, such as blacklists, in order to resist workers' demands. The owners of fifty tailoring firms, including many of the largest in the city, endorsed the agreement. Henceforth, employers refused to recognize the union of tailors or to conduct negotiations with it.[89]

Employers in St. Petersburg and Moscow achieved greater coordination and unity in this period than in 1905–1907, and their collective opposition soon made itself felt on the strike movement. Not since 1905 had strikes acquired such massive proportions, and yet there was one notable difference. Whereas about 70 percent of the strikes over economic demands in 1905 had ended with the workers' full or partial victory, only about one-third of the strikes in the first half of 1914 had a favorable outcome for the workers. These data apply to economic strikes by factory workers in the country as a whole, but comparable trends characterized strike outcomes in St. Petersburg and Moscow.[90]

Petersburg workers generally, and the capital's metalworkers in particular, led the country's prewar strike movement. Apart from a great many strikes conducted over political issues, the major demands put forward by factory workers centered around wages and hours. For the first time since November 1905, Petersburg metalworkers conducted a campaign for an eight-hour or, in some cases, nine-hour workday. Demands concerning the internal factory order, including such issues as working conditions, fines, polite treatment, and the dismissal of unpopular supervisory personnel, also appeared frequently on strike petitions of this period. In addition, some workers demanded employer recognition of elected representatives at the shop and enterprise levels, or the recognition of trade unions as collective bargaining agents.

By 1912 the demand for shop and factory representatives had a considerable history behind it, extending back to the 1905 revolution, and in certain industries even earlier. During 1906–1907, workers sometimes won the right to elect enterprise-level representatives, but in the Stolypin period most employers rescinded these concessions and withdrew recognition of factory and shop delegates. Almost immediately following the Lena protests, workers resumed their campaign for enterprise-level representation. This campaign, which continued up to the outbreak of the First World War, engaged the attention of diverse workers and assumed several different forms. As in 1905, the metalworkers were

---

[89]Oliunina, *Portnovskii promysel v Moskve*, pp. 312–316; *Vestnik portnykh*, no. 6–7 (January 2, 1914), pp. 22–23. Member firms included the largest workshops in the city, such as Mandl' and Soldatskii.

[90]Balabanov, *Ot 1905*, p. 193; Balabanov, *Rabochee dvizhenie*, p. 14.

the first to call for elected factory representatives. They based their demand on the June 1903 law on factory elders. Workers had never been enthusiastic about this highly restrictive law, but in 1905–1907 some employers had invoked it as legal sanction for the election of workers' representatives at the factory level.

In late 1911 the Petersburg metalworkers' union moved to reintroduce factory elders in the hope of transforming these councils into centers for union activity. The metalworkers' campaign did not gather momentum until May and June 1912.[91] During the next year and a half, a variety of workers in the capital and in Moscow demanded the introduction of factory elders, including metalworkers, printers, bakers, railroad workers, telephone and telegraph employees, and others.[92]

The campaign to implement a law that had been on the books for nearly a decade encountered strong opposition from industrialists in both cities. The May 1912 convention of the Petersburg Society of Factory Owners explicitly prohibited members from introducing councils of elders. Consequently, only a few plants, such as the Nevskii, Siemens-Halske, Vulkan, and Novyi Aivaz factories, permitted the election of elders.[93] The Moscow Society of Factory Owners also blocked the implementation of the 1903 law. The Society's official organ devoted to labor problems, *Rabochee dvizhenie: Biulleten'*, reported with satisfaction in 1913 that "friendly resistance on the part of factory owners evidently had its effect, and demands for a council of factory elders are now made rather rarely."[94]

The attempt to revive the 1903 law on factory elders was part of a broader effort to achieve organization and collective representation at the enterprise level. Whereas some workers called for factory elders, others simply demanded employer recognition of their elected representatives *(vybornye* or *upolnomochennye)*. Strike petitions by Petersburg printers, bakers, metalworkers, jewelers, woodworkers, and Moscow printers, tram park workers, and others included this

---

[91]Workers in numerous Petersburg metalworking plants put forward this demand. See, for example, *Pravda*, no. 35 (June 9 [22], 1912), p. 12 (Obukhov plant); no. 28 (June 1 [14], 1912), p. 10 (Russian-American metalworking plant, Rechkin wagonworks); no. 19 (May 22 [June 4], 1912), pp. 12–13 (Admiralteiskii plant). Other issues of *Pravda* in May and June 1912 carry numerous other references to this demand by metalworkers.

[92]*Pravda*, no. 28 (June 1 [14], 1912); no. 56 (26) (March 8, 1913), p. 3; no. 97 (301) (April 28, 1913), p. 5; no. 129 (333) (June 7, 1913), p. 3.

[93]*Severnaia pravda*, no. 30 (September 6, 1913), p. 7; Bulkin, *Na zare*, p. 250.

[94]*Rabochee dvizhenie: Biulleten'*, no. 17 (January-June 1913), p. 14; Bulkin, *Na zare*, pp. 403–404.

demand.[95] The Petersburg printers' union observed that workers seldom elected representatives without employer approval, although they frequently included this demand in lists of grievances.[96] The situation was thus quite different from that in 1905, when workers had taken matters into their own hands and elected representatives regardless of employer consent.

Unions did not initiate most of the strikes in the prewar period, but they were sometimes drawn into labor-management conflicts once these had already gotten under way. Trade union leaders often complained that workers failed to consult the union before declaring a strike, and the Petersburg metalworkers' union threatened in late 1913 to withhold funds from workers who struck without union approval.[97]

Once striking workers turned to the union for advice and assistance, the issue of union representation frequently became a major point of contention between labor and management. Metalworkers and printers in both cities put forward this demand on numerous occasions.[98] Workers at the Robert Krug factory in St. Petersburg, for example, presented a petition to the employer in the spring of 1913 demanding that all negotiations be conducted with the directing board of the union of metalworkers; other points in the petition included a nine-hour workday and the dismissal of an unpopular foreman.[99] The demand for union representation also played a part in strikes waged by salesclerks, woodworkers, leatherworkers, tailors, bakers, textile workers, and others.[100] The radical and

[95]There are numerous instances of this demand reported in contemporary police documents and the radical press. See, for example, TsGAOR, DPOO, f. 102, opis' 122, d. 61, ch. 2, t. 1, 1913, p. 1; *Luch*, no. 146 (232) (June 23, 1913), p. 3; *Novaia rabochaia gazeta*, no. 49 (October 5, 1913), p. 3; *Pravda*, no. 13 (May 6 [21], 1912), p. 11; no. 15 (May 10 [23], 1912), p. 9; no. 4 (April 26 [May 9], 1912), p. 12; no. 24 (228) (January 30, 1913), p. 3; no. 25 (229) (January 31, 1913), p. 4; no. 26 (230) (February 1, 1913), p. 3; no. 98 (202) (April 30, 1913), p. 3; no. 144 (348) (June 26, 1913), p. 4; *Za pravdu*, no. 41 (November 21, 1913), p. 3.

[96]*Novoe pechatnoe delo*, no. 4 (April 11, 1913), p. 3.

[97]*Put' pravdy*, no. 1 (January 22, 1914), p. 3.

[98]*Novaia rabochaia gazeta*, no. 66 (October 25, 1913), p. 3; no. 28 (September 10, 1913), p. 3; no. 76 (November 6, 1913), p. 31; *Pravda*, no. 146 (350) (June 28, 1913), p. 3; *Za pravdu*, no. 46 (November 28, 1913), p. 3; *Rabochaia pravda*, no. 6 (July 19, 1913), p. 3; *Severnaia pravda*, no. 4 (August 9, 1913), p. 3; *Luch*, no. 147 (233) (June 29, 1913), p. 3; TsGAOR, f. 6860, ed. kh. 431, p. 7.

[99]TsGIA, f. 150, opis' 1, d. 667, p. 298.

[100]*Luch*, no. 79 (165) (April 4, 1913), p. 3; no. 82 (168) (April 9, 1913), p. 3; no. 98 (184) (April 30, 1913), p. 3; *Pravda*, no. 30 (234) (February 6, 1913), p. 3; no. 36 (240) (February 13, 1913), p. 3; *Rabochaia pravda*, no. 10 (July 24, 1913), p. 4; *Za pravdu*, no. 35 (November 14, 1913), p. 3; *Severnaia rabochaia gazeta*, no. 20 (March 3, 1914), p. 3.

labor press, moreover, carried articles reminding workers of the importance of concluding collective agreements negotiated by their own representatives from the union.[101]

In large-scale industries, such as metalworking, union intervention was confined to small firms that did not belong to the Society of Factory Owners. The Petersburg metalworkers' union participated in forty-one conflicts between September and December 1913. This was only a small percentage of the disputes that arose in these months. In October alone, Petersburg metalworkers were involved in a total of forty conflicts over workplace issues.[102] Of the forty-one conflicts in which the union took part, it had advance consultation with the strikers in only twelve. In five of these twelve conflicts, the union board entered into negotiation with the employer—all of them small firms. Out of these five cases, three ended to the full satisfaction of the workers and one with partial satisfaction; the outcome of the fifth dispute is not known.[103] There were, in addition, a number of strikes in which the union became actively involved after a work stoppage had already commenced. Workers at the Russo-Baltiiskii and Erikson plants, for example, insisted upon negotiations through union representatives in strikes conducted during October and November 1913.[104] The record of union involvement in labor-management disputes was somewhat better in predominantly artisanal trades such as baking and tailoring,[105] but even here the overall picture was discouraging.

The case of the Moscow metalworkers' union illustrates the interaction among organized workers, employers, and government authorities in the prewar years. The metalworkers' union had been closed by the police in 1907, and subsequent efforts to reregister during the Stolypin years did not succeed. Beginning with the Lena massacre, metalworkers once again stood in the forefront of the city's strike movement, and soon afterward new attempts were made to organize a metalworkers' union in Moscow. The first application for registra-

---

[101]See, for example, *Za pravdu*, no. 7 (October 11, 1913), "Kollektivnyi dogovor i Peterburgskie bulochniki."

[102]Bulkin, *Na zare*, p. 406.

[103]*Put' pravdy*, no. 1 (January 22, 1914), p. 3.

[104]*Za pravdu*, no. 48 (November 30, 1913), p. 3; *Novaia rabochaia gazeta*, no. 78 (November 9, 1913), p. 3.

[105]*Proletarskaia pravda*, no. 12 (30) (January 16, 1914), p. 3; *Vestnik portnykh*, no. 6–7 (January 2, 1914), p. 13.

tion was rejected in early 1913, but a revised version of the charter obtained official approval in late April 1913.[106]

The union, called "Workers' Solidarity," proved an immediate success. By mid-August 1913, three and one-half months after registration, the union had drawn nearly two thousand members, or about 6 percent of the Moscow workers in this industry.[107] The predecessor union of 1907 had attracted 14 percent of the city's metalworkers after recruiting for an entire year. Considering the short period of recruitment and the rapid rate of growth, this union was highly successful. The industry contained a solid core of workers who remained receptive to the appeals of organized labor and enlisted in trade union ranks.

When a vigorous strike movement developed among metalworkers in June and July 1913, striking workers at five Moscow plants asked the union to represent them in negotiations with the factory administration.[108] Citing the March 1906 law and the union's own charter,[109] the union attempted to intervene on behalf of workers. But Moscow factory owners refused to cooperate. Their objections were set forth in the *Biulleten'* of the Moscow Society of Factory Owners:

This union [Workers' Solidarity], composed of 440 members, attempted from the outset of its activities to take into its hands the leadership of the strike movement of Moscow metalworkers. . . . In order to conduct the strike struggle more successfully, the leaders of Workers' Solidarity turned to the administration of factories where strikes were in progress with a proposal to conduct negotiations with the workers through the mediation of responsible union members. However, members of the Society of Factory Owners rejected this mediation. Their motive for this was the small authority of the new union over workers because it had been in existence only several weeks and had only several hundred members. As a result, the decisions of the union could not be binding for the majority of workers in Moscow metalworking factories. . . . Our Society takes into consideration the inevitability of the organization of workers into large professional units whose activity under normal circumstances makes economic strike struggle more rational. And at the moment when the union achieves the necessary stability, the Society will agree to the proposal for mediation by the workers' unions.[110]

---

[106]Z. Shchap, *Moskovskie metallisty v professional'nom dvizhenii* (Moscow, 1927), p. 146.

[107]*Novaia rabochaia gazeta*, no. 8 (August 17, 1913), p. 3. Labor force data are from the 1912 Moscow city census, *Statisticheskii ezhegodnik goroda Moskvy i Moskovskoi gubernii*, pp. 69, 71.

[108]Ibid.

[109]Shchap, *Moskovskie metallisty*, p. 222.

[110]*Rabochee dvizhenie: Biulleten'*, no. 18 (July-December 1913), p. 29.

The union's attempt to intervene in strikes also alarmed the police, and on August 16 the Moscow Bureau on Unions withdrew the organization's legal status on the grounds that it had become a strike center under Social Democratic leadership.[111] In its subsequent brief to the state Senate appealing the Bureau's decision, the union denied these allegations and insisted that both the March 1906 law and the union's own charter gave Workers' Solidarity the right to perform a conciliatory function in resolving labor disputes.[112] And indeed, the union at the time espoused no revolutionary ideology, but aspired merely to defend the workers' economic interests by legal means.

The experience of the Moscow metalworkers' union typifies the pattern of worker-employer-state interaction in these years. Workers drew the conclusion from this and other incidents that factory owners and the government colluded to prevent unions from performing their legal and rightful functions. *Metallist* [The Metalworker], the organ of the Petersburg metalworkers' union, expressed these sentiments in an article that appeared soon after the Moscow union was declared illegal:

Russian employers who often decry the anarchy of the strike movement, and [who are] allegedly sympathetic to the more organized forms of the movement, in practice use all their powers to oppose the organization of workers, preferring chaos, atomization, and elemental spontaneity *[buntarstvo]*. The workers' press reports that the fate of the [Moscow metalworkers'] union was decided on the day following a meeting of the Moscow Society of Factory Owners where the eminent merchants let it be known to those whose business it was to know that intervention by the union in strikes was undesirable. But to interfere with the union's activity without closing it down was found to be impossible, and so the [government] administration carried out the procedure common in such cases: a raid, arrests, searches, and as a result of all this police terror—closure [of the union].[113]

In a similar vein, the Petersburg Menshevik daily, *Novaia rabochaia gazeta* [New Workers' Newspaper], observed, "the Moscow manufacturers are refusing to enter into relations with the Moscow union of metalworkers, which is trying to introduce into the strike movement consciousness and organization. Yet the

[111]Shchap, *Moskovskie metallisty*, p. 162; *Novaia rabochaia gazeta*, no. 22 (September 3, 1913), p. 2.

[112]The entire text of the union's brief appears in Shchap, *Moskovskie metallisty*, pp. 219–223.

[113]*Metallist*, no. 3 (31) (August 24, 1913), p. 2.

[government] administration, aiding the capitalists, is closing this organization without any serious reason."[114]

The Bolshevik legal newspaper in the capital, *Pravda,* aptly characterized the situation as early as January 1913. Trade unions, it asserted, confronted a curious dilemma. At a time of growing strike activity, unions were at a standstill because they were permitted, though often with considerable difficulty, to resume their legal status but were not permitted to engage in activity. Attempts to achieve economic improvement by orderly means, through collective labor contracts negotiated by union representatives, were obstructed by employers and punished by government authorities.[115]

This, indeed, was the crux of the issue for trade unionists in the prewar years. For the first time since mid-1907 they could establish legal organizations and newspapers, openly recruit members, and resume their efforts, cut short half a decade earlier, to erect a mass-based labor movement. Yet as soon as the unions began to perform the basic functions for which they were constituted—most notably, the quest for improvement in the terms and conditions of labor—trade unionists found their efforts thwarted and the very existence of their organizations threatened. To be sure, unions had also faced closure for involvement in labor-management disputes during the Stolypin years. But after April 1912, the context of industrial relations had been transformed by the explosive combination of a resurgent strike movement and mounting discontent in educated circles of urban Russian society.

The predicament experienced by organized workers might have had different political consequences were it not for another important circumstance in the prewar years. The opportunities for legal association and a labor and radical press again brought thousands of workers into sustained contact with radical activists. These encounters had a decisive influence over the politics of organized workers on the eve of the First World War.

[114]*Novaia rabochaia gazeta,* no. 5 (August 13, 1913), pp. 1–2.
[115]*Pravda,* no. 11 (215) (January 15, 1913), p. 1.

Chapter 10

The Radicalization of Labor, 1912–1914

> There are no parallel unions in Russia. In St. Petersburg
> and in Moscow the trade unions are united. The fact is
> that in the unions there is a complete predominance of
> *pravdisty*.
>
> *V. I. Lenin, July 1914*[1]

The relationship between Social Democracy and the trade unions took a new turn on the eve of the Lena massacre. The Prague Conference, convened unilaterally by Lenin in January 1912, marked a transition in the Bolshevik approach toward legal opportunities, inaugurating a new phase in this party's relationship to trade unions.[2] The conference instructed party workers to redirect their focus because the

new upsurge of the working-class movement makes possible the further development of organizational forms of party work along the lines indicated therein, i.e., by the formation

---

[1]V. I. Lenin, *Sochineniia*, 3rd ed., 30 vols. (Moscow, 1928–1937), vol 17, p. 551.

[2]The Prague Conference arrogated to itself the title of Sixth All-Russian Conference of the RSDRP, and thereby ended the fiction of party unity that had been maintained since the Fourth "Unification" Congress in 1906. Henceforth, the Bolsheviks and the Mensheviks constituted two separate parties. Only two non-Bolshevik delegates were present at the Prague Conference. The representatives from Moscow were F. I. Goloshchekin, G. E. Zinov'ev, and R. V. Malinovskii. A. S. Romanov represented the party's *oblast'* organization in the Moscow Industrial Region. Both Malinovskii and Romanov were employed by the secret police. The representatives from St.

of illegal Social Democratic nuclei surrounded by as wide a network as possible of every kind of workers' association. . . . It is essential for the maximum possible initiative to be shown in the organization of Social Democratic work in legally existing associations.[3]

These legal opportunities, Lenin elaborated lest his followers misunderstand, included reading rooms, libraries, and recreational societies as well as trade unions, trade union publications, and election campaigns to municipal bodies and the State Duma.

In summoning the party to seize legal opportunities, Lenin faced the familiar problem of ensuring party unity and control within larger, nonparty, legal labor organizations. He resolved this difficulty by resorting to the idea of party cells originally proposed by M. Borisov in 1905 and revived in early 1908. Borisov, it will be recalled, had recommended that Bolsheviks become "unofficial agents" in trade unions, forming party cells within these organizations to conduct agitation and strengthen party influence.

Following the Prague Conference, party cells became a basic feature of the Bolshevik approach to union-party relations in the prewar period.[4] Through the creation of these exclusively Bolshevik cells within legal organizations, party members attempted to draw nonparty people into the party orbit and to fortify the party's influence over union affairs. A Central Committee resolution in 1913 put the situation plainly:

Social Democrats must attract into all workers' societies the broadest possible circles of workers, inviting into membership all workers without distinction according to party views. But the Social Democrats within these societies must organize party groups [cells] and through long, systematic work within all these societies establish the very closest relations between them and the Social Democratic Party.[5]

Soon after the Lena massacre, Bolsheviks in both St. Petersburg and Moscow began to take a strong interest in the union movement that was beginning to revive. In early June 1912, the newly legalized Bolshevik newspaper *Pravda* carried a front-page article entitled "How to Organize a Trade Union," by an

---

Petersburg were P. A. Zalutskii and P. Onufriev. In all, there were fourteen voting delegates at the conference. Lenin, *Sochineniia*, 15:651.

[3]Ibid, 15:382–83.

[4]Thomas Taylor Hammond, *Lenin on Trade Unions and Revolution 1893-1917* (New York, 1957), pp. 69–73.

[5]Ibid., p. 72.

unidentified author, "A. M." The three-part article furnished a detailed guide to the formation and legal registration of unions, including advice on ways to organize union meetings that would go "smoothly, interestingly, and leave a good impression."[6] The article was indicative of the new party attitude toward unions. Menshevik "liquidators," whose focus on legal organizations had earlier aroused Lenin's vitriolic attack, were now joined in these organizations by an active and determined group of Bolsheviks.

Yet there remained a basic difference in the approach of the two branches of Social Democracy toward trade unions and other legal workers' organizations in which the Bolsheviks now became involved. As Lenin asserted at the Prague Conference and in his subsequent writings, legal organizations were important and useful because they served as instrumentalities in the hands of dedicated revolutionaries. Trade unions, cultural societies, insurance councils, and the Duma should be utilized as channels for the dissemination of Bolshevik propaganda and for recruitment into the party.

The Mensheviks did not share this narrow view of legal labor organizations. They continued to believe that workers' associations would raise the cultural, material, and political level of Russian workers, enabling them to perform their role as class-conscious participants in the revolutionary overthrow of the tsarist autocracy and the transition from capitalism to socialism. During the Stolypin years, the Mensheviks counseled workers to bide their time in legal clubs and cultural organizations until trade unions could once again emerge and recapture their earlier momentum, which had been so impressive, and in the Menshevik view so promising. Profoundly influenced by Western European models and experiences, the Mensheviks were eager to build a mass-membership, legal labor movement on Russian soil.[7] They never lost sight of the eventual goal of revolution, but Menshevik *praktiki* focused their attention on reestablishing the unions and achieving a variety of workplace improvements, including the introduction of many of the same reforms in the conduct of labor-management relations that had been at the core of union activities since the inception of these organizations in 1905.[8]

[6]*Pravda,* no. 34 (June 8, 1912), p. 1; no. 35 (June 9, 1912), p. 1.

[7]See *Novaia rabochaia gazeta,* no. 15 (August 25, 1913), p. 2, for an article by A. V. Gorskii [A. E. Diuba] which evokes the views of the German labor leaders A. Bebel and K. Liebknecht as a model for Russian trade unionists.

[8]For Menshevik views on trade unions, see *Nasha zaria,* which served as a forum for Menshevik discussion of strategy and tactics. The Menshevik position on legal labor organizations was reiterated at the August 1912 Vienna Conference held in response to the January 1912 Bolshevik Prague Conference.

The Bolsheviks, by contrast, advocated a militant strike policy designed to culminate in a general strike and the overthrow of the autocratic system. For Bolshevik activists, the future development of a legal labor movement was far less important than the immediate goal of a revolution, and they regarded trade unions as adjuncts in this struggle.

Tactical issues and more fundamental differences over labor strategy both played a part in union conflicts during the prewar years. The intense political battles that took place over the leadership and direction of these organizations centered around the two branches of Russian Social Democracy. For the first time, Menshevik hegemony in Petersburg and Moscow trade unions was effectively challenged by the Bolsheviks, whose new policy toward legal organizations established at the Prague Conference brought them into intense union activity. Other political parties that had earlier drawn a following in the union movement retained only a dwindling influence over organized workers in the prewar period. The Socialist Revolutionaries maintained a foothold in no more than a handful of unions; the liberal Kadets were influential only in unions involving sales-clerical and service groups, such as the Moscow unions of salesclerks, waiters, and cooks. As for the syndicalists, they left no trace of their influence in the unions, despite the inroads they had made in earlier years.

By late 1913 eight years of Menshevik predominance over the organized labor movement had come to an end, and Bolsheviks had assumed the leadership over many workers' associations. The longtime Menshevik union activist Sher has described this dramatic development:

In early 1912 the overwhelming majority of the unions were under the influence of the *Luchisty* [Mensheviks]; at the end of 1913, on the contrary, a number of very large and influential unions came under the influence of *Pravdisty* [Bolsheviks]. This change, which came about with extreme rapidity [and] for many almost unexpectedly, took place in an atmosphere of savage fratricidal struggle.[9]

BOLSHEVIK ASCENDANCY IN WORKERS' ORGANIZATIONS

At the founding meeting of the newly registered Petersburg metalworkers' union on April 21, 1913, an unexpected event took place: the seven or eight hundred

[9] V. Sh-r [Sher], "Nashe professional'noe dvizhenie za dva poslednikh goda," *Bor'ba*, no. 4 (April 28, 1914), p. 21. For similar public acknowledgments of the situation, see G. Rakitin [V. O. Tsederbaum], "Rabochaia massa i rabochaia intelligentsiia," *Nasha zaria*, no. 9 (1913), pp. 57–58; B. I Gorev, "Demagogiia ili marksizm?" *Nasha zaria*, no. 6 (1914), pp. 80 ff.

workers present at the gathering elected a Bolshevik majority to the union's interim directing board.[10] The Bolshevik victory in this important Petersburg union made a profound impression on contemporaries because, as Bulkin put it,

the metalworkers' union was one of the few organizations where Mensheviks, by virtue of tradition, still felt comparatively secure. In the course of a number of years they had controlled the union apparatus, had created cadres of union activists, had become known to a broad mass of unionized workers as people who could get things done; all this created for [the Mensheviks] a position in the union and strengthened their influence.[11]

Four months later, the union held a second election for a permanent board. The Mensheviks felt confident that the Bolsheviks would fail to keep control over the union, for it was well known that among the Bolsheviks elected to the directing board in April, not one had any previous experience in trade union affairs.[12] Nevertheless, on August 25, between 1,800 and 3,000 workers (out of the union's 5,600 members) attended a second meeting, which elected a Bolshevik directing board.[13] According to reports published by the Bolshevik press—

[10]*Luch*, no. 92 (178) (April 23, 1914), p. 2, states that 710 people were present at the meeting; *Pravda*, no. 92 (296) (April 23, 1913), p. 7, states that 800 attended. Accounts of the political composition of this temporary board differ. According to F. Bulkin, *Na zare profdvizheniia: Istoriia Peterburgskogo soiuza metallistov 1906-1914 gg.* (Moscow and Leningrad, 1924), p. 262, thirteen of the twenty-six full and candidate members were Bolsheviks. The information he provides shows that seven of the twelve full members and six of the fourteen candidate members were Bolsheviks. The report furnished by the Petersburg Okhrana on the election gave somewhat different results. According to this report, there was a total of twenty-five members (full and candidate): thirteen Bolsheviks, five Mensheviks, one Socialist Revolutionary, and six nonparty people. Of the full members of the directing board, six were described as Bolsheviks—but they are not the same six as those noted by Bulkin. Seven of the fourteen candidate members are listed as belonging to the Bolshevik party slate. *Tsentral'nyi gosudarstvennyi arkhiv Oktiabr'skoi revoliutsii* (TsGAOR), DPOO, f. 102, opis' 14, d. 17, ch. 57, 1913, pp. 15 ff.

[11]Bulkin, *Na zare*, p. 261; *Nash put'*, no. 6 (August 31, 1913), p. 2.

[12]Bulkin, *Na zare*, p. 263; TsGAOR, DPOO, f. 102, d. 17, opis' 14, ch. 57, 1913, p. 15, Okhrana report of June 13, 1913.

[13]Varying estimates of the attendance can be found in the contemporary press. *Severnaia pravda*, no. 21 (August 27, 1913), p. 3, reported that three thousand workers attended; *Novaia rabochaia gazeta*, no. 16 (August 27, 1913), p. 3, also reported three thousand, but subsequently revised this figure downward to eighteen hundred (ibid., no. 26 [September 7, 1913], p. 4). According to the Okhrana, two thousand union members attended the meeting, including twenty-five women. TsGAOR, DPOO, f. 102, d. 17, opis' 14, ch. 57, 1913, p. 28.

and not contradicted by Menshevik accounts—the slate of Menshevik candidates received only 100–150 votes.[14]

Prior to the election, both parties conducted intensive organizational and propaganda campaigns. On the appointed day, representatives of each group stood at the entrance of the meeting hall and distributed their party's newspaper *(Pravda* and *Luch* respectively) to union members. Admission was based on presentation of a valid membership card and an invitation to the meeting, a procedure supervised by the police. Heated debates preceded the vote, with speakers rising to defend each slate of candidates.[15]

Regrettably, we know little about the content of the debate or those who attended the meeting. Some contemporary Mensheviks have suggested that young and newly unionized workers supported the Bolsheviks, and that older, experienced trade unionists voted for Menshevik candidates.[16] The available evidence, limited though it is, indicates that Bolshevik electoral support on this occasion must have included a cross section of the union membership.

Following the reregistration of the Petersburg metalworkers' union in March 1913, many members of the predecessor union, closed in August 1912, promptly rejoined. The new union sought to attract them by offering an exemption from the initial membership fee and eligibility for all union benefits, provided that dues had been paid until the closing of the old union. As of June 1, 1913, there were about 1,800 union members, of whom about 600, or one-third, had belonged to the previous union.[17] Between June 1 and December 31, 1913, another 1,300 former union members rejoined the organization, and in January 1914 the union's correspondent to *Pravda* reported that a total of 2,000 members (out of 9,000) had belonged to the previous union.[18] Had the return rate been more or less continuous, then an average of 186 former union members

[14]*Severnaia pravda,* no. 21 (August 27, 1913), p. 3. *Novaia rabochaia gazeta,* no. 26 (September 7, 1913), p. 4, reported that votes for the directing board were not actually counted at the meeting, so that any specific numbers given were arbitrary. This report acknowledged, however, that the "majority" favored the Bolshevik slate. According to *Istoriia rabochikh Leningrada,* vol. 1 (Leningrad, 1972), p. 444, the Menshevik slate received 200 votes.

[15]*Severnaia pravda,* no. 21 (August 27, 1913), p. 3; TsGAOR, DPOO, f. 102, d. 17, opis' 14, ch. 57, 1913, pp. 28–32. The text of this Okhrana report on the meeting is reproduced in Bulkin, *Na zare,* pp. 270–272. This appears to be the most detailed extant report of the August 25 election.

[16]F. Bulkin, "Rabochaia samodeiatel'nost i rabochaia demagogiia," *Nasha zaria,* no. 3 (1914), pp. 59–60. As part of a general discussion, V. Sher suggested that a generational struggle was taking place in many unions. V. Sh-r [Sher], "Nashe professional'noe dvizhenie," *Bor'ba,* no. 4, p. 17.

[17]*Pravda,* no. 27 (331) (June 5, 1913), p. 3.

[18]*Proletarskaia pravda,* no. 15 (33) (January 19, 1914), p. 1.

would have reentered union rolls each month from June through December 1913. In fact, however, the influx of returnees slowed down during the fall of 1913, suggesting that the bulk of those who rejoined did so during the summer months.[19]

When the election meeting took place in late August 1913, the union's nominal membership had reached 5,600. In the first two weeks of June, 77 former members had rejoined;[20] assuming that at least 186 workers had re-enlisted during each month prior to the meetings (June, July, and August), then there were 1,158 members of the predecessor union on the rolls at the time of the August 25 gathering, or about 21 percent of the total. Some of these former members must have attended the August 25 election meeting. Even if only two-fifths of them were actually present—the same proportion that attended from the total membership—then some 463 former members were in the union hall when the election took place. Their number may have been even higher, since these workers had previous experience with union affairs and might be expected to show up on such a critical occasion.

The Menshevik slate received only 100–150 votes. This was almost certainly fewer votes than the number of old union members participating in the election. A good proportion of the members of the previous union—perhaps as many as three out of four—must have cast their ballots for the Bolshevik candidates. Recent union recruits were not the only ones to support the Bolsheviks in this important election. Police surveillance over admission to the meeting, moreover, rules out the possibility that the Bolsheviks manipulated the election by sending nonmembers to participate in the vote. An Okhrana report asserts that only a few nonmembers succeeded in gaining admission.[21]

Many factors played a part in the Bolshevik victory over the Mensheviks in the metalworkers' union. One of the most important circumstances was the discontent workers felt with the policies and actions of the Menshevik leadership toward the strike movement. In the months following the Lena massacre, the strike movement had revived, affecting St. Petersburg metalworkers more than any other group in the capital. Menshevik leaders of the union viewed this resurgence with caution, and they repeatedly urged workers to refrain from unplanned strikes against a well-organized opponent. This policy proved unpopular among many workers, as Bulkin related in the 1920s:

[19]*Metallist*, no. 8 (32) (September 18, 1913), p. 12.
[20]*Pravda*, no. 133 (337) (June 12, 1913), p. 3.
[21]TsGAOR, DPOO, f. 102, d. 17, opis' 14, ch. 57, 1913, p. 28.

We have already mentioned that the old union with its leanings toward liquidationism sowed distrust among the masses for union work. The workers did not perceive it as a leader of their struggle with capital. Among this mass [that the union] alienated, a reaction against the union was beginning to grow. The spirit of gradualism and extreme timidity, a desire to protect the union from being closed . . . at the price of any compromise, including giving up the leadership of the economic struggle, in other words, doing all [those things] which the liquidators had been propagating in the union with such zeal—all of this not only worked against [the union's] popularity and influence in the growing movement of Petersburg metalworkers, but . . . was undermining its authority in the eyes of the masses.[22]

The August 1913 election in the Petersburg metalworkers' union forced both the Bolsheviks and the Mensheviks to formulate a programmatic position for trade unions. The Mensheviks stressed the necessity for unions to impose discipline, organization, and restraint on the strike movement, whereas the Bolsheviks endorsed active union participation in the increasingly militant strike struggle—a tactic designed to build momentum toward a general strike that would finally bring an end to autocratic rule.[23] In the summer of 1913 metalworkers were little inclined to embrace the cautionary rhetoric of Menshevik labor leaders, whereas the Bolshevik position corresponded to the mood of many workers. The astute Menshevik observer of labor politics in the capital, Iulii Martov [Iu. O. Tsederbaum], described the situation in a rejoinder to Bulkin, one of the defeated "liquidator" leaders of the Petersburg metalworkers' union:

It is against you, comrade Bulkin, against you and people like you who have been leading the workers' movement in recent years, that this "mutiny" is directed, and it has its own deep roots. You should not be discouraged by the fact that the worker-romanticist who is misled by *"pravdism"* curses Potresov, accuses Cherevanin of treason, threatens to kill Ezhov, etc., without, perhaps, ever having read these writers. . . . He says "Ezhov," but means that very skepticism with which the worker-Marxists [Mensheviks] reacted to the talk of an "uprising" likely to take place any autumn. . . . He swears at Cherevanin but remembers the [Menshevik] calls for organization, the severe criticism of "guerilla tactics" *[partizanstvo]*, the struggle against "compulsive striking" *[stachechnyi azart]*, the admonitions not to ignore the real interrelations of social forces, the appeals to deepen the theoretical foundation of their political positions. This is a mutiny against the Dement'evs, Gvozdevs, Chirkins, Romanovs, Bulkins, Kabtsanovs as representatives of

[22]Bulkin, *Na zare*, p. 265.
[23]See the discussion in Sher, "Nashe professional'noe dvizhenie," *Bor'ba*, no. 4, p. 22.

the entire, and in the capital rather dense, stratum of Marxist-workers who have tried and are trying to "liquidate" the infantile-romantic stage of the Russian workers' movement.[24]

The elections to the metalworkers' union in 1913 inaugurated a new phase in the history of labor politics. For the first time, union officers were supported on the sole basis of factional affiliation, regardless of experience or ability. Whereas the two factions of Social Democracy and the Socialist Revolutionaries had formerly competed on an individual basis for positions on the union board, now rank-and-file unionists voted for entire slates of candidates identified with a particular political orientation. The Mensheviks deplored this development, accusing the Bolsheviks of "factionalism" and destruction of the mass base on which union strength ultimately rested.[25] What the Mensheviks portrayed as divisive factionalism, the Bolsheviks insisted was a natural and inevitable phase in union development, involving the defeat of "liquidator" neutrality by true Marxism—a battle which the Bolsheviks claimed to discern in other European labor movements as well.[26]

The struggle waged between Bolsheviks and Mensheviks in the trade union arena involved more than a contest for hegemony over organized workers.[27] Concrete issues growing out of contrasting conceptions of the labor movement underlay the bitter contest over union leadership. In one organization after another, Bolsheviks gained support in elections for union officers—a development extending to diverse groups in both St. Petersburg and Moscow and indicative of certain generalized conditions affecting the outlook of broad and varied strata of the prewar labor movement.

In contrast to the Petersburg metalworkers' union, the Moscow tailors' organization drew its membership from artisanal workers employed in small shops. Yet Bolshevik ascendancy can also be charted among the tailors, who established the city's second largest union—a union reputed to have the "most revolutionary mood" in Moscow during the prewar period.[28] The Moscow

[24]L. Martov, "Otvet Bulkinu," *Nasha zaria*, no. 3 (1914), p. 68. The individuals referred to in the quotation are labor leaders who rose from the ranks of the workers themselves, all associated with the Menshevik "liquidator" position on trade unions.

[25]See, for example, the letter from Gvozdev in *Novaia rabochaia gazeta*, no. 65 (October 25, 1913), p. 1; *Luch*, no. 92 (178) (April 23, 1913), p. 1.

[26]*Pravda*, no. 100 (304) (May 3, 1913), p. 2.

[27]Sher suggests that a struggle for power was a basis for the conflict within labor organizations. Sh-r [Sher], "Nashe professional'noe dvizhenie," *Bor'ba*, no. 4, p. 22.

[28]E. Ignat'ev, "Stranitsy proshlogo," in *Nakanune velikoi revoliutsii*, ed. N. Ovsiannikov (Moscow, 1922), p. 158.

tailors had a long history of unionization dating back to 1905, and even during the Stolypin period they managed to build a thriving organization under adverse conditions. The tailors reregistered their union in November 1912, after a one-year lapse in operations, and from then on the organization expanded rapidly. In July 1914 it reported a nominal membership of 2,460 workers, about 4 percent of the city's labor force in the tailoring trades.[29]

Mensheviks and Socialist Revolutionaries dominated the union's board following its reestablishment in 1912, and under their direction the union organized a wide range of activities and engaged the Menshevik lawyer and labor activist A. M. Nikitin to provide legal services for members.[30] During 1913, however, a change took place in the political orientation of the union's leadership. Bolshevik tailors formed a party cell in accordance with instructions at the Prague Conference, and by February 1914 the Bolsheviks had won a majority on the union board. The new leadership promptly dismissed Nikitin as legal counsel for reasons of political incompatibility, and replaced him with a Bolshevik lawyer. Five months later, in July 1914, the eleven-member board included ten Bolsheviks and one left SR.[31] Mensheviks had been completely excluded from the leadership. During the spring of 1914 representatives of the tailors' union actively participated in citywide Social Democratic and trade union work, where their advocacy of the Bolshevik position earned them a reputation for exceptional militancy.[32]

Bolshevik ascendancy can also be charted in the Petersburg union of tailors. At the union's general meeting on March 25, 1914, the Bolshevik slate of candidates was chosen in full. According to an account published in the Bolshevik press, 450 of the union's nearly 1,000 members attended the meeting, but only 120 voted for the opposing (Menshevik) slate.[33] Similarly, members of the Petersburg union of tavern employees assembled on February 23, 1914, to

[29]N. Shevkov, *Moskovskie shveiniki do fevral'skoi revoliutsii* (Moscow, 1927), pp. 31–32. According to the 1912 Moscow census, there were 62,729 workers in the city's apparel trades. *Statisticheskii ezhegodnik goroda Moskvy i Moskovskoi gubernii za 1914-1925 gg.*, vyp. 2: *Statisticheskie dannye po gorudu Moskve* (Moscow, 1927), pp. 68–72.

[30]*Luch*, no. 59 (145) (March 12, 1913), p. 4. Nikitin received one hundred rubles annually for his services to the union.

[31]TsGAOR, DPOO, f. 102, d. 5, ch. 46, L. B. 1914, pp. 111, 155; DPOO, f. 102, d. 5, ch. 46, L. B. pr. II, 1914, p. 26; Shevkov, *Moskovskie shveiniki*, p. 35. According to Shevkov, the replacement for Nikitin was a Bolshevik lawyer, Kurskii.

[32]TsGAOR, DPOO, f. 102, d. 5, ch. 46, L. B. pr. I, 1914, p. 258.

[33]*Put' pravdy*, no. 48 (March 28, 1914), p. 3; for a list of candidates sponsored by *Pravda* in this union, see ibid., no. 44 (March 25, 1914), p. 3.

choose union officers. Here, too, the entire slate of Bolshevik candidates was elected.[34]

Even in unions where Bolshevik victories were less dramatic, and where Mensheviks and Socialist Revolutionaries managed to retain significant leadership positions, the Bolsheviks still made impressive, if less complete, gains in the struggle for control. The Mensheviks had held a majority in the Moscow metalworkers' union "Workers' Solidarity" until its suppression in August 1913. A successor union calling itself "Unity" finally obtained registration on December 31, 1913, and held its first general meeting at the beginning of March 1914, when a directing board was elected. Seven of the fifteen new union officers belonged to the Bolshevik faction. Four of these were outspoken Bolshevik "conciliators" who supported the party's general position but took exception to Lenin's policy on factional conflict with the Mensheviks.[35] Constituting a majority of Bolshevik supporters in Moscow, the "conciliators" differed from the *pravdisty,* or strict followers of Lenin, by demanding a reunited Social Democratic party and collaboration with Mensheviks who accepted both legal and illegal methods of struggle. With less than a majority on the directing board of the Moscow metalworkers' union in 1914, the Bolsheviks could not claim hegemony over this important group of organized workers, as did their Petersburg counterparts. Still, the party had expanded its influence among metalworkers, a key group in the city's labor movement.

The powerful printers' unions in both cities seemed impregnable Menshevik strongholds, with their carefully cultivated worker intelligentsia and long history of organization. It was a remarkable event, therefore, when in 1913 the Bolsheviks began to penetrate the leadership of the Moscow and Petersburg printers' unions.

In September 1913 the Menshevik-controlled printers' journal in the capital, *Novoe pechatnoe delo,* published an anonymous but candid report concerning the Moscow printers' union.[36] The author, "O. Aksident," wrote that the Moscow

[34]*Put' pravdy,* no. 27 (March 4, 1914), p. 3.

[35]Three of the four conciliators on the union board belonged to a revolutionary group in the Lefortovo district of Moscow, an area with large metalworking establishments. The Lefortovo group, led by G. I. Lomov [G. I. Oppokov], resisted domination by party regulars and maintained an independent position throughout this period, particularly on the issue of party unity. One of the four, S. I. Sokolov, was concurrently serving as an informer for the Moscow Okhrana. Lomov was the union's legal consultant. *Severnaia rabochaia gazeta,* no. 21 (March 5, 1914), p. 4; TsGAOR, f. 102, d. 5, ch. 46, L. B., pr. I, p. 30; f. 102, d. 5, ch. 46, L. B. pp. 101, 214; f. 6935, opis' 5, d. 124, p. 50.

[36]*Novoe pechatnoe delo,* no. 10 (September 21, 1913), pp. 10–11.

union was plagued by a "heavy atmosphere created by factional disagreements." Work in the union, he continued, "is difficult because of the influence of elements that are deliberately and strongly exploiting the existing disagreements." One divisive element, the writer explained, was the worker-correspondent from the Moscow printers' union to the Bolshevik newspaper *Severnaia pravda*. This individual was rebuked by the union's board for his factional activities, despite the fact that "many members" of the board considered themselves supporters of *Severnaia pravda*.

Growing Bolshevik influence in the Petersburg union of printers drew a public response from the Menshevik leadership of the organization in June 1913. Responding to Bolshevik appeals for the election of "true democrats" to the board, the Mensheviks strongly criticized the recent election in the Petersburg metalworkers' union and warned that the election of officers should be based on service to the organization and not on factional affiliation, an argument that favored Mensheviks, who were often union activists of long standing.[37] By the fall of 1913 the struggle within the union had grown more intense and acrimonious, provoking an editorial in the printers' union journal calling for unity. The editors further suggested a code of conduct for members—an indication of the deteriorating atmosphere within the union. Members were urged to maintain "adherence to polite methods of criticism of [other] world views, applying logical arguments, and not harsh phrases which do not convince but only cause conflict within the organization."[38] Soon afterward, at a general union meeting to discuss the question of workers' insurance councils instituted by the law of June 23, 1912, the Bolsheviks advocated a citywide insurance council among printing workers, while the Mensheviks favored enterprise-level councils. The meeting voted to support the Bolshevik proposal, thereby inflicting a serious defeat on the Menshevik leaders of the union. A report in the Bolshevik press stated that young printers at the meeting were an important factor in winning support for the Bolshevik position.[39]

Finally, in late April 1914, members of the Petersburg printers' union elected Bolshevik candidates to nine of the eighteen full seats on the directing board and eight of the twelve candidate seats.[40] Thus, 57 percent of the thirty union officers were Bolshevik candidates supported by *Pravda*—a testimony to the party's

---

[37]*Novoe pechatnoe delo*, no. 6 (June 27, 1913), p. 2.

[38]*Nashe pechatnoe delo*, no. 1 (November 1, 1913), p. 1.

[39]*Za pravdu*, no. 33 (November 12, 1913), p. 3.

[40]*Put' pravdy*, no. 72 (April 27, 1914), p. 3; no. 76 (May 3, 1914), p. 3. Curiously, the Bolshevik electoral victory in April is not noted in *Istoriia rabochikh Leningrada*, vol. 1, p. 445.

strength among some of the most skilled, educated, and urbanized workers in the Petersburg labor force. A subsequent election in late June 1914 sustained the Bolshevik position on this union's board.

Workers' clubs and recreational societies, many of them dating from the Stolypin years, were also drawn into the political struggle between the two branches of Russian Social Democracy. The Moscow Society for Popular Recreation, originally founded by Kadets, was taken over by Mensheviks in 1912, and a member of the Menshevik Initiative Group in Moscow, the lawyer O. I. Rozenfel'd, was elected the Society's president. Under Menshevik auspices, the Society held lectures, literary and musical events, and theatre excursions for workers.[41]

Beginning in the spring of 1914, Moscow Bolsheviks took steps to wrest control of the Society from the Mensheviks. A clandestine meeting of pro-Bolshevik trade unionists resolved to utilize the Society for Bolshevik party purposes and to elect only "Marxists," that is, Bolsheviks, to the directing board.[42] Over the next six months, Bolsheviks gradually displaced the Menshevik leadership of the Society. By December 1914 Rozenfel'd had been removed from the presidency and replaced by a Bolshevik, I. S. Komarov, who also served as an informer for the Okhrana. Another Bolshevik, L. K. Sokol'ev, became the secretary of the Society, thus completing the party's domination.[43]

The largest workers' club in the capital, "Science and Life," witnessed a similar shift in leadership. This club had attracted 946 members (768 men and 178 women) by February 1914, of whom 53 percent were also members of a trade union.[44] The first general meeting of the membership, held in January 1914, elected officers by slate, following the example of the Petersburg metalworkers' union. When the vote was taken, the Bolshevik slate received more votes than the SR slate and the mixed (mainly Menshevik) slate combined.

At a second general meeting of the club in early February 1914, attended by three hundred members, the Bolsheviks again won all the seats for full members

[41]*Luch*, no. 84 [170] (April 11, 1913), p. 4. The full title of this organization is the Society for Assistance to General Educational Popular Recreation.

[42]TsGAOR, DPOO, f. 102, d. 5, ch. 46, L. B. pr. I, 1914, p. 192. The meeting was held in May 1914.

[43]TsGAOR, DPOO, f. 102, d. 5, ch. 46, 1916, p. 10.

[44]Of the 505 club members who also belonged to a union, 462 were men and 43 were women. V. P., "Sredi peterburgskikh rabochikh: K kulturno-prosvetitel'nykh obshchestvakh," *Bor'ba*, no. 2 (March 18, 1914), p. 32.

of the directing board, while a mixed slate won in the contest for candidate members. A third meeting of rank-and-file members in late March 1914, preceded by vigorous agitation, again gave the Bolsheviks a majority.[45]

During the first half of 1914, factional disputes extended to virtually all organized activity among workers. When Petersburg trade unions formed a joint commission in January 1914 to plan the observance of International Women's Day (February 23), the group could not function, because the seven Bolsheviks refused to work together with the five Mensheviks.[46] The Petersburg club "Source of Light and Knowledge" reported in late 1913 that Bolsheviks and Mensheviks fought over every policy issue arising in the organization.[47]

With the establishment of insurance councils, both the Mensheviks and the Bolsheviks directed their attention to these new and promising centers for legal activity. The councils rapidly became the largest associations of workers in the country's history. By June 1914 there were 344 councils representing 378,000 workers in Moscow province, and 176 councils representing 164,000 workers in Petersburg province.[48] In December 1912 the Mensheviks began publication of a special journal, *Strakhovanie rabochikh* [Workers' Insurance], designed to provide information on the insurance law and assist workers in utilizing the councils to their best advantage.[49] Unwilling to stand by while their opponents preempted the insurance campaign, Bolsheviks began publication of their own journal, *Voprosy strakhovaniia* [Insurance Questions], in October 1913.[50]

The appearance of the Bolshevik journal precipitated a heated debate in many Petersburg unions and clubs. Since the journals depended on workers' organizations for financial contributions and a distribution network, both publications were eager to solicit their endorsement. In the late fall of 1913, when Bolshevik labor support was generally increasing, the party's journal won an endorsement from many Petersburg organizations, including the unions of woodworkers, marble and granite workers, gold- and silversmiths, and the club

---

[45]*Bor'ba*, no. 4 (April 28, 1914), pp. 40–41. *Put'pravdy*, no. 9 (January 31, 1914), p. 3; Ibid., no. 57 (April 10, 1914), p. 3.

[46] "Zhenskii den'," *Bor'ba*, no. 2 (March 18, 1914), p. 34.

[47]*Novaia rabochaia gazeta*, no. 115 (December 24, 1913), p. 3; *Za pravdu*, no. 4 (October 5, 1913), p. 3. In December 1913 the Mensheviks still held a majority on the club's directing board.

[48]G. A. Arutiunov, *Rabochee dvizhenie v Rossii v period novogo revoliutsionnogo pod"ema 1910–1914 gg.* (Moscow, 1975), p. 258.

[49]*Strakhovanie rabochikh* continued publication until February 1917, and thereafter under the title *Strakhovanie rabochikh i sotsial'naia politika*, which appeared until July 1918.

[50]*Voprosy strakhovaniia* continued publication until March 1918.

"Source of Light and Knowledge."[51] The Petersburg metalworkers' union also gave financial support to the Bolshevik journal, but the decision generated opposition within union ranks, and eventually the directing board voted to allocate one hundred rubles to the Menshevik insurance journal as well.[52] The election of an all-Bolshevik board did not eliminate the presence within the metalworkers' union of Menshevik supporters, who continued to press their influence over union affairs. The Petersburg textile workers' union also voted to assist both the Bolshevik and the Menshevik insurance publications.[53]

When the Petersburg union of gold- and silversmiths debated the question of support for the two journals, one issue emerged which may have disposed workers in this and other organizations to support the Bolsheviks. Some workers criticized the Menshevik organ because it was "written in the language of the intelligentsia and incomprehensible to the semiliterate masses."[54] This objection touched on a genuine difference between the two publications and probably contributed to the workers' perception of the Mensheviks as a party of intellectuals, whereas the Bolsheviks projected a more proletarian image.

Elections to the Petersburg citywide Insurance Council and the Petersburg Province Insurance Bureau dealt the Mensheviks a further defeat. The Mensheviks had adopted a critical attitude toward the Bolshevik demand for citywide and all-Russian insurance organizations on the grounds that factory-level councils should be strengthened before broader-based councils were established. The Bolshevik suggestion for a citywide council generated considerable enthusiasm among workers, however. When elections for a citywide council were held in the capital on March 2, 1914, forty-seven worker-electors participated in the election. Thirty-five of them voted for the Bolshevik slate of candidates; twelve supported the Menshevik slate.[55]

---

[51]On the woodworkers' union, *Za pravdu*, no. 25 (November 1, 1913), p. 3; on the marble and granite workers' union, *Pravda truda*, no. 20 (October 9, 1913), p. 2; on the gold- and silversmiths' union, *Golos zolotoserebrianikov i bronzovshchikov*, no. 3 (October 2, 1913), p. 3; on the club "Source of Light and Knowledge," *Za pravdu*, no. 5 (October 6, 1913), p. 3.

[52]*Metallist*, no. 11 (35) (November 16, 1913), p. 14.

[53]*Novaia rabochaia gazeta*, no. 58 (October 16, 1913), pp. 3–4; *Za pravdu*, no. 10 (October 15, 1913), p. 2, incorrectly reports that the board voted support only for the Bolshevik insurance journal. The union of sales employees in food stores voted 6 to 2 not to support the Bolshevik organ in February 1914. It is uncertain whether they decided to support the Menshevik organ. *Put' pravdy*, no. 14 (February 6, 1914), p. 3.

[54]*Golos zolotoserebrianikov i bronzovshchikov*, no. 3 (October 2, 1913), p. 2; also quoted in *Pravda truda*, no. 20 (October 9, 1913), p. 2.

[55]*Put' pravdy*, no. 27 (March 4, 1914), p. 2.

On April 13, 1914, elections took place for the Petersburg Province Insurance Bureau. The assembled electors voted "almost unanimously" for the slate of candidates proposed by the Bolsheviks. Nevertheless, the Bolshevik slate included one non-Bolshevik, V. D. Rubtsov, and he received the highest number of votes among the individual candidates.[56] Bolsheviks also won elections for worker representatives to insurance councils in many individual factories. At the Putilov plant, a Bolshevik slate was elected in November 1913.[57] Thus, the newly established insurance councils, which exemplified Menshevik hopes for progress toward a legal mass-based workers' movement, provided the Bolsheviks with yet another source of popular support.

At the Fourth Congress of Commercial Employees, held in 1913, a Social Democratic contingent led by the Bolshevik Duma deputy and police informant Roman Malinovskii attempted to displace the traditional Kadet leadership over these unions. The Bolshevik editor of *Voprosy strakhovaniia*, D. Antoshkin, was a candidate for chairman of the congress. He was defeated by Alexander Kerensky by a vote of 142 to 96. But on other congress committees, Bolsheviks won a majority. Their influence prompted the authorities to disperse the congress before it had officially concluded.[58]

Under Bolshevik direction, prewar labor organizations began to assume dual functions. On the one hand, they continued to perform the duties for which they were granted legal status by the government. Behind the screen of legality, however, they conducted illegal revolutionary work and carried on political and party functions, such as the dissemination of SD literature and illegal publications and the organization of political protests and demonstrations. Meetings of party members and sympathizers and party recruitment took place under union cover, and in some cases, delegates to party conferences and congresses were elected there.[59] To be sure, party activities had been covertly carried on in unions during the Stolypin years. But there was an important difference in the prewar period. Now the Bolsheviks, rather than the Mensheviks, were using trade unions as a surrogate for the much beleaguered party underground, and the Bolsheviks propagated the idea that unions should serve, above all, as organizational bases in the growing revolutionary movement led by the Bolshevik party.

[56]*Put' pravdy*, no. 61 (April 15, 1914), pp. 2–3.

[57]*Za pravdu*, no. 45 (November 27, 1913), p. 3; *Istoriia rabochikh Leningrada*, vol. 1, p. 442.

[58]*Pravda*, no. 149 (353) (July 2, 1913), p. 1; no. 150 (354) (July 3, 1913), p. 1.

[59]TsGAOR, DPOO, f. 102, d. 5, ch. 46, L. B.; DPOO, f. 102, d. 5, ch. 46, L. B., pr. I; DPOO, f. 102, d. 5, ch. 46, L. B., pr. II; DPOO, f. 102, d. 5, ch. 46, L. B., pr. III, 1914.

The Bolsheviks' advocacy of a militant strike policy facilitated their ascendancy among organized workers who had become impatient with the more cautionary approach of Menshevik labor leaders. This policy coincided with the mood of many workers, particularly in the capital, where the strike movement acquired massive dimensions. During the first six months of 1914, strikers in St. Petersburg province accounted for more than one-half of all the strikers in the country as a whole. Metalworkers in the capital stood at the forefront of the strike movement, constituting 63 percent of the strikers in the city between 1912 and 1914.[60]

As the strike movement intensified during 1914 the Bolsheviks found themselves in an increasingly anomalous situation. During the struggle to defeat their adversaries in the trade unions, they had exhorted workers to mount an aggressive strike offensive against employers. But once they assumed union leadership, they confronted the problem of asserting direction over a largely uncontrolled and uncontrollable strike movement—a situation which anticipated by three years the relationship between the Bolsheviks and the Petrograd masses in the June and July days of 1917.[61] Having aroused the workers' impatience for decisive and far-reaching solutions to their problems, the Bolsheviks found themselves caught in both instances between popular aspirations on the one hand and the necessity for tactical restraint on the other. The full implications of this dilemma had only begun to emerge when the First World War interrupted the progress of the workers' movement in July 1914.

The Bolshevik officers of the Petersburg metalworkers' union who took over in August 1913 soon found themselves facing this problem as they attempted to implement their policy of strike support in the turbulent metalworking industry. The union was rarely consulted by workers prior to the declaration of a strike,[62] and even when consulted, it encountered stiff opposition from employers, who rejected union efforts to serve as a collective bargaining agent. At the Lessner plant in 1913, for example, it was not until the eighty-second day of the strike that workers requested the union to intervene with employers to settle the dispute by means of arbitration. Union representatives approached the factory

[60]Arutiunov, *Rabochee dvizhenie*, pp. 384–385.

[61]Alexander Rabinowitch, *Prelude to Revolution: The Petrograd Bolsheviks and the July 1917 Uprising* (Bloomington, Ind.), 1968.

[62]*Za pravdu*, no. 28 (November 5, 1913), p. 4. For further discussion of this point, see the section "Employers, Trade Unions, and Industrial Conflicts," in chapter 9 above.

administration, which refused to cooperate. After one hundred days the strike ended in defeat for the workers.[63] As in earlier years, the union was able to intervene successfully only in conflicts involving small enterprises where the employer did not belong to the Society of Factory Owners.

After taking office, the new Bolshevik leaders of the metalworkers' union encouraged the strike movement, but sought to give it some direction and cohesion by withholding benefits from strikers who acted without consulting the union.[64] In January 1914 an amendment to the union charter was adopted which barred the union from giving assistance to strikers who acted without the prior approval of the organization. Some members opposed the amendment, arguing that the union should support every action taken by the working class to improve conditions. But a majority disagreed, and the amendment was adopted, giving the board the right to make exceptions in individual cases.[65]

Despite such restrictions, the union budget reflected the Bolsheviks' commitment to use union resources in support of striking workers. In 1911 only 7.8 percent of the union's income went to support strikes; in 1912, under the impact of the Lena events, the percentage rose to 30.6 percent; but in 1913, following the reestablishment of the union in March and the installation of a Bolshevik directing board, the union allocated 48.3 percent of its income to assist striking workers.[66]

Although union strike funds had already been authorized by the government in 1907 in those cases when the work stoppage conformed to the provisions of the law of December 2, 1905, the authorities used such support as grounds for depriving unions of their legal status. This had earlier made the Menshevik leadership cautious about participating in the strike movement, a restraint largely disregarded by prewar Bolshevik labor activists. Consequently, one year after its reregistration, the Petersburg metalworkers' union was closed by the authorities (April 1, 1914).[67] At the time of its suppression, the organization had attracted eleven thousand nominal members. The union's rapid growth, its radical leader-

---

[63]*Zhivaia zhizn'*, no. 3 (July 13, 1913), p. 3; M. Balabanov, *Rabochee dvizhenie v Rossii v gody pod"ema 1912–1914 gg.* (Leningrad, 1927), p. 54.

[64]Sher, "Nashe professional'noe dvizhenie," *Bor'ba*, no. 4, p. 22.

[65]*Put' pravdy*, no. 1 (January 22, 1914), p. 3.

[66]Bulkin, *Na zare*, pp. 318, 320.

[67]*Put' pravdy*, no. 52 (April 2, 1914), p. 3.

ship, and its intervention in the mounting strike movement alarmed the government and led to its closing.[68]

SOCIAL DEMOCRATS AND CITYWIDE LABOR ORGANIZATIONS

The history of citywide trade union organizations in Moscow and St. Petersburg further illustrates the pattern of growing Bolshevik influence. It will be recalled that between 1905 and 1907 the Central Bureau of Trade Unions in both cities played a major role in the workers' movement. Bolsheviks had gained a firm position in the Moscow Bureau by 1907 and taken control of the trade union journal, *Professional*, published under the Bureau's aegis. Toward the end of 1907 the Bureau gradually disintegrated following the widespread destruction of trade unions. Bolshevik efforts to revive the Moscow Bureau in 1911 had failed, because the trade union movement still had not recovered from a prolonged period of inactivity.

In January and February 1913 a group calling itself the Consultative Commission for Organizing a Central Bureau of Trade Unions met several times in Moscow, but evidently failed to establish a Central Bureau.[69] A year later, in March 1914, representatives of ten Moscow trade unions assembled once again to discuss the formation of a Central Bureau.[70] At this meeting the question of representation provoked a sharp exchange of views. Some unionists asserted that the general membership or the board of each trade union should elect representatives to the Central Bureau, while others pressed for the election of representatives by "Marxist," that is, Bolshevik, groups within the trade unions. Two leading Bolshevik unionists, D. V. Golubin and A. A. Poskrebukhin—both secret agents of the Okhrana—argued that only an election by "Marxist" groups would ensure the reliable political orientation of representatives, since some union boards were dominated by liquidators, liberals, or parties even further to

---

[68]*Put' pravdy*, no. 53 (April 3, 1914), p. 3. The union of metalworkers was closed for alleged violation of Articles 33–35 of the law of March 4, 1906, concerning the disturbance of public order.

[69]TsGAOR, DPOO, f. 102, d. 5, ch. 47, L. B. 1913, p. 5.

[70]TsGAOR, DPOO, f. 102, d. 5, ch. 46, L. B. 1914, p. 222. Among the unions represented at this meeting were the printers, tailors, woodworkers, confectioners, sales employees, waiters, pursemakers, and textile workers.

the right. After prolonged discussion, the meeting voted to leave the question of representation to the discretion of individual unions.[71]

In mid-March 1914 forty people gathered for the first meeting of the Moscow Central Bureau, but the meeting had to be postponed when it turned out that many unions had failed to send their representatives.[72] A second meeting convened soon afterward, but the Bureau never actually functioned, because by the end of May all except one member had been arrested by the police. Another general meeting of trade unionists subsequently resolved to resurrect the Bureau, but this effort also failed,[73] and Moscow remained without a Central Bureau until after the outbreak of the First World War. Only in September 1914 did representatives of eleven trade unions—all of them Bolshevik with the exception of the printers' union—finally reestablish the Bureau.[74]

In the absence of a Central Bureau, trade unionists devised a substitute arrangement to maintain regular channels for communication and coordination. During the spring of 1914 trade union representatives assembled weekly under the cover of excursions organized by the Society for Popular Recreation. A record of these gatherings is preserved in the archives of the Moscow Okhrana, whose secret agents were among the regular participants.

On a typical Sunday, the Society for Popular Recreation arranged an excursion for workers to a locale in the vicinity of Moscow. Sometimes as many as three hundred workers attended these outings.[75] Following afternoon tea, a group of workers would separate from the others to hold a meeting. The excursions provided an opportunity for large general meetings of Moscow trade union representatives as well as meetings of individual unions. Attendance at these meetings fluctuated from week to week. The regular participants included representatives from the unions of tailors, printers, plumbers, woodworkers, shoemakers, sales employees, and the Moscow Society of Consumer Cooperatives. A majority of those attending the clandestine Sunday meetings considered themselves Social Democrats, judging by the issues they discussed and the resolutions that were adopted. Here, as in the individual unions, Bolsheviks

[71]TsGAOR, DPOO, f. 102, d. 5, ch. 46, L. B. 1914, p. 234.

[72]TsGAOR, DPOO, f. 102, d. 5, ch. 46, L. B. pr. I, 1914, p. 19.

[73]Ibid., p. 232.

[74]T. V. Sapronov, *Iz istorii rabochego dvizheniia (po lichnym vospominaniiam)* (Moscow, 1925), p. 40.

[75]TsGAOR, DPOO, f. 102, d. 5, ch. 46, L. B., pr. I, 1914, p. 253.

commanded far greater support than the Mensheviks, whose influence dwindled significantly by the spring of 1914.[76]

Efforts to revive a Central Bureau of Trade Unions in Petersburg also failed during the prewar period. Local union activists attempted to reestablish a Central Bureau in anticipation of May Day in 1913. Representatives were assembled from the Petersburg (Bolshevik) Committee, the Central Initiative Group of Mensheviks, and local Socialist Revolutionary groups, as well as the city's unions. The Bureau was short-lived, however, and on May 5, 1913, the police arrested its members at a clandestine meeting.[77] During the summer of 1913, once again in response to plans for a strike, representatives of trade unions gathered to reestablish an illegal coordinating center. The first meeting was planned for late July in the woods outside the city, but the police received advance notice of the assembly from a secret informant and prevented the meeting from taking place. A second meeting, scheduled for early August, gathered at the appointed location, only to be arrested by the police. Twenty-one people were taken into custody, representing nearly all the unions operating in St. Petersburg at the time.[78]

The Petersburg Central Bureau, like its Moscow counterpart, could not surmount the intense repression to which it was subjected. Nor did Petersburg unionists succeed in arranging regular weekly excursions to provide an organizing center for the city's labor movement as a whole. In the capital, the legal Social Democratic and labor press, together with the Social Democratic Duma faction, served instead as the locus for organization and leadership in the trade unions. Unlike the illegal central bureaus of trade unions which faltered in the prewar years, the press and the Duma faction enjoyed legal if tenuous status until the outbreak of the First World War.

SOCIAL DEMOCRATS AND THE PRESS

Soon after the Prague Conference, the Bolsheviks hastened to establish a legal, daily, Social Democratic newspaper in St. Petersburg. *Pravda* [Truth] began

---

[76]Ibid., pp. 253 ff., 263, 269.

[77]Leningradskii gosudarstvennyi istoricheskii arkhiv (LGIA), f. 287, opis' 1, d. 68a, p. 169; TsGAOR, DPOO, f. 102, opis' 14, d. 17, ch. 57, 1913, p. 5.

[78]TsGAOR, DPOO, f. 102, opis' 122, d. 61, ch. 2, t. 2, pp. 178, 179; LGIA, f. 287, opis' 1, d. 16, p. 131. Missing from this gathering were representatives from the unions of marbleworkers and bakers.

publication on April 22, 1912, and despite police harassment and frequent modifications of the title, it appeared until the beginning of the First World War.[79] Written in simple, direct language intelligible to literate workers, it focused more on practical than on theoretical issues, giving extensive coverage to strikes, unions, and government policies in the capital, other major industrial centers, and abroad, as well as detailed advice on such problems as legalizing a trade union or obtaining permission for a public lecture.[80]

Competing with *Pravda* was the Menshevik daily newspaper, *Luch* [Light] and its numerous successor publications, which first appeared in September 1912 and continued until July 1914.[81] Initially conveying a more "intelligentsia" tone than its Bolshevik counterpart, the Menshevik daily also proved popular among workers and was often found along with *Pravda* in trade unions, clubs, and even certain taverns. Like *Pravda,* it presented detailed information concerning all aspects of labor and the party's view of tactics and strategy for the workers' movement.

The circulation of *Luch* was about sixteen thousand per issue, considerably fewer than the Bolshevik daily, which had a press run of about forty thousand.[82] But the two Social Democratic newspapers reached many more workers than these figures suggest. According to a report by the chief of the Moscow Okhrana, "advanced and conscious workers" formed groups in factories and sales-clerical establishments where they read the legal SD press aloud to their less conscious (and often less literate) fellow workers.[83] In this manner, the SD legal press reached an audience of tens of thousands of workers with information

---

[79]Six hundred and thirty-six issues of *Pravda* and its successor publications appeared in 1912–1914. The newspaper was closed eight times, 152 issues were confiscated by the authorities, and the editors were fined on thirty-five occasions. *Istoriia rabochikh Leningrada,* vol. 1, p. 436.

[80]*Pravda truda,* no. 5 (September 15, 1913), p. 3; *Pravda,* no. 18 (222) (January 23, 1913), p. 3. In May 1914, *Pravda* devoted a supplementary issue exclusively to the subject of trade unions, including contributions from many worker-correspondents. On *Pravda*'s coverage of unions, see *Bol'shevistskaia pechat' 1894–1917 gg.* (Moscow, 1962), pp. 329–334.

[81]*Luch* appeared from September 1912 to July 1913 (nos. 1–236); *Novaia zhizn'* appeared from July 11 to August 1, 1913 (nos. 1–19); *Novaia rabochaia gazeta* appeared from August 8 to January 23, 1914 (nos. 1–136); *Severnaia rabochaia gazeta* appeared from January 30 to May 1, 1914 (nos. 1–69); *Nasha rabochaia gazeta* appeared from May to July 1914 (nos. 1–55).

[82]*Trudovaia pravda,* no. 25 (June 26, 1914), p. 2. Data are for the period October 1913 to June 1914. According to a letter of March 10, 1914, written by V. Krakov to V. Lenin and intercepted by the police, the average circulation of *Pravda* was 20–30,000 per issue. "Bor'ba za rabochuiu pechat' nakanune mirovoi voiny," *Krasnyi arkhiv,* no. 3 (64) (1914), p. 140.

[83]TsGAOR, DPOO, f. 102, d. 34, opis' 13, pr. 3, 1912, pp. 128–129.

about the labor movement presented from a Social Democratic perspective. In early 1913 Socialist Revolutionaries in the capital also began publication of their own organ, *Trudovoi golos* [Labor's Voice], but it never matched the circulation or popularity of the SD press.[84]

The two daily SD newspapers encountered intermittent police persecution, including confiscation and the arrest of the editorial staff. Nevertheless, both organs stubbornly continued publication, taking advantage of the precarious atmosphere of the prewar years. An Okhrana report of January 1913 attributed major accomplishments to the press and the Duma faction in changing the consciousness of workers and organizing them for action.[85] It credited them, in particular, with taking over and expanding many of the functions formerly performed by the party underground. The report noted that the press spread Social Democratic ideas, gave the party view of events, disseminated party directives, published letters from workers, described strikes, printed names of strikebreakers, and collected funds for those arrested or exiled. To this can be added the role of the SD press and the labor press in fortifying among workers a sense of their class identity and the commonality of their interests, transcending a specialized occupation or a particular enterprise. In a period when trade unions foundered and the party underground was chronically disabled by arrests, the workers' press became one of the most important means for strengthening class solidarity.

Data on group contributions to the Social Democratic press by three key groups—metalworkers, textile workers, and printers—show a pattern of Bolshevik ascendancy similar to the one we have observed in workers' organizations. The number of group contributions to the Bolshevik press by metal and textile workers and printers increased substantially between 1912 and 1914. By contrast, group contributions to the Menshevik press grew at a far slower rate (except for contributions by the printers' unions in both cities), and in some instances (the Petersburg and Moscow textile workers' unions), the number of contributions increased hardly at all (table 41). Organized workers were not the only ones to make these contributions, but readers of the radical press—usually the more educated and politically conscious workers—included many trade union members.

The same trend toward growing Bolshevik influence over the daily SD press

---

[84]*Trudovoi golos* appeared from February 17 to July 23, 1913, followed by *Zhivaia mysl'* (August 17-September 6, 1913) and *Zavetnaia mysl'* (September 28, 1913-October 22, 1913).

[85]TsGAOR, DPOO, f. 102. d. 341, 1913, pp. 8–10.

Table 41

Workers' Group Contributions to the Social Democratic Press,
St. Petersburg and Moscow, 1912–1914

NUMBER OF GROUP CONTRIBUTIONS, WITH RUBLE AMOUNT WHERE KNOWN

	1912		1913		1914 (JAN.-JULY)	
	Bolshevik Press	Menshevik Press	Bolshevik Press	Menshevik Press	Bolshevik Press	Menshevik Press
St. Petersburg						
Metalworkers	126	33	538	156	755	178
	(883r)	(364r)	(3,258r)	(1,010r)	(7,142r)	(1,525r)
Textile workers	11	0	40	2	55	2
Printers	55	5	120	38	209	141
Moscow						
Metalworkers	1	7	15	12	31	2
	(6r)	(20r)	(76r)	(74r)	(392r)	(41r)
Textile workers	—	—	7	1	11	1
Printers	—	1	—	2	9	19

Source: N. A. Kurasova and S. A. Livshits, "Gruppovye denezhnye sbory rabochikh na 'Pravdu' i gazety drugikh politicheskikh napravlenii (1912–1914 gg.)," in *Rossiiskii proletariat: oblik, bor'ba, gegemoniia*, ed. L. M. Ivanov et al. (Moscow, 1970), pp. 209–240, especially pp. 221, 230, 233. In addition to group contributions, there were many individual contributions not included in this table.

can be seen in trade union and other workers' publications of the prewar years. The Bolsheviks founded two labor newspapers in Moscow, both of them under the leadership of the Bolshevik Duma deputy Malinovskii. The first, *Nash put'* [Our Path], a general workers' newspaper modeled after *Pravda*, appeared in the summer of 1913. The idea originated in a letter sent to *Pravda* by a group of Moscow workers in late 1912 calling for a local Bolshevik organ.[86] The public response was enthusiastic, and contributions poured in from workers in Moscow (who contributed 3,000 rubles) and the surrounding Central Industrial Region (contributions totaling 2,700 rubles).[87]

On June 27, 1913, the Bolshevik Central Committee in St. Petersburg gave approval for the establishment of *Nash put'*, and the first issue appeared about two months afterward. During its short-lived existence (sixteen issues appeared, but some were confiscated by the censor), the newspaper acquired genuine popularity among broad strata of Moscow workers and received additional contributions totaling three thousand rubles.[88] Some workers, such as the employees at the bookstore Nauka (Science), sent 1 percent of their monthly wages to the fund for *Nash put'* and another 1 percent to the Menshevik newspaper *Luch*.[89] The Bolshevik labor organ clearly had widespread support, and when the police finally closed it, 29,000 workers struck in protest.[90]

Following the suppression of *Nash put'*, Moscow workers were without a local labor publication for another nine months. In February 1914 the Bolsheviks again took the initiative, and under Malinovskii's leadership a group of union and party representatives founded a trade union journal, *Rabochii trud*

[86]A. Usagin [A. Gin], "Bol'shevistskaia pechat' v Moskve v epokhu 'Zvezdy' i 'Pravdy,' *Proletarskaia revoliutsiia*, no. 14 (1923), p. 407. For a detailed discussion of the history of *Nash put'*, see G. M. Derenkovskii, "Rabochaia gazeta 'Nash put','" in *Bol'shevistskaia pechat' i rabochii klass Rossii v gody revoliutsionnogo pod"ema 1910–1914 gg.* (Moscow, 1965).

[87]*Ocherki istorii Moskovskikh organizatsii KPSS* (Moscow, 1966), p. 163. Illustrative of the contributions to *Nash put'* are the following, reported in *Pravda*, no. 3 (207) (January 4, 1913), p. 4: group contributions from printers at the firm Zako, teapackers at the Perlov firm, typesetters at the Grossman and Vindel'shtein printing houses, a group of workers in the Bronnitskii district, workers at the Danilovskii manufacturing plant, a group of waiters, and others, totaling 143 rubles, 63 kopecks.

[88]"K istorii," in *Put' k Oktiabriu: Sbornik statei, vospominanii i dokumentov*, ed. S. I. Chernomordik, 3:84.

[89]*Luch*, no. 41 (127) (February 19, 1914), p. 1.

[90]*Izvestiia obshchestva zavodchikov i fabrikantov Moskovskogo promyshlennogo raiona*, no. 4 (October 1913), p. 14.

[Workers' Toil].[91] The conciliatory tendency of many Moscow Bolsheviks was reflected in the decision to give the journal a Bolshevik orientation and also to open its pages to contributions from both Bolsheviks and Mensheviks.[92] Moreover, a committee of trade union representatives was established to supervise the editorial board composed of local Bolshevik intelligentsia and to ensure genuine worker control over the journal, an arrangement suggesting that tensions may have existed between worker-activists and the party intelligentsia.[93]

In mid-June 1914 the first issue of *Rabochii trud* appeared, followed by three more—two of them confiscated by the police.[94] Trade unions (particularly the unions of tailors, plumbers, printers, woodworkers, bakers, and metalworkers) provided a distribution network for the paper,[95] and despite its brief existence it elicited considerable worker support and undoubtedly helped to strengthen the Bolshevik position in the labor movement.

Moscow Mensheviks also attempted to establish a local trade union organ in early 1914, but the project came to naught. The Menshevik lawyer O. I. Rozenfel'd organized a meeting of trade unionists, which declared itself an "initiative group" to organize a local newspaper. A subsequent meeting of trade union and club representatives was planned but apparently failed to take place.[96] The Menshevik project made no further progress. A similar project launched by Bolsheviks in St. Petersburg also failed in the spring of 1913, though many unions made substantial contributions to finance the project, to be called *Rabochii golos* [Workers' Voice].[97]

[91]Representatives of the following unions attended the meeting: tailors, shoemakers, printers, plumbers, textile workers, bakers, sales employees, and two workers' clubs. TsGAOR, DPOO, f. 102, d. 5, ch. 46, L. B., 1914, pp. 142, 153, 155–157, 161.

[92]Ibid., pp. 142, 156.

[93]Ibid., p. 142.

[94]Although the first issue was subject to confiscation, copies were concealed by various unions and subsequently distributed. TsGAOR, DPOO, f. 102, d. 5, ch. 46, L. B., pr. I, 1914, p. 292. The second issue of *Rabochii trud* appeared on June 21. Ten thousand copies were to be distributed, primarily through the unions (tailors, plumbers, woodworkers, bakers, metalworkers). Ibid., p. 289. But of that issue, 7,000 copies were confiscated and only 3,000 copies actually reached the workers. E. Ignat'ev, "Stranitsy proshlogo," in *Nakanune velikoi revoliutsii*, ed. N. Ovsiannikov (Moscow, 1922), p. 161. Two more issues were published, and only the third number escaped confiscation by the police. *Ocherki istorii Moskovskikh organizatsii KPSS*, p. 178.

[95]TsGAOR, DPOO, f. 102, d. 5, ch. 46, L. B., pr. I, 1914, p. 289.

[96]TsGAOR, DPOO, f. 102, d. 5, ch. 46, L. B., 1914, p. 96.

[97]*Pravda* reported the following contributions in issue no. 30 (234) (February 6, 1913), p. 4: textile workers' union, 125 rubles; leatherworkers' union, 100 rubles; tailors' union, 130 rubles; carriage-

The prewar period also witnessed efforts to revive individual trade union publications in St. Petersburg and Moscow, with very different consequences in the two cities. Between January 1912 and July 1914, seventeen different trade union publications appeared in St. Petersburg, only six of them established prior to 1912.[98] By contrast, Moscow had only one trade union journal during this period, published by the unionized sales-clerical employees.[99] The Petersburg authorities, unlike their counterparts in Moscow, had to contend with the presence of the Duma and the glare of public opinion as well as a far more turbulent strike movement. These circumstances helped to restrain measures designed to suppress legal trade union journals—measures taken by the Moscow authorities with relative impunity.

The seventeen trade union organs in St. Petersburg covered a broad range of industries and occupations (printers, tailors, metal, textile, wood and leather workers, and sales-clerical personnel), and in some instances appeared regularly over a period of several years. The five journals that survived for only three months or fewer had been established in the spring of 1914, when administrative measures against the press became more severe. The typical pressrun for a trade union journal was three thousand copies, some of them distributed to other cities.[100]

Trade union publications generally reflected the political orientation of the union they represented. Following the April 1913 election in the Petersburg metalworkers' union, the new directing board installed Bolsheviks on the editorial board of the union journal, *Metallist*. For several months the Mensheviks also continued to occupy positions on the editorial board and to publish articles opposing the politicization *[partiinost']* of trade unions.[101] Lenin personally intervened to protest the continuation of Menshevik participation in *Metallist*, and by August 1913 the journal was under exclusive Bolshevik control.[102]

---

makers' union, 100 rubles; woodworkers' union, 40 rubles. For a detailed history of this project, see I. S. Rozental', " 'Pravda' i professional'naia pechat' 1912–1914 gg.," in *Bolshevistskaia pechat' i rabochii klass Rossii* (Moscow, 1965).

[98]A complete list of these publications can be found in Ia. S. Roginskii, *Russkaia profsoiuznaia periodicheskaia pechat' 1905–1917 gg.* (Moscow, 1957), pp. 64–65.

[99]This journal was the *Vestnik torgovykh sluzhashchikh*, which appeared between September 1912 and March 1914. Ibid., p. 65.

[100]*Tekstil'nyi rabochii*, no. 2 (March 1914), p. 6. In a few instances, such as the Petersburg metalworkers' union journal, *Metallist*, the pressrun was as high as 12,000. Rozental', " 'Pravda,' " in *Bol'shevistskaia pechat'*, p. 105.

[101]G. Baturskii, "Soiuzy i partiia," *Metallist*, no. 4 (28) (June 3, 1913), p. 4.

[102]Rozental', " 'Pravda,' " in *Bol'shevistskaia pechat'*, pp. 103–105; Bulkin, *Na zare*, pp. 432–433.

The legal SD and trade union press in the capital, and to a lesser extent in Moscow, served to strengthen the Bolshevik position in the organized labor movement. Popular and widely read publications such as *Pravda* and *Voprosy strakhovaniia* helped to build a Bolshevik image among workers—the image of a competent, well-organized, and hard working party capable of an impressive range of activity under adverse conditions. This image was fortified by the presence of a number of outstanding labor leaders in Bolshevik ranks. None was more important in this respect than Malinovskii, a police agent whose activities as a labor leader and Bolshevik deputy in the Fourth State Duma further enhanced party fortunes in those years.

SOCIAL DEMOCRATIC LABOR LEADERS AND THE SECRET POLICE

Elections to the Fourth State Duma in the fall of 1912 represented an important turning point in the Bolshevik struggle for hegemony over the labor movement. Bolsheviks did extremely well in the elections, winning six of the nine contests in the workers' curiae, including all the major industrial centers (St. Petersburg, Moscow, Kharkov, Ekaterinoslav, Vladimir, and Kostroma provinces). The Mensheviks succeeded in electing seven deputies to the Duma, but only three from the workers' curiae. Petersburg workers chose as their deputy the metal-worker A. E. Badaev, a party member since 1904 and a loyal but colorless Bolshevik follower. Most significant of all was the election from the Moscow workers' curia of the Bolshevik metalworker and longtime trade unionist Malinovskii. Malinovskii's brief but dazzling career in the Fourth State Duma epitomized Bolshevik tactics and accomplishments in the prewar period.

A recent convert to Bolshevism, Malinovskii was concurrently employed as a secret agent of the Okhrana.[103] Approval for Malinovskii's candidacy was secured at the highest governmental levels, and his campaign for the Duma was

---

[103]There is some basis for suspecting that Malinovskii may have been serving as a double agent and that Lenin may have known of his connections with the Okhrana. For a discussion of this point and Malinovskii's association with the police, see Bertram Wolfe, *Three Who Made a Revolution* (New York, 1964), pp. 556–557; A. P. Martynov, *Moia sluzhba v otdel'nom korpuse zhandarmov* (Stanford, Calif., 1972), pp. 229–236; *Padenie tsarskogo rezhima: Stenograficheskie otchety doprosov i pokazanii, dannykh v 1917 g.* (Moscow and Leningrad, 1926), vol. 3, p. 281; Ralph Carter Elwood, *Roman Malinovsky: A Life Without a Cause* (Newtonville, Massachusetts, 1977), pp. 64–67.

conducted with cooperation from the authorities.[104] Taking advantage of his earlier Menshevik associations, Malinovskii adopted a conciliatory position on the question of factional disputes within the Social Democratic party, and this strengthened the support for his candidacy in Moscow labor circles where conciliatory views enjoyed popularity. It is doubtful, in fact, whether Malinovskii would have been elected without the assistance he received from such local Mensheviks as A. M. Nikitin, the well-known and influential lawyer who served as legal counsel for many unions and was himself a Social Democratic candidate to the Fourth Duma from the second city curia.

The election of a Duma deputy from the workers' curia took place in the following manner. In accordance with electoral procedures for the workers' curia, workers first voted at their factories and shops for ninety-four delegates who, in turn, voted for nine electors. Then the worker-electors participated in the plenary session of the electoral assembly along with electors from other curiae to choose Duma deputies. The election of a Social Democratic deputy under these circumstances required exceptional discipline and coordination among the workers at each stage of the process.

The strategy for Malinovskii's election was carefully prepared in advance by a group of Moscow Social Democrats that included representatives of both factions. They organized a meeting of the ninety-four delegates elected at the factory level and presented them with a slate of Social Democratic candidates, urging them to vote only for SD workers in the next stage of the electoral process. The meeting, held with the covert approval of the police, yielded the desired results, and on the following day workers on this slate were chosen as electors.[105] In the final stage of the election, all of the electors united behind Malinovskii, who succeeded in being elected a Duma deputy from Moscow. This show of solidarity behind Social Democratic candidates at each stage of the electoral process testifies to the base of support that the party had cultivated over many years among the more articulate and politically aware elements of the city's working class.

---

[104]Technically, Malinovskii was disqualified by law from standing as a candidate for the Duma because he had a criminal record for theft and did not have the required length of employment. With the connivance of the authorities, these difficulties were overcome.

[105]For a discussion of the election by a participant, see F. Tikhomirov, "Zamoskvorech'e v gody tsarizma," in *Krasnoe Zamoskvorech'e: Sbornik revoliutsionnykh vospominanii k dniu desiatiletiia oktiabr'skoi revoliutsii,* ed. K. V. Ostrovitianov (Moscow, 1927), pp. 11 ff. See also L. Martov, "Raskol v sotsial-demokraticheskoi fraktsii," *Nasha zaria,* no. 10–11 (1913), pp. 90–91, and *Luch,* no. 16 (October 4, 1912), p. 2.

Following his election, Malinovskii observed in private correspondence: "The single merit of the Duma is that from its tribune we can openly defend the demands of the working class, and by doing so we can contribute to the dissemination of our ideas to the broad masses."[106] Accordingly, he exploited his position to the fullest extent, taking advantage of the legal immunity from prosecution granted a Duma deputy. Having begun his career in Petersburg unions, Malinovskii displayed a special interest in the organized labor movement and helped to carry out the party's Prague Conference resolutions. During visits to Moscow, he held frequent consultations with trade unionists, and as we have seen, he assisted in the establishment of two workers' newspapers. In the Duma itself, Malinovskii rose on various occasions to speak on behalf of legal labor organizations, and when the Duma was not in session he traveled around Moscow province, meeting with workers, discussing their problems, reporting on activities of the Duma, and urging workers to participate in trade unions and factory insurance councils.[107]

Malinovskii's popularity extended beyond the confines of his Moscow constituency. More than any other member of the Social Democratic Duma faction, he used this important forum to promote the interests of workers under the banner of Bolshevism, and his eloquent oratory and forceful leadership soon earned him a unique and respected position in a broad circle of workers and Social Democratic activists. Malinovskii's working-class background—he was a lathe operator by occupation—represented a further asset for the Bolsheviks, enabling them to project a more proletarian image than that of their Menshevik competitors. In his energetic activities on behalf of the Bolshevik party, Malinovskii enjoyed the protection of the secret police. He entered regular employment for the Okhrana in the spring of 1910, under the code name "Portnoi," with an impressive monthly salary of one hundred rubles[108]—two or three times the earnings of a highly skilled lathe operator. Until his forced resignation and flight from Russia in May 1914, Malinovskii played a dual role in the workers'

[106]This statement was made in a letter to I. F. Burykin which was intercepted by the secret police. The letter was dated December 3, 1912. TsGAOR, DPOO, f. 102, d. 307, 1913, p. 2.

[107]See, for example, TsGAOR, DPOO, f. 102, d. 5, ch. 47, L. B., 1913, p. 4; DPOO, f. 102, d. 341, t. 5, 1912; DPOO, f. 102, d. 307, 1913; DPOO, f. 102, d. 5, ch. 46, L. B., 1914, p. 156; DP, opis' 14, d. 307, 1913, pr. II, p. 200; *Pravda*, no. 134 (338) (June 13, 1913), p. 2.

[108]B. K. Erenfel'd, "Delo Malinovskogo," *Voprosy istorii*, no. 1 (July 1965), p. 109. For other accounts of Malinovskii's career, see Elwood, *Roman Malinovsky;* Wolfe, *Three Who Made a Revolution;* Martynov, *Moia sluzhba; Padenie tsarskogo rezhima*, 3:281.

movement, which, as Lenin acknowledged in 1917, had both negative and positive effects:

In 1912 a provocateur, Malinovskii, joined the Central Committee [of the party]. He ruined dozens and dozens of the best and most devoted comrades, subjecting them to prison and hastening the death of many of them. . . . In order to win our confidence, Malinovskii, as a member of the party Central Committee and a Duma Deputy, had to assist us in establishing legal newspapers which, even under tsarist conditions, were able to carry on the work against Menshevik opportunism, preach the basics of Bolshevism covertly [as was] appropriate [given the situation]. Dispatching dozens and dozens of the best Bolshevik activists to prison and to death with one hand, with the other hand Malinovskii had to contribute to the education of many tens of thousands of new Bolsheviks through the legal press.[109]

On balance, Malinovskii did more to win support for the Bolshevik party among workers than any other labor leader in Russia during the prewar years. His accomplishments were so impressive that his employers in the secret police became uneasy, and some, such as the head of the Moscow Okhrana, A. P. Martynov, felt that Malinovskii had eluded the control of his police supervisors.[110]

Malinovskii's dual career as labor leader and Okhrana secret agent was spectacular but far from unique. Secret agents were ubiquitous in the organized labor movement, and these men stood at the very center of organized activity, providing direction, leadership, and continuity. One former activist has written that "Poskrebukhin, Nikolaev, Sokolov, Maros, Romanov, Marakushev, and a series of others . . . were the spirit [dusha] of one or another group or organization. Their reports, compared with the reports of others, give a full and truthful picture of what existed."[111] The position they occupied in various organizations made these informants as indispensable to the trade union movement as to the secret police.

Many secret agents remained active over a period of years, providing uninterrupted service for all concerned. Of the eighteen Moscow secret agents functioning in December 1916, nine began their work for the Okhrana in 1912. Among them were some of the city's most outstanding Social Democratic labor

[109]Erenfel'd, "Delo Malinovskogo," pp. 107–108.
[110]Martynov, Moia sluzhba, p. 233.
[111]I. Menitskii, Rabochee dvizhenie i sotsial-demokraticheskoe podpol'e Moskvy v voennye gody (1914–1917 gg.) (Moscow, 1923), p. 1.

activists during these years: S. I. Sokolov, A. Poskrebukhin, A. N. Nikolaev, S. A. Regekampf.[112] Three of these four agents belonged to the Bolshevik party, and while serving their police employers they also helped to facilitate Bolshevik ascendancy in the trade unions by providing continuous and capable leadership over a prolonged period.

Little is known about the people who served in the union movement as secret agents for the Okhrana.[113] One of the most intriguing figures is A. Poskrebukhin, born a *meshchanin* in Tula province in 1887.[114] Reporting to the police from 1912 on under the code name "Evgenii," Poskrebukhin stood at the center of party and trade union work in Moscow. Politically, he belonged to the Bolshevik faction, but like many Moscow Bolsheviks, he advocated a conciliatory position toward those Mensheviks willing to engage in underground activity. He participated in the Bolshevik regional party committee, the Bolshevik leadership group, and the City Committee for a party congress in the spring of 1914.

Poskrebukhin was also a leader of the union of sales employees, a large and active union with a substantial Social Democratic contingent among the rank and file. He attended nearly all citywide trade union meetings in 1913–1914, as well as meetings of Marxist student groups and workers' clubs, and he played a leading part in the two workers' publications founded in Moscow during these years. "In a word," wrote the trade unionist Timofei Sapronov, "he had the entire Moscow organization in his hands and through him in the hands of the Okhrana."[115] Elsewhere, Sapronov described Poskrebukhin's position in the workers' movement:

The author of these lines [Sapronov], in those days a young activist, used to look up to Poskrebukhin; and in general all the young comrades treated him as a star of definite magnitude. He held all the communication lines between Moscow and Piter [St. Petersburg] in his hands. All the meetings took place only after he had been informed; and as a result, he could arrange police raids in a manner and on a date that most suited his

---

[112]S. B. Chlenov, *Moskovskaia okhranka i ee sekretnye sotrudniki,* pp. 18–19.

[113]Evidence on this important subject is extremely limited. Soviet scholars tend to avoid the subject because of the embarrassing light it sheds on police infiltration into the Bolshevik party. Police archives that might provide information on the informants' background and careers have not been made available to Western scholars. Consequently, our knowledge of the personal history of Okhrana agents is at most fragmentary.

[114]I. Menitskii, *Revoliutsionnoe dvizhenie voennykh godov (1914–1917 gg.)* (Moscow, 1924), vol. 1, p. 371.

[115]Sapronov, *Iz istorii rabochego dvizheniia,* p. 23.

fancy. This is precisely what he was doing, and it never crossed anybody's mind that inside this activist there sat a Judas.[116]

For five years (1912–1917) Poskrebukhin maintained his dual life as Bolshevik union activist and Okhrana secret agent, and he helped to provide uninterrupted and experienced leadership in a labor movement chronically incapacitated by the arrest and flight of its principal figures.[117]

S. I. Sokolov, a metalworker, was elected to the directing board of the first Moscow metalworkers' union in 1906.[118] Beginning his Okhrana career in 1912 under the pseudonym "Konduktor," Sokolov reported to the police about the metalworkers' union, and more generally about union and party affairs. He, too, belonged to the Bolshevik party and gave continuous leadership for many years, ending with the outbreak of the revolution. Sokolov has been described as an individual who was "energetic, informed, and accurate in his reports [to the police]."[119]

A. N. Nikolaev, known to the police as "Andreev," was a Bolshevik printer who worked in the Moscow printers' union beginning in 1910 and subsequently held various leadership positions among the organized printers.[120] In the spring of 1913 he was elected to the directing board of the printers' union and the citywide printers' insurance council. He also participated in the Bolshevik party group in the Zamoskvorech'e district of Moscow and in the workers' club "Enlightenment," and after the outbreak of the First World War he continued his activities among Moscow printers.[121]

Another leading police agent, A. S. Romanov, served the Okhrana under the code name "Pelageia" or "Polia."[122] Romanov was of peasant origin from Vladimir province and a bookbinder by profession. At the age of twenty-eight, in 1909, he was arrested and agreed to work as a secret agent. Prior to that he had attended Maxim Gorky's party school on Capri and had established himself

---

[116]T. V. Sapronov, "Iz zapisok maliara," in *Nakanune velikoi revoliutsii,* ed. Ovsiannikov, pp. 54–55.

[117]Menitskii, *Rabochee dvizhenie,* p. 189. Poskrebukhin was arrested soon after the February Revolution and executed on June 20, 1918.

[118]Z. Shchap, *Moskovskie metallisty v professional'nom dvizhenii: Ocherki po istorii Moskovskogo soiuza metallistov* (Moscow, 1927), p. 65.

[119]Menitskii, *Rabochee dvizhenie,* p. 190. Sokolov was executed by the Bolsheviks in 1918.

[120]Menitskii, *Revoliutsionnoe dvizhenie,* 1:369–370.

[121]Ibid. Nikolaev's fate is not known.

[122]Ibid., pp. 374–375.

as a leading worker-Bolshevik. On returning to Russia he entered full-time party work in the Moscow region and attended the Prague Conference in 1912 as a Moscow representative (another was Malinovskii). Following the Prague Conference he became involved in efforts to revive the Moscow printers' union, most likely in response to party directives issued at the conference. The group to which he belonged failed to establish a union, possibly because of his betrayal, and he took no further part in union affairs. Nevertheless, as a member of the party's regional bureau of the Central Industrial Region, he was involved in many aspects of the workers' movement.[123]

In the important Petersburg metalworkers' union, one of the oldest and most trusted labor activists was a police agent. I. P. Sesitskii joined the union's directing board in 1908 as the delegated representative of the Petersburg Bolshevik Party Committee. In April 1913 Sesitskii was elected president of the Petersburg metalworkers' union. Bulkin described him as "a man of little culture, [who] had a weak grasp of the problems involved in trade union work and mechanically carried out party directives."[124] His term as union president was short-lived because he proved inept in performing his responsibilities, but he remained a member of the union's board.

The Mensheviks also had their share of police agents, although in far smaller numbers than the Bolsheviks. Important unions such as the Petersburg and Moscow metalworkers often contained two highly placed agents, one representing each branch of Russian Social Democracy. Thus, in addition to Sesitskii, the Petersburg metalworkers' union included V. M. Abrosimov, a peasant from Tver province who served as the union's secretary in 1912. Abrosimov was elected to the board when the union reopened in April 1913, and became the organization's secretary in May 1913. Like many Okhrana agents, he acquired a leading role in the union. In the words of a contemporary, Abrosimov was "an outstanding worker, and he enjoyed great popularity at the time as a good orator who knew how to approach the masses and how to explain in popular terms the heart of the matter."[125] Abrosimov served not only in the metalworkers' union but also in the workers' club "Education," where he was elected to the organization's directing board in the spring of 1913, and in the Workers' Group of the Military-Industrial Committee during the First World War. These positions enabled him

---

[123]Menitskii, *Rabochee dvizhenie*, p. 187. Romanov remained active until the February Revolution, when he was arrested. He was executed by the Bolsheviks in 1918.

[124]Bulkin, *Na zare*, p. 283.

[125]Ibid., p. 282.

to provide the police with extensive information on various aspects of the workers' movement up to the outbreak of the revolution.

The Moscow metalworkers' union, like its Petersburg counterpart, also included a highly placed Menshevik agent. A peasant from Vladimir province who had finished primary school, A. K. Marakushev was a senior (he was forty years old in 1912) and respected Social Democrat in Moscow.[126] He took part in the 1905 revolution and had been arrested on numerous occasions. Following his fifth arrest in February 1911, he agreed to inform on his fellow activists, a task he diligently pursued under the code name "Bosiak." A member of the Menshevik faction, Marakushev worked in the metalworkers' union, in the Lefortovo SD group (which had a pronounced conciliator orientation), and in trade union and party affairs. He enjoyed great popularity and trust among workers, and was elected by three unions (metalworkers, shoemakers, and pursemakers) as representative to the International Socialist Congress in the summer of 1914, a gathering which never took place because of the outbreak of the First World War. In 1916 Marakushev was again elected to the board of the Moscow metalworkers' union.[127]

The Moscow printers' union harbored agents belonging to both branches of Social Democracy. Whereas Nikolaev represented the Bolsheviks, V. M. Buksin was a leading exponent of the Menshevik position.[128] A peasant from Smolensk province, Buksin went to work at Moscow's Mamontov printing firm in 1910 at the age of fifteen. One year later, he began his career as an Okhrana agent under the code name "Voskresenskii," and served until the outbreak of the February Revolution. As might be expected of a printer, he had attended rural school and was equipped to assume a range of responsible posts despite his youth. During the prewar period he joined the board of the Moscow printers' union and was elected vice-president of the union in the spring of 1914. He also sat on the directing board of the Society for Popular Enlightenment and served as a delegate from the Mamontov firm to the printers' citywide insurance council.[129] Buksin took an active part in Menshevik party affairs and reported extensively on a wide variety of organizations and individuals, including his own brother.

In the prewar period, virtually every major union had one or more highly

[126]Menitskii, *Revoliutsionnoe dvizhenie*, 1:362–364.

[127]Ibid., p. 363. Prior to his execution in July 1918, Marakushev commented, "The historian will judge and understand our dirty work." Ibid.

[128]Ibid., p. 363.

[129]*Put' pravdy*, no. 65 (April 19, 1914), p. 5.

placed informers with close connections to the Bolshevik or, less frequently, to the Menshevik party. One writer on the subject has noted that it was "not uncommon to have party organizations and groups of a highly conspiratorial character, where 50 to 75 percent of the members were 'secret agents' of the Okhrana."[130] Many of these people also served as agents in the major legal labor organizations, where they occupied positions on the union directing boards, and held key posts as secretary or president of the organization. The large Moscow unions of metalworkers, woodworkers, and sales employees, for example, each had three informants; the printers' union had two informants; the Moscow union of tailors had one.[131]

The presence of so many Okhrana agents raises some intriguing questions. What tactical objectives did the Okhrana seek to accomplish through its secret agents? What effect did the agents have on the struggle between Bolsheviks and Mensheviks for hegemony over the organized labor movement? Did widespread police penetration of union and party groups help or hinder the anti-autocratic cause?

The evidence on police motives is contradictory. The Okhrana adopted a policy of *divide et impera* in an attempt to create a permanent rift between the two SD factions and weaken the influence of Social Democracy.[132] A police report dated June 15, 1914, noted with alarm that "there is a marked increase in the new conciliatory movement among workers in the rank and file of Social Democracy who are extremely dissatisfied with the political fervor and factional infighting between the *pravdisty* and the liquidators."[133] In the SD faction of the Fourth Duma and other party affairs, Okhrana agents such as Malinovskii helped to widen the breach between Bolsheviks and Mensheviks. Interestingly, however, this was not always the case.

Two of the Okhrana's principal agents in Moscow, Poskrebukhin and Mar-

---

[130]M. A. Osorgin, *Okhrannoe otdelenie i ego sekrety* (Moscow, 1917), p. 20.

[131]The agents in these unions were as follows: metalworkers' union, Marakushev, Sokolov, Lychagin; woodworkers' union, Golubin, Komarov, Lychagin (who also served in the metalworkers' union); sales employees' union, Poskrebukhin, Muranov, Golubev; printers' union, Buksin, Nikolaev; tailors' union, Komarov. The most important workers' clubs and recreational societies, especially those with strong Social Democratic influence, also had well-placed informers. For example, the Society for Popular Enlightenment had a Menshevik, A. I. Mironov, as its secretary. An Okhrana agent, Mironov also served on the board of the workers' club "Enlightenment."

[132]For evidence on this point, see *Padenie tsarskogo rezhima*, 3:286.

[133]M. A. Tsiavlovskii, ed., *Bol'sheviki: Dokumenty po istorii bol'shevizma s 1903 po 1916 god byvsh. Moskovskogo okhrannogo otdeleniia* (Moscow, 1918), p. 145.

akushev, supported the cause of party unity. Poskrebukhin, a Bolshevik, worked closely with Mensheviks in the trade unions and favored collaboration between the parties. Indeed, the Moscow Menshevik group regarded him as something of an ally and decided to support his candidacy as delegate to the International Socialist Congress from the Society for Popular Recreation.[134] The Menshevik Marakushev also advocated reconciliation, and belonged to the group of Moscow *partiitsy* who assigned major importance to the goal of unification.

The chief of the Moscow Okhrana, Martynov, evidently believed that through his highly placed secret agents he could control the revolutionary movement in Moscow. Perhaps the conciliatory stance adopted by his agents was regarded as indispensable for reaching prominence in the Moscow labor movement, where unification sentiments were particularly strong among rank-and-file workers. Martynov's strategy was to utilize his agents not merely to liquidate labor and revolutionary groups but to neutralize others through deliberate inactivity. The party leader Romanov, for example, kept party work to a minimum throughout this period on instructions from Martynov.[135]

Regardless of police strategy, highly placed agents had to display some accomplishments to maintain their credibility as labor leaders. Men like Malinovskii, Poskrebukhin, Marakushev, Sesitskii, and Abrosimov were compelled to pursue their responsibilities energetically in various organizations. The evidence suggests that they made many contributions to the workers' cause. Secret agents helped to establish and direct trade unions and to promote other legal workers' organizations and publications.

For the Bolsheviks, whose party unknowingly harbored many police agents within its ranks, infiltration represented both a liability and an advantage. On the one hand, agents were in a position to inform against fellow workers, and for this reason the Bolshevik underground organization fared poorly during the prewar period. On the other hand, the police had a vested interest in retaining their key agents in positions of influence and authority. Consequently, a number of prominent Bolsheviks who happened to be serving as informers remained active throughout these years, providing stability and continuity in party leadership of the trade unions—a circumstance that strengthened the Bolshevik position in the labor movement generally.

Police agents who belonged to the Bolshevik party helped to divert unions from legal to illegal methods of struggle and to promote the party position

[134]TsGAOR, DPOO, f. 102, d. 5, ch. 46, L. B., pr. I, 1914, p. 282.
[135]Martynov, *Moia sluzhba*, p. 226.

within these organizations. Perhaps the Okhrana viewed this as a means of reducing the mass appeal of potentially powerful labor associations and of containing dissident elements within smaller and more manageable conspiratorial organizations under party domination. Bolshevik ascendancy in many unions during 1913–1914 did, in fact, accelerate the overlap of party and labor leadership and activities—a process that culminated in the virtual fusion of party and union groups during the First World War. But Bolshevik appeals, disseminated so effectively by men like Malinovskii and Poskrebukhin, also fortified the conviction of many organized workers that revolutionary solutions were indispensable for the resolution of labor problems. Through their involvement in the legal labor movement, Okhrana agents helped to undermine the workers' confidence in gradualism and prepare the ground for the events of 1917.

INTERPRETATIONS OF BOLSHEVIK ASCENDANCY

On July 16–17, 1914, all the factions and nationality groups of the Russian Social Democratic Workers' Party gathered in Brussels for a conference to promote party unity, held under the auspices of the International Socialist Bureau. Lenin's memorandum to the conference, delivered by his personal emissary Inessa Armand, stated that four-fifths of the "conscious Russian workers" supported the Bolsheviks, a claim based on elections to the Fourth Duma, workers' contributions to the legal press, and the leadership of trade unions.[136] Lenin cited Bolshevik achievements in all three areas, noting in particular:

There are no parallel unions in Russia. In St. Petersburg and in Moscow the trade unions are united. The fact is that in the unions there is a complete predominance of *pravdisty*. Of the thirteen trade unions in Moscow, there is not one that is liquidator. Of the twenty trade unions in St. Petersburg that have been listed in our workers' calendar including information on membership, only the unions of [industrial] draftsmen, pharmacists, and office clerks are liquidator, and half the printers' union. In all other unions, [including] the

---

[136]Lenin, *Sochineniia*, 17:543. Lenin's information on trade unions in the capital came from a letter written on June 27, 1914, by A. S. Enukidze, in which the Georgian Bolshevik noted that "liquidators" held control in three unions (accounting clerks, draftsmen, and pharmacists) and in the workers' club *"Znanie i svet."* According to Enukidze, the Socialist Revolutionaries dominated the Petersburg union of leatherworkers, a fact which Lenin chose to ignore in his report to the Brussels Conference. TsGAOR, DPOO, f. 102, d. 5, ch. 102, L. B., 1914, p. 58.

metalworkers, textile workers, tailors, woodworkers, salesclerks, and others, there is the fullest predominance of *pravdisty*.[137]

While accurately describing the trend toward Bolshevik ascendancy in the organized labor movement, Lenin's statement exaggerated the party's actual accomplishments. Worker support for Bolshevik leadership dramatically increased in 1913–1914, but did not reach the proportions Lenin claimed. Nor did labor support for the Bolsheviks represent an endorsement of Lenin's position on all of the controversial issues that were debated at the time. Indeed, contemporary Social Democrats were careful to draw a distinction between "Bolsheviki" and "Pravdisty." The latter term applied to strict followers of Lenin who adhered to his pronouncements on the subject of party unity, whereas "Bolsheviki" accepted the general tactical approach prescribed at the Prague Conference but rejected Lenin's position on the issue of intraparty unity and cooperation with the Mensheviks. A majority of the Moscow party followers, including a number of leading trade unionists, were "Bolsheviki." In June 1914 they explicitly repudiated Lenin's policy on factional struggle and endorsed a resolution calling for a general party congress of the RSDRP, including all factions willing to accept both legal and illegal methods of struggle.[138]

It cannot be said, therefore, that the Bolshevik ascendancy in the trade unions and elsewhere signified a complete acceptance of Lenin's views by Petersburg and Moscow workers who voted for Bolshevik candidates, contributed to the Bolshevik press, and in other ways supported party activities. Indeed, the meaning of this support was a subject of heated debate among contemporaries. The question—then as now—was how to account for the sudden and pronounced shift in the political preferences of organized workers.

In his report to the Brussels Conference in July 1914, Lenin ascribed Bolshevik ascendancy in the labor movement to the workers' growing revolutionary consciousness.[139] Mensheviks did not accept this explanation for the precipitous

[137]Lenin, *Sochineniia*, 17:551.

[138]TsGAOR, DPOO, f. 102, d. 5, ch. 46, L. B., pr. I, 1914, p. 253. Poskrebukhin reported the text of the resolution as follows: "We, Marxists in Moscow, sixty people, recognizing the necessity of a general party congress, give our delegate to the Vienna congress a mandate: to insist on the necessity for a general party congress with all tendencies [factions] that recognize the resolutions of the congresses of 1903, 1908, and 1910 and who are working in local areas." Another secret agent present at the meeting reported that the resolution was adopted by a vote of 26 to 19 with 9 abstentions, fewer than the sixty representatives noted in the above resolution. Ibid., p. 259. Lenin himself had criticized the Moscow Bolsheviks on earlier occasions. See, for example, his letter to M. Gorky written at the end of January 1913 in Lenin, *Sochineniia*, 16:276–278.

[139]Lenin, *Sochineniia*, 17:549.

decline in their party's popularity among organized workers. Yet there was no consensus among Mensheviks seeking to account for their dismal showing in the organizations that had been the focus of much of their effort and hope during the preceding nine years.

At the time, Menshevik worker-intellectuals such as Bulkin, a displaced leader of the Petersburg metalworkers' union, attributed Bolshevik ascendancy to the penetration of intellectuals who manipulated the rank and file, taking advantage of their ignorance, inexperience, and "slave psychology."[140] In his view, Bolshevik intellectuals used the labor movement for factional purposes, diverting workers from their own constructive tasks and destroying the unity necessary for concerted action. As to the leadership of trade unions, the generation of worker-activists to which Bulkin himself belonged, he wrote in the spring of 1914, "The whole group of broadly educated workers—who could have been the pride of any Western European party—move around in organizational circles permeated with an atmosphere of factionalism and, as a result, give up their strength, their intellect, their energy, and their knowledge in the service of the factionalist Moloch."[141]

Replying to Bulkin and others like him, the Menshevik leader Martov disputed the claim that intellectuals had acquired a dominant role in trade unions.[142] The revolutionary intelligentsia had long departed from the organized labor movement, he argued. Their place was taken by a new Bolshevik "intellectual lumpenproletariat," whose influence derived from the workers' psychological need for a "strong power" over them. Their elemental rebelliousness, Martov asserted, led workers to vent frustration against "liquidators" and the worker-intelligentsia advocating Western European models of struggle instead of the real targets—the employers and the government. In his view, Bolshevism fulfilled a psychological craving, which in the absence of Lenin's party would have been satisfied by some other group appealing to the immature romanticism of many workers.[143]

The Menshevik labor activist Sher provided still another explanation, tracing the Bolshevization of unions to a combination of two circumstances.[144] First,

[140]Bulkin, "Rabochaia samodeiatel'nost'," p. 60. For further elaboration of Bulkin's views, see his article "Raskol fraktsii i zadachi rabochikh," *Nasha zaria*, no. 6 (1914), pp. 42–51.

[141]Bulkin, "Rabochaia samodeiatel'nost'," p. 61.

[142]Martov, "Otvet Bulkinu," p. 67.

[143]Ibid., pp. 67–68.

[144]For Sher's views, see his four-part essay, "Nashe professional'noe dvizhenie za dva poslednikh goda," in *Bor'ba*, no. 1 (February 22, 1914), no. 2 (March 18, 1914); no. 3 (April 9, 1914); no. 4 (April 28, 1914).

Sher detected a change in the composition of trade unionists following the influx of new members in 1913. These new members entered trade unions from strike committees, where they had acquired their formative experience. Young and unaccustomed to the rigors of planned struggle and "Western European practices," they quickly clashed with the older trade unionists.[145] Partly a generational struggle, partly a clash of methods and approach, the conflict between the two groups would, under ordinary conditions, have yielded eventually to cooperation under the banner of Social Democracy. But a second major factor in the situation—the presence of two highly factionalized political groups struggling for hegemony over the trade unions—prevented a resolution of the conflict. Factional conflicts were thus imposed on the unions from outside by political groups with minimal programmatic differences but a common ambition for control over organized labor.[146] The generational tensions between new and old union members became an important element in the parties' competition for domination over the trade union movement.

Sher was not alone among the Mensheviks in identifying young workers as the pro-Bolshevik element in legal labor organizations. Two other Menshevik commentators, V. Levitskii [V. O. Tsederbaum] and B. I. Gorev [B. I. Gol'dman], writing in the journal *Nasha zaria*, emphasized that these youthful workers had entered urban factories and shops fresh from the countryside, bringing with them the "primitiveness of the peasant world view."[147] These ignorant, semipeasant workers, who came to maturity in the years following the 1905 revolution, were said to display impulsiveness, disorganization, spontaneity, and an indiscriminate hatred for all of bourgeois society—attitudes that made them receptive to the Bolsheviks' extremist political slogans ("the more radical, the better," as Levitskii put it).[148] Thus the Bolsheviks won "easy 'victories' in trade unions and other workers' organizations" by adapting themselves to "the primitive level of consciousness of the masses and to the young workers' no less primitive understanding of their class tasks."[149]

In sum, leading contemporary Mensheviks took issue with Lenin's assertion that organized workers had acquired a self-conscious class and revolutionary

[145]*Bor'ba*, no. 3, p. 17.

[146]*Bor'ba*, no. 4, pp. 21–23.

[147]Rakitin, "Rabochaia massa," pp. 52–60; Gorev, "Demogogiia ili Marksizm?" pp. 30–41. F. Bulkin also notes the presence of young peasant recruits among Bolshevik supporters. See his essay "Raskol fraktsii," p. 49. Levitskii and Rakitin were both pseudonyms for V. O. Tsederbaum.

[148]Rakitin, "Rabochaia massa," p. 53.

[149]Ibid., p. 57.

perspective. They put forward, instead, explanations emphasizing the role of Bolshevik intellectuals (Bulkin), the "romantic elemental rebelliousness" of workers (Martov), and their youth and semipeasant outlook (Sher, Levitskii, and Gorev).

Contemporary interpretations reappear in later writings of both Soviet and Western scholars. Key aspects of Bulkin's analysis can be found in Perlman's study, *A Theory of the Labor Movement*,[150] which stresses the role of radical intellectuals in diverting Russian workers from economic to political objectives. Elements of the Martov-Levitskii-Gorev-Sher interpretations, moreover, are incorporated into Haimson's essay on social stability in urban Russia. Haimson attributes pro-Bolshevik sentiments to the psychological disposition of workers who were "impatient, romantic, singularly responsive to maximalist appeals,"[151] attitudes which he ascribes to the distress caused by the recent entry of young workers into the urban labor force. He identifies two groups of younger workers: "the younger generation of the cities, the urban youths who had grown to working age since the Revolution of 1905," and the young peasant-workers who reacted to the oppression of factory life with "elemental rebelliousness."[152] Like Sher, he discerns a generational struggle within labor organizations between young, inexperienced workers, who flowed from strike committees into unions, and the older, "more sober" generation of Menshevik labor activists. The Bolsheviks, Haimson argues, "managed to stir up and exploit the workers' embittered mood."[153] Finally, Lenin's analysis, linking Bolshevik ascendancy to the workers' growing class and revolutionary consciousness, forms the basis for Soviet scholarship on the prewar period.

Turning first to the Menshevik interpretations, we find that the upsurge in legal opportunities, beginning in 1912, did bring intelligentsia party activists back into the labor movement. But frequent complaints by workers about the dearth of intellectuals indicate that they were often in short supply.[154] The leadership of labor organizations did not pass into their hands, as Bulkin and

---

[150]Selig Perlman, *A Theory of the Labor Movement* (New York, 1949).

[151]Leopold Haimson, "The Problem of Social Stability in Urban Russia, 1905–1917," *Slavic Review,* pt. 1, 23, no. 4 (December 1964), p. 636.

[152]Ibid., p. 634. It is my understanding that in his forthcoming study of this period, Professor Haimson places considerably less stress on the recent rural background of workers as a major radicalizing influence.

[153]Ibid., p. 638.

[154]TsGAOR, DPOO, f. 102, d. 5, ch. 46, L. B., 1914, p. 111, for evidence of complaints by Moscow metalworkers regarding the paucity of intellectuals in the organized labor movement.

Perlman have argued. With few exceptions, union officers arose out of the ranks of the workers themselves, and as we have seen, union boards showed little hesitation in dispensing with the services of sympathetic intellectuals, such as lawyers, whose party affiliation no longer coincided with that of the union majority.

During the prewar years, intelligentsia organizers were far less in evidence than during the earlier period of intense labor activism in 1905–1907. Following the pattern established during the intervening Stolypin years, worker-activists and not intellectuals provided leadership for trade unions and other legal organizations. But whereas a pro-Menshevik generation of worker-leaders with a legalist and gradualist outlook had dominated the unions in 1907–1911, militant pro-Bolshevik workers were elected to union boards in 1913 and early 1914.

The youth of trade unionists and their inclination for generational struggle against older, more experienced labor leaders has been borne out by some of the evidence. In a number of important Petersburg unions, conflicts erupted between young, inexperienced trade unionists and older, seasoned labor activists. Generational struggle represented one component of the contentious atmosphere in some Petersburg unions. But if young, inexperienced trade unionists in the capital tended to support the Bolsheviks, they were certainly not the only ones to do so. The Bolshevization of numerous prewar organizations in the capital could not have occurred without the participation of a broad spectrum of workers, including some who had many years' experience in the organized labor movement. More important still, a trend toward Bolshevik ascendancy has also been documented in Moscow, but in this city generational struggle played no discernable role.

Rank-and-file supporters of the Bolsheviks included both younger and older workers, but what about those elected to union offices? A large group of Bolshevik officers in the youngest age cohort (under the age of twenty-one) would lend support to the interpretation emphasizing generational struggle. Regrettably, the evidence on union officers is too fragmentary to establish a profile of members of directing boards. But what little data there are show that the new generation of union leaders included workers of widely varying ages, many of them in their late twenties and older.[155]

---

[155]In the Moscow union movement, for example, these included I. S. Abramov, age 30, treasurer of the tailors' union; T. V. Sapronov, age 27, president of the construction workers' union; P. F. Fedotov, age 25, secretary of the shoemakers' union; K. E. Balitskii, age 29, treasurer of the

Nor did the Bolsheviks owe their ascendancy to recent peasant recruits into the labor force who brought with them a semipeasant outlook. As we have seen, skilled workers provided the social basis for the union movement. Although most skilled workers had been born in the countryside, they frequently arrived in the city in their early or middle teens to begin an apprenticeship. Skilled workers, to a greater extent than other segments of the labor force, were inclined to relinquish their rural habits, demeanor, and customs and acquire instead a new identity as urban workers.

It was not the disorientation connected with recent entry into an urban labor force that was characteristic of the skilled workers in trade unions, but assimilation, reorientation, and self-redefinition. Skilled groups, including artisans, displayed a sense of collective identity that came from long-term or permanent residence in a city and prolonged experience of employment in an urban labor force. Their self-perception as permanent urban workers made it possible for them to envision new forms of collective struggle that were incomprehensible to recent peasant recruits.

In the prewar years, as earlier, trade unionism flourished among workers in artisanal shops. The Petersburg tailors' union showed exceptionally "energetic activity," while the Moscow tailors were reputed to have had "the most revolutionary mood" of any union in the city.[156] The Bolsheviks attracted an enthusiastic following among tailors in both cities. The bulk of the membership in the Moscow tailors' union fell between the ages of twenty-two and thirty-five.[157] By the age of twenty-one, workers in the tailoring trades had already become experienced adult workers, and they cannot be included among the disoriented recruits to the urban labor force identified by Levitskii, Gorev, and Haimson as the backbone of Bolshevik support. On balance, the evidence raises serious doubts about the explanatory power of interpretations based primarily on the

---

metalworkers' union *Edinenie;* I. Ia. Volkov, age 29, member of the board of the metalworkers' union *Edinenie;* S. S. Vanisiforov, age 22, secretary of the metalworkers' union *Edinenie;* and A. A. Poskrebukhin, age 27, leader of the sales employees' union. S. I. Solokov, a leader of the metalworkers' union *Edinenie* and secretary in August 1914, was a party member from 1904, and although his exact age is unknown, he must have been at least in his late twenties by 1914. Poskrebukhin and Sokolov, both central figures in Moscow trade union organizations, also served as secret agents of the Okhrana. All ages are given for the year 1914.

[156]*Rabochee dvizhenie: Biulleten',* no. 17 (1913), p. 48; E. Ignat'ev, "Stranitsy proshlogo," in *Nakanune velikoi revoliutsii,* ed. Ovsiannikov, p. 158.

[157]*Proletarskaia pravda,* no. 10 (December 18, 1913), p. 3; see above, chapter 4, for discussion of the age of union members.

age and peasant outlook of Bolshevik supporters in the organized labor movement.

Soviet scholars, adhering to Lenin's pronouncements, portray class-conscious workers in the unions supporting Lenin and the Bolshevik party.[158] The premise that pro-Bolshevik unionists were followers of Lenin cannot be maintained in view of the strong conciliationist tendency in Moscow. The workers who voted for Bolshevik candidates in union elections were drawn to the Bolshevik slate because this party offered an alternative to the Mensheviks' cautious and moderate approach to labor problems. A growing number of workers, eager for redress of their grievances, had concluded that the Menshevik vision of an open, mass-based, legal labor movement was deceptive and futile under autocratic conditions. They sought, instead, a bolder and more immediate means of attaining justice from employers and the state. In contrast to the Mensheviks, the Bolsheviks were responsive to the workers' increasingly radical disposition.

THE RADICALIZATION OF LABOR: AN ANALYSIS

What stands out in the years 1912–1914 is the way the government and employers blocked workers from making concrete gains, while at the same time allowing them to organize collectively. The government, facing pressure for reform and disunited internally over the appropriate response to renewed labor unrest, adopted a vacillating position toward the union movement. Unions were again permitted to acquire legal status and to commence operations. But as soon as these organizations attempted to perform their central functions, such as collective representation in industrial disputes, the authorities imposed harsh and crippling repression.

Employers, now more extensively and effectively organized than ever before, mounted strong resistance to the workers' demands and refused to recognize unions or other workers' representatives. All of this unfolded against the background of a strike movement that month by month showed increasing militance and a corresponding failure to secure workers' demands. The unions, representing only a small minority of the workers in most industries and occupations, attempted to intervene in industrial conflicts and to promote collective bargain-

---

[158] Arutiunov, *Rabochee dvizhenie;* E. E. Kruze, *Peterburgskie rabochie v 1912–1914 godakh* (Moscow and Leningrad).

ing. But employers rejected these efforts, and even the modest, union-sponsored proposal for factory elders encountered implacable opposition.

Unionized workers were enraged in the prewar period by their inability, in spite of the union revival and a vigorous strike movement, to win tangible improvements. Taken in isolation, of course, the failure to make concrete gains does not furnish an adequate explanation for the radicalization of workers in this period. In 1907–1911, when conditions deteriorated and labor struggles also registered little success, workers did not turn to radical ideas. On the contrary, in these years many trade unionists embraced legalist and gradualist methods of struggle.

It was not intense and pervasive repression and employer resistance that turned workers in a radical direction, but a situation fraught with contradictory tendencies that made workers aware of their organizational potential without permitting them to derive tangible benefits from it. This served to undermine the workers' willingness to persist in an effort to build a legal mass labor movement and to seek reforms in the conduct of labor-management relations. Their anger, frustration, and disillusionment opened the way to revolutionary mobilization.

The Bolsheviks proved remarkably adept at turning these circumstances to their advantage. Their success in the prewar labor movement, the result of a shrewd combination of party policies and activities, foreshadowed their performance in the interrevolutionary months between February and October 1917. Two features of Bolshevik conduct in the prewar years were especially important: their organizational skills and their responsiveness to the varied and even contradictory aspirations among workers.

The Bolsheviks' "organizational weapon," as it has been called, took several forms.[159] The Prague Conference had instructed party workers to form Bolshevik cells within legal organizations to maximize party influence. Party activists subsequently established cells in a number of unions, and these assisted a relatively small number of party members and sympathizers to plan and coordinate their actions within a larger, mass-membership organization. In the Moscow tailors' union, for example, a twelve-member Bolshevik cell formed in late 1913 played an important role in promoting this party's position on the union's directing board.

The Bolshevik methods of electing union officers by a slate of candidates also proved advantageous to the party. First introduced in the Petersburg metal-

---

[159]Philip Selznick, *The Organizational Weapon: A Study of Bolshevik Strategy and Tactics* (New York, 1952).

workers' union in April 1913, this procedure was subsequently adopted by many other workers' organizations. The Mensheviks disapproved of election by slate and attempted to resist its introduction, but rank-and-file members often voted to adopt this method, which involved the selection of an entire roster of candidates drawn up by one party or another.

Workers seem to have welcomed the opportunity to express their political preferences unambiguously, and as we have seen, they frequently voted for the Bolsheviks, whose refusal to join a mixed slate forced the membership to make a clear-cut political choice. Through the introduction of this electoral procedure, the Bolsheviks accelerated the transition in union leadership. Overnight, they took control of such large unions as the Petersburg metalworkers, avoiding the possibility of sharing union offices with their political adversaries. In late 1913, Martov candidly observed:

I am dejected by the story of the Union of Metalworkers, which exposes our weakness even more than we are used to. It is altogether likely that in the course of this season our positions in Petersburg will be squeezed back even further. But that is not what is awful [skverno]. What is worse is that from an organizational point of view, Mensheviks—despite the newspaper [the legal Menshevik organ, Luch], despite everything that has been done during the past two years—remain a weak little circle.[160]

From an organizational point of view, the Mensheviks were decidedly less competent than the Bolsheviks, who proved remarkably adept in taking advantage of opportunities presented by the Duma elections, the legal press, the insurance law, and the proliferation of workers' associations. The prewar Bolsheviks were far from the disciplined and centralized party depicted by Soviet scholars. Yet party activists were more skillful than their competitors in utilizing the existing situation to promote their party's cause, an endeavor that succeeded because of the workers' growing radical disposition.

In their struggle for hegemony during the prewar period, the Bolsheviks also benefited from the presence of influential labor activists whose continuous service in the workers' movement was sometimes a consequence of their concurrent service in the tsarist Okhrana. Secret agents—more ubiquitous in Bolshevik than in Menshevik ranks—decimated the party underground in these years, but frequently made a genuine contribution to the Bolshevik cause in legal labor organizations. The Bolshevik activists Malinovskii, Poskrebukhin, Sokolov, and

---

[160]Haimson, "The Problem of Social Stability," pt. 1, p. 632. Haimson is citing a letter from the Nikolaevsky Collection Archive, written by Martov to Potresov on September 15, 1913.

Nikolaev directed the day-to-day struggles in the labor movement during the prewar years, enhancing the party's reputation for effective and decisive leadership.

Just as Lenin had appropriated the "Bolshevik" or "majority" label for his faction in 1903, so the prewar Bolsheviks appropriated terminology calculated to create a favorable impression among the rank and file. They called themselves the "true democrats" in trade unions, and designated their slate of candidates the "Marxist" slate. And although Bolsheviks and Mensheviks both included a large contingent of intellectuals and professionals, the Bolsheviks succeeded in conveying a more proletarian image. With the help of men like Malinovskii, a respected leader and a genuine worker, the Bolsheviks impressed many supporters as a party of and for workers. The Mensheviks, by contrast, were sometimes criticized for their remoteness from ordinary workers, an image reinforced by the intellectual tone of such publications as the insurance journal *Strakhovanie rabochikh*.

While accusing the Mensheviks of succumbing to reformist tactics, the Bolsheviks diligently attended to questions of immediate concern to workers. The pages of *Pravda* and *Voprosy strakhovanii* exemplify the practical side of Bolshevik activity. Here workers found detailed advice on how to register a trade union, obtain official permission for a public meeting, and organize around the insurance law. At the same time, however, the Bolsheviks argued that only a revolutionary overthrow of the tsarist regime would enable workers to achieve redress of their grievances. Consequently, the Bolsheviks advocated a militant strike movement—to culminate in a general strike—as a means of hastening the revolution and the downfall of the autocracy. The contradictoriness of the Bolshevik position was precisely the party's strength. At one and the same time, the Bolsheviks utilized opportunities for winning tangible improvements while arguing that amelioration was impossible under prevailing political arrangements. Conditions in the prewar period gave credence to the Bolshevik message, and many workers concluded that incremental improvements could not be achieved under the autocratic system.

The Bolsheviks cannot be credited with having radicalized workers; the disposition to embrace radical solutions arose out of the workers' own experiences with employers and the state. But the party gave tactical and ideological expression to those experiences, calling for the abandonment of a gradualist approach and the adoption instead of revolutionary methods to end tsarist rule. The Bolshevik advocacy of a militant strike struggle coincided with the mood of many unionized workers, and party efforts to transform unions into adjuncts of the revolutionary movement appeared to be a logical consequence of the unions' inability to represent and defend the workers' collective interests openly and legally. The leftward trend among organized workers on the eve of the First World War foreshadowed by two and a half years developments during the interrevolutionary months of 1917 when the Bolsheviks once again displayed their skill in harnessing popular disillusionment to party fortunes.

Conclusion

From the turn of the nineteenth century onward, highly diverse groups of Petersburg and Moscow workers attempted to establish collective organizations for the purpose of asserting and defending their rights at the workplace and in society at large. Harsh and restrictive policies of the tsarist regime severely limited the opportunities for collective association prior to 1905, but on the eve of the First Russian Revolution a variety of organizations (both legal and illegal) drew the participation of workers, including artisanal guilds, mutual aid societies, strike and factory committees, party groups, and most important, the government-sponsored Zubatov societies and Gapon Assembly, the country's first open, mass-based labor associations.

Following the outbreak of the 1905 revolution, Petersburg and Moscow workers took steps to create their own independent organizations. By the end of the year they had formed a multitude of factory committees and trade unions, and the Soviets of Workers' Deputies. Although the soviets and most factory committees disappeared at the end of 1905, trade unions remained an active and influential force on the labor scene in subsequent years.

The promulgation of the March 4, 1906, law legalizing trade unions and employers' associations inaugurated a new era in the history of Russia's organized labor movement. Trade unions proliferated rapidly, and thousands of Petersburg and Moscow workers added their names to union rolls. In a matter of months, one out of ten workers in each city had joined a trade union, and in some industries and trades more than half of the labor force entered union ranks by the spring of 1907. Attracting hundreds or even thousands of members, unions developed an elaborate organizational infrastructure and conducted an impressive array of activities.

Sobered by the failure of the revolution and eager to take advantage of the opportunity to create open, mass-membership organizations, trade unionists showed an inclination to utilize legal and gradualist methods for dealing with industrial conflicts during the peak period of unionization between March 1906 and June 1907. A generation of working-class leaders rose through union ranks, and organized workers acquired firsthand experience with democratic institutions and practices, even venturing, after some hesitation, into the realm of electoral politics. Profoundly influenced by Western European labor movements, trade unionists popularized, and in certain cases implemented, new procedures and institutions, such as collective bargaining, collective representation, arbitration, and permanent workers' committees at the enterprise level. To an extent previously unacknowledged in the literature, these activities yielded some remarkable achievements.

The progress of trade unionism was cut short by the Stolypin "coup d'état" of June 3, 1907, which marked the onset of a half decade of severe and repressive government policies toward labor. Faced with government persecution, employer retribution, and a deepening economic recession, the trade unions swiftly fell into disarray. Despite workers' efforts to make use of other legal opportunities for collective association—clubs, educational and cultural societies, consumers' and producers' cooperatives—organizational activity remained extremely limited until 1912. A small core of organized workers, committed to a legal and gradualist approach, bided their time in labor associations during the Stolypin years, awaiting an opportunity to revive the once-promising trade unions. When this opportunity arose, it produced consequences few of them had anticipated.

A sharp reversal in the political outlook and allegiances of organized workers took place on the eve of the First World War, a period of economic expansion, trade union revival, and renewed popular unrest. Workers sought to resurrect the union movement, but they failed to recapture the earlier momentum of these organizations. By mid-1914 many organized workers showed a growing disposition to embrace revolutionary solutions to labor problems, thus anticipating by two and one-half years the radicalization (and Bolshevization) of the workers' movement between February and October 1917.

Trade unions occupied an important place in Russian working-class life before 1917, just as they did in other European countries making the transition from an agrarian to an industrial economy. But whereas in Western Europe, despite variations from country to country, trade unions contributed to the workers' tendency to reach an accommodation (if only partially) with the status quo, in Russia the situation was very different. At their inception in 1905, Petersburg and Moscow trade unions were extensively involved in the revolutionary movement, and by 1914 they had again become vehicles not for accommodation but for revolutionary struggle. The evolution of these organizations— their brief and impressive progress and their subsequent failure—exemplifies the broader pattern of social and political relations in urban Russia, bringing into focus the changing outlook and allegiances of workers in the closing years of autocratic rule.

The intense and varied associational activities of Petersburg and Moscow workers both reflected and shaped their conception of themselves and their relationship to those who ruled them, those who employed them, and those who sought to recruit them into a political movement. This study has drawn attention to two major developments in workers' attitudes and collective behavior between 1900 and 1914. First, workers acquired new images of their collective identity, enabling them to find bases of solidarity and to create organizations for collective action. Second, workers began to see their relationship with superordinate authorities—employers and the state—in a new light. This, in turn, led them to put forward unprecedented claims and to utilize novel methods of struggle at the workplace and in society and the polity. The history of organized labor between 1905 and 1914 centers around the reception of these claims and the consequences when they were not met.

IDENTITY AND ORGANIZATION

Organization presupposes the existence of bases of commonality, that is, a shared identity or common sense of purpose. In Western European societies, workers who formed trade unions frequently found bases of solidarity in preexisting organizations such as guilds and mutual aid societies. When they began to unionize during the First Revolution, Russian workers also benefited from antecedent experiences acquired in pre-1905 organizations. Some factory groups found it possible to unionize rapidly and effectively in 1905–1907 because of their prior involvement in a Zubatov society or the Gapon Assembly. Artisanal groups with a strong record of participation in mutual aid societies—such as the Petersburg printers—also proved to be early and enthusiastic trade unionists. Underground party groups served, to some extent, as a training ground for future labor leaders. But Russian workers lacked a legacy of preindustrial organizations comparable to their Western European counterparts, and it is precisely the absence of this legacy that places the collective endeavors of Petersburg and Moscow workers in a special light.

Where, then, did Russian workers find bases of commonality? One important source of identity was a shared position in the work hierarchy. The lines of stratification among Petersburg and Moscow workers were numerous at the beginning of the twentieth century, but the most significant demarcation can be drawn horizontally across all sectors of the labor force, corresponding, above all, to the acquisition of a skilled occupation. There were many varieties of skilled workers. Some were employed in artisanal workshops, others could be found in a factory setting, while still others labored in shops and service occupations. Their specialized skill set these workers apart from the bulk of the laboring population, giving them a sense of dignity and status relative to other, less qualified workers, as well as a different appearance, demeanor, and life style.

Skilled groups tended to have a more clearly developed self-image as urban workers than their unskilled or semiskilled counterparts. Their separation from the countryside was often more complete, and they had greater contact with city life and more independence, both on the job and outside it. As in Western Europe at an earlier time, they were the ones who most readily participated in labor organizations, and from their ranks emerged working-class leaders from the turn of the century onward.

The skilled workers who predominated in the union movement were generally literate, urbanized, and nearly always male; most had entered the labor force at a young age to serve an apprenticeship, and they often performed tasks that relied mainly or exclusively on hand labor, with little division of labor. Those employed in small or medium-sized factories, or small workshops, retail firms, or service establishments, generally had a higher propensity to join a trade union than workers in large firms. In large enterprises, workers with a strong disposition to unionize often labored in a small-scale *immediate* work environment, that is, a relatively small shop within a big factory.

In the metalworking shop, for example, workers developed informal social networks, traditions, and rudimentary forms of organization (such as shop elders) that facilitated collective association. Metalfitters, lathe operators, and patternmakers—groups with a consistently high recruitment rate—spent their workday in the relatively small and even intimate shop environment, where workers came to know each other and to find bases of solidarity. The first major associational effort launched by metalworkers during the 1905 revolution—the factory committee movement—arose on this foundation.

A small-scale work environment proved conducive to collective organization, even in occupations and trades where firms were widely dispersed. In fact, the dispersion of workers in a multitude of small firms may have accelerated collective endeavors among artisanal, sales-clerical, service, and construction groups who were otherwise unable to conduct a coordinated struggle against employers. The small enterprise had another advantage as well, one which helps to account for the high recruitment rate of the workers employed there. Whereas large factories were subject to extensive and disruptive fluctuations in the labor force, in small firms the labor force remained relatively stable, even during the massive influx of new workers into the expanding urban economy beginning in the winter of 1909–1910. Tens of thousands of peasants flowed into the cities on the eve of the First World War, many of them finding employment in large factories that relied primarily on unskilled (and often female) labor. The new workers—many of them sojourners in the city, with strong continuing ties to the countryside—had a profoundly disruptive effect on the labor force in large enterprises, and this in turn interfered with union recruitment at these factories in the prewar years.

Unskilled and semiskilled workers were, on the whole, ill equipped to comprehend or to handle the tasks of unionization. They made their most impressive showing in the union movement during 1905, when the revolutionary upheavals mobilized groups that elsewhere have been among the last to participate in collective organizations. When unionizing ventures among unskilled or semiskilled groups achieved a modicum of success and continuity, these workers often had previous experience in a Zubatov society or the Gapon Assembly. In other cases, they were assisted by intelligentsia activists. Their participation in the union movement declined after 1907, and few rejoined the unions in the prewar years.

The skilled workers who provided the backbone for the union movement often displayed a preference for craft-based organizations. Craft unions predominated in Petersburg and Moscow during the 1905 revolution, and they retained an important place in the union movement until the outbreak of the First World

War and even afterward.[1] Artisanal groups formed unions along craft lines, as did many "factory artisans" and a wide range of other skilled workers in diverse sectors of the urban economy. Industrial unions also made an appearance beginning in 1905. By 1914, a majority of the unionized workers belonged to industrial unions, although in some cases these organizations were internally structured to accommodate the needs of specialized subgroups. The continuing vitality of craft consciousness was only one manifestation of the narrow parochial allegiances that promoted unification among Petersburg and Moscow workers. The related, though distinct, phenomena of factory and district patriotism also drew workers together in collective associations from the turn of the century onward.

The articulation of parochial allegiances did not, however, preclude a simultaneous identification with a broader collectivity—the working class. Class consciousness and craft consciousness emerged more or less simultaneously during 1905, and the workers who in one context (a trade union) exhibited intense craft loyalty were capable in another context (the soviets and the Central Bureaus of Trade Unions) of a class perspective. And if some industrial groups, such as the metalworkers, manifested class consciousness, so too did the partially artisanal printers, many tailors, bakers, salesclerks, and others in nonindustrial employment.

The sociological implications of these findings can be summarized briefly. This study lends support to the view that in transitional societies labor activism has been closely correlated, as Tilly and others have asserted, with long-term urban roots and a distinct social identity, frequently based on an occupational specialization.[2] A Durkheimian approach, linking labor activism to deracination and disorientation, does not account for the social bases of the union movement in St. Petersburg and Moscow.

Furthermore, this study has emphasized the importance of the workplace in generating solidarity among workers and facilitating collective organization. But in contrast to Marx and his Soviet successors, this investigation has shown that

[1] On this point, see William G. Rosenberg, "Workers and Workers' Control in the Russian Revolution," *History Workshop*, no. 5 (Spring 1978), and Steve Smith, "Craft Consciousness, Class Consciousness: Petrograd 1917," *History Workshop*, no. 11 (Spring 1981).

[2] Charles Tilly, "Collective Violence in European Perspective," in *A History of Violence in America: Historical and Comparative Perspectives*, ed. Hugh Davis Graham and Ted Robert Gurr (New York, 1969), p. 11.

the propensity for unionization did not coincide with employment in a large-scale enterprise and an elaborate division of labor. On the contrary, the most consistently active unionized groups proceeded from small or medium-sized firms or from small shops within a larger enterprise, and they performed skilled work based entirely or primarily on hand labor, with little division of labor. This was the case not only among artisanal workers but also among "factory artisans" with a strong disposition for unionization.

The problematical nature of the Marxist argument becomes especially apparent when we consider the role of artisanal workers in the organized labor movement. In both St. Petersburg and Moscow, artisans numbered among the leading trade unionists from 1905 on, just as they had in Western European countries at an earlier time. The groups relegated by Marx and Soviet historians to the so-called backward ranks of the labor force, because they belonged to the preindustrial economic order, thus stood in the forefront of the movement to form collective organizations in tsarist Russia. How can the labor activism of artisanal workers be explained?

Unlike Western European artisans, Russia's artisanal workers lacked a strong tradition of guild organization or cooperation in mutual aid societies. The highly restricted membership of these organizations on the eve of 1905 cannot account for the widespread disposition among artisans to form trade unions during the revolution and afterward. In the absence of corporate traditions as deeply rooted as those in Western Europe, Russian artisans nevertheless had a variety of shop customs and informal networks that contributed to their solidarity.

In Western European societies, artisans have historically turned to trade unions in self-defense following the advent of a factory system. In Russia as well, adverse economic trends induced artisanal groups to take defensive action through collective organization. The effort by some Petersburg and Moscow artisans to restrict entry into the trade and to curtail the spread of subcontracting and the concomitant deterioration of skill requirements by means of trade union organization bears close similarity to the conduct of artisanal groups in Western Europe at an earlier time. In addition, we have seen that artisanal workers displayed many of the same attributes (skill, urbanization, literacy) and labored under the same workplace conditions that help to account for the broader pattern of unionization among skilled groups.

Finally, this study has shown that although some factory groups, such as the metalworkers, developed a class perspective in 1905, class consciousness was scarcely confined to industrial workers. The partially artisanal printers, the salesclerks, and various artisanal groups provided enthusiastic support for the first class-based organization—the soviet—and subsequently promoted regional and national consolidation of the union movement. Thus, if industrial workers had a special disposition to adopt a class perspective, as Marx and others have assumed, they were certainly not the only ones to do so. Conversely, we have seen that skilled factory groups exhibited strong craft and other particularistic allegiances.

Images of class and craft affected the collective behavior of widely heterogeneous groups of skilled workers in all branches of the urban economy, and from the point of view of contemporaries the "working class" encompassed a far broader range of workers than most historical accounts have disclosed. To be sure, factory workers in major industries such as metalworking occupied a position of exceptional importance and influence in the labor movement, often setting the pace for others. But artisans, sales-clerical groups, and even service workers took an active part in virtually all types of voluntary association and collective activity. They, too, considered themselves part of the "working class," and were so regarded by their fellow workers.

The social bases of labor activism in Petersburg and Moscow trade unions conform to many of the same patterns found in Western European societies undergoing the transition from an agrarian to an industrial economy. What distinguished Russia was not the social composition of the workers who participated in these organizations, but the conflation of stages. Industrial workers entered Russia's organized labor movement more or less simultaneously with artisanal groups, craft and industrial unions arose almost synchronously, and craft and class consciousness developed together in the course of 1905 and afterward. This telescoping of phases that elsewhere occurred sequentially was a characteristic feature of all aspects of the Petersburg and Moscow union movements. In no respect was this exceptional feature of Russian labor more evident than in the workers' formulation and articulation of new claims during 1905 and the years that followed.

WORKERS' CLAIMS AND CONCEPTIONS OF RIGHTS

New expectations and approaches to labor problems only gain acceptance among workers once a break with tradition has taken place. As Moore has noted in his study of Germany, three developments must take place before moral outrage is likely to produce a basic critique or rejection of the status quo:

workers must reject paternalistic expectations, they must perceive their suffering as caused by human agents rather than an inevitable order of things, and their escape to traditional forms of security must be blocked.[3] What is distinctive about Russia in comparison with the German case analyzed by Moore is the suddenness, intensity, and simultaneity of these developments during 1905, a situation heightened still further by the presence of radical intellectuals eager to implant among workers a new world view.

On the eve of Bloody Sunday, most workers still retained their faith in the beneficent paternalism of the Tsar. The events of January 9, 1905, undermined this faith, and the government's subsequent inaction destroyed it altogether. By the end of the year, workers had not only broken with paternalistic expectations; many had also reached the conclusion that their enemies were "employers, officialdom, and the Tsar."[4]

"I was born again," wrote the Petersburg metalworker Buzinov, recalling the abruptness and totality of the changes in his consciousness after the catastrophe of January 9.[5] In the months that followed, Buzinov and others like him listened with unprecedented interest and receptivity to the appeals of politically minded intellectuals. At the same time, workers drew the conclusion that improvements in their lives could only be attained by their own independent collective efforts, rather than through the intervention of the Tsar. The workers' growing awareness of their collective potential in 1905 marked the beginning of an organized labor movement in tsarist Russia, and the workers most actively involved in these new organizations came from the ranks of skilled labor where the severance of ties with the countryside, and hence the loss of traditional forms of security, had proceeded the furthest.

What is important about 1905 is not merely that workers broke with traditional expectations, but that they generated new claims.[6] Partly on their own, partly under the influence of radical intellectuals, Petersburg and Moscow work-

---

[3]Barrington Moore, Jr., *Injustice: The Social Bases of Obedience and Revolt* (White Plains, N.Y., 1978).

[4]V. Voitinskii, *Gody pobed i porazhenii*, Book 1:*1905-yi god* (Berlin, Petersburg, and Moscow, 1923), p. 114.

[5]Aleksei Buzinov, *Za Nevskoi zastavoi* (Moscow and Leningrad, 1930), p. 40.

[6]The notion of claims that I am discussing here bears close resemblance to what Tilly has called "proactive" claims, that is, demands which have not previously been exercised, as opposed both to "competitive" claims "to resources also claimed by other group," and to "reactive" claims "to reassert established claims when someone else challenges or violates them." Charles Tilly, *From Mobilization to Revolution* (Reading, Mass., 1978), pp. 144–147. This distinction is an important one

ers put forward demands that entailed fundamental and far-reaching changes in the existing autocratic system. From the outset, these claims involved a dualistic conception of workers' rights, which centered, on the one hand, around the rights of citizenship and, on the other, around the right to extensive (even exclusive) worker control. The development of the workers' movement from 1905 to the Bolshevik seizure of power in October 1917 bears the imprint of this duality.

Even though informed by paternalistic expectations with respect to the Tsar, the Gapon petition carried to the Winter Palace on January 9, 1905, already included provisions calling for the rights of citizenship, that is, individual civil rights as well as the collective rights of labor to strike and to form trade unions. These demands became central during the 1905 revolution, when they were incorporated into a broader campaign for civil and constitutional reform. But whereas the two battles—for civil rights and for the collective rights of labor—had been fought sequentially in many Western European countries at an earlier period, they occurred simultaneously in Russia during the 1905 revolution, and workers played a leading part in advancing both claims.

The workers' claims to citizenship arose out of a basic struggle to attain tangible material improvements and the dignity and respect to which they felt entitled. They put forward the demands for freedom of assembly, speech, the press, association, and the right to strike, not as abstract ideals, but as indispensable preconditions for collective self-defense against the depredations of industrial life. In advancing these claims, workers envisioned a democratic alternative to the prevailing autocratic system of rule. They called for a constituent assembly and for the full and equal participation of workers in political life.

At the inception of the 1905 revolution, workers put forward another set of claims of an emphatically sweeping nature, involving the right to control key aspects of decision making. Claims for worker control first appeared at the time of the factory committee movement in early 1905, and initially focused on control over workplace decisions such as hiring, firing, apprenticeship, and the determination of wage rates. These demands impinged upon the most fundamental employer prerogatives, and, as Giddens has observed, they helped to

because it draws attention to situations in which workers generate new demands and to those cases when they seek to reclaim rights which they believe to have been violated. On this issue see also Charles Tilly, "Revolutions and Collective Violence," in *Macropolitical Theory*, ed. Fred I. Greenstein and Nelson W. Polsby (Reading, Mass., 1975).

"bring into the open the connections between political power in the polity as such, and the broader 'political' subordination of the working class within the economic order."[7] In 1905 a mounting revolutionary crisis and the penetration of radical activists into the workers' milieu rapidly made these connections explicit, integrating them into a political ideology and extending the concept of control beyond the factory and the workshop to the society and the polity as a whole. This radical transformative vision found its fullest expression in the Soviets of Workers' Deputies formed in October and November 1905.

Where did workers acquire this vision? I have argued that in the aftermath of Bloody Sunday workers began to see their painful and degrading position in a new way. Their lack of participatory power and elementary rights came suddenly into sharp relief, producing in them a desire for a complete reversal of the existing arrangements—for direct and comprehensive control over decisions affecting their lives. Radical intellectuals, especially Social Democrats, gave political shape and coherence to these aspirations. The image of a future society disseminated by the Social Democrats resonated closely with the workers' own popular imagination, which created an alternative to the present in the form of an upside-down world where the last became the first and the powerless the all-powerful.

This conception of future arrangements, enunciated during 1905, receded from the scene in the years that followed. It was not until after the February Revolution had finally and irrevocably destroyed the autocratic regime that the vision of worker control in society and the polity once again acquired mass appeal. Between 1906 and 1914, however, workers in St. Petersburg and Moscow were preoccupied not with the struggle for control but with the quest for citizenship. Although the revolution of 1905 had failed to produce a democratic system of rule, it did yield modest civil and constitutional reforms. The October Manifesto, together with the laws of December 2, 1905, and March 4, 1906 (legalizing certain categories of strikes and trade unions, respectively), accorded workers the rights of citizenship for the first time. These reforms constituted, as it were, a new social contract between state and society, adding legal entitlement to the workers' already strong belief in the justice of their claims.

Despite their cynical and suspicious attitude toward the government and the incompleteness of the reforms, workers hastened to take advantage of the

[7]Anthony Giddens, *The Class Structure of the Advanced Societies* (New York, 1975), p. 206.

opportunity to exercise and extend their rights. But these efforts, notwithstanding the brief efflorescence of trade unionism in 1906 and early 1907, encountered formidable obstacles from the government and employers. The changing political orientation of the organized labor movement from 1906 to the First World War was shaped, above all, by the workers' struggle to attain recognition of civil and collective rights and by their response when these efforts failed.

WORKERS, EMPLOYERS, AND THE STATE

In a country where autocratic rule persisted until 1917, the state exerted far-reaching—even decisive—influence over the organized labor movement. The progress of trade unions depended upon the willingness of the government, and to a lesser extent employers, "to meet the challenge from below," as Bendix has put it,[8] and to accord workers the civil and collective rights they demanded.

There was no consensus in official circles regarding the appropriate strategy toward labor. Two positions—one favoring relative social autonomy for labor and management, and the other stressing a combination of government intervention and repression—were debated from the turn of the century onward. Weakened first by urban and then by rural rebellion, the government briefly implemented the former approach between 1905 and mid-1907. But this strategy failed to gain solid and lasting support in government circles, and after June 1907 these modest reforms gave way to a half-decade of highly repressive policies toward labor.

On the eve of the First World War, faced once again with mounting popular unrest, the government wavered in its approach to the labor movement, allowing legal trade unions to reemerge but subjecting them to intermittent repression. As a result, workers who anticipated a revival of the labor movement and had hoped to conduct an effective campaign for improvements in the workplace found that their efforts were blocked. As de Tocqueville and others have noted,[9] disappointment and frustration serve to enrage people and to drive them in a radical direction.

[8]Reinhard Bendix, *Work and Authority in Industry* (Berkeley, 1974), p. 441.

[9]Alexis de Tocqueville, *The Old Regime and the French Revolution,* trans. Stuart Gilbert (New York, 1955), p. 177; James C. Davies, "Toward a Theory of Revolution," *American Sociological Review* 27, no. 1 (February 1962), pp. 5–15; Ted Robert Gurr, *Why Men Rebel* (Princeton, N.J., 1969).

It was not conditions of full-scale repression during the Stolypin years that radicalized workers, therefore, but government vacillation toward labor combined with employer resistance.[10] The government's ambivalent stance toward the organized labor movement in the prewar years helped to propel workers in a leftward direction, yet state policies in Imperial Germany also displayed considerable ambiguity after 1890. Where the two governments differed was in their basic tolerance toward legal labor organizations. After 1890, German workers proceeded along a reformist path under Social Democratic auspices, combining the rhetoric of revolutionary Marxism with the struggle for tangible incremental improvements won through collective organization. The continuing prospect of economic improvement played a decisive role in discouraging German workers from embracing drastic solutions that called for a fundamental transformation of society. Roth has described this situation as "negative integration," that is, political and social isolation combined with economic and partial cultural inclusion of workers into German society.[11]

Unlike its counterpart in Germany, the tsarist government would not permit a trade union movement to become rooted in Russian soil or to conduct an open and moderately successful struggle against employers for improved wages, hours, and working conditions. Had the tsarist regime pursued such a policy, it is conceivable that organized workers might have moved toward some kind of partial reconciliation with the autocratic system, as they showed tentative signs of doing in 1906–1907.

What stood in the way of the reforms in government policy advocated by some ministerial circles was the chronic and overriding fear of social instability. Having failed to integrate new entrepreneurial elements into political life, the government relied on an increasingly attenuated social base of political power in the closing decades of autocratic rule. The swift and impressive progress of the union movement in 1905–1907 and its penetration by radical intellectuals deeply alarmed the authorities, who feared it would threaten the precarious social and political equilibrium in urban Russia.

Government policies after June 1907 relegated workers to a position of extreme exclusion, a situation further exacerbated by employers. Relying on

---

[10]The general observation that intermittent repression produces explosive social consequences is made by Gaetano Mosca, *The Ruling Class,* trans. Hannah D. Kahn (New York, 1939), p. 191, and Moore, *Injustice,* p. 483.

[11]Guenther Roth, *Social Democrats in Imperial Germany: A Study in Working-Class Isolation and National Integration* (Totawa, N.J., 1963).

their own newly established organizations, employers attempted to resist workers' efforts to introduce reforms in the conduct of labor-management relations. Again, it was only during a brief period in 1905–1907 that some employers—usually those at an organizational disadvantage compared with workers—consented to recognize trade unions and to settle disputes by means of arbitration and permanent grievance committees. Highly diverse groups of organized workers sought to win employer cooperation throughout the period from 1905 to 1914, but apart from a few concessions extracted in the aftermath of the First Russian Revolution, these endeavors had no lasting effect. At the workplace, as in society at large, workers encountered severe and, in the prewar years, seemingly insurmountable obstacles when they sought—often by legal means—to unite collectively for a better life. Working-class isolation was thus far more complete than in Germany during the same period because, apart from a brief interlude in 1905–1907, Russian workers proved unable to defend their economic rights.

In contrast to some applications of integration theory, this study has emphasized the dualism inherent in the workers' outlook—a dualism which first emerges clearly from workers' statements and actions during 1905 but which originated, as I have suggested, in Russian working-class life. It is not simply that workers strove for "legitimacy" and acceptance and then rebelled when this failed to materialize. To be sure, indignation, disappointment, and frustration helped to strengthen the appeal among workers of a radical transformative vision. Yet the claims for control underlying this vision were rooted in the very same milieu that generated demands for civil and collective rights. Both of these conceptions could coexist among workers in the final years of autocratic rule because each of them bore a close organic connection to cultural attitudes that were formed, in large measure, by workers' relations with superordinate authorities and, from 1905 on, with political parties and intellectuals.

PARTIES, INTELLECTUALS, AND ORGANIZED WORKERS

Well before the 1905 revolution, political parties and intelligentsia activists had already established limited contact with rank-and-file workers through radical circles, underground groups, and the Zubatov and Gapon experiments. From 1905 on, these encounters acquired new scope, proceeding for the most part through the medium of trade unions and other voluntary associations.

The Social Democrats, to a greater extent than other parties and groups

(Socialist Revolutionaries, syndicalists, and the liberal Kadets), presided over the formation of the union movement and remained an important presence there in the years that followed. Far from being an isolated band of underground revolutionaries between 1905 and 1914, as they are sometimes portrayed, Social Democratic activists established extensive and sustained contact with rank-and-file workers through legal voluntary associations.

Utilizing the trade unions, the legal labor press, and other organizational channels, Social Democrats conveyed to workers several key themes: proletarian solidarity, the irreconcilability of class interests, and the interconnection between economic and political struggle. These ideas influenced the ways that workers thought and acted in 1905 and afterward, accelerating the development of class consciousness, conflict consciousness, and the politicization of the labor movement.

Most important, Social Democrats (together with other politically minded intelligentsia organizers) assisted workers in extending their horizons beyond the workshop or factory gates to the society and the polity as a whole. They also imparted to workers the powerful, if often amorphous, image of a socialist society—an image of future arrangements which represented an extension and elaboration of the workers' own inclination to wrest control from employers over the key decisions of factory life. In these respects, an outside agency was required to transpose workers' grievances and aspirations to the broader framework of social and political institutions.

But if radical intellectuals carried workers' claims beyond the workplace, the workers themselves were not without their own ideas. Throughout the period from 1905 to 1914, organized workers displayed a strong independent cast of mind in their repeated preference for craft-based unions and their insistence on union-sponsored mutual aid programs, notwithstanding the objections of their radical mentors. Their relationship with intelligentsia activists was mutually initiated in 1905, and it retained a reciprocal character as each group adapted to and learned from the outlook and priorities of the other. Interaction between the two groups was not a one-way street, as Lenin and others have implied, and the Bolsheviks, as well as Mensheviks and others, made many adjustments to meet the needs and demands of workers whom they sought to reach and to recruit into a political movement.

The two factions of Social Democracy—the Mensheviks and the Bolsheviks—presented workers with contrasting approaches to labor problems, which reinforced the workers' dualistic conception of their rights. The Mensheviks never relinquished the long-term strategic goals of revolution and a future socialist society, but they advocated the short-term utilization of legal methods to build a mass-based, Western European type of labor movement, and they encouraged workers to defend and extend their basic civil and collective rights, which Mensheviks viewed as a precondition for the self-emancipation of the working class.

The Bolsheviks, by contrast, were less concerned with issues pertaining to citizenship, and they remained chronically fearful of independent (nonparty) labor organizations. They focused on the mobilization of workers in a revolutionary movement under party leadership, and sought to utilize trade unions to that end. In the prewar years and again in 1917, the Bolsheviks helped to strengthen among workers the commitment to a radical transformative vision and to turn workers' discontent to the party's advantage.

The two factions of Social Democracy drew their support from widely heterogeneous groups within the organized labor movement. Party *praktiki* did not confine their attention to factory workers; they devoted a good deal of energy to reaching such groups as bakers, tailors, carpenters, gold- and silversmiths, and salesclerks. Soviet historians have generally asserted that the Mensheviks found a following among the so-called backward elements of the labor force, while the Bolsheviks attracted the support of factory groups, including metal and textile workers. As this study has disclosed, however, the Mensheviks established a very broad base within the labor movement from 1905 to 1913, including support from the metalworkers' unions in both cities as well as numerous other factory and nonfactory groups. The Bolsheviks achieved some of their most enthusiastic and militant followers among bakers, tailors, and other artisans, together with some segments of the industrial population. In Russia as in Western Europe at an earlier time, radical ideas and socialist ideologies struck a responsive chord among skilled nonfactory groups and "factory artisans"—workers with a relatively well defined social identity, a sense of pride and independence, and a belief in their right to a better life.

LOOKING AHEAD

The complex and varied tendencies among organized workers in the closing decades of autocratic rule did not disappear following the overthrow of the tsarist regime in February 1917. During the months between the February and October revolutions, the same dualistic conception of rights and diverse bases of solidarity and consciousness continued to influence the outlook and allegiances of workers and their organizational activity. Just as significant lines of continuity have been discerned before and during 1905, so the developments preceding 1917 set the stage for the revolutionary upheavals that eventually brought the Bolsheviks to power. Drawing upon their earlier organizational experiences, workers promptly reestablished factory committees, trade unions, and soviets after the February Revolution, and attempted to win recognition of their rights, long denied by the autocratic regime.

The advent of dual power—the Provisional Government and the soviets—carried forward in a new form the still-unresolved ambiguity in workers' conceptions of their rights dating from 1905. Whereas the Provisional Government held out the promise of a full realization of workers' civil and collective rights, the soviets embodied—as Lenin so quickly recognized—a radical transformative vision of social and political organization in which workers, together with other lower-class groups, exercised decisive control over the country's future. Originating in the realm of ideology, the two conceptions now acquired concrete institutional reality on a national scale.

The mounting crisis in 1917 and the growing radicalization and Bolshevization of Petersburg and Moscow workers was the outcome of a constellation of social and political forces that replicated many of the features of earlier crises in 1905 and on the eve of the First World War. Once again angered and disappointed when their expectations were unmet, workers gravitated to the one party whose vision of the future promised, at last, to turn the world upside down, making the last into the first, the weak into the truly powerful.

Appendix I

St. Petersburg and Moscow Trade Unions, 1905

ST. PETERSBURG, 1905

Union	Founding Date	Adoption of Charter
Chemical		
Union of Workers in the Russian-American Rubber Manufactory	November	n.d.
Communications		
Union of Postmen	n.d. (September)	n.d.
Construction		
Union of Stucco Molders*	November	n.d.
Union of Workers in the Cement Industry	November	n.d.
Union of Plumbers*	November	n.d.
Food		
Union of Bakers and Confectioners*	October	December
Union of Tobacco Workers	November	November
Union of Workers in Candy Factories	November	n.d.
Government		
Union of Employees in the Petersburg City Treasury	November	n.d.
Union of Employees in the Offices of the City Courts	n.d. (November)	n.d.
Union of Employees and Workers in the Institutions of the Petersburg City Administration	November	n.d.
Union of Workers in State Wine Cellars	December	n.d.
Metal		
St. Petersburg General Workers' Union (Smesovist)	April (March)	April
Union of Workers in the Nevskii Shipbuilding and Machine Plant (Union of Metalworkers)	none (July)	none

ST. PETERSBURG, 1905

Union	Founding Date	Adoption of Charter
Union of Port and Shipyard Workers	November	November
Union of Workers in the Metal Industry in the Firms of Odner, Beyer, Westinghouse, Armaturnyi, Galkin, Glebov, Richter, and others	November (September)	November
Union of Workers of the Obukhov Plant	November	none
Union of Workers in the Workshops of the Firm of Artur Koppel'	n.d. (November)	n.d.
Metal—Nonferrous		
Union of Journeymen and Apprentices in the Watchmaking Craft*	November (April)	November
Union of Workers in the Gold and Silver Trade*	November (October)	November
Union of Workers in the Bronze Smelting Trade*	November (October)	November
Paper		
Union of Workers in the Manufacture of Cardboard and Cardboard Products	November	n.d.
Union of Envelope Makers	November	n.d.
Printing		
Union of Workers in the Printing Trade	April (January)	June
Affiliated with this union:		
Union of Employees in the Periodical Press in the City of St. Petersburg	October	November
Union of Bookbinders, Stitchers, and Men and Women Folders	November	n.d.

ST. PETERSBURG, 1905

Union	Founding Date	Adoption of Charter
Union of Employees and Workers in Zincographics	November	n.d.
Union of Lithographers	October	October
Sales and Clerical		
Union of Office Clerks and Bookkeepers	July (February)	July
Union of Salesclerks	September (March)	September
Union of Pharmacists	April	n.d.
Union of Workers in the Pharmaceutical Trade	November	n.d.
Union of Employees in Notary Offices	November	n.d.
Union of Employees in Banking and Credit Institutions	November	November
Union of Bookstore Employees	November	n.d.
Union of Employees in Insurance and Transportation Companies	November	n.d.
Service		
Union of Chimney Sweeps	September	n.d.
Union of Barbers	November (October)	n.d.
Union of Cooks	November	n.d.
Union of Workers in the Tavern Trade	November	November
Union of Gardeners	November	November
Union of Building Superintendents and Doormen	November	November
Union of Household Servants	December (November)	n.d.
Union of Floor Polishers	November	none
Union of Funeral Torch Bearers	n.d. (November)	n.d.
Union of Bath Attendants	December	n.d.
Union of Newspaper Deliverers	(Functioning in November)	n.d.

ST. PETERSBURG, 1905

Union	Founding Date	Adoption of Charter
Technical		
Union of Master Craftsmen and Technicians in Factory Industries	October	n.d.
Union of Draftsmen	November (October)	November
Union of Electricians	n.d. (November)	n.d.
Union of Workers in the Lighting Industry	November	November
Textiles		
Union of Textile Workers	November (October)	November
Union of Dyers	November	November
Union of Workers in the Lace and Galloon Weaving Trade	November	n.d.
Transportation		
Union Center of the All-Russian Union of Railroad Employees and Workers in St. Petersburg	n.d. (July)	n.d.
Union of Cabmen and Draymen	December (November)	December
Wood		
Union of Woodworkers*	November (March)	December
Union of Workers in the Furniture and Upholstery Trade*	November	November
Union of Woodcarvers in Industrial Enterprises Specializing in Decorative Work	n.d. (December)	n.d.
Miscellaneous		
Central Workers' Union (Ushakovist)	October (July)	n.d.
Union of Women Workers (Ushakovist)	October	n.d.
All-Russian Union of Worker-Photographers*	November (July)	November
Union of Orchestra Personnel	November (October)	n.d.

ST. PETERSBURG, 1905

Union	Founding Date	Adoption of Charter
Union of Middle- and Lower-level Medical Personnel (this union split into two separate unions, shown below)	November	none
Union of Middle-level Medical Personnel	December (November)	December
Union of Lower-level Medical Personnel	December (November)	December
Union of Workers in the Manufacture of Beds	November	n.d.

MOSCOW, 1905

Union	Founding Date	Adoption of Charter
Apparel and Leather		
Union of Pursemakers*	May	n.d.
Union of Workers in the Manufacture of Shoes*	n.d. (November)	n.d.
Union of Boot and Shoe Makers*	November (October)	December
Union of Tailors*	November	November
Union of Workers in All Trades of Clothing Manufacture*	November	November
Union of Men and Women Workers in the Glovemaking Trade in the City of Moscow*	November (October)	n.d.
Union of Workers in the Manufacture of Leather Luggage*	December	n.d.
Union of Workers in the Manufacture of Harnesses and Saddles for the Military*	December	n.d.
Chemical		
Union of Workers in the Manufacture of Perfume	November	n.d.

MOSCOW, 1905

Union	Founding Date	Adoption of Charter
Communications		
All-Russian Union of Postal and Telegraph Employees	October (July)	October
Union of Telephone Operators and Employees	November	n.d.
Construction		
Union of Industrial Construction Workers	November	November
The above union was a federation of autonomous craft unions:		
Union of Carpenters*	November	none
Union of Stucco Molders*	November	none
Union of House Painters*	October	none
Union of Marble Workers*	November	none
Union of Plumbing and Heating Workers*	December	December
Food		
Union of Bakers*	November (March)	n.d.
Union of Workers in the Tobacco Industry	September	n.d.
Union of Sausage Makers*	November	n.d.
Union of Teapacking Workers	November	November
Union of Candymakers	November (October)	November
Government		
Corporation of Employees of the Moscow City Administration	February	September
Corporation of Workers and Lower-level Employees in the Moscow City Administration	July (April)	October
Corporation of Middle-level Technicians Employed by the Moscow City Administration	September	n.d.
Corporation of City Engineers	October	n.d.

MOSCOW, 1905

Union	Founding Date	Adoption of Charter
Corporation of Hospital Workers	October	n.d.
Metal		
Moscow Union of Machine Workers (Zubatovist)	1901	1902
Union of Workers in the Manufacture of Beds in the Firms of Krymov and Turkin	October	n.d.
Union of Metalfitters in the Construction Trades*	November	n.d.
Union of Workers in Metal Rolling Shops	November	n.d.
Union of Workers in Mechanical, Surgical, and Tool Production	November	n.d.
Union of Blacksmiths	November (October)	n.d.
Union of Metalworkers	December (October)	none
Metal—Nonferrous		
Union of Copper Workers in Artisanal Enterprises*	October	n.d.
Union of Jewelry, Gold-Silver, and Bronze Journeymen*	November (July)	November
Union of Workers in the Manufacture of Gold Thread*	November	none
Union of Tinsmiths*	November	n.d.
Paper		
Union of Workers in the Manufacture of Wallpaper	August	n.d.
Printing		
Society of Typographical Workers (Zubatovist)	1903 (liquidated summer 1905)	1903
Moscow Union of Typo-Lithographical Workers for the Struggle to Improve Conditions of Labor	1903	1903

MOSCOW, 1905

Union	Founding Date	Adoption of Charter
Moscow Union of Workers in the Printing Trade	October	October
Fund for the Assistance of Workers in the Printing Trade	July	July
Union of Proofreaders (in early December joined Union of Workers in the Printing Trade)	November	n.d.
Sales and Clerical		
Union of Pharmacy Employees	May	n.d.
First Union of Sales Employees	November (March)	n.d.
Second Union of Sales Employees	none (March)	none
Union of Hired Workers in Trade and Industry	May	n.d.
Union of Employees in the Sale of Foodstuffs (in October helped to form and joined "In Unity, Strength")	June (March)	n.d.
Union of Sales-Clerical Employees ("In Unity, Strength")	October (March)	November
Affiliated with this union:		
Union of Hardware Store Employees	November	n.d.
Union of Music Shop Employees	November	n.d.
Union of Metalware Shop Employees	November	n.d.
Union of Employees in Dry Goods and Grocery Stores	November	n.d.
Union of Employees in Stationery, Notion, and Toy Stores	November	n.d.
Union of Employees in Furrier Shops	December	n.d.
Union of Cashiers	December	n.d.
Union of Hired Workers in the Book Trade	October	November

MOSCOW, 1905

Union	Founding Date	Adoption of Charter
Union of Employees in Credit Institutions	October	November
Union of Office Clerks and Bookkeepers	October	n.d.
Union of Employees in Lumberyards	October	n.d.
Union of Employees in Insurance and Transportation Institutions	November	n.d.
Union of Newspaper Vendors	November	n.d.
Union of Butchershop Employees	November	n.d.
Union of Employees in the Sale of Meat and Fish	November	n.d.

Service

Union	Founding Date	Adoption of Charter
Mutual Aid Society of Waiters and Other Tavern and Hotel Personnel	1902 (began to function as a trade union in October 1905)	1902
Union of Barbers	November (May)	n.d.
Union of Employees in Beer Halls	October	November
Union of Building Superintendents	November	n.d.
Union of Household Servants	November	November
Union of Gardeners	November	n.d.
Union of Cooks	November	none
Union of Window Washers	November	n.d.
Union of Chimney Sweeps	December	n.d.

Technical

Union	Founding Date	Adoption of Charter
Union of Middle-level Technicians (until October, Mutual Aid Society of Russian Technicians)	October (August)	December
Union of Electricians	November	n.d.

MOSCOW, 1905

Union	Founding Date	Adoption of Charter
Textiles		
Union of Textile Workers (Zubatovist)	1902	1902
Union of Ribbonweavers	August	n.d.
Union of Engravers and Operators of Roller Printers†	October	n.d.
Union of Workers in the Textile Industry	November (October)	November
Union of Workers in Dyeing and Dressing Enterprises	November (October)	n.d.
Union of Workers in Machine Embroidery	November	n.d.
Union of Workers in the Manufacture of Velvet	November	n.d.
Transportation		
All-Russian Union of Railroad Employees and Workers	April (February)	April
Union of Railway Employees of the Moscow Junction, under the Moscow Committee of the RSDRP	May (February)	n.d.
Union of Workers in the Workshops of the Brest Railroad	October (May)	n.d.
Union of Workers in the Workshops of the Kazan Railroad	November	n.d.
Wood		
Union of Carpenters*	September	October
Union of Workers in Toy Factories	November	n.d.
Union of Turners in Umbrella Shops*	November	November
Union of Box Makers	n.d. (November)	n.d.
Union of Parquetry Makers*	n.d. (November)	n.d.

MOSCOW, 1905

Union	Founding Date	Adoption of Charter
Miscellaneous		
Union of Church Artists	December (Summer)	December
Union of Middle-level Medical, Veterinary, and Nursing Personnel	November	n.d.
Union of Lower-level Medical Personnel	November	n.d.

Sources for Appendix I:

Dmitriev, K. [P. N. Kolokol'nikov]. *Professional'nye soiuzy v Moskve.* [St. Petersburg, 1906.]

Engelstein, Laura. *Moscow, 1905: Working-Class Organization and Political Conflict.* Stanford, Calif., 1982.

Materialy po istorii professional'nogo dvizheniia v Peterburge za 1905–1907 gg. Leningrad, 1926.

Milonov, Iu. K. *Kak voznikli professional'nye soiuzy v Rossii.* Moscow, 1929.

Obshcheprofessional'nye organy 1905–1907 gg. Vypusk 1: *Moskovskie zhurnaly 1905 g.* Moscow, 1926.

Pushkareva, I. M. *Zheleznodorozhniki Rossii v burzhuazno-demokraticheskikh revoliutsiiakh.* Moscow, 1975.

Ramazov, R. G. "Sozdanie profsoiuzov Peterburgskogo proletariata i ikh deiatel'nost' v pervoi russkoi revoliutsii." Candidate dissertation, Higher School on Trade Unions. Moscow, 1975.

Sviatlovskii, V. V. *Professional'noe dvizhenie v Rossii.* St. Petersburg, 1907.

Tiurin, S. P. *Moskovskoe tsentral'noe biuro professional'nykh soiuzov.* Moscow, 1913.

In addition, information was drawn from the contemporary labor and political press.

Note: The founding date refers to the occasion of the first general meeting when the workers reached a collective decision to found the union. This meeting was sometimes preceded by the formation of a small initiative group which functioned, in some cases, for weeks or even months before the founding meeting took place. The date of the establishment of an initiative group, where known, appears in parentheses. The evidence confirming the existence of some unions is extremely limited and is sometimes based on the fact that a union sent a representative to the Central Bureau of Trade Unions or the All-Russian Conference of Trade Unions.

*An asterisk indicates a union designated as artisanal.

†Existed in the late 1890s as a mutual aid society.

Appendix II

St. Petersburg and Moscow Trade Unions,
March 1906–May 1907

Union	Registration Date	Closing Date	Peak Nominal Membership
Apparel and Leather			
Union of Men and Women Tailors and Furriers*	March 28, 1906	July 27, 1906 (but continued to function)	1,514
Union of Workers in the Shoe and Bootmaking Trade*	May 3, 1906	July 28, 1906 (but continued to function)	1,200
Union of Leather Workers	July 14, 1906	n.d.	771
Union of of Hat and Cap Makers*	July 14, 1906	n.d.	n.d.
Union of Men and Women Workers in the Manufacture of Knitted Hosiery*	August 9, 1906	(In 1908 joined the Union of Textile Workers)	85
Union of Master Furriers*	January 30, 1907	n.d.	n.d.
Narvskii Union of Men and Women Tailors*	April 17, 1907	n.d.	n.d.
Union of Men and Women Workers in the Mechanized Manufacture of Shoes in the City of St. Petersburg	Unregistered (functioning May 1906)	—	n.d.
Union of Seamstresses*	Unregistered	—	n.d.
Union of Milliners*	Unregistered	—	n.d.
Chemical			
Union of Men and Women Workers in All Branches of Rubber Production	July 14, 1906	n.d.	n.d.

Union of Workers in the Industrial Processing of Fats, Namely Soapmaking, Stearin Manufacture, etc.	July 14, 1906	n.d.	120
Union of Workers in the Manufacture of Tallow, Soap, and Stearin	May 15, 1907	n.d.	n.d.
Union of Workers in Glass Factories and Mirror Workshops	Unregistered (founded July 22, 1906)	—	97
Union of Workers in the Manufacture of Gunpowder and Explosives	August 9, 1906	n.d.	500
Construction			
Union of Architectural and Construction Workers*	May 31, 1906	n.d.	3,730
Union of Plumbers*	May 31, 1906	n.d.	200
Union of Marble and Granite Workers*	July 14, 1906	n.d.	374
Same—reregistration*	May 15, 1907	—	n.d.
Food			
Union of Workers in Factories Producing Candy, Chocolate, and Cakes	May 31, 1906	n.d.	n.d.
Union of Workers in Factories Producing Cakes, Chocolate, and Candy	June 12, 1906	n.d.	998
Same—reregistration	May 12, 1907	1910	n.d.
Union of Workers in the Tobacco Industry	July 14, 1906	n.d.	450
Same—reregistration	May 8, 1907	n.d.	500

ST. PETERSBURG, MARCH 1906–MAY 1907

Union	Registration Date	Closing Date	Peak Nominal Membership
Union of Workers in the Bread Baking and Pastry Making Trade*	July 14, 1906	Late July 1906	4,140
Union of Master Craftsmen in the Bread, Roll Baking, and Pastry Making Trades*	March 20, 1907	July 1907	n.d.
Union of Workers in the Manufacture of Sausages in the City of St. Petersburg*	April 10, 1907	n.d.	n.d.
Metal			
Union of Workers in the Metal Industry (Gaponist)	July 14, 1906	n.d.	n.d.
Same—reregistration	April 17, 1907	1910	n.d.
Union of Metalworkers	Applied for registration April 11, 1906, but neither approved nor rejected	July 28, 1906 (but continued to function)	10,700
Same—reregistration	May 15, 1907	March 1912	n.d.
Union of Workers in Blacksmith Enterprises	September 20, 1906	n.d.	n.d.
Same—reregistration	February 13, 1907	—	300
Union of Port and Shipyard Workers	May 15, 1907	(In 1907 joined Union of Metal Workers)	300

	Charter submitted to Ministry of Internal Affairs, January 1906		
St. Petersburg Workers' Union (Smesovist)		(April 15, 1907, joined Union of Metal Workers)	393
Union of Patternmakers	May 1906	n.d.	300
Metal—Nonferrous			
Union of Workers in the Manufacture of Tin Lamps*	August 9, 1906	n.d.	n.d.
Same—reregistration*	May 29, 1907	n.d.	n.d.
Union of Journeymen and Salesclerks in the Watchmaking Craft*	September 20, 1906	n.d.	202
Same—reregistration*	May 15, 1907	April 1913	n.d.
Union of Workers in the Gold, Silver, and Bronze Trade*	May 1, 1907	—	1,110
Union of Workers in the Bronze Smelting Trade and Tinsmiths*	Unregistered	—	n.d.
Paper			
Union of Workers in the Manufacture of Wallpaper	July 14, 1906	n.d.	240
Same—reregistration	April 3, 1907	n.d.	n.d.
Union of Workers in the Manufacture of Writing and Printing Paper	July 14, 1906	n.d.	310
Same—reregistration	April 17, 1907	n.d.	n.d.
Union of Workers in the Manufacture of Cardboard and Cardboard Products	May 22, 1907	May 8, 1912	120

ST. PETERSBURG, MARCH 1906–MAY 1907

Union	Registration Date	Closing Date	Peak Nominal Membership
Printing			
Union of Workers in the Printing Trade	August 9, 1906	Late 1906 (but continued to function)	12,000
Same—reregistration	August 17, 1907	October 16, 1907	n.d.
Mutual Fund Aid of Master Craftsmen Operating Typographical Machines	May 1, 1907	n.d.	n.d.
Union of Lithographic Workers	January 30, 1907	July 31, 1907	566
Sales and Clerical			
Union of Hired Workers in the St. Petersburg Book Trade	June 1906	n.d.	129
Union of Salesclerks	July 14, 1906	December 28, 1906	2,688
Union of Workers in the Sale of State Monopoly Beverages	August 9, 1906	n.d.	n.d.
Union of Employees in Printing Establishments	February 28, 1907	n.d.	n.d.
Union of Office Clerks and Bookkeepers	April 17, 1907	n.d.	2,000
Union of Pharmacy Employees	April 17, 1907	—	n.d.
Union of Employees in the Sale of Textile Goods	May 15, 1907	n.d.	n.d.

Union of Employees in the Sale of Foodstuffs	May 15, 1907	n.d.	n.d.
Union of Workers in the Pharmaceutical Trade	Unregistered	—	30
Service			
Union of Gardeners	May 3, 1906	n.d.	200
Union of Chimney Sweeps	July 14, 1906	n.d.	n.d.
Union of Journeymen Barbers	February 13, 1907	n.d.	102
First Association of Cooks in the City and Province of St. Petersburg	April 17, 1907	n.d.	400
Union of Laundresses	Unregistered	—	n.d.
Union of Bath Attendants	Unregistered	—	n.d.
Union of Building Superintendents and Doormen	Unregistered	—	n.d.
Technical			
Union of Workers and Employees in Lighting and Electrical Enterprises (formed by a merger of the Union of Electricians and the Union of Workers in Lighting Enterprises)	July 14, 1906	n.d.	181
Union of Draftsmen	July 14, 1906	n.d.	252
Union of Master Craftsmen and Technicians in Factory Industries	July 14, 1906	n.d.	n.d.
Union of Technicians	April 10, 1907	n.d.	85

ST. PETERSBURG, MARCH 1906–MAY 1907

Union	Registration Date	Closing Date	Peak Nominal Membership
Textiles			
Union of Workers in Dyeing Factories and Workshops	August 9, 1906	n.d.	251
Union of Men and Women Textile Workers in the Northern Industrial Region	May 15, 1907	—	4,000
Union of Workers in the Lace and Galloon Weaving Trade	Unregistered	—	n.d.
Transportation			
Union of Cabmen	July 14, 1906	n.d.	123
Union of Workers Loading Furnaces	July 14, 1906	n.d.	1,100
All-Russian Union of Railroad Employees and Workers	Unregistered	—	n.d.
Union of Workers on the Warsaw Railway	Unregistered	—	n.d.
Union of Employees on the Steam-Powered Trams of the Nevskaia Suburban Railway	Unregistered	—	n.d.
Wood			
Union of Woodworkers*	July 14, 1906	July 1906 (but continued to function)	1,965

Same—reregistration	May 14, 1907	July 1914	n.d.
Union of Workers in the Furniture Upholstery Trade*	July 14, 1906	n.d.	n.d.
Union of Workers in Cooperage and Barrel Making	August 9, 1906	n.d.	n.d.
Miscellaneous			
Union of Lower-level Medical Personnel	May 30, 1906	n.d.	500
Union of Workers in the Manufacture of Carriages*	May 31, 1906	n.d.	163
Union of Women Workers in Felt and Straw Hat Making and the Manufacture of Decorative Flower Accessories*	July 14, 1906	n.d.	n.d.
Union of Workers in the Manufacture of Musical Instruments*	July 14, 1906	n.d.	n.d.
Union of Middle-level Medical Personnel	Unregistered	—	n.d.
Union of Orchestra Musicians	Unregistered	—	n.d.
Union of Worker-Photographers*	Unregistered	—	200

MOSCOW, MARCH 1906–MAY 1907

Union	Registration Date	Closing Date	Peak Nominal Membership
Apparel and Leather			
Moscow Union of Workers in the Manufacture of Hats*	May 8, 1906	March 6, 1907	222
Union of Workers in the Fur Wetting and Dyeing Industry	May 27, 1906	October 2, 1907	n.d.
Union of Workers in the Leather Industry in the Moscow Industrial Region	June 20, 1906	—	627
Union of Men and Women Workers in the Manufacture of Clothing in the Moscow Industrial Region*	June 20, 1906	May 17, 1907	3,415
Union of Men and Women Workers in the Manufacture of Leather Gloves*	July 4, 1906	—	n.d.
Union of Master Craftsmen in the Manufacture of Hats*	August 1, 1906	n.d.	n.d.
Union of Workers in Suitcase, Trunk, and Leather Case Workshops*	August 19, 1906	December 11, 1907	500
Union of Workers in the Manufacture of Purses*	August 26, 1906	May 13, 1908	249
Union of Workers in the Manufacture of Hats in the Moscow Region and Kostroma Province*	September 26, 1906	n.d.	n.d.
Union of Workers in the Manufacture of Shoes in the Moscow Industrial Region*	November 20, 1906	n.d.	500

Chemical

Union of Workers in the Manufacture of Perfume in the City of Moscow	May 27, 1906	n.d.	692
Union of Workers in the Manufacture of Crystal in the Moscow Industrial Region	June 20, 1906	n.d.	750
Union of Chemical Workers in the Moscow Industrial Region	Denied registration May 1907	—	n.d.

Construction

Union of Architectural and Construction Workers in the Moscow Industrial Region*	May 8, 1906	June 26, 1907	1,200
Union of Plumbing and Heating Workers in the City of Moscow*	May 8, 1906	—	1,154
Union of Workers in Pictorial, Decorative, and Ornamental Work in the Moscow Industrial Region*	May 27, 1906	n.d.	n.d.
Union of Marble and Granite Workers in the Moscow Industrial Region*	June 20, 1906	n.d.	300
Union of Workers in Decorative Stucco Molding in Construction*	November 7, 1906	October 20, 1907	n.d.

Food

Union of Tea Packing Workers in the City of Moscow	May 8, 1906	February 15, 1907	2,000
Union of Moscow Bakers*	May 8, 1906	July 26, 1906	4,000

MOSCOW, MARCH 1906–MAY 1907

Union	Registration Date	Closing Date	Peak Nominal Membership
Union of Workers in the Moscow Bread-Baking Industry*	Denied registration March 8, 1908 (charter submitted February 1907)	—	n.d.
Union of Tobacco Workers in the City of Moscow	May 27, 1906	n.d.	1,218
Union of Workers in the Manufacture of Sausages*	May 27, 1906	April 17, 1907	n.d.
Union of Workers in the Manufacture of Confections	July 4, 1906	December 22, 1908	1,626
Union of Workers in Vodka Distilleries	November 7, 1906	May 1, 1908	n.d.
Government			
Union of Workers and Lower-level Employees in Enterprises of the Moscow City Administration	May 8, 1906	January 2, 1908	2,800
Metal			
Union of Metalworkers in the Moscow Industrial Region	May 8, 1906	February 15, 1907	4,725
Union of Metalfitters in the Construction Trades in the City of Moscow*	May 8, 1906	n.d.	393

Union of Workers in the Manufacture of Agricultural Implements in the Moscow Industrial Region	July 18, 1906	n.d.	n.d.
Union of Workers in the Metallurgical and Machine-building Industry	October 24, 1906	July 10, 1907	n.d.
Metal—Nonferrous			
Union of Tinsmiths in the City of Moscow*	May 8, 1906	n.d.	n.d.
Union of Journeyman Workers in Precious Metals*	July 4, 1906	February 1, 1907	1,296
Paper			
Union of Workers in the Manufacture of Cardboard and Cardboard Products	June 20, 1906	July 18, 1906	n.d.
Union of Workers in the Manufacture of Wallpaper in the Moscow Industrial Region	August 1, 1906	October 30, 1907	350
Printing			
Union of Workers in the Printing Trade	April 28, 1906	August 1, 1906	n.d.
Moscow Union of Typo-Lithographical Workers	May 8, 1906	—	n.d.
Union of Workers in the Graphic Arts in the Moscow Industrial Region	August 26, 1906	June 12, 1907	8,000
Sales and Clerical			
The Moscow Union of Office Clerks and Bookkeepers	April 28, 1906	February 1, 1907	1,500
The First Union of Sales Employees in Moscow	May 8, 1906	November 2, 1909	752

MOSCOW, MARCH 1906–MAY 1907

Union	Registration Date	Closing Date	Peak Nominal Membership
Union of Employees in Stores and Offices in the Wholesale and Retail Trade in Pharmaceutical Supplies	May 8, 1906	n.d.	250
Union of Employees in Book Enterprises in the City of Moscow	June 9, 1906	n.d.	167
Union of Sales-Clerical Employees ("In Unity, Strength")	June 20, 1906	December 19, 1906	900
Union of Employees in Meat, Fish, and Vegetable Markets in the City of Moscow	June 20, 1906	n.d.	200
Union of Employees in Flour, Wine, and Colonial Goods Shops in the City of Moscow	July 18, 1906	July 24, 1907	n.d.
Union of Workers in Accounting	September 25, 1906	n.d.	n.d.
Union of Employees in Credit Institutions in the City of Moscow	September 25, 1906	n.d.	n.d.
Mutual-Aid Society of Employees in Sales and Industrial Enterprises	November 1, 1906	n.d.	n.d.
Union of Employees in Insurance and Transportation Institutions	Unregistered	—	n.d.
Union of Newspaper Vendors	Unregistered	—	n.d.
Russian Pharmacists' Union	(1885)	n.d.	159

Service			
Union of Moscow Window Washers	March 28, 1906	n.d.	n.d.
Union of Cooks in the Moscow Industrial Region	April 11, 1906	—	483
Union of Male and Female Household Servants in the City of Moscow	May 8, 1906	September 18, 1907	200
Union of Gardening Workers in the City of Moscow	June 20, 1906	n.d.	n.d.
Union of Men and Women Workers in Laundering Enterprises in the City of Moscow	August 19, 1906	n.d.	n.d.
Union of Barbers in the Moscow Region	August 19, 1906	—	351
Union of Floor Polishers	October 24, 1906	November 13, 1907	150
The Moscow Mutual Aid Society of Waiters and Other Employees in All Enterprises of the Tavern Trade	September 12, 1906	—	2,618
Union of Employees in Beer Stalls in the City of Moscow	November 7, 1906	October 10, 1907	200
Union of Bath Attendants	Unregistered	—	n.d.
Technical			
Union of Technicians in the Moscow Industrial Region	May 8, 1906	November 20, 1907	452
Union of Workers in Electrical Engineering in Moscow	May 8, 1906	December 11, 1907	90

Union	Registration Date	Closing Date	Peak Nominal Membership
Textiles			
Union of Workers in the Weaving and Knitting Industry in the City of Moscow	May 27, 1906	July 24, 1907	450
Union of Textile Workers in the Moscow Industrial Region	June 9, 1906	July 24, 1907	2,382
Union of Workers in the Dyeing and Dressing Industry	June 20, 1906	July 24, 1907	1,400
Union of Master Craftsmen in the Manufacture of Fringes*	December 5, 1906	n.d.	n.d.
Union of Ribbon Weavers	Denied registration November 1906	—	367
Union of Engravers and Operators of Roller Printers	Unregistered	—	n.d.
Transportation			
All-Russian Union of Railroad Employees and Workers	Unregistered	—	n.d.
Union of Workers in the Workshops of the Brest Railroad	Unregistered	—	n.d.
Union of Workers in the Workshops of the Kazan Railroad	Unregistered	—	n.d.
Union of Workers in the Moscow Railroad Junction	Unregistered (founded August 1906)	—	1,311

Wood

Union of Workers in the Decorative Woodworking Industry in the Moscow Industrial Region*	May 8, 1906	March 6, 1907	1,500
Miscellaneous			
Union of Workers in Carriage Production in the City of Moscow*	June 20, 1906	n.d.	n.d.
Old Believers' Union of Gonfalon Bearers of the Cathedrals of the Rogozhskoe Old Believers' Cemetery	July 18, 1906	—	n.d.
Union of Worker-Photographers*	August 19, 1906	n.d.	119
Union of Button and Hook Makers in the Moscow Industrial Region*	November 20, 1906	—	400

Sources for Appendix II:

TsGAOR, DPOO, f. 102, op. 00, d. 17, ch. 46, 1916; DPOO, f. 102, op. 00, d. 1000, ch. 14, t. 1, 1905; DPOO, f. 111, op. 5, d. 263, 1909.

Gol'dberg, G. *K istorii professional'nogo dvizheniia v Rossii: Sostoianie soiuzov nakanune Vtoroi Gosudarstvennoi Dumy.* St. Petersburg, 1907.

Milonov, Iu. K., ed. *Moskovskoe professional'noe dvizhenie v gody pervoi revoliutsii.* Moscow, [1925].

Tiurin, S. P. *Moskovskoe tsentral'noe biuro professional'nykh soiuzov.* Moscow, 1913.

In addition, information was drawn from the contemporary labor and political press.

Note: The notation "n.d." in the "Closing Date" column indicates that the closing date of the union is unknown. Where no date is shown, the union retained its legal status in the years that followed.

*An asterisk indicates a union designated as artisanal.

Appendix III

St. Petersburg and Moscow Employers' Organizations, 1906–1907

ST. PETERSBURG, MARCH 1906–MAY 1907

Organization	Date of Registration
Manufacturing	
Society of Factory Owners	September 1906
Society of Printing Firm Owners	October 1906
Union of Owners of Typographical Firms	December 1906
Professional Society of Employers in the Lumber Industry	January 1907
Society of Tailoring Shop Owners	June 1907
Professional Society of Owners of Brickmaking Factories	May 1907
Society of Owners of Gold, Silver, and Jewelry Workshops	n.d.
Union of Bakery Owners	n.d.
Commerce	
Union of Merchants on Vasil'evskii Island and in the Peterburgskaia and Vyborgskaia Districts	May 1906
Professional Society of Tobacco Merchants	August 1906

ST. PETERSBURG, MARCH 1906–MAY 1907

Organization	Date of Registration
Union of Beer Merchants	February 1907
Russian Commercial Society	n.d.
Union of Merchants of Butter and Milk Products	n.d.
Union of Iron Merchants	n.d.

Transportation

Professional Society of Employers in Drayage Enterprises	July 1906
Union of Owners of Tugboats on the Rumiantsevskaia Pier	n.d.

Service

Union of Tavern Owners (Unlicensed to Sell Spirits)	n.d.
Central Bureau of the Wine, Vodka, Beer and Tavern Industry	n.d.

MOSCOW, MARCH 1906–MAY 1907

Organization	Date of Registration
Manufacturing	
All-Russian Society of Employers in the Flax Industry	May 1906
Society of Factory Owners in the Central Industrial Region	August 1906
Society of Bread Bakery Owners in the City of Moscow	August 1906
Society of Factory Owners in the Perfume Industry	September 1906
Society of Factory Owners in the Candy Industry	September 1906
Society of Owners of Tailoring Shops	December 1906
Society of Owners of Typographical-Lithographical Firms	December 1906
Society of Owners of Sausagemaking Firms	March 1907
Society of Owners of Brickmaking Enterprises	May 1907
Society of Owners of Printing Enterprises	October 1907
Commerce	
Society of Tobacco Merchants	August 1906
Society of Merchants in Colonial Trade	September 1906
Society of Retail Merchants in the Sale of Textiles, Linen, and Haberdashery	January 1907

MOSCOW, MARCH 1906–MAY 1907

Organization	Date of Registration
Transportation	
Society of Employers in Drayage Enterprises	June 1906
Service	
Mutual Aid Society of Tavern Owners in Moscow	May 1906
Mutual Aid Society of Bathhouse Owners in Moscow	February 1907
Construction	
Society of Subcontractors in the Construction Industry	April 1906

Sources for Appendix III:
TsGAOR, DPOO, f. 102, op. 00, d. 17, ch. 46, 1916; DPOO, f. 102, op. 00, d. 1000, ch. 14, t. 1, 1905.
TsGIA, f. 150, op. 1, d. 54.
Materialy po istorii professional'nogo dvizheniia v Peterburge za 1905–1907 gg. Leningrad, 1926. p. 251.

Appendix IV

St. Petersburg and Moscow Trade Unions, June 1907–1911

ST. PETERSBURG, JUNE 1907–1911

Union	Registration Date	Closing Date	Peak Nominal Membership
Apparel and Leather			
Union of Men and Women Workers in the Manufacture of Knitted Hosiery	August 9, 1906	(In 1908 joined Union of Textile Workers)	85
Union of Workers in the Shoe and Boot Making Trade*	July 24, 1907	n.d.	987
Union of Workers in the Manufacture of Leather Goods (Leather Case Makers)*	August 28, 1907	—	300
Union of Workers in Tanning and the Manufacture of Leather Goods	November 13, 1907	—	1,273
Union of Tailoring Workers*	November 1907	March 18, 1908	n.d.
Union of Men and Women Workers in the Tailoring Trade*	October 20, 1908	—	1,019
Chemical			
Union of Glass Workers	June 15, 1908	n.d.	175
Union of Mirror Makers	n.d.	n.d.	139
Construction			
Union of Marble and Granite Workers*	May 15, 1907	—	301
Union of Architectural and Construction Workers*	October 1907	May 27, 1914	1,215

Union of Plumbers*	September 18, 1907	n.d.	400
Food			
Union of Workers in the Manufacture of Sausages in the City of St. Petersburg*	April 10, 1907	n.d.	n.d.
Union of Workers in the Tobacco Industry	May 8, 1907	n.d.	576
Union of Workers in the Manufacture of Cakes, Chocolate and Candy	May 12, 1907	1910	825
Union of Workers in the Baking and Pastry Making Industry*	August 28, 1907	January 18, 1914	1,195
Metal			
Union of Workers in Blacksmith Enterprises	February 13, 1907	—	219
Union of Workers in the Metal Industry (Gaponist)	April 17, 1907	1910	n.d.
Union of Workers in the Metalworking Industry	May 15, 1907	March 1912	9,791
Union of Workers in Metal†	December 9, 1908	August 21, 1912	n.d.
Metal—Nonferrous			
Union of Workers in the Gold, Silver, and Bronze Trade*	May 1, 1907	—	480
Union of Journeymen and Salesclerks in the Watchmaking Craft*	May 15, 1907	April 1913	237
Union of Workers in the Manufacture of Tin Lamps*	May 29, 1907	n.d.	n.d.

ST. PETERSBURG, JUNE 1907–1911

Union	Registration Date	Closing Date	Peak Nominal Membership
Paper			
Union of Workers in the Manufacture of Wallpaper	April 3, 1907	n.d.	255
Union of Workers in the Manufacture of Writing and Printing Paper	April 17, 1907	n.d.	395
Union of Workers in the Manufacture of Cardboard and Cardboard Products	May 22, 1907	May 8, 1912	518
Printing			
Union of Workers in the Printing Trade	April 17, 1907	October 16, 1907	7,500
Union of Workers in the Graphic Arts	January 8, 1908	December 14, 1910	5,666
Union of Workers in the Printing Industry	June 5, 1911	March 6, 1912	1,510
Mutual Aid Fund of Master Craftsmen Operating Typographical Machines	May 1, 1907	n.d.	156
Sales and Clerical			
Union of Employees in Printing Establishments	February 28, 1907	n.d.	69
Union of Office Clerks and Bookkeepers	April 17, 1907	n.d.	565
Union of Pharmacy Employees	April 17, 1907	—	n.d.

Union of Employees in the Sale of Textile Goods	May 15, 1907	n.d. ⎫	800
Union of Employees in the Sale of Foodstuffs	May 15, 1907	n.d. ⎬	n.d.
Union of Employees in the Sale of Commercial and Surgical Apparatus in Warehouses and Stores	n.d. (functioning in 1908)	n.d.	n.d.
Union of Employees in the Sale of Household Goods	n.d. (functioning in 1908)	n.d.	n.d.
Union of Workers in the Wine Trade	June 24, 1907	n.d.	n.d.
Mutual Aid Society of Employees in Wallpaper Factories and Stores	n.d.	n.d.	86
Service			
First Association of Cooks in the City and Province of St. Petersburg	April 17, 1907	n.d.	n.d.
Technical			
Union of Technicians	April 10, 1907	n.d.	77
Union of Master Craftsmen and Technicians in Factory Industries	June 15, 1907	n.d.	n.d.
Union of Draftsmen	July 24, 1907	—	300
Textiles			
Union of Workers in Dyeing Factories and Workshops	August 9, 1906	n.d.	111
Union of Men and Women Textile Workers in the Northern Industrial Region	May 15, 1907	—	2,257

ST. PETERSBURG, JUNE 1907–1911

Union	Registration Date	Closing Date	Peak Nominal Membership
Transportation			
Union of Cabmen	July 14, 1906	n.d.	101
Wood			
Union of Woodworkers*	May 15, 1907	July 1914	1,699
Union of Workers in Cooperage and Barrel Making	August 14, 1907	n.d.	300
Narvskoe Union of Woodworkers*	August 1910	n.d.	30
Miscellaneous			
Union of Workers in the Manufacture of Carriages*	July 24, 1907	—	305
Union of Worker-Photographers*	September 18, 1907	n.d.	375

MOSCOW, JUNE 1907–1911

Union	Registration Date	Closing Date	Peak Nominal Membership
Apparel and Leather			
Union of Workers in the Fur Wetting and Dyeing Industry	May 27, 1906	October 2, 1907	n.d.
Union of Workers in the Leather Industry in the Moscow Industrial Region	June 20, 1906	—	1,500
Union of Men and Women Workers in the Manufacture of Leather Gloves*	July 4, 1906	—	210
Union of Workers in Suitcase, Trunk, and Leather Case Workshops*	August 19, 1906	December 11, 1907	n.d.
Union of Workers in the Manufacture of Purses*	August 26, 1906	May 13, 1908	n.d.
Union of Workers in the Manufacture of Shoes in the Moscow Industrial Region*	November 20, 1906	n.d.	88
Union of Dressmakers, Tailors, and Furriers in the City of Moscow*	February 1908	October 31, 1911	596
Moscow Union of Artisanal Wallet and Purse Makers*	August 28, 1908	—	150
Construction			
Union of Plumbing and Heating Workers*	May 8, 1906	—	311

MOSCOW, JUNE 1907–1911

Union	Registration Date	Closing Date	Peak Nominal Membership
Union of Marble and Granite Workers in the Moscow Industrial Region*	June 20, 1906	n.d.	11
Union of Workers in Decorative Stucco Molding in Construction*	November 7, 1906	October 20, 1907	n.d.
Food			
Union of Workers in the Manufacture of Confections	July 4, 1906	December 22, 1908	n.d.
Union of Workers in Vodka Distilleries	November 7, 1906	May 1, 1908	n.d.
Moscow Union of Sausage-Making Enterprises*	1907	—	n.d.
Union of Tea Packing Workers in the City of Moscow	1909	—	200
Government			
Union of Workers and Lower-level Employees of the Moscow City Administration	May 8, 1906	January 2, 1908	n.d.
Metal			
Union of Metalworkers in Enterprises of the Moscow City Administration	Early 1909	October 12, 1909	249

Union of Workers in Physical and Mechanical Engineering	1909	1909	n.d.
Union of Workers in the Machine Industry of Kolomenskii *uezd*	1909	July 1912	250
Metal—Nonferrous			
Union of Tinsmiths*	May 8, 1906	n.d.	n.d.
Union of Jewelry, Sacramental Objects, and Copper Production*	1908	n.d.	450
Paper			
Union of Workers in the Manufacture of Wallpaper	August 1, 1906	October 30, 1907	n.d.
Printing			
Moscow Union of Typo-Lithographical Workers	May 8, 1906	—	n.d.
Ivan Fedorov Union of Printing Workers	November 10, 1908	July 1910	1,258
Sales and Clerical			
Russian Pharmacists' Union	(1885)	—	n.d.
The First Union of Sales Employees in Moscow	May 8, 1906	November 2, 1909	2,483
Union of Workers in Accounting	September 25, 1906	n.d.	74
Mutual Aid Society of Sales Employees	1907	—	195
Union of Dining Room Employees in Sales-Industrial Enterprises in the Upper Trading Rows of Moscow	1907	—	692

MOSCOW, JUNE 1907–1911

Union	Registration Date	Closing Date	Peak Nominal Membership
Moscow Union of Bookkeepers	1907	—	n.d.
Union of Employees in Fur Enterprises in the City of Moscow	1909	—	n.d.
Moscow Mutual Aid Society of Employees in the Cattle Trade	1910	—	n.d.
Union for the Organization of Congresses of Bookkeepers	1911	—	n.d.
Service			
Union of Cooks in the Moscow Industrial Region	April 11, 1906	—	1,464
Union of Male and Female Household Servants in the City of Moscow	May 8, 1906	September 18, 1907	356
Union of Barbers in the Moscow Region	August 19, 1906	—	305
Union of Floor Polishers	October 24, 1906	November 13, 1907	n.d.
Moscow Mutual Aid Society of Waiters and Other Employees in All Enterprises of the Tavern Trade	September 12, 1906	—	460
Union of Employees in Beer Stalls in the City of Moscow	November 7, 1906	October 10, 1907	n.d.

Technical			
Union of Technicians in the Moscow Industrial Region	May 8, 1906	November 20, 1907	n.d.
Union of Workers in Electrical Engineering in Moscow	May 8, 1906	December 11, 1907	n.d.
Union of Electricians	1908	—	n.d.
Textiles			
Union of Textile Workers in the Moscow Industrial Region	June 9, 1906	July 24, 1907 (but continued to function)	n.d.
Union of Textile Workers	July 1908	—	867
Wood			
Union of Joiners and Turners*	Mid-1908	n.d.	63
Miscellaneous			
Old Believers' Union of Gonfalon Bearers of the Cathedrals of the Rogozhskoe Old Believers' Cemetery	July 18, 1906	—	140

MOSCOW, JUNE 1907–1911

Union	Registration Date	Closing Date	Peak Nominal Membership
Union of Worker-Photographers*	August 19, 1906	n.d.	61
Union of Button and Hook Makers in the Moscow Industrial Region*	November 20, 1906	—	n.d.

Sources for Appendix IV:

TsGAOR, DPOO, f. 102, op. 00, d. 17, ch. 46, 1916; DPOO, f. 102, op. 12, d. 5, ch. 47, L.B., 1912; DPOO, f. 111, op. 5, d. 263, 1909.

TsGIA, f. 23, op. 29, d. 40; f. 23, op. 29, d. 44.

In addition, information was drawn from the contemporary labor and political press.

Note: The notation "n.d." in the "Closing Date" column indicates that the closing date of the union is unknown; where no date is shown, the union retained its legal status in the years that followed.

*An asterisk indicates unions designated as artisanal.

†A fictitious union, created and registered in case the Union of Workers in the Metalworking Industry was closed. Began to function only in April 1912.

Appendix V

St. Petersburg and Moscow Trade Unions,
1912–1914

ST. PETERSBURG, 1912–1914

Union	Registration Date	Closing Date	Peak Nominal Membership
Apparel and Leather			
Union of Workers in the Manufacture of Leather Goods (Leather Case Makers)*	August 28, 1907	—	101
Union of Workers in Tanning and the Manufacture of Leather Goods	November 13, 1907	—	1,000
Union of Men and Women Workers in the Tailoring Trade*	October 20, 1908	—	973
Chemical			
Union of Glass Workers	Being organized July 1912	n.d.	n.d.
Union of Rubber Workers	Being organized early 1914	—	n.d.
Construction			
Union of Marble and Granite Workers*	May 15, 1907	—	320
Union of Architectural and Construction Workers*	October 1907	May 27, 1914	435
Union of Plumbing and Heating Workers*	April 15, 1914	—	n.d.

Food

Union of Workers in the Baking and Pastry Making Industry*	August 28, 1907	January 18, 1914	1,700
Union of Workers in the Production of Baked Goods*	May 13, 1914	—	800
Union of Candymakers	Charter submitted December 1913	—	n.d.
Union of Workers in the Meat Industry	Charter submitted second time on June 20, 1914	—	n.d.

Metal

Union of Workers in Blacksmith Enterprises	February 13, 1907	—	200
Union of Workers in the Metalworking Industry	May 15, 1907	March 1912	n.d.
Union of Workers in Metal†	December 9, 1908	August 21, 1912	2,510
Union of Metalworkers	March 26, 1913	April 1, 1914	11,000
Union of Workers in Metal Products	Charter submitted September 24, 1913, denied January 17, 1914	—	n.d.

Metal—Nonferrous

Union of Workers in the Gold, Silver, and Bronze Trade*	May 1, 1907	—	484
Union of Journeymen and Salesclerks in the Watchmaking Craft*	May 15, 1907	April 1913	n.d.

ST. PETERSBURG, 1912–1914

Union	Registration Date	Closing Date	Peak Nominal Membership
Union of Workers in Watchmaking*	Charter rejected July 1912	—	n.d.
Paper			
Union of Workers in the Manufacture of Cardboard and Cardboard Products	May 22, 1907	May 8, 1912	n.d.
Union of Workers in the Cardboard and Paper Goods Industry	February 12, 1913	—	514
Printing			
Union of Workers in the Printing Industry	June 5, 1911	March 6, 1912	1,510
Same—reregistration	August 7, 1912	July 1914	3,870
Sales and Clerical			
Union of Pharmacy Employees	April 17, 1907	—	n.d.
Union of Employees in the Sale of Textile Goods	May 6, 1912	—	1,500
Union of Sales Employees in Enterprises Selling Foodstuffs	May 15, 1913	—	800
Union of Sales Employees in Enterprises Selling Household Goods	May 25, 1913	—	500

Union of Accounting Clerks in Sales and Sales-Manufacturing Enterprises	n.d.	n.d.	1,000
"The Assembly of St. Petersburg Bookkeepers" Union	Charter rejected March 19, 1913	—	n.d.
Union of Druggists	Being organized July 1913	—	n.d.
Service			
Union of Employees in the Tavern Trade	September 24, 1913	—	1,075
Union of Workers Employed in Wine Cellars	Being organized July 1913	—	n.d.
Union of Men and Women Workers in the Laundry and Dyeing Industry	Charter rejected June 1914	—	n.d.
Technical			
Union of Draftsmen	July 24, 1907	—	127
Union of Electrical Workers	Charter rejected January 17, 1914	—	n.d.
Textiles			
Union of Men and Women Textile Workers in the Northern Industrial Region	May 15, 1907	—	1,500
Transportation			
Union of Cabmen	Being organized July 1912	—	n.d.

ST. PETERSBURG, 1912–1914

Union	Registration Date	Closing Date	Peak Nominal Membership
Union of Clerical Employees of the Petersburg Tram	Charter submitted October 1913	—	n.d.
Union of Port Employees and Workers	April 4, 1914	—	n.d.
Wood			
Union of Woodworkers*	May 15, 1907	July 1914	1,200
Same—reregistration*	June or July 1914	—	n.d.
Miscellaneous			
Union of Workers in the Manufacture of Carriages*	July 24, 1907	—	330

MOSCOW, 1912–1914

Union	Registration Date	Closing Date	Peak Nominal Membership
Apparel and Leather			
Union of Workers in the Leather Industry in the Moscow Industrial Region	June 20, 1906	—	220
Union of Men and Women Workers in the Manufacture of Leather Gloves*	July 4, 1906	—	n.d.

Moscow Union of Artisanal Wallet and Purse Makers*	August 28, 1908	n.d.	—
Union of Men and Women Workers in the Tailoring Industry in the City of Moscow*	November 1912	2,460	—
Union of Workers in the Manufacture of Shoes*	February or March 1913	300	—
Chemical			
Union of Workers in the Manufacture of Glass and China in the Moscow Industrial Region	May 1914	320	—
Construction			
Union of Plumbing and Heating Workers*	May 8, 1906	n.d.	—
Union of Architectural and Construction Workers in the Moscow Industrial Region*	July 7, 1914	225	—
Union of Repair Workers*	Unregistered	n.d.	n.d.
Food			
Moscow Union of Sausage-Making Enterprises*	1907	n.d.	—
Union of Tea Packing Workers in the City of Moscow	1909	94	—
Union of Workers in the Bread Baking Industry in the City of Moscow*	March 11, 1913	1,725	—
Union of Workers in the Manufacture of Confections	March 1914	800	—

MOSCOW, 1912–1914

Union	Registration Date	Closing Date	Peak Nominal Membership
Union of Workers in the Tobacco Industry in the City of Moscow	Unregistered	n.d.	n.d.
Metal			
Union of Metal Workers under the name "Workers' Solidarity"	April 22, 1913	August 16, 1913	1,960
Union of Metal Workers under the name "Unity"	December 31, 1913	—	1,300
Metal—Nonferrous			
Union of Workers in the City of Moscow in the Manufacture of Artifacts in Precious Metals*	December 31, 1913	—	1,000
Printing			
Moscow Union of Typo-Lithographical Workers	May 8, 1906	—	n.d.
Union of Printing Workers	March 7, 1913	November 24, 1914	4,000
Sales and Clerical			
Mutual Aid Society of Sales Employees	1907	—	700
Union of Dining Room Employees in Sales-Industrial Enterprises in the Upper Trading Rows of Moscow	1907	—	n.d.

Moscow Union of Bookkeepers	1907	n.d.	—
Union of Employees in Fur Enterprises in the City of Moscow	1909	n.d.	—
Moscow Mutual Aid Society of Employees in the Cattle Trade	1910	n.d.	—
Union for the Organization of Congresses of Bookkeepers	1911	n.d.	—
Service			
Union of Cooks in the Moscow Industrial Region	April 11, 1906	1,061	—
Union of Barbers in the Moscow Region	August 19, 1906	150	—
Moscow Mutual Aid Society of Waiters and Other Employees in All Enterprises of the Tavern Trade	September 12, 1906	627	—
Technical			
Union of Electricians	1908	n.d.	—
Union of Mechanics and Master Craftsmen	Unregistered	n.d.	n.d.
Textiles			
Union of Textile Workers	July 1908	342	—
Union of Master Pattern Weavers in the City of Moscow	1914	n.d.	—
Wood			
Moscow Union of Woodworkers*	November 20, 1912	450	—

MOSCOW, 1912–1914

Union	Registration Date	Closing Date	Peak Nominal Membership
Union of Box Makers	Unregistered	n.d.	n.d.
Miscellaneous			
Old Believers' Union of Gonfalon Bearers of the Cathedrals of the Rogozhskoe Old Believers' Cemetery	July 18, 1906	—	n.d.
Union of Button and Hook Makers in the Moscow Industrial Region*	November 20, 1906	—	n.d.

Sources for Appendix V:

TsGAOR, DPOO, f. 102, op. 00, d. 17, ch. 46, 1916.

TsGIA, f. 23, op. 29, d. 40; f. 23, op. 29, d. 44.

Istoriia rabochikh Leningrada, 1703–fevral' 1917. Volume 1. Leningrad, 1972.

Oliunina, E. A. *Portnovskii promysel' v Moskve i v derevniakh Moskovskoi i Riazanskoi gubernii.* Moscow, 1914.

Sapronov, T. V. *Iz istorii rabochego dvizheniia (po lichnym vospominaniiam).* Moscow, 1925.

In addition, information was drawn from the contemporary labor and political press.

Note: The notation "n.d." in the "Closing Date" column indicates that the closing date of the union is unknown; where no date is shown, the union retained its legal status.

*An asterisk indicates a union designated as artisanal.

†A fictitious union, created and registered in case the Union of Workers in the Metalworking Industry was closed. Began to function only in April 1912.

Selected Bibliography

I. ARCHIVAL SOURCES

Tsentral'nyi gosudarstvennyi arkhiv oktiabr'skoi revoliutsii (TsGAOR) (Central State Archive of the October Revolution)

fond 63, Otdelenie po okraneniiu obshchestvennoi bezopasnosti i poriadka v gorode Moskve (Okhrannoe otdelenie)

fond 102, Departament politsii

fond 111, Otdelenie po okhraneniiu obshchestvennoi bezopasnosti i poriadka v. S.-Peterburge (Okhrannoe otdelenie)

fond 518, Soiuz soiuzov

fond 523, Konstitutsionno-demokraticheskaia partiia

fond 6860, Istprof pri TsK Soiuza metallistov

fond 6865, Istprof pri TsK Soiuza zheleznodorozhnikov

fond 6935, Istprof pri Vsesoiuznom tsentral'nom sovete professional'nykh soiuzov

Tsentral'nyi gosudarstvennyi arkhiv goroda Moskvy (TsGAgM) (Central State Archive of the City of Moscow)

fond 2005, Fabrichnyi inspektor 10 uchasta Moskovskoi gubernii

fond 2069, Moskovskii profsoiuz rabotnikov pechatnogo dela

Tsentral'nyi gosudarstvennyi istoricheskii arkhiv (TsGIA) (Central State Historical Archive)

fond 23, Ministerstvo torgovli i promyshlennosti

fond 150, Petrogradskoe obshchestvo zavodchikov i fabrikantov

fond 229, Kantseliariia Ministerstva putei soobshcheniia

fond 273, Upravlenie zheleznykh dorog

fond 560, Obshchaia kantseliariia Ministerstva finansov

fond 1278, Gosudarstvennaia duma

fond 1284, Departament obshchikh del Ministerstva vnutrennikh del

fond 1289, Glavnoe upravlenie pocht i telegrafov Ministerstva vnutrennikh del

fond 1405, Ugolovnyi kassatsiionnyi departament Senata

Leningradskii gosudarstvennyi istoricheskii arkhiv (LGIA) (Leningrad State Historical Archive)

fond 287, Petrogradskoe osoboe gorodskoe po delam ob obshchestvakh prisutstvie

Nikolaevsky Collection, Hoover Institution on War, Revolution and Peace

No. 91, Letter from Iu. Larin

No. 109, Box 5, Document 58, Letter from St. Petersburg.

II. BOOKS, ARTICLES, AND UNPUBLISHED WORKS

Abramovich, N. *Revoliutsionnoe podpol'e i okhrannoe otdelenie.* Petrograd, 1917.

Ainzaft, S. S. *Istoriia rabochego i professional'nogo dvizheniia derevoobdelochnikov do revoliutsii 1917 g.* Moscow, 1928.

———. "K istorii professional'nogo dvizheniia torgovo-promyshlennykh sluzhashchikh." *Vestnik truda,* no. 2 (39) (1924), pp. 222–230.

———. *Pervyi etap professional'nogo dvizheniia v Rossii. (1905–1907 gg.).* Moscow, 1925.

————. "Pervyi etap rossiiskogo profdvizheniia (1905–1907 gg.)." *Vestnik truda,* no. 4 (31) (1923), pp. 132–156.

————. *Professional'noe dvizhenie v Rossii v 1905–1907 gg. Szhatyi ocherk.* Moscow, 1925.

Aluf, A. S. *Bol'shevizm i men'shevizm v professional'nom dvizhenii.* Moscow, 1926.

Aluf, A. S., ed. *Materialy po istorii professional'nogo dvizheniia meditsinskikh rabotnikov. Sbornik 2.* Moscow, 1926.

Alymov, V. "K voprosu o polozhenii truda v remeslennom proizvodstve." *Narodnoe khoziaistvo,* Book 6 (November–December 1904), pp. 1–27.

Aminzade, Ronald. *Class, Politics and Early Industrial Capitalism: A Study of Mid-Nineteenth-Century Toulouse.* Albany, N.Y., 1981.

Anderson, Barbara. *Internal Migration During Modernization in Late Nineteenth-Century Russia.* Princeton, N.J., 1980.

Andronov, F. I. "Iz istorii professional'nogo dvizheniia izvozchikov v Peterburga." *Krasnaia letopis',* no. 1 (12) (1925), pp. 111–115.

Anskii, A., ed. *Professional'noe dvizhenie v Petrograde v 1917 g. Ocherki i materialy.* Leningrad, 1928.

Antonov, M. *Professional'nye soiuzy.* St. Petersburg, 1907.

Antonova, S. I. *Vliianie stolypinskoi agrarnoi reformy na izmeneniia v sostave rabochego klassa. Po materialam Moskovskoi gubernii, 1906–1913 gg.* Moscow, 1951.

Antoshkin, D. V. *Ocherk dvizheniia sluzhashchikh v Rossii.* Moscow, 1921.

————. *Professional'noe dvizhenie sluzhashchikh 1917–1924 gg.* Moscow, 1927.

————. *Professional'noe dvizhenie v Rossii.* 2d ed. Moscow, 1924.

Anufriev, V. M., P. I. Dorovatskii, and N. I. Roganov. *Iz istorii profdvizheniia rabotnikov torgovli.* Moscow, 1958.

Anweiler, Oskar. *The Soviets: The Russian Workers, Peasants, and Soldiers Councils.* Translated by Ruth Hein. New York, 1974.

Arbuzov, S. *Polozhenie russkoi poligraficheskoi promyshlennosti.* Moscow, 1921.

Aronson, G. Ia. *Men'shevizm v 1905 g.* (Typewritten.) [New York, 196?].

Arskii, K. N. *Kak rabochim soiuzy ustraivat'.* Moscow, 1905.

Arutiunov, G. A. *Rabochee dvizhenie v Rossii v periode novogo revoliutsionnogo pod"ema 1910–1914 gg.* Moscow, 1975.

Ascher, Abraham. *Pavel Axelrod and the Development of Menshevism.* Cambridge, Mass., 1972.

Avrekh, A. Ia. *Tsarizm i tret'eiiun'skaia sistema.* Moscow, 1966.

Badaev, A. E. *Bol'sheviki v gosudarstvennoi dume. Bol'shevistskaia fraktsiia IV gosudarstvennoi dumy i revoliutsionnoe dvizhenie v Peterburge. Vospominaniia.* Leningrad, 1929.

———. "Bol'shevistskaia fraktsiia IV gosudarstvennoi dumy i revoliutsionnoe dvizhenie v Petrograde." *Krasnaia letopis',* no. 3 (30) (1929), pp. 202–244.

Baevskii, D. A. *Istoriia rabochikh pechati v Rossii.* Moscow, 1923.

Balabanov, M. S. *Fabrichnye zakony. Sbornik zakonov, rasporiazhenii i raz"iasnenii po voprosam russkogo fabrichnogo zakonodatel'stva.* St. Petersburg, 1909.

———. *Istoriia rabochikh kooperatsii v Rossii (1864–1917).* Kiev, 1923.

———. *Ocherk istorii revoliutsionnogo dvizheniia v Rossii.* Leningrad, 1929.

———. *Ot 1905 k 1917 godu. Massovoe rabochee dvizhenie.* Moscow and Leningrad, 1927.

———. *Rabochee dvizhenie v Rossii v gody pod"ema 1912–1914 gg.* Leningrad, 1927.

Bater, James H. *St. Petersburg: Industrialization and Change.* London, 1976.

Bazilevich, K. V. *Ocherki po istorii professional'nogo dvizheniia rabotnikov sviazi. 1905–1906 gg.* Moscow, 1925.

Beliavskii, R. N. *Ocherki po istorii professional'nogo dvizheniia v Rossii.* Moscow, 1918.

Belin, A. [A. A. Evdokimov]. *Professional'noe dvizhenie torgovykh sluzhashchikh v Rossii.* Moscow, 1906.

———. "Vtoraia konferentsiia professional'nykh rabochikh soiuzov." *Bez zaglaviia,* no. 13 (April 13, 1906), pp. 17–23.

———. "Zametki o professional'nom dvizhenii rabochikh (Pis'mo iz Moskvy)." *Bez zaglaviia,* no. 6 (Feb. 26, 1906), pp. 239–242.

Belin, A., ed. *Spravochnye svedeniia ob ob"edineniiu professional'nykh rabochikh soiuzov v Rossii.* Moscow, 1906.

Belousov, I. A. *Ushedshaia Moskva: Zapiski po lichnym vospominaniiam s nachala 1870 godov.* Moscow, 1927.

Belousov, V. V. *Izuchenie truda v tabachnom proizvodstve.* Petrograd, 1921.

Bendix, Reinhard. *Nation-Building and Citizenship: Studies of Our Changing Social Order.* New enlarged edition. Berkeley, Los Angeles, and London, 1977.

————. *Work and Authority in Industry: Ideologies of Management in the Course of Industrialization.* Berkeley, Los Angeles, and London, 1974.

Bendix, Reinhard, and Seymour Martin Lipset, eds. *Class, Status, and Power: A Reader in Social Stratification.* Glencoe, Ill., 1953.

Berlin, P. A. *Russkaia burzhuaziia v staroe i novoe vremia.* Moscow, 1922.

Bernshtein-Kogan, S. *Chislennost', sostav i polozhenie Peterburgskikh rabochikh. Opyt statisticheskogo issledovaniia.* St. Petersburg, 1910.

Beshkin, G., ed. *Legal'naia sotsial-demokraticheskaia literatura v Rossii za 1906–1914 gody.* Moscow, 1924.

Bibikov, Iu. K., and V. F. Malyshkin. *Vozniknovenie i deiatel'nost' profsoiuzov Peterburga (1905–1907 gg.).* Moscow, 1955.

Bibikov, Iu. K., V. F. Malyshkin, and E. Shalaeva. *Profsoiuzy Petrograda do Velikoi Oktiabr'skoi sotsialisticheskoi revoliutsii (1907–1917 gody). Iz istorii profsoiuznogo dvizheniia v SSSR.* Moscow, 1957.

Blackwell, William L. *The Beginnings of Russian Industrialization 1800–1860.* Princeton, N.J., 1968.

Blauner, Robert. *Alienation and Freedom: The Factory Worker and His Industry.* Chicago, 1964.

Blek, A. "Usloviia truda na Peterburgskikh zavodakh po dannym 1901 g." *Arkhiv istorii truda v Rossii,* Book 2 (1921), pp. 65–85.

Bogdanov, N. [Fedosov]. *Organizatsiia stroitel'nykh rabochikh Rossii i drugikh stran.* Moscow, 1919.

Bogdanov-Evdokimov, F. "Zubatovshchina v Moskve." *Vestnik truda,* no. 9 (November 1923).

Bol'sheviki vo glave pervoi russkoi revoliutsii 1905–1907 godov. Moscow, 1956.

Bol'shevistskaia pechat' i rabochii klass Rossii v gody revoliutsionnogo pod''ema 1910–1914 gg. Moscow, 1965.

Bol'shevistskaia pechat'. Kratkie ocherki istorii 1894–1917 gg. Moscow, 1962.

Bol'shevistskaia periodicheskaia pechat' (dekabr' 1900–oktiabr' 1917). Bibliograficheskii ukazatel'. Moscow, 1964.

Bonnell, Victoria E. "Introduction" to T. Sapronov, *Iz istorii rabochego dvizheniya (po lichnym vospominaniyam).* Newtonville, Mass., 1976.

————. "Radical Politics and Organized Labor in Pre-Revolutionary Moscow, 1905–1914." *Journal of Social History,* vol. 12, no. 2 (March 1979), pp. 282–300.

————. "Trade Unions, Parties, and the State in Tsarist Russia: A Study of Labor Politics in St. Petersburg and Moscow." *Politics and Society,* vol. 9, no. 3 (1980), pp. 299–322.

————, ed. *The Russian Worker: Life and Labor under the Tsarist Regime.* Berkeley, Los Angeles, and London, 1983.

"Bor'ba so stachechnym dvizheniem nakanune mirovoi voiny." *Krasnyi arkhiv,* vol. 3 (34) (1929), pp. 95–125.

Borshchenko, I. L. *Vozniknovenie profsoiuzov v Rossii i ikh deiatel'nost' v 1905–1917 godakh.* Moscow, 1961.

Borshchevskii, A., S. Reshetov, and N. Chistov, eds. *Moskovskie pechatniki v 1905 godu.* Moscow, 1925.

Bratskaia mogila: biograficheskii sovlar' umershikh i pogibshikh chlenov Moskovskoi organizatsii R. K. P. 2 vols. Moscow, 1922–1923.

Brodskii, N. L., et al. *Tekstil'shchik (Istoriia, byt, bor'ba). Khrestomatiia.* Moscow, 1925.

Brooks, Jeffrey. "Readers and Reading at the End of the Tsarist Era," in *Literature and Society in Imperial Russia, 1800–1914.* Edited by William Mills Todd III. Stanford, Calif., 1978.

Bulkin, F. A. [F. A. Semenov]. *Na zare profdvizheniia: Istoriia Peterburgskogo soiuza metallistov 1906–1914 gg.* Moscow and Leningrad, 1924.

————. "Rabochaia samodeiatel'nost' i rabochaia demogogiia." *Nasha zaria,* no. 3 (1914), pp. 55–64.

————. "Raskol' fraktsii i zadachi rabochikh." *Nasha zaria,* no. 6 (1914), pp. 42–51.

————. *Soiuz metallistov i departament politsii.* Leningrad, 1923.

————. *Soiuz metallistov 1906–1918 gg.* Moscow, 1926.

Bulkin-Semenov, F. *V bor'be za soiuz metallistov.* Leningrad, 1926.

See also F. Semenov-Bulkin.

Burdzhalov, E. N. *Vtoraia russkaia revoliutsiia.* Vol. 1: *Vosstanie v Petrograde.* Moscow, 1967. Vol. 2: *Moskva—Front—Periferiia.* Moscow, 1971.

Buzinov, A. *Za Nevskoi zastavoi: Zapiski rabochego.* Moscow and Leningrad, 1930.

Ch., Iu. [P. A. Garvi,]. "Professional'nye soiuzy i vybory v Gosudarstvennoi Dume." *Otkliki,* vyp. 1 (December 17, 1906), pp. 49–59.

Chaadaeva, O., ed. "Iiul'skie stachki i demonstratsii 1914 g." *Krasnyi arkhiv,* no. 4 (95) (1939), pp. 137–155.

Chebarin, A. *Moskva v revoliutsii 1905–1907 godov.* Moscow, 1955.

Chekin, A. *Proiskhozhdenie i razvitie profdvizheniia v Rossii.* Moscow, 1926.

Chermenskii, E. D. *Burzhuaziia i tsarizm v pervoi russkoi revoliutsii.* Moscow, 1970.

——. *Fevral'skaia burzhuazno-demokraticheskaia revoliutsiia 1917 g. v Rossii.* Moscow, 1959.

——. "Tzarizm i tret'eiunskaia Duma." *Voprosy istorii,* no. 1 (January 1973), pp. 30–47.

Chernomordik, S. I., ed. *Piatyi god.* 2 vols. Moscow, 1925.

——. *Put' k oktiabriu. Sbornik statei, vospominanii i dokumentov.* 5 vols. Moscow, 1923–1926.

Chislennost' i sostav rabochikh v Rossii na osnovanii dannykh pervoi vseobshchei perepisi naseleniia Rossiiskoi Imperii 1897 g. 2 vols. St. Petersburg, 1906.

Chistov, N. "Moskovskie pechatniki v revoliutsii 1905 goda." *Katorga i ssylka,* no. 73 (1931), pp. 132–144.

Chlenov, S. B. *Moskovskaia okhranka i ee sekretnye sotrudniki.* Moscow, 1919.

Dalalo, V., ed. "Bor'ba za rabochuiu pechat' nakanune mirovoi voiny." *Krasnyi arkhiv,* no. 3 (64) (1934), pp. 139–143.

Davidovich, M. *Peterburgskii tekstil'nyi rabochii.* Chast' 1. Moscow, 1919.

Davies, James C. "Toward a Theory of Revolution." *American Sociological Review,* vol. 27, no. 1 (February 1962), pp. 5–15.

Deiateli soiuza sovetskikh sotsialisticheskikh respublik ob Oktiabr'skoi revoliutsii. Avtografii i biografii. Moscow, 192[7].

Derenkovskii, G. M. "Vseobshchaia stachka i sovety rabochikh deputatov v iiule 1906 g." *Istoricheskie zapiski,* vol. 77 (1965), pp. 108–153.

Derenkovskii, G. M., et al., eds. *Vtoroi period revoliutsii. 1906–1907 gody.* 4 vols. Moscow, 1957–1965.

Deutscher, Isaac. *Soviet Trade Unions.* London and New York, 1950.

Dinamo. 25 let revoliutsionnoi bor'by. Moscow, 1923.

Dmitriev, K. [P. N. Kolokol'nikov,]. *Iz praktiki professional'nogo dvizheniia v Rossii.* Odessa, 1907.

——. *Professional'nye soiuzy v Moskve.* [St. Petersburg], 190[6].

——. "Vtoraia konferentsiia professional'nykh soiuzov." *Otkliki sovremennosti,* no. 4 (May 25, 1906), pp. 62–76.

See also P. N. Kolokol'nikov.

Dorovatovskii, P. *Soiuz transportnykh rabochikh: Ocherk istorii Leningradskoi organizatsii 1905–1918 gg.* Leningrad, 1927.

Dorovatovskii, P., and V. Zlotin. *Professional'noe dvizhenie v gody imperialisticheskoi voiny.* Leningrad, 1927.

Eliiasson, L. S., ed. *Zakony ob otnosheniiakh predprinimatelei i rabochikh v oblasti fabrichno-zavodskoi promyshlennosti.* St. Petersburg, 1908.

El'nitskii, A. E. *Istoriia rabochego dvizheniia v Rossii.* 4th ed. Moscow, 1925.

———. *Pervye shagi rabochego dvizheniia v Rossii.* Berlin, [1918].

Elwood, Ralph Carter. *Roman Malinovsky: A Life Without a Cause.* Newtonville, Mass., 1977.

———. *Russian Social Democracy in the Underground: A Study of the RSDRP in the Ukraine, 1907–1914.* Assen, The Netherlands, 1974.

Emmons, Terrence. "Russia's Banquet Campaign." *California Slavic Studies,* vol. 10 (1977), pp. 45–86.

Engelstein, Laura. *Moscow, 1905: Working-Class Organization and Political Conflict.* Stanford, Calif., 1982.

Erenfel'd, B. K. "Delo Malinovskogo." *Voprosy istorii,* no. 1 (July 1965), pp. 106–116.

Erman, L. K. *Intelligentsiia v pervoi Russkoi revoliutsii.* Moscow, 1966.

Ermanskii, A. "Soiuzy rabotodatelei." *Sovremennyi mir,* Book 12 (December 1909), pp. 25–45.

Essen, M. M., ed. *VKP (b) o profsoiuzakh. Sbornik reshenii i postavlenii s"ezdov, konferentsii i plenumov TSK VKP (b).* Moscow, 1933.

Evdokimov, A. A. See Belin, A.

Evgenii [E. Maevskii]. "Peterburgskii sovet rabochikh deputatov (ocherk vozniknoveniia)." *Otkliki sovremennosti,* no. 5 (1906), pp. 1–11.

Evsenin, I. *Ot fabrikanta k krasnomu oktiabriu. Iz istorii odnoi fabriki.* Moscow, 1927.

Ezhov, V., ed. *Pamiatnaia kniga rabochego.* Chast' 1. *Ekonomicheskaia.* St. Petersburg, 1918.

Fabrichno-zavodskie predpriiatiia v Rossiiskoi imperii (iskliuchaia Finlandiiu). 2d ed. Petrograd, 1914.

Freze, G. *Opyt rabochego predstavitel'stva i upravlenii fabrikoi.* Translated from the German by L. Liven. Moscow, 1913.

Galai, Shmuel. *The Liberation Movement in Russia 1900–1905.* Cambridge, England, 1973.

Galenson, Walter, ed. *Comparative Labor Movements.* New York, 1952.

Gaponenko, L. S. *Rabochii klass Rossii v 1917 godu.* Moscow, 1970.

Gardins, F. *Professional'nye soiuzy v rabochem dvizhenii.* Translated by O. Dilevskaia. Moscow, 1906.

Garvi, P. A. *Professional'nye soiuzy, ikh organizatsiia i deiatel'nost'.* 2d ed. Petrograd, 1917.

———. *Professional'nye soiuzy v Rossii v pervye gody revoliutsii (1917–1921).* New York, 1958.

———. *Revoliutsionnye siluety.* New York, 1962.

———. *Vospominaniia. Peterburg—1906 g.* New York, 1961.

———. *Vospominaniia Sotsial-demokrata. Stati o zhizni i deiatel'nosti P. A. Garvi.* New York, 1946.

See also Iu. Ch.

Gerschenkron, Alexander. "Agrarian Politics and Industrialization—Russia 1861–1917." *The Cambridge Economic History of Europe.* Vol. 6, part 2 (Cambridge, England, 1965), pp. 706–800.

———. *Economic Backwardness in Historical Perspective: A Book of Essays.* Cambridge, Mass., 1966.

Giddens, Anthony. *The Class Structure of the Advanced Societies.* New York, Hagerstown, San Francisco, and London, 1975.

Giliarovskii, V. A. *Moskva i moskvichi. Ocherki staromoskovskogo byta.* Moscow, 1955.

Girinis, S. V. *Lenin i professional'noe dvizhenie.* Moscow, 1924.

Glavneishie predvaritel'nye dannye perepisi g. Moskvy 31 ianvaria 1902 g. Vyp. 1–6. Moscow, 1902–1907.

Glavneishie predvaritel'nye dannye perepisi g. Moskvy 6 marta 1912 g. Vyp. 1. Moscow, 1913.

Glickman, Rose. *Russian Factory Women: Workplace and Society* 1880–1914. Berkeley and Los Angeles, 1984.

Gol'dberg, G. *K istorii professional'nogo dvizheniia v Rossii: Sostoianie soiuzov nakanune Vtoroi Gosudarstvennoi Dumy.* St. Petersburg, 1907.

Golubev, I. "Vospominaniia o Peterburgskom soiuze metallistov (1907–1908)." *Krasnaia letopis',* no. 8 (1923), pp. 234–236.

Gordon, G. "K voprosu o polozhenii detei voobshche i remeslennykh i torgovykh uchenikov v chastnosti." *Trudovaia pomoshch',* no. 1 (January 1908), pp. 230–239.

Gordon, M. *Professional'noe dvizhenie v epokhu russkoi revoliutsii 1905–1907 gg.* Leningrad, 1925.

Gordon, M., ed. *Iz istorii professional'nogo dvizheniia sluzhashchikh v Peterburge: Pervyi etap (1904–1919).* Leningrad, 1925.

Gordon, Manya. *Workers Before and After Lenin.* New York, 1941.

Gorev, B. I. "Demagogia ili marksizm?" *Nasha zaria,* no. 6 (1914), pp. 30–41.

Gosudarstvennaia Duma: Chetvertyi sozyv. Stenograficheskie otchety 1912–1913 gg. St. Petersburg, 1913–1914.

Grave, B. B. *K istorii klassovoi bor'by v Rossii v gody imperialisticheskoi voiny. Iiul' 1914 g.-fevral' 1917 g. Proletariat i burzhuaziia.* Moscow and Leningrad, 1926.

Grave, B. B., ed. *Burzhuaziia nakanune fevral'skoi revoliutsii.* Moscow, 1927.

Grave, B. B., M. V. Nechkina, A. M. Pankratova, and K. F. Sidorov, eds. *Ocherki istorii proletariata SSSR.* Moscow, 1931.

Grinevich, V. "Ocherk razvitiia professional'nogo dvizheniia v S.-Peterburge." *Obrazovanie,* vol. 15, no. 8 (August 1906), pp. 208–226; and no. 9 (September 1906), pp. 226–255.

———. *Professional'noe dvizhenie rabochikh v Rossii.* St. Petersburg, 1908.

Gruzdev, S. M. *Trud i bor'ba shveinikov v Petrograde 1905–1916 gg.* Leningrad, 1929.

Gudvan, A. M. *Normirovka truda torgovo-promyshlennykh sluzhashchikh.* Petrograd, 1917.

———. *Ocherki po istorii dvizheniia sluzhashchikh v Rossii.* Chast' 1: *Do revoliutsii 1905 goda.* Moscow, 1925.

———. *Prikazchichii vopros. Zhizn' i trud prikazchikov.* Odessa, 1905.

Gurevich, A. I. *Lenin i professional'nye soiuzy.* Moscow, 1924.

Gurevich, S. A. *Radikal'naia burzhuaziia i professional'nye soiuzy.* St. Petersburg, 1907.

Gurr, Ted Robert. *Why Men Rebel.* Princeton, N.J., 1969.

Haimson, Leopold. "The Problem of Social Stability in Urban Russia, 1905–1917." *Slavic Review,* part 1, vol. 23, no. 4 (December 1964), pp. 619–642; part 2, vol. 24, no. 1 (March 1965), pp. 1–22.

———. *The Russian Marxists and the Origins of Bolshevism.* Cambridge, Mass., 1955.

Hammond, Thomas Taylor. *Lenin on Trade Unions and Revolution 1893–1917.* New York, 1957.

Hanagan, Michael Patrick. *The Logic of Solidarity: Artisans and Industrial Workers in Three French Towns 1871–1914.* Urbana, Chicago, and London, 1980.

Harcave, Sidney. *The Russian Revolution of 1905.* London, 1970.

Iakovlev, V. *1905 v Moskve. Istoriko-revoliutsionnyi ocherk.* Moscow, 1955.

Iakub, R. "Iz zhizni Moskovskikh professional'nykh soiuzov v 1911 godu." *Vestnik truda,* no. 8–9 (23–24) (August–September 1922), pp. 189–198.

Iretskii, V. Ia. *Okhranka (stranitsa russkoi istorii).* Petrograd, [1917].

Istoriia Leningradskogo soiuza rabochikh poligraficheskogo proizvodstva. Book 1: *(1904–1907).* Leningrad, 1925.

Istoriia Moskvy. 6 vols. Moscow, 1952–1959.

Istoriia odnogo soiuza. Moscow, 1907.

Istoriia profsoiuzov SSSR. Uchebnoe posobie. Chast' 1: *1905–1937.* 2d ed. Moscow, 1977.

Istoriia Putilovskogo zavoda. 1801–1917. Moscow, 1961.

Istoriia rabochego klassa Leningrada. Vyp. 2. Leningrad, 1963.

Istoriia rabochikh Leningrada, 1703–fevral' 1917. Volume 1. Leningrad, 1972.

Istoriia soveta rabochikh deputatov g. S.-Peterburga. St. Petersburg, 1906.

Ivanov, B. I. "Bor'ba rabochikh-pishchevikov za khleb i prodovol'stvie nakanune oktiabria 1917 g." *Istoricheskii arkhiv,* no. 3 (1957), pp. 185–198.

―――. *Professional'noe dvizhenie rabochikh khlebo-pekarno-konditerskogo proizvodstva Petrograda i gubernii (s 1903–1917 g.).* Moscow, 1920.

Ivanov, L. M. et al., eds. *Rossiiskii proletariat: oblik, bor'ba, gegemoniia.* Moscow, 1970.

Iz epokhi "Zvezdy" i "Pravdy" (1911–1914). Moscow, 1921.

Izveshchenie o konferentsii organizatsii R.S.-D.R.P. [Vienna], 1912.

Johnson, Chalmers. *Revolutionary Change.* Boston, 1966.

Johnson, Robert Eugene. *Peasant and Proletarian: The Working Class of Moscow in the Late Nineteenth Century.* New Brunswick, N.J., 1979.

―――. "Peasant Migration and the Russian Working Class: Moscow at the End of the Nineteenth Century." *Slavic Review,* vol. 35, no. 4 (December 1976), pp. 652–664.

"K 4-mu vserossiiskomu s"ezdu organizatsii torgovo-promyshlennykh sluzhashchikh." *Vestnik truda,* no. 8 (October 1923), pp. 263–273.

Kabanov, P. I. *Rabochee i profsoiuznoe dvizhenie v Moskve v 1905–1907 godakh.* Moscow, 1955.

Kabo, E. O. *Ocherki rabochego byta. Opyt monograficheskogo issledovaniia domashnego rabochego byta.* Vol. 1. Moscow, 1928.

Kanatchikov, S. I. *Iz istorii moego bytiia.* Book 1. Moscow and Leningrad, 1929.

Karlova, L. A. *Istoriia zavoda "Dinamo."* Vol. 1: *"Dinamo" na putiakh k Oktiabriu.* Moscow, 1961.

Kaplun, S. I. *Polozhenie rabochego klassa. Bibliograficheskii ukazatel'.* Moscow, 1927.

Kats, A. "Glavneishie momenty rabochego dvizheniia Rossii v 1905 godu." *Vestnik truda,* no. 12 (61) (1925), pp. 60–73.

Kats, A., and Iu. Milonov, eds. *1905: Professional'noe dvizhenie.* Moscow and Leningrad, 1926.

Kautskii, K. [Karl Kautsky]. *Professional'noe dvizhenie i politicheskaia partiia proletariata.* St. Petersburg, 1905.

———. *Vozniknovenie rabochego klassa.* St. Petersburg, 1905.

Kedrov, A. *Rabochie soiuzy v zapadnoi Evrope.* Moscow, 1905.

Keep, John L. H. *The Rise of Social Democracy in Russia.* Oxford, 1963.

———. *The Russian Revolution: A Study in Mass Mobilization.* New York, 1976.

Kerr, Clark, and Abraham Siegel. "The Interindustry Propensity to Strike—An International Comparison," in *Industrial Conflict,* edited by Arthur Kornhauser et al. New York, 1954.

Kheisin, M. L. *Professional'nye rabochie soiuzy (sushchnost', organizatsiia i sredstva bor'by). S prilozheniem prakticheskikh ukazanii ob organizatsii soiuzov.* St. Petersburg, 1907.

Khokhlov, K. *Zasada: Istoriia razgroma pervoi rabochei gazety v Moskve.* Moscow, 1929.

Khromov, P. A. *Ekonomika Rossii perioda promyshlennogo kapitalizma.* Moscow, 1963.

Kir'ianov, Iu. I. "Ekonomicheskoe polozhenie rabochego klassa Rossii nakanune revoliutsii 1905–1907 gg." *Istoricheskie zapiski,* no. 98 (1977), pp. 147–189.

———. *Zhiznennyi uroven' rabochikh Rossii.* Moscow, 1979.

Kir'ianov, Iu. I, and L. M. Shalaginova. "Materialy fondov komissii Istprofov kak istochnik po istorii rabochego klassa Rossii." *Voprosy istorii,* no. 5 (May 1978), pp. 137–146.

Kirillov, V. S. *Bol'sheviki vo glave massovykh politicheskikh stachek v period pod"ema revoliutsii 1905–1907 gg.* Moscow, 1961.

Kirpichnikov, S. D. "L. I. Lutugin i soiuz soiuzov." *Byloe,* no. 6 (34) (1925), pp. 134–146.

K[irpichnikov], S. D. *Soiuz soiuzov.* St. Petersburg, 1906.

Koenker, Diane. *Moscow Workers and the 1917 Revolution.* Princeton, N.J., 1981.

Kolokol'nikov, P. N. *Professional'noe dvizhenie i soiuzy v Rossii.* St. Petersburg, 1909.

———. *Professional'noe dvizhenie v Rossii.* Petrograd, 1918.

Kolokol'nikov, P., and S. Rapoport, eds. *1905–1907 gg. v professional'nom dvizhenii: I i II Vserossiiskie konferentsii professional'nykh soiuzov.* Moscow, 1925.

See also K. Dmitriev.

Kol'tsov, D. *Professional'nye soiuzy i rabochaia partiia.* St. Petersburg, 1906.

Kolychev, A. A. "K voprosu ob uregulirovanii polozheniia remeslennykh rabotnikov." *Vestnik znaniia,* no. 3 (1904), pp. 65–69.

Kommunisticheskaia partiia Sovetskogo Soiuza v rezoliutsiiakh i resheniiakh s"ezdov, konferentsii i plenumov Ts.K. 1898–1954. Moscow, 1953–1954.

Kondrat'ev, V. A., and V. I. Nevzorov, eds. *Iz istorii fabrik i zavodov Moskvy i Moskovskoi gubernii (konets XVIII-nachalo XX v.). Obzor dokumentov.* Moscow, 1968.

Korbut, M. "Strakhovaia kampaniia 1912–1914 gg." *Proletarskaia revoliutsiia,* no. 2 (73) (1928), pp. 96–117.

Kovalenskii, M. N., and E. A. Morokhovets. *Russkaia revoliutsiia v sudebnykh protsessakh i memuarakh.* Vol. 4. Moscow, 1925.

Krivosheina, E. *Peterburgskii sovet rabochikh deputatov v 1905 godu.* Moscow, 1926.

Kruze, E. E. *Peterburgskie rabochie v 1912–1914 godakh.* Moscow and Leningrad, 1961.

———. *Polozhenie rabochego klassa Rossii v 1900–1914 gg.* Leningrad, 1976.

Kudelli, P. F., and G. L. Shidlovskii, eds. *1905: Vospominaniia chlenov SPB soveta rabochikh deputatov.* Leningrad, 1926.

Kurskaia, A. S. *Proizvodstvo chasov v Moskve i Moskovskoi gubernii. Materialy k istorii kustarnoi promyshlennosti v Rossii.* Moscow, 1914.

LaFarg, P. [Paul LaFargue]. *Professional'noe dvizhenie v Germanii.* Moscow, 1905.

Laverychev, V. Ia. *Po tu storonu barrikad (Iz istorii bor'by Moskovskoi burzhuazii s revoliutsiei).* Moscow, 1967.

————. *Tsarizm i rabochii vopros v Rossii 1861–1917 gg.* Moscow, 1972.

Lavrinovich, Iu. *Rabochie soiuzy.* St. Petersburg, 1905.

Lebedev, N. I. *Russkii tekstil'shchik. v rabochem dvizhenii.* 2 vols. Moscow, 1924.

————. *Tekstil'shchiki v 1905 godu.* Moscow, 1925.

Leiderov, I. P. "Profsoiuzy Peterburga v 1905 godu." *Voprosy istorii,* no. 10 (1955), pp. 18–30.

Lenin, V. I. *V. I. Lenin o professional'nom dvizhenii. Stat'i i rechi.* Moscow, 1925.

————. *V. I. Lenin o profsoiuzakh 1894–1922.* Moscow, 1970.

————. *Selected Works.* 3 vols. New York, 1967.

————. *Sochineniia.* 3rd ed. 30 vols. Moscow, 1928–1937.

Leont'ev, V. V. *Ob izuchenii polozheniia rabochikh. Priemy issledovaniia i materialy.* St. Petersburg, 1912.

Lerner, E., ed. *Fabzavkomy i profsoiuzy: Sbornik statei.* 2d ed. Moscow, 1925.

Levitskii, V. [V. O. Tsederbaum]. *Kak rabochie dobivalis' prava koalitsii.* St. Petersburg, 1914.

See also G. Rakitin.

Lidtke, Vernon. *The Outlawed Party. Social Democracy in Germany, 1878–1890.* Princeton, N.J., 1966.

Lipset, Seymour Martin. *Political Man: The Social Bases of Politics.* Garden City, N.Y., 1963.

Lipset, Seymour Martin, Martin Trow, and James S. Coleman. *Union Democracy.* Glencoe, Ill., 1956.

Liskner, M. L. *Istoriia professional'nogo dvizheniia leningradskikh rabotnikov lechebno-sanitarnogo, aptechnogo, veterinarnogo dela.* Vol. 1. Leningrad, 1925.

Listovki Moskovskoi organizatsii bol'shevikov 1914–1925. Moscow, 1954.

Listovki Peterburgskikh bol'shevikov RSDRP, 1902–1917. 2 vols. Leningrad, 1939.

Lozinskii, E. *Itogi i perspektivy rabochego dvizheniia.* St. Petersburg, 1909.

Lur'e, E. S. *Organizatsiia i organizatsii torgovo-promyshlennykh interesov v Rossii.* St. Petersburg, 1913.

Lur'e, M., ed. "Tsarizm v bor'be s rabochim dvizheniem v gody pod"ema." *Krasnyi arkhiv,* no. 1 (74) (1936), pp. 37–65.

Mann, M. *Consciousness and Action Among the Western Working Class.* London, 1973.

Margolin, S. O. "Usloviia truda v remeslennoi i domashnei promyshlennosti."

Vestnik fabrichnogo zakonodatel'stva professional'noi gigieny, no. 2 (February 1905), pp. 40–51.

Marshall, T. H. *Class, Citizenship and Social Development.* New York, 1965.

Martov, L. "Otvet Bulkinu." *Nasha zaria,* no. 3 (1914), pp. 64–70.

———. "Raskol v sotsial-demokraticheskoi fraktsii." *Nasha zaria,* no. 10–11 (1913), pp. 89–101.

———. *Razvitie krupnoi promyshlennosti i rabochee dvizhenie v Rossii.* Leningrad, 1923.

Martov, L., P. Maslov, and A. Potresov, eds. *Obshchestvennoe dvizhenie v Rossii v nachale XX veka.* 5 vols. St. Petersburg, 1909–1914.

Martynov, A. P. *Moia sluzhba v otdel'nom korpuse zhandarmov. Vospominaniia.* Stanford, Calif., 1972.

Marx, Karl. *Capital: A Critique of Political Economy.* Vol. 1. New York, 1977.

———. *Economic and Philosophic Manuscripts of 1844.* Moscow, 1961.

———. *Karl Marx: Selected Writings.* Edited by David McLellen. Oxford, 1977.

Marx, Karl, and Friedrich Engels. *Basic Writings on Politics and Philosophy.* Edited by Louis S. Feuer. New York, 1959.

———. *The German Ideology.* Edited, with an introduction, by C. J. Arthur. New York, 1970.

Materialy ob ekonomicheskom polozhenii i professional'noi organizatsii Peterburgskikh rabochikh po metallu. St. Petersburg, 1909.

Materialy po istorii professional'nogo dvizheniia v Peterburge za 1905–1907 gg.: Sbornik. Leningrad, 1926.

Materialy po istorii professional'nogo dvizheniia v Rossii. 5 vols. Moscow, 1924–1927.

Mendelsohn, Ezra. *Class Struggle in the Pale: The Formative Years of the Jewish Workers' Movement in Tsarist Russia.* Cambridge, England, 1970.

Menitskii, I. *Rabochee dvizhenie i sotsial-demokraticheskoe podpol'e Moskvy v voennye gody (1914–1917).* Moscow, 1923.

———. *Revoliutsionnoe dvizhenie voennykh godov (1914–1917): Ocherki i materialy.* 2 vols. Moscow, 1924–1925.

———. *Russkoe rabochee dvizhenie i RSDRP nakanune voiny (1912–1914 gg.).* Moscow, 1923.

Mikhailov, M. "Ianvarskie vybory po rabochei kurii v gorode Peterburge." *Otkliki* (April 2, 1907), pp. 65–78.

———. "Vybory vo vtoruiu Dumu v Peterburgskoi rabochei kurii." *Otzvuki* (August 1907), pp. 41–51.

Miliukov, Paul. *Political Memoirs 1905–1917.* Edited by Arthur P. Mendel. Ann Arbor, Mich., 1967.

Miller, Margaret Stevenson. *The Economic Development of Russia 1905–1914, with Special Reference to Trade, Industry and Finance.* London, 1967.

Milonov, Iu. K. *Kak voznikli professional'nye soiuzy v Rossii.* 2d ed. Moscow, 1929.

———. "Partiia i professional'nye soiuzy v 1905 godu (Svodka vazhneishikh faktov i dokumentov)." *Proletarskaia revoliutsiia,* no. 1 (48) (1926), pp. 93–118.

Milonov, Iu. K., ed. *Moskovskoe professional'noe dvizhenie v gody pervoi revoliutsii.* Moscow, [1925].

———. *Professional'nye soiuzy v SSSR v proshlom i nastoiashem 1905–1917–1927.* Moscow, 1927.

———. *Putevoditel' po rezoliutsiiam vserossiiskikh s"ezdov i konferentsii professional'nykh soiuzov.* Moscow, 1924.

Milonov, Iu. K., and M. Rakovskii. *Istoriia Moskovskogo professional'nogo soiuza rabochikh derevoobdelochnikov.* Vyp. 1. Moscow, 1928.

Mitel'man, M., B. Glebov, and A. Ul'ianskii. *Istoriia Putilovskogo zavoda 1801–1917.* 3rd ed. Moscow, 1961.

Moore, Barrington, Jr. *Injustice: The Social Bases of Obedience and Revolt.* White Plains, N.Y., 1978.

———. *Social Origins of Dictatorship and Democracy: Lord and Peasant in the Making of the Modern World.* Boston, 1966.

Morozov-Vorontsov, N., ed. *Zamoskvorech'e v 1905 g. Sbornik vospominanii, dokumentov i fotografii.* Moscow, 1925.

Moskovskoe professional'noe dvizhenie v gody pervoi revoliutsii. K dvadtsatiletniu 1905 goda. Sbornik I. Moscow, 1926.

Moskovskie pishcheviki do ob"edineniia (1917–1921 gg.). Sbornik statei i vospominanii. Moscow, 1928.

Moss, Bernard H. *The Origins of the French Labor Movement: The Socialism of Skilled Workers, 1830–1914.* Berkeley, Los Angeles, London, 1976.

Muranovskii, Sh. P. *Moskovskii soiuz rabochikh portnykh v 1917 g.* Moscow, 1927.

Muromskii, K. *Byt i nuzhdy torgovo-promyshlennykh sluzhashchikh.* Moscow, 1906.

Nedrov, A. *Rabochii vopros.* St. Petersburg, 1906.

Nelidov, N. *Viktor Pavlovich Nogin (tovarishch "Makar"). Kratkii bibliograficheskii ocherk.* Moscow, n.d.

Nevskii, V. I. "Vybor v komissiiu senatora Shidlovskogo (1905 g.)." *Arkhiv istorii truda v Rossii,* Book 3 (1922), pp. 78–90.

Nevskii, V. I., ed. *Istoriko-revoliutsionnyi sbornik.* 2 vols. Moscow and Leningrad, 1924.

———. *1905. Sovetskaia pechat' i literatura o sovetakh.* Moscow, 1925.

Nikitin, A. M., ed. *Otdykh torgovo-promyshlennykh sluzhashchikh (po dannym ankety 1909 g.).* Vypusk I: *Usloviia prazdnichnoi torgovli do izdaniia zakona 15 noiabria 1906 g. o normal'nom otdykhe sluzhashchikh v torgovo-promyshlennykh zavedeniiakh.* Moscow, 1912.

Nikol'skii, D. P. "O neobkhodimosti inspektsii dlia fabrichno-remeslennykh zavedenii." *Meditsinskaia beseda,* no. 9 (May 1904), pp. 244–254.

Nogin, V. "1906–1907 gg." *Vestnik truda,* no. 3 (March 1924).

Noyes, P. H. *Organization and Revolution: Working-Class Associations in the German Revolutions of 1848–1849.* Princeton, N.J., 1966.

Obshcheprofessional'nye organy 1905–1907 gg. Vypusk 1: *Moskovskie zhurnaly 1905 goda "Biulleten' Muzeia sodeistviia trudu" i "Materialy po professional'nomu dvizheniiu rabochikh."* Moscow, 1926.

Obshchestvo zavodchikov i fabrikantov Moskovskogo promyshlennogo raiona v 1912 g. Moscow, 1913.

Obzor po gorodu Moskve (za 1904–1909 gg.). Moscow, 1906–1911.

Ocherki istorii Moskovskikh organizatsii KPSS, 1883–1965. Moscow, 1966.

Oliunina, E. A. *Portnovskii promysel v Moskve i v derevniakh Moskovskoi i Riazanskoi gubernii: Materialy k istorii domashnei promyshlennosti v Rossii.* Moscow, 1914.

Ol'minskii, M. A., and M. A. Savelev, eds. *Pravda. Ezhednevnaia gazeta g. 1–4. 25 apr. (5 maia) 1912–26 okt (8 noiabria) 1917.* Moscow, 1927–1935.

Olson, Mancur. *The Logic of Collective Action: Public Goods and the Theory of Groups.* Cambridge, Mass., and London, 1975.

Orlov, B. P. *Poligraficheskaia promyshlennost' Moskvy. Ocherk razvitiia do 1917 goda.* Moscow, 1953.

Osokin, E., ed. "Iz zapisnoi knizhki arkhivista: k istorii Moskovskoi bol'shevistskoi pechati v gody revoliutsionnogo pod"ema (1913–1914 gg.)." *Krasnyi arkhiv,* no. 2 (105) (1941), pp. 168–178.

Osorgin, M. A. *Okhrannoe otdelenie i ego sekrety*. Moscow, 1917.

Ostrovitianov, K. V., ed. *Krasnoe zamoskvorech'e: Sbornik revoliutsionnykh vospominanii k dniu desiatiletiia oktiabr'skoi revoliutsii*. Moscow, 1927.

Ovsiannikov, N. *Na zare rabochego dvizheniia v Moskve*. Moscow, 1919.

Ovsiannikov, N., ed. *Nakanune velikoi revoliutsii. Sbornik statei, zametok i vospominanii*. Moscow, 1922.

Ozerov, I. Kh. *Politika po rabochemu voprosu v Rossii za poslednie gody*. Moscow, 1906.

Padenie tsarskogo rezhima: Stenograficheskie otchety doprosov i pokazanii, dannykh v 1917 g. 7 vols. Moscow and Leningrad, 1924–1926.

Panin, M. "Rabochii s"ezd i ego protivniki." *Otgoloski*, sbornik 4 (1907), pp. 22–38.

Pankratova, A. *Fabzavkomy Rossii v bor'be za sotsialisticheskuiu fabriku*. Moscow, 1923.

Pavlov, F. P. *Za desiat' let praktiki (Otryvki iz vospominanii, vpechatlenii i nabliudenii iz fabrichnoi zhizni)*. Moscow, 1901.

Pazhitnov, K. A. *Nekotorye itogi i perspektivy v oblasti rabochego voprosa v Rossii*. St. Petersburg, 1910.

———. *Polozhenie rabochego klassa v Rossii*. St. Petersburg, 1906.

———. *Problema remeslennykh tsekhov v zakonodatel'stve russkogo absoliutizma*. Moscow, 1952.

Perepis' Moskvy 1902 goda. Chast' 1: *Naselenie*. Vyp. 2. Moscow, 1906.

Perlman, Selig. *A Theory of the Labor Movement*. New York, 1949.

Pervaia konferentsiia professional'nykh soiuzov rabochikh po metallu Moskovskogo promyshlennogo raiona. Moscow, 1907.

Pervaia oblastnaia konferentsiia professional'nykh soiuzov rabochikh po obrabotke voloknistykh veshchestv Moskovskogo promyshlennogo raiona. Moscow, 1907.

Pervaia russkaia revoliutsiia. Ukazatel' literatury. Moscow, 1930.

Peterburgskie bol'sheviki v period pod"ema pervoi russkoi revoliutsii 1905–1907 gg. Sbornik dokumentov i materialov. Leningrad, 1955.

Petrograd po perepisi 15 dekabria 1910 g. Chast' 1 and 2. Petrograd, 1915.

Pipes, Richard. *Social Democracy and the St. Petersburg Labor Movement, 1855–1897*. Cambridge, Mass., 1963.

Pis'ma P. B. Akselroda i Iu. O. Martova. Netherlands, 1967.

Podvoiskii, N. *Pervyi sovet rabochikh deputatov (Ivanovo-Voznesenskii–1905 g.)*. Moscow, 1925.

Pogozhev, A. V. *Uchet, chislennost' i sostav rabochikh v Rossii: Materialy po statistike truda.* St. Petersburg, 1906.

Pogozhev, A. V., ed. *Adresnaia kniga fabrichno-zavodskoi i remeslennoi promyshlennosti vsei Rossii.* St. Petersburg, 1905.

Pokrovskaia, M. I. *Po podvalam, cherdakam i uglovym kvartiram Peterburga.* St. Petersburg, 1903.

Pokrovskii, M. N., ed. *1905. Istoriia revoliutsionnogo dvizheniia v otdel'nykh ocherkakh.* 3 vols. Moscow and Leningrad, 1925–1927.

Polianskii, V., ed. "Pamiatnaia zapiska o rabochikh gazetakh v Peterburge." *Krasnyi arkhiv,* no. 3 (10) (1925), pp. 286–299.

Portugalov, V. "Nasha 'konstitutsiia' i professional'noe dvizhenie rabochikh." *Bez zaglaviia,* no. 4 (February 12, 1906), pp. 145–151.

———. "O nashei rabochei professional'noi presse." *Bez zaglaviia,* no. 16 (May 1906), pp. 122–128.

Pospielovsky, Dmitry. *Russian Police Trade Unionism: Experiment or Provocation?* London, 1971.

Professional'noe dvizhenie Moskovskikh pishchevikov v gody pervoi revoliutsii. Sbornik 1. Moscow, 1927.

Professional'noe dvizhenie rabochikh pishchevikov za desiat' let (1917–1927 gg.). Moscow, 1927.

Professional'noe dvizhenie rabochikh khimikov i stekol'shchikov 1905–1918 gg. Materialy po istorii soiuza. Edited by Iu. K. Milonov. Moscow, 1928.

Profsoiuzy i revoliutsiia 1905 g. Moscow, 1931.

Profsoiuzy Moskvy. Ocherki istorii. Moscow, 1975.

Profsoiuzy SSSR. Dokumenty i materialy v chetyrekh tomakh 1905–1963 gg. Vol. 1: *Profsoiuzy v bor'be za sverzhenie samoderzhaviia i ustanovlenie diktatury proletariata (1905–1917 gg.).* Moscow, 1963.

Profsoiuzy—V. I. Leninu. Dokumenty i materialy. Moscow, 1961.

Prokhorovskaia Trekhgornaia manufaktura v Moskve. 1799–1899 gg. Istoriko-statisticheskii ocherk. Moscow, 1900.

Prokopovich, S. N. *Biudzhety Peterburgskikh rabochikh.* St. Petersburg, 1909.

———. *K rabochemu voprosu v Rossii.* St. Petersburg, 1905.

———. *Rabochee dvizhenie na zapade. Opyt kriticheskogo issledovaniia.* St. Petersburg, 1899.

———. *Soiuzy rabochikh i ikh zadachi.* [St. Petersburg], [1905].

Protokoly pervoi vserossiiskoi konferentsii soiuzov rabochikh pechatnogo dela. St. Petersburg, 1907.

Pushkareva, I. M. *Zheleznodorozhniki Rossii v burzhuazno-demokraticheskikh revoliutsiiakh.* Moscow, 1975.

Putilovets v trekh revoliutsiiakh. Sbornik materialov po istorii Putilovskogo zavoda. Leningrad, 1933.

Rabinowitch, Alexander. *The Bolsheviks Come to Power: The Revolution of 1917 in Petrograd.* New York, 1976.

————. *Prelude to Revolution: The Petrograd Bolsheviks and the July 1917 Uprising.* Bloomington, Ind., 1968.

Rabochee dvizhenie v Petrograde v 1912–1917 gg. Dokumenty i materialy. Leningrad, 1958.

Rabochee dvizhenie v Rossii v 1901–1904 gg. Sbornik dokumentov. Leningrad, 1975.

Rabochii klass i rabochee dvizhenie v Rossii. 1861–1917 gg. Moscow, 1966.

Rabochii vopros v komissii V. N. Kokovtsova v 1905 g. N.p., 1926.

Rakitin, G. [V. O. Tsederbaum]. "Rabochaia massa i rabochaia intelligentsiia." *Nasha zaria,* no. 9 (1913), pp. 52–60.

See also V. Levitskii.

Ramazov, R. G. "Sozdanie profsoiuzov Peterburgskogo proletariata i ikh deiatel'nost' v pervoi russkoi revoliutsii." Candidate dissertation, Higher School on Trade Unions. Moscow, 1975.

Rapoport, S., and R. Iakub. *Sistematicheskii uzkatel' literatury po professional'nomu dvizheniiu v Rossii.* Vyp. I. Moscow, 1923.

Rashin, A. G. *Formirovanie rabochego klassa Rossii: Istoriko-ekonomicheskie ocherki.* Moscow, 1958.

Reichman, Henry Frederick. "Russian Railwaymen and the Revolution of 1905." Ph.D. dissertation, University of California, Berkeley, 1977.

Remeslenniki i remeslennoe upravlenie v Rossii. Petrograd, 1916.

"Remeslennye zavedeniia v 1910 g." *Vestnik finansov, promyshlennosti i torgovli,* no. 29 (1916), pp. 99–100.

Revoliutsiia 1905–1907 godov v Rossii i profsoiuzy: Sbornik statei. Moscow, 1975.

Rimlinger, Gaston V. "Autocracy and the Factory Order in Early Russian Industrialization." *Journal of Economic History,* vol. 20, no. 1 (March 1960), pp. 67–92.

————. "The Management of Labor Protest in Tsarist Russia 1870–1905." *International Review of Social History,* vol. 5, part 2 (1960), pp. 226–248.

Rodionova, E. I. *Ocherki istorii professional'nogo dvizheniia meditsinskikh rabotnikov*. Moscow, 1962.

Roginskii, Ia. S. *Russkaia profsoiuznaia periodicheskaia pechat' 1905–1907 gg. Bibliograficheskii ukazatel'*. Moscow, 1957.

Romanov, F. A. *Vozniknovenie i deiatel'nost' profsoiuzov tekstil'shchikov (1905–1907 gody)*. [Moscow], 1955.

Roosa, Ruth Amende. "Russian Industrialists and 'State Socialism,' 1906–1917." *Soviet Studies*, vol. 23, no. 3 (January 1972), pp. 395–417.

———. "Workers' Insurance Legislation and the Role of the Industrialists in the Period of the Third State Duma." *Russian Review*, vol. 34, no. 4 (October 1975), pp. 410–452.

Rosenberg, William G. "Workers and Workers' Control in the Russian Revolution." *History Workshop*, no. 5 (Spring 1978), pp. 89–97.

Rossiiskaia kommunisticheskaia partiia (bol'shevikov) v rezoliutsiiakh ee s"ezdov i konferentsii (1898–1921 gg.). Moscow, 1922.

Roth, Guenther. *The Social Democrats in Imperial Germany: A Study in Working-Class Isolation and National Integration*. Totowa, N.J., 1963.

Rozen, M. *Ocherki polozheniia torgovo-promyshlennogo proletariata v Rossii*. St. Petersburg, 1907.

Rozenfel'd, O. *Istoriia professional'nogo dvizheniia v Rossii. Sinkhronisticheskie tablitsy*. 3rd ed. Moscow, 1924.

Rozhkov, N. A., and A. V. Sokolov [Stanislav Vol'skii]. *O 1905 gode. Vospominaniia*. Moscow, 1925.

Rudanovskii, A. P. *Professional'nye soiuzy, ikh organizatsiia, programma i taktika*. Moscow, 1906.

Sablinsky, Walter. "The All-Russian Railroad Union and the Beginning of the General Strike in October 1905," in *Revolution and Politics in Russia: Essays in Memory of B. I. Nikolaevsky*. Edited by Alexander and Janet Rabinowitch and Ladis K. D. Kristof. Bloomington, Ind., and London, 1972.

———. *The Road to Bloody Sunday: Father Gapon and the St. Petersburg Massacre of 1905*. Princeton, N.J., 1976.

S.-Peterburg po perepisi 15 dekabria 1900 g. Vyp. 2. St. Petersburg, 1903.

Samoilov, D. *O rabochikh professional'nykh soiuzakh*. Moscow, 1906.

Sapronov, T. V. *Iz istorii rabochego dvizheniia (po lichnym vospominaniiam)*. Moscow, 1925.

Sapronov, T. V., ed. *Iubileinyi sbornik. Po istorii dvizheniia stroitel'nykh rabochikh Moskvy*. Moscow, 1922.

Sbornik materialov po istorii soiuza stroitelei, 1906–1926. Leningrad, 1926.

Schapiro, Leonard. *The Communist Party of the Soviet Union.* New York, 1971.

Schneiderman, Jeremiah. *Sergei Zubatov and Revolutionary Marxism: The Struggle for the Working Class in Tsarist Russia.* Ithaca, N.Y., London, 1976.

———. "The Tsarist Government and the Labor Movement, 1898–1903: The Zubatovshchina." Ph.D. dissertation, University of California, Berkeley, 1966.

Schorske, Carl E. *German Social Democracy 1905–1917: The Development of the Great Schism.* New York, 1972.

Schwarz, Solomon. *Lénine et le mouvement syndical.* Paris, 1935.

———. *The Russian Revolution of 1905: The Workers' Movement and the Formation of Bolshevism and Menshevism.* Chicago and London, 1967.

Scott, Joan Wallach. *The Glassworkers of Carmaux: French Craftsmen and Political Action in a Nineteenth Century City.* Cambridge, Mass., 1974.

Sef, S. E. *Burzhuaziia v 1905 godu.* Moscow and Leningrad, 1926.

Selznick, Philip. *The Organizational Weapon: A Study of Bolshevik Strategy and Tactics.* New York, 1952.

Semanov, S. N. *Peterburgskie rabochie nakanune pervoi russkoi revoliutsii.* Moscow and Leningrad, 1966.

Semenov-Bulkin, F. [F. A. Bulkin]. "Ekonomicheskaia bor'ba rabochikh metallistov v 1905–1906 gg." *Trud v Rossii,* no. 1 (1925), pp. 3–17.

———. "Ekonomicheskoe polozhenie rabochikh metallistov do 1905 g." *Arkhiv istorii truda v Rossii,* Book 9 (1923), pp. 77–98.

———. "Smesovshchina." *Trud v Rossii,* no. 1 (1925), pp. 153–170.

See also F. A. Bulkin.

Severianin [A. N. Bykov]. "Polozhenie promyshlennosti i predprinimatel'skoe ob"edinenie." *Russkaia mysl',* vol. 29 (October 1908), pp. 138–148.

Severianin, P. "Soiuz rabochikh pechatnogo dela." *Bez zaglaviia,* no. 14 (April 1906), pp. 52–62.

Sewell, William G. *Work and Revolution in France: The Language of Labor from the Old Regime to 1848.* Cambridge, England, 1980.

Sh-r, V. [V. Sher]. "Nashe professional'noe dvizhenie za dva poslednikh goda." *Bor'ba,* no. 1 (February 22, 1914), pp. 17–22; no. 2 (March 18, 1914), pp. 12–16; no. 3 (April 9, 1914), pp. 15–19; no. 4 (April 28, 1914), pp. 18–23.

Shalaeva, E. I., and I. P. Leiberov. "Profsoiuzy Peterburga v 1905 godu." *Voprosy istorii,* no. 10 (October 1955), pp. 18–30.

Shatilova, T. I. *Ocherk istorii Leningradskogo soiuza khimikov (1905–1918 gg.).* Leningrad, 1927.

Shchap, Z. *Moskovskie metallisty v professional'nom dvizhenii. Ocherki po istorii Moskovskogo soiuza metallistov.* Moscow, 1927.

Shelymagin, I. I. *Zakonodatel'stvo o fabrichno-zavodskom trude v Rossii 1900–1917.* Moscow, 1952.

Shenlank, B. *Soiuzy podmaster'ev vo Frantsii.* Moscow, 1905.

Sher, V. V. *Istoriia professional'nogo dvizheniia rabochikh pechatnogo dela v Moskve.* Moscow, 1911.

See also V. Sh-r.

Shevkov, N. *Moskovskie shveiniki do fevral'skoi revoliutsii.* Moscow, 1927.

Shippel', M. *Professional'nye soiuzy.* Rostov-na-Donu, 1905.

Shuster, U. A. *Peterburgskie rabochie v 1905–1907 gg.* Leningrad, 1976.

Shuvalov, I. *Rabochee i professional'noe dvizhenie na bumazhnykh fabrikakh 1750–1914.* Moscow, 1926.

Sidorov, A. L., et al., eds. *Vysshii pod"em revoliutsii. Noiabr'–dekabr' 1905–1907 gg.* 4 vols. Moscow, 1955–1957.

Sidorov, N. I., ed. *1905 god v Peterburge.* Vypusk 2: *Sovet rabochikh deputatov. Sbornik materialov.* Leningrad, 1925.

Sindeev, I. *Professional'noe dvizhenie rabochikh-stroitelei v 1917 g.* Moscow, 1927.

Skachkov, I., ed. *Materialy po istorii professional'nogo dvizheniia rabochikh poligraficheskogo proizvodstva v Rossii.* Moscow, 1925.

Skocpol, Theda. *States and Social Revolutions: A Comparative Analysis of France, Russia, and China.* Cambridge, England, 1979.

Skopinskii, A. V. *Iznanka professional'nykh soiuzov.* Vilna, 1908.

Smelser, Neil J. *Social Change in the Industrial Revolution: An Application of Theory to the British Cotton Industry.* Chicago, 1959.

———. *Theory of Collective Behavior.* New York, 1963.

———. "Toward a Theory of Modernization," in *Social Change: Sources, Patterns, and Consequences.* Edited by Eva Etzioni-Halevy and Amitai Etzioni. New York, 1973.

Smith, Steve. "Craft Consciousness, Class Consciousness: Petrograd, 1917." *History Workshop,* no. 11 (Spring 1981), pp. 33–58.

Somov, S. I. "Iz istorii sotsialdemokraticheskogo dvizheniia v Peterburge v 1905 godu (Lichnye vospominaniia)." *Byloe,* no. 4 (16) (April 1907), pp. 22–55; no. 5 (17) (May 1907), pp. 152–178.

————. *Professional'nye soiuzy i sotsialdemokraticheskaia partiia.* St. Petersburg, 1907.

Sovremennoe khoziaistvo goroda Moskvy. Moscow, 1913.

Spisok fabrik i zavodov evropeiskoi Rossii. St. Petersburg, 1903.

Spisok fabrik i zavodov Moskvy i Moskovskoi gubernii. Moscow, 1916.

Spisok fabrik i zavodov Rossii, 1910 g. Po ofitsial'nym dannym fabrichnogo, podatnogo i gornogo nadzora. Moscow, St. Petersburg, and Warsaw, n.d.

Spisok fabrik i zavodov Rossiiskoi imperii. Sostavlennyi po ofitsial'nym svedeniiam. St. Petersburg, 1912.

Statisticheskii atlas goroda Moskvy. Territoriia, sostav naseleniia, gramotnost' i zaniatiia. Moscow, 1911.

Statisticheskii ezhegodnik goroda Moskvy. Moscow, 1908–1916.

Statisticheskii ezhegodnik goroda Moskvy i Moskovskoi gubernii za 1914–1925 gg. Vypusk 2: *Statisticheskie dannye po gorodu Moskve.* Moscow, 1927.

Statisticheskii sbornik za 1913–1917 gg. Moscow, 1921.

Steinberg, Mark David. "Moscow Printing Workers: The September Strikes of 1903 and 1905." Seminar paper, University of California, Berkeley, Spring 1980.

Suny, Ronald G. "Labor and Liquidators: Revolutionaries and the 'Reaction' in Baku, May 1908–April 1912," *Slavic Review,* vol. 34, no. 2 (June 1975), pp. 319–340.

Surh, Gerald Dennis. "Petersburg Workers in 1905: Strikes, Workplace Democracy, and the Revolution." Ph.D. dissertation, University of California, Berkeley, 1979.

————. "Petersburg's First Mass Labor Organization: The Assembly of Russian Workers and Father Gapon," *Russian Review,* part 1, vol. 40, no. 3 (July 1981), pp. 241–262; part 2, vol. 40, no. 4 (October 1981), pp. 412–441.

Svavitskii, V. A., and V. Sher. *Ocherk polozheniia rabochikh pechatnogo dela v Moskve (Po dannym ankety, proizvedennoi obshchestvom rabochikh graficheskikh iskusstv v 1907 godu).* St. Petersburg, 1909.

Sviatlovskii, V. V. *Istoriia professional'nogo dvizheniia v Rossii ot vozniknoveniia rabochego klassa do kontsa 1917 g.* Leningrad, 1925.

————. "Iz istorii kass i obshchestv vzaimopomoshchi rabochikh." *Arkhiv istorii truda v Rossii,* Book 4 (1922), pp. 32–46.

————. *Polozhenie voprosa o rabochikh organizatsiiakh v inostrannykh gosudarstvakh.* Vypusk 2. 2d ed. St. Petersburg, 1906.

————. *Professional'noe dvizhenie v Rossii.* St. Petersburg, 1907.

————. *Professional'nye rabochie soiuzy na zapade*. St. Petersburg, 1907.

————. *Professional'nye soiuzy i uchrezhdeniia*. St. Petersburg, 1908.

————. *Sovremennoe zakonodatel'stvo o professional'nykh rabochikh soiuzakh. Frantsiia. Bel'giia. Angliia. Avstraliia. Germaniia. Rossiia*. St. Petersburg, 1907.

————. ed. *Ukazatel' literatury po professional'nomu rabochemu dvizheniiu*. St. Petersburg, 1906.

Svirskii, A. I. *Zapiski rabochego*. Moscow, 1919.

Svod otchetov fabrichnykh inspektorov za [1900–1914]. St. Petersburg, 1900–1915.

Svod otchetov professional'nykh obshchestv za 1906–1907 gg. St. Petersburg, 1911.

Svodnyi biulleten' po gorodu Moskve za 1901–1914. Moscow, 1902–1916.

Swain, G. R. "Bolsheviks and the Metal Workers on the Eve of the First World War." *Journal of Contemporary History*, vol. 16, no. 2 (April 1981), pp. 273–291.

Thompson, E. P. "Eighteenth-Century English Society: Class Struggle Without Class?" *Social History*, vol. 3, no. 2 (May 1978), pp. 133–165.

————. *The Making of the English Working Class*. New York, 1964.

Tikhomirov, L. A. *Rabochii vopros (prakticheskie sposoby ego resheniia)*. Moscow, 1909.

Tilly, Charles. *From Mobilization to Revolution*. Reading, Mass., 1978.

————. "Revolutions and Collective Violence," in *Macropolitical Theory*. Edited by Fred I. Greenstein and Nelson W. Polsby. Reading, Mass., 1975, pp. 483–556.

————. "Collective Violence in European Perspective," in *A History of Violence in America: Historical and Comparative Perspectives*. Edited by Hugh Davis Graham and Ted Robert Gurr. New York, 1969.

Tilly, Charles, and Lynn Lees. "Le Peuple de juin 1848." *Annales: économies, sociétés, civilizations* 29 (September–October 1974), pp. 1061–1091.

Timofeev, P. *Chem zhivet zavodskii rabochii*. St. Petersburg, 1906.

————. "Ocherki zavodskoi zhizni." *Russkoe bogatstvo*, no. 9 (September 1905), pp. 19–34; no. 10 (October 1905), pp. 71–91.

————. "Zavodskie budni. Iz zapisok rabochego," *Russkoe bogatstvo*, no. 8 (August 1903), pp. 30–53; no. 9 (September 1903), pp. 175–199.

Tiurin, S. P. *Moskovskoe tsentral'noe biuro professional'nykh soiuzov*. Moscow, 1913.

See also S. P. Turin.

Tobias, Henry J. *The Jewish Bund in Russia: From Its Origins to 1905*. Stanford, Calif., 1972.

Tocqueville, Alexis de. *The Old Regime and the French Revolution.* Translated by Stuart Gilbert. New York, 1955.

Torgazhev, B. P. *Professional'noe dvizhenie i sotsialdemokratiia.* Moscow, 1907.

Totomiants, V. K. *Kooperatsiia v Rossii.* Prague, 1922.

Touraine, Alain. *La Conscience Ouvrière.* Paris, 1966.

Traugott, Mark. "The Mobile Guard in the French Revolution of 1848." *Theory and Society,* vol. 9, no. 5 (September 1980), pp. 683–720.

Trotsky, Leon. *1905.* Translated by Anya Bostock. New York, 1972.

———. *The Russian Revolution.* Edited by F. W. Dupee. Garden City, N. Y., 1959.

Trusova, N. S. *Revoliutsionnoe dvizhenie v Rossii vesnoi i letom 1905 goda: aprel'-sentiabr'.* 2 vols. Moscow, 1957–1961.

Trusova, N. S. et al., eds. *Nachalo pervoi russkoi revoliutsii: Ianvar'–mart 1905 goda.* Moscow, 1955.

Trudy pervogo vserossiiskogo s"ezda po remeslennoi promyshlennosti v Peterburge. Vol. 3. St. Petersburg, 1900.

"Tsarizm v bor'be s rabochim dvizheniem v gody pod"ema." *Krasnyi arkhiv,* vol. 1 (74) (1936), pp. 37–65.

Tsiavlovskii, M. A., ed. *Bolsheviki. Dokumenty po istorii bol'shevizma s 1903 po 1916 god byvsh. Moskovskogo okhrannogo otdeleniia.* Moscow, 1918.

Tsytsarin, V. "Vospominaniia metallista." *Vestnik truda,* no. 12 (61) (December 1925), pp. 34–40.

Tugan-Baranovsky, M. I. *The Russian Factory in the 19th Century.* Translated from the third Russian edition by Arthur Levin and Claora S. Levin, under the supervision of Gregory Grossman. Homewood, Ill., 1970.

Tunnel'. *Nakanune suda. Ocherk ekonomicheskoi i politicheskoi bor'by pochtovo-tele-grafnykh sluzhashchikh Rossii.* Moscow, 1908.

Turin, S. P. *From Peter the Great to Lenin: A History of the Russian Labour Movement with Special Reference to Trade Unionism.* London, 1935.
See also S. P. Tiurin.

Ulam, Adam. *The Bolsheviks: The Intellectual and Political History of the Triumph of Communism in Russia.* New York, 1965.

———. *The Unfinished Revolution: An Essay on the Sources of Influence of Marxism and Communism.* New York, 1964.

Umbreit, P. *Znachenie i zadachi tsentral'nykh biuro professional'nykh soiuzov.* St. Petersburg, 1906.

Utkin, A. I. "Ekonomicheskoe polozhenie Moskovskikh rabochikh posle pervoi russkoi revoliutsii." *Vestnik Moskovskogo universiteta: Istoriia*, no. 1 (January–February 1974), pp. 41–53.

V pomoshch' rabochemu. Sbornik statei o professional'nom i kooperativnom dvizhenii. Vypusk 1. [Moscow, 1907].

Vallier, Ivan, ed. *Comparative Methods in Sociology: Essays on Trends and Applications.* Berkeley, Los Angeles, London, 1971.

Vasil'ev, P. "Ushakovshchina." *Trud v Rossii*, no. 1 (1925), pp. 143–152.

Vasil'ev-Iuzhin, M. I. *Moskovskii sovet rabochikh deputatov v 1905 g.* Moscow, 1925.

———. "Moskovskii sovet rabochikh deputatov v 1905 i podgotovka im vooruzhennogo vosstaniia." *Proletarskaia revoliutsiia*, no. 4 (39) (1925), pp. 84–124; no. 5 (40) (1925), pp. 92–133.

Vecher vospominanii po istorii Moskovskogo soiuza kozhevnikov, 4 ianvaria 1925. Moscow, [1926].

Voinova, K. "Iiul'skie dni 1914 g. v Moskve (Khronika sobytii)." *Proletarskaia revoliutsiia*, no. 7 (30) (1924), pp. 215–223.

Voitinskii, V. S. *Gody pobed i porazhenii.* Book 1, *1905-yi god.* Berlin, Petersburg, and Moscow, 1923.

Volobuev, P. *Proletariat i burzhuaziia Rossii v 1917 g.* Moscow, 1964.

Volodarskaia, A. M. "Poroninskoe soveshchanie TsK RSDRP s partiinymi rabotnikami v 1913 g." *Istoricheskie zapiski*, no. 59 (1957), pp. 125–181.

Von Laue, Theodore H. *Sergei Witte and the Industrialization of Russia.* New York, 1963.

Vostrikov, N. I. *Bor'ba za massy: Gorodskie srednie sloi nakanune oktiabria.* Moscow, 1970.

Vsia Rossiia. Adres-kalendar'. God III. Moscow, 1912.

Vtoraia konferentsiia professional'nykh soiuzov: Doklady i protokoly. St. Petersburg, 1906.

Vtoroi period revoliutsii: 1906–1907 gody. Moscow, 1957.

Vtoroi s"ezd R.S.D.R.P., iiul'–avgust 1903 goda. Protokoly. Moscow, 1959.

Walkin, Jacob. "The Attitude of the Tsarist Government Toward the Labor Problem." *American Slavic and East European Review*, vol. 13, no. 2 (April 1954), pp. 163–184.

———. *The Rise of Democracy in Pre-Revolutionary Russia: Political and Social Institutions Under the Last Three Czars.* New York, 1962.

Webb, Sydney, and Beatrice Webb. *The History of Trade Unionism*. Revised edition. London, 1950.

———. *Teoriia i praktika angliiskogo tred-iunionizma. V perevode s angliiskogo Vladimira Il'ina (V. Ul'ianova-Lenina)*. Moscow, 1925.

———. *Teoriia i praktika angliiskogo tred-iunionizma (Industrial Democracy)*. *Perevod s angliiskogo*. 2 vols. St. Petersburg, 1900–1901.

Wildman, Allan K. *The Making of a Workers' Revolution: Russian Social Democracy, 1891–1903*. Chicago and London, 1967.

Wilensky, Harold L. *Intellectuals in Labor Unions: Organizational Pressures on Professional Roles*. Glencoe, Ill., 1956.

Wolfe, Bertram. *Three Who Made a Revolution: A Biographical History*. New York, 1964.

Za marksistko-leninskuiu istoriiu profdvizheniia. Moscow, 1932.

Zaiats, M. *Tekstili v gody pervoi revoliutsii (1905–1907 gg.): Materialy po istorii professional'nogo dvizheniia tekstil'shchikov tsentral'no-promyshlennogo raiona*. Moscow, 1925.

Zakon 4-go marta 1906 goda o soiuzakh i obshchestvakh s posleduiushchimi k nemu raz'iasneniiami Pravitel'stvuiushchego senata i Ministerstva vnutrennikh del. St. Petersburg, 1906.

Zaverzin, P. P. *Rabota tainoi politsii. Chast' 1: O rozyske. Chast' 2: Vospominaniia*. Paris, 1924.

———. *Zhandarmy i revoliutsionery; vospominaniia*. Paris, 1930.

Zheleznodorozhniki i revoliutsiia. Moscow and Leningrad, 1925.

Zheleznodorozhniki v 1905 g. (ocherki iz istorii soiuza). Moscow, 1922.

Zelnik, Reginald E. "Russian Bebels: An Introduction to the Memoirs of Semen Kanatchikov and Matvei Fisher." *Russian Review*, part 1, vol. 35, no. 3 (July 1976), pp. 249–289; part 2, vol. 36, no. 4 (October 1976), pp. 417–447.

———. *Labor and Society in Tsarist Russia: The Factory Workers of St. Petersburg, 1855–1870*. Stanford, Calif., 1971.

Zil'berg, I. *Professional'noe dvizhenie sluzhashchikh farmatsevtsev. Period pervoi russkoi revoliutsii*. Moscow, 1930.

Zinin, G. V. "Shkola i fabrika." *Zavety*, no. 4 (April 1913).

III. BIBLIOGRAPHY OF PERIODICAL PRESS

A. PUBLICATIONS OF TRADE UNION AND EMPLOYERS' ORGANIZATIONS

Biulleten' Obshchestva zavodchikov i fabrikantov (St. Petersburg), June 1910-July 1912, nos. 1–3.

Biulleten' Muzeia sodeistviia trudu (Moscow), 16–26 November 1905, nos. 1–2.

Bulochnik (Moscow), February-March 1906, nos. 1–3.

Bulochnik (St. Petersburg), May 1908, no. 1.

Chasovshchik (St. Petersburg), February 1907, no. 1.

Chelnok (St. Petersburg), September 1907, no. 1.

Edinstvo (St. Petersburg), February 1909-April 1910, nos. 1–17.

Fabrichnaia zhizn' (St. Petersburg), February 1910-July 1911, nos. 1–7.

Fabrichnyi (Moscow), May 1907, no. 1.

Fabrichnyi stanok (St. Petersburg), May-September 1908, nos. 1–5.

Fabrichnyi vestnik (St. Petersburg), May-December 1909, nos. 1–5.

Golos bulochnika i konditera (St. Petersburg), July 1910-November 1911, nos. 1–11; August-October 1912, nos. 1–13.

Golos farmatsevta (St. Petersburg), February-May 1906, nos. 1–4.

Golos krasil'shchika (St. Petersburg), August 1907, no. 1.

Golos pechatnika (St. Petersburg), August-December 1906, nos. 1–17.

Golos pechatnogo truda (Moscow), November 1916-April 1917, nos. 1–4.

Golos portnogo (St. Petersburg), May 1910-April 1911, nos. 1–7.

Golos prikazchika (St. Petersburg), April-October 1906, nos. 1–14.

Golos tabachnika (St. Petersburg), December 1906-February 1907, nos. 1–3.

Golos tkacha (St. Petersburg), October 1906-January 1907, nos. 1–3.

Golos truda (Kharkov), December 1908-January 1909, nos. 1–4.

Golos zheleznodorozhnikov (St. Petersburg), November 1907, no. 1.

Golos zhizni (St. Petersburg), June 1910-March 1911, nos. 1–5.

Golos zoloteserebriannikov i bronzovshchikov (St. Petersburg), July-September 1913, nos. 1–4.

Izvestiia Obshchestva zavodchikov i fabrikantov Moskovskogo promyshlennogo raiona (Moscow), July 1913-December 1916 (monthly).

Konfetchik (St. Petersburg), November-December 1906, nos. 1–2.

Kozhevnik (St. Petersburg), February-December 1907, nos. 1–4; March-April 1911, nos. 1–6.

Krasil'shchik (St. Petersburg), February-March 1907, nos. 1–2.

Kuznets (St. Petersburg), February 1907-March 1908, nos. 1–8.

Listok bulochnikov i konditerov (St. Petersburg), April 1906-March 1907, nos. 1–11.

Listok dlia rabochikh portnykh, portnikh i skorniakov (St. Petersburg), December 1905, no. 1; January-December 1906, nos. 1–20; February-March 1907, nos. 1–6.

Listok dlia remeslennykh rabochikh. Prilozhenie k No. 1 zhurnala "Nadezhda" (St. Petersburg), July 1908.

Listok professional'nogo obshchestva rabochikh po obrabotke metallov (Moscow), December 1906.

Listok rabochikh po obrabotke dereva (St. Petersburg), June-November 1907, nos. 1–6.

Lokomotiv (St. Petersburg), March-May 1907, nos. 1–5.

Materialy po professional'nomu dvizheniiu rabochikh (Moscow), February 1906, no. 1.

Metallist (St. Petersburg), September 1911-June 1914, nos. 1–45.

Molniia (St. Petersburg), April 1907, no. 1; January 1908, nos. 4–5.

Nadezhda (St. Petersburg), July-October 1908, nos. 1–3.

Nash golos (St. Petersburg), March-April 1908, nos. 1–2.

Nash put' (Moscow), May 1910-January 1911, nos. 1–8.

Nash put' (St. Petersburg), June 1910-August 1911, nos. 1–21.

Nashe pechatnoe delo (St. Petersburg), November 1913-November 1916, nos. 1–36.

Nashe vremia (Moscow), April 1911, no. 1.

Novoe pechatnoe delo (St. Petersburg), June-December 1911, nos. 1–13; December 1912-September 1913, nos. 1–10.

Ocherednoi (Moscow), March 1907, nos. 1–2.

Parovoz (Moscow), October-November 1907, nos. 1–2.

Pechatnik (Moscow), April-July 1906, nos. 1–8.

Pechatnoe delo (Moscow), September 1906-June 1907, nos. 1–30.

Pechatnoe delo (St. Petersburg), November 1908-May 1911, nos. 1–37; January-June 1912, nos. 1–6.

Pechatnoe slovo (Moscow), November 1906-June 1907, nos. 1–3.

Pechatnyi vestnik (St. Petersburg), May-December 1905, nos. 1–19; February-March 1906, nos. 1–5.

Peterburgskii kozhevnik (St. Petersburg), December 1908-January 1909, nos. 1–2.

Peterburgskii sapozhnik (St. Petersburg), March-August 1906, nos. 1–3.

Pod"em (Moscow), October-November 1907, nos. 1–2.

Portnoi (St. Petersburg), April-October 1907, nos. 1–8; March 1908, nos. 1–2.

Professional (Moscow), April-May 1907, nos. 1–5.

Professional'noe dvizhenie (St. Petersburg), May 1907, no. 1.

Professional'nyi soiuz (St. Petersburg), November 1905-July 1906, nos. 1–21.

Professional'nyi vestnik (St. Petersburg), January 1907-October 1909, nos. 1–26.

Proletarii igly (St. Petersburg), April-May 1914, nos. 1–3.

Rabochee delo (Moscow), May-October 1909, nos. 1–7.

Rabochee dvizhenie. Biulleten'. Obshchestvo zavodchikov i fabrikantov (Moscow), 1907–1913, nos. 1–18.

Rabochie vedomosti (Petrograd), August-November 1916, nos. 1–3.

Rabochii po kozhe (St. Petersburg), December 1906, no. 1.

Rabochii po metallu (St. Petersburg), June 1906, no. 1; August 1906-November 1907, nos. 1–24.

Rabochii trud (Moscow), June-July 1914, nos. 1–4.

Russkii pechatnik (Moscow), January 1909-September 1910, nos. 1–21.

Semafor (St. Petersburg), July 1906, no. 1.

Slovo remeslennika (Nizhni-Novgorod), March-April 1907, nos. 1–5.

Stanok (St. Petersburg), February-April 1908, nos. 1–3.

Stanok tekstil'shchika (St. Petersburg), November 1908-February 1909, nos. 1–2.

Tekstil'noe delo (St. Petersburg), November 1907, no. 1.

Tekstil'nyi rabochii (St. Petersburg), January-March 1914, nos. 1–2.

Tekstil'shchik (St. Petersburg), December 1915-March 1916.

Ternii truda (St. Petersburg), November 1906, no. 1.

Tkach (St. Petersburg), June-October 1906, nos. 1–8.

Trud pechatnika (St. Petersburg), October 1907, no. 1.

Trud tabachnika (St. Petersburg), May 1907, nos. 1–2.

Vestnik pechatnikov (St. Petersburg), April-July 1906, nos. 1–13; February-March 1907, nos. 1–8.

Vestnik portnykh (St. Petersburg), June 1911-March 1914, nos. 1–8.

Vestnik rabochikh po obrabotke metalla (St. Petersburg), May-June 1908, nos. 1–3.

Vestnik rabotnits i rabochikh voloknistykh proizvodstv (St. Petersburg), February-July 1907, nos. 1–6.

Vestnik torgovykh sluzhashchikh (Moscow), September 1912-March 1914, nos. 1–6.

Vestnik zolotoserebrianikov i bronzovshchikov (St. Petersburg), December 1906-June 1907, nos. 1–9.

Zheleznodorozhnaia zhizn' (Moscow), October 1906, nos. 1–2.

Zhizn' kozhevnika (St. Petersburg), May 1914, no. 1.

Zhizn' pechatnika (St. Petersburg), May-October 1907, nos. 1–16.

Zhizn' pekarei (St. Petersburg), May-November 1913, March-May 1914, nos. 1–5.

Zhizn' prikazchika (Moscow), November 1906-March 1907, nos. 1–13.

Zhizn' tabachnika (St. Petersburg), July-August 1907, nos. 1–2.

B. POLITICAL PARTY PRESS

Bez zaglaviia (St. Petersburg), January-May 1906, nos. 1–16.

Bor'ba (Moscow), November-December 1905, nos. 1–9.

Bor'ba (St. Petersburg), February-July 1914, nos. 1–7.

Delo naroda (St. Petersburg), May 1906, nos. 1–9.

Ekho (St. Petersburg), June-July 1906, nos. 1–14.

Golos truda (St. Petersburg), June-July 1906, nos. 1–16.

Luch' (St. Petersburg), September 1912-July 1913, nos. 1–118, 120–236.

Nash put' (Moscow), August-September 1913, nos. 1–16.

Nasha rabochaia gazeta (St. Petersburg), May-July 1914, nos. 1–55.

Nasha zaria (St. Petersburg), January 1910-November 1914 (monthly).

Novaia rabochaia gazeta (St. Petersburg), August 1913-June 1914, nos. 1–136.

Novaia zhizn' (St. Petersburg), October-December 1905, nos. 1–28.

Otgoloski (St. Petersburg), April 1907, no. 4.

Otkliki (St. Petersburg), December 1906-April 1907, nos. 1–3.

Otkliki sovremennosti (St. Petersburg), March-June 1906, nos. 1–5.

Otzvuki (St. Petersburg), August 1907, no. 1.

Pravda (Rabochaia pravda, Severnaia pravda, Pravda truda, Za trud, Proletarskaia pravda, Put' pravdy, Trudovaia pravda) (St. Petersburg), April 1912-July 1914 (daily).

Proletarii (Geneva), May-November 1905, nos. 1–26.

Rabotnitsa (St. Petersburg), February-June 1914, nos. 1–7.

Severnaia rabochaia gazeta (St. Petersburg), January-May 1914, nos. 1–59, 61–69.

Volna (St. Petersburg), April-May 1906, nos. 1–25.

Vozrozhdenie (Moscow), 1908, no. 1; 1909, nos. 1–12; 1910, nos. 1–11.

Vpered (St. Petersburg), May-June 1906, nos. 1–17.

Zhivaia zhizn' (St. Petersburg), July-August 1913, nos. 1–19.

INDEX